1988 Suppleme

to

CONSTITUTIONAL LAW

CASES AND MATERIALS

By

EDWARD L. BARRETT, Jr.

Professor of Law, University of California, Davis

WILLIAM COHEN

C. Wendell and Edith M. Carlsmith
Professor of Law, Stanford University

SEVENTH EDITION

Westbury, New York
THE FOUNDATION PRESS, INC.
1988

B. & C. Cs. Const.Law 7th Ed. UCB
1988 Supp.

TABLE OF CONTENTS

TABLE OF CONTENTS

PART II
ALLOCATION OF GOVERNMENTAL POWERS: THE NATION AND THE STATES; THE PRESIDENT, THE CONGRESS, AND THE COURTS

CHAPTER 4
THE SCOPE OF NATIONAL POWER

SECTION 3. THE SCOPE OF NATIONAL POWER TODAY

A. The Commerce Power

CHAPTER 5

THE SCOPE OF STATE POWER—REGULATION

SECTION 2. IMPLIED RESTRICTIONS OF THE COMMERCE CLAUSE—
PRODUCTION AND TRADE

A. Restricting Importation and Insulating In-State Business
From Out-of-State Competition

TABLE OF CONTENTS

TABLE OF CONTENTS

vii

PART III

GOVERNMENT AND THE INDIVIDUAL: THE PROTECTION OF LIBERTY AND PROPERTY UNDER THE DUE PROCESS AND EQUAL PROTECTION CLAUSES

CHAPTER 10

THE DUE PROCESS, CONTRACT, AND JUST COMPENSATION CLAUSES AND THE REVIEW OF THE REASONABLENESS OF LEGISLATION

SECTION 1. ECONOMIC REGULATORY LEGISLATION

A. The Rise and Fall of Due Process

TABLE OF CONTENTS

TABLE OF CONTENTS

E.   Education

CHAPTER 12

DEFINING THE SCOPE OF "LIBERTY" AND "PROPERTY" PROTECTED BY THE DUE PROCESS CLAUSE—THE PROCEDURAL DUE PROCESS CASES

SECTION 1.   WHAT CONSTITUTES A DEPRIVATION OF LIBERTY OR PROPERTY WHICH MANDATES THE PROVISION OF A HEARING?

CHAPTER 13

APPLICATION OF THE POST CIVIL WAR AMENDMENTS TO PRIVATE CONDUCT: CONGRESSIONAL POWER TO ENFORCE THE AMENDMENTS

SECTION 2.   APPLICATION OF THE CONSTITUTION TO PRIVATE CONDUCT

A.   Private Performance of "Government" Functions

C.   Government Financing, Regulation and Authorization of Private Conduct

2.   Government Financial Assistance to Private Activities

TABLE OF CONTENTS

PART IV

CONSTITUTIONAL PROTECTION OF EXPRESSION AND CONSCIENCE

CHAPTER 14

GOVERNMENTAL CONTROL OF THE CONTENT OF EXPRESSION

Section 2. Intermezzo: An Introduction to the Concepts of Vagueness, Overbreadth and Prior Restraint

A. Vagueness and Overbreadth

Section 3. Speech Conflicting With Other Community Values: Government Control of the Content of Speech

A. Protection of Individual Reputation and Privacy

TABLE OF CONTENTS

SECTION 3. THE NON-TRADITIONAL FORUM

A. Speech Activities in Public Property Other Than Parks and Streets

CHAPTER 16

PROTECTION OF PENUMBRAL FIRST AMENDMENT RIGHTS

SECTION 1. SYMBOLIC SPEECH

TABLE OF CONTENTS

SECTION 2. COMPELLED AFFIRMATION OF BELIEF

TABLE OF CONTENTS

*

TABLE OF CASES

Principal cases are in italic type. Cases discussed are in roman type. References are to Pages.

*

1988 Supplement

to

CONSTITUTIONAL LAW

CASES AND MATERIALS

*

Part I

THE CONSTITUTION AND THE COURTS: THE JUDICIAL FUNCTION IN CONSTITUTIONAL CASES

Chapter 2

JUDICIAL REVIEW

SECTION 1. THE LEGITIMACY OF JUDICIAL REVIEW

Page 36. Replace Note (4):

(4) The theory of judicial review expounded in Marbury v. Madison, coupled with the orthodox theory of the declaratory nature of judicial decisionmaking, requires that new constitutional decisions be applied to govern conduct that preceded the decisions. In a significant number of cases beginning in 1965, however, the Supreme Court applied newly announced constitutional rules governing criminal procedure prospectively only, to avoid wholesale release of prisoners whose convictions violated the new rule. Linkletter v. Walker, 381 U.S. 618 (1965) (rule requiring exclusion of illegally seized evidence, established by Mapp v. Ohio, 367 U.S. 643 (1961), is inapplicable to convictions challenged on collateral review). The standards for measuring prospective and retroactive application became increasingly controversial, as the court declined to apply new constitutional criminal procedure rules, even in cases on direct appeal, to events that preceded the decision. E.g., Desist v. United States, 394 U.S. 244 (1969) (new interpretation of fourth amendment applicable only to police activity that occurred after the date of the decision). In a dissenting opinion, Justice Harlan argued that increasing use of the technique of prospective constitutional adjudication was inconsistent with the premises of judicial review.

"If we do not resolve all cases before us on direct review in light of our best understanding of constitutional principles, it is difficult to see why we should adjudicate any case at all. . . . In truth, the Court's assertion of power to disregard current law in adjudicating cases before us that have not already run the full course of appellate review, is quite simply an assertion that our constitutional function is not one of adjudication but in effect of

1

legislation." Mackey v. United States, 401 U.S. 667, 675, 691 (1971) (Harlan, J., dissenting).

In Griffith v. Kentucky, 479 U.S. 314 (1987), citing Justice Harlan, the Court decided that all new rules for the conduct of criminal prosecutions would be applied to all cases pending on direct review, with no exceptions.[1]

> "Unlike a legislature, we do not promulgate new rules of constitutional criminal procedure on a broad basis. Rather, the nature of judicial review requires that we adjudicate specific cases, and each case usually becomes the vehicle for announcement of a new rule. But after we have decided a new rule in the cases selected, the integrity of judicial review requires that we apply that rule to all similar cases pending on direct review."

Despite the concern that prospective application of new constitutional decisions is inconsistent with the "integrity of judicial review," in a footnote to the *Griffith* decision the Court reaffirmed earlier cases, not involving criminal procedure, that applied new rules of constitutional law prospectively "[w]here a decision of this Court could produce substantial inequitable results if applied retroactively." Cipriano v. City of Houma, 395 U.S. 701, 706 (1969) (rule invalidating property ownership requirements for voting in bond elections). See also Lemon v. Kurtzman, 411 U.S. 192 (1973) (rule forbidding state compensation of religious schools for educational services); Gosa v. Mayden, 413 U.S. 665 (1973) (rule forbidding court martial for non-service connected crimes); Marks v. United States, 430 U.S. 188 (1977) (relaxed constitutional standards governing prosecution for obscenity); Northern Pipeline Construction Co. v. Marathon Pipe Line Co., 458 U.S. 50 (1982) (decision declaring federal bankruptcy court unconstitutional because judges lacked tenure during good behavior).

---

[1] The Court did not resolve the continuing controversy over the retroactive application of new constitutional decisions to criminal convictions that had become final, but that are challenged collaterally through the federal writ of habeas corpus. The extent to which new constitutional criminal procedure rules will be applied in those cases turns, practically, on the question whether habeas corpus is available to a prisoner whose counsel did not raise the question at the criminal trial. Compare Reed v. Ross, 468 U.S. 1 (1984) with Smith v. Murray, 477 U.S. 527 (1986).

Chapter 3

THE JURISDICTION OF FEDERAL COURTS IN CONSTITUTIONAL CASES

SECTION 1. SUPREME COURT REVIEW OF STATE COURT DECISIONS

A. HISTORY AND STRUCTURE

Page 48. Replace note, "The Current Jurisdiction of the Supreme Court to Review State Court Decisions":

THE CURRENT JURISDICTION OF THE SUPREME COURT TO REVIEW STATE COURT DECISIONS

In 1916 and 1925, Congress had provided that the Supreme Court would have discretion, on writ of certiorari, whether or not to review the majority of state cases deciding federal questions. Between 1925 and 1988, however (when most of the cases in this book were decided), two categories of state court decisions were subject to obligatory review on appeal—if a state statute was held constitutional, or if a federal statute or treaty was held unconstitutional. In 1988, Congress eliminated these appeals, as well as most appeals from decisions of lower federal courts. The current statute provides in substance for discretionary Supreme Court review of all state court decisions turning on issues of federal law:

28 U.S.C. § 1257.

"Final judgments or decrees rendered by the highest court of a State in which a decision could be had may be reviewed by the Supreme Court by writ of certiorari where the validity of a treaty or statute of the United States is drawn in question or where the validity of a statute of any State is drawn in question on the ground of its being repugnant to the Constitution, treaties or laws of the United States, or where any title, right, privilege, or immunity is specially set up or claimed under the Constitution or the treaties or statutes of, or any commission held or authority exercised under, the United States."

The requirement that the state court's decision be "final" has been carried forward from the Judiciary Act of 1789. The Court's current flexible definition of that requirement is discussed in Cox Broadcasting Corp. v. Cohn, 420 U.S. 469, 476–487 (1975). The requirement that the decision be of the highest state court "in which a decision could be had" also stems from the 1789 Judiciary Act. This provision can permit

3

review of the decision of inferior state courts, if further appeals within the state system are not possible. For example, Thompson v. Louisville, 362 U.S. 199 (1960), reviewed the decision of a police court.

C. THE DISTINCTION BETWEEN OBLIGATORY AND DISCRETIONARY JURISDICTION

Pages 56–64. Delete Subsection C, "The Distinction between Obligatory and Discretionary Jurisdiction":

SECTION 2. CONSTITUTIONAL LITIGATION INITIATED IN THE FEDERAL COURTS

A. JURISDICTION OF FEDERAL COURTS IN CASES INVOLVING FEDERAL LAW ISSUES

Pages 65–66. Replace sentence running from page 65 to page 66, and footnote 3:

Decisions of the courts of appeals are reviewable in the Supreme Court by certiorari.[3]　28 U.S.C. § 1254.

B. ENFORCEMENT OF FEDERAL RIGHTS IN SUITS AGAINST STATE OFFICERS: THE ELEVENTH AMENDMENT

Page 76. Add to end of footnote 2:

Papasan v. Allain, 478 U.S. 265 (1986) illustrates the difficulty of distinguishing between prospective relief for a continuing wrong, permitted by the doctrine of Ex Parte Young, and retroactive relief for a past wrong, prohibited by Edelman v. Jordan. Plaintiffs challenged the pattern of Mississippi school financing on two theories: (1) that the state had failed to meet its trust obligation to hold federal land grants in trust for education; (2) that the disparity in allocation to school districts violated the equal protection clause. The Court held that the first claim was barred by the eleventh amendment because plaintiffs sought to remedy the "past" loss of the trust corpus, but that the second claim was permissible because plaintiffs sought to remedy a "continuing violation" of the Constitution.

Page 76. Add to end of next to last paragraph of note:

Parden was overruled in Welch v. State Department of Highways and Public Transportation, 107 S.Ct. 2941 (1987). Neither the Jones Act (establishing damage actions for injured seamen) nor the Federal Employers Liability Act contain an express Congressional statement permitting suit against states who own vessels or railroads. Accordingly, the eleventh amendment barred suit by an injured railroad worker or seaman.

[3] Prior to 1988, decisions of courts of appeals holding state statutes unconstitutional, and decisions of lower federal courts holding federal statutes unconstitutional in proceedings where the United States was a party, were reviewable by appeal.

Page 76. Replace last paragraph of note:

In Atascadero State Hospital v. Scanlon, 473 U.S. 234 (1985), the Court concluded that the Rehabilitation Act of 1973, which provides remedies against "any recipient of Federal assistance," contained only a general authorization of federal court suits and did not abrogate eleventh amendment sovereign immunity. Justice Brennan, in a lengthy dissent, reiterated his position that the eleventh amendment does not establish sovereign immunity. For the first time, that position gained the endorsement of three other Justices (Marshall, Blackmun, and Stevens), who joined his dissent.

The majority in *Scanlon* stated, as had previous opinions of the Court, that the eleventh amendment creates a constitutional rule of sovereign immunity. The basis of the decision, however, was that Congress had not "unequivocally" expressed its intention to abrogate eleventh amendment immunity. When that intention has been "unequivocally" expressed, are there limits to Congress' power to remove the Eleventh Amendment's bar to suits against unconsenting states? The following case deals with that question.

Page 78. Add ahead of last sentence in note:

While it partially overruled *Parden,* in Welch v. State Department of Highways and Public Transportation, 107 S.Ct. 2941 (1987), the Court "assume[d], without deciding or intimating a view of the question, that the authority of Congress to subject unconsenting States to suit in federal court is not confined to section 5 of the Fourteenth Amendment." A footnote to Justice Powell's plurality opinion in *Welch* said, concerning this question:

> "The argument for such an authority starts from the proposition that the Constitution authorizes Congress to regulate matters within the admiralty and maritime jurisdiction, either under the Commerce Clause or the Necessary and Proper Clause. . . . By ratifying the Constitution, the argument runs, the States necessarily consented to suit in federal court with respect to enactments under either Clause."

C. NON–CONSTITUTIONAL RESTRICTIONS ON FEDERAL COURT INJUNCTIONS

Page 83. Replace last paragraph of note and Trainor v. Hernandez with the following:

The Court has been divided on the question of the application of *Younger* rules to state enforcement of its laws through civil and administrative proceedings. The issue is whether many of the restraints previously imposed by the doctrine of exhaustion of administrative remedies, and the Anti-Injunction Act, will be reintroduced by *Younger* and "Our Federalism."

PENNZOIL CO. v. TEXACO, INC.

—— U.S. ——, 107 S.Ct. 1519, 95 L.Ed.2d 1 (1987).

Justice Powell delivered the opinion of the Court.

The principal issue in this case is whether a federal district court lawfully may enjoin a plaintiff who has prevailed in a trial in state court from executing the judgment in its favor pending appeal of that judgment to a state appellate court.

I

Getty Oil Co. and appellant Pennzoil Co. negotiated an agreement under which Pennzoil was to purchase about three-sevenths of Getty's outstanding shares for $110 a share. Appellee Texaco, Inc. eventually purchased the shares for $128 a share. On February 8, 1984, Pennzoil filed a complaint against Texaco in the Harris County District Court, a state court located in Houston, Texas, the site of Pennzoil's corporate headquarters. The complaint alleged that Texaco tortiously had induced Getty to breach a contract to sell its shares to Pennzoil; Pennzoil sought actual damages of $7.53 billion and punitive damages in the same amount. On November 19, 1985, a jury returned a verdict in favor of Pennzoil, finding actual damages of $7.53 billion and punitive damages of $3 billion. The parties anticipated that the judgment, including prejudgment interest, would exceed $11 billion.

. . . By recording an abstract of a judgment in the real property records of any of the 254 counties in Texas, a judgment creditor can secure a lien on all of a judgment debtor's real property located in that county. . . . If a judgment creditor wishes to have the judgment enforced by state officials so that it can take possession of any of the debtor's assets, it may secure a writ of execution from the clerk of the court that issued the judgment. . . . But the judgment debtor "may suspend the execution of the judgment by filing a . . . bond for at least the amount of the judgment, interest, and costs." . . .

. . .

. . . The amount of the bond required . . . would have been more than $13 billion. It is clear that Texaco would not have been able to post such a bond. Accordingly, "the business and financial community concluded that Pennzoil would be able, under the lien and bond provisions of Texas law, to commence enforcement of any judgment entered on the verdict before Texaco's appeals had been resolved."

. . .

Texaco did not argue to the trial court that the judgment, or execution of the judgment, conflicted with federal law. Rather, . . . Texaco filed this action in the United States District Court for the Southern District of New York in White Plains, New York, the site of Texaco's corporate headquarters. Texaco alleged that the Texas proceedings violated rights secured to Texaco by the Constitution and various federal statutes. . . .

. . .

. . . [T]he court issued a preliminary injunction.

On appeal, the Court of Appeals for the Second Circuit affirmed. . . .

     . . .

. . . We reverse.

II

The courts below should have abstained under the principles of federalism enunciated in Younger v. Harris, 401 U.S. 37 (1971). Both the District Court and the Court of Appeals failed to recognize the significant interests harmed by their unprecedented intrusion into the Texas judicial system. . . .

A

The first ground for the *Younger* decision was "the basic doctrine of equity jurisprudence that courts of equity should not act, and particularly should not act to restrain a criminal prosecution, when the moving party has an adequate remedy at law." Id., at 43. The Court also offered a second explanation for its decision:

> "This underlying reason . . . is reinforced by an even more vital consideration, the notion of 'comity,' that is, a proper respect for state functions, a recognition of the fact that the entire country is made up of a Union of separate state governments, and a continuance of the belief that the National Government will fare best if the States and their institutions are left free to perform their separate functions in their separate ways. . . . The concept does not mean blind deference to 'States' Rights' any more than it means centralization of control over every important issue in our National Government and its courts. The Framers rejected both these courses. What the concept does represent is a system in which there is sensitivity to the legitimate interests of both State and National Governments, and in which the National Government, anxious though it may be to vindicate and protect federal rights and federal interests, always endeavors to do so in ways that will not unduly interfere with the legitimate activities of the States." Id., at 44.

This concern mandates application of *Younger* abstention not only when the pending state proceedings are criminal, but also when certain civil proceedings are pending, if the State's interests in the proceeding are so important that exercise of the federal judicial power would disregard the comity between the States and the National Government. E.g., Huffman v. Pursue, Ltd., 420 U.S. 592, 603–605 (1975).

Another important reason for abstention is to avoid unwarranted determination of federal constitutional questions. When federal courts interpret state statutes in a way that raises federal constitutional questions, "a constitutional determination is predicated on a reading of the statute that is not binding on state courts and may be discredited at any time—thus essentially rendering the federal-court decision advisory and the litigation underlying it meaningless." Moore v. Sims, 442 U.S. 415, 428 (1979). See Trainor v. Hernandez, 431 U.S. 434, 445 (1977).[9] This concern has special significance in this case. Because Texaco chose not to present to the Texas courts the constitutional claims asserted in this case, it is impossible to be certain that the governing Texas statutes and procedural rules actually raise these claims. Moreover, the Texas Constitution contains an "open courts" provision . . . that appears to address Texaco's claims more specifically than the Due Process Clause of the Fourteenth Amendment. Thus, when this case was filed in Federal Court, it was entirely possible that the Texas courts would have resolved this case on state statutory or constitutional grounds, without reaching the federal constitutional questions Texaco raises in this case. As we have noted, *Younger* abstention in situations like this "offers the opportunity for narrowing constructions that might obviate the constitutional problem and intelligently mediate federal constitutional concerns and state interests." Moore v. Sims, supra, at 429–430.

Texaco's principal argument against *Younger* abstention is that exercise of the District Court's power did not implicate a "vital" or "important" state interest. This argument reflects a misreading of our precedents. This Court repeatedly has recognized that the States have important interests in administering certain aspects of their judicial systems. E.g., Trainor v. Hernandez, supra, at 441; Middlesex County Ethics Comm. v. Garden State Bar Assn., 457 U.S. 423, 432 (1982). In Juidice v. Vail, 430 U.S. 327 (1977), we held that a federal court should have abstained from adjudicating a challenge to a State's contempt process. The Court's reasoning in that case informs our decision today:

> "A State's interest in the contempt process, through which it vindicates the regular operation of its judicial system, so long as that system itself affords the opportunity to pursue federal claims within it, is surely an important interest. Perhaps it is not quite as important as is the State's interest in the enforcement of its criminal laws, *Younger,* supra, or even its interest in the maintenance of a quasi-criminal proceeding such as was involved in *Huffman,* supra. But we think it is of sufficiently great import to require application of the principles of those cases." Id., at 335.

Our comments on why the contempt power was sufficiently important to justify abstention also are illuminating: "Contempt in these cases, serves, of course, to vindicate and preserve the private interests

---

[9] In some cases, the probability that any federal adjudication would be effectively advisory is so great that this concern alone is sufficient to justify abstention, even if there are no pending state proceedings in which the question could be raised. See Railroad Comm'n of Texas v. Pullman Co., 312 U.S. 496 (1941). Because appellant has not argued in this Court that *Pullman* abstention is proper, we decline to address Justice Blackmun's conclusion that *Pullman* abstention is the appropriate disposition of this case. We merely note that considerations similar to those that mandate *Pullman* abstention are relevant to a court's decision whether to abstain under *Younger.* Cf. Moore v. Sims, 442 U.S. 415, 428 (1979). The various types of abstention are not rigid pigeonholes into which federal courts must try to fit cases. Rather, they reflect a complex of considerations designed to soften the tensions inherent in a system that contemplates parallel judicial processes.

of competing litigants, . . . but its purpose is by no means spent upon purely private concerns. It stands in aid of the authority of the judicial system, so that its orders and judgments are not rendered nugatory." Id., at 336, n. 12 (citations omitted).

The reasoning of *Juidice* controls here. That case rests on the importance to the States of enforcing the orders and judgments of their courts. There is little difference between the State's interest in forcing persons to transfer property in response to a court's judgment and in forcing persons to respond to the court's process on pain of contempt. Both *Juidice* and this case involve challenges to the processes by which the State compels compliance with the judgments of its courts.[12] Not only would federal injunctions in such cases interfere with the execution of state judgments, but they would do so on grounds that challenge the very process by which those judgments were obtained. So long as those challenges relate to pending state proceedings, proper respect for the ability of state courts to resolve federal questions presented in state court litigation mandates that the federal court stay its hand.[13]

B

Texaco also argues that *Younger* abstention was inappropriate because no Texas court could have heard Texaco's constitutional claims within the limited time available to Texaco. But the burden on this point rests on the federal plaintiff to show "that state procedural law barred presentation of its claims." Moore v. Sims, 442 U.S., at 432. See Younger v. Harris, 401 U.S., at 45 (" 'The accused should first set up and rely upon his defense in the state courts, even though this involves a challenge of the validity of some statute, unless it plainly appears that this course would not afford adequate protection' ") (quoting Fenner v. Boykin, 271 U.S. 240, 244 (1926)).

Moreover, denigrations of the procedural protections afforded by Texas law hardly come from Texaco with good grace, as it apparently made no effort under Texas law to secure the relief sought in this case of Middlesex County Ethics Comm. v. Garden State Bar Assn., supra, at 435 (rejecting on similar grounds an assertion about the inhospitability of state procedures to federal claims). Article VI of the United States Constitution declares that "the Judges in every State shall be bound" by the Federal Constitution, laws, and treaties. We cannot assume that state judges will interpret ambiguities in state procedural law to bar presentation of federal claims. Cf. Ohio Civil Rights Comm'n v.

---

[12] Thus, contrary to Justice Stevens' suggestion, the State of Texas has an interest in this proceeding "that goes beyond its interest as adjudicator of wholly private disputes." Our opinion does not hold that *Younger* abstention is always appropriate whenever a civil proceeding is pending in a state court. Rather, as in *Juidice*, we rely on the State's interest in protecting "the authority of the judicial system, so that its orders and judgments are not rendered nugatory," 430 U.S., at 336, n. 12 (citations omitted).

[13] Texaco also suggests that abstention is unwarranted because of the absence of a state judicial proceeding with respect to which the Federal District Court should have abstained. Texaco argues that "the Texas judiciary plays no role" in execution of judgments. We reject this assertion. There is at least one pending judicial proceeding in the state courts; the lawsuit out of which Texaco's constitutional claims arose is now pending before a Texas Court of Appeals in Houston, Texas. . . .

Dayton Christian Schools, Inc., 477 U.S. ___, ___ (1986) (assuming that a state administrative commission would construe its own statutory mandate "in the light of federal constitutional principles"). Accordingly, when a litigant has not attempted to present his federal claims in related state court proceedings, a federal court should assume that state procedures will afford an adequate remedy, in the absence of unambiguous authority to the contrary.

The "open courts" provision of the Texas Constitution . . . has considerable relevance here. This provision has appeared in each of Texas' six constitutions, dating back to the Constitution of the Republic of Texas in 1836. . . . According to the Texas Supreme Court, the provision "guarantees all litigants . . . the right to their day in court." . . . "The common thread of the Texas Supreme Court's decisions construing the open courts provision is that the legislature has no power to make a remedy by due course of law contingent on an impossible condition." Nelson v. Krusen, 678 S.W.2d 918, 921 (Tex. 1984). In light of this demonstrable and longstanding commitment of the Texas Supreme Court to provide access to the state courts, we are reluctant to conclude that Texas courts would have construed state procedural rules to deny Texaco an effective opportunity to raise its constitutional claims.

Against this background, Texaco's submission that the Texas courts were incapable of hearing its constitutional claims is plainly insufficient. . . . Texaco has failed to meet its burden on this point.

In sum, the lower courts should have deferred on principles of comity to the pending state proceedings. They erred in accepting Texaco's assertions as to the inadequacies of Texas procedure to provide effective relief. It is true that this case presents an unusual fact situation, never before addressed by the Texas courts, and that Texaco urgently desired prompt relief. But we cannot say that those courts, when this suit was filed, would have been any less inclined than a federal court to address and decide the federal constitutional claims. Because Texaco apparently did not give the Texas courts an opportunity to adjudicate its constitutional claims, and because Texaco cannot demonstrate that the Texas courts were not then open to adjudicate its claims, there is no basis for concluding that the Texas law and procedures were so deficient that *Younger* abstention is inappropriate. Accordingly, we conclude that the District Court should have abstained.

III

. . . We are not unmindful of the unique importance to Texaco of having its challenges to that judgment authoritatively considered and resolved. We of course express no opinion on the merits of those challenges. Similarly, we express no opinion on the claims Texaco has raised in this case against the Texas bond and lien provisions, nor on the possibility that Texaco now could raise these claims in the Texas courts. Today we decide only that it was inappropriate for the District Court to entertain these claims. If, and when, the Texas courts render a final decision on any federal issue presented by this litigation, review may be sought in this Court in the customary manner.

IV

The judgment of the Court of Appeals is reversed. The case is remanded to the District Court with instructions to vacate its order and dismiss the complaint. The judgment of this Court shall issue forthwith.

It is so ordered.

Justice Scalia, with whom Justice O'Connor joins, concurring.

I join the opinion of the Court. I write separately only to indicate that I do not believe that the so-called *Rooker-Feldman* doctrine deprives the Court of jurisdiction to decide Texaco's challenge to the constitutionality of the Texas stay and lien provisions. In resolving that challenge, the Court need not decide any issue either actually litigated in the Texas courts or inextricably intertwined with issues so litigated. Under these circumstances, I see no jurisdictional bar to the Court's decision in this case.

Justice Brennan, with whom Justice Marshall joins, concurring in the judgment.

Texaco's claim that the Texas bond and lien provisions violate the Fourteenth Amendment is without merit. While Texaco cannot, consistent with due process and equal protection, be arbitrarily denied the right to a meaningful opportunity to be heard on appeal, this right can be adequately vindicated even if Texaco were forced to file for bankruptcy.

I believe that the Court should have confronted the merits of this case. I wholeheartedly concur with Justice Stevens' conclusion that a creditor's invocation of a State's postjudgment collection procedures constitutes action under color of state law within the meaning of 42 U.S.C. section 1983.

I also agree with his conclusion that the District Court was not required to abstain under the principles enunciated in Younger v. Harris, 401 U.S. 37 (1971). I adhere to my view that *Younger* is, in general, inapplicable to civil proceedings, especially when a plaintiff brings a section 1983 action alleging violation of federal constitutional rights. See Huffman v. Pursue, Ltd., 420 U.S. 592, 613 (1975) (Brennan, J., dissenting) (*Younger* held "that federal courts should not interfere with pending state *criminal* proceedings, except under extraordinary circumstances") (emphasis in original)); Juidice v. Vail, 430 U.S. 327, 342 (1977) (Brennan, J., dissenting) ("In congressional contemplation, the pendency of state civil proceedings was to be wholly irrelevant. The very purpose of section 1983 was to interpose the federal courts between the States and the people, as guardians of the people's federal rights'") (quoting Mitchum v. Foster, 407 U.S. 225, 242 (1972)).

The State's interest in this case is negligible. The State of Texas— not a party in this appeal—expressly represented to the Court of Appeals that it "has no interest in the underlying action," except in its fair adjudication. The court identifies the State's interest as enforcing "the authority of the judicial system, so that its orders and judgments are not rendered nugatory." Yet, the District Court found that "Pennzoil publicly admitted that Texaco's assets are sufficient to satisfy the judgment even without liens or a bond." . . .

Indeed, the interest in enforcing the bond and lien requirement is privately held by Pennzoil, not by the State of Texas. . . . Pennzoil was free to waive the bond and lien requirements under Texas law, without asking the State of Texas for permission. . . . The State's decision to grant private parties unilateral power to invoke, or not invoke, the State's bond and lien provisions demonstrates that the State has no independent interest in the enforcement of those provisions.

Texaco filed this section 1983 suit claiming only violations of *federal* statutory and constitutional law. In enacting section 1983, Congress "created a specific and unique remedy, enforceable in a federal court of equity, that could be frustrated if the federal court were not empowered to enjoin a state court proceeding." Mitchum v. Foster, supra, at 237. Today the Court holds that this section 1983 suit should be filed instead in Texas courts, offering to Texaco the unsolicited advice to bring its claims under the "open courts" provision of the Texas Constitution. This "blind deference to 'States' Rights' " hardly shows "sensitivity to the legitimate interests of *both* State *and National* Governments".*

Furthermore, I reject Pennzoil's contention that District of Columbia Court of Appeals v. Feldman, 460 U.S. 462 (1983), and Rooker v. Fidelity Trust Co., 263 U.S. 413 (1923), forbid collateral review in this instance. In *Rooker* and *Feldman,* the Court held that lower federal courts lack jurisdiction to engage in appellate review of state court determinations. In this case, however, Texaco filed the section 1983 action only to protect its federal constitutional right to a meaningful opportunity for appellate review, not to challenge the merits of the Texas suit. Texaco's federal action seeking a stay of judgment pending appeal is therefore an action " 'separable from and collateral to' " the merits of the state court judgment. Nationalist Socialist Party v. Skokie, 432 U.S. 43, 44 (1977) (quoting Cohen v. Beneficial Loan Corp., 337 U.S. 541, 546 (1949)).

* Although the Court's opinion is based on a rather diffuse rationale, I read the opinion as narrowly limited by the unique factual circumstances of the case. The Court is responding to "an unusual fact situation, never before addressed by the Texas courts," or by this Court. The Court bases is holding on several dependent considerations. First, the court acknowledges that today's extension of the *Younger* doctrine applies only "when certain civil proceedings are pending, if the State's interest in the proceeding are so important that exercise of the federal judicial power would disregard the comity between the States and the National Government." Second, the Court emphasizes that in this instance "it is impossible to be certain that the governing Texas statutes and procedural rules actually raise Texaco's claims," and that the Texas Constitution contains an "open courts" provision "that appears to address Texaco's claims more specifically" than the Federal Constitution. Third, the Court heavily relies on the State's particular interest in enforcing bond and lien requirements to prevent state court judgments, which have been already pronounced, from being rendered "nugatory." The unique and extraordinary circumstances of this case should limit its influence in determining the outer limits of the *Younger* doctrine.

While I agree with Justice Stevens that Texaco's claim is "plainly without merit," my reasons for so concluding are different. . . .

. . .

Given the particular facts of this case, I would reverse the judgment of the Court of Appeals, and remand the case with instructions to dismiss the complaint.

Justice Marshall, concurring in the judgment.

. . . Were I to reach the merits I would reverse for the reasons stated in the concurring opinions of Justices Brennan and Stevens, in which I join. But I can find no basis for the District Court's unwarranted assumption of jurisdiction over the subject matter of this lawsuit, and upon that ground alone I would reverse the decision below.

. . .

. . . It is a well-settled principle that federal appellate review of judgments rendered by state courts can only occur in this Court, on appeal or by writ of certiorari. See District of Columbia Court of Appeals v. Feldman, 460 U.S. 462, 482 (1983); Rooker v. Fidelity Trust Co., 263 U.S. 413, 416 (1923); see also Atlantic Coast Line R. Co. v. Locomotive Engineers, 398 U.S. 281, 296 (1970). . . . It is said, however, that this principle applies only to review of the substance of state judgments, and that the federal action now before us involved solely a constitutional challenge to procedures for enforcement of the state judgment, totally apart from the merits of the state-court action itself. In the circumstances of the present case I find this asserted distinction completely unconvincing.

As we have said, "if the constitutional claims presented to a United States district court are inextricably intertwined" with the merits of a judgment rendered in state court, "then the district court is in essence being called upon to review the state-court decision. This the district court may not do." District of Columbia Court of Appeals v. Feldman, supra, at 483–484, n. 16. While the question whether a federal constitutional challenge is inextricably intertwined with the merits of a state-court judgment may sometimes be difficult to answer, it is apparent, as a first step, that the federal claim is inextricably intertwined with the state-court judgment if the federal claim succeeds only to the extent that the state court wrongly decided the issues before it. . . .

. . .

. . . [T]he courts below, by asking whether Texaco was frivolous in asserting that the trial court erred or whether Texaco should have prevailed in the Texas trial court, undertook a review of the merits of judgments rendered by a state court. As the Court of Appeals recognized, the issuance of an injunction depended upon the finding that Texaco had significant claims to asset in its state-court appeal. Because determination of Texaco's claim for an injunction *necessarily* involved some review of the merits of its state appeal, Texaco's constitutional claims were inextricably intertwined with the merits of the Texas judgment, and thus the District Court lacked jurisdiction over Texaco's complaint in the first instance.

. . .

Justice Blackmun, concurring in the judgment.

. . .

I conclude . . . that this case presents an example of the "narrowly limited 'special circumstances,' " Zwickler v. Koota, 389 U.S. 241, 248 (1967), quoting Propper v. Clark, 337 U.S. 472, 492 (1949), where the District Court should have abstained under the principles announced in Railroad Comm'n of Texas v. Pullman Co., 312 U.S. 496 (1941). . . . If the extensive briefing by the parties on the numerous Texas statutes and constitutional provisions at issue here suggests anything, it is that on the unique facts of *this* case "unsettled questions of state law must be resolved before a substantial federal constitutional question can be decided," Hawaii Housing Authority v. Midkiff, 467 U.S. 229, 236 (1984), because "the state courts may interpret the challenged state statutes so as to eliminate, or at least to alter materially, the constitutional question presented." Ohio Bureau of Employment Services v. Hodory, 431 U.S. 471, 477 (1977). The possibility of such a state law resolution of this dispute seems to me still to exist.

Justice Stevens, with whom Justice Marshall joins, concurring in the judgment.

In my opinion Texaco's claim that the Texas judgment lien and supersedeas bond provisions violate the Fourteenth Amendment is plainly without merit. The injunction against enforcement of those provisions must therefore be dissolved. I rest my analysis on this ground because I cannot agree with the grounds upon which the Court disposes of the case. In my view the District Court and the Court of Appeals were correct to hold that a creditor's invocation of a State's post-judgment collection procedures constitutes action "under color of" state law within the meaning of 42 U.S.C. section 1983,[1] and that there is no basis for abstention in this case.[2]

. . .

[1] See Lugar v. Edmondson Oil Co., 457 U.S. 922 (1982), and cases cited at 932–933. In *Lugar,* the Court explained that "a private party's joint participation with state officials in the seizure of disputed property is sufficient to characterize that party as a 'state actor' for purposes of the Fourteenth Amendment." Id., at 941. We reached this conclusion based on the rule that a person "may fairly be said to be a state actor . . . because he is a state official, because he acted together with or has obtained significant aid from state officials, or because his conduct is otherwise chargeable to the State." Id., at 937. This reasoning allows no distinction between a litigant's prejudgment and postjudgment involvement.

[2] As the Court of Appeals explained: "The state interests at stake in this proceeding differ in both kind and in degree" from the cases in which the Court has held *Younger* abstention appropriate. As Justice Brennan's analysis points out, the issue of whether "proceedings implicate important state interests" is quite distinct from the question of whether there is an ongoing proceeding. See Middlesex Ethics Comm. v. Garden State Bar Assn., 457 U.S. 423, 432 (1982). Although we have often wrestled with deciding whether a particular exercise of state enforcement power implicates an "important state interest," see Younger v. Harris, 401 U.S. 37 (1971) (criminal statute); Huffman v. Pursue, Ltd., 420 U.S. 592 (1975) (obscenity regulation); Juidice v. Vail, 430 U.S. 327 (1977) (contempt proceedings); Trainor v. Hernandez, 431 U.S. 434 (1977) (welfare fraud action); Moore v. Sims, 442 U.S. 415 (1979) (child abuse regulation); Middlesex Ethics Comm., supra, (bar disciplinary proceedings); Ohio Civil Rights Comm. v. Dayton Chris-

SECTION 3.   CASES AND CONTROVERSIES AND JUSTICIABILITY

B.   STANDING

---

3.   Taxpayer and Citizen Standing

Page 115.   Add at end of subsection:

BOWEN v. KENDRICK, 108 S.Ct. ___ (1987).   The Court held that taxpayers had standing to challenge a federal grant program, both on its face and as applied, on the ground that it violated the establishment clause.   (For the Court's discussion of the merits, see infra page ___.) On the standing issue, Chief Justice Rehnquist's opinion said:

". . . In Flast v. Cohen, 392 U.S. 83 (1968), we held that federal taxpayers have standing to raise Establishment Clause claims against exercises of congressional power under the taxing and spending power of Art. I, section 8, of the Constitution.   Although we have considered the problem of standing and Article III limitations on federal jurisdiction many times since then, we have consistently adhered to *Flast* and the narrow exception it created to the general rule against taxpayer standing established in Frothingham v. Mellon, 262 U.S. 447 (1923).   Accordingly, in this case there is no dispute that appellees have standing to raise their challenge to the AFLA on its face.   What is disputed, however, is whether appellees also have standing to challenge the statute as applied.   The answer to this question turns on our decision in Valley Forge Christian College v. American United for Separation of Church and State, Inc., 454 U.S. 464 (1982).   . . . Appellants . . . contend that . . . a challenge to the AFLA 'as applied' is really a challenge to executive action, not to an exercise of congressional authority under the Taxing and Spending Clause.   We do not think, however, that appellees' claim that AFLA funds are being used improperly by individual grantees is any less a challenge to congressional taxing and spending power simply because the funding authorized by Congress has flowed through and been administered by the Secretary.   Indeed, *Flast* itself was a suit against the Secretary of HEW, who had been given the authority

tian Schools, Inc., 477 U.S. ___ (1986) (antidiscrimination laws), we have invariably required that the State have a *substantive* interest in the ongoing proceeding, an interest that goes beyond its interest as adjudicator of wholly private disputes.   By abandoning this critical limitation, the Court cuts the *Younger* doctrine adrift from its original doctrinal moorings which dealt with the States' interest in enforcing their criminal laws, and the federal courts' longstanding reluctance to interfere with such proceedings.   See *Huffman,* supra, at 604.

under the challenged statute to administer the spending program that Congress had created. In subsequent cases, . . . we have not questioned the standing of taxpayer plaintiffs to raise Establishment Clause challenges, even when their claims raised questions about the administratively made grants. . . . This is not a case like *Valley Forge,* where the challenge was to an exercise of executive authority pursuant to the Property Clause of Art. IV, section 3, see 454 U.S., at 480, or Schlesinger v. Reservists Committee to Stop the War, 418 U.S. 208, 228 (1974), where the plaintiffs challenged the executive decision to allow Members of Congress to maintain their status as officers of the Armed Forces Reserve. . . . Nor is this, as we stated in *Flast,* a challenge to 'an incidental expenditure of tax funds in the administration of an essentially regulatory statute.' 392 U.S., at 102. The AFLA is at heart a program of disbursement of funds pursuant to Congress' taxing and spending powers, and appellees' claims call into question how the funds authorized by Congress are being disbursed pursuant to the AFLA's statutory mandate. In this case there is thus a sufficient nexus between the taxpayer's standing as a taxpayer and the congressional exercise of taxing and spending power, notwithstanding the role the Secretary plays in administering the statute."

E. POLITICAL QUESTIONS

Page 135. Add after Baker v. Carr:

DAVIS v. BANDEMER, 478 U.S. 109 (1986). The Court concluded that a claim that a "political gerrymander" violated the equal protection clause did not constitute a political question. Justice White's opinion for the Court reasoned that cases adjudicating the constitutionality of racial gerrymanders established that constitutional claims to denial of representation were justiciable. Justice O'Connor, joined by Chief Justice Burger and Justice Rehnquist, dissented on this issue. The dissent argued that the Court did not provide judicially manageable standards for judging the validity of political gerrymanders under the equal protection clause, and that decision under the Court's standards involved non-judicial policy questions. (On the constitutional standards applicable to political gerrymanders, see the report of this case infra at page 272.)

Part II

ALLOCATION OF GOVERNMENTAL POWERS: THE NATION AND THE STATES; THE PRESIDENT, THE CONGRESS, AND THE COURTS

Chapter 4

THE SCOPE OF NATIONAL POWER

SECTION 3. THE SCOPE OF NATIONAL POWER TODAY

A. THE COMMERCE POWER

Page 223. Add ahead of B. The Taxing Power:

RUSSELL v. UNITED STATES

471 U.S. 858, 105 S.Ct. 2455, 85 L.Ed.2d 829 (1985).

Justice Stevens delivered the opinion for the Court.

The question presented is whether 18 U.S.C. § 844(i) applies to a two-unit apartment building that is used as rental property.

Petitioner owns an apartment building located at 4530 South Union, Chicago, Illinois. He earned rental income from it and treated it as business property for tax purposes. In early 1983, he made an unsuccessful attempt to set fire to the building and was consequently indicted for violating § 844(i). Following a bench trial, petitioner was convicted and sentenced to 10 years' imprisonment. The District Court and the Court of Appeals both rejected his contention that the building was not commercial or business property, and therefore was not capable of being the subject of an offense under § 844(i).

Section 844(i) uses broad language to define the offense. It provides:

"Whoever maliciously damages or destroys, or attempts to damage or destroy, by means of fire or an explosive, any building,

17

vehicle, or other real or personal property used in interstate or foreign commerce or in any activity affecting interstate or foreign commerce shall be imprisoned for not more than ten years or fined not more than $10,000, or both . . .."

The reference to "any building . . . used . . . in any activity affecting interstate or foreign commerce" expresses an intent by Congress to exercise its full power under the Commerce Clause.

The legislative history indicates that Congress intended to exercise its full power to protect "business property." Moreover, after considering whether the bill as originally introduced would cover bombings of police stations or churches, the bill was revised to eliminate the words "for business purposes" from the description of covered property. Even after that change, however, the final Report on the bill emphasized the "very broad" coverage of "substantially all business property." In the floor debates on the final bill, although it was recognized that the coverage of the bill was extremely broad, the Committee Chairman, Representative Celler, expressed the opinion that "the mere bombing of a private home even under this bill would not be covered because of the question whether the Congress would have the authority under the Constitution." In sum, the legislative history suggests that Congress at least intended to protect all business property, as well as some additional property that might not fit that description, but perhaps not every private home.

By its terms, however, the statute only applies to property that is "used" in an "activity" that affects commerce. The rental of real estate is unquestionably such an activity. We need not rely on the connection between the market for residential units and "the interstate movement of people," to recognize that the local rental of an apartment unit is merely an element of a much broader commercial market in rental properties. The congressional power to regulate the class of activities that constitute the rental market for real estate includes the power to regulate individual activity within that class.

Petitioner was renting his apartment building to tenants at the time he attempted to destroy it by fire. The property was therefore being used in an activity affecting commerce within the meaning of § 844(i).

The judgment of the Court of Appeals is affirmed.

Chapter 5

THE SCOPE OF STATE POWER—
REGULATION

SECTION 2. IMPLIED RESTRICTIONS OF THE COMMERCE CLAUSE—PRODUCTION AND TRADE

A. RESTRICTING IMPORTATION AND INSULATING IN-STATE BUSINESS FROM OUT–OF–STATE COMPETITION

Page 280. Add ahead of B. Requiring Business Operations to be Performed in the Home State:

BROWN–FORMAN DISTILLERS CORPORATION v. NEW YORK STATE LIQUOR AUTHORITY, 476 U.S. 573 (1986). New York requires every liquor distiller or producer that sells liquor to wholesalers within the State to sell at a price that is no higher than the lowest price the distiller charges wholesalers anywhere in the United States. Distillers must file a price schedule before the 25th day of each month, with the prices effective on the first day of the second following month. All sales to any wholesalers in New York during the month for which the schedule is in effect must be at those prices. Twenty other states have similar affirmation laws.

Brown-Forman Distillers offered promotional allowances to its wholesalers with the amount dependent on the volume of purchases. Other states with price controls like those in New York did not regard the promotional allowances as discounts. New York, however, prohibited such payments.

The Court, in an opinion by Justice Marshall, held that the New York statute violated the commerce clause, stating in part:

"This Court has adopted what amounts to a two-tiered approach to analyzing state economic regulation under the Commerce Clause. When a state statute directly regulates or discriminates against interstate commerce, or when its effect is to favor in-state economic interests over out-of-state interests, we have generally struck down the statute without further inquiry. See, e.g., Philadelphia v. New Jersey, 437 U.S. 617 (1978); . . . When, however, a statute has only indirect effects on interstate commerce and regulates evenhandedly, we have examined whether the State's interest is legitimate and whether the burden on interstate commerce clearly exceeds the local benefits. Pike v. Bruce Church, Inc., 397 U.S. 137, 142 (1970). We have also recognized that there is no clear line separating the category of state regulation that is virtually *per se* invalid under the Commerce Clause, and the category subject to the Pike v. Bruce Church balancing approach. In either situation the critical consideration is the overall effect of the statute on both local and interstate activity. See Raymond Motor Transportation, Inc. v. Rice, 434 U.S. 429, 440–441 (1978).

. . .

"This Court has once before examined the extraterritorial effects of a New York affirmation statute. In Joseph E. Seagram & Sons, Inc. v. Hostetter, 384 U.S. 35 (1966), the Court considered the constitutionality, under the Commerce and Supremacy Clauses, of the predecessor to New York's current affirmation law. That law differed from the present version in that it required the distiller to affirm that its prices during a given month in New York would be no higher than the lowest price at which the item had been sold elsewhere during the *previous* month. The Court recognized in that case, as we have here, that the most important issue was whether the statute regulated out-of-state transactions. Id., at 42–43. It concluded, however, that '[t]he mere fact that [the statute] is geared to appellants' pricing policies in other States is not sufficient to invalidate the statute.' The Court distinguished *Seelig*, supra, by concluding that any effects of New York's ABC Law on a distiller's pricing policies in other States were 'largely matters of conjecture,' ibid.

. . .

"We agree with appellants . . . that a 'prospective' statute such as . . . New York's liquor affirmation statute, regulates out-of-state transactions in violation of the Commerce Clause. Once a distiller has posted prices in New York, it is not free to change its prices elsewhere in the United States during the relevant month. Forcing a merchant to seek regulatory approval in one State before undertaking a transaction in another directly regulates interstate commerce. Edgar v. MITE Corp., 457 U.S., at 642 (plurality opinion); see also Baldwin v. G.A.F. Seelig, Inc., 294 U.S. at 522 (regulation tending to 'mitigate the consequences of competition between the states' constitutes direct regulation). While New York may regulate the sale of liquor within its borders, and may seek low prices for its residents, it may not 'project its legislation into [other States] by regulating the price to be paid' for liquor in those States. Id., at 521.

"That the ABC Law is addressed only to sales of liquor in New York is irrelevant if the 'practical effect' of the law is to control liquor prices in other States. Southern Pacific Co. v. Arizona ex rel. Sullivan, 325 U.S. 761, 775 (1945). We cannot agree with New York that the practical effects of the affirmation law are speculative. It is undisputed that once a distiller's posted price is in effect in New York, it must seek the approval of the New York State Liquor Authority before it may lower its price for the same item in other States . . . ..

"Moreover, the proliferation of state affirmation laws following this Court's decision in *Seagram* has greatly multiplied the likelihood that a seller will be subjected to inconsistent obligations in different States.

The ease with which New York's lowest-price regulation can interfere with a distiller's operations in other States is aptly demonstrated by the controversy that gave rise to this lawsuit. By defining the 'effective price' of liquor differently from other States, New York can effectively force appellant to abandon its promotional allowance program in States in which that program is legal, or force those other States to alter their own regulatory schemes in order to permit appellant to lower its New York prices without violating the affirmation laws of those States. Thus New York has 'project[ed] its legislation' into other States, and directly regulated commerce therein, in violation of *Seelig,* supra.[6]"

Justice Brennan took no part in the consideration or decision of the case. Justice Blackmun signed the majority opinion and filed a concurring opinion. Justices Stevens, White, and Rehnquist dissented.

C. PRESERVING RESOURCES FOR IN–STATE CONSUMPTION

Page 295. Add ahead of D. Preserving State-owned Resources For In-State Use:

MAINE v. TAYLOR

477 U.S. 131, 106 S.Ct. 2440, 91 L.Ed.2d 110 (1986).

Justice Blackmun delivered the opinion of the Court.

Once again, a little fish has caused a commotion. See Hughes v. Oklahoma, 441 U.S. 322 (1979) . . . The fish in this case is the golden shiner, a species of minnow commonly used as live bait in sport fishing.

Appellee Robert J. Taylor operates a bait business in Maine. Despite a Maine statute prohibiting the importation of live baitfish,[1] he arranged to have 158,000 live golden shiners delivered to him from outside the State. The shipment was intercepted, and a federal grand jury in the District of Maine indicted Taylor for violating and conspiring to violate the Lacey Act Amendments of 1981, 95 Stat. 1073, 16 U.S.C. §§ 3371–3378. Section 3(a)(2)(A) of those Amendments, 16 U.S.C. § 3372(a)(2)(A), makes it a federal crime "to import, export, transport, sell, receive, acquire, or purchase in interstate or foreign commerce . . . any fish or wildlife taken, possessed, transported, or sold in violation of any law or regulation of any State or in violation of any foreign law."

Taylor moved to dismiss the indictment on the ground that Maine's import ban unconstitutionally burdens interstate commerce and there-

---

[6] While we hold that New York's prospective price affirmation statute violates the Commerce Clause, we do not necessarily attach constitutional significance to the difference between a prospective statute and the retrospective statute at issue in *Seagram.* Indeed, one could argue that the effects of the statute in *Seagram,* do not differ markedly from the effects of the statute at issue in the present case. If there is a conflict between today's decision and the *Seagram* decision, however, there will be time enough to address that conflict should a case arise involving a retrospective statute. Because no such statute is before us now, we need not consider the continuing validity of *Seagram.*

[1] "A person is guilty of importing live bait if he imports into this State any live fish, including smelts, which are commonly used for bait fishing in inland waters." Me.Rev.Stat.Ann., Tit. 12, § 7613 (1981).

fore may not form the basis for a federal prosecution under the Lacey Act. Maine, pursuant to 28 U.S.C. § 2403(b), intervened to defend the validity of its statute, arguing that the ban legitimately protects the State's fisheries from parasites and non-native species that might be included in shipments of live baitfish. The District Court found the statute constitutional and denied the motion to dismiss. 585 F.Supp. 393 (Me.1984). Taylor then entered a conditional plea of guilty pursuant to Federal Rule of Criminal Procedure 11(a)(2), reserving the right to appeal the District Court's ruling on the constitutional question. The Court of Appeals for the First Circuit reversed, agreeing with Taylor that the underlying state statute impermissibly restricts interstate trade. 752 F.2d 757 (1985). Maine appealed. . . .

. . .

II

. . .

The District Court and the Court of Appeals both reasoned correctly that, since Maine's import ban discriminates on its face against interstate trade, it should be subject to the strict requirements of Hughes v. Oklahoma, notwithstanding Maine's argument that those requirements were waived by the Lacey Act Amendments of 1981. It is well established that Congress may authorize the States to engage in regulation that the Commerce Clause would otherwise forbid. See, e.g., Southern Pacific Co. v. Arizona, 325 U.S. 761, 769 (1945). But because of the important role the Commerce Clause plays in protecting the free flow of interstate trade, this Court has exempted state statutes from the implied limitations of the Clause only when the congressional direction to do so has been "unmistakably clear." South-Central Timber Development, Inc. v. Wunnicke, 467 U.S. 82, 91 (1984). The 1981 amendments of the Lacey Act clearly provide for federal enforcement of valid state and foreign wildlife laws, but Maine identifies nothing in the text or legislative history of the amendments that suggests Congress wished to validate state laws that would be unconstitutional without federal approval.

. . .

. . . Maine's ban on the importation of live baitfish thus is constitutional only if it satisfies the requirements ordinarily applied under Hughes v. Oklahoma to local regulation that discriminates against interstate trade: the statute must serve a legitimate local purpose, and the purpose must be one that cannot be served as well by available nondiscriminatory means.

III

The District Court found after an evidentiary hearing that both parts of the *Hughes* test were satisfied, but the Court of Appeals disagreed. We conclude that the Court of Appeals erred in setting aside the findings of the District Court. To explain why, we need to discuss the proceedings below in some detail.

A

The evidentiary hearing on which the District Court based its conclusions was one before a magistrate. Three scientific experts testified for the prosecution and one for the defense. The prosecution experts testified that live baitfish imported into the State posed two significant threats to Maine's unique and fragile fisheries. First, Maine's population of wild fish—including its own indigenous golden shiners—would be placed at risk by three types of parasites prevalent in out-of-state baitfish, but not common to wild fish in Maine. Second, non-native species inadvertently included in shipments of live baitfish could disturb Maine's aquatic ecology to an unpredictable extent by competing with native fish for food or habitat, by preying on native species, or by disrupting the environment in more subtle ways.

The prosecution experts further testified that there was no satisfactory way to inspect shipments of live baitfish for parasites or commingled species. According to their testimony, the small size of baitfish and the large quantities in which they are shipped made inspection for commingled species "a physical impossibility." Parasite inspection posed a separate set of difficulties because the examination procedure required destruction of the fish. Although statistical sampling and inspection techniques had been developed for salmonids (i.e., salmon and trout), so that a shipment could be certified parasite-free based on a standardized examination of only some of the fish, no scientifically accepted procedures of this sort were available for baitfish.

Appellee's expert denied that any scientific justification supported Maine's total ban on the importation of baitfish. He testified that none of the three parasites discussed by the prosecution witnesses posed any significant threat to fish in the wild, and that sampling techniques had not been developed for baitfish precisely because there was no need for them. He further testified that professional baitfish farmers raise their fish in ponds that have been freshly drained to ensure that no other species is inadvertently collected.

Weighing all the testimony, the magistrate concluded that both prongs of the *Hughes* test were satisfied, and accordingly that appellee's motion to dismiss the indictment should be denied. Appellee filed objections, but the District Court, after an independent review of the evidence, reached the same conclusions. First, the court found that Maine "clearly has a legitimate and substantial purpose in prohibiting the importation of live bait fish," because "substantial uncertainties" surrounded the effects that baitfish parasites would have on the State's unique population of wild fish, and the consequences of introducing non-native species were similarly unpredictable. 585 F.Supp., at 397. Second, the court concluded that less discriminatory means of protecting against these threats were currently unavailable, and that, in particular, testing procedures for baitfish parasites had not yet been devised. Id., at 398. Even if procedures of this sort could be effective, the court found that their development probably would take a considerable amount of time. Id., at 398, n. 11.

Although the Court of Appeals did not expressly set aside the District Court's finding of a legitimate local purpose, it noted that several factors "cast doubt" on that finding. 752 F.2d, at 762. First, Maine was apparently the only State to bar all importation of live baitfish. See, id., at 761. Second, Maine accepted interstate shipments of other freshwater fish, subject to an inspection requirement. Third, "an aura of economic protectionism" surrounded statements made in 1981 by the Maine Department of Inland Fisheries and Wildlife in opposition to a proposal by appellee himself to repeal the ban. Ibid. Finally, the court noted that parasites and non-native species could be transported into Maine in shipments of non-baitfish, and that nothing prevented fish from simply swimming into the State from New Hampshire. Id., at 762, n. 12.

Despite these indications of protectionist intent, the Court of Appeals rested its invalidation of Maine's import ban on a different basis, concluding that Maine had not demonstrated that any legitimate local purpose served by the ban could not be promoted equally well without discriminating so heavily against interstate commerce. Specifically, the court found it "difficult to reconcile" Maine's claim that it could not rely on sampling and inspection with the State's reliance on similar procedures in the case of other freshwater fish. Id., at 762.

Following the reversal of appellee's conviction, Maine and the United States petitioned for rehearing on the ground that the Court of Appeals had improperly disregarded the District Court's findings of fact. The court denied the petitions, concluding that, since the unavailability of a less discriminatory alternative "was a mixed finding of law and fact," a reviewing court "was free to examine carefully the factual record and to draw its own conclusions." Id., at 765.

B

Although the proffered justification for any local discrimination against interstate commerce must be subjected to "the strictest scrutiny," Hughes v. Oklahoma, 441 U.S., at 337, the empirical component of that scrutiny, like any other form of factfinding, " 'is the basic responsibility of district courts, rather than appellate courts,' " Pullman-Standard v. Swint, 456 U.S. 273, 291 (1982), quoting DeMarco v. United States, 415 U.S. 449, 450, n. (1974). As this Court frequently has emphasized, appellate courts are not to decide factual questions *de novo*, reversing any findings they would have made differently. . . . We note, . . . that no broader review is authorized here simply because this is a constitutional case, or because the factual findings at issue may determine the outcome of the case. . . .

No matter how one describes the abstract issue whether "alternative means could promote this local purpose as well without discriminating against interstate commerce," Hughes v. Oklahoma, 441 U.S., at 336, the more specific question whether scientifically accepted techniques exist for the sampling and inspection of live baitfish is one of fact, and the District Court's finding that such techniques have not been devised cannot be characterized as clearly erroneous. Indeed, the record probably could not support a contrary finding. Two prosecution witnesses testified to the lack of such procedures, and appellee's expert conceded the point, although he disagreed about the need for such tests. . . .

. . .

More importantly, we agree with the District Court that the "abstract possibility," of developing acceptable testing procedures, particularly when there is no assurance as to their effectiveness, does not make those procedures an "[a]vailable . . . nondiscriminatory alternativ[e]," *Hunt,* 432 U.S., at 353, for purposes of the Commerce Clause. A State must make reasonable efforts to avoid restraining the free flow of commerce across its borders, but it is not required to develop new and unproven means of protection at an uncertain cost. Appellee, of course, is free to work on his own or in conjunction with other bait dealers to develop scientifically acceptable sampling and inspection procedures for golden shiners; if and when such procedures are developed, Maine no longer may be able to justify its import ban. The State need not join in those efforts, however, and it need not pretend they already have succeeded.

C

Although the Court of Appeals did not expressly overturn the District Court's finding that Maine's import ban serves a legitimate local purpose, appellee argues as an alternative ground for affirmance that this finding should be rejected. After reviewing the expert testimony presented to the magistrate, however, we cannot say that the District Court clearly erred in finding that substantial scientific uncertainty surrounds the effect that baitfish parasites and non-native species could have on Maine's fisheries. Moreover, we agree with the District Court that Maine has a legitimate interest in guarding against imperfectly understood environmental risks, despite the possibility that they may ultimately prove to be negligible. "[T]he constitutional principles underlying the commerce clause cannot be read as requiring the State of Maine to sit idly by and wait until potentially irreversible environmental damage has occurred or until the scientific community agrees on what disease organisms are or are not dangerous before it acts to avoid such consequences." 585 F.Supp., at 397.

Nor do we think that much doubt is cast on the legitimacy of Maine's purposes by what the Court of Appeals took to be signs of protectionist intent. Shielding in-state industries from out-of-state competition is almost never a legitimate local purpose, and state laws that amount to "simple economic protectionism" consequently have been subject to a "virtually *per se* rule of invalidity." Philadelphia v. New Jersey, 437 U.S. 617, 624 (1978); accord, e.g., Minnesota v. Clover Leaf Creamery Co., 449 U.S. 456, 471 (1981).[19] But there is little reason

[19] This rule has been applied not only to laws motivated solely by a desire to protect local industries from out-of-state competition, but also to laws that respond to legitimate local concerns by discriminating arbitrarily against interstate trade, for "the evil of protectionism can reside in legislative means a well as legislative ends." Philadelphia v.

in this case to believe that the legitimate justifications the State has put forward for its statute are merely a sham or a "*post hoc* rationalization." *Hughes,* 441 U.S., at 338, n. 20. In suggesting to the contrary, the Court of Appeals relied heavily on a 3-sentence passage near the end of a 2000-word statement submitted in 1981 by the Maine Department of Inland Fisheries and Wildlife in opposition to appellee's proposed repeal of the State's ban on the importation of live baitfish:

> "[W]e can't help asking why we should spend our money in Arkansas when it is far better spent at home? It is very clear that much more can be done here in Maine to provide our sportsmen with safe, home-grown bait. There is also the possibility that such an industry could develop a lucrative export market in neighboring states."

752 F.2d, at 760, quoting Baitfish Importation: The Position of the Maine Department of Inland Fisheries and Wildlife, App. 294, 309–310. We fully agree with the magistrate that "[t]hese three sentences do not convert the Maine statute into an economic protectionism measure." As the magistrate pointed out, the context of the statements cited by appellee "reveals [they] are advanced not in direct support of the statute, but to counter the argument that inadequate bait supplies in Maine requires acceptance of the environmental risks of imports. Instead, the Department argues, Maine's own bait supplies can be increased." Furthermore, the comments were made by a state administrative agency long after the statute's enactment, and thus constitute weak evidence of legislative intent in any event.

The other evidence of protectionism identified by the Court of Appeals is no more persuasive. The fact that Maine allows importation of salmonids, for which standardized sampling and inspection procedures are available, hardly demonstrates that Maine has no legitimate interest in prohibiting the importation of baitfish, for which such procedures have not yet been devised. Nor is this demonstrated by the fact that other States may not have enacted similar bans, especially given the testimony that Maine's fisheries are unique and unusually fragile. Finally, it is of little relevance that fish can swim directly into Maine from New Hampshire. As the magistrate explained: "The

New Jersey, 437 U.S. 617, 626 (1978). The Court has held, for example, that New Jersey may not conserve the disposal capacity of its landfill sites by banning importation of wastes, see *ibid.,* and that Oklahoma may not fight depletion of its population of natural minnows by prohibiting their commercial exportation, see Hughes v. Oklahoma, 441 U.S. 322 (1979). In each case, out-of-state residents were forced to bear the brunt of the conservation program for no apparent reason other than that they lived and voted in other States. See Philadelphia v. New Jersey, supra, at 629; *Hughes,* supra, at 337–338, and n. 20. Not all intentional barriers to interstate trade are protectionist, however, and the Commerce Clause "is not a guaranty of the right to import into a state whatever one may please, absent a prohibition by Congress, regardless of the effects of the importation upon the local community." Robertson v. California, 328 U.S. 440, 458 (1946). Even overt discrimination against interstate trade may be justified where, as in this case, out-of-state goods or services are particularly likely for some reason to threaten the health and safety of a State's citizens or the integrity of its natural resources, and where "outright prohibition of entry, rather than some intermediate form of regulation, is the only effective method of protecti[on]." Lewis v. BT Investment Managers, Inc., 447 U.S. 27, 43 (1980).

impediments to complete success . . . cannot be a ground for preventing a state from using its best efforts to limit [an environmental] risk."

IV

The Commerce Clause significantly limits the ability of States and localities to regulate or otherwise burden the flow of interstate commerce, but it does not elevate free trade above all other values. As long as a State does not needlessly obstruct interstate trade or attempt to "place itself in a position of economic isolation," Baldwin v. G.A.F. Seelig, Inc., 294 U.S. 511, 527 (1935), it retains broad regulatory authority to protect the health and safety of its citizens and the integrity of its natural resources. The evidence in this case amply supports the District Court's findings that Maine's ban on the importation of live baitfish serves legitimate local purposes that could not adequately be served by available nondiscriminatory alternatives. This is not a case of arbitrary discrimination against interstate commerce; the record suggests that Maine has legitimate reasons, "apart from their origin, to treat [out-of-state baitfish] differently," Philadelphia v. New Jersey, 437 U.S., at 627. The judgment of the Court of Appeals setting aside appellee's conviction is therefore reversed.

It is so ordered.

Justice Stevens, dissenting.

There is something fishy about this case. Maine is the only State in the Union that blatantly discriminates against out-of-state baitfish by flatly prohibiting their importation. Although golden shiners are already present and thriving in Maine (and, perhaps not coincidentally, the subject of a flourishing domestic industry), Maine excludes golden shiners grown and harvested (and, perhaps not coincidentally, sold) in other States. This kind of stark discrimination against out-of-state articles of commerce requires rigorous justification by the discriminating State. "When discrimination against commerce of the type we have found is demonstrated, the burden falls on the State to justify it both in terms of the local benefits flowing from the statute and the unavailability of nondiscriminatory alternatives adequate to preserve the local interests at stake." Hunt v. Washington Apple Advertising Comm'n, 432 U.S. 333, 353 (1977).

Like the District Court, the Court concludes that uncertainty about possible ecological effects from the possible presence of parasites and nonnative species in shipments of out-of-state shiners suffices to carry the State's burden of proving a legitimate public purpose. The Court similarly concludes that the State has no obligation to develop feasible inspection procedures that would make a total ban unnecessary. It seems clear, however, that the presumption should run the other way. Since the State engages in obvious discrimination against out-of-state commerce, it should be put to its proof. Ambiguity about dangers and alternatives should actually defeat, rather than sustain, the discriminatory measure.

This is not to derogate the State's interest in ecological purity. But the invocation of environmental protection or public health has never been thought to confer some kind of special dispensation from the general principle of nondiscrimination in interstate commerce. "A different view, that the ordinance is valid simply because it professes to be a health measure, would mean that the Commerce Clause of itself imposes no restraints on state action other than those laid down by the Due Process Clause, save for the rare instance where a state artlessly discloses an avowed purpose to discriminate against interstate goods." Dean Milk Co. v. Madison, 340 U.S. 349, 354 (1951). If Maine wishes to rely on its interest in ecological preservation, it must show that interest, and the infeasibility of other alternatives, with far greater specificity. Otherwise, it must further that asserted interest in a manner far less offensive to the notions of comity and cooperation that underlie the Commerce Clause.

Significantly, the Court of Appeals, which is more familiar with Maine's natural resources and with its legislation than we are, was concerned by the uniqueness of Maine's ban. That Court felt as I do, that Maine's unquestionable natural splendor notwithstanding, the State has not carried its substantial burden of proving why it cannot meet its environmental concerns in the same manner as other States with the same interest in the health of their fish and ecology. . . .

———

D. PRESERVING STATE–OWNED RESOURCES FOR IN– STATE USE

Page 308. Add ahead of E. Limits on Business Entry:

NEW ENERGY CO. OF INDIANA v. LIMBACH, 108 S.Ct. 1803 (1988). An Ohio taxing statute awarded a tax credit against the Ohio motor vehicle fuel sales tax for each gallon of ethanol sold (as a component of gasohol) by fuel dealers, but only if the ethanol was produced in Ohio or in a state that granted similar tax advantages to ethanol produced in Ohio. New Energy produced ethanol in Indiana, a state which gave a direct subsidy to local ethanol producers but no tax exemption. New Energy challenged the constitutionality of Ohio imposing a tax on the ethanol it sold in Ohio on grounds that the Ohio tax scheme discriminated against interstate commerce, a contention upheld by the Court. Ohio contended that in any event its tax scheme was valid under the market participant doctrine. The Court responded as follows:

"Appellees contend that even if § 5735.145(B) is discriminatory, the discrimination is not covered by the Commerce Clause because of the so-called market participant doctrine. That doctrine differentiates between a State's acting in its distinctive governmental capacity, and a State's acting in the more general capacity of a market participant; only the former is subject to the limitations of the negative Commerce Clause. See Hughes v. Alexandria Scrap Corp., 426 U.S. 794, 806–810 (1976). Thus, for example, when a

State chooses to manufacture and sell cement, its business methods, including those that favor its residents, are of no greater constitutional concern than those of a private business. See Reeves, Inc. v. Stake, 447 U.S. 429, 438–439 (1980).

"The market participant doctrine has no application here. The Ohio action ultimately at issue is neither its purchase nor its sale of ethanol, but its assessment and computation of taxes—a primeval governmental activity. To be sure, the tax credit scheme has the purpose and effect of subsidizing a particular industry, as do many dispositions of the tax laws. That does not transform it into a form of state participation in the free market. Our opinion in *Alexandria Scrap*, supra, a case on which appellees place great reliance, does not remotely establish such a proposition. There we examined, and upheld against Commerce Clause attack on the basis of the market-participant doctrine, a Maryland cash subsidy program that discriminated in favor of in-state auto-hulk processors. The purpose of the program was to achieve the removal of unsightly abandoned autos from the State, 426 U.S., at 796–797, and the Court characterized it as proprietary rather than regulatory activity, based on the analogy of the State to a private purchaser of the auto hulks, id., at 808–810. We have subsequently observed that subsidy programs unlike that of *Alexandria Scrap* might not be characterized as proprietary. See *Reeves, Inc.,* supra, at 440, n. 14. We think it clear that Ohio's assessment and computation of its fuel sales tax, regardless of whether it produces a subsidy, cannot plausibly be analogized to the activity of a private purchaser."

E. LIMITS ON BUSINESS ENTRY

Page 315. Add ahead of F. Interstate Mobility of Persons:

CTS CORP. v. DYNAMICS CORP. OF AMERICA
___ U.S. ___, 107 S.Ct. 1637, 95 L.Ed.2d 67 (1987).

Justice Powell delivered the opinion of the Court.

This case presents the questions whether the Control Share Acquisitions Chapter of the Indiana Business Corporation Law, Ind.Code § 23–1–42–1 et seq. (Supp.1986), is preempted by the Williams Act, 82 Stat. 454, as amended, 15 U.S.C. §§ 78m(d)–(e) and 78n(d)–(f) (1982 ed. and Supp. III), or violates the Commerce Clause of the Federal Constitution, Art. I, § 8, cl. 3.

I

A

On March 4, 1986, the Governor of Indiana signed a revised Indiana Business Corporation Law, Ind.Code § 23–1–17–1 et seq. (Supp. 1986). That law included the Control Share Acquisitions Chapter

(Indiana Act or Act). Beginning on August 1, 1987, the Act will apply
to any corporation incorporated in Indiana, § 23–1–17–3(a), unless the
corporation amends its articles of incorporation or bylaws to opt out of
the Act, § 23–1–42–5. Before that date, any Indiana corporation can
opt into the Act by resolution of its board of directors. § 23–1–17–3(b).
The Act applies only to "issuing public corporations." The term
"corporation" includes only businesses incorporated in Indiana. See
§ 23–1–20–5. An "issuing public corporation" is defined as:

> "a corporation that has:

>> "(1) one hundred (100) or more shareholders;

>> "(2) its principal place of business, its principal office, or
substantial assets within Indiana; and

>> "(3) either:

>>> "(A) more than ten percent (10%) of its shareholders
resident in Indiana;

>>> "(B) more than ten percent (10%) of its shares owned
by Indiana residents; or

>>> "(C) ten thousand (10,000) shareholders resident in
Indiana." § 23–1–42–4(a).

The Act focuses on the acquisition of "control shares" in an issuing
public corporation. Under the Act, an entity acquires "control shares"
whenever it acquires shares that, but for the operation of the Act,
would bring its voting power in the corporation to or above any of three
thresholds: 20%, 33⅓%, or 50%. § 23–1–42–1. An entity that acquires control shares does not necessarily acquire voting rights. Rather, it gains those rights only "to the extent granted by resolution
approved by the shareholders of the issuing public corporation." § 23–
1–42–9(a). Section 9 requires a majority vote of all disinterested
shareholders holding each class of stock for passage of such a resolution. § 23–1–42–9(b). The practical effect of this requirement is to
condition acquisition of control of a corporation on approval of a
majority of the pre-existing disinterested shareholders.

The shareholders decide whether to confer rights on the control
shares at the next regularly scheduled meeting of the shareholders, or
at a specially scheduled meeting. The acquiror can require management of the corporation to hold such a special meeting within 50 days if
it files an "acquiring person statement," requests the meeting, and
agrees to pay the expenses of the meeting. See § 23–1–42–7. If the
shareholders do not vote to restore voting rights to the shares, the
corporation may redeem the control shares from the acquiror at fair
market value, but it is not required to do so. § 23–1–42–10(b). Similarly, if the acquiror does not file an acquiring person statement with the
corporation, the corporation may, if its bylaws or articles of incorporation so provide, redeem the shares at any time after 60 days after the
acquiror's last acquisition. § 23–1–42–10(a).

B

On March 10, 1986, appellee Dynamics Corporation of America (Dynamics) owned 9.6% of the common stock of appellant CTS Corporation, an Indiana corporation. On that day, six days after the Act went into effect, Dynamics announced a tender offer for another million shares in CTS; purchase of those shares would have brought Dynamics' ownership interest in CTS to 27.5%. Also on March 10, Dynamics filed suit in the United States District Court for the Northern District of Illinois, alleging that CTS had violated the federal securities laws in a number of respects no longer relevant to these proceedings. On March 27, the Board of Directors of CTS, an Indiana corporation, elected to be governed by the provisions of the Act, see § 23–1–17–3.

Four days later, on March 31, Dynamics moved for leave to amend its complaint to allege that the Act is pre-empted by the Williams Act, 15 U.S.C. §§ 78m(d)–(e) and 78n(d)–(f) (1982 ed. and Supp. III), and violates the Commerce Clause, Art. I, § 8, cl. 3. Dynamics sought a temporary restraining order, a preliminary injunction, and declaratory relief against CTS's use of the Act. On April 9, the District Court ruled that the Williams Act pre-empts the Indiana Act and granted Dynamics' motion for declaratory relief. . . . A week later, on April 17, the District Court issued an opinion accepting Dynamics' claim that the Act violates the Commerce Clause. This holding rested on the court's conclusion that "the substantial interference with interstate commerce created by the [Act] outweighs the articulated local benefits so as to create an impermissible indirect burden on interstate commerce." The District Court certified its decisions on the Williams Act and Commerce Clause claims as final under Fed.Rule Civ.Proc. 54(b).

CTS appealed the District Court's holdings on these claims to the Court of Appeals for the Seventh Circuit. . . . On April 23, . . . the Court of Appeals issued an order affirming the judgment of the District Court. The opinion followed on May 28. 794 F.2d 250 (1986).

. . .

Both Indiana and CTS filed jurisdictional statements. We noted probable jurisdiction under 28 U.S.C. § 1254(2), 479 U.S. ___ (1986), and now reverse.

. . .

II

The first question in this case is whether the Williams Act pre-empts the Indiana Act. . . .

. . .

In our view, the possibility that the Indiana Act will delay some tender offers is insufficient to require a conclusion that the Williams Act pre-empts the Act. The longstanding prevalence of state regulation in this area suggests that, if Congress had intended to pre-empt all state laws that delay the acquisition of voting control following a tender offer, it would have said so explicitly. The regulatory conditions that the Act places on tender offers are consistent with the text and the purposes of the Williams Act. Accordingly, we hold that the Williams Act does not pre-empt the Indiana Act.

III

As an alternative basis for its decision, the Court of Appeals held that the Act violates the Commerce Clause of the Federal Constitution. We now address this holding. On its face, the Commerce Clause is nothing more than a grant to Congress of the power "[t]o regulate Commerce . . . among the several States . . .," Art. I, § 8, cl. 3. But it has been settled for more than a century that the Clause prohibits States from taking certain actions respecting interstate commerce even absent congressional action. See, e.g., Cooley v. Board of Wardens, 12 How. * 299 (1852). The Court's interpretation of "these great silences of the Constitution," H.P. Hood & Sons, Inc. v. Du Mond, 336 U.S. 525, 535 (1949), has not always been easy to follow. Rather, as the volume and complexity of commerce and regulation has grown in this country, the Court has articulated a variety of tests in an attempt to describe the difference between those regulations that the Commerce Clause permits and those regulations that it prohibits. See, e.g., Raymond Motor Transportation, Inc. v. Rice, 434 U.S. 429, 441, n. 15 (1978).

A

The principal objects of dormant Commerce Clause scrutiny are statutes that discriminate against interstate commerce. See, e.g., Lewis v. BT Investment Managers, Inc., 447 U.S. 27, 36–37 (1980); Philadelphia v. New Jersey, 437 U.S. 617, 624 (1978). See generally Regan, The Supreme Court and State Protectionism: Making Sense of the Dormant Commerce Clause, 84 Mich.L.Rev. 1091 (1986). The Indiana Act is not such a statute. It has the same effects on tender offers whether or not the offeror is a domiciliary or resident of Indiana. Thus, it "visits its effects equally upon both interstate and local business," Lewis v. BT Investment Managers, Inc., supra, at 36.

Dynamics nevertheless contends that the statute is discriminatory because it will apply most often to out-of-state entities. This argument rests on the contention that, as a practical matter, most hostile tender offers are launched by offerors outside Indiana. But this argument avails Dynamics little. "The fact that the burden of a state regulation falls on some interstate companies does not, by itself, establish a claim of discrimination against interstate commerce." Exxon Corp. v. Governor of Maryland, 437 U.S. 117, 126 (1978). See Minnesota v. Clover Leaf Creamery Co., 449 U.S. 456, 471–472 (1981) (rejecting a claim of discrimination because the challenged statute "regulate[d] evenhandedly . . . without regard to whether the [commerce came] from outside the State"); Commonwealth Edison Co. v. Montana, 453 U.S. 609, 619 (1981) (rejecting a claim of discrimination because the "tax burden [was] borne according to the amount . . . consumed and not according to any distinction between in-state and out-of-state consumers"). Because nothing in the Indiana Act imposes a greater burden on out-of-state offerors than it does on similarly situated Indiana offerors, we reject the contention that the Act discriminates against interstate commerce.

B

This Court's recent Commerce Clause cases also have invalidated statutes that adversely may affect interstate commerce by subjecting activities to inconsistent regulations. E.g., Brown-Forman Distillers Corp. v. New York State Liquor Authority, 476 U.S. ___, ___ (1986); Edgar v. MITE Corp., 457 U.S., at 642 (plurality opinion of White, J.); Kassel v. Consolidated Freightways Corp., 450 U.S. 662, 671 (1981) (plurality opinion of Powell, J.). See Southern Pacific Co. v. Arizona, 325 U.S. 761, 774 (1945) (noting the "confusion and difficulty" that would attend the "unsatisfied need for uniformity" in setting maximum limits on train lengths); Cooley v. Board of Wardens, supra, at * 319 (stating that the Commerce Clause prohibits States from regulating subjects that "are in their nature national, or admit only of one uniform system, or plan of regulation"). The Indiana Act poses no such problem. So long as each State regulates voting rights only in the corporations it has created, each corporation will be subject to the law of only one State. No principle of corporation law and practice is more firmly established than a State's authority to regulate domestic corporations, including the authority to define the voting rights of shareholders. See Restatement (Second) of Conflict of Laws § 304 (1971) (concluding that the law of the incorporating State generally should "determine the right of a shareholder to participate in the administration of the affairs of the corporation"). Accordingly, we conclude that the Indiana Act does not create an impermissible risk of inconsistent regulation by different States.

C

The Court of Appeals did not find the Act unconstitutional for either of these threshold reasons. Rather, its decision rested on its view of the Act's potential to hinder tender offers. We think the Court of Appeals failed to appreciate the significance for Commerce Clause analysis of the fact that state regulation of corporate governance is regulation of entities whose very existence and attributes are a product of state law. As Chief Justice Marshall explained:

> "A corporation is an artificial being, invisible, intangible, and existing only in contemplation of law. Being the mere creature of law, it possesses only those properties which the charter of its creation confers upon it, either expressly, or as incidental to its very existence. These are such as are supposed best calculated to effect the object for which it was created." Trustees of Dartmouth College v. Woodward, 4 Wheat. 518, 636 (1819).

See First National Bank of Boston v. Bellotti, 435 U.S. 765, 822–824 (1978) (Rehnquist, J., dissenting). Every State in this country has enacted laws regulating corporate governance. By prohibiting certain transactions, and regulating others, such laws necessarily affect certain aspects of interstate commerce. This necessarily is true with respect to corporations with shareholders in States other than the State of incorporation. Large corporations that are listed on national exchanges, or even regional exchanges, will have shareholders in many States and shares that are traded frequently. The markets that facilitate this national and international participation in ownership of corporations are essential for providing capital not only for new enterprises but also for established companies that need to expand their businesses. This beneficial free market system depends at its core upon the fact that a corporation—except in the rarest situations—is organized under, and governed by, the law of a single jurisdiction, traditionally the corporate law of the State of its incorporation.

These regulatory laws may affect directly a variety of corporate transactions. Mergers are a typical example. In view of the substantial effect that a merger may have on the shareholder's interests in a corporation, many States require supermajority votes to approve mergers. See, e.g., MBCA § 73 (requiring approval of a merger by a majority of all shares, rather than simply a majority of votes cast); RMBCA § 11.03 (same). By requiring a greater vote for mergers than is required for other transactions, these laws make it more difficult for corporations to merge. State laws also may provide for "dissenters' rights" under which minority shareholders who disagree with corporate decisions to take particular actions are entitled to sell their shares to the corporation at fair market value. See, e.g., MBCA § 80–81; RMBCA § 13.02. By requiring the corporation to purchase the shares of dissenting shareholders, these laws may inhibit a corporation from engaging in the specified transactions.

It thus is an accepted part of the business landscape in this country for States to create corporations, to prescribe their powers, and to define the rights that are acquired by purchasing their shares. A State has an interest in promoting stable relationships among parties involved in the corporations it charters, as well as in ensuring that investors in such corporations have an effective voice in corporate affairs.

There can be no doubt that the Act reflects these concerns. The primary purpose of the Act is to protect the shareholders of Indiana corporations. It does this by affording shareholders, when a takeover offer is made, an opportunity to decide collectively whether the resulting change in voting control of the corporation, as they perceive it, would be desirable. A change of management may have important effects on the shareholders' interests; it is well within the State's role as overseer of corporate governance to offer this opportunity. The autonomy provided by allowing shareholders collectively to determine whether the takeover is advantageous to their interests may be especially beneficial where a hostile tender offer may coerce shareholders into tendering their shares.

Appellee Dynamics responds to this concern by arguing that the prospect of coercive tender offers is illusory, and that tender offers generally should be favored because they reallocate corporate assets into the hands of management who can use them most effectively. See generally Easterbrook and Fischel, The Proper Role of a Target's Management in Responding to a Tender Offer, 94 Harv.L.Rev. 1161 (1981). As indicated, Indiana's concern with tender offers is not groundless. Indeed, the potentially coercive aspects of tender offers have been recognized by the Securities and Exchange Commission, see SEC Release No. 21079, p. 86,916, and by a number of scholarly commentators, see, e.g., Bradley & Rosenzweig, Defensive Stock Repurchases, 99 Harv.L.Rev. 1377, 1412–1413 (1986); Macey & McChesney, A Theoretical Analysis of Corporate Greenmail, 95 Yale L.J. 13, 20–22 (1985); Lowenstein, 83 Colum.L.Rev., at 307–309. The Constitution does not require the States to subscribe to any particular economic theory. We are not inclined "to second-guess the empirical judgments of lawmakers concerning the utility of legislation," Kassel v. Consolidated Freightways Corp., 450 U.S., at 679 (Brennan, J., concurring in judgment). In our view, the possibility of coercion in some takeover bids offers additional justification for Indiana's decision to promote the autonomy of independent shareholders.

Dynamics argues in any event that the State has " 'no legitimate interest in protecting the nonresident shareholders.' " Brief for Appellee Dynamics Corp. of America 21 (quoting Edgar v. MITE Corp., 457 U.S., at 644). Dynamics relies heavily on the statement by the *MITE* Court that "[i]nsofar as the . . . law burdens out-of-state transactions, there is nothing to be weighed in the balance to sustain the law." 457 U.S., at 644. But that comment was made in reference to an Illinois law that applied as well to out-of-state corporations as to in-state corporations. We agree that Indiana has no interest in protecting nonresident shareholders *of nonresident corporations.* But this Act applies only to corporations incorporated in Indiana. We reject the contention that Indiana has no interest in providing for the shareholders of its corporations the voting autonomy granted by the Act. Indiana has a substantial interest in preventing the corporate form from becoming a shield for unfair business dealing. Moreover, unlike the Illinois statute invalidated in *MITE,* the Indiana Act applies only to corporations that have a substantial number of shareholders in Indiana. See Ind.Code § 23–1–42–4(a)(3) (Supp.1986). Thus, every application of the Indiana Act will affect a substantial number of Indiana residents, whom Indiana indisputably has an interest in protecting.

D

Dynamics' argument that the Act is unconstitutional ultimately rests on its contention that the Act will limit the number of successful tender offers. There is little evidence that this will occur. But even if true, this result would not substantially affect our Commerce Clause analysis. We reiterate that this Act does not prohibit any entity— resident or nonresident—from offering to purchase, or from purchasing, shares in Indiana corporations, or from attempting thereby to gain control. It only provides regulatory procedures designed for the better protection of the corporations' shareholders. We have rejected the "notion that the Commerce Clause protects the particular structure or methods of operation in a . . . market." Exxon Corp. v. Governor of Maryland, 437 U.S., at 127. The very commodity that is traded in the securities market is one whose characteristics are defined by state law. Similarly, the very commodity that is traded in the "market for corporate control"—the corporation—is one that owes its existence and attributes to state law. Indiana need not define these commodities as other States do; it need only provide that residents and nonresidents have equal access to them. This Indiana has done. Accordingly, even if the Act should decrease the number of successful tender offers for Indiana corporations, this would not offend the Commerce Clause.

IV

On its face, the Indiana Control Share Acquisitions Chapter even-handedly determines the voting rights of shares of Indiana corporations. The Act does not conflict with the provisions or purposes of the Williams Act. To the limited extent that the Act affects interstate commerce, this is justified by the State's interests in defining the attributes of shares in its corporations and in protecting shareholders. Congress has never questioned the need for state regulation of these matters. Nor do we think such regulation offends the Constitution. Accordingly, we reverse the judgment of the Court of Appeals.

It is so ordered.

Justice Scalia, concurring in part and concurring in the judgment.

I join Parts I, III–A, and III–B of the Court's opinion. However, having found, as those Parts do, that the Indiana Control Share Acquisitions Chapter neither "discriminates against interstate commerce," nor "create[s] an impermissible risk of inconsistent regulation by different States." I would conclude without further analysis that it is not invalid under the dormant Commerce Clause. While it has become standard practice at least since Pike v. Bruce Church, Inc., 397 U.S. 137 (1970), to consider, in addition to these factors, whether the burden on commerce imposed by a state statute "is clearly excessive in relation to the putative local benefits," id., at 142, such an inquiry is ill suited to the judicial function and should be undertaken rarely if at all. This case is a good illustration of the point. Whether the control shares statute "protects shareholders of Indiana corporations," or protects incumbent management seems to me a highly debatable question, but it is extraordinary to think that the constitutionality of the Act should depend on the answer. Nothing in the Constitution says that the protection of entrenched management is any less important a "putative local benefit" than the protection of entrenched shareholders, and I do not know what qualifies us to make that judgment—or the related judgment as to how effective the present statute is in achieving one or the other objective—or the ultimate (and most ineffable) judgment as to whether, given importance-level x, and effectiveness-level y, the worth of the statute is "outweighed" by impact-on-commerce z.

One commentator has suggested that, at least much of the time, we do not in fact mean what we say when we declare that statutes which neither discriminate against commerce nor present a threat of multiple and inconsistent burdens might nonetheless be unconstitutional under a "balancing" test. See Regan, The Supreme Court and State Protectionism: Making Sense of the Dormant Commerce Clause, 84 Mich.L. Rev. 1091 (1986). If he is not correct, he ought to be. As long as a State's corporation law governs only its own corporations and does not discriminate against out-of-state interests, it should survive this Court's scrutiny under the Commerce Clause, whether it promotes shareholder welfare or industrial stagnation. Beyond that, it is for Congress to prescribe its invalidity.

I also agree with the Court that the Indiana control shares Act is not pre-empted by the Williams Act . . . ..

I do not share the Court's apparent high estimation of the beneficence of the state statute at issue here. But a law can be both economic folly and constitutional. The Indiana Control Shares Acquisition Chapter is at least the latter. I therefore concur in the judgment of the Court.

Justice White, with whom Justice Blackmun and Justice Stevens join as to Part II, dissenting.

The majority today upholds Indiana's Control Share Acquisitions Chapter, a statute which will predictably foreclose completely some tender offers for stock in Indiana corporations. I disagree with the conclusion that the Chapter is neither pre-empted by the Williams Act nor in conflict with the Commerce Clause. The Chapter undermines the policy of the Williams Act by effectively preventing minority shareholders, in some circumstances, from acting in their own best interests by selling their stock. In addition, the Chapter will substantially burden the interstate market in corporate ownership, particularly if other States follow Indiana's lead as many already have done. The Chapter, therefore, directly inhibits interstate commerce, the very economic consequences the Commerce Clause was intended to prevent. The opinion of the Court of Appeals is far more persuasive than that of the majority today, and the judgment of that court should be affirmed.

. . .

The Commerce Clause was included in our Constitution by the Framers to prevent the very type of economic protectionism Indiana's Control Share Chapter represents:

. . .

The State of Indiana, in its brief, admits that at least one of the Chapter's goals is to protect Indiana Corporations. . . . A state law which permits a majority of an Indiana corporation's stockholders to prevent individual investors, including out-of-state stockholders, from selling their stock to an out-of-state tender offeror and thereby frustrate any transfer of corporate control, is the archetype of the kind of state law that the Commerce Clause forbids.

Unlike state blue sky laws, Indiana's Control Share Acquisitions Chapter regulates the purchase and sale of stock of Indiana corporations in interstate commerce. Indeed, as noted above, the Chapter will inevitably be used to block interstate transactions in such stock. Because the Commerce Clause protects the "interstate market" in such securities, Exxon Corp. v. Governor of Maryland, 437 U.S. 117, 127 (1978), and because the Control Share Chapter substantially interferes with this interstate market, the Chapter clearly conflicts with the Commerce Clause.

With all due respect, I dissent.

BENDIX AUTOLITE CORP. v. MIDWESCO ENTERPRISES, INC.

___ U.S. ___, 108 S.Ct. ___, ___ L.Ed.2d ___ (1988).

Justice Kennedy delivered the opinion of the Court.

Ohio recognizes a four-year statute of limitations in actions for breach of contract or fraud. The statute is tolled, however, for any period that a person or corporation is not "present" in the state. To be present in Ohio, a foreign corporation must appoint an agent for service of process, which operates as consent to the general jurisdiction of the Ohio courts. Applying well-settled constitutional principles, we find the Ohio statute that suspends limitations protection for out-of-state entities is a violation of the Commerce Clause.

I

Underlying the constitutional question presented by the Ohio statute of limitations rules is a rather ordinary contract dispute. In 1974, Midwesco Enterprises, Inc., agreed with Bendix Autolite Corporation to deliver and install a boiler system at a Bendix facility in Fostoria, Ohio. Dissatisfied with the work, Bendix claimed that the boiler system had been installed improperly and that it was insufficient to produce the quantity of steam specified in the contract. This diversity action was filed against Midwesco in the United States District Court for the Northern District of Ohio in 1980. Bendix is a Delaware corporation with its principal place of business in Ohio; Midwesco is an Illinois corporation with its principal place of business in Illinois.

When Midwesco asserted the Ohio statute of limitations as a defense, Bendix responded that the statutory period had not elapsed because under Ohio law running of the time is suspended, or tolled, for claims against entities that are not within the State and have not designated an agent for service of process. Midwesco replied that this tolling provision violated both the Commerce Clause and the Due Process Clause of the Fourteenth Amendment.

The District Court dismissed the action, finding that the Ohio tolling statute constituted an impermissible burden on interstate commerce. The Court of Appeals for the Sixth Circuit affirmed. . . . We now affirm.

II

Where the burden of a state regulation falls on interstate commerce, restricting its flow in a manner not applicable to local business and trade, there may be either a discrimination that renders the regulation invalid without more, or cause to weigh and assess the State's putative interests against the interstate restraints to determine if the burden imposed is an unreasonable one. See Brown-Forman Distillers Corp. v. New York State Liquor Authority, 476 U.S. 573, 578–579 (1986). The Ohio statute before us might have been held to be a discrimination that invalidates without extended inquiry. We choose, however, to assess the interests of the State, to demonstrate that its legitimate sphere of regulation is not much advanced by the statute while interstate commerce is subject to substantial restraints. We find that the burden imposed on interstate commerce by the tolling statute exceeds any local interest that the State might advance.

The burden the tolling statute places on interstate commerce is significant. Midwesco has no corporate office in Ohio, is not registered to do business there, and has not appointed an agent for service of process in the State. To gain the protection of the limitations period, Midwesco would have had to appoint a resident agent for service of process in Ohio and subject itself to the general jurisdiction of the Ohio courts. This jurisdiction would extend to any suit against Midwesco, whether or not the transaction in question had any connection with Ohio. The designation of an agent subjects the foreign corporation to the general jurisdiction of the Ohio courts in matters to which Ohio's tenuous relation would not otherwise extend. Cf. World-Wide Volkswagen Corp. v. Woodson, 444 U.S. 286 (1980). The Ohio statutory scheme thus forces a foreign corporation to choose between exposure to the general jurisdiction of Ohio courts or forfeiture of the limitations defense, remaining subject to suit in Ohio in perpetuity. Requiring a foreign corporation to appoint an agent for service in all cases and to defend itself with reference to all transactions, including those in which it did not have the minimum contacts necessary for supporting personal jurisdiction, is a significant burden. See Asahi Metal Industry Co. v. Superior Court, 480 U.S. ___, ___ (1987).

Although statute of limitations defenses are not a fundamental right, Chase Securities Corp. v. Donaldson, 325 U.S. 304, 314 (1945), it is obvious that they are an integral part of the legal system and are relied upon to project the liabilities of persons and corporations active in the commercial sphere. The State may not withdraw such defenses on conditions repugnant to the Commerce Clause. Where a State denies ordinary legal defenses or like privileges to out-of-state persons or corporations engaged in commerce, the State law will be reviewed under the Commerce Clause to determine whether the denial is discriminatory on its face or an impermissible burden on commerce. The State may not condition the exercise of the defense on the waiver or relinquishment of rights that the foreign corporation would otherwise retain. Cf. Dahnke-Walker Milling Co. v. Bondurant, 257 U.S. 282 (1921); Allenberg Cotton Co. v. Pittman, 419 U.S. 20 (1974).

The ability to execute service of process on foreign corporations and entities is an important factor to consider in assessing the local interest in subjecting out-of-state entities to requirements more onerous than those imposed on domestic parties. It is true that serving foreign corporate defendants may be more arduous than serving domestic corporations or foreign corporations with a designated agent for service, and we have held for Equal Protection purposes that a State rationally may make adjustments for this difference by curtailing limitations protection for absent foreign corporations. G.D. Searle & Co. v. Cohn, 455 U.S. 404 (1982). Nevertheless, State interests that are legitimate for equal protection or due process purposes may be insufficient to withstand Commerce Clause scrutiny.

In the particular case before us, the Ohio tolling statute must fall under the Commerce Clause. Ohio cannot justify its statute as a means of protecting its residents from corporations who become liable for acts done within the State but later withdraw from the jurisdiction, for it is conceded by all parties that the Ohio long arm statute would have permitted service on Midwesco throughout the period of limitations. The Ohio statute of limitations is tolled only for those foreign corporations that do not subject themselves to the general jurisdiction of Ohio courts. In this manner the Ohio statute imposes a greater burden on out-of-state companies than it does on Ohio companies, subjecting the activities of foreign and domestic corporations to inconsistent regulations. CTS Corp. v. Dynamics Corp. of America, 481 U.S. __, __ (1987).

The suggestion that Midwesco had the simple alternatives of designating an agent for service of process in its contract with Bendix or tendering an agency appointment to the Ohio Secretary of State is not persuasive. Initially, there is no statutory support for either option, and it is speculative that either device would have satisfied the Ohio requirements for the continued running of the limitations period. In any event, a designation with the Ohio Secretary of State of an agent for the service of process likely would have subjected Midwesco to the general jurisdiction of Ohio courts over transactions in which Ohio had no interest. As we have already concluded, this exaction is an unreasonable burden on commerce.

. . .

Affirmed.

———

Justice Scalia, concurring in judgment.

I cannot confidently assess whether the Court's evaluation and balancing of interests in this case is right or wrong. Although the Court labels the effect of exposure to the general jurisdiction of Ohio's courts "a significant burden" on commerce, I am not sure why that is. In precise terms, it is the burden of defending in Ohio (rather than some other forum) any lawsuit having all of the following features: (1) the plaintiff desires to bring it in Ohio, (2) it has so little connection to Ohio that service could not otherwise be made under Ohio's long-arm statute, and (3) it has a great enough connection to Ohio it is not subject to dismissal on *forum non conveniens* grounds. The record before us supplies no indication as to how many suits fit this description (even the present suit is not an example since appellee was subject to long-arm service), and frankly I have no idea how one would go about estimating the number. It may well be "significant," but for all we know it is "negligible."

A person or firm that takes the other alternative, by declining to appoint a general agent for service, will remain theoretically subject to suit in Ohio (as the Court says) "in perpetuity"—at least as far as the statute of limitations is concerned. But again, I do not know how we assess how significant a burden this is, unless anything that is theoretically perpetual must be significant. It seems very unlikely that anyone would intentionally wait to sue later rather than sooner—not only because the prospective defendant may die or dissolve, but also because prejudgment interest is normally not awarded, and the staleness of evidence generally harms the party with the burden of proof. The likelihood of an unintentionally delayed suit brought under this provision that could not be brought without it seems not enormously large. Moreover, whatever the likelihood is, it does not seem terribly plausible that any real-world deterrent effect on interstate transactions will be produced by the incremental cost of having to defend a *delayed* suit rather than a *timely* suit. But the point is, it seems to me we can do no more than speculate.

On the other side of the scale, the Court considers the benefit of the Ohio scheme to local interests. These are, presumably, to enable the preservation of claims against defendants who have placed themselves beyond the personal jurisdiction of Ohio Courts, and (by encouraging appointment of an agent) to facilitate service upon out-of-state defendants who might otherwise be difficult to locate. See G.D. Searle & Co. v. Cohn, 455 U.S. 404, 410 (1982) (it is "a reasonable assumption that unrepresented foreign corporations, as a general rule, may not be so easy to find and serve"). We have no way of knowing how often these ends are in fact achieved, and the Court thus says little about them except to call them "an important factor to consider."

Having evaluated the interests on both sides as roughly as this, the Court then proceeds to judge which is more important. This process is ordinarily called "balancing," Pike v. Bruce Church, Inc., 397 U.S. 137, 142 (1970), but the scale analogy is not really appropriate, since the interests on both sides are incommensurate. It is more like judging whether a particular line is longer than a particular rock is heavy. All I am really persuaded of by the Court's opinion is that the burdens the Court labels "significant" are more determinative of its decision than the benefits it labels "important." Were it not for the brief implication that there is here a discrimination unjustified by *any* state interest I suggest an opinion could as persuasively have been written coming out the opposite way. We sometimes make similar "balancing" judgments in determining how far the needs of the State can intrude upon the liberties of the individual, see, e.g., Boos v. Barry, 485 U.S. ___, ___ (1988), but that is of the essence of the courts' function as the nonpolitical branch. Weighing the governmental interests of a State against the needs of interstate commerce is, by contrast, a task squarely within the responsibility of Congress, see U.S.Const., Art. I, § 8, cl. 3, and "ill suited to the judicial function." CTS Corp. v. Dynamics Corp. of America, 481 U.S. ___, ___ (1987) (Scalia, J., concurring in part and concurring in judgment).

I would therefore abandon the "balancing" approach to these negative commerce clause cases, first explicitly adopted 18 years ago in Pike v. Bruce Church, Inc., supra, and leave essentially legislative judgments to the Congress. Issues already decided I would leave untouched, but would adopt for the future an anaylsis more appropriate to our role and our abilities. This does no damage to the interests protected by the doctrine of *stare decisis*. Since the outcome of any particular still-undecided issue under the current methodolgy is in my view not predictable—except within the broad range that would in any event come out the same way under the test I would apply—no expectations can possibly be upset. To the contrary, the ultimate objective of the rule of *stare decisis* will be furthered. Because the outcome of the test I would apply is considerably more clear, confident expectations will more readily be able to be entertained.

In my view, a state statute is invalid under the Commerce Clause if, and only if, it accords discriminatory treatment to interstate commerce in a respect not required to achieve a lawful state purpose. When such a validating purpose exists, it is for Congress and not us to determine it is not significant enough to justify the burden on commerce. The Ohio tolling statute, Ohio Rev. Code Ann. § 2305.15 (Supp. 1987), is on its face discriminatory because it applies only to out-of-state corporations. That facial discrimination cannot be justified on the basis that "it advances a legitimate local purpose that cannot be adequately served by reasonable nondiscriminatory alternatives," New Energy Co. of Indiana v. Limbach, 486 U.S. ___, ___ (1988). A tolling statute that operated only against persons beyond the reach of Ohio's long-arm statute, or against all persons that could not be found for mail service, would be narrowly tailored to advance the legitimate purpose of preserving claims; but the present statute extends the time for suit even against corporations which (like appellee) are fully suable within Ohio, and readily reachable through the mails.

Because the present statute discriminates against interstate commerce by applying a disadvantageous rule against nonresidents for no valid state purpose that requires such a rule, I concur in the judgment that the Ohio statute violates the Commerce Clause.

Chief Justice Rehnquist, dissenting.

This case arises because of two peculiar, if not unique, rules of Ohio law. The first is that even though a foreign corporation may be subject to process under the state "long arm" statute, it is nonetheless not "present" in the State for purposes of tolling the statute of limitations. The second is that a foreign corporation installing machinery or equipment sold by it in interstate commerce is not required to appoint a statutory agent in order to transact business in Ohio. Ohio Rev. Code § 1703.02 (Supp. 1987). The Court dwells heavily upon the first peculiarity of Ohio law, but makes no mention of the second.

Midwesco agreed to deliver and install a boiler system at a Bendix plant in Fostoria, Ohio. On the basis of the sparse record before us, it is fair to say that while the sale may have been a transaction in interstate commerce, there is no reason at all to think that the installation was such. Cases such as Allenberg Cotton Co. v. Pittman, 419 U.S. 20 (1974), and Dahnke-Walker Milling Co. v. Bondurant, 257 U.S. 282 (1921), on which the Court relies, deal with transactions respecting goods which are "in the stream of interstate commerce." 419 U.S., at 30. A State may not require licensure of a foreign corporation which seeks only to engage in this sort of transaction. But a State may require licensure when a foreign corporation engages in intrastate commerce. Eli Lilly & Co. v. Sav-On-Drugs, Inc., 366 U.S. 276 (1961). And where a foreign corporation is engaged in both interstate and intrastate commerce in a particular commodity, a State may require licensure in order to sue in connection with an intrastate aspect of the business. Union Brokerage Co. v. Jensen, 322 U.S. 202 (1944).

Thus, Midwesco's immunity from Ohio's requirement that foreign corporations appoint a statutory agent before doing business in the State is not by reason of any federal constitutional right, but by reason of a provision of the Ohio statutes. And if Ohio could have insisted that Midwesco appoint a statutory agent before it engaged in that portion of its transaction with Bendix which was intrastate commerce, I see no reason why it may not also treat Midwesco as it would treat any other entity which has done intrastate business in Ohio, incurred liability, and thereafter withdrawn from the State. Ohio seeks to do no more, I think, when it applies its tolling statute to Bendix's action against Midwesco under these circumstances. I see no discrimination against interstate commerce here, and I would reverse the judgment of the Court of Appeals.

———

SECTION 3. EFFECT OF OTHER CONSTITUTIONAL PROVISIONS ON STATE REGULATORY POWER

———

A. THE PRIVILEGES AND IMMUNITIES CLAUSE OF ARTICLE IV, SECTION 2

———

Page 323. Add ahead of B. The Twenty-first Amendment:

SUPREME COURT OF VIRGINIA v. FRIEDMAN

___ U.S. ___, 108 S.Ct.___, ___ L.Ed.2d ___ (1988).

Justice Kennedy delivered the opinion of the Court.

Qualified lawyers admitted to practice in other States may be admitted to the Virginia bar "on motion," that is, without taking the bar examination which Virginia otherwise requires. The State conditions such admission on a showing, among other matters, that the applicant is a permanent resident of Virginia. The question for decision is whether this residency requirement violates the Privileges and Immunities Clause of the United States Constitution, Art. IV, § 2. We hold that it does.

I

Myrna E. Friedman was admitted to the Illinois bar by examination in 1977 and to the District of Columbia bar by reciprocity in 1980. From 1977 to 1981, she was employed by the Department of the Navy in Arlington, Virginia, as a civilian attorney, and from 1982 until 1986, she was an attorney in private practice in Washington, D.C. In January 1986, she became associate general counsel for ERC International, Inc., a Delaware corporation. Friedman practices and maintains her offices at the company's principal place of business in Vienna, Virginia. Her duties at ERC International include drafting contracts and advising her employer and its subsidiaries on matters of Virginia law.

From 1977 to early 1986, Friedman lived in Virginia. In February 1986, however, she married and moved to her husband's home in Cheverly, Maryland. In June 1986, Friedman applied for admission to the Virginia bar on motion.

The applicable rule, promulgated by the Supreme Court of Virginia pursuant to statute, is Rule 1A:1. The Rule permits admission on motion of attorneys who are licensed to practice in another jurisdiction, provided the other jurisdiction admits Virginia attorneys without examination. The applicant must have been licensed for at least five years and the Virginia Supreme Court must determine that the applicant:

"(a) Is a proper person to practice law.

"(b) Has made such progress in the practice of law that it would be unreasonable to require him to take an examination.

"(c) Has become a permanent resident of the Commonwealth.

"(d) Intends to practice full time as a member of the Virginia bar."

In a letter accompanying her application, Friedman alerted the Clerk of the Virginia Supreme Court to her change of residence, but argued that her application should nevertheless be granted. Friedman gave assurance that she would be engaged full-time in the practice of law in Virginia, that she would be available for service of process and court appearances, and that she would keep informed of local rules. She also asserted "that there appears to be no reason to discriminate against my petition as a nonresident for admission to the Bar on motion," that her circumstances fit within the purview of this Court's decision in Supreme Court of New Hampshire v. Piper, 470 U.S. 274 (1985), and that accordingly she was entitled to admission under the Privileges and Immunities Clause of the Constitution Art. IV, § 2.

The Clerk wrote Friedman that her request had been denied. He explained that because Friedman was no longer a permanent resident of the Commonwealth of Virginia, she was not eligible for admission to the Virginia bar pursuant to Rule 1A:1. He added that the court had concluded that our decision in *Piper,* which invalidated a residency requirement imposed on lawyers who had passed a State's bar examination, was "not applicable" to the "discretionary requirement in Rule 1A:1 of residence as a condition of admission by reciprocity."

Friedman then commenced this action, against the Supreme Court of Virginia and its Clerk, in the United States District Court for the Eastern District of Virginia. She alleged that the residency requirement of Rule 1A:1 violated the Privileges and Immunities Clause. The District Court entered summary judgment in Friedman's favor, holding that the requirement of residency for admission without examination violates the Clause.*

The Court of Appeals for the Fourth Circuit unanimously affirmed. 822 F.2d 423 (1987). . . .

The Supreme Court of Virginia and its Clerk filed a timely notice of appeal. We noted probable jurisdiction, 484 U.S. ___ (1987), and we now affirm.

II

Article IV, § 2, of the Constitution provides that the "Citizens of each State shall be entitled to all Privileges and Immunities of Citizens in the several States." The provision was designed "to place the citizens of each State upon the same footing with citizens of other States, so far as the advantages resulting from citizenship in those States are concerned." Paul v. Virginia, 8 Wall. 168, 180 (1869). See also Toomer v. Witsell, 334 U.S. 385, 395 (1948) (the Privileges and Immunities Clause "was designed to insure to a citizen of State A who ventures into State B the same privileges which the citizens of State B enjoy"). The Clause "thus establishes a norm of comity without specifying the particular subjects as to which citizens of one State coming within the jurisdiction of another are guaranteed equality of treatment." Austin v. New Hampshire, 420 U.S. 656, 660 (1975).

---

* The District Court did not address Friedman's claims that the residency requirement of Rule 1A:1 also violates the Commerce Clause and the Equal Protection Clause of the Fourteenth Amendment. The Court of Appeals did not pass on these contentions either, and our resolution of Friedman's claim that the residency requirement violates the Privileges and Immunities Clause makes it unnecessary for us to reach them.

While the Privileges and Immunities Clause cites the term "Citizens," for analytic purposes citizenship and residency are essentially interchangeable. See United Building & Construction Trades Council v. Mayor of Camden, 465 U.S. 208, 216 (1984). When examining claims that a citizenship or residency classification offends privileges and immunities protections, we undertake a two-step inquiry. First, the activity in question must be "sufficiently basic to the livelihood of the Nation' . . . as to fall within the purview of the Privileges and Immunities Clause . . . ." Id., at 221–222, quoting Baldwin v. Montana Fish & Game Comm'n, 436 U.S. 371, 388 (1978). For it is " '[o]nly with respect to those "privileges" and "immunities" bearing on the vitality of the Nation as a single entity' that a State must accord residents and nonresidents equal treatment." Supreme Court of New Hampshire v. Piper, 470 U.S., at 279, quoting *Baldwin,* supra, at 383. Second, if the challenged restriction deprives nonresidents of a protected privilege, we will invalidate it only if we conclude that the restriction is not closely related to the advancement of a substantial State interest. *Piper,* supra, at 284. Appellants assert that the residency requirement offends neither part of this test. We disagree.

A

Appellants concede, as they must, that our decision in *Piper* establishes that a nonresident who takes and passes an examination prescribed by the State, and who otherwise is qualified for the practice of law, has an interest in practicing law that is protected by the Privileges and Immunities Clause. Appellants contend, however, that the discretionary admission provided for by Rule 1A:1 is not a privilege protected by the Clause for two reasons. First, appellants argue that the bar examination "serves as an adequate, alternative means of gaining admission to the bar." In appellants' view, "[s]o long as any applicant may gain admission to a State's bar, without regard to residence, by passing the bar examination," the State cannot be said to have discriminated against nonresidents "as a matter of fundamental concern." Second, appellants argue that the right to admission on motion is not within the purview of the Clause because, without offense to the Constitution, the State could require all bar applicants to pass an examination. Neither argument is persuasive.

We cannot accept appellants' first theory because it is quite inconsistent with our precedents. We reaffirmed in *Piper* the well-settled principle that " 'one of the privileges which the Clause guarantees to citizens of State A is that of doing business in State B on terms of substantial equality with the citizens of that State.' " *Piper,* supra, at 280, quoting Toomer v. Witsell, supra, at 396. See also *United Building & Construction Trades Council,* supra, at 219 ("Certainly, the pursuit of a common calling is one of the most fundamental of those privileges protected by the Clause"). After reviewing our precedents, we explicitly held that the practice of law, like other occupations considered in those cases, is sufficiently basic to the national economy to be deemed a privilege protected by the Clause. See *Piper,* supra, at 280–281. The clear import of *Piper* is that the Clause is implicated whenever, as is the case here, a State does not permit qualified nonresidents to practice law within its borders on terms of substantial equality with its own residents.

Nothing in our precedents, moreover, supports the contention that the Privileges and Immunities Clause does not reach a State's discrimination against nonresidents when such discrimination does not result in their total exclusion from the State. In Ward v. Maryland, 12 Wall. 418 (1871), for example, the Court invalidated a statute under which residents paid an annual fee of $12 to $150 for a license to trade foreign goods, while nonresidents were required to pay $300. Similarly, in *Toomer,* supra, the Court held that nonresident fishermen could not be required to pay a license fee one hundred times the fee charged to residents. In Hicklin v. Orbeck, 437 U.S. 518 (1978), the Court invalidated a statute requiring that residents be hired in preference to nonresidents for all positions related to the development of the State's oil and gas resources. Indeed, as the Court of Appeals correctly noted, the New Hampshire rule struck down in *Piper* did not result in the total exclusion of nonresidents from the practice of law in that State. 822 F.2d, at 427 (citing *Piper,* supra, at 277, n. 2).

Further, we find appellants' second theory—that Virginia could constitutionally require that all applicants to its bar take and pass an examination—quite irrelevant to the question whether the Clause is applicable in the circumstances of this case. A State's abstract authority to require from resident and nonresident alike that which it has chosen to demand from the nonresident alone has never been held to shield the discriminatory distinction from the reach of the Privileges and Immunities Clause. Thus, the applicability of the Clause to the present case no more turns on the legality *vel non* of an examination requirement than it turned on the inherent reasonableness of the fees charged to nonresidents in *Toomer* and *Ward.* The issue instead is whether the State has burdened the right to practice law, a privilege protected by the Privileges and Immunities Clause, by discriminating among otherwise equally qualified applicants solely on the basis of citizenship or residency. We conclude it has.

B

Our conclusion that the residents requirement burdens a privilege protected by the Privileges and Immunities Clause does not conclude the matter, of course; for we repeatedly have recognized that the Clause, like other constitutional provisions, is not an absolute. See, e.g., *Piper,* supra, at 284; *United Building & Construction Trades Council,* 465 U.S., at 222; *Toomer,* 334 U.S., at 396. The Clause does not preclude disparity in treatment where substantial reasons exist for the discrimination and the degree of discrimination bears a close relation to such reasons. See *United Building & Construction Trades Council,* supra, at 222. In deciding whether the degree of discrimination bears a sufficiently close relation to the reasons proffered by the State, the Court has considered whether, within the full panoply of legislative choices otherwise available to the State, there exist alternative means of furthering the State's purpose without implicating constitutional concerns. See *Piper*, 470 U.S., at 284.

Appellants offer two principal justifications for the Rule's requirement that applicants seeking admission on motion reside within the Commonwealth of Virginia. First, they contend that the residence requirement assures, in tandem with the full-time practice requirement, that attorneys admitted on motion will have the same commitment to service and familiarity with Virginia law that is possessed by applicants securing admission upon examination. Attorneys admitted on motion, appellants argue, have "no personal investment" in the jurisdiction; consequently, they "are entitled to no presumption that they will willingly and actively participate in bar activities and obligations, or fulfill their public service responsibilities to the State's client community." Second, appellants argue that the residency requirement facilitates enforcement of the full-time practice requirement of Rule 1A:1. We find each of these justifications insufficient to meet the State's burden of showing that the discrimination is warranted by a substantial State objective and closely drawn to its achievement.

We acknowledge that a bar examination is one method of assuring that the admitted attorney has a stake in her professional licensure and a concomitant interest in the integrity and standards of the bar. A bar examination, as we know judicially and from our own experience, is not a casual or lighthearted exercise. The question, however, is whether lawyers who are admitted in other States and seek admission in Virginia are less likely to respect the bar and further its interests solely because they are nonresidents. We cannot say this is the case. While *Piper* relied on an examination requirement as an indicium of the nonresident's commitment to the bar and to the State's legal profession, see *Piper,* supra, at 285, it does not follow that when the State waives the examination it may make a distinction between residents and nonresidents.

Friedman's case proves the point. She earns her living working as an attorney in Virginia, and it is of scant relevance that her residence is located in the neighboring State of Maryland. It is indisputable that she has a substantial stake in the practice of law in Virginia. Indeed, despite appellants' suggestion at oral argument that Friedman's case is "atypical," the same will likely be true of all nonresident attorneys who are admitted on motion to the Virginia bar, in light of the State's requirement that attorneys so admitted show their intention to maintain an office and a regular practice in the State. See Application of Brown, 213 Va. 282, 286, n. 3, 191 S.E.2d 812, 815, n. 3 (1972) (interpreting full-time practice requirement of Rule 1A:1). This requirement goes a long way toward ensuring that such attorneys will have an interest in the practice of law in Virginia that is at least comparable to the interest we ascribed in *Piper* to applicants admitted upon examination. Accordingly, we see no reason to assume that nonresident attorneys who, like Friedman, seek admission to the Virginia bar on motion will lack adequate incentives to remain abreast of changes in the law or to fulfill their civic duties.

Further, to the extent that the State is justifiably concerned with ensuring that its attorneys keep abreast of legal developments, it can protect these interests through other equally or more effective means that do not themselves infringe constitutional protections. While this Court is not well-positioned to dictate specific legislative choices to the State, it is sufficient to note that such alternatives exist and that the State, in the exercise of its legislative prerogatives, is free to implement them. The Supreme Court of Virginia could, for example, require mandatory attendance at periodic continuing legal education courses. See *Piper,* supra, at 285, n. 19. The same is true with respect to the State's interest that the nonresident bar member does her share of volunteer and *pro bono* work. A "nonresident bar member, like the resident member, could be required to represent indigents and perhaps to participate in formal legal-aid work." *Piper,* supra, at 287 (footnote omitted).

We also reject appellants' attempt to justify the residency restriction as a necessary aid to the enforcement of the full-time practice requirement of Rule 1A:1. Virginia already requires, pursuant to the full-time practice restriction of Rule 1A:1, that attorneys admitted on motion maintain an office for the practice of law in Virginia. As the Court of Appeals noted, the requirement that applicants maintain an office in Virginia facilitates compliance with the full-time practice requirement in nearly the identical manner that the residency restriction does, rendering the latter restriction largely redundant. 822 F.2d, at 429. The office requirement furnishes an alternative to the residency requirement that is not only less restrictive, but also is fully adequate to protect whatever interest the State might have in the full-time practice restriction.

III

We hold that Virginia's residency requirement for admission to the State's bar without examination violates the Privleges and Immunities Clause. The nonresident's interest in practicing law on terms of substantial equality with those enjoyed by residents is a privilege protected by the Clause. A State may not discriminate against nonresidents unless it shows that such discrimination bears a close relation to the achievement of substantial State objectives. Virginia has failed to make this showing. Accordingly, the judgment of the Court of Appeals is affirmed.

It is so ordered.

Chief Justice Rehnquist, with whom Justice Scalia joins, dissenting.

Three Terms ago the Court invalidated a New Hampshire Bar rule which denied admission to an applicant who had passed the state bar examination because she was not, and would not become, a resident of the State. Supreme Court of New Hampshire v. Piper, 470 U.S. 274 (1985). In the present case the Court extends the reasoning of *Piper* to invalidate a Virginia Bar rule allowing admission on motion without examination to qualified applicants, but restricting the privilege to those applicants who have become residents of the State.

For the reasons stated in my dissent in *Piper,* I also disagree with the Court's decision in this case. I continue to believe that the Privileges and Immunities Clause of Article IV, § 2, does not require States to ignore residency when admitting lawyers to practice in the way that they must ignore residency when licensing traders in foreign goods, Ward v. Maryland, 12 Wall, 418 (1871), or when licensing commercial shrimp fishermen, Toomer v. Witsell, 334 U.S. 385 (1948).

I think the effect of today's decision is unfortunate even apart from what I believe is its mistaken view of the Privileges and Immunities Clause. Virginia's rule allowing admission on motion is an ameliorative provision, recognizing the fact that previous practice in another State may qualify a new resident of Virginia to practice there without the necessity of taking another bar examination. The Court's ruling penalizes Virginia, which has at least gone part way towards accommodating the present mobility of our population, but of course leaves untouched the rules of those States which allow no reciprocal admission on motion. Virginia may of course retain the privilege of admission on motion without enforcing a residency requirement even after today's decision, but it might also decide to eliminate admission on motion altogether.

B. THE TWENTY–FIRST AMENDMENT

Page 327. Add ahead of Capital Cities Cable, Inc. v. Crisp:

BROWN–FORMAN DISTILLERS CORP. v. NEW YORK STATE LIQUOR AUTHORITY, 476 U.S. 573 (1986). This case involved an attack on a New York law requiring liquor distillers to sell liquor in the state at a price no higher than the lowest price charged for similar sales in other states. The commerce clause issue is discussed supra, p. 19. New York also contended that the twenty-first amendment validated its statute. The Court rejected this defense, saying:

"New York finally contends that the Twenty-first Amendment, which bans the importation or possession of intoxicating liquors into a State 'in violation of the laws thereof,' saves the ABC Law from invalidation under the Commerce Clause. That Amendment gives the States wide latitude to regulate the importation and distribution of liquor within their territories, California Liquor Dealers Assn. v. Midcal Aluminum, Inc., 445 U.S. 97, 107 (1980). Therefore, New York argues, its ABC Law, which regulates the sale of alcoholic beverages within the State, is a valid exercise of the State's authority.

"It is well settled that the Twenty-first Amendment did not entirely remove state regulation of alcohol from the reach of the Commerce Clause. See Bacchus Imports, Ltd. v. Dias, 468 U.S. 263 (1984). Rather, the Twenty-first Amendment and the Commerce Clause 'each must be considered in light of the other and in the context of the issues and interests at stake in any concrete case.' Hostetter v. Idlewild Bon

Voyage Liquor Corp., 377 U.S. 324, 332 (1964). Our task, then, is to reconcile the interests protected by the two constitutional provisions.

"New York has a valid constitutional interest in regulating sales of liquor within the territory of New York. Section 2 of the Twenty-first Amendment, however, speaks only to state regulation of the 'transportation or importation into any State . . . for delivery or use therein' of alcoholic beverages. That Amendment, therefore, gives New York only the authority to control sales of liquor in New York, and confers no authority to control sales in other states. The Commerce Clause operates with full force whenever one State attempts to regulate the transportation and sale of alcoholic beverages destined for distribution and consumption in a foreign country, *Idlewild Bon Voyage Liquor Corp.,* supra, or another State. Our conclusion that New York has attempted to regulate sales in other States of liquor that will be consumed in other States therefore disposes of the Twenty-first Amendment issue.

"Moreover, New York's affirmation law may interfere with the ability of other States to exercise their own authority under the Twenty-first Amendment. Once a distiller has posted prices in New York, it is not free to lower them in another State, even in response to a regulatory directive by that State, without risking forfeiture of its license in New York. New York law, therefore, may force other States either to abandon regulatory goals or to deprive their citizens of the opportunity to purchase brands of liquor that are sold in New York. New York's reliance on the Twenty-first Amendment is therefore misplaced. . . ."

Page 330. Add ahead of Section 4. Preemption of State Legislation by Federal Legislation—The Impact of the Supremacy Clause:

324 LIQUOR CORP. v. DUFFY, 479 U.S. 335 (1987). The Court held that a New York statute requiring retailers to charge at least 112 percent of the posted wholesale price for liquor, but permitting wholesalers to sell to retailers at less than the posted price violated the Sherman Act. It then addressed the question whether the twenty-first amendment immunized the state law from the Sherman Act, saying:

"The States' Twenty-first Amendment powers, though broad, are circumscribed by other provisions of the Constitution. See Larkin v. Grendel's Den, Inc., 459 U.S. 116, 122, n. 5 (1982) (Establishment Clause); Craig v. Boren, 429 U.S. 190, 204–209 (1976) (Equal Protection Clause); Wisconsin v. Constantineau, 400 U.S. 433, 436 (1971) (procedural due process); Department of Revenue v. James Beam Co., 377 U.S. 341, 345–346 (1964) (Export-Import Clause). Although § 2 directly qualifies the federal commerce power, the Court has rejected the view that 'the Twenty-first Amendment has somehow operated to "repeal" the Commerce Clause wherever regulation of intoxicating liquors is concerned.' Hostetter v. Idlewild Liquor Corp., 377 U.S. 324 331–332 (1964). Instead the Court has engaged in a 'pragmatic effort to harmonize state and federal powers.' *Midcal*, supra, 445 U.S., at 109. The question in each case is whether the interests implicated by a state regulation are so closely related to the powers reserved by the Twenty-first Amendment that the regulation may prevail, notwithstanding that its requirements directly conflict with express federal policies. Capital Cities Cable, Inc. v. Crisp, 467 U.S. 691, 714 (1984)."

The Court then went on to find that there were no adequate state interests protected here to override the federal statute. Two justices dissented.

Chapter 6

THE SCOPE OF STATE POWER—TAXATION

SECTION 2. THE GENERAL SCOPE OF THE LIMITATIONS
IMPOSED ON STATE TAXATION OF INTERSTATE AND
FOREIGN COMMERCE BY THE COMMERCE AND
IMPORT-EXPORT CLAUSES

Page 344. Replace Armco, Inc. v. Hardesty with the following:

NEW ENERGY CO. OF INDIANA v. LIMBACH

___ U.S. ___, 108 S.Ct. 1803, ___ L.Ed.2d ___ (1988).

Justice Scalia delivered the opinion of the Court.

Appellant New Energy Company of Indiana has challenged the constitutionality of Ohio Rev.Code Ann. § 5735.145(B) (1986), a provision that awards a tax credit against the Ohio motor vehicle fuel sales tax for each gallon of ethanol sold (as a component of gasohol) by fuel dealers, but only if the ethanol is produced in Ohio or in a State that grants similar tax advantages to ethanol produced in Ohio. The question presented is whether § 5735.145(B) discriminates against interstate commerce in violation of the Commerce Clause, U.S.Const., Art. I, § 8, cl. 3.

I

Ethanol, or ethyl alcohol, is usually made from corn. In the last decade it has come into widespread use as an automotive fuel, mixed with gasoline in a ratio of 1:9 to produce what is called gasohol. The interest in ethanol emerged in reaction to the petroleum market dislocations of the early 1970's. The product was originally promoted as a means of achieving energy independence while providing a market for surplus corn; more recently, emphasis has shifted to its environmental advantages as a replacement for lead in enhancing fuel octane. See United States Department of Agriculture, Ethanol: Economic and Policy Tradeoffs 1 (1988). Ethanol was, however (and continues to be), more expensive than gasoline, and the emergence of ethanol production on a commercial scale dates from enactment of the first federal subsidy, in the form of an exemption from federal motor fuel excise taxes, in 1978. See Energy Tax Act of 1978, Pub.L. 95–618, § 221, 92 Stat. 3185, codified, as amended, at 26 U.S.C. §§ 4041, 4081 (1982 ed. and Supp. IV). Since then, many States, particularly those in the grain-producing areas of the country, have enacted their own ethanol subsidies. See

53

United States General Accounting Office, Importance and Impact of Federal Alcohol Fuel Tax Incentives 5 (1984). Ohio first passed such a measure in 1981, providing Ohio gasohol dealers a credit of so many cents per gallon of ethanol used in their product against the Ohio motor vehicle fuel sales tax payable on both ethanol and gasoline. This credit was originally available without regard to the source of the ethanol. See Act of June 10, 1981, § 1, 1981–1982 Ohio Leg.Acts 1693, 1731–1732. In 1984, however, Ohio enacted § 5735.145(B), which denies the credit to ethanol coming from States that do not grant a tax credit, exemption, or refund to ethanol from Ohio, or, if a State grants a smaller tax advantage than Ohio's, granting only an equivalent credit to ethanol from that State.

Appellant is an Indiana limited partnership that manufactures ethanol in South Bend, Indiana, for sale in several States, including Ohio. Indiana repealed its tax exemption for ethanol, effective July 1, 1985, see Act of Mar. 5, 1984, §§ 4, 5, 8, 1984 Ind.Acts 189, 194–195, at which time it also passed legislation providing a direct subsidy to Indiana ethanol producers (the sole one of which was appellant). See Ind.Code §§ 4–4–10.1 to 4–4–10.8 (Supp.1987). Thus, by reason of Ohio's reciprocity provision, appellant's ethanol sold in Ohio became ineligible for the Ohio tax credit. Appellant sought declaratory and injunctive relief in the Court of Common Pleas of Franklin County, Ohio, alleging that § 5735.145(B) violated the Commerce Clause by discriminating against out-of-state ethanol producers to the advantage of in-state industry. The court denied relief, and the Ohio Court of Appeals affirmed. A divided Ohio Supreme Court initially reversed, finding that § 5735.145(B) discriminated without adequate justification against products of out-of-state origin, and shielded Ohio producers from out-of-state competition. The Ohio Supreme Court then granted appellees' motion for rehearing and reversed itself, a majority of the court finding that the provision was not protectionist or unreasonably burdensome. 32 Ohio St.3d 206, 513 N.E.2d 258 (1987). . . .

II

It has long been accepted that the Commerce Clause not only grants Congress the authority to regulate commerce among the States, but also directly limits the power of the States to discriminate against interstate commerce. See, e.g., Hughes v. Oklahoma, 441 U.S. 322, 326 (1979); H.P. Hood & Sons, Inc. v. Du Mond, 336 U.S. 525, 534–535 (1949); Welton v. Missouri, 91 U.S. 275 (1876). This "negative" aspect of the Commerce Clause prohibits economic protectionism—that is, regulatory measures designed to benefit in-state economic interests by burdening out-of-state competitors. See, e.g., Bacchus Imports, Ltd. v. Dias, 468 U.S. 263, 270–273 (1984); *H.P. Hood & Sons,* supra, at 532–533; Guy v. Baltimore, 100 U.S. 434, 443 (1880). Thus, state statutes that clearly discriminate against interstate commerce are routinely struck down, see, e.g., Sporhase v. Nebraska ex rel. Douglas, 458 U.S. 941 (1982); Lewis v. BT Investment Managers, Inc., 447 U.S. 27 (1980); Dean Milk Co. v. Madison, 340 U.S. 349 (1951), unless the discrimination is demonstrably justified by a valid factor unrelated to economic protectionism, see, e.g., Maine v. Taylor, 477 U.S. 131 (1986).

The Ohio provision at issue here explicitly deprives certain products of generally available beneficial tax treatment because they are made in certain other States, and thus on its face appears to violate the cardinal requirement of nondiscrimination. Appellees argue, however, that the availability of the tax credit to some out-of-state manufacturers (those in States that give tax advantages to Ohio-produced ethanol) shows that the Ohio provision, far from discriminating against interstate commerce, is likely to promote it, by encouraging other States to enact similar tax advantages that will spur the interstate sale of ethanol. We rejected a similar contention in an earlier "reciprocity" case, Great Atlantic & Pacific Tea Co. v. Cottrell, 424 U.S. 366 (1976). The regulation at issue there permitted milk from out of State to be sold in Mississippi only if the State of origin accepted Mississippi milk on a reciprocal basis. Mississippi put forward, among other arguments, the assertion that "the reciprocity requirement is in effect a free-trade provision, advancing the identical national interest that is served by the Commerce Clause." Id., at 378. In response, we said that "Mississippi may not use the threat of economic isolation as a weapon to force sister States to enter into even a desirable reciprocity agreement." Id., at 379. More recently, we characterized a Nebraska reciprocity requirement for the export of ground water from the State as "facially discriminatory legislation" which merited " 'strictest scrutiny.' " Sporhase v. Nebraska ex rel. Douglas, supra, at 958, quoting Hughes v. Oklahoma, supra, at 337.

It is true that in *Cottrell* and *Sporhase* the effect of a State's refusal to accept the offered reciprocity was total elimination of all transport of the subject product into or out of the offering State; whereas in the present case the only effect of refusal is that the out-of-state product is placed at a substantial commercial disadvantage through discriminatory tax treatment. That makes no difference for purposes of Commerce Clause analysis. In the leading case of Baldwin v. G.A.F. Seelig, Inc., 294 U.S. 511 (1935), the New York law excluding out-of-state milk did not impose an absolute ban, but rather allowed importation and sale so long as the initial purchase from the dairy farmer was made at or above the New York State-mandated price. In other words, just as the appellant here, in order to sell its product in Ohio, only has to cut its profits by reducing its sales price below the market price sufficiently to compensate the Ohio purchaser-retailer for the forgone tax credit, so also the milk wholesaler-distributor in *Baldwin*, in order to sell its product in New York, only had to cut its profits by increasing its purchase price above the market price sufficiently to meet the New York-prescribed minimum. We viewed the New York law as "an economic barrier against competition" that was "equivalent to a rampart of customs duties." Id., at 527. Similarly, in Hunt v. Washington Apple Advertising Comm'n, 432 U.S. 333, 349–351 (1977), we found invalid under the Commerce Clause a North Carolina statute that did not exclude apples from other States, but merely imposed additional costs upon Washington sellers and deprived them of the commercial advantage of their distinctive grading system. The present law likewise imposes an economic disadvantage upon out-of-state sellers; and the promise to remove that if reciprocity is accepted no more justifies disparity of treatment than it would justify categorical exclusion. We have indicated that reciprocity requirements are not *per se* unlawful. See *Cottrell,* supra, at 378. But the case we cited for that proposition, Kane v. New Jersey, 242 U.S. 160, 167–168 (1916), discussed a context in which, if a State offered the reciprocity did not accept it, the consequence was, to be sure, *less favored* treatment for its citizens, but nonetheless treatment that complied with the minimum requirements of the Commerce Clause. Here, quite to the contrary, the threat used to induce Indiana's acceptance is, in effect, taxing a product made by its manufacturers at a rate higher than the same product made by Ohio manufacturers, without (as we shall see) justification for the disparity.

Appellees argue that § 5735.145(B) should not be considered discrimination against interstate commerce because its practical scope is so limited. Apparently only one Ohio ethanol manufacturer exists (appellee South Point Ethanol) and only one out-of-state manufacturer (appellant) is clearly disadvantaged by the provision. Our cases, however, indicate that where discrimination is patent, as it is here, neither a widespread advantage to in-state interests nor a widespread disadvantage to out-of-state competitors need be shown. For example, in *Bacchus Imports, Ltd. v. Dias,* supra, we held unconstitutional under the Commerce Clause a special exemption from Hawaii's liquor tax for certain locally produced alcoholic beverages (okolehao and fruit wine), even though other locally produced alcoholic beverages were subject to the tax. 468 U.S., at 265, 271. And in *Lewis v. BT Investment Managers, Inc.,* supra, we held unconstitutional a Florida statute that excluded from certain business activities in Florida not all out-of-state entities, but only out-of-state bank holding companies, banks, or trust companies. In neither of these cases did we consider the size or number of the in-state businesses favored or the out-of-state businesses disfavored relevant to our determination. Varying the strength of the bar against economic protectionism according to the size and number of in-state and out-of-state firms affected would serve no purpose except the creation of new uncertainties in an already complex field.

. . .

It has not escaped our notice that the appellant here, which is eligible to receive a cash subsidy under Indiana's program for in-state ethanol producers, is the potential beneficiary of a scheme no less discriminatory than the one that it attacks, and no less effective in conferring a commercial advantage over out-of-state competitors. To believe the Indiana scheme is valid, however, is not to believe that the Ohio scheme must be valid as well. The Commerce Clause does not prohibit all state action designed to give its residents an advantage in the marketplace, but only action of that description *in connection with the State's regulation of interstate commerce.* Direct subsidization of domestic industry does not ordinarily run afoul of that prohibition; discriminatory taxation of out-of-state manufactures does. Of course, even if the Indiana subsidy were invalid, retaliatory violation of the

Commerce Clause by Ohio would not be acceptable. See *Cottrell*, 424 U.S., at 379–380.

III

Our cases leave open the possibility that a State may validate a statute that discriminates against interstate commerce by showing that it advances a legitimate local purpose that cannot be adequately served by reasonable nondiscriminatory alternatives. See, e.g., Maine v. Taylor, 477 U.S., at 138, 151; Sporhase v. Nebraska ex rel. Douglas, 458 U.S., at 958; Hughes v. Oklahoma, 441 U.S., at 336–337; Dean Milk Co. v. Madison, 340 U.S., at 354. This is perhaps just another way of saying that what may appear to be a "discriminatory" provision in the constitutionally prohibited sense—that is, a protectionist enactment—may on closer analysis not be so. However it be put, the standards for such justification are high. Cf. Philadelphia v. New Jersey, 437 U.S. 617, 624 (1978) ("[W]here simple economic protectionism is effected by state legislation, a virtually *per se* rule of invalidity has been erected"); Hughes v. Oklahoma, 441 U.S., at 337 ("[F]acial discrimination by itself may be a fatal defect" and "[a]t a minimum . . . invokes the strictest scrutiny").

Appellees advance two justifications for the clear discrimination in the present case: health and commerce. As to the first, they argue that the provision encourages use of ethanol (in replacement of lead as a gasoline octane-enhancer) to reduce harmful exhaust emissions, both in Ohio itself and in surrounding States whose polluted atmosphere may reach Ohio. Certainly the protection of health is a legitimate state goal, and we assume for purposes of this argument that use of ethanol generally furthers it. But § 5735.145(B) obviously does not, except perhaps by accident. As far as ethanol use in Ohio itself is concerned, there is no reason to suppose that ethanol produced in a State that does not offer tax advantages to ethanol produced in Ohio is less healthy, and thus should have its importation into Ohio suppressed by denial of the otherwise standard tax credit. And as far as ethanol use outside Ohio is concerned, surely that is just as effectively fostered by other States' subsidizing ethanol production or sale in some fashion other than giving a tax credit to Ohio-produced ethanol; but these helpful expedients do not qualify for the tax credit. It could not be clearer that health is not the purpose of the provision, but is merely an occasional and accidental effect of achieving what is its purpose, favorable tax treatment for Ohio-produced ethanol. Essentially the same reasoning also responds to appellees' second (and related) justification for the discrimination, that the reciprocity requirement is designed to increase commerce in ethanol by encouraging other States to enact ethanol subsidies. What is encouraged is not ethanol subsidies in general, but only favorable treatment for Ohio-produced ethanol. In sum, appellees' health and commerce justifications amount to no more than implausible speculation, which does not suffice to validate this plain discrimination against products of out-of-state manufacture.

. . . .

For the reasons stated, judgment of the Ohio Supreme Court is Reversed.

Page 348.   Add ahead of Note:

For further consideration of the problems in *Western and Southern Life Insurance Co.,* see Metropolitan Life Insurance Co. v. Ward, 470 U.S. 869, set out infra p. 194.

For a case holding that an exemption in a sales and use tax statute was invalid under the equal protection clause because it favored residents of the state, see Williams v. Vermont, 472 U.S. 14, set out infra p. 204.

Page 348.   Add to first paragraph of Note:

For a recent case dealing with the statute, see Burlington Northern Railroad Co. v. Oklahoma Tax Comm., 107 S.Ct. 1855 (1987).

Page 366.   Add to Note:

In R.J. Reynolds Tobacco Co. v. Durham County, 479 U.S. 130 (1986) the Court held that North Carolina could impose a nondiscriminatory ad valorem property tax on imported goods stored under bond in a customs warehouse and destined for domestic manufacture and sale. The Court said that the tax seemed indistinguishable from the tax in *Michelin* and did not violate the import-export clause.

Page 371.   Add at end of page:

WARDAIR CANADA, INC. v. FLORIDA DEPARTMENT OF REVENUE, 477 U.S. 1 (1986).   Florida in 1983 applied its tax on aviation fuel to the full amount of the fuel purchased in the state even though the fuel was used largely in interstate or foreign commerce. Wardair, a Canadian corporation operating charter flights between Canada and the United States, brought suit challenging the constitutionality of the tax.   The Court upheld the tax, basically on the ground that the federal government had permitted the states to impose such taxes and hence the dormant commerce clause analysis did not apply.

SECTION 3.   JURISDICTION TO TAX AND APPORTIONMENT

B.   SALES AND USE TAXES

Page 390.   Add at end of page:

D.H. HOLMES CO., LTD. v. McNAMARA, 108 S.Ct. 1619 (1988). D.H. Holmes, a Louisiana corporation with 13 department stores in Louisiana, had merchandizing catalogs printed outside Louisiana and mailed directly to residents of that state.   Louisiana imposed its use tax on all catalogs shipped to Louisiana residents.   Holmes asserted that imposition of the tax was forbidden by the Commerce Clause.   The Supreme Court unanimously rejected that assertion.   It said that the tax complied with the four prongs of the *Complete Auto* formula. It was fairly apportioned because it provided a credit against its use tax for sales taxes paid to other states. It did not discriminate against interstate commerce—its rate was the same as that of the sales tax imposed upon goods purchased in the state. It was fairly related to benefits provided by the state. And Holmes' substantial business activities in the state provided an adequate nexus with Louisiana.

Chapter 7

INTERGOVERNMENTAL RELATIONSHIPS WITHIN THE FEDERAL SYSTEM

SECTION 1. INTERGOVERNMENTAL TAX IMMUNITY

B. STATE IMMUNITY

Page 398. Replace Massachusetts v. United States with the following:

SOUTH CAROLINA v. BAKER

__ U.S. __, 108 S.Ct. 1355, 99 L.Ed.2d 592 (1988).

Justice Brennan delivered the opinion of the Court.

Section 310(b)(1) of the Tax Equity and Fiscal Responsibility Act of 1982 (TEFRA), Pub.L. 97–248, 96 Stat. 596, 26 U.S.C. section 103(j)(1), removes the federal income tax exemption for interest earned on publicly offered long-term bonds issued by state and local governments unless those bonds are issued in registered form. This original jurisdiction case presents the issues whether section 310(b)(1) of TEFRA either (1) violates the Tenth Amendment and constitutional principles of federalism by compelling States to issue bonds in registered form or (2) violates the doctrine of intergovernmental tax immunity by taxing the interest earned on unregistered state bonds.

I

. . .

In 1982, Congress enacted TEFRA, which contains a variety of provisions, including section 310, designed to reduce the federal deficit by promoting compliance with the tax laws. . . . Unregistered bonds apparently became a focus of attention because they left no paper trail and thus facilitated tax evasion. . . .

. . .

Because section 310 aims to address the tax evasion concerns posed generally by unregistered bonds, it covers not only state bonds but also bonds issued by the United States and private corporations. . . . Section 310(b)(1) completes this statutory scheme by denying the federal income tax exemption for interest earned on state bonds to owners of long-term publicly offered state bonds that are not issued in registered form.

. . .

[Part II of the opinion appears infra, page 80.]

III

South Carolina contends that . . . section 310 unconstitutionally violates the doctrine of intergovernmental tax immunity because it imposes a tax on the interest earned on a state bond. We agree with South Carolina that section 310 is inconsistent with Pollock v. Farmers' Loan & Trust Co., 157 U.S. 429 (1895), which held that any interest earned on a state bond was immune from federal taxation.

The Secretary and the Master, however, suggest that we should uphold the constitutionality of section 310 without explicitly overruling *Pollock* because section 310 does not abolish the tax exemption for state bond interest entirely but rather taxes the interest on state bonds only if the bonds are not issued in the form Congress requires. In our view, however, this suggestion implicitly rests on a rather mischievous proposition of law. If, for example, Congress imposed a tax that applied exclusively to South Carolina and levied the tax directly on the South Carolina treasury, we would be obligated to adjudicate the constitutionality of that tax even if Congress allowed South Carolina to escape the tax by restructuring its state government in a way Congress found more to its liking. The United States cannot convert an unconstitutional tax into a constitutional one simply by making the tax conditional. Whether Congress could have imposed the condition by direct regulation is irrelevant; Congress cannot employ unconstitutional means to reach a constitutional end. Under *Pollock,* a tax on the interest income derived from any state bond was considered a direct tax on the State and thus unconstitutional. 157 U.S., at 585–586. If this constitutional rule still applies, Congress cannot threaten to tax the interest on state bonds that do not conform to congressional dictates. We thus decline to follow a suggestion that would force us to embrace implicitly a proposition of law far more controversial than the current validity of *Pollock*'s ban on taxing state bond interest, and proceed to address whether *Pollock* should be explicitly overruled.

Under the intergovernmental tax immunity jurisprudence prevailing at the time, *Pollock* did not represent a unique immunity limited to income derived from state bonds. Rather, *Pollock* merely represented one application of the more general rule that neither the federal nor the state governments could tax income an individual directly derived from any contract with another government. Not only was it unconstitutional for the Federal Government to tax a bondowner on the interest she received on any state bond, but it was also unconstitutional to tax a state employee on the income earned from his employment contract, Collector v. Day, 11 Wall. 113 (1871), to tax a lessee on income derived from lands leased from a State, Burnet v. Coronado Oil, 285 U.S. 393 (1932), or to impose a sales tax on proceeds a vendor derived from selling a product to a state agency, Indian Motorcycle Co. v. United States, 283 U.S. 570 (1931). Income derived from the same kinds of contracts with the Federal Government were likewise immune from taxation by the States. . . . Cases concerning the tax immunity of income derived from state contracts freely cited principles established in federal tax immunity cases, and vice versa. . . .

This general rule was based on the rationale that any tax on income a party received under a contract with the government was a tax on the contract and thus a tax "on" the government because it burdened the government's power to enter into the contract. . . .

Thus, although a tax was collected from an independent private party, the tax was considered to be "on" the government because the tax burden might be passed on to it through the contract. This reasoning was used to determine the basic scope of both federal and state tax immunities with respect to all types of government contracts.[10]. . . The commonality of the rationale underlying all these immunities for government contracts was highlighted by *Indian Motorcycle,* supra. In that case, the Court reviewed the then current status of intergovernmental tax immunity doctrine, observing that a tax on interest earned on a state or federal bond was unconstitutional because it would burden the exercise of the government's power to borrow money and that a tax on the salary of state or Federal Government employee was unconstitutional because it would burden the government's power to obtain the employee's services. Id., at 576–578. It then concluded that under the same principle a sales tax imposed on a vendor for a sale to a state agency was unconstitutional because it would burden the sale transaction. Id., at 579.

The rationale underlying *Pollock* and the general immunity for government contract income has been thoroughly repudiated by modern intergovernmental immunity caselaw. In Graves v. New York ex rel. O'Keefe, 306 U.S. 466 (1939), the Court announced, "The theory . . . that a tax on income is legally or economically a tax on its source, is no longer tenable." Id., at 480. . . .

---

[10] The sources of the state and federal immunities are, of course, different: the state immunity arises from the constitutional structure and a concern for protecting state sovereignty whereas the federal immunity arises from the Supremacy Clause. The immunities have also differed somewhat in their underlying political theory and in their doctrinal contours. Many of this Court's opinions have suggested that the Constitution should be interpreted to confer a greater tax immunity on the Federal Government than on States because all the people of the States are represented in the Federal Government whereas all the people of the Federal Government are not represented in individual States. Helvering v. Gerhardt, 304 U.S. 405, 412 (1938); McCulloch v. Maryland, 4 Wheat. 316, 435–436 (1819); New York v. United States, 326 U.S. 572, 577, and n. 3 (1946) (Opinion of Frankfurter, J.). In fact, the federal tax immunity has always been greater than the States' immunity. The Federal Government, for example, possesses the power to enact statutes immunizing those with whom it deals from state taxation even if intergovernmental tax immunity doctrine would not otherwise confer an immunity. See, e.g., Graves v. New York ex rel. O'Keefe, 306 U.S. 466, 478 (1939). The States lack any such power. Also, although the Federal Government has always enjoyed blanket immunity from any state tax considered to be "on" the government under the prevailing methodology, the States have never enjoyed immunity from all federal taxes considered to be "on" a State. To some, Garcia v. San Antonio Metropolitan Transit Authority, 469 U.S. 528 (1985), may suggest further limitations on state tax immunity. We need not, however, decide here the extent to which the scope of the federal and state immunities differ or the extent, if any, to which States are currently immune from direct nondiscriminatory federal taxation. It is enough for our purposes that federal and state tax immunity cases have always shared the identical methodology for determining whether a tax is "on" a government, and that this identity has persisted even though the methodology for both federal and state immunities has changed as intergovernmental tax immunity doctrine shifted into the modern era.

. . .

With the rationale for conferring a tax immunity on parties dealing with another government rejected, the government contract immunities recognized under prior doctrine were, one by one, eliminated. Overruling Burnet v. Coronado Oil, 285 U.S. 393 (1932), and Gillespie v. Oklahoma, 257 U.S. 501 (1922), the Court upheld the constitutionality of a federal tax on net income a corporation derived from a state lease in Helvering v. Mountain Producers Corp., 303 U.S. 376 (1938). See also Oklahoma Tax Comm'n v. Texas Co., 336 U.S. 342 (1949) (upholding constitutionality of federal tax on gross income derived from state lease). Later, the Court explicitly overruled Collector v. Day, 11 Wall. 113 (1871), and upheld the constitutionality of a nondiscriminatory state tax on the salary of a federal employee. Graves v. New York ex rel. O'Keefe, 306 U.S. 466 (1939). . . . The only premodern tax immunity for parties to government contracts that has so far avoided being explicitly overruled is the immunity for recipients of governmental bond interest. That this Court has yet to overrule *Pollock* explicitly, however, is explained not by any distinction between the income derived from government bonds and the income derived from other government contracts, but by the historical fact that Congress has always exempted state bond interest from taxation by statute, beginning with the very first federal income tax statute. Act of Oct. 3, 1913, ch. 16, section II(B), 38 Stat. 168.

In sum, then, under current intergovernmental tax immunity doctrine the States can never tax the United States directly but can tax any private parties with whom it does business, even though the financial burden falls on the United States, as long as the tax does not discriminate against the United States or those with whom it deals. . . . The rule with respect to state tax immunity is essentially the same, . . . except that at least some nondiscriminatory federal taxes can be collected directly from the States even though a parallel state tax could not be collected directly from the Federal Government.[13]

We thus confirm that subsequent caselaw has overruled the holding in *Pollock* that state bond interest is immune from a nondiscriminatory federal tax. We see no constitutional reason for treating persons who receive interest on government bonds differently than persons who receive income from other types of contracts with the government, and

[13] All federal activities are immune from direct state taxation . . . but at least some state activities have always been subject to direct federal taxation. For a time, only the States' governmental, as opposed to proprietary, activities enjoyed tax immunity, . . . but this distinction was subsequently abandoned as untenable by all eight justices participating in New York v. United States, 326 U.S. 572 (1946). . . . Two justices reasoned that any nondiscriminatory tax on a State was constitutional, even if directly collected from the State. See id., at 582–584 (Frankfurter, J., joined by Rutledge, J.). Four other justices declined to hold that every nondiscriminatory tax levied directly on a State would be constitutional . . . 326 U.S., at 587 (Stone, C.J., concurring, joined by Reed, Murphy and Burton, JJ.) . . . We need not concern ourselves here, however, with the extent to which, if any, States are currently immune from direct federal taxation. See supra, n. 10. For our purposes, the important principle *New York* reaffirms is that the issue whether a nondiscriminatory federal tax might nonetheless violate state tax immunity does not even arise unless the Federal Government seeks to collect the tax directly from a State.

no tenable rationale for distinguishing the costs imposed on States by a tax on state bond interest from the costs imposed by a tax on the income from any other state contract. . . .

. . . .

TEFRA section 310 thus clearly imposes no direct tax on the States. The tax is imposed on and collected from bondholders, not States, and any increased administrative costs incurred by States in implementing the registration system are not "taxes" within the meaning of the tax immunity doctrine. . . .

IV

. . . [B]ecause a nondiscriminatory federal tax on the interest earned on state bonds does not violate the intergovernmental tax immunity doctrine, we uphold the constitutionality of section 310, overrule the exceptions to the Special Master's Report, and approve his recommendation to enter judgment for the defendant.

It is so ordered.

Justice Kennedy took no part in the consideration or decision of this case.

[Concurring opinions by Justice Scalia and Chief Justice Rehnquist appear infra, page 82. A concurring opinion by Justice Stevens is omitted.]

Justice O'Connor, dissenting.

The Court today overrules a precedent that it has honored for nearly a hundred years and expresses a willingness to cancel the constitutional immunity that traditionally has shielded the interest paid on state and local bonds from federal taxation. Henceforth the ability of state and local governments to finance their activities will depend in part on whether Congress voluntarily abstains from tapping this permissible source of additional income tax revenue. I believe that state autonomy is an important factor to be considered in reviewing the National Government's exercise of its enumerated powers. . . . I dissent from the decision to overrule Pollock v. Farmers' Loan & Trust Co., 157 U.S. 429 (1895), and I would invalidate Congress' attempt to regulate the sovereign States by threatening to deprive them of this tax immunity, which would increase their dependence on the National Government.

. . . .

I do not think the Court's bipartite test adequately accommodates the constitutional concerns raised by the prospect of applying the federal income tax to the interest paid on state and local bonds. This Court has a duty to inquire into the devastating effects that such an innovation would have on state and local governments. Although Congress has taken a relatively less burdensome step in subjecting only income from bearer bonds to federal taxation, the erosion of state sovereignty is likely to occur a step at a time. "If there is any danger, it lies in the tyranny of small decisions—in the prospect that Congress will nibble away at state sovereignty, bit by bit, until someday essentially nothing is left but a gutted shell." L. Tribe, American Constitutional Law 381 (2d ed. 1988).

. . . If this Court is the States' sole protector against the threat of crushing taxation, it must take seriously its responsibility to sit in judgment of federal tax initiatives. I do not think that the Court has lived up to its constitutional role in this case. The Court has failed to enforce the constitutional safeguards of state autonomy and self-sufficiency that may be found in the Tenth Amendment and the Guarantee Clause, as well as in the principles of federalism implicit in the Constitution. I respectfully dissent.

SECTION 2. INTERGOVERNMENTAL REGULATORY IMMUNITY

B. STATE IMMUNITY

Page 408. Replace pages 408–425 (*National League of Cities, United Transportation Union,* EEOC v. Wyoming, and *Hodel*):

STATE IMMUNITY FROM FEDERAL REGULATION—1976–1985

Maryland v. Wirtz was overruled in the five to four decision of the Court in National League of Cities v. Usery, 426 U.S. 833 (1976). 1974 amendments to the Fair Labor Standards Act extended the Act's maximum hour and minimum wage provisions to employees of the states and their political subdivisions. The Court held that the Act could not constitutionally be applied to state employees performing traditional governmental functions. Justice Rehnquist's opinion for the Court relied on the statement in the footnote to the *Fry* opinion that Congress could not "exercise power in a fashion that impairs the States' integrity or their ability to function effectively in a federal system." Applying the Fair Labor Standards Act to state employees would impose costs and limit flexibility. The Court concluded that "insofar as the challenged amendments operate to directly displace the States' freedom to structure integral operations in areas of traditional government functions, they are not within the authority granted Congress by" the Commerce Clause. Justice Blackmun joined the Court's opinion, but admitted in a concurrence that he was "not untroubled by certain possible implications of the Court's opinion." He explained that he joined the Court's opinion because he read it to adopt "a balancing approach" that permitted federal regulation "where the federal interest is demonstrably greater and where state . . . compliance with imposed federal standards would be essential." Justice Brennan's dissent, joined by Justices White and Marshall, argued that "restraints upon exercise by Congress of its plenary commerce power lies in the political process and not in the judicial process. . . . [T]he political branches of our Government are structured to protect the interests of the States, as well as the Nation as a whole, and . . . the States are fully able to protect their own interests . . .." Justice Stevens' dissent emphasized the absence of standards distinguishing invalid federal regulation and "federal regulation of state activities that I consider unquestionably permissible."

In Hodel v. Virginia Surface Mining and Reclamation Association, Inc., 452 U.S. 264 (1981), the Court summarized three requirements that *National League of Cities* challenges to federal legislation must meet in order to succeed. "First, there must be a showing that the challenged statute regulates the 'states as states.' . . . Second, the federal regulation must address matters that are indisputably 'attribute[s] of state sovereignty.' . . . And, third, it must be apparent that the States' compliance with the federal law would directly impair their ability 'to structure integral operations in areas of traditional governmental functions.'" (The Court also mentioned in a footnote the possibility that a challenged federal law would be valid, even if all three requirements were satisfied, under the balancing test suggested by Justice Blackmun's concurrence in *National League of Cities.*)

In United Transportation Union v. Long Island Railroad Co., 455 U.S. 678 (1982), the Court was unanimous, concluding that a state-owned railroad was not immune from application of the labor provisions of the Railway Labor Act, because operation of a railroad was not a "traditional" state function. In Equal Employment Opportunity Commission v. Wyoming, 460 U.S. 226 (1983), however, the Court divided five to four with Justice Blackmun joining the four *National League of Cities* dissenters to form the majority. The Court upheld a 1974 amendment to the Age Discrimination in Employment Act extending the Act to state employees. The case arose out of the involuntary retirement of a state game warden at age 55, which violated provisions of the Act forbidding involuntary retirement prior to age 70. Justice Brennan's opinion for the Court concluded that state compliance with the Act would be less costly than, and would not impair flexibility to the same degree as, the minimum wage and maximum hour provisions at issue in *National League of Cities.* The prohibitions of the Age Discrimination Act thus involved federal intrusion that was "sufficiently less serious" and did not impair states' ability to structure their integral operations—a question that "must depend . . . on considerations of degree."

GARCIA v. SAN ANTONIO METROPOLITAN TRANSIT AUTHORITY

469 U.S. 528, 105 S.Ct. 1005, 83 L.Ed.2d 1016 (1985).

Justice Blackmun delivered the opinion of the Court.

We revisit in these cases an issue raised in National League of Cities v. Usery, 426 U.S. 833 (1976). In that litigation, this Court, by a sharply divided vote, ruled that the Commerce Clause does not empower Congress to enforce the minimum-wage and overtime provisions of the Fair Labor Standards Act (FLSA) against the States "in areas of traditional governmental functions." Id., at 852. Although *National League of Cities* supplied some examples of "traditional governmental functions," it did not offer a general explanation of how a "traditional" function is to be distinguished from a "nontraditional" one. Since then, federal and state courts have struggled with the task, thus imposed, of identifying a traditional function for purposes of state immunity under the Commerce Clause.

In the present cases, a Federal District Court concluded that municipal ownership and operation of a mass-transit system is a traditional governmental function and thus, under *National League of Cities,* is exempt from the obligations imposed by the FLSA. Faced with the identical question, three Federal Courts of Appeals and one state appellate court have reached the opposite conclusion.

Our examination of this "function" standard applied in these and other cases over the last eight years now persuades us that the attempt to draw the boundaries of state regulatory immunity in terms of "traditional governmental function" is not only unworkable but is inconsistent with established principles of federalism and, indeed, with those very federalism principles on which *National League of Cities* purported to rest. That case, accordingly, is overruled.

I

. . .

The FLSA obligations of public mass-transit systems like SATS were expanded in 1974 when Congress provided for the progressive repeal of the surviving overtime exemption for mass-transit employees. Fair Labor Standards Amendments of 1974, § 21(b), 88 Stat. 68. Congress simultaneously brought the States and their subdivisions further within the ambit of the FLSA by extending FLSA coverage to virtually all state and local-government employees. §§ 6(a)(1) and (6), 88 Stat. 58, 60, 29 U.S.C. §§ 203(d) and (x). SATS complied with the FLSA's overtime requirements until 1976, when this Court, in *National League of Cities,* supra, overruled *Maryland v. Wirtz,* and held that the FLSA could not be applied constitutionally to the "traditional governmental functions" of state and local governments. Four months after *National League of Cities* was handed down, SATS informed its employees that the decision relieved SATS of its overtime obligations under the FLSA.

. . .

. . . After initial argument, the cases were restored to our calendar for reargument, and the parties were requested to brief and argue the following additional question:

"Whether or not the principles of the Tenth Amendment as set forth in National League of Cities v. Usery, 426 U.S. 833 (1976), should be reconsidered?" . . .

II

. . .

The controversy in the present cases has focused on the third *Hodel* requirement—that the challenged federal statute trench on "traditional governmental functions.". . .

Thus far, this Court itself has made little headway in defining the scope of the governmental functions deemed *protected* under *National League of Cities*. In that case the Court set forth examples of protected and unprotected functions, see 426 U.S., at 851, 854, n. 18, but provided no explanation of how those examples were identified. The only other case in which the Court has had occasion to address the problem is *Long Island*. We there observed: "The determination of whether a federal law impairs a state's authority with respect to 'areas of traditional [state] functions' may at times be a difficult one." 455 U.S., at 684, quoting National League of Cities, 426 U.S., at 852. The accuracy of that statement is demonstrated by this Court's own difficulties in *Long Island* in developing a workable standard for "traditional governmental functions." We relied in large part there on "the *historical reality* that the operation of railroads is not among the functions *traditionally* performed by state and local governments," but we simultaneously disavowed "a static historical view of state functions generally immune from federal regulation." 455 U.S., at 686 (first emphasis added; second emphasis in original). . . . Finally, having disclaimed a rigid reliance on the historical pedigree of state involvement in a particular area, we nonetheless found it appropriate to emphasize the extended historical record of federal involvement in the field of rail transportation. Id., at 687–689.

Many constitutional standards involve "undoubte[d] . . . gray areas," Fry v. United States, 421 U.S. 542, 558 (1975) (dissenting opinion), and, despite the difficulties that this Court and other courts have encountered so far, it normally might be fair to venture the assumption that case-by-case development would lead to a workable standard for determining whether a particular governmental function should be immune from federal regulation under the Commerce Clause. . . .

. . .

The distinction the Court discarded as unworkable in the field of tax immunity has proved no more fruitful in the field of regulatory immunity under the Commerce Clause. Neither do any of the alternative standards that might be employed to distinguish between protected and unprotected governmental functions appear manageable. We rejected the possibility of making immunity turn on a purely historical standard of "tradition" in *Long Island*, and properly so. The most obvious defect of a historical approach to state immunity is that it prevents a court from accommodating changes in the historical functions of States, changes that have resulted in a number of once-private functions like education being assumed by the States and their subdivisions. At the same time, the only apparent virtue of a rigorous historical standard, namely, its promise of a reasonably objective measure for state immunity, is illusory. Reliance on history as an organizing principle results in linedrawing of the most arbitrary sort; the genesis of state governmental functions stretches over a historical continuum from before the Revolution to the present, and courts would have to decide by fiat precisely how longstanding a pattern of state involvement had to be for federal regulatory authority to be defeated.

A nonhistorical standard for selecting immune governmental functions is likely to be just as unworkable as is a historical standard. The goal of identifying "uniquely" governmental functions, for example, has been rejected by the Court in the field of government tort liability in part because the notion of a "uniquely" governmental function is unmanageable. See Indian Towing Co. v. United States, 350 U.S. 61, 64–68 (1955); see also Lafayette v. Louisiana Power & Light Co., 435 U.S. 389, 433 (1978) (dissenting opinion). Another possibility would be to confine immunity to "necessary" governmental services, that is, services that would be provided inadequately or not at all unless the government provided them. Cf. Flint v. Stone Tracy Co., 220 U.S., at 172. The set of services that fits into this category, however, may well be negligible. The fact that an unregulated market produces less of some service than a State deems desirable does not mean that the State itself must provide the service; in most if not all cases, the State can "contract out" by hiring private firms to provide the service or simply by providing subsidies to existing suppliers. It also is open to question how well equipped courts are to make this kind of determination about the workings of economic markets.

We believe, however, that there is a more fundamental problem at work here, a problem that explains why the Court was never able to provide a basis for the governmental/proprietary distinction in the intergovernmental tax immunity cases and why an attempt to draw similar distinctions with respect to federal regulatory authority under *National League of Cities* is unlikely to succeed regardless of how the distinctions are phrased. The problem is that neither the governmental/proprietary distinction nor any other that purports to separate out important governmental functions can be faithful to the role of federalism in a democratic society. The essence of our federal system is that within the realm of authority left open to them under the Constitution, the States must be equally free to engage in any activity that their citizens choose for the common weal, no matter how unorthodox or unnecessary anyone else—including the judiciary—deems state involvement to be. Any rule of state immunity that looks to the "traditional," "integral," or "necessary" nature of governmental functions inevitably invites an unelected federal judiciary to make decisions about which state policies it favors and which ones it dislikes. . . .

We therefore now reject, as unsound in principle and unworkable in practice, a rule of state immunity from federal regulation that turns on a judicial appraisal of whether a particular governmental function is "integral" or "traditional." Any such rule leads to inconsistent results at the same time that it disserves principles of democratic self-governance, and it breeds inconsistency precisely because it is divorced from those principles. If there are to be limits on the Federal Government's power to interfere with state functions—as undoubtedly there are—we must look elsewhere to find them. We accordingly return to the underlying issue that confronted this Court in *National League of Cities*—the manner in which the Constitution insulates States from the reach of Congress' power under the Commerce Clause.

III

The central theme of *National League of Cities* was that the States occupy a special position in our constitutional system and that the scope of Congress' authority under the Commerce Clause must reflect that position. Of course, the Commerce Clause by its specific language does not provide any special limitation on Congress' actions with respect to the States. See EEOC v. Wyoming, 460 U.S. 226, 248 (1983) (concurring opinion). It is equally true, however, that the text of the Constitution provides the beginning rather than the final answer to every inquiry into questions of federalism. . . .

What has proved problematic is not the perception that the Constitution's federal structure imposes limitations on the Commerce Clause, but rather the nature and content of those limitations. One approach to defining the limits on Congress' authority to regulate the States under the Commerce Clause is to identify certain underlying elements of political sovereignty that are deemed essential to the States' "separate and independent existence." Lane County v. Oregon, 7 Wall. 71, 76 (1869). This approach obviously underlay the Court's use of the "traditional governmental function" concept in *National League of Cities*. It also has led to the separate requirement that the challenged federal statute "address matters that are indisputably 'attribute[s]' of state sovereignty.'" Hodel, 452 U.S., at 288, quoting National League of Cities, 426 U.S., at 845. In *National League of Cities* itself, for example, the Court concluded that decisions by a State concerning the wages and hours of its employees are an "undoubted attribute of state sovereignty." 426 U.S., at 845. The opinion did not explain what aspects of such decisions made them such an "undoubted attribute," and the Court since then has remarked on the uncertain scope of the concept. See EEOC v. Wyoming, 460 U.S., at 238, n. 11. The point of the inquiry, however, has remained to single out particular features of a State's internal governance that are deemed to be intrinsic parts of state sovereignty.

We doubt that courts ultimately can identify principled constitutional limitations on the scope of Congress' Commerce Clause powers over the States merely by relying on *a priori* definitions of state sovereignty. In part, this is because of the elusiveness of objective criteria for "fundamental" elements of state sovereignty, a problem we have witnessed in the search for "traditional governmental functions." There is, however, a more fundamental reason: the sovereignty of the States is limited by the Constitution itself. A variety of sovereign powers, for example, are withdrawn from the States by Article I, § 10. Section 8 of the same Article works an equally sharp contraction of state sovereignty by authorizing Congress to exercise a wide range of legislative powers and (in conjunction with the Supremacy Clause of

Article VI) to displace contrary state legislation. See *Hodel,* 452 U.S., at 290–292. By providing for final review of questions of federal law in this Court, Article III curtails the sovereign power of the States' judiciaries to make authoritative determinations of law. See Martin v. Hunter's Lessee, 1 Wheat. 304 (1816). Finally, the developed application, through the Fourteenth Amendment, of the greater part of the Bill of Rights to the States limits the sovereign authority that States otherwise would possess to legislate with respect to their citizens and to conduct their own affairs.

The States unquestionably do "retai[n] a significant measure of sovereign authority." EEOC v. Wyoming, 460 U.S., at 269 (Powell, J., dissenting). They do so, however, only to the extent that the Constitution has not divested them of their original powers and transferred those powers to the Federal Government. . . .

. . .

When we look for the States' "residuary and inviolable sovereignty," The Federalist No. 39, p. 285 (B. Wright ed. 1961) (J. Madison), in the shape of the constitutional scheme rather than in predetermined notions of sovereign power, a different measure of state sovereignty emerges. Apart from the limitation on federal authority inherent in the delegated nature of Congress' Article I powers, the principal means chosen by the Framers to ensure the role of the States in the federal system lies in the structure of the Federal Government itself. It is no novelty to observe that the composition of the Federal Government was designed in large part to protect the States from overreaching by Congress.[11] The Framers thus gave the States a role in the selection both of the Executive and the Legislative Branches of the Federal Government. The States were vested with indirect influence over the House of Representatives and the Presidency by their control of electoral qualifications and their role in presidential elections. U.S. Const., Art. I, § 2, and Art. II, § 1. They were given more direct influence in the Senate, where each State received equal representation and each Senator was to be selected by the legislature of his State. Art. I, § 3. The significance attached to the States' equal representation in the Senate is underscored by the prohibition of any constitutional amendment divesting a State of equal representation without the State's consent. Art. V.

The extent to which the structure of the Federal Government itself was relied on to insulate the interests of the States is evident in the views of the Framers. James Madison explained that the Federal Government "will partake sufficiently of the spirit [of the States], to be disinclined to invade the rights of the individual States, or the prerogatives of their governments." The Federalist No. 46, p. 332 (B. Wright ed. 1961). Similarly, James Wilson observed that "it was a favorite object in the Convention" to provide for the security of the States

[11] See, e.g., J. Choper, Judicial Review and the National Political Process 175–184 (1980); Wechsler, The Political Safeguards of Federalism: The Role of the States in the Composition and Selection of the National Government, 54 Colum.L.Rev. 543 (1954); La Pierre, The Political Safeguards of Federalism Redux: Intergovernmental Immunity and the States as Agents of the Nation, 60 Wash.U.L.Q. 779 (1982).

against federal encroachment and that the structure of the Federal Government itself served that end. 2 Elliot, at 438–439. Madison placed particular reliance on the equal representation of the States in the Senate, which he saw as "at once a constitutional recognition of the portion of sovereignty remaining in the individual States, and an instrument for preserving that residuary sovereignty." The Federalist No. 62, p. 408 (B. Wright ed. 1961). He further noted that "the residuary sovereignty of the States [is] implied *and secured* by that principle of representation in one branch of the [federal] legislature" (emphasis added). The Federalist No. 43, p. 315 (B. Wright ed. 1961). See also M'Culloch v. Maryland, 4 Wheat. 316, 435 (1819). In short, the Framers chose to rely on a federal system in which special restraints on federal power over the States inhered principally in the workings of the National Government itself, rather than in discrete limitations on the objects of federal authority. State sovereign interests, then, are more properly protected by procedural safeguards inherent in the structure of the federal system than by judicially created limitations on federal power.

The effectiveness of the federal political process in preserving the States' interests is apparent even today in the course of federal legislation. On the one hand, the States have been able to direct a substantial proportion of federal revenues into their own treasuries in the form of general and program-specific grants in aid. The federal role in assisting state and local governments is a longstanding one; Congress provided federal land grants to finance state governments from the beginning of the Republic, and direct cash grants were awarded as early as 1887 under the Hatch Act. In the past quarter-century alone, federal grants to States and localities have grown from $7 billion to $96 billion. As a result, federal grants now account for about one-fifth of state and local government expenditures. The States have obtained federal funding for such services as police and fire protection, education, public health and hospitals, parks and recreation, and sanitation. Moreover, at the same time that the States have exercised their influence to obtain federal support, they have been able to exempt themselves from a wide variety of obligations imposed by Congress under the Commerce Clause. For example, the Federal Power Act, the National Labor Relations Act, the Labor-Management Reporting and Disclosure Act, the Occupational Safety and Health Act, the Employee Retirement Insurance Security Act, and the Sherman Act all contain express or implied exemptions for States and their subdivisions. The fact that some federal statutes such as the FLSA extend general obligations to the States cannot obscure the extent to which the political position of the States in the federal system has served to minimize the burdens that the States bear under the Commerce Clause.

We realize that changes in the structure of the Federal Government have taken place since 1789, not the least of which has been the substitution of popular election of Senators by the adoption of the Seventeenth Amendment in 1913, and that these changes may work to alter the influence of the States in the federal political process. Nonetheless, against this background, we are convinced that the fundamental limitation that the constitutional scheme imposes on the Commerce Clause to protect the "States as States" is one of process rather than one of result. Any substantive restraint on the exercise of Commerce Clause powers must find its justification in the procedural nature of this basic limitation, and it must be tailored to compensate for possible failings in the national political process rather than to dictate a "sacred province of state autonomy." EEOC v. Wyoming, 460 U.S., at 236.

Insofar as the present cases are concerned, then, we need go no further than to state that we perceive nothing in the overtime and minimum-wage requirements of the FLSA, as applied to SAMTA, that is destructive of state sovereignty or violative of any constitutional provision. SAMTA faces nothing more than the same minimum-wage and overtime obligations that hundreds of thousands of other employers, public as well as private, have to meet.

. . .

IV

This analysis makes clear that Congress' action in affording SAMTA employees the protections of the wage and hour provisions of the FLSA contravened no affirmative limit on Congress' power under the Commerce Clause. The judgment of the District Court therefore must be reversed.

Of course, we continue to recognize that the States occupy a special and specific position in our constitutional system and that the scope of Congress' authority under the Commerce Clause must reflect that position. But the principal and basic limit on the federal commerce power is that inherent in all congressional action—the built-in restraints that our system provides through state participation in federal governmental action. The political process ensures that laws that unduly burden the States will not be promulgated. In the factual setting of these cases the internal safeguards of the political process have performed as intended.

These cases do not require us to identify or define what affirmative limits the constitutional structure might impose on federal action affecting the States under the Commerce Clause. See Coyle v. Oklahoma, 221 U.S. 559 (1911). We note and accept Justice Frankfurter's observation in New York v. United States, 326 U.S. 572, 583 (1946):

> "The process of Constitutional adjudication does not thrive on conjuring up horrible possibilities that never happen in the real world and devising doctrines sufficiently comprehensive in detail to cover the remotest contingency. Nor need we go beyond what is required for a reasoned disposition of the kind of controversy now before the Court."

Though the separate concurrence providing the fifth vote in *National League of Cities* was "not untroubled by certain possible implications" of the decision, 426 U.S., at 856, the Court in that case attempted to articulate affirmative limits on the Commerce Clause power in terms of core governmental functions and fundamental attributes of state sovereignty. But the model of democratic decisionmaking the Court there identified underestimated, in our view, the solicitude of the national political process for the continued vitality of the States. Attempts by other courts since then to draw guidance from this model have proved it both impracticable and doctrinally barren. In sum, in *National League of Cities* the Court tried to repair what did not need repair.

We do not lightly overrule recent precedent. We have not hesitated, however, when it has become apparent that a prior decision has departed from a proper understanding of congressional power under the Commerce Clause. See United States v. Darby, 312 U.S. 100, 116–117 (1941). Due respect for the reach of congressional power within the federal system mandates that we do so now.

National League of Cities v. Usery, 426 U.S. 833 (1976), is overruled. The judgment of the District Court is reversed, and these cases are remanded to that court for further proceedings consistent with this opinion.

It is so ordered.

Justice Powell, with whom The Chief Justice, Justice Rehnquist, and Justice O'Connor join, dissenting.

The Court today, in its 5–4 decision, overrules National League of Cities v. Usery, 426 U.S. 833 (1976), a case in which we held that Congress lacked authority to impose the requirements of the Fair Labor Standards Act on state and local governments. Because I believe this decision substantially alters the federal system embodied in the Constitution, I dissent.

I

There are, of course, numerous examples over the history of this Court in which prior decisions have been reconsidered and overruled. There have been few cases, however, in which the principle of *stare decisis* and the rationale of recent decisions were ignored as abruptly as we now witness.[1] The reasoning of the Court in *National League of Cities,* and the principle applied there, have been reiterated consistently over the past eight years. Since its decision in 1976, *National League of Cities* has been cited and quoted in opinions joined by every member of the present Court. Hodel v. Virginia Surface Mining & Recl. Assn., 452 U.S. 264, 287–293 (1981); United Transportation Union v. Long Island R. Co., 455 U.S. 678, 684–686 (1982); FERC v. Mississippi, 456 U.S. 742, 764–767 (1982). . . .

. . . .

Whatever effect the Court's decision may have in weakening the application of *stare decisis,* it is likely to be less important than what the Court has done to the Constitution itself. A unique feature of the United States is the *federal* system of government guaranteed by the

---

[1] *National League of Cities,* following some changes in the composition of the Court, had overruled Maryland v. Wirtz, 392 U.S. 183 (1968). Unlike *National League of Cities,* the rationale of *Wirtz* had not been repeatedly accepted by our subsequent decisions.

Constitution and implicit in the very name of our country. Despite some genuflecting in Court's opinion to the concept of federalism, today's decision effectively reduces the Tenth Amendment to meaningless rhetoric when Congress acts pursuant to the Commerce Clause.

.   .   .

    .   .   .

II

    .   .   .

B

Today's opinion does not explain how the States' role in the electoral process guarantees that particular exercises of the Commerce Clause power will not infringe on residual State sovereignty.[7] Members of Congress are elected from the various States, but once in office they are members of the federal government. Although the States participate in the Electoral College, this is hardly a reason to view the President as a representative of the States' interest against federal encroachment. We noted recently "the hydraulic pressure inherent within each of the separate Branches to exceed the outer limits of its power . . . ." Immigration and Naturalization Service v. Chadha, 462 U.S. 919, — (1983). The Court offers no reason to think that this pressure will not operate when Congress seeks to invoke its powers under the Commerce Clause, notwithstanding the electoral role of the States.[9]

[7] Late in its opinion, the Court suggests that after all there may be some "affirmative limits the constitutional structure might impose on federal action affecting the States under the Commerce Clause." The Court asserts that "[i]n the factual setting of these cases the internal safeguards of the political process have performed as intended." The Court does not explain the basis for this judgment. Nor does it identify the circumstances in which the "political process" may fail and "affirmative limits" are to be imposed. Presumably, such limits are to be determined by the Judicial Branch even though it is "unelected." Today's opinion, however, has rejected the balancing standard and suggests no other standard that would enable a court to determine when there has been a malfunction of the "political process." The Court's failure to specify the "affirmative limits" on federal power, or when and how these limits are to be determined, may well be explained by the transparent fact that any such attempt would be subject to precisely the same objections on which it relies to overrule *National League of Cities.*

[9] At one time in our history, the view that the structure of the federal government sufficed to protect the States might have had a somewhat more practical, although not a more logical, basis. Professor Wechsler, whose seminal article in 1954 proposed the view adopted by the Court today, predicated his argument on assumptions that simply do not accord with current reality. Professor Wechsler wrote: "National action has . . . always been regarded as exceptional in our polity, an intrusion to be justified by some necessity, the special rather than the ordinary case." Wechsler, The Political Safeguards of Federalism: The Role of the States in the Composition and Selection of the National Government, 54 Colum.L.Rev. 543, 544 (1954). Not only is the premise of this view clearly at odds with the proliferation of national legislation over the past 30 years, but "a variety of structural and political changes in this century have combined to make Congress particularly *insensitive* to state and local values." Advisory Comm'n on Intergovernmental Relations [ACIR], Regulatory Federalism: Policy, Process, Impact and Reform 50 (1984). The adoption of the Seventeenth Amendment (providing for direct election of senators), the weakening of political parties on the local level, and the rise of

. . . The fact that Congress generally does not transgress constitutional limits on its power to reach State activities does not make judicial review any less necessary to rectify the cases in which it does do so.[12] The States' role in our system of government is a matter of constitutional law, not of legislative grace. "The powers not delegated to the United States by the Constitution, nor prohibited by it to the States, are reserved to the States, respectively, or to the people." U.S. Const., Amend. 10.

More troubling than the logical infirmities in the Court's reasoning is the result of its holding, i.e., that federal political officials, invoking the Commerce Clause, are the sole judges of the limits of their own power. This result is inconsistent with the fundamental principles of our constitutional system. See, e.g., The Federalist No. 78 (Hamilton). At least since *Marbury v. Madison* it has been the settled province of the federal judiciary "to say what the law is" with respect to the constitutionality of acts of Congress. 1 Cranch 137, 177 (1803). In rejecting the role of the judiciary in protecting the States from federal overreaching, the Court's opinion offers no explanation for ignoring the teaching of the most famous case in our history.

national media, among other things, have made Congress increasingly less representative of State and local interests, and more likely to be responsive to the demands of various national constituencies. Id., at 50–51. As one observer explained, "As Senators and members of the House develop independent constituencies among groups such as farmers, businessmen, laborers, environmentalists, and the poor, each of which generally supports certain national initiatives, their tendency to identify with state interests and the positions of state officials is reduced." Kaden, "Federalism in the Courts: Agenda for the 1980s," in ACIR, The Future of Federalism in the '80s, at 97 (1981).

See also Kaden, Politics, Money, and State Sovereignty: The Judicial Role, 79 Colum.L. Rev. 847 (1979) (changes in political practices and the breadth of national initiatives mean that the political branches "may no longer be as well suited as they once were to the task of safeguarding the role of the states in the federal system and protecting the fundamental value of federalism") and ACIR, Regulatory Federalism, supra, at 1–24 (detailing the "dramatic shift" in kind of federal regulation applicable to the States over the past two decades). Thus, even if one were to ignore the numerous problems with the Court's position in terms of constitutional theory, there would remain serious questions as to its factual premises.

[12] This Court has never before abdicated responsibility for assessing the constitutionality of challenged action on the ground that affected parties theoretically are able to look out for their own interests through the electoral process. As the Court noted in *National League of Cities,* a much stronger argument as to inherent structural protections could have been made in either Buckley v. Valeo, 424 U.S. 1 (1976) or Myers v. United States, 272 U.S. 52 (1926), than can be made here. In these cases, the President signed legislation that limited his authority with respect to certain appointments and thus arguably "it was no concern of this Court that the law violated the Constitution." 426 U.S., at 841–842 n. 12. The Court nevertheless held the laws unconstitutional because they infringed on presidential authority, the President's consent notwithstanding. The Court does not address this point; nor does it cite any authority for its contrary view.

III

A

. . .

. . . Far from being "unsound in principle," judicial enforcement of the Tenth Amendment is essential to maintaining the federal system so carefully designed by the Framers and adopted in the Constitution.

B

. . .

The Framers believed that the separate sphere of sovereignty reserved to the States would ensure that the States would serve as an effective "counterpoise" to the power of the federal government. The States would serve this essential role because they would attract and retain the loyalty of their citizens. The roots of such loyalty, the Founders thought, were found in the objects peculiar to state government. For example, Hamilton argued that the States "regulat[e] all those personal interests and familiar concerns to which the sensibility of individuals is more immediately awake . . .." The Federalist No. 17, p. 107. Thus, he maintained that the people would perceive the States as "the immediate and most visible guardian of life and property," a fact which "contributes more than any other circumstance to impressing upon the minds of the people affection, esteem and reverence towards the government." Ibid. Madison took the same position, explaining that "the people will be more familiarly and minutely conversant" with the business of state governments, and "with the members of these, will a greater proportion of the people have the ties of personal acquaintance and friendship, and of family and party attachments . . .." The Federalist No. 46, p. 316. Like Hamilton, Madison saw the States' involvement in the everyday concerns of the people as the source of their citizens' loyalty. Ibid. See also Nagel, Federalism as a Fundamental Value: National League of Cities in Perspective, 1981 Sup.Ct.Rev. 81 (1981).

Thus, the harm to the States that results from federal overreaching under the Commerce Clause is not simply a matter of dollars and cents. *National League of Cities,* 426 U.S., at 846–851. Nor is it a matter of the wisdom or folly of certain policy choices. Rather, by usurping functions traditionally performed by the States, federal overreaching under the Commerce Clause undermines the constitutionally mandated balance of power between the States and the federal government, a balance designed to protect our fundamental liberties.

. . .

IV

The question presented in this case is whether the extension of the FLSA to the wages and hours of employees of a city-owned transit system unconstitutionally impinges on fundamental state sovereignty. . . .

I return now to the balancing test approved in *National League of Cities* and accepted in *Hodel, Long Island R. Co.,* and FERC v. Mississippi. The Court does not find in this case that the "federal interest is demonstrably greater." 426 U.S., at 856 (Blackmun, J., concurring). No such finding could have been made, for the state interest is compelling. The financial impact on States and localities of displacing their control over wages, hours, overtime regulations, pensions, and labor relations with their employees could have serious, as well as unanticipated, effects on state and local planning, budgeting, and the levying of taxes. As we said in *National League of Cities,* federal control of the terms and conditions of employment of State employees also inevitably "displaces state policies regarding the manner in which [States] will structure delivery of those governmental services that citizens require." Id., at 847.

The Court emphasizes that municipal operation of an intracity mass transit system is relatively new in the life of our country. It nevertheless is a classic example of the type of service traditionally provided by local government. It is *local* by definition. It is indistinguishable in principle from the traditional services of providing and maintaining streets, public lighting, traffic control, water, and sewerage systems. Services of this kind are precisely those "with which citizens are more 'familiarly and minutely conversant.' " The Federalist, No. 46, p. 316. State and local officials of course must be intimately familiar with these services and sensitive to their quality as well as cost. Such officials also know that their constituents and the press respond to the adequacy, fair distribution, and cost of these services. It is this kind of state and local control and accountability that the Framers understood would insure the vitality and preservation of the federal system that the Constitution explicitly requires. See *National League of Cities,* supra, at 847–852.

V

. . .

As I view the Court's decision today as rejecting the basic precepts of our federal system and limiting the constitutional role of judicial review, I dissent.

Justice Rehnquist, dissenting.

I join both Justice Powell's and Justice O'Connor's thoughtful dissents. Justice Powell's reference to the "balancing test" approved in *National League of Cities* is not identical with the language in that case, which recognized that Congress could not act under its commerce power to infringe on certain fundamental aspects of state sovereignty that are essential to "the States' separate and independent existence." Nor is either test, or Justice O'Connor's suggested approach, precisely congruent with Justice Blackmun's views in 1976, when he spoke of a balancing approach which did not outlaw federal power in areas "where the federal interest is demonstrably greater." But under any one of these approaches the judgment in this case should be affirmed, and I do not think it incumbent on those of us in dissent to spell out further the fine points of a principle that will, I am confident, in time again command the support of a majority of this Court.

Justice O'Connor, with whom Justice Powell and Justice Rehnquist join, dissenting.

The Court today surveys the battle scene of federalism and sounds a retreat. Like Justice Powell, I would prefer to hold the field and, at the very least, render a little aid to the wounded. I join Justice Powell's opinion. I also write separately to note my fundamental disagreement with the majority's views of federalism and the duty of this Court.

. . .

. . . [M]any of this Court's decisions acknowledge that the means by which national power is exercised must take into account concerns for state autonomy. . . . The operative language of these cases varies, but the underlying principle is consistent: state autonomy is a relevant factor in assessing the means by which Congress exercises its powers.

This principle requires the Court to enforce affirmative limits on federal regulation of the States to complement the judicially crafted expansion of the interstate commerce power. *National League of Cities v. Usery* represented an attempt to define such limits. The Court today rejects *National League of Cities* and washes its hands of all efforts to protect the States. In the process, the Court opines that unwarranted federal encroachments on state authority are and will remain " 'horrible possibilities that never happen in the real world.' " There is ample reason to believe to the contrary.

. . .

The problems of federalism in an integrated national economy are capable of more responsible resolution than holding that the States as States retain no status apart from that which Congress chooses to let them retain. The proper resolution, I suggest, lies in weighing state autonomy as a factor in the balance when interpreting the means by which Congress can exercise its authority on the States as States. It is insufficient, in assessing the validity of congressional regulation of a State pursuant to the commerce power, to ask only whether the same regulation would be valid if enforced against a private party. That reasoning, embodied in the majority opinion, is inconsistent with the spirit of our Constitution . . . ..

It has been difficult for this Court to craft bright lines defining the scope of the state autonomy protected by *National League of Cities*. Such difficulty is to be expected whenever constitutional concerns as important as federalism and the effectiveness of the commerce power come into conflict. Regardless of the difficulty, it is and will remain the duty of this Court to reconcile these concerns in the final instance. That the Court shuns the task today by appealing to the "essence of federalism" can provide scant comfort to those who believe our federal system requires something more than a unitary, centralized government. I would not shirk the duty acknowledged by *National League of Cities* and its progeny, and I share Justice Rehnquist's belief that this Court will in time again assume its constitutional responsibility.

I respectfully dissent.

Page 430. Add as a footnote to the end of the opinion for the Court in Federal Energy Regulatory Commission v. Mississippi:

* In Puerto Rico v. Branstad, 107 S.Ct. 2802 (1987), the Court held that a federal court could order a governor to deliver up a fugitive, overruling Kentucky v. Dennison on this point. Justice Marshall's opinion for the Court said, in part:

"It has long been a settled principle that federal courts may enjoin unconstitutional action by state officials. . . . The fundamental premise of the holding in *Dennison*—'that the States and the Federal Government in all circumstances must be viewed as coequal sovereigns—is not representative of the law today.' FERC v. Mississippi, 456 U.S. 742, 761 (1982).

. . .

"Kentucky v. Dennison is the product of another time. The conception of the relation between the States and the Federal Government there announced is fundamentally incompatible with more than a century of constitutional development. Yet this decision has stood while the world of which it was a part has passed away. We conclude that it may stand no longer."

Page 432. Add at end of section:

SOUTH CAROLINA v. BAKER
___ U.S. ___, 108 S.Ct. 1355, 99 L.Ed.2d 592 (1988).

Justice Brennan delivered the opinion of the Court.

[The facts in this case, portions of the opinion other than part II, and the dissent of Justice O'Connor appear *supra*, page 60.]

II

[The Court assumed that a provision of the Internal Revenue Code taxing bearer bonds issued by States was, "[f]or the purposes of Tenth Amendment analysis . . . as if it directly regulated States by prohibiting outright the issuance of bearer bonds."]

A

The Tenth Amendment limits on Congress' authority to regulate state activities are set out in Garcia v. San Antonio Metropolitan Transit Authority, 469 U.S. 528 (1985). *Garcia* holds that the limits are structural, not substantive—i.e., that States must find their protection from congressional regulation through the national political process, not through judicially defined spheres of unregulable state activity. Id., at 537–554. South Carolina contends that the political process failed here because Congress had no concrete evidence quantifying the tax evasion attributable to unregistered state bonds and relied instead on anecdotal evidence that taxpayers have concealed taxable income using bearer bonds. It also argues that Congress chose an ineffective remedy by requiring registration because most bond sales are handled by brokers who must file information reports regardless of the form of the bond and because beneficial ownership of registered bonds need not necessarily be recorded.

Although *Garcia* left open the possibility that some extraordinary defects in the national political process might render congressional regulation of state activities invalid under the Tenth Amendment, the Court in *Garcia* had no occasion to identify or define the defects that might lead to such invalidation. See id., at 556. Nor do we attempt any definitive articulation here. It suffices to observe that South Carolina has not even alleged that it was deprived of any right to participate in the national political process or that it was singled out in a way that left it politically isolated and powerless. Cf. United States v. Carolene Products Co., 304 U.S. 144, 152, n. 4 (1938). Rather, South Carolina argues that the political process failed here because section 310(b)(1) was "imposed by the vote of an uninformed Congress relying upon incomplete information." But nothing in *Garcia* or the Tenth Amendment authorizes courts to second-guess the substantive basis for congressional legislation. . . . Where, as here, the national political process did not operate in a defective manner, the Tenth Amendment is not implicated.

B

[It is argued] that section 310 is invalid because it commandeers the state legislative and administrative process by coercing States into enacting legislation authorizing bond registration and into administering the registration scheme. They cite FERC v. Mississippi, 456 U.S. 742 (1982), which left open the possibility that the Tenth Amendment might set some limits on Congress' power to compel States to regulate on behalf of federal interests, id., at 761–764. The extent to which the Tenth Amendment claim left open in *FERC* survives *Garcia* or poses constitutional limitations independent of those discussed in *Garcia* is far from clear. We need not, however, address that issue because we find the claim discussed in *FERC* inapplicable to section 310.

. . .

Because, by hypothesis, section 310 effectively prohibits issuing unregistered bonds, it presents the very situation *FERC* distinguished from a commandeering of state regulatory machinery: the extent to which the Tenth Amendment "shields the States from generally applicable federal regulations." 456 U.S., at 759. Section 310 regulates state activities; it does not, as did the statute in *FERC*, seek to control or influence the manner in which States regulate private parties. [It is argued] that section 310 has commandeered the state legislative and administrative process because many state legislatures had to amend a substantial number of statutes in order to issue bonds in registered form and because state officials had to devote substantial effort to determine how best to implement a registered bond system. Such "commandeering" is, however, an inevitable consequence of regulating a state activity. Any federal regulation demands compliance. That a State wishing to engage in certain activity must take administrative and sometimes legislative action to comply with federal standards

regulating that activity is a commonplace that presents no constitutional defect. After *Garcia*, for example, several States and municipalities
had to take administrative and legislative action to alter the employment practices or raise the funds necessary to comply with the wage
and overtime provisions of the Federal Labor Standards Act. Indeed,
even the pre-*Garcia* line of Tenth Amendment cases recognized that
Congress could constitutionally impose federal requirements on States
that States could meet only by amending their statutes. . . .

**Justice Scalia, concurring in part and concurring in the judg-
ment.**

I join in the Court's judgment, and in its opinion except for Part II.
I do not join the latter because, as observed by the Chief Justice, it
unnecessarily casts doubt upon FERC v. Mississippi, 456 U.S. 742
(1982), and because it misdescribes the holding in Garcia v. San Antonio
Metropolitan Transit Authority, 469 U.S. 528 (1985). I do not read
Garcia as adopting—in fact I read it as explicitly disclaiming—the
proposition attributed to it in today's opinion, that the "national
political process" is the States' only constitutional protection, and that
nothing except the demonstration of "some extraordinary defects" in
the operation of that process can justify judicial relief. We said in
Garcia: "These cases do not require us to identify or define what
affirmative limits *the constitutional structure* might impose on federal
action affecting the States under the Commerce Clause. See Coyle v.
Oklahoma, 221 U.S. 559 (1911)." See 469 U.S., at 556 (emphasis added).
I agree only that that structure does not prohibit what the Federal
Government has done here.

Concurrence in the Judgment of Chief Justice Rehnquist.

. . . [I]n my view the Court unnecessarily casts doubt on the
protective scope of the Tenth Amendment in the course of upholding
section 310(b)(1).

. . .

. . . I see no need . . ., as the majority does, to discuss the
possibility of defects in the national political process that spawned
TEFRA, nor to hypothesize that the Tenth Amendment concerns voiced
in FERC v. Mississippi, 456 U.S. 742 (1982), may not have survived
Garcia v. San Antonio Metropolitan Transit Authority, 469 U.S. 528
(1985). Those issues, intriguing as they may be, are of no moment in
the present case and are best left unaddressed until clearly presented.

STATE REGULATORY IMMUNITY AND THE EXERCISE
OF OTHER CONGRESSIONAL POWERS

In National League of Cities v. Usery, the Court had reserved the
question whether its analysis of state immunity applied when Congressional powers other than the commerce power were exercised. One
question expressly reserved in *National League of Cities*—whether
states could claim immunity from the exercise of Congressional power
under § 5 of the fourteenth amendment and § 2 of the fifteenth

amendment—was given a negative answer in City of Rome v. United States, 446 U.S. 156 (1980). (See casebook, p. 1020, at p. 1025.)

A second question reserved—whether Congress could, by withholding funds appropriated to the states, command the states indirectly to do that which could not be commanded directly—was not answered in later cases. In his dissent in *National League of Cities,* Justice Brennan commented that Congress might "accomplish its objectives . . . by conditioning grants of federal funds upon compliance with federal minimum wage and overtime standards." Later, in a summary per curiam opinion, the Court affirmed a lower court decision that Congress could condition health care grants on the requirement that the state make and enforce standards for health care providers. North Carolina v. Califano, 435 U.S. 962 (1978).

Justice Blackmun's opinion for the Court in Federal Energy Regulatory Commission v. Mississippi deliberately avoided making "a definitive choice between competing views of federal power to compel state regulatory activity." Does his opinion in Garcia v. San Antonio Metropolitan Transit Authority still leave that question open? Assuming that Congressional power to compel states to enact and enforce federal regulatory policies is limited, can that limit be ignored if the compulsion takes the form of a conditional federal grant?

For analysis of the wide range of constitutional problems related to conditional federal spending, see Rosenthal, *Conditional Federal Spending and the Constitution,* 39 Stanford Law Review 1103 (1987).

SOUTH DAKOTA v. DOLE

___ U.S. ___, 107 S.Ct. 2793, 97 L.Ed.2d 171 (1987).

Chief Justice Rehnquist delivered the opinion of the Court.

Petitioner South Dakota permits persons 19 years of age or older to purchase beer containing up to 3.2% alcohol. S.D. Codified Laws section 35–6–27 (1986). In 1984 Congress enacted 23 U.S.C. section 158 (1982 ed., Supp. III) ("section 158"), which directs the Secretary of Transportation to withhold a percentage of federal highway funds otherwise allocable from States "in which the purchase or public possession of any alcoholic beverage by a person who is less than twenty-one years of age is lawful." The State sued in United States District Court seeking a declaratory judgment that section 158 violates the constitutional limitations on congressional exercise of the spending power and violates the Twenty-first Amendment to the United States Constitution. The District Court rejected the State's claims, and the Court of Appeals . . . affirmed.

In this Court, the parties direct most of their efforts to defining the proper scope of the Twenty-first Amendment. . . . South Dakota asserts that the setting of minimum drinking ages is clearly within the "core powers" reserved to the States under section 2 of the Amendment. . . . The Secretary in response asserts that the Twenty-first Amendment is simply not implicated by section 158; the plain language of section 2 confirms the States' broad power to impose restrictions on the sale and distribution of alcoholic beverages but does not confer on them any power to permit sales that Congress seeks to prohibit. . . .

. . . Despite the extended treatment of the question by the parties, however, we need not decide in this case whether that Amendment would prohibit an attempt by Congress to legislate directly a national minimum drinking age. Here, Congress has acted indirectly under its spending power to encourage uniformity in the States' drinking ages. As we explain below, we find this legislative effort within constitutional bounds even if Congress may not regulate drinking ages directly.

. . . Incident to [the spending] power, Congress may attach conditions on the receipt of federal funds, and has repeatedly employed the power "to further broad policy objectives by conditioning receipt of federal moneys upon compliance by the recipient with federal statutory and administrative directives." Fullilove v. Klutznick, 448 U.S. 448, 474 (1980) (Opinion of Burger, C.J.). . . . The breadth of this power was made clear in United States v. Butler, 297 U.S. 1, 66 (1936), where the Court, resolving a longstanding debate over the scope of the Spending Clause, determined that "the power of Congress to authorize expenditure of public moneys for public purposes is not limited by the direct grants of legislative power found in the Constitution." Thus, objectives not thought to be within Article I's "enumerated legislative fields," id., at 65, may nevertheless be attained through the use of the spending power and the conditional grant of federal funds.

The spending power is of course not unlimited, Pennhurst State School and Hospital v. Halderman, 451 U.S. 1, 17, and n. 13 (1981), but is instead subject to several general restrictions articulated in our cases. The first of these limitations is derived from the language of the Constitution itself: the exercise of the spending power must be in pursuit of "the general welfare." . . . In considering whether a particular expenditure is intended to serve general public purposes, courts should defer substantially to the judgment of Congress.[2] Second, we have required that if Congress desires to condition the States' receipt of federal funds, it "must do so unambiguously . . . ., enabling the States to exercise their choice knowingly, cognizant of the consequences of their participation." Pennhurst State School v. Halderman, supra, at 17. Third, our cases have suggested (without significant elaboration) that conditions on federal grants might be illegitimate if they are unrelated "to the federal interest in particular national projects or programs." Massachusetts v. United States, 435 U.S. 444, 461 (1978) (plurality opinion). . . . Finally, we have noted that other constitutional provisions may provide an independent bar to the conditional grant of federal funds. Lawrence County v. Lead-Deadwood School Dist., 469 U.S. 256, 269–270 (1985); Buckley v. Valeo, 424 U.S. 1, 91 (1976) (per curiam); King v. Smith, 392 U.S. 309, 333, n. 34 (1968).

---

[2] The level of deference to the congressional decision is such that the Court has more recently questioned whether "general welfare" is a judicially enforceable restriction at all. See Buckley v. Valeo, 424 U.S. 1, 90–91 (1976) (per curiam).

South Dakota does not seriously claim that section 158 is inconsistent with any of the first three restrictions mentioned above. We can readily conclude that the provision is designed to serve the general welfare, especially in light of the fact that "the concept of welfare or the opposite is shaped by Congress. . . ." . . . Congress found that the differing drinking ages in the States created particular incentives for young persons to combine their desire to drink with their ability to drive, and that this interstate problem required a national solution. The means it chose to address this dangerous situation were reasonably calculated to advance the general welfare. The conditions upon which States receive the funds, moreover, could not be more clearly stated by Congress. . . . And the State itself, rather than challenging the germaneness of the condition to federal purposes, admits that it "has never contended that the congressional action was . . . unrelated to a national concern in the absence of the Twenty-first Amendment." Indeed, the condition imposed by Congress is directly related to one of the main purposes for which highway funds are expended—safe interstate travel. . . .[3] This goal of the interstate highway system had been frustrated by varying drinking ages among the States. A presidential commission appointed to study alcohol-related accidents and fatalities on the Nation's highways concluded that the lack of uniformity in the States' drinking ages created "an incentive to drink and drive" because "young persons commute to border States where the drinking age is lower." Presidential Commission on Drunk Driving, Final Report 11 (1983). By enacting section 158, Congress conditioned the receipt of federal funds in a way reasonably calculated to address this particular impediment to a purpose for which the funds are expended.

The remaining question about the validity of section 158—and the basic point of disagreement between the parties—is whether the Twenty-first Amendment constitutes an "independent constitutional bar" to the conditional grant of federal funds. . . . Petitioner, relying on its view that the Twenty-first Amendment prohibits *direct* regulation of drinking ages by Congress, asserts that "Congress may not use the spending power to regulate that which it is prohibited from regulating directly under the Twenty-first Amendment." But our cases show that this "independent constitutional bar" limitation on the spending power is not of the kind petitioner suggests. United States v. Butler, 297 U.S., at 66, for example, established that the constitutional limitations on Congress when exercising its spending power are less exacting than those on its authority to regulate directly.

We have also held that a perceived Tenth Amendment limitation on congressional regulation of state affairs did not concomitantly limit

---

[3] Our cases have not required that we define the outer bounds of the "germameness" or "relatedness" limitation on the imposition of conditions under the spending power. Amici urge that we take this occasion to establish that a condition on federal funds is legitimate only if it relates directly to the purpose of the expenditure to which it is attached. Because the petitioner has not sought such a restriction, and because we find any such limitation on conditional federal grants satisfied in this case in any event, we do not address whether conditions less directly related to the particular purpose of the expenditure might be outside the bonds of the spending power.

the range of conditions legitimately placed on federal grants. In Oklahoma v. Civil Service Comm'n, 330 U.S. 127 (1947), the Court considered the validity of the Hatch Act insofar as it was applied to political activities of state officials whose employment was financed in whole or in part with federal funds. The State contended that an order under this provision to withhold certain federal funds unless a state official was removed invaded its sovereignty in violation of the Tenth Amendment. Though finding that "the United States is not concerned with, and has no power to regulate, local political activities as such of state officials," the Court nevertheless held that the Federal Government "does have power to fix the terms upon which its money allotments to states shall be disbursed." Id., at 143. The Court found no violation of the State's sovereignty because the State could, and did, adopt "the 'simple expedient' of not yielding to what she urges is federal coercion. The offer of benefits to a state by the United States dependent upon cooperation by the state with federal plans, assumedly for the general welfare, is not unusual." Id., at 143–144 (citation omitted). See also Steward Machine Co. v. Davis, 301 U.S. 548, 595 (1937) ("There is only a condition which the state is free at pleasure to disregard or to fulfill") . . .

These cases establish that the "independent constitutional bar" limitation on the spending power is not, as petitioner suggests, a prohibition on the indirect achievement of objectives which Congress is not empowered to achieve directly. Instead, we think that the language in our earlier opinions stands for the unexceptionable proposition that the power may not be used to induce the States to engage in activities that would themselves be unconstitutional. Thus, for example, a grant of federal funds conditioned on invidiously discriminatory state action or the inaction of cruel and unusual punishment would be an illegitimate exercise of the Congress' broad spending power. But no such claim can be or is made here. Were South Dakota to succumb to the blandishments offered by Congress and raise its drinking age to 21, the State's action in so doing would not violate the constitutional rights of anyone.

Our decisions have recognized that in some circumstances the financial inducement offered by Congress might be so coercive as to pass the point at which "pressure turns into compulsion." Steward Machine Co. v. Davis, supra, at 590. Here, however, Congress has directed only that a State desiring to establish a minimum drinking age lower than 21 lose a relatively small percentage of certain federal highway funds. Petitioner contends that the coercive nature of this program is evident from the degree of success it has achieved. We cannot conclude, however, that a conditional grant of federal money of this sort is unconstitutional simply by reason of its success in achieving the congressional objective.

When we consider, for a moment, that all South Dakota would lose if she adheres to her chosen course as to a suitable minimum drinking age is 5% of the funds otherwise obtainable under specified highway grant programs, the argument as to coercion is shown to be more rhetoric than fact. As we said a half century ago in Steward Machine Co. v. Davis:

> "Every rebate from a tax when conditioned upon conduct is in some measure a temptation. But to hold that motive or temptation is equivalent to coercion is to plunge the law in endless difficulties. The outcome of such a doctrine is the acceptance of a philosophical determinism by which choice becomes impossible. Till now the law has been guided by a robust common sense which assumes the freedom of the will as a working hypothesis in the solution of its problems." Id., at 589–590.

Here Congress has offered relatively mild encouragement to the States to enact higher minimum drinking ages than they would otherwise choose. But the enactment of such laws remains the prerogative of the States not merely in theory but in fact. Even if Congress might lack the power to impose a national minimum drinking age directly, we conclude that encouragement to state action found in section 158 is a valid use of the spending power. Accordingly, the judgment of the Court of Appeals is

Affirmed.

Justice Brennan, dissenting.

I agree with Justice O'Connor that regulation of the minimum age of purchasers of liquor falls squarely within the ambit of those powers reserved to the States by the Twenty-first Amendment. Since States possess this constitutional power, Congress can not condition a federal grant in a manner that abridges this right. The Amendment, itself, strikes the proper balance between federal and state authority. I therefore dissent.

Justice O'Connor, dissenting.

The Court today upholds the National Minimum Drinking Age Amendment, . . . as a valid exercise of the Spending Power . . . But section 158 is not a condition on spending reasonably related to the expenditure of federal funds and cannot be justified on that ground. Rather, it is an attempt to regulate the sale of liquor, an attempt that lies outside Congress' power to regulate commerce because it falls within the ambit of section 2 of the Twenty-first Amendment.

My disagreement with the Court is relatively narrow on the Spending Power issue . . .

. . . [T]he Court's application of the requirement that the condition imposed be reasonably related to the purpose for which the funds are expended, is cursory and unconvincing. . . . [E]stablishment of a minimum drinking age of 21 is not sufficiently related to interstate highway construction to justify so conditioning funds appropriated for that purpose.

. . .

. . . The Court reasons that Congress wishes that the roads it builds may be used safely, that drunk drivers threaten highway safety, and that young people are more likely to drive while under the influence of alcohol under existing law than would be the case if there were a uniform national drinking age of 21. It hardly needs saying, however, that if the purpose of section 158 is to deter drunken driving, it is far too over- and under-inclusive. It is over-inclusive because it stops teenagers from drinking even when they are not about to drive on interstate highways. It is under-inclusive because teenagers pose only a small part of the drunken driving problem in this Nation. . . .

When Congress appropriates money to build a highway, it is entitled to insist that the highway be a safe one. But it is not entitled to insist as a condition of the use of highway funds that the State impose or change regulations in other areas of the State's social and economic life because of an attenuated or tangential relationship to highway use or safety. Indeed, if the rule were otherwise, the Congress could effectively regulate almost any area of a State's social, political, or economic life on the theory that use of the interstate transportation system is somehow enhanced. If, for example, the United States were to condition highway moneys upon moving the state capital, I suppose it might argue that interstate transportation is facilitated by locating local governments in places easily accessible to interstate highways— or, conversely, that highways might become overburdened if they had to carry traffic to and from the state capital. In my mind, such a relationship is hardly more attenuated than the one which the Court finds supports section 158.

. . . .

. . . The *Butler* Court saw the Agricultural Adjustment Act for what it was—an exercise of regulatory, not spending, power. The error in *Butler* was not the Court's conclusion that the Act was essentially regulatory, but rather its crabbed view of the extent of Congress' regulatory power under the Commerce Clause. The Agricultural Adjustment Act was regulatory but it was regulation that today would likely be considered within Congress' Commerce Power. . . .

. . . If the Spending Power is to be limited only by Congress' notion of the general welfare, the reality, given the vast financial resources of the Federal Government, is that the Spending Clause gives "power to the Congress to tear down the barriers, to invade the states' jurisdiction, and to become a parliament of the whole people, subject to no restrictions save such as are self-imposed." United States v. Butler, supra, at 78. This, of course, as *Butler* held, was not the Framers' plan and it is not the meaning of the Spending Clause.

. . .

Of the other possible sources of congressional authority for regulating the sale of liquor only the Commerce Power comes to mind. But in my view, the regulation of the age of the purchasers of liquor, just as the regulation of the price at which liquor may be sold, falls squarely within the scope of those powers reserved to the States by the Twenty-first Amendment. . . .

. . .

. . . Congress simply lacks power under the Commerce Clause to displace state regulation of this kind. . . . The immense size and power of the Government of the United States ought not obscure its fundamental character. It remains a Government of enumerated powers. McCulloch v. Maryland, 4 Wheat. 316, 405 (1819). Because . . . section 158 . . . cannot be justified as an exercise of any power delegated to the Congress, it is not authorized by the Constitution. The Court errs in holding it to be the law of the land, and I respectfully dissent.

Chapter 8

SEPARATION OF POWERS

SECTION 2. CONGRESSIONAL INTERFERENCE WITH PRESIDENTIAL PREROGATIVES

A. THE LEGISLATIVE VETO

Page 464. Add at end of subsection:

ALASKA AIRLINES, INC. v. BROCK, 107 S.Ct. 1476 (1987). The Airline Deregulation Act of 1978, contains provisions requiring airlines to give a "first right of hire" to airline employees dislocated by deregulation of commercial air carriers. The Secretary of Labor was authorized to issue regulations implementing these provisions, subject to a legislative veto of the regulations. The Court held that the invalid legislative veto provision was severable, and the statutory duty to hire was valid.

B. APPOINTMENT OF "OFFICERS OF THE UNITED STATES"

Pages 464–467. Replace Buckley v. Valeo with the following:

MORRISON v. OLSON

___ U.S. ___, 108 S.Ct. 2597, ___ L.Ed.2d ___ (1988).

Chief Justice Rehnquist delivered the opinion of the Court.

This case presents us with a challenge to the independent counsel provisions of the Ethics in Government Act of 1978, 28 U.S.C.A. §§ 49, 591 et seq. (Supp.1988). We hold today that these provisions of the Act do not violate the Appointments Clause of the Constitution, Art. II, § 2, cl. 2, or the limitations of Article III, nor do they impermissibly interfere with the President's authority under Article II in violation of the constitutional principle of separation of powers.

I

Briefly stated, Title VI of the Ethics of Government Act (Title VI or the Act), 28 U.S.C.A. §§ 591–599 (Supp.1988), allows for the appoint-

90

ment of an "independent counsel" to investigate and, if appropriate, prosecute certain high ranking government officials for violations of federal criminal laws. The Act requires the Attorney General, upon receipt of information that he determines is "sufficient to constitute grounds to investigate whether any person [covered by the Act] may have violated any Federal criminal law," to conduct a preliminary investigation of the matter. When the Attorney General has completed this investigation, or 90 days has elapsed, he is required to report to a special court (the Special Division) created by the Act "for the purpose of appointing independent counsels." 28 U.S.C.A. § 49 (Supp.1988). If the Attorney General determines that "there are no reasonable grounds to believe that further investigation is warranted," then he must notify the Special Division of this result. In such a case, "the division of the court shall have no power to appoint an independent counsel." § 592(b)(1). If, however, the Attorney General has determined that there are "reasonable grounds to believe that further investigation or prosecution is warranted," then he "shall apply to the division of the court for the appointment of an independent counsel." The Attorney General's application to the court "shall contain sufficient information to assist the [court] in selecting an independent counsel and in defining that independent counsel's prosecutorial jurisdiction." § 592(d). Upon receiving this application, the Special Division "shall appoint an appropriate independent counsel and shall define that independent counsel's prosecutorial jurisdiction." § 593(b).

With respect to all matters within the independent counsel's jurisdiction, the Act grants the counsel "full power and independent authority to exercise all investigative and prosecutorial functions and powers of the Department of Justice, the Attorney General, and any other officer or employee of the Department of Justice." § 594(a). The functions of the independent counsel include conducting grand jury proceedings and other investigations, participating in civil and criminal court proceedings and litigation, and appealing any decision in any case in which the counsel participates in an official capacity. §§ 594(a)(1)–(3). Under § 594(a)(9), the counsel's powers include "initiating and conducting prosecutions in any court of competent jurisdiction, framing and signing indictments, filing informations, and handling all aspects of any case, in the name of the United States." The counsel may appoint employees, § 594(c), may request and obtain assistance from the Department of Justice, § 594(d), and may accept referral of matters from the Attorney General if the matter falls within the counsel's jurisdiction as defined by the Special Division, § 594(e). The Act also states that an independent counsel "shall, except where not possible, comply with the written or other established policies of the Department of Justice respecting enforcement of the criminal laws." § 594(f). In addition, whenever a matter has been referred to an independent counsel under the Act, the Attorney General and the Justice Department are required to suspend all investigations and proceedings regarding the matter. § 597(a). An independent counsel has "full authority to dismiss matters within [his] prosecutorial jurisdiction without conducting an investigation or at any subsequent time before prosecution, if to do so would be consistent" with Department of Justice policy. § 594(g). Two statutory provisions govern the length of an independent counsel's tenure in office. The first defines the procedure for removing an independent counsel. Section 596(a)(1) provides:

> "An independent counsel appointed under this chapter may be removed from office, other than by impeachment and conviction, only by the personal action of the Attorney General and only for good cause, physical disability, mental incapacity, or any other condition that substantially impairs the performance of such independent counsel's duties."

If an independent counsel is removed pursuant to this section, the Attorney General is required to submit a report to both the Special Division and the Judiciary Committees of the Senate and the House "specifying the facts found and the ultimate grounds for such removal." § 596(a)(2). Under the current version of the Act, an independent counsel can obtain judicial review of the Attorney General's action by filing a civil action in the United States District Court for the District of Columbia. Members of the Special Division "may not hear or determine any such civil action or any appeal of a decision in any such civil action." The reviewing court is authorized to grant reinstatement or "other appropriate relief." § 596(a)(3).

The other provision governing the tenure of the independent counsel defines the procedures for "terminating" the counsel's office. Under § 596(b)(1), the office of an independent counsel terminates when he notifies the Attorney General that he has completed or substantially completed any investigations or prosecutions undertaken pursuant to the Act. In addition, the Special Division, acting either on its own or on the suggestion of the Attorney General, may terminate the office of an independent counsel at any time if it finds that "the investigation of all matters within the prosecutorial jurisdiction of such independent counsel . . . have been completed or so substantially completed that it would be appropriate for the Department of Justice to complete such investigations and prosecutions." § 596(b)(2).

Finally, the Act provides for Congressional oversight of the activities of independent counsels. An independent counsel may from time to time send Congress statements or reports on his activities. § 595(a)(2). The "appropriate committees of the Congress" are given oversight jurisdiction in regard to the official conduct of an independent counsel, and the counsel is required by the Act to cooperate with Congress in the exercise of this jurisdiction. § 595(a)(1). The counsel is required to inform the House of Representatives of "substantial and credible information which [the counsel] receives . . . that may constitute grounds for an impeachment." § 595(c). In addition, the Act gives certain Congressional Committee Members the power to "request in writing that the Attorney General apply for the appointment of an independent counsel." § 592(g)(1). The Attorney General is required to respond to this request within a specified time but is not required to accede to the request. § 592(g)(2).

The proceedings in this case provide an example of how the Act works in practice. In 1982, two subcommittees of the House of Representatives issued subpoenas directing the Environmental Protection Agency (EPA) to produce certain documents relating to the efforts of the EPA and the Land and Natural Resources Division of the Justice Department to enforce the "Superfund Law." At that time, appellee Olson was the Assistant Attorney General for the Office of Legal Counsel (OLC), appellee Schmults was Deputy Attorney General, and appellee Dinkins was the Assistant Attorney General for the Land and Natural Resources Division. Acting on the advice of the Justice Department, the President ordered the Administrator of EPA to invoke executive privilege to withhold certain of the documents on the ground that they contained "enforcement sensitive information." The Administrator obeyed this order and withheld the documents. In response, the House voted to hold the Administrator in contempt, after which the Administrator and the United States together filed a lawsuit against the House. The conflict abated in March 1983, when the Administration agreed to give the House committees limited access to the documents.

The following year, the House Judiciary Committee began an investigation into the Justice Department's role in the controversy over the EPA documents. During this investigation, appellee Olson testified before a House subcommittee on March 10, 1983. Both before and after that testimony, the Department complied with several Committee requests to produce certain documents. Other documents were at first withheld, although these documents were eventually disclosed by the Department after the Committee learned of their existence. In 1985, the majority members of the Judiciary Committee published a lengthy report on the Committee's investigation. Report on Investigation of the Role of the Department of Justice in the Withholding of Environmental Protection Agency Documents from Congress in 1982–83, H.R.Rep. No. 99–435 (1985). The report not only criticized various officials in the Department of Justice for their role in the EPA executive privilege dispute, but it also suggested that appellee Olson had given false and misleading testimony to the subcommittee on March 10, 1983, and that appellees Schmults and Dinkins had wrongfully withheld certain documents from the Committee, thus obstructing the Committee's investigation. The Chairman of the Judiciary Committee forwarded a copy of the report to the Attorney General with a request, pursuant to 28 U.S.C. § 592(c), that he seek the appointment of an independent counsel to investigate the allegations against Olson, Schmults, and Dinkins.

The Attorney General directed the Public Integrity Section of the Criminal Division to conduct a preliminary investigation. The Section's report concluded that the appointment of an independent counsel was warranted to investigate the Committee's allegations with respect to all three appellees. After consulting with other Department officials, however, the Attorney General chose to apply to the Special Division for the appointment of an independent counsel solely with respect to appellee Olson. The Attorney General accordingly requested appointment of an independent counsel to investigate whether Olson's

March 10, 1983, testimony "regarding the completeness of [OLC's] response to the Judiciary Committee's request for OLC documents, and regarding his knowledge of EPA's willingness to turn over certain disputed documents to Congress, violated 18 U.S.C. § 1505, § 1001, or any other provision of federal criminal law." Attorney General Report, at 2–3. The Attorney General also requested that the independent counsel have authority to investigate "any other matter related to that allegation." Id., at 11.

On April 23, 1986, the Special Division appointed James C. McKay as independent counsel . . .

McKay later resigned as independent counsel, and on May 29, 1986, the Division appointed appellant Morrison as his replacement . . .

. . .

. . . [I]n May and June 1987, appellant caused a grand jury to issue and serve subpoenas ad testificandum and duces tecum on appellees. All three appellees moved to quash the subpoenas, claiming, among other things, that the independent counsel provisions of the Act were unconstitutional and that appellant accordingly had no authority to proceed. On July 20, 1987, the District Court upheld the constitutionality of the Act and denied the motions to quash. . . .

A divided Court of Appeals reversed. . . . We now reverse.

II

. . .

III

The Appointments Clause of Article II, reads as follows:

"[The President] shall nominate, and by and with the Advice and Consent of the Senate, shall appoint Ambassadors, other public Ministers and Consuls, Judges of the supreme Court, and all other Officers of the United States, whose Appointments are not herein otherwise provided for, and which shall be established by Law: but the Congress may by Law vest the Appointment of such inferior Officers, as they think proper, in the President alone, in the Courts of Law, or in the Heads of Departments." U.S. Const., Art. II, § 2, cl. 2

The parties do not dispute that "[t]he Constitution for purposes of appointment . . . divides all its officers into two classes." United States v. Germaine, 99 U.S. 508, 509 (1879). As we stated in Buckley v. Valeo, 424 U.S. 1, 132 (1976), "[p]rincipal officers are selected by the President with the advice and consent of the Senate. Inferior officers Congress may allow to be appointed by the President alone, by the heads of departments, or by the Judiciary." The initial question is, accordingly, whether appellant is an "inferior" or a "principal" officer. If she is the latter, as the Court of Appeals concluded, then the Act is in violation of the Appointments Clause.

The line between "inferior" and "principal" officers is one that is far from clear, and the Framers provided little guidance into where it should be drawn. . . . We need not attempt here to decide exactly where the line falls between the two types of officers, because in our view appellant clearly falls on the "inferior officer" side of that line. Several factors lead to this conclusion.

First, appellant is subject to removal by a higher Executive Branch official. Although appellant may not be "subordinate" to the Attorney General (and the President) insofar as she possesses a degree of independent discretion to exercise the powers delegated to her under the Act, the fact that she can be removed by the Attorney General indicates that she is to some degree "inferior" in rank and authority. Second, appellant is empowered by the Act to perform only certain, limited duties. An independent counsel's role is restricted primarily to investigation and, if appropriate, prosecution for certain federal crimes. Admittedly, the Act delegates to appellant "full power and independent authority to exercise all investigative and prosecutorial functions and powers of the Department of Justice," § 594(a), but this grant of authority does not include any authority to formulate policy for the Government or the Executive Branch, nor does it give appellant any administrative duties outside of those necessary to operate her office. The Act specifically provides that in policy matters appellant is to comply to the extent possible with the policies of the Department. § 594(f).

Third, appellant's office is limited in jurisdiction. Not only is the Act itself restricted in applicability to certain federal officials suspected of certain serious federal crimes, but an independent counsel can only act within the scope of the jurisdiction that has been granted by the Special Division pursuant to a request by the Attorney General. Finally, appellant's office is limited in tenure. There is concededly no time limit on the appointment of a particular counsel. Nonetheless, the office of independent counsel is "temporary" in the sense that an independent counsel is appointed essentially to accomplish a single task, and when that task is over the office is terminated, either by the counsel herself or by action of the Special Division. Unlike other prosecutors, appellant has no ongoing responsibilities that extend beyond the accomplishment of the mission that she was appointed for and authorized by the Special Division to undertake. In our view, these factors relating to the "ideas of tenure, duration . . . and duties" of the independent counsel, *Germaine,* supra, at 511, are sufficient to establish that appellant is an "inferior" officer in the constitutional sense.

This conclusion is consistent with our few previous decisions that considered the question of whether a particular government official is a "principal" or an "inferior" officer. In United States v. Eaton, 169 U.S. 331 (1898), for example, we approved Department of State regulations that allowed executive officials to appoint a "vice-consul" during the temporary absence of the consul, terming the "vice-consul" a "subordinate officer" notwithstanding the Appointment Clause's specific reference to "Consuls" as principal officers. As we stated, "Because the subordinate officer is charged with the performance of the duty of the superior for a limited time and under special and temporary conditions he is not thereby transformed into the superior and permanent official." Id., at 343. In Ex parte Siebold, 100 U.S. 371 (1880), the Court found that federal "supervisor[s] of elections," who were charged with various duties involving oversight of local congressional elections, see id., at 379–380, were inferior officers for purposes of the Clause. In Go-Bart Importing Co. v. United States, 282 U.S. 344, 352–353 (1931), we held that "United States commissioners are inferior officers." Id., at 352. These commissioners had various judicial and prosecutorial powers, including the power to arrest and imprison for trial, to issue warrants, and to institute prosecutions under "laws relating to the elective franchise and civil rights." Id., at 353, n. 2. All of this is consistent with our reference in United States v. Nixon, 418 U.S. 683, 694, 696 (1974), to the office of Watergate Special Prosecutor—whose authority was similar to that of appellant, see id., at 694, n. 8—as a "subordinate officer."

This does not, however, end our inquiry under the Appointments Clause. Appellees argue that even if appellant is an "inferior" officer, the Clause does not empower Congress to place the power to appoint such an officer outside the Executive Branch. They contend that the Clause does not contemplate congressional authorization of "interbranch appointments," in which an officer of one branch is appointed by officers of another branch. The relevant language of the Appointments Clause is worth repeating. It reads: ". . . but the Congress may by Law vest the Appointment of such inferior Officers, as they think proper, in the President alone, in the courts of Law, or in the Heads of Departments." On its face, the language of this "excepting clause" admits of no limitation on innerbranch appointments. Indeed, the inclusion of "as they think proper" seems clearly to give Congress significant discretion to determine whether it is "proper" to vest the appointment of, for example, executive officials in the "courts of Law." We recognized as much in one of our few decisions in this area, Ex parte Siebold, supra, where we stated:

> "It is no doubt usual and proper to vest the appointment of inferior officers in that department of the government, executive or judicial, or in that particular executive department to which the duties of such officers appertain. But there is no absolute requirement to this effect in the Constitution; and, if there were, it would be difficult in many cases to determine to which department an office properly belonged. . . .

> ". . ." 100 U.S., at 397–398.

Our only decision to suggest otherwise, Ex parte Hennen, 13 Pet. 230 (1839), from which the first sentence in the above quotation from Siebold was derived, was discussed in Siebold and distinguished as "not intended to define the constitutional power of Congress in this regard, but rather to express the law or rule by which it should be governed." 100 U.S., at 398. Outside of these two cases, there is very little, if any, express discussion of the propriety of interbranch appointments in our decisions, and we see no reason now to depart from the holding of *Siebold* that such appointments are not proscribed by the excepting clause.

We also note that the history of the clause provides no support for appellees' position. . . . [T]here was little or no debate on the question of whether the Clause empowers Congress to provide for interbranch appointments, and there is nothing to suggest that the Framers intended to prevent Congress from having that power.

We do not mean to say that Congress' power to provide for interbranch appointments of "inferior officers" is unlimited. In addition to separation of powers concerns, which would arise if such provisions for appointment had the potential to impair the constitutional functions assigned to one of the branches, *Siebold* itself suggested that Congress' decision to vest the appointment power in the courts would be improper if there was some "incongruity" between the functions normally performed by the courts and the performance of their duty to appoint. 100 U.S., at 398 ("the duty to appoint inferior officers, when required thereto by law, is a constitutional duty of the courts; and in the present case there is no such incongruity in the duty required as to excuse the courts from its performance, or to render their acts void"). In this case, however, we do not think it impermissible for Congress to vest the power to appoint independent counsels in a specially created federal court. . . . We have recognized that courts may appoint private attorneys to act as prosecutor for judicial contempt judgments. See Young v. United States ex rel. Vuittion et Fils S.A., 481 U.S. ___ (1987). In Go-Bart Importing Co. v. United States, 282 U.S. 344 (1931), we approved court appointment of United States commissioners, who exercised certain limited prosecutorial powers. Id., at 353, n. 2. In *Siebold,* as well, we indicated that judicial appointment of federal marshals, who are "executive officer[s]," would not be inappropriate. Lower courts have also upheld interim judicial appointments of United States Attorneys, see United States v. Solomon, 216 F.Supp. 835 (SDNY 1963), and Congress itself has vested the power to make these interim appointments in the district courts, see 28 U.S.C.A. § 546(d) (Supp.1988). Congress of course was concerned when it created the office of independent counsel with the conflicts of interest that could arise in situations when the Executive Branch is called upon to investigate its own high-ranking officers. If it were to remove the appointing authority from the Executive Branch, the most logical place to put it was in the Judicial Branch. In the light of the Act's provision making the judges of the Special Division ineligible to participate in any matters relating to an independent counsel they have appointed, 28 U.S.C. § 49(f), we do not think that appointment of the independent counsels by the court runs afoul of the constitutional limitation on "incongruous" interbanch appointments.

IV

Appellees next contend that the powers vested in the Special Division by the Act conflict with Article III of the Constitution. We have long recognized that by the express provision of Article III, the judicial power of the United States is limited to "Cases" and "Controversies." See Muskrat v. United States, 219 U.S. 346, 356 (1911). As a general rule, we have broadly stated that "executive or administrative duties of a nonjudicial nature may not be imposed on judges holding office under Art. III of the Constitution." Buckley, 424 U.S., at 123 (citing United States v. Ferreira, 13 How. 40 (1852); Hayburn's Case, 2 Dall. 409 (1792)). The purpose of this limitation is to help ensure the independence of the Judicial Branch and to prevent the judiciary from encroaching into areas reserved for the other branches. . . . With this in mind, we address in turn the various duties given to the Special Division by the Act.

Most importantly, the Act vests in the Special Division the power to choose who will serve as independent counsel and the power to define his or her jurisdiction. § 593(b). Clearly, once it is accepted that the Appointments Clause gives Congress the power to vest the appointment of officials such as the independent counsel in the "courts of Law," there can be no Article III objection to the Special Division's exercise of that power, as the power itself derives from the Appointments Clause, a source of authority for judicial action that is independent of Article III. Appellees contend, however, that the Division's Appointments Clause powers do not encompass the power to define the independent counsel's jurisdiction. We disagree. In our view, Congress' power under the Clause to vest the "Appointment" of inferior officers in the courts may, in certain circumstances, allow Congress to give the courts some discretion in defining the nature and scope of the appointed official's authority. Particularly when, as here, Congress creates a temporary "office" the nature and duties of which will by necessity vary with the factual circumstances giving rise to the need for an appointment in the first place, it may vest the power to define the scope of the office in the court as an incident to the appointment of the officer pursuant to the Appointments Clause. This said, we do not think that Congress may give the Division *unlimited* discretion to determine the independent counsel's jurisdiction. In order for the Division's definition of the counsel's jurisdiction to be truly "incidental" to its power to appoint, the jurisdiction that the court decides upon must be demonstrably related to the factual circumstances that gave rise to the Attorney General's investigation and request for the appointment of the independent counsel in the particular case.

The Act also vests in the Special Division various powers and duties in relation to the independent counsel that, because they do not involve appointing the counsel or defining her jurisdiction, cannot be said to derive from the Division's Appointments Clause authority. These duties include granting extensions for the Attorney General's preliminary investigation, § 592(a)(3); receiving the report of the Attorney General at the conclusion of his preliminary investigation, §§ 592(b)(1), 593(c)(2)(B); referring matters to the counsel upon request, § 594(e);[18] receiving reports from the counsel regarding expenses in-

---

[18] In our view, this provision does not empower the court to expand the original scope of the counsel's jurisdiction; that may be done only upon request of the Attorney General

curred, § 594(h)(1)(A); receiving a report from the Attorney General following the removal of an independent counsel, § 596(a)(2); granting attorney's fees upon request to individuals who were investigated but not indicted by an independent counsel, § 593(f); receiving a final report from the counsel, § 594(h)(1)(B); deciding whether to release the counsel's final report to Congress or the public and determining whether any protective orders should be issued, § 594(h)(2); and terminating an independent counsel when his task is completed, § 596(b)(2).

Leaving aside for the moment the Division's power to terminate an independent counsel, we do not think that Article III absolutely prevents Congress from vesting these other miscellaneous powers in the Special Division pursuant to the Act. . . . [T]he powers granted by these provisions are themselves essentially ministerial. The Act simply does not give the Division the power to "supervise" the independent counsel in the exercise of her investigative or prosecutorial authority. And, the functions that the Special Division is empowered to perform are not inherently "executive"; indeed, they are directly analogous to functions that federal judges perform in other contexts . . .

We are more doubtful about the Special Division's power to terminate the office of the independent counsel pursuant to § 596(b)(2). As appellees suggest, the power to terminate, especially when exercised by the Division on its own motion, is "administrative" to the extent that it requires the Special Division to monitor the progress of proceedings of the independent counsel and come to a decision as to whether the counsel's job is "completed." § 596(b)(2). It also is not a power that could be considered typically "judicial," as it has few analogues among the court's more traditional powers. Nonetheless, we do not, as did the Court of Appeals, view this provision as a significant judicial encroachment upon executive power or upon the prosecutorial discretion of the independent counsel.

. . . [I]t is the duty of federal courts to construe a statute in order to save it from constitutional infirmities, . . . and to that end we think a narrow construction is appropriate here. The termination provisions of the Act do not give the Special Division anything approaching the power to remove the counsel while an investigation or court proceeding is still underway—this power is vested solely in the Attorney General. As we see it, "termination" may occur only when the duties of the counsel are truly "completed" or "so substantially completed" that there remains no need for any continuing action by the independent counsel. It is basically a device for removing from the public payroll an independent counsel who has served her purpose, but is unwilling to acknowledge the fact. So construed, the Special Division's power to terminate does not pose a sufficient threat of judicial intrusion into matters that are more properly within the Executive's authority to require that the Act be invalidated as inconsistent with Article III.

pursuant to section 593(c)(2). At most, section 594(e) authorizes the court simply to refer matters that are "relate[d] to the independent counsel's prosecutorial jurisdiction" as already defined.

. . .

We emphasize . . . that the Special Division has no authority to take any action or undertake any duties that are not specifically authorized by the Act. The gradual expansion of the authority of the Special Division might in another context be a bureaucratic success story, but it would be one that would have serious constitutional ramifications. The record in other cases involving independent counsels indicate that the Special Division has at times given advisory opinions or issued orders that are not directly authorized by the Act. . . . The propriety of the Special Division's actions in these instances is not before us as such, but we nonetheless think it appropriate to point out not only that there is no authorization for such actions in the Act itself, but that the division's exercise of unauthorized powers risks the transgression of the constitutional limitations of Article III that we have just discussed.

V

We now turn to consider whether the Act is invalid under the constitutional principle of separation of powers. Two related issues must be addressed: The first is whether the provision of the Act restricting the Attorney General's power to remove the independent counsel to only those instances in which he can show "good cause," taken by itself, impermissibly interferes with the President's exercise of his constitutionally appointed functions. The second is whether, taken as a whole, the Act violates the separation of powers by reducing the President's ability to control the prosecutorial powers wielded by the independent counsel.

A

Two Terms ago we had occasion to consider whether it was consistent with the separation of powers for Congress to pass a statute that authorized a government official who is removable only by Congress to participate in what we found to be "executive powers." Bowsher v. Synar, 478 U.S. 714, 730 (1986). We held in Bowsher that "Congress cannot reserve for itself the power of removal of an officer charged with the execution of the laws except by impeachment." Id., at 726. A primary antecedent for this ruling was our 1925 decision in Myers v. United States, 272 U.S. 52 (1926). *Myers* had considered the propriety of a federal statute by which certain postmasters of the United States could be removed by the President only "by and with the advice and consent of the Senate." There too, Congress' attempt to involve itself in the removal of an executive official was found to be sufficient grounds to render the statute invalid. As we observed in *Bowsher,* the essence of the decision in *Myers* was the judgment that the Constitution prevents Congress from "draw[ing] to itself . . . the power to remove or the right to participate in the exercise of that power. To do this would be to go beyond the words and implications of the [Appointments Clause] and to infringe the constitutional principle of the separation of governmental powers." *Myers,* supra, at 161.

Unlike both *Bowsher* and *Myers,* this case does not involve an attempt by Congress itself to gain a role in the removal of executive officials other than its established powers of impeachment and conviction. The Act instead puts the removal power squarely in the hands of the Executive Branch; an independent counsel may be removed from office, "only by the personal action of the Attorney General, and only for good cause." § 596(a)(1). There is no requirement of congressional approval of the Attorney General's removal decision, though the decision is subject to judicial review. § 596(a)(3). In our view, the removal provisions of the Act make this case more analogous to Humphrey's Executor v. United States, 295 U.S. 602 (1935), and Weiner v. United States, 357 U.S. 349 (1958), than to *Myers* or *Bowsher.*

In *Humphrey's Executor,* the issue was whether a statute restricting the President's power to remove the commissioners of the Federal Trade Commission only for "inefficiency, neglect of duty, or malfeasance in office" was consistent with the Constitution. 295 U.S., at 619. We stated that whether Congress can "condition the [President's power of removal] by fixing a definite term and precluding a removal except for cause, will depend upon the character of the office." Id., at 631. Contrary to the implication of some dicta in *Myers,*[24] the President's power to remove government officials simply was not "all-inclusive in respect of civil officers with the exception of the judiciary provided for by the Constitution." 295 U.S., at 629. At least in regard to "quasi-legislative" and "quasi-judicial" agencies such as the FTC,[25] "[t]he authority of Congress, in creating [such] agencies, to require them to act in discharge of their duties independently of executive control . . . includes, as an appropriate incident, power to fix the period during which they shall continue in office, and to forbid their removal except for cause in the meantime." Ibid. In *Humphrey's Executor,* we found it "plain" that the Constitution did not give the President "illimitable power of removal" over the officers of independent agencies. Ibid. Were the President to have the power to remove FTC commissioners at will, the "coercive influence" of the removal power would "threate[n] the independence of [the] commission." Id., at 630.

Similarly, in *Wiener* we considered whether the President had unfettered discretion to remove a member of the War Claims Commission, which had been established by Congress in the War Claims Act of 1948, 62 Stat. 1240. The Commission's function was to receive and

[24] The Court expressly disapproved of any statements in *Myers* that "are out of harmony" with the views expressed in *Humphrey's Executor.* 295 U.S., at 626. We recognized that the only issue actually decided in *Myers* was that "the President had power to remove a postmaster of the first class, without the advice and consent of the Senate as required by act of Congress." 295 U.S., at 626.

[25] See id., at 627–628. We described the FTC as "an administrative body created by Congress to carry into effect legislative policies embodied in the statute in accordance with the legislative standard therein prescribed, and to perform other specified duties as a legislative or as a judicial aid." Such an agency was not "an arm or an eye of the executive," and the commissioners were intended to perform their duties "without executive leave and . . . free from executive control." Id., at 628. As we put it at the time, the powers of the FTC were not "purely" executive, but were "quasi-legislative or quasi-judicial." Ibid.

adjudicate certain claims for compensation from those who had suffered personal injury or property damage at the hands of the enemy during World War II. Commissioners were appointed by the President, with the advice and consent of the Senate, but the statute made no provision for the removal of officers, perhaps because the Commission itself was to have a limited existence. As in *Humphrey's Executor,* however, the Commissioners were entrusted by Congress with adjudicatory powers that were to be exercised free from executive control. In this context, "Congress did not wish to have hang over the Commission the Damocles' sword of removal by the President for no reason other than that he preferred to have on that Commission men of his own choosing." 357 U.S., at 356. Accordingly, we rejected the President's attempt to remove a Commissioner "merely because he wanted his own appointees on [the] Commission," stating that "no such power is given to the President directly by the Constitution, and none is impliedly conferred upon him by statute." Ibid.

Appellees contend that *Humphrey's Executor* and *Wiener* are distinguishable from this case because they did not involve officials who performed a "core executive function." They argue that our decision in *Humphrey's Executor* rests on a distinction between "purely executive" officials and officials who exercise "quasi-legislative" and "quasi-judicial" powers. In their view, when a "purely executive" official is involved, the governing precedent is *Myers,* not *Humphrey's Executor.* See *Humphrey's Executor,* 295 U.S., at 628. And, under *Myers,* the President must have absolute discretion to discharge "purely" executive officials at will. See Myers, 272 U.S., at 132–134.[26]

We undoubtedly did rely on the terms "quasi-legislative" and "quasi-judicial" to distinguish the officials involved in *Humphrey's Executor* and *Wiener* from those in *Myers,* but our present considered view is that the determination of whether the Constitution allows Congress to impose a "good cause"-type restriction on the President's power to remove an official cannot be made to turn on whether or not that official is classified as "purely executive."[27] The analysis contained in our removal cases is designed not to define rigid categories of those officials who may or may not be removed at will by the President,[28] but to ensure that Congress does not interfere with the Presi-

[26] This same argument was raised by the Solicitor General in Bowsher v. Synar, 478 U.S. 714 (1986), although as Justice White noted in dissent in that case, the argument was clearly not accepted by the Court at that time. Id., at 738–739, and nn. 1–3.

[27] Indeed, this Court has never held that the Constitution prevents Congress from imposing limitations on the President's power to remove all executive officials simply because they wield "executive" power. *Myers* itself expressly distinguished cases in which Congress had chosen to vest the appointment of "inferior" executive officials in the head of a department. See 272 U.S., at 161–163, 164. In such a situation, we saw no specific constitutional impediment to congressionally imposed restrictions on the President's removal powers. . . .

[28] The difficulty of defining such categories of "executive" or "quasi-legislative" officials is illustrated by a comparison of our decisions in cases such as *Humphrey's Executor,* Buckley v. Valeo, 424 U.S. 1, 140–141 (1976), and *Bowsher,* supra, at ___. In *Buckley,* we indicated that the functions of the Federal Election Commission are "administrative," and "more legislative and judicial in nature," and are "of kinds usually performed by independent regulatory agencies or by some department in the Executive Branch under

dent's exercise of the "executive power" and his constitutionally appointed duty to "take care that the laws be faithfully executed" under Article II. *Myers* was undoubtedly correct in its holding, and in its broader suggestion that there are some "purely executive" officials who must be removable by the President at will if he is to be able to accomplish his constitutional role.[29] See 272 U.S., at 132–134. But as the Court noted in *Wiener,*

> "The assumption was short-lived that the *Myers* case recognized the President's inherent constitutional power to remove officials no matter what the relation of the executive to the discharge of their duties and no matter what restrictions Congress may have imposed regarding the nature of their tenure." 357 U.S., at 352.

At the other end of the spectrum from *Myers,* the characterization of the agencies in *Humphrey's Executor* and *Wiener* as "quasi-legislative" or "quasi-judicial" in large part reflected our judgment that it was not essential to the President's proper execution of his Article II powers that these agencies be headed up by individuals who were removable at will. We do not mean to suggest that an analysis of the functions served by the officials at issue is irrelevant. But the real question is whether the removal restrictions are of such a nature that they impede the President's ability to perform his constitutional duty, and the functions of the officials in question must be analyzed in that light.

Considering for the moment the "good cause" removal provision in isolation from the other parts of the Act at issue in this case, we cannot say that the imposition of a "good cause" standard for removal by itself unduly trammels on executive authority. There is no real dispute that the functions performed by the independent counsel are "executive" in the sense that they are law enforcement functions that typically have been undertaken by officials within the Executive Branch. As we noted above, however, the independent counsel is an inferior officer

---

the direction of an Act of Congress." 424 U.S., at 140–141. In *Bowsher,* we found that the functions of the Comptroller General were "executive" in nature, in that he was required to "exercise judgment concerning facts that affect the application of the Act," and he must "interpret the provisions of the Act to determine precisely what budgetary calculations are required." 478 U.S., at 733. Compare this with the description of the FTC's powers in *Humphrey's Executor,* which we stated "occupie[d] no place in the executive department": "The [FTC] is an administrative body created by Congress to carry into effect legislative policies embodied in the statute in accordance with the legislative standard therein prescribed, and to perform other specified duties as a legislative or as a judicial aid." 295 U.S., at 628. As Justice White noted in his dissent in *Bowsher,* it is hard to dispute that the powers of the FTC at the time of *Humphrey's Executor* would at the present time be considered "executive," at least to some degree. See 478 U.S., at 761, n. 3.

[29] The dissent says that the language of Article II vesting the executive power of the United States in the President requires that every officer of the United States exercising any part of that power must serve at the pleasure of the President and be removable by him at will. This rigid demarcation—a demarcation incapable of being altered by law in the slightest degree, and applicable to tens of thousands of holders of offices neither known nor foreseen by the framers—depends upon an extrapolation from general constitutional language which we think is more than the text will bear. It is also contrary to our holding in United States v. Perkins, 116 U.S. 483 (1886), decided more than a century ago.

under the Appointments Clause, with limited jurisdiction and tenure and lacking policymaking or significant administrative authority. Although the counsel exercises no small amount of discretion and judgment in deciding how to carry out her duties under the Act, we simply do not see how the President's need to control the exercise of that discretion is so central to the functioning of the Executive Branch as to require as a matter of constitutional law that the counsel be terminable at will by the President.

Nor do we think that the "good cause" removal provision at issue here impermissibly burdens the President's power to control or supervise the independent counsel, as an executive official, in the execution of her duties under the Act. This is not a case in which the power to remove an executive official has been completely stripped from the President, thus providing no means for the President to ensure the "faithful execution" of the laws. Rather, because the independent counsel may be terminated for "good cause," the Executive, through the Attorney General, retains ample authority to assure that the counsel is competently performing her statutory responsibilities in a manner that comports with the provisions of the Act. Although we need not decide in this case exactly what is encompassed within the term "good cause" under the Act, the legislative history of the removal provision also makes clear that the Attorney General may remove an independent counsel for "misconduct." See H.R. Conf. Rep. No. 100–452, p. 37 (1987). Here, as with the provision of the Act conferring the appointment authority of the independent counsel on the special court, the congressional determination to limit the removal power of the Attorney General was essential, in the view of Congress, to establish the necessary independence of the office. We do not think that this limitation as it presently stands sufficiently deprives the President of control over the independent counsel to interfere impermissibly with his constitutional obligation to ensure the faithful execution of the laws.

B

The final question to be addressed is whether the Act, taken as a whole, violates the principle of separation of powers by unduly interfering with the role of the Executive Branch. Time and again we have reaffirmed the importance in our constitutional scheme of the separation of governmental powers into the three coordinate branches. See, e.g., Bowsher v. Synar, 478 U.S., at 725 (citing *Humphrey's Executor,* 295 U.S., at 629–630). As we stated in Buckley v. Valeo, 424 U.S. 1 (1976), the system of separated powers and checks and balances established in the Constitution was regarded by the Framers as "a self-executing safeguard against the encroachment or aggrandizement of one branch at the expense of the other." Id., at 122. We have not hesitated to invalidate provisions of law which violate this principle. See id., at 123. On the other hand, we have never held that the Constitution requires that the three Branches of Government "operate with absolute independence." United States v. Nixon, 418 U.S., at 707; see also Nixon v. Administrator of General Services, 433 U.S. 425, 442 (1977) (citing James Madison in The Federalist No. 47, and Joseph

Story in 1 Commentaries on the Constitution § 525 (M. Bigelow, 5th ed. 1905)).   In the often-quoted words of Justice Jackson,

> "While the Constitution diffuses power the better to secure liberty, it also contemplates that practice will integrate the dispersed powers into a workable government.   It enjoins upon its branches separateness but interdependence, autonomy but reciprocity."   Youngstown Sheet & Tube Co. v. Sawyer, 343 U.S. 579, 635 (1952) (concurring opinion).

We observe first that this case does not involve an attempt by Congress to increase its own powers at the expense of the Executive Branch.   Cf. Commodity Futures Trading Comm'n v. Schor, 478 U.S., at 856.   Unlike some of our previous cases, most recently Bowsher v. Synar, this case simply does not pose a "dange[r] of congressional usurpation of Executive Branch functions."   478 U.S., at 727; see also INS v. Chadha, 462 U.S. 919, 958 (1983).   Indeed, with the exception of the power of impeachment—which applies to all officers of the United States—Congress retained for itself no powers of control or supervision over an independent counsel.   The Act does empower certain members of Congress to request the Attorney General to apply for the appointment of an independent counsel, but the Attorney General has no duty to comply with the request, although he must respond within a certain time limit.   § 529(g).   Other than that, Congress' role under the Act is limited to receiving reports or other information and oversight of the independent counsel's activities, § 595(a), functions that we have recognized generally as being incidental to the legislative function of Congress.   See McGrain v. Daugherty, 273 U.S. 135, 174 (1927).

Similarly, we do not think that the Act works any *judicial* usurpation of properly executive functions.   As should be apparent from our discussion of the Appointments Clause above, the power to appoint inferior officers such as independent counsels is not in itself an "executive" function in the constitutional sense, at least when Congress has exercised its power to vest the appointment of an inferior office in the "courts of Law."   We note nonetheless that under the Act the Special Division has no power to appoint an independent counsel *sua sponte;* it may only do so upon the specific request of the Attorney General, and the courts are specifically prevented from reviewing the Attorney General's decision not to seek appointment, § 592(f).   In addition, once the court has appointed a counsel and defined her jurisdiction, it has no power to supervise or control the activities of the counsel.   As we pointed out in our discussion of the Special Division in relation to Article III, the various powers delegated by the statute to the Division are not supervisory or administrative, nor are they functions that the Constitution requires be performed by officials within the Executive Branch.   The Act does give a federal court the power to review the Attorney General's decision to remove an independent counsel, but in our view this is a function that is well within the traditional power of the judiciary.

Finally, we do not think that the Act "impermissibly undermine[s]" the powers of the Executive Branch, *Schor,* supra, at 856, or "disrupts the proper balance between the coordinate branches [by] prevent[ing] the Executive Branch from accomplishing its constitutionally assigned functions," Nixon v. Administrator of General Services, supra, at 443. It is undeniable that the Act reduces the amount of control or supervision that the Attorney General and, through him, the President exercises over the investigation and prosecution of a certain class of alleged criminal activity. . . . Nonetheless, the Act does give the Attorney General several means of supervising or controlling the prosecutorial powers that may be wielded by an independent counsel. . . . Notwithstanding the fact that the counsel is to some degree "independent" and free from Executive supervision to a greater extent than other federal prosecutors, in our view these features of the Act give the Executive Branch sufficient control over the independent counsel to ensure that the President is able to perform his constitutionally assigned duties.

VI

In sum, we conclude today that it does not violate the Appointments Clause for Congress to vest the appointment of independent counsels in the Special Division; that the powers exercised by the Special Division under the Act do not violate Article III; and that the Act does not violate the separation of powers principle by impermissibly interfering with the functions of the Executive Branch. The decision of the Court of Appeals is therefore

Reversed.

Justice Kennedy took no part in the consideration or decision of this case.

Justice Scalia, dissenting.

. . .

II

. . . [W]hile I will subsequently discuss why our appointments and removal jurisprudence does not support today's holding, I begin with a consideration of the fountainhead of that jurisprudence, the separation and equilibration of powers.

. . .

. . . It seems to me . . . that the decision of the Court of Appeals invalidating the present statute must be upheld on fundamental separation-of-powers principles if the following two questions are answered affirmatively: (1) Is the conduct of a criminal prosecution (and of an investigation to decide whether to prosecute) the exercise of purely executive power? (2) Does the statute deprive the President of the United States of exclusive control over the exercise of that power? Surprising to say, the Court appears to concede an affirmative answer to both questions, but seeks to avoid the inevitable conclusion that since the statute vests some purely executive power in a person who is not the President of the United States it is void.

. . .

. . . [I]t is ultimately irrelevant *how much* the statute reduces presidential control. The case is over when the Court acknowledges, as it must, that "[i]t is undeniable that the Act reduces the amount of control or supervision that the Attorney General and, through him, the President exercises over the investigation and prosecution of a certain class of alleged criminal activity." . . .

. . .

Is it unthinkable that the President should have such exclusive power, even when alleged crimes by him or his close associates are at issue? No more so than that Congress should have the exclusive power of legislation, even when what is at issue is its own exemption from the burdens of certain laws. . . . No more so than that this Court should have the exclusive power to pronounce the final decision on justiciable cases and controversies, even those pertaining to the constitutionality of a statute reducing the salaries of the Justices. . . . A system of separate and coordinate powers necessarily involves an acceptance of exclusive power that can theoretically be abused. . . . While the separation of powers may prevent us from righting every wrong, it does so in order to ensure that we do not lose liberty. The checks against any Branch's abuse of its exclusive powers are twofold: First, retaliation by one of the other Branch's use of *its* exclusive powers: Congress, for example, can impeach the Executive who willfully fails to enforce the laws; the Executive can decline to prosecute under unconstitutional statutes . . .; and the courts can dismiss malicious prosecutions: Second, and ultimately, there is the political check that the people will replace those in the political branches . . . who are guilty of abuse. Political pressures produced special prosecutors—for Teapot Dome and for Watergate, for example—long before this statute created the independent counsel. . . .

. . .

III

. . .

Because appellant (who all parties and the Court agree is an officer of the United States) was not appointed by the President with the advice and consent of the Senate, but rather by the Special Division of the United States Court of Appeals, her appointment is constitutional only if (1) she is an "inferior" officer within the meaning of the above clause, and (2) Congress may vest her appointment in a court of law.

. . .

That "inferior" means "subordinate" is . . . consistent with what little we know about the evolution of the Appointments Clause. . . .

. . .

The independent counsel is not even subordinate to the President. . . .

Because appellant is not subordinate to another officer, she is not an "inferior" officer and her appointment other than by the President with the advice and consent of the Senate is unconstitutional.

IV

. . . [T]he restrictions upon the removal of the independent counsel also violate our established precedent dealing with that specific subject. . . .

. . .

Since our 1935 decision in Humphrey's Executor v. United States, 295 U.S. 602—which was considered by many at the time the product of an activist, anti-New Deal court bent on reducing the power of President Franklin Roosevelt—it has been established that the line of permissible restriction upon removal of principal officers lies at the point at which the powers exercised by those officers are no longer purely executive. . . .

One can hardly grieve for the shoddy treatment given today to *Humphrey's Executor,* which, after all, accorded the same indignity (with much less justification) to Chief Justice Taft's opinion 10 years earlier in Myers v. United States, supra—gutting, in six quick pages devoid of textual or historical precedent for the novel principle it set forth . . . *Humphrey's Executor* at least had the decency formally to observe the constitutional principle that the President had to be the repository of *all* executive power, see 295 U.S., at 627–628, which, as *Myers* carefully explained, necessarily means that he must be able to discharge those who do not perform executive functions according to his liking. . . .

V

. . .

Under our system of government, the primary check against prosecutorial abuse is a political one. The prosecutors who exercise this awesome discretion are selected and can be removed by a President, whom the people have trusted enough to elect. Moreover, when crimes are not investigated and prosecuted fairly, nonselectively, with a reasonable sense of proportion, the President pays the cost in political damage to his administration. . . .

. . .

. . . [The Court] extends into the very heart of our most significant constitutional function the "totality of the circumstances" mode of analysis that this Court has in recent years become fond of. Taking all things into account, we conclude that the power taken away from the President here is not really *too* much. . . .

The ad hoc approach to constitutional adjudication has real attraction, even apart from its work-saving potential. It is guaranteed to produce a result, in every case, that will make a majority of the Court happy with the law. The law is, by definition, precisely what the majority thinks, taking all things into account, it *ought* to be. I prefer to rely upon the judgment of the wise men who constructed our system, and of the people who approved it, and of two centuries of history that have shown it to be sound. Like it or not, that judgment says, quite plainly, that "[t]he executive Power shall be vested in a President of the United States."

SECTION 3. PRESIDENTIAL AND CONGRESSIONAL IMMUNITIES

Page 474. Add to footnote 1:

In Mitchell v. Forsyth, 472 U.S. 511 (1985), four of the seven Justices participating concluded that the Attorney General did not share the President's absolute immunity in authorizing a warrantless wiretap on national security grounds. A different majority concluded that the Attorney General's qualified immunity protected him from civil liability in the absence of proof of violation of "clearly established statutory or constitutional rights." In this case, the former Attorney General was not liable, because the legality of warrantless national security wiretaps was an open question at the time he acted.

Part III

GOVERNMENT AND THE INDIVIDUAL: THE PROTECTION OF LIBERTY AND PROPERTY UNDER THE DUE PROCESS AND EQUAL PROTECTION CLAUSES

Chapter 10

THE DUE PROCESS, CONTRACT, AND JUST COMPENSATION CLAUSES AND THE REVIEW OF THE REASONABLENESS OF LEGISLATION

SECTION 1. ECONOMIC REGULATORY LEGISLATION

A. THE RISE AND FALL OF DUE PROCESS

Page 542. Add ahead of State Courts and Business Regulations:

NATIONAL RAILROAD PASSENGER CORP. v. ATCHISON, TOPEKA AND SANTA FE RAILWAY CO., 470 U.S. 451 (1985). Under the Act setting up Amtrak service, railroads seeking to shed their intercity rail passenger obligations entered into contracts with Amtrak. One section of the contract provided that the right of railroad employees to travel on Amtrak trains for free or reduced fares should be as determined by Amtrak. Amtrak immediately cut back on employee pass privileges and a long dispute followed with Congress finally providing that employees who held passes at the time of the takeover should get passes, with the railroads paying to Amtrak a fare about 25% of that charged as normal fare to ticket-buying passengers. The railroads sued Amtrak, alleging that the requirement that they reimburse Amtrak for pass travel violated the due process clause. They argued principally that they had a contractual right against the United States and that the Act imposing the charge on them impaired an obligation of the United States under this contract.

The Court, in an opinion by Justice Marshall joined by all Justices except Justice Powell who did not sit, rejected the railroads' claims and upheld the legislation. Most of the opinion talks about obligations of contracts and discusses the issue within the context of cases involving

110

claims that states had violated the contract clause, even though the Court recognizes that the issues are not the same. The following two excerpts from the long opinion do raise the question whether the contract clause, like the equal protection clause, is to be held as binding the federal government under the due process clause of the 5th amendment.

"To prevail on a claim that federal economic legislation unconstitutionally impairs a private contractual right, the party complaining of unconstitutionality has the burden of demonstrating, first, that the statute alters contractual rights or obligations. See United States Trust Co. v. New Jersey, 431 U.S., at 17–21. If an impairment is found, the reviewing court next determines whether the impairment is of constitutional dimension. If the alteration of contractual obligations is minimal, the inquiry may end at this stage, Allied Structural Steel Co. v. Spannaus, 438 U.S. 234, 245 (1978); if the impairment is substantial, a court must look more closely at the legislation, ibid.; see also Energy Reserves Group, Inc., 459 U.S., at 411. When the contract is a private one, and when the impairing statute is a federal one, this next inquiry is especially limited, and the judicial scrutiny quite minimal. The party asserting a Fifth Amendment due process violation must overcome a presumption of constitutionality and 'establish that the legislature has acted in an arbitrary and irrational way.' Pension Benefit Guaranty Corp. v. R.A. Gray & Co., 467 U.S. 717, 729 (1984) (quoting Usery v. Turner Elkhorn Mining Co., 428 U.S., at 15).[25]

"The starting point for our inquiry is therefore whether the 1979 and 1981 pass-rider amendments impaired the private contractual rights that the railroads obtained under the Basic Agreements. We must first consider what rights vested in the railroads pursuant to the Basic Agreements and then examine the way in which the 1979 and 1981 amendments altered those rights."

. . .

"Initially, it is far from evident that the railroads have a private contractual right to be free from all obligations to make financial payments to subsidize Amtrak, which is the way in which the railroads view any payments in excess of Amtrak's incremental costs. . . .

"Even were the Court of Appeals correct that the railroads have a private contractual right not to pay more than the incremental cost of the passes, we disagree with the Court of Appeals' conclusion that the Due Process Clause limited Congress' power to choose a different reimbursement scheme in this case. Under the Fifth Amendment's Due Process Clause, Congress remained free to 'adjust the burdens and benefits of economic life,' as long as it did so in a manner that was neither arbitrary nor irrational. Pension Benefit Guaranty Corp. v.

[25] When the court reviews state economic legislation the inquiry will not necessarily be the same. As we made clear in Pension Benefit Guaranty Corp. v. R.A. Gray & Co., 467 U.S., at 732–733 (1984), we have never held that the principles embodied in the Fifth Amendment's due process guarantee are coextensive with the prohibitions against state impairment of contracts under the Contract Clause, and, we observed, to the extent the standards differ, a less searching inquiry occurs in the review of federal economic legislation.

R.A. Gray & Co., 467 U.S., at 729, (quoting Usery v. Turner Elkhorn Mining Co., 428 U.S., at 15). Moreover, in the determination whether economic legislation that substantially alters contractual rights and duties violates due process, the burden of proving irrationality rests squarely on the party asserting a due process violation. When it performed this due process inquiry, the court below erred both in placing the burden of proof on Amtrak to defend the legislation and in defining the standard of review as rigorously as it did.

"Had it applied the correct standard, the Court of Appeals would have found that the railroads have not met their burden of proof. . . .

. . .

"Having concluded that the Basic Agreements relieved the railroads only of the direct and onerous responsibilities they had borne as common carriers, and having further concluded that the provision of free and partial-fare passes was not among those responsibilities, we conclude that the 1979 and 1981 amendments to the Act did not impair private contractual rights acquired by the railroads as parties to the Basic Agreements. The amendments imposed new obligations on the railroads and in no respect infringed the railroads' existing contractual rights. But even if the payment of more than the incremental cost of pass privileges indirectly subsidizes Amtrak operations in violation of a private contractual right, Congress' decision to assess the railroads is rational and reasoned, and the railroads have failed to demonstrate a due process violation. We therefore reverse the Court of Appeals insofar as it ruled to the contrary."

. . .

BOWEN v. PUBLIC AGENCIES OPPOSED TO SOCIAL SECURITY ENTRAPMENT, 477 U.S. 41 (1986): In 1950 Congress enacted Section 418 of the Social Security Act authorizing voluntary participation by the states and their subdivisions in the social security system, and permitting termination of coverage on two years notice. In 1983 Congress amended Section 418 providing no state may withdraw from the system after April 20, 1983, including those who had given advance notice for withdrawal after that date. The Court upheld the revision, saying that the right to terminate coverage given originally did not constitute a property right and so its elimination did not violate the due process clause of the fifth amendment.

C. THE JUST COMPENSATION CLAUSE OF THE FIFTH AMENDMENT—WHAT DOES IT ADD TO THE DUE PROCESS LIMITATION?

Page 571. Add ahead of Ruckelshaus v. Monsanto Co.:

F.C.C. v. FLORIDA POWER CORP., 107 S.Ct. 1107 (1987). Congress in the Pole Attachments Act authorized the Federal Communications Commission to regulate the rates, terms, and conditions of agreements made by power companies to cable television operators who sought to use the power company poles for their wires. The power company here had entered into a pole attachment agreement with a cable company at a price and the F.C.C. issued an order requiring a substantial reduction in that price.

The Court distinguished the *Loretto* case and upheld the regulation. It said that in this case, unlike *Loretto,* the power company was not required to enter into an agreement with the cable company and so there was no taking. The situation was similar then to public regulation of the rates charged by public utilities and clearly constitutional.

Page 576. Add ahead of San Diego Gas & Electric Co. v. City of San Diego:

KEYSTONE BITUMINOUS COAL ASS'N v. DeBENEDICTIS
___ U.S. ___, 107 S.Ct. 1232, 94 L.Ed.2d 472 (1987).

Justice Stevens, delivered the opinion of the Court.

In Pennsylvania Coal Co. v. Mahon, 260 U.S. 393 (1922), the Court reviewed the constitutionality of a Pennsylvania statute that admittedly destroyed "previously existing rights of property and contract." Writing for the Court, Justice Holmes explained:

> "Government hardly could go on if to some extent values incident to property could not be diminished without paying for every such change in the general law. As long recognized, some values are enjoyed under an implied limitation and must yield to the police power. But obviously the implied limitation must have its limits, or the contract and due process clauses are gone. One fact for consideration in determining such limits is the extent of the diminution. When it reaches a certain magnitude, in most if not in all cases there must be an exercise of eminent domain and compensation to sustain the act. So the question depends upon the particular facts."

In that case the "particular facts" led the Court to hold that the Pennsylvania Legislature had gone beyond its constitutional powers when it enacted a statute prohibiting the mining of anthracite coal in a manner that would cause the subsidence of land on which certain structures were located.

Now, 65 years later, we address a different set of "particular facts," involving the Pennsylvania Legislature's 1966 conclusion that the Commonwealth's existing mine subsidence legislation had failed to protect the public interest in safety, land conservation, preservation of affected municipalities' tax bases, and land development in the Commonwealth. Based on detailed findings, the legislature enacted the Bituminous Mine Subsidence and Land Conservation Act (the "Subsidence Act" or the "Act"), Pa.Stat.Ann., Tit. 52, § 1406.1 et seq. (Purdon Supp.1986). Petitioners contend, relying heavily on our decision in *Pennsylvania Coal,* that § 4 and § 6 of the Subsidence Act and certain implementing regulations violate the Takings Clause, and that § 6 of the Act violates the Contracts Clause of the Federal Constitution. The District Court and the Court of Appeals concluded that *Pennsylvania Coal* does not control for several reasons and that our subsequent cases make it clear that neither § 4 nor § 6 is unconstitutional on its face. We agree.

I

Coal mine subsidence is the lowering of strata overlying a coal mine, including the land surface, caused by the extraction of underground coal. This lowering of the strata can have devastating effects. It often causes substantial damage to foundations, walls, other structural members, and the integrity of houses and buildings. Subsidence frequently causes sinkholes or troughs in land which make the land difficult or impossible to develop. Its effect on farming has been well documented—many subsided areas cannot be plowed or properly prepared. Subsidence can also cause the loss of groundwater and surface ponds. In short, it presents the type of environmental concern that has been the focus of so much federal, state, and local regulation in recent decades.

Despite what their name may suggest, neither of the "full extraction" mining methods currently used in western Pennsylvania enables miners to extract all subsurface coal; considerable amounts need to be left in the ground to provide access, support, and ventilation to the mines. Additionally, mining companies have long been required by various Pennsylvania laws and regulations, the legitimacy of which is not challenged here, to leave coal in certain areas for public safety reasons. Since 1966, Pennsylvania has placed an additional set of restrictions on the amount of coal that may be extracted; these restrictions are designed to diminish subsidence and subsidence damage in the vicinity of certain structures and areas.

Pennsylvania's Subsidence Act authorizes the Pennsylvania Department of Environmental Resources (DER) to implement and enforce a comprehensive program to prevent or minimize subsidence and to regulate its consequences. Section 4 of the Subsidence Act, Pa.Stat. Ann., Tit. 52, § 1406.4 (Purdon Supp.1986), prohibits mining that causes subsidence damage to three categories of structures that were in place on April 17, 1966: public buildings and noncommercial buildings generally used by the public; dwellings used for human habitation; and cemeteries. Since 1966 the DER has applied a formula that generally requires 50% of the coal beneath structures protected by § 4 to be kept in place as a means of providing surface support. Section 6 of the Subsidence Act, 52 Pa.Stat.Ann., Tit. 52, § 1406.6 (Purdon Supp.1986), authorizes the DER to revoke a mining permit if the removal of coal causes damage to a structure or area protected by § 4 and the operator has not within six months either repaired the damage, satisfied any claim arising therefrom, or deposited a sum equal to the reasonable cost of repair with the DER as security.

II

In 1982, petitioners filed a civil rights action in the United States District Court for the Western District of Pennsylvania seeking to enjoin officials of the DER from enforcing the Subsidence Act and its implementing regulations. The petitioners are an association of coal mine operators, and four corporations that are engaged, either directly or through affiliates, in underground mining of bituminous coal in western Pennsylvania. The members of the association and the corporate petitioners own, lease, or otherwise control substantial coal reserves beneath the surface of property affected by the Subsidence Act. The defendants in the action, respondents here, are the Secretary of the Commonwealth of Pennsylvania, the Chief of DER's Division of Mine Subsidence, and the Chief of DER's Section on Mine Subsidence Regulation.

The complaint alleges that Pennsylvania recognizes three separate estates in land: The mineral estate; the surface estate; and the "support estate." Beginning well over 100 years ago, land owners began severing title to underground coal and the right of surface support while retaining or conveying away ownership of the surface estate. It is stipulated that approximately 90% of the coal that is or will be mined by petitioners in western Pennsylvania was severed from the surface in the period between 1890 and 1920. When acquiring or retaining the mineral estate, petitioners or their predecessors typically acquired or retained certain additional rights that would enable them to extract and remove the coal. Thus, they acquired the right to deposit wastes, to provide for drainage and ventilation, and to erect facilities such as tipples, roads, or railroads, on the surface. Additionally, they typically acquired a waiver of any claims for damages that might result from the removal of the coal.

In the portions of the complaint that are relevant to us, petitioners alleged that both § 4 of the Subsidence Act, as implemented by the 50% rule, and § 6 of the Subsidence Act, constitute a taking of their private property without compensation in violation of the Fifth and Fourteenth Amendments. They also alleged that § 6 impairs their contractual agreements in violation of Article I, § 10 of the Constitution. The parties entered into a stipulation of facts pertaining to petitioners' facial challenge, and filed cross motions for summary judgment on the facial challenge. The District Court granted respondent's motion.

.   .   .

The Court of Appeals affirmed . . . 771 F.2d 707, 715 (1985). . . .

. . . We granted certiorari, 475 U.S. ___ (1986), and now affirm.

III

Petitioners assert that disposition of their takings claim calls for no more than a straightforward application of the Court's decision in

Pennsylvania Coal Co. v. Mahon. Although there are some obvious similarities between the cases, we agree with the Court of Appeals and the District Court that the similarities are far less significant than the differences, and that *Pennsylvania Coal* does not control this case.

. . .

The [Pennsylvania Coal] company . . . appealed to this Court, asserting that the impact of the statute was so severe that "a serious shortage of domestic fuel is threatened." The company explained that until the Court ruled, "no anthracite coal which is likely to cause surface subsidence can be mined," and that strikes were threatened throughout the anthracite coal fields. In its argument in this Court, the Company contended that the Kohler Act was not a bona fide exercise of the police power, but in reality was nothing more than " 'robbery under the forms of law' " because its purpose was "not to protect the lives or safety of the public generally but merely to augment the property rights of a favored few."

Over Justice Brandeis' dissent, this Court accepted the company's argument. In his opinion for the Court, Justice Holmes first characteristically decided the specific case at hand in a single, terse paragraph:

"This is the case of a single private house. No doubt there is a public interest even in this, as there is in every purchase and sale and in all that happens within the commonwealth. Some existing rights may be modified even in such a case. Rideout v. Knox, 148 Mass. 368. But usually in ordinary private affairs the public interest does not warrant much of this kind of interference. A source of damage to such a house is not a public nuisance even if similar damage is inflicted on others in different places. The damage is not common or public. Wesson v. Washburn Iron Co., 13 Allen, 95, 103. The extent of the public interest is shown by the statute to be limited, since the statute ordinarily does not apply to land when the surface is owned by the owner of the coal. Furthermore, it is not justified as a protection of personal safety. That could be provided for by notice. Indeed the very foundation of this bill is that the defendant gave timely notice of its intent to mine under the house. On the other hand the extent of the taking is great. It purports to abolish what is recognized in Pennsylvania as an estate in land—a very valuable estate—and what is declared by the Court below to be a contract hitherto binding the plaintiffs. If we were called upon to deal with the plaintiffs' position alone, we should think it clear that the statute does not disclose a public interest sufficient to warrant so extensive a destruction of the defendant's constitutionally protected rights." 260 U.S., at 413–414.

Then—uncharacteristically—Justice Holmes provided the parties with an advisory opinion discussing "the general validity of the Act." In the advisory portion of the Court's opinion, Justice Holmes rested on two propositions, both critical to the Court's decision. First, because it served only private interests, not health or safety, the Kohler Act could not be "sustained as an exercise of the police power." Id., at 414.

Second, the statute made it "commercially impracticable" to mine "certain coal" in the areas affected by the Kohler Act.

The holdings and assumptions of the Court in *Pennsylvania Coal* provide obvious and necessary reasons for distinguishing *Pennsylvania Coal* from the case before us today. The two factors that the Court considered relevant, have become integral parts of our takings analysis. We have held that land use regulation can effect a taking if it "does not substantially advance legitimate state interests, . . . or denies an owner economically viable use of his land." Agins v. Tiburon, 447 U.S. 255, 260 (1980) (citations omitted); see also Penn Central Transportation Co. v. New York City, 438 U.S. 104, 124 (1978). Application of these tests to petitioners' challenge demonstrates that they have not satisfied their burden of showing that the Subsidence Act constitutes a taking. First, unlike the Kohler Act, the character of the governmental action involved here leans heavily against finding a taking; the Commonwealth of Pennsylvania has acted to arrest what it perceives to be a significant threat to the common welfare. Second, there is no record in this case to support a finding, similar to the one the Court made in *Pennsylvania Coal,* that the Subsidence Act makes it impossible for petitioners to profitably engage in their business, or that there has been undue interference with their investment-backed expectations.

The Public Purpose

Unlike the Kohler Act, which was passed upon in *Pennsylvania Coal,* the Subsidence Act does not merely involve a balancing of the private economic interests of coal companies against the private interests of the surface owners. The Pennsylvania Legislature specifically found that important public interests are served by enforcing a policy that is designed to minimize subsidence in certain areas. Section 2 of the Subsidence Act provides:

> "This act shall be deemed to be an exercise of the police powers of the Commonwealth for the protection of the health, safety and general welfare of the people of the Commonwealth, by providing for the conservation of surface land areas which may be affected in the mining of bituminous coal by methods other than 'open pit' or 'strip' mining, to aid in the protection of the safety of the public, to enhance the value of such lands for taxation, to aid in the preservation of surface water drainage and public water supplies and generally to improve the use and enjoyment of such lands and to maintain primary jurisdiction over surface coal mining in Pennsylvania." Pa.Ann.Stat., Tit. 52, § 1406.2 (Purdon Supp.1986).

The District Court and the Court of Appeals were both convinced that the legislative purposes set forth in the statute were genuine, substantial, and legitimate, and we have no reason to conclude otherwise.

. . .

Thus, the Subsidence Act differs from the Kohler Act in critical and dispositive respects. With regard to the Kohler Act, the Court believed that the Commonwealth had acted only to ensure against damage to some private landowners' homes. Justice Holmes stated that if the private individuals needed support for their structures, they should not have "take[n] the risk of acquiring only surface rights." 260 U.S., at 416. Here, by contrast, the Commonwealth is acting to protect the public interest in health, the environment, and the fiscal integrity of the area. That private individuals erred in taking a risk cannot estop the State from exercising its police power to abate activity akin to a public nuisance. . . .

. . .

The Court's hesitance to find a taking when the state merely restrains uses of property that are tantamount to public nuisances is consistent with the notion of "reciprocity of advantage" that Justice Holmes referred to in *Pennsylvania Coal.* Under our system of government, one of the state's primary ways of preserving the public weal is restricting the uses individuals can make of their property. While each of us is burdened somewhat by such restrictions, we, in turn, benefit greatly from the restrictions that are placed on others. See Penn Central Transportation Co. v. New York City, 438 U.S., at 144–150 (Rehnquist, J., dissenting); cf. California Reduction Co. v. Sanitary Reduction Works, 199 U.S. 306, 322 (1905). These restrictions are "properly treated as part of the burden of common citizenship." Kimball Laundry Co. v. United States, 338 U.S. 1, 5 (1949). Long ago it was recognized that "all property in this country is held under the implied obligation that the owner's use of it shall not be injurious to the community," Mugler v. Kansas, 123 U.S., at 665; see also Beer Co. v. Massachusetts, 97 U.S. 25, 32 (1878), and the Takings Clause did not transform that principle to one that requires compensation whenever the State asserts its power to enforce it. See *Mugler,* 123 U.S., at 664.

In Agins v. Tiburon, we explained that the "determination that governmental action constitutes a taking, is, in essence, a determination that the public at large, rather than a single owner, must bear the burden of an exercise of state power in the public interest," and we recognized that this question "necessarily requires a weighing of private and public interests." 447 U.S., at 260–261. As the cases discussed above demonstrate, the public interest in preventing activities similar to public nuisances is a substantial one, which in many instances has not required compensation. The Subsidence Act, unlike the Kohler Act, plainly seeks to further such an interest. Nonetheless, we need not rest our decision on this factor alone, because petitioners have also failed to make a showing of diminution of value sufficient to satisfy the test set forth in *Pennsylvania Coal* and our other regulatory takings cases.

Diminution of Value and Investment-Backed Expectations

The second factor that distinguishes this case from *Pennsylvania Coal* is the finding in that case that the Kohler Act made mining of "certain coal" commercially impracticable. In this case, by contrast, petitioners have not shown any deprivation significant enough to satisfy the heavy burden placed upon one alleging a regulatory taking. For this reason, their takings claim must fail.

In addressing petitioners' claim we must not disregard the posture in which this case comes before us. The District Court granted summary judgment to respondents only on the facial challenge to the Subsidence Act. . . .

. . .

. . . Petitioners thus face an uphill battle in making a facial attack on the Act as a taking.

The hill is made especially steep because petitioners have not claimed, at this stage, that the Act makes it commercially impracticable for them to continue mining their bituminous coal interests in western Pennsylvania. Indeed, petitioners have not even pointed to a single mine that can no longer be mined for profit. The only evidence available on the effect that the Subsidence Act has had on petitioners' mining operations comes from petitioners' answers to respondents' interrogatories. Petitioners described the effect that the Subsidence Act had from 1966–1982 on 13 mines that the various companies operate, and claimed that they have been required to leave a bit less than 27 million tons of coal in place to support § 4 areas. The total coal in those 13 mines amounts to over 1.46 billion tons. See App. 284. Thus § 4 requires them to leave less than 2% of their coal in place. But, as we have indicated, nowhere near all of the underground coal is extractable even aside from the Subsidence Act. The categories of coal that must be left for § 4 purposes and other purposes are not necessarily distinct sets, and there is no information in the record as to how much coal is actually left in the ground *solely* because of § 4. We do know, however, that petitioners have never claimed that their mining operations, or even any specific mines, have been unprofitable since the Subsidence Act was passed. Nor is there evidence that mining in any specific location affected by the 50% rule has been unprofitable.

Instead, petitioners have sought to narrowly define certain segments of their property and assert that, when so defined, the Subsidence Act denies them economically viable use. They advance two alternative ways of carving their property in order to reach this conclusion. First, they focus on the specific tons of coal that they must leave in the ground under the Subsidence Act, and argue that the Commonwealth has effectively appropriated this coal since it has no other useful purpose if not mined. Second, they contend that the Commonwealth has taken their separate legal interest in property—the "support estate."

Because our test for regulatory taking requires us to compare the value that has been taken from the property with the value that remains in the property, one of the critical questions is determining how to define the unit of property "whose value is to furnish the denominator of the fraction." Michelman, Property, Utility, and Fairness: Comments on the Ethical Foundations of "Just Compensation" Law, 80 Harv.L.Rev. 1165, 1192 (1967).

" 'Taking' jurisprudence does not divide a single parcel into discrete segments and attempt to determine whether rights in a particular segment have been entirely abrogated. In deciding whether a particular governmental action has effected a taking, this Court focuses rather both on the character of the action and on the nature of the interference with rights *in the parcel as a whole* —here the city tax block designated as the 'landmark site.' " 438 U.S., at 130–131.

Similarly, in Andrus v. Allard, 444 U.S. 51 (1979), we held that "where an owner possesses a full 'bundle' of property rights, the destruction of one 'strand' of the bundle is not a taking because the aggregate must be viewed in its entirety." Id., at 65–66. Although these verbal formulizations do not solve all of the definitional issues that may arise in defining the relevant mass of property, they do provide sufficient guidance to compel us to reject petitioners' arguments.

The Coal in Place

The parties have stipulated that enforcement of the DER's 50% rule will require petitioners to leave approximately 27 million tons of coal in place. Because they own that coal but cannot mine it, they contend that Pennsylvania has appropriated it for the public purposes described in the Subsidence Act.

This argument fails for the reason explained in *Penn Central* and *Andrus*. The 27 million tons of coal do not constitute a separate segment of property for takings law purposes. Many zoning ordinances place limits on the property owner's right to make profitable use of some segments of his property. A requirement that a building occupy no more than a specified percentage of the lot on which it is located could be characterized as a taking of the vacant area as readily as the requirement that coal pillars be left in place. Similarly, under petitioners' theory one could always argue that a set-back ordinance requiring that no structure be built within a certain distance from the property line constitutes a taking because the footage represents a distinct segment of property for takings law purposes. Cf. Gorieb v. Fox, 274 U.S. 603 (1927) (upholding validity of set-back ordinance) (per Holmes, J.). There is no basis for treating the less than 2% of petitioners' coal as a separate parcel of property.

. . .

When the coal that must remain beneath the ground is viewed in the context of any reasonable unit of petitioners' coal mining operations and financial-backed expectations, it is plain that the petitioners have not come close to satisfying their burden of proving that they have been denied the economically viable use of that property. The record indicates that only about 75% of petitioners' underground coal can be profitably mined in any event, and there is no showing that petitioners' reasonable "investment-backed expectations" have been materially affected by the additional duty to retain the small percentage that must be used to support the structures protected by § 4.[27]

[27] We do not suggest that the State may physically appropriate relatively small amounts of private property for its own use without paying just compensation. The question here is whether there has been any taking at all when no coal has been physically appropriated, and the regulatory program places a burden on the use of only a small fraction of the property that is subjected to regulation. See generally n. 18, supra.

The Support Estate

Pennsylvania property law is apparently unique in regarding the support estate as a separate interest in land that can be conveyed apart from either the mineral estate or the surface estate. Petitioners therefore argue that even if comparable legislation in another State would not constitute a taking, the Subsidence Act has that consequence because it entirely destroys the value of their unique support estate. It is clear, however, that our takings jurisprudence forecloses reliance on such legalistic distinctions within a bundle of property rights. For example, in *Penn Central,* the Court rejected the argument that the "air rights" above the terminal constituted a separate segment of property for Takings Clause purposes. 438 U.S., at 130. Likewise, in Andrus v. Allard, we viewed the right to sell property as just one element of the owner's property interest. 444 U.S., at 65–66. In neither case did the result turn on whether state law allowed the separate sale of the segment of property.

. . .

Thus, in practical terms, the support estate has value only insofar as it protects or enhances the value of the estate with which it is associated. Its value is merely a part of the entire bundle of rights possessed by the owner of either the coal or the surface. Because petitioners retain the right to mine virtually all of the coal in their mineral estates, the burden the Act places on the support estate does not constitute a taking. Petitioners may continue to mine coal profitably even if they may not destroy or damage surface structures at will in the process.

But even if we were to accept petitioners' invitation to view the support estate as a distinct segment of property for "takings" purposes, they have not satisfied their heavy burden of sustaining a facial challenge to the Act. . . . The record is devoid of any evidence on what percentage of the purchased support estates, either in the aggregate or with respect to any individual estate, has been affected by the Act. Under these circumstances, petitioners' facial attack under the takings clause must surely fail.

IV

In addition to their challenge under the Takings Clause, petitioners assert that § 6 of the Subsidence Act violates the Contracts Clause by not allowing them to hold the surface owners to their contractual waiver of liability for surface damage. Here too, we agree with the Court of Appeals and the District Court that the Commonwealth's strong public interests in the legislation are more than adequate to justify the impact of the statute on petitioners' contractual agreements.

. . .

As we explained more fully above, the Subsidence Act plainly survives scrutiny under our standards for evaluating impairments of private contracts. The Commonwealth has determined that in order to deter mining practices that could have severe effects on the surface, it is not enough to set out guidelines and impose restrictions, but that imposition of liability is necessary. By requiring the coal companies either to repair the damage or to give the surface owner funds to repair the damage, the Commonwealth accomplishes both deterrence and restoration of the environment to its previous condition. We refuse to second guess the Commonwealth's determinations that these are the most appropriate ways of dealing with the problem. We conclude, therefore, that the impairment of petitioners' right to enforce the damage waivers is amply justified by the public purposes served by the Subsidence Act.

The judgment of the Court of Appeals is affirmed.

Chief Justice Rehnquist, with whom Justice Powell, Justice O'Connor, and Justice Scalia join, dissenting.

More than 50 years ago, this Court determined the constitutionality of Pennsylvania's Kohler Act as it affected the property interests of coal mine operators. Pennsylvania Coal Co. v. Mahon, 260 U.S. 393 (1922). The Bituminous Mine Subsidence and Land Conservation Act approved today effects an interference with such interests in a strikingly similar manner. The Court finds at least two reasons why this case is different. First, we are told, "the character of the governmental action involved here leans heavily against finding a taking." Second, the Court concludes that the Subsidence Act neither "makes it impossible for petitioners to profitably engage in their business," nor involves "undue interference with [petitioners'] investment-backed expectations." Neither of these conclusions persuades me that this case is different, and I believe that the Subsidence Act works a taking of petitioners' property interests. I therefore dissent.

I

In apparent recognition of the obstacles presented by *Pennsylvania Coal* to the decision it reaches, the Court attempts to undermine the authority of Justice Holmes' opinion as to the validity of the Kohler Act, labeling it "uncharacteristically . . . advisory." I would not so readily dismiss the precedential value of this opinion. . . .

. . .

I accordingly approach this case with greater deference to the language as well as the holding of *Pennsylvania Coal* than does the Court. Admittedly, questions arising under the Just Compensation Clause rest on ad hoc factual inquiries, and must be decided on the facts and circumstances in each case. See Penn Central Transportation Co. v. New York City, supra, at 124; United States v. Central Eureka Mining Co., supra, at 168. Examination of the relevant factors presented here convinces me that the differences between them and those in *Pennsylvania Coal* verge on the trivial.

II

The Court first determines that this case is different from *Pennsylvania Coal* because "the Commonwealth of Pennsylvania has acted to arrest what it perceives to be a significant threat to the common welfare." In my view, reliance on this factor represents both a misreading of *Pennsylvania Coal* and a misunderstanding of our precedents.

A

The Court opines that the decision in *Pennsylvania Coal* rested on the fact that the Kohler Act was "enacted solely for the benefit of private parties," and "served only private interests." A review of the Kohler Act shows that these statements are incorrect. The Pennsylvania legislature passed the statute "as remedial legislation, designed to cure existing evils and abuses." 274 Pa., at 495, 118 A., at 492 (quoting the Act). These were *public* "evils and abuses," identified in the preamble as "wrecked and dangerous streets and highways, collapsed public buildings, churches, schools, factories, streets, and private dwellings, broken gas, water and sewer systems, the loss of human life. . . ." Id., at 496, 118 A., at 493. The Pennsylvania Supreme Court recognized that these concerns were "such as to create an emergency, properly warranting the exercise of the police power. . . ." Id., at 497, 118A., at 493. There can be no doubt that the Kohler Act was intended to serve public interests.

. . .

The Subsidence Act rests on similar public purposes. These purposes were clearly stated by the legislature: "[T]o aid in the protection of the safety of the public, to enhance the value of [surface area] lands for taxation, to aid in the preservation of surface water drainage and public water supplies and generally to improve the use and enjoyment of such lands. . . ." Pa.Stat.Ann., Title 52, § 1406.2 (Purdon Supp. 1986). The Act's declaration of policy states that mine subsidence "has seriously impeded land development . . . has caused a very clear and present danger to the health, safety and welfare of the people of Pennsylvania [and] erodes the tax base of the affected municipalities." §§ 1406.3(2), (3), (4). The legislature determined that the prevention of subsidence would protect surface structures, advance the economic future and well-being of Pennsylvania, and ensure the safety and welfare of the Commonwealth's residents. Thus, it is clear that the Court has severely understated the similarity of purpose between the Subsidence Act and the Kohler Act. The public purposes in this case are not sufficient to distinguish it from *Pennsylvania Coal.*

B

The similarity of the public purpose of the present Act to that in *Pennsylvania Coal* does not resolve the question of whether a taking has occurred; the existence of such a public purpose is merely a necessary prerequisite to the government's exercise of its taking power. See Hawaii Housing Authority v. Midkiff, 467 U.S. 229, 239–243, 245 (1984); Berman v. Parker, 348 U.S. 26, 32–33 (1954). The *nature* of these purposes may be relevant, for we have recognized that a taking does not occur where the government exercises its unquestioned authority to prevent a property owner from using his property to injure others without having to compensate the value of the forbidden use. See Goldblatt v. Hempstead, 369 U.S. 590 (1962); Hadacheck v. Sebastian 239 U.S. 394 (1915); Mugler v. Kansas, 123 U.S. 623 (1887). See generally Penn Central Transportation Co. v. New York City, 438 U.S., at 144–146 (Rehnquist, J., dissenting). The Court today indicates that this "nuisance exception" alone might support its conclusion that no taking has occurred. . . . This statute is not the type of regulation that our precedents have held to be within the "nuisance exception" to takings analysis.

. . .

Thus, our cases applying the "nuisance" rationale have involved at least two narrowing principles. First, nuisance regulations exempted from the Fifth Amendment have rested on discrete and narrow purposes. The Subsidence Act, however, is much more than a nuisance statute. The central purposes of the Act, though including public safety, reflect a concern for preservation of buildings, economic development, and maintenance of property values to sustain the Commonwealth's tax base. We should hesitate to allow a regulation based on essentially economic concerns to be insulated from the dictates of the Fifth Amendment by labeling it nuisance regulation.

Second, and more significantly, our cases have never applied the nuisance exception to allow complete extinction of the value of a parcel of property. Though nuisance regulations have been sustained despite a substantial reduction in value, we have not accepted the proposition that the State may completely extinguish a property interest or prohibit all use without providing compensation. . . .

Here, petitioners' interests in particular coal deposits have been completely destroyed. By requiring that defined seams of coal remain in the ground § 4 of the Subsidence Act has extinguished any interest one might want to acquire in this property, for " 'the right to coal consists in the right to mine it.' " *Pennsylvania Coal,* supra, at 414, quoting Commonwealth ex rel. Keator v. Clearview Coal Co., 256 Pa. 328, 331, 100 A. 820, 820 (1917). Application of the nuisance exception in these circumstances would allow the State not merely to forbid one "particular use" of property with many uses but to extinguish *all* beneficial use of petitioners' property.

Though suggesting that the purposes alone are sufficient to uphold the Act, the Court avoids reliance on the nuisance exception by finding that the Subsidence Act does not impair petitioners' investment backed expectations or ability to profitably operate their businesses. This conclusion follows mainly from the Court's broad definition of the "relevant mass of property" which allows it to ascribe to the Subsidence Act a less pernicious effect on the interests of the property owner. The need to consider the effect of regulation on some identifiable segment of property makes all important the admittedly difficult task of defining the relevant parcel. See Penn Central Transportation Co. v. New York City, 438 U.S., at 149, n. 13 (Rehnquist, J., dissenting). For the reasons explained below, I do not believe that the Court's opinion adequately performs this task.

III

The *Pennsylvania Coal* Court found it sufficient that the Kohler Act rendered it "commercially impracticable to mine certain coal." 260 U.S., at 414. The Court observes that this language is best understood as a conclusion that certain coal mines could not be operated at a profit. Petitioners have not at this stage of the litigation rested their claim on similar proof; they have not "claimed that their mining operations, or even any specific mines, have been unprofitable since the Subsidence Act was passed." The parties have, however, stipulated for purposes of this facial challenge that the Subsidence Act requires petitioners to leave in the ground 27 million tons of coal, without compensation therefor. Petitioners also claim that the Act extinguishes their purchased interests in support estates which allow them to mine the coal without liability for subsidence. We are thus asked to consider whether these restrictions are such as to constitute a taking.

A

. . .

In this case, enforcement of the Subsidence Act and its regulations will require petitioners to leave approximately 27 million tons of coal in place. There is no question that this coal is an identifiable and separable property interest. Unlike many property interests, the "bundle" of rights in this coal is sparse. " 'For practical purposes, the right to coal consists in the right to mine it.' " Pennsylvania Coal, 260 U.S., at 414, quoting Commonwealth ex rel. Keater v. Clearview Coal Co., 256 Pa. 328, 331, 100 A. 820, 820 (1917). From the relevant perspective— that of the property owners—this interest has been destroyed every bit as much as if the government had proceeded to mine the coal for its own use. The regulation, then, does not merely inhibit one strand in the bundle, cf. Andrus v. Allard, supra, but instead destroys completely any interest in a segment of property. In these circumstances, I think it unnecessary to consider whether petitioners may operate individual mines or their overall mining operations profitably, for they have been denied all use of 27 million tons of coal. I would hold that § 4 of the Subsidence Act works a taking of these property interests.

B

Petitioners also claim that the Subsidence Act effects a taking of their support estate. Under Pennsylvania law, the support estate, the surface estate, and the mineral estate are "three distinct estates in land which can be held in fee simple separate and distinct from each other. . . ." Captline v. County of Allegheny, 74 Pa.Commw. 85, 91, 459 A.2d 1298, 1301 (1983), cert. denied, 466 U.S. 904 (1984). . . .

I see no reason for refusing to evaluate the impact of the Subsidence Act on the support estate alone, for Pennsylvania has clearly defined it as a separate estate in property. The Court suggests that the practical significance of this estate is limited, because its value "is merely part of the bundle of rights possessed by the owner of either the coal or the surface." Though this may accurately describe the usual state of affairs, I do not understand the Court to mean that one holding the support estate alone would find it worthless, for surely the owners of the mineral or surface estates would be willing buyers of this interest. Nor does the Court suggest that the owner of both the mineral and support estates finds his separate interest in support to be without value. In these circumstances, where the estate defined by state law is both severable and of value in its own right, it is appropriate to consider the effect of regulation on that particular property interest.

When held by owners of the mineral estate, the support estate "consists of the right to remove the strata of coal and earth that undergird the surface . . ." 771 F.2d, at 715. Purchase of this right, therefore, shifts the risk of subsidence to the surface owner. Section 6 of the Subsidence Act, by making the coal mine operator strictly liable for any damage to surface structures caused by subsidence, purports to place this risk on the holder of the mineral estate regardless of whether the holder also owns the support estate. Operation of this provision extinguishes the petitioners' interests in their support estates, making worthless what they purchased as a separate right under Pennsylvania law. Like the restriction on mining particular coal, this complete interference with a property right extinguishes its value, and must be accompanied by just compensation.

IV

In sum, I would hold that Pennsylvania's Bituminous Mine Subsidence and Land Conservation Act effects a taking of petitioners' property without providing just compensation. Specifically, the Act works to extinguish petitioners' interest in at least 27 million tons of coal by requiring that coal to be left in the ground, and destroys their purchased support estates by returning to them financial liability for subsidence. I respectfully dissent from the Court's decision to the contrary.[9]

HODEL v. IRVING, 107 S.Ct. 2076 (1987). Towards the end of the last century Congress enacted acts which divided the communal reservations of Indian tribes into individual allotments for Indians and unallotted lands for non-Indian settlement. Until this policy was ended

[9] Because I would find § 6 of the Subsidence Act unconstitutional under the Fifth Amendment, I would not reach the Contracts Clause issue addressed by the Court, ante, at 29–33.

in 1934 many Indians received allotments of land held in trust by the United States. The land could not be alienated and over time through laws of succession parcels became splintered into multiple undivided interests in land, with some parcels having hundreds and many having dozens of owners. As time went on the situation became worse with nobody having a sufficient interest in the land as the inheritance laws increased the number of owners. In 1983 Congress sought to deal with this problem by providing that no undivided fractional interest within a tribal reservation shall descend "by intestacy or devise but shall escheat to that tribe if such interest represents 2 per centum or less of the total acreage in such tract and has earned to its owner less than $100 in the preceding year before it is due to escheat."

Indians who were heirs or devisees of interests in land which fell under the statute brought suit claiming that they had been deprived of property without just compensation. The Court agreed, saying, in part:

". . . [T]he regulation here amounts to virtually the abrogation of the right to pass on a certain type of property—the small undivided interest—to one's heirs. In one form or another, the right to pass on property—to one's family in particular—has been part of the Anglo-American legal system since feudal times. See United States v. Perkins, 163 U.S. 625, 627–628 (1896). . . . Even the United States concedes that total abrogation of the right to pass property is unprecedented and likely unconstitutional. Moreover, this statute effectively abolishes both descent and devise of these property interests even when the passing of the property to the heir might result in consolidation of property—as for instance when the heir already owns another undivided interest in the property. . . . Since the escheatable interests are not, as the United States argues, necessarily *de minimis,* nor, as it also argues, does the availability of *inter vivos* transfer obviate the need for descent and devise, a *total* abrogation of these rights cannot be upheld. . . .

"In holding that complete abolition of both the descent and devise of a particular class of property may be a taking, we reaffirm the continuing vitality of the long line of cases recognizing the States', and where appropriate, the United States', broad authority to adjust the rules governing the descent and devise of property without implicating the guarantees of the Just Compensation Clause. . . . The difference in this case is the fact that both descent and devise are completely abolished; indeed they are abolished even in circumstances when the governmental purpose sought to be advanced, consolidation of ownership of Indian lands, does not conflict with the further descent of the property."

———

NOLLAN v. CALIFORNIA COASTAL COMMISSION
___ U.S. ___, 107 S.Ct. 3141, 97 L.Ed.2d 677 (1987).

Justice Scalia delivered the opinion of the Court.

James and Marilyn Nollan appeal from a decision of the California Court of Appeal ruling that the California Coastal Commission could condition its grant of permission to rebuild their house on their transfer to the public of an easement across their beachfront property. 177 Cal. App.3d 719, 223 Cal.Rptr. 28 (1986). The California Court rejected their claim that imposition of that condition violates the Takings Clause of the Fifth Amendment, as incorporated against the States by the Fourteenth Amendment. We noted probable jurisdiction. 479 U.S. ___ (1986).

I

The Nollans own a beach front lot in Ventura County, California. A quarter-mile north of their property is Faria County Park, an oceanside public park with a public beach and recreation area. Another public beach area, known locally as "the Cove," lies 1,800 feet south of their lot. A concrete seawall approximately eight feet high separates the beach portion of the Nollans' property from the rest of the lot. The historic mean high tide line determines the lot's oceanside boundary.

The Nollans originally leased their property with an option to buy. The building on the lot was a small bungalow, totaling 504 square feet, which for a time they rented to summer vacationers. After years of rental use, however, the building had fallen into disrepair, and could no longer be rented out. The Nollans' option to purchase was conditioned on their promise to demolish the bungalow and replace it. In order to do so, under California Public Resources Code sections 30106, 30212, and 30600 (West 1986), they were required to obtain a coastal development permit from the California Coastal Commission. On February 25, 1982, they submitted a permit application to the Commission in which they proposed to demolish the existing structure and replace it with a three-bedroom house in keeping with the rest of the neighborhood. The Nollans were informed that their application had been placed on the administrative calendar, and that the Commission staff had recommended that the permit be granted subject to the condition that they allow the public an easement to pass across a portion of their property bounded by the mean high tide line on one side, and their seawall on the other side. This would make it easier for the public to get to Faria County Park and the Cove. The Nollans protested imposition of the condition, but the Commission overruled their objections and granted the permit subject to their recordation of a deed restriction granting the easement.

On June 3, 1982, the Nollans filed a petition for writ of administrative mandamus asking the Ventura County Superior Court to invalidate the access condition. They argued that the condition could not be imposed absent evidence that their proposed development would have a direct adverse impact on public access to the beach. The court agreed, and remanded the case to the Commission for a full evidentiary hearing on that issue. On remand, the Commission held a public hearing, after which it made further factual findings and reaffirmed its imposition of the condition. It found that the new house would increase blockage of the view of the ocean, thus contributing to the development of "a 'wall' of residential structures" that would prevent the public "psychological-ly . . . from realizing a stretch of coastline exists nearby that they have every right to visit." The new house would also increase private use of the shorefront. These effects of construction of the house, along with other area development, would cumulatively "burden the public's ability to traverse to and along the shorefront." Therefore the Commission could properly require the Nollans to offset that burden by providing additional lateral access to the public beaches in the form of an easement across their property. The Commission also noted that it had similarly conditioned 43 out of 60 coastal development permits along the same tract of land, and that of the 17 not so conditioned, 14 had been approved when the Commission did not have administrative regulations in place allowing imposition of the condition, and the remaining 3 had not involved shorefront property.

The Nollans filed a supplemental petition for a writ of administrative mandamus with the Superior Court, in which they argued that imposition of the access condition violated the Takings Clause of the Fifth Amendment, as incorporated against the States by the Fourteenth Amendment. The Superior Court ruled in their favor on statutory grounds,. . . .

The Commission appealed to the California Court of Appeal. While that appeal was pending, the Nollans satisfied the condition on their option to purchase by tearing down the bungalow and building the new house, and bought the property. They did not notify the Commission that they were taking that action. The Court of Appeal reversed the Superior Court. 177 Cal.App.3d 719, 223 Cal.Rptr. 28 (1986). . . . It also ruled that that requirement did not violate the Constitution under the reasoning of an earlier case of the Court of Appeal, Grupe v. California Coastal Comm'n, 166 Cal.App.3d 148, 212 Cal.Rptr. 578 (1985). In that case, the court had found that so long as a project contributed to the need for public access, even if the project standing alone had not created the need for access, and even if there was only an indirect relationship between the access exacted and the need to which the project contributed, imposition of an access condition on a development permit was sufficiently related to burdens created by the project to be constitutional. . . . The Court of Appeal ruled that the record established that that was the situation with respect to the Nollans' house. 177 Cal.App.3d, at 722–723, 223 Cal.Rptr., at 30–31. It ruled that the Nollans' taking claim also failed because, although the condition diminished the value of the Nollans' lot, it did not deprive them of all reasonable use of their property. . . . Since, in the Court of Appeal's view, there was no statutory or constitutional obstacle to imposition of the access condition, the Superior Court erred in granting the writ of mandamus. The Nollans appealed to this Court, raising only the constitutional question.

II

Had California simply required the Nollans to make an easement across their beachfront available to the public on a permanent basis in order to increase public access to the beach, rather than conditioning their permit to rebuild their house on their agreeing to do so, we have no doubt there would have been a taking. To say that the appropriation of a public easement across a landowner's premises does not constitute the taking of a property interest but rather, (as Justice Brennan contends) "a mere restriction on its use," is to use words in a manner that deprives them of all their ordinary meaning. Indeed, one of the principal uses of the eminent domain power is to assure that the government be able to require conveyance of just such interests, so long as it pays for them. J. Sackman, 1 Nichols on Eminent Domain section 2.11 (Rev.3d ed. 1985), 2 id., section 5.015; see 1 id., section 1.42 9, 2 id., section 6.14. Perhaps because the point is so obvious, we have never been confronted with a controversy that required us to rule upon it, but our cases' analysis of the effect of other governmental action leads to the same conclusion. We have repeatedly held that, as to property reserved by its owner for private use, "the right to exclude others is 'one of the most essential sticks in the bundle of rights that are commonly characterized as property.'" Loretto v. Teleprompter Manhattan CATV Corp., 458 U.S. 419, 433 (1982), quoting Kaiser Aetna v. United States, 444 U.S. 164, 176 (1979). In Loretto we observed that where governmental action results in "a permanent physical occupation" of the property, by the government itself or by others, see 458 U.S., at 432–433, n. 9, "our cases uniformly have found a taking to the extent of the occupation, without regard to whether the action achieves an important public benefit or has only minimal economic impact on the owner," id., at 434–435. We think a "permanent physical occupation" has occurred, for purposes of that rule, where individuals are given a permanent and continuous right to pass to and fro, so that the real property may continuously be traversed, even though no particular individual is permitted to station himself permanently upon the premises.

. . .

Given, then, that requiring uncompensated conveyance of the easement outright would violate the Fourteenth Amendment, the question becomes whether requiring it to be conveyed as a condition for issuing a land use permit alters the outcome. We have long recognized that land use regulation does not effect a taking if it "substantially advances legitimate state interests" and does not "deny an owner economically viable use of his land," Agins v. Tiburon, 447 U.S. 255, 260 (1980). See also Penn Central Transportation Co. v. New York City, 438 U.S. 104, 127 (1978) ("a use restriction may constitute a 'taking' if not reasonably necessary to the effectuation of a substantial government purpose"). Our cases have not elaborated on the standards for determining what constitutes a "legitimate state interest" or what type of connection between the regulation and the state interest satisfies the requirement that the former "substantially advance" the latter.[3] They have made clear, however, that a broad range of governmental purposes and regulations satisfies these requirements. See Agins v. Tiburon, supra, at 260–262 (scenic zoning); Penn Central Transportation Co. v. New York City, supra (landmark preservation); Euclid v. Ambler Realty Co., 272 U.S. 365 (1926) (residential zoning); Laitos and Westfall, Government Interference with Private Interests in Public Resources, 11 Harv. Envtl.L.Rev. 1, 66 (1987). The Commission argues that among these permissible purposes are protecting the public's ability to see the beach, assisting the public in overcoming the "psychological barrier" to using the beach created by a developed shorefront, and preventing congestion on the public beaches. We assume, without deciding, that this is so—in which case the Commission unquestionably would be able to deny the Nollans their permit outright if their new house (alone, or by reason of the cumulative impact produced in conjunction with other construction) would substantially impede these purposes, unless the denial would interfere so drastically with the Nollans' use of their property as to constitute a taking. See Penn Central Transportation Co. v. New York City, supra.

The Commission argues that a permit condition that serves the same legitimate police-power purpose as a refusal to issue the permit should not be found to be a taking if the refusal to issue the permit would not constitute a taking. We agree. Thus, if the Commission attached to the permit some condition that would have protected the public's ability to see the beach notwithstanding construction of the new house—for example, a height limitation, a width restriction, or a ban on fences—so long as the Commission could have exercised its police power (as we have assumed it could) to forbid construction of the house altogether, imposition of the condition would also be constitutional. Moreover (and here we come closer to the facts of the present case), the condition would be constitutional even if it consisted of the requirement that the Nollans provide a viewing spot on their property for

---

[3] Contrary to Justice Brennan's claim our opinions do not establish that these standards are the same as those applied to due process or equal-protection claims. To the contrary, our verbal formulations in the takings field have generally been quite different. We have required that the regulation "substantially advance" the "legitimate state interest" sought to be achieved, Agins v. Tiburan, 447 U.S. 255, 260 (1980), not that "the State *could rationally have decided*' the measure adopted might achieve the State's objective." Quoting Minnesota v. Clover Leaf Creamery Co., 449 U.S. 456, 466 (1981). Justice Brennan relies principally on an equal protection case, Minnesota v. Clover Leaf Creamery Co., supra, and two substantive due process cases, Williamson v. Lee Optical of Oklahoma, Inc., 348 U.S. 483, 487–488 (1955) and Day-Brite Lighting, Inc. v. Missouri, 342 U.S. 421, 423 (1952), in support of the standards he would adopt. But there is no reason to believe (and the language of our cases gives some reason to disbelieve) that so long as the regulation of property is at issue the standards for takings challenges, due process challenges, and equal protection challenges are identical; any more than there is any reason to believe that so long as the regulation of speech is at issue the standards for due process challenges, equal protection challenges, and First Amendment challenges are identical. Goldblatt v. Hempstead, 369 U.S. 590 (1962), does appear to assume that the inquiries are the same, but that assumption is inconsistent with the formulations of our later cases.

passersby with whose sighting of the ocean their new house would interfere. Although such a requirement, constituting a permanent grant of continuous access to the property, would have to be considered a taking if it were not attached to a development permit, the Commission's assumed power to forbid construction of the house in order to protect the public's view of the beach must surely include the power to condition construction upon some concession by the owner, even a concession of property rights, that serves the same end. If a prohibition designed to accomplish that purpose would be a legitimate exercise of the police power rather than a taking, it would be strange to conclude that providing the owner an alternative to that prohibition which accomplishes the same purpose is not.

The evident constitutional propriety disappears, however, if the condition substituted for the prohibition utterly fails to further the end advanced as the justification for the prohibition. When that essential nexus is eliminated, the situation becomes the same as if California law forbade shouting fire in a crowded theater, but granted dispensations to those willing to contribute $100 to the state treasury. While a ban on shouting fire can be a core exercise of the State's police power to protect the public safety, and can thus meet even our stringent standards for regulation of speech, adding the unrelated condition alters the purpose to one which, while it may be legitimate, is inadequate to sustain the ban. Therefore, even though, in a sense, requiring a $100 tax contribution in order to shout fire is a lesser restriction on speech than an outright ban, it would not pass constitutional muster. Similarly here, the lack of nexus between the condition and the original purpose of the building restriction converts that purpose to something other than what it was. The purpose then becomes, quite simply, the obtaining of an easement to serve some valid governmental purpose, but without payment of compensation. Whatever may be the outer limits of "legitimate state interests" in the takings and land use context, this is not one of them. In short, unless the permit condition serves the same governmental purpose as the development ban, the building restriction is not a valid regulation of land use but "an out-and-out plan of extortion." J.E.D. Associates, Inc. v. Atkinson, 121 N.H. 581, 584, 432 A.2d 12, 14–15 (1981); see Brief for United States as Amicus Curiae 22, and n. 20. See also Loretto v. Teleprompter Manhattan CATV Corp., 458 U.S., at 439, n. 17.

III

The Commission claims that it concedes as much, and that we may sustain the condition at issue here by finding that it is reasonably related to the public need or burden that the Nollans' new house creates or to which it contributes. We can accept, for purposes of discussion, the Commission's proposed test as to how close a "fit" between the condition and the burden is required, because we find that this case does not meet even the most untailored standards. The Commission's principal contention to the contrary essentially turns on a play on the word "access." The Nollans' new house, the Commission found, will interfere with "visual access" to the beach. That in turn (along with other shorefront development) will interfere with the desire of people who drive past the Nollans' house to use the beach, thus creating a "psychological barrier" to "access." The Nollans' new house will also, by a process not altogether clear from the Commission's opinion but presumably potent enough to more than offset the effects of the psychological barrier, increase the use of the public beaches, thus creating the need for more "access." These burdens on "access" would be alleviated by a requirement that the Nollans provide "lateral access" to the beach.

Rewriting the argument to eliminate the play on words makes clear that there is nothing to it. It is quite impossible to understand how a requirement that people already on the public beaches be able to walk across the Nollans' property reduces any obstacles to viewing the beach created by the new house. It is also impossible to understand how it lowers any "psychological barrier" to using the public beaches, or how it helps to remedy any additional congestion on them caused by construction of the Nollans' new house. We therefore find that the Commission's imposition of the permit condition cannot be treated as an exercise of its land use power for any of these purposes. Our conclusion of this point is consistent with the approach taken by every other court that has considered the question, with the exception of the California state courts. . . .

Justice Brennan argues that imposition of the access requirement is not irrational. In his version of the Commission's argument, the reason for the requirement is that in its absence, a person looking toward the beach from the road will see a street of residential structures including the Nollans' new home and conclude that there is no public beach nearby. If, however, that person sees people passing and repassing along the dry sand behind the Nollans' home, he will realize that there is a public beach somewhere in the vicinity. The Commission's action, however, was based on the opposite factual finding that the wall of houses completely blocked the view of the beach and that a person looking from the road would not be able to see it at all.

Even if the Commission had made the finding that Justice Brennan proposes, however, it is not certain that it would suffice. We do not share Justice Brennan's confidence that the Commission "should have little difficulty in the future in utilizing its expertise to demonstrate a specific connection between provisions for access and burdens on access," that will avoid the effect of today's decision. We view the Fifth Amendment's property clause to be more than a pleading requirement, and compliance with it to be more than an exercise in cleverness and imagination. As indicated earlier, our cases describe the condition for abridgement of property rights through the police power as a "*substantial* advancing" of a legitimate State interest. We are inclined to be particularly careful about the adjective where the actual conveyance of property is made a condition to the lifting of a land use restriction, since in that context there is heightened risk that the purpose is avoidance of the compensation requirement, rather than the stated police power objective.

We are left, then, with the Commission's justification for the access requirement unrelated to land use regulation:

"Finally, the Commission notes that there are several existing provisions of pass and repass lateral access benefits already given by past Faria Beach Tract applicants as a result of prior coastal permit decisions. The access required as a condition of this permit is part of a comprehensive program to provide continuous public access along Faria Beach as the lots undergo development or redevelopment."

That is simply an expression of the Commission's belief that the public interest will be served by a continuous strip of publicly accessible beach along the coast. The Commission may well be right that it is a good idea, but that does not establish that the Nollans (and other coastal residents) alone can be compelled to contribute to its realization. Rather, California is free to advance its "comprehensive program," if it wishes, by using its power of eminent domain for this "public purpose", see U.S. Const., Amdt. V; but if it wants an easement across the Nollans' property, it must pay for it.

Reversed.

Justice Brennan, with whom Justice Marshall joins, dissenting.

Appellants in this case sought to construct a new dwelling on their beach lot that would both diminish visual access to the beach and move private development closer to the public tidelands. The Commission reasonably concluded that such "buildout," both individually and cumulatively, threatens public access to the shore. It sought to offset this encroachment by obtaining assurance that the public may walk along the shoreline in order to gain access to the ocean. The Court finds this an illegitimate exercise of the police power, because it maintains that there is no reasonable relationship between the effect of the development and the condition imposed.

The first problem with this conclusion is that the Court imposes a standard of precision for the exercise of a State's police power that has been discredited for the better part of this century. Furthermore, even under the Court's cramped standard, the permit condition imposed in this case directly responds to the specific type of burden on access created by appellants' development. Finally, a review of those factors deemed most significant in takings analysis makes clear that the Commission's action implicates none of the concerns underlying the Takings Clause. The Court has thus struck down the Commission's reasonable effort to respond to intensified development along the California coast, on behalf of landowners who can make no claim that their reasonable expectations have been disrupted. The Court has, in short, given appellants a windfall at the expense of the public.

I

The Court's conclusion that the permit condition imposed on appellants is unreasonable cannot withstand analysis. First, the Court demands a degree of exactitude that is inconsistent with our standard for reviewing the rationality of a state's exercise of its police power for the welfare of its citizens. Second, even if the nature of the public access condition imposed must be identical to the precise burden on access created by appellants, this requirement is plainly satisfied.

A

There can be no dispute that the police power of the States encompasses the authority to impose conditions on private development. . . . It is also by now commonplace that this Court's review of the rationality of a State's exercise of its police power demands only that the State "*could rationally have decided*" that the measure adopted might achieve the State's objective. Minnesota v. Clover Leaf Creamery Co., 449 U.S. 456, 466 (1981) (emphasis in original). . . .

The Court finds fault with this measure because it regards the condition as insufficiently tailored to address the precise type of reduction in access produced by the new development. The Nollans' development blocks visual access, the Court tells us, while the Commission seeks to preserve lateral access along the coastline. Thus, it concludes, the State acted irrationally. Such a narrow conception of rationality, however, has long since been discredited as a judicial arrogation of legislative authority.

"To make scientific precision a criterion of constitutional power would be to subject the State to an intolerable supervision hostile to the basic principles of our Government." Sproles v. Binford, 286 U.S. 374, 388 (1932). Cf. Keystone Bituminous Coal Assn. v. DeBenedictis, 480 U.S. ___, ___, n. 21 (1987) ("The Takings Clause has never been read to require the States or the courts to calculate whether a specific individual has suffered burdens . . . in excess of the benefits received"). . . .

. . .

. . . The Commission's determination that certain types of development jeopardize public access to the ocean, and that such development should be conditioned on preservation of access, is the essence of responsible land use planning. The Court's use of an unreasonably demanding standard for determining the rationality of state regulation in this area thus could hamper innovative efforts to preserve an increasingly fragile national resource.

B

Even if we accept the Court's unusual demand for a precise match between the condition imposed and the specific type of burden on access created by the appellants, the State's action easily satisfies this requirement. First, the lateral access condition serves to dissipate the impression that the beach that lies behind the wall of homes along the shore is for private use only. It requires no exceptional imaginative powers to find plausible the Commission's point that the average person passing along the road in front of a phalanx of imposing permanent residences, including the appellants' new home, is likely to conclude that this particular portion of the shore is not open to the public. If, however, that person can see that numerous people are passing and repassing along the dry sand, this conveys the message that the beach is in fact open for use by the public. Furthermore, those persons who go down to the public beach a quarter-mile away will be able to look down the coastline and see that persons have continuous access to the tidelands, and will observe signs that proclaim the public's right of access over the dry sand. The burden produced by the diminution in visual access— the impression that the beach is not open to the public—is thus directly alleviated by the provision for public access over the dry sand. The Court therefore has an unrealistically limited conception of what measures could reasonably be chosen to mitigate the burden produced by a diminution of visual access.

. . .

The Court is therefore simply wrong that there is no reasonable relationship between the permit condition and the specific type of burden on public access created by the appellants' proposed development. Even were the Court desirous of assuming the added responsibility of closely monitoring the regulation of development along the California coast, this record reveals rational public action by any conceivable standard.

II

The fact that the Commission's action is a legitimate exercise of the police power does not, of course, insulate it from a takings challenge, for when "regulation goes too far it will be recognized as a taking." Pennsylvania Coal Co. v. Mahon, 260 U.S. 393, 415 (1922). Conventional takings analysis underscores the implausibility of the Court's holding, for it demonstrates that this exercise of California's police power implicates none of the concerns that underlie our takings jurisprudence.

. . .

Standard Takings Clause analysis thus indicates that the Court employs its unduly restrictive standard of police power rationality to find a taking where neither the character of governmental action nor the nature of the private interest affected raise any takings concern. The result is that the Court invalidates regulation that represents a reasonable adjustment of the burdens and benefits of development along the California coast.

III

The foregoing analysis makes clear that the State has taken no property from appellants. Imposition of the permit condition in this case represents the State's reasonable exercise of its police power. The Coastal Commission has drawn on its expertise to preserve the balance between private development and public access, by requiring that any project that intensifies development on the increasingly crowded California coast must be offset by gains in public access. Under the normal standard for review of the police power, this provision is eminently reasonable. Even accepting the Court's novel insistence on a precise quid pro quo of burdens and benefits, there is a reasonable relationship between the public benefit and the burden created by appellants' development. The movement of development closer to the ocean creates the prospect of encroachment on public tidelands, because of fluctuation in the mean high tide line. The deed restriction ensures that disputes about the boundary between private and public property will not deter the public from exercising its right to have access to the sea.

Furthermore, consideration of the Commission's action under traditional takings analysis underscores the absence of any viable takings claim. The deed restriction permits the public only to pass and repass along a narrow strip of beach, a few feet closer to a seawall at the periphery of appellants' property. Appellants almost surely have enjoyed an increase in the value of their property even with the restriction, because they have been allowed to build a significantly larger new home with garage on their lot. Finally, appellants can claim the disruption of no expectation interest, both because they have no right to exclude the public under state law, and because, even if they did, they had full advance notice that new development along the coast is conditioned on provisions for continued public access to the ocean. Fortunately, the Court's decision regarding this application of the Commission's permit program will probably have little ultimate impact

. . . ..

With respect to the permit condition program in general, the Commission should have little difficulty in the future in utilizing its expertise to demonstrate a specific connection between provisions for access and burdens on access produced by new development. . . . As Congress has declared, "The key to more effective protection and use of the land and water resources of the coastal [is for the states to] develo[p] land and water use programs for the coastal zone, including unified policies, criteria, standards, methods, and processes for dealing with land and water use decisions of more than local significance." 16 U.S.C. section 1451(i). This is clearly a call for a focus on the overall impact of development on coastal areas. State agencies therefore require considerable flexibility in responding to private desires for development in a way that guarantees the preservation of public access to the coast. They should be encouraged to regulate development in the context of the overall balance of competing uses of the shoreline. The Court today does precisely the opposite, overruling an eminently reasonable exercise of an expert state agency's judgment, substituting its own narrow view of how this balance should be struck. Its reasoning is hardly suited to the complex reality of natural resource protection in the twentieth century. I can only hope that today's decision is an aberration, and that a broader vision ultimately prevails.

I dissent.

Justice Blackmun, dissenting.

. . .

I disagree with the Court's rigid interpretation of the necessary correlation between a burden created by development and a condition imposed pursuant to the State's police power to mitigate that burden. The land-use problems this country faces require creative solutions. These are not advanced by an "eye for an eye" mentality. The close nexus between benefits and burdens that the Court now imposes on permit conditions creates an anomaly in the ordinary requirement that a State's exercise of its police power need be no more than rationally based. See, e.g., Minnesota v. Clover Leaf Creamery Co., 449 U.S. 456, 466 (1981). In my view, the easement exacted from appellants and the problems their development created are adequately related to the governmental interest in providing public access to the beach. Coastal development by its very nature makes public access to the shore generally more difficult. Appellants' structure is part of that general development and, in particular, it diminishes the public's visual access to the ocean and decreases the public's sense that it may have physical access to the beach. These losses in access can be counteracted, at least in part, by the condition on appellants' construction permitting public passage that ensures access along the beach. Traditional takings analysis compels the conclusion that there is no taking here. The governmental action is a valid exercise of the police power, and, so far as the record reveals, has a nonexistent economic effect on the value of appellants' property. No investment-backed expectations were diminished. It is significant that the Nollans had notice of the easement before they purchased the property and that public use of the beach had been permitted for decades. For these reasons, I respectfully dissent.

Justice Stevens, with whom Justice Blackmun joins, dissenting.

The debate between the Court and Justice Brennan illustrates an extremely important point concerning government regulation of the use of privately owned real estate. Intelligent, well-informed public officials may in good faith disagree about the validity of specific types of land use regulation. Even the wisest lawyers would have to acknowledge great uncertainty about the scope of this Court's takings jurisprudence. Yet, because of the Court's remarkable ruling in First English Evangelical Lutheran Church v. Los Angeles County, 482 U.S. ___ (1987), local governments and officials must pay the price for the necessarily vague standards in this area of the law.

In his dissent in San Diego Gas & Electric Co. v. San Diego, 450 U.S. 621 (1981), Justice Brennan proposed a brand new constitutional rule. He argued that a mistake such as the one that a majority of the Court believes that the California Coastal Commission made in this case should automatically give rise to pecuniary liability for a "temporary taking." Id., at 653–661. Notwithstanding the unprecedented chilling effect that such a rule will obviously have on public officials charged with the responsibility for drafting and implementing regulations designed to protect the environment and the public welfare, six Members of the Court recently endorsed Justice Brennan's novel proposal. See First English Evangelical Lutheran Church, supra. I write today to identify the severe tension between that dramatic development in the law and the view expressed by Justice Brennan's dissent in this case that the public interest is served by encouraging state agencies to exercise considerable flexibility in responding to private desires for development in a way that threatens the preservation of public resources. I like the hat that Justice Brennan has donned today better than the one he wore in San Diego, and I am persuaded that he has the better of the legal arguments here. Even if his position prevailed in this case, however, it would be of little solace to land-use planners who would still be left guessing about how the Court will react to the next case, and the one after that. As this case demonstrates, the rule of liability created by the Court in First English is a short-sighted one. Like Justice Brennan, I hope "that a broader vision ultimately prevails."

I respectfully dissent.

BOWEN v. GILLIARD, 107 S.Ct. 3008 (1987): In 1975 federal statutes governing the Aid to Families with Dependent Children (AFDC) program required, as a condition of eligibility, that applicants for assistance assign to the State any right to receive child support payments for any family member included in the family unit, but a recipient of aid (the amount of which is determined by the number and income of persons in the family unit) could exclude a child for whom support payments were being made from the family unit if it was financially advantageous to do so, even though the child continued to live with the family. The Deficit Reduction Act of 1984 (DEFRA) amended the AFDC program to require families to include in the filing unit all children living in the same home, including those for whom support payments were being received. Under a separate amendment, the first $50 per month of child support collected by the state must be remitted to the family and not counted as income in determining its benefit level. Thus, if the assigned support exceeded $50 plus the difference in the benefit level resulting from adding the child to the family unit, the family would suffer financially as compared with its total income prior to the amendment. In a class action, the Federal District Court held that North Carolina's implementing regulations were in conformance with the statute, but that the 1984 statutory scheme violated the due process clause of the fifth amendment and its equal protection component, as well as the takings clause of that amendment.

The equal protection issue will be discussed infra. On the takings issue the Court, in an opinion by Justice Stevens, upheld the statute. Justices Brennan, Marshall, and Blackmun, dissented on the equal protection issue and did not discuss the takings issue.

In reaching its conclusion, the Court said, in part: "Some perspective on the issue is helpful here. Had no AFDC program ever existed until 1984, and had Congress then instituted a program that took into account support payments that a family receives, it is hard to believe that we would seriously entertain an argument that the new benefit program constituted a taking. Yet, somehow, once benefits are in place and Congress sees a need to reduce them in order to save money and to distribute limited resources more fairly, the 'taking' label seems to have a bit more plausibility. For legal purposes though, the two situations are identical. See Bowen v. Public Agencies Opposed to Social Security Entrapment, 477 U.S. ___ (1986). Congress is not, by virtue of having instituted a social welfare program, bound to continue it at all, much less at the same benefit level. Thus, notwithstanding the technical legal arguments that have been advanced, it is imperative to recognize that the amendments at issue merely incorporate a definitional element into an entitlement program. It would be quite strange indeed if, by virtue of an offer to *provide* benefits to needy families through the entirely voluntary AFDC program, Congress or the States were deemed to have *taken* some of those very family members' property.

"The basic requirement that the AFDC filing unit must include all family members living in the home, and therefore that support payments made on behalf of a member of the family must be considered in determining that family's level of benefits, does not even arguably take anyone's property. The family members other than the child for whom the support is being paid certainly have no taking claim, since it is clear that they have no protected property rights to continued benefits at the same level. See *Public Agencies Opposed to Social Security Entrapment,* supra. Nor does the simple inclusion of the support income in the benefit calculation have any legal effect on the child's right to have it used for his or her benefit. To the extent that a child has the right to have the support payments used in his 'best interest,' he or she fully retains that right. Of course, the effect of counting the support payments as part of the filing unit's income often reduces the family's resources, and hence increases the chances that sharing of the support money will be appropriate. But given the unquestioned premise that the Government has a right to reduce AFDC benefits generally, that result does not constitute a taking of private property without just compensation.

"The only possible legal basis for appellees' takings claim, therefore, is the requirement that an applicant for AFDC benefits must assign the support payments to the State, which then will remit the amount collected to the custodial parent to be used for the benefit of the entire family. This legal transformation in the status of the funds, the argument goes, modifies the child's interest in the use of the money so dramatically that it constitutes a taking of the child's property. As a practical matter, this argument places form over substance, and labels over reality. Although it is true that money which was earmarked for a specific child's or children's 'best interest' becomes a part of a larger fund available for all of the children, the difference between these concepts is . . . more theoretical than practical.
. . .

"The law does not require any custodial parent to apply for AFDC benefits. Surely it is reasonable to presume that a parent who does make such an application does so because she or he is convinced that the family as a whole—as well as *each* child committed to her or his custody—will be better off with the benefits than without. In making such a decision, the parent is not taking a child's property without just compensation; nor is the State doing so when it responds to that decision by supplementing the collections of support money with additional AFDC benefits."

Page 576. Add in lieu of San Diego Gas & Electric Co. v. City of San Diego:

FIRST ENGLISH EVANGELICAL LUTHERAN CHURCH OF GLENDALE v. COUNTY OF LOS ANGELES

___ U.S. ___, 107 S.Ct. 2378, 96 L.Ed.2d 250 (1987).

Chief Justice Rehnquist delivered the opinion of the Court.

In this case the California Court of Appeal held that a landowner who claims that his property has been "taken" by a land-use regulation may not recover damages for the time before it is finally determined that the regulation constitutes a "taking" of his property. We disagree, and conclude that in these circumstances the Fifth and Fourteenth Amendments to the United States Constitution would require compensation for that period.

In 1957, appellant First English Evangelical Lutheran Church purchased a 21–acre parcel of land in a canyon along the banks of the Middle Fork of Mill Creek in the Angeles National Forest. The Middle Fork is the natural drainage channel for a watershed area owned by the National Forest Service. Twelve of the acres owned by the church are flat land, and contained a dining hall, two bunkhouses, a caretaker's lodge, an outdoor chapel, and a footbridge across the creek. The church operated on the site a campground, known as "Lutherglen," as a retreat center and a recreational area for handicapped children.

In July 1977, a forest fire denuded the hills upstream from Lutherglen, destroying approximately 3,860 acres of the watershed area and creating a serious flood hazard. Such flooding occurred on February 9 and 10, 1978, when a storm dropped 11 inches of rain in the watershed. The runoff from the storm overflowed the banks of the Mill Creek, flooding Lutherglen and destroying its buildings.

In response to the flooding of the canyon, appellee County of Los Angeles adopted Interim Ordinance No. 11,855 in January 1979. The ordinance provided that "[a] person shall not construct, reconstruct, place or enlarge any building or structure, any portion of which is, or will be, located within the outer boundary lines of the interim flood protection area located in Mill Creek Canyon. . . ." The ordinance was effective immediately because the county determined that it was "required for the immediate preservation of the public health and safety. . . ." The interim flood protection area described by the ordinance included the flat areas on either side of Mill Creek on which Lutherglen had stood.

The church filed a complaint in the Superior Court of California a little more than a month after the ordinance was adopted. As subsequently amended, the complaint alleged two claims against the county and the Los Angeles County Flood Control District. The first alleged that the defendants were liable under Cal.Gov't Code Ann. § 835 (West 1980) for dangerous conditions on their upstream properties that contributed to the flooding of Lutherglen. As a part of this claim, appellant also alleged that "Ordinance No. 11,855 denies [appellant] all use of Lutherglen." The second claim sought to recover from the Flood District in inverse condemnation and in tort for engaging in cloud seeding during the storm that flooded Lutherglen. Appellant sought damages under each count for loss of use of Lutherglen. The defendants moved to strike the portions of the complaint alleging that the county's ordinance denied all use of Lutherglen, on the view that the California Supreme Court's decision in Agins v. Tiburon, 24 Cal.3d 266, 598 P.2d 25 (1979), aff'd on other grounds, 447 U.S. 255 (1980), rendered the allegation "entirely immaterial and irrelevant[, with] no bearing upon any conceivable cause of action herein." . . .

In Agins v. Tiburon, supra, the Supreme Court of California decided that a landowner may not maintain an inverse condemnation suit in the courts of that State based upon a "regulatory" taking. 24 Cal.3d, at 275–277, 598 P.2d, at 29–31. In the court's view, maintenance of such a suit would allow a landowner to force the legislature to exercise its power of eminent domain. Under this decision, then, compensation is not required until the challenged regulation or ordinance has been held excessive in an action for declaratory relief or a writ of mandamus and the government has nevertheless decided to continue the regulation in effect. Based on this decision, the trial court in the present case granted the motion to strike the allegation that the church had been denied all use of Lutherglen. It explained that "a careful re-reading of the *Agins* case persuades the Court that when an ordinance, even a non-zoning ordinance, deprives a person of the total use of his lands, his challenge to the ordinance is by way of declaratory relief or possibly mandamus." Because the appellant alleged a regulatory taking and sought only damages, the allegation that the ordinance denied all use of Lutherglen was deemed irrelevant.

On appeal, the California Court of Appeal read the complaint as one seeking "damages for the uncompensated taking of all use of Lutherglen by County Ordinance No. 11,855. . . ." It too relied on the California Supreme Court's decision in *Agins* in rejecting the cause of action, ... It accordingly affirmed the trial court's decision to strike the allegations concerning appellee's ordinance. The Supreme Court of California denied review.

This appeal followed, and we noted probable jurisdiction. Appellant asks us to hold that the Supreme Court of California erred in Agins v. Tiburon in determining that the Fifth Amendment, as made applicable to the States through the Fourteenth Amendment, does not require compensation as a remedy for "temporary" regulatory takings—those regulatory takings which are ultimately invalidated by the courts. Four times this decade, we have considered similar claims and have found ourselves for one reason or another unable to consider the merits of the *Agins* rule. See MacDonald, Sommer & Frates v. Yolo County, 477 U.S. 340 (1986); Williamson County Regional Planning Comm'n v. Hamilton Bank, 473 U.S. 172 (1985); *San Diego Gas &*

Electric Co., supra; Agins v. Tiburon, supra. For the reasons explained below, however, we find the constitutional claim properly presented in this case, and hold that on these facts the California courts have decided the compensation question inconsistently with the requirements of the Fifth Amendment.

I

Concerns with finality left us unable to reach the remedial question in the earlier cases where we have been asked to consider the rule of *Agins.* See *MacDonald, Sommer & Frates,* supra, at 351 (summarizing cases). In each of these cases, we concluded either that regulations considered to be in issue by the state court did not effect a taking, Agins v. Tiburon, supra, at 263, or that the factual disputes yet to be resolved by state authorities might still lead to the conclusion that no taking had occurred. *MacDonald, Sommer & Frates,* supra, at 352–353; *Williamson County,* supra, at 191; San Diego Gas & Electric Co., supra, at 631–623. Consideration of the remedial question in those circumstances, we concluded, would be premature.

The posture of the present case is quite different. Appellant's complaint alleged that "Ordinance No. 11,855 denies [it] all use of Lutherglen," and sought damages for this deprivation. In affirming the decision to strike this allegation, the Court of Appeal assumed that the complaint sought "damages for the uncompensated *taking* of all use of Lutherglen by County Ordinance No. 11,855." It relied on the California Supreme Court's *Agins* decision for the conclusion that "the remedy for a *taking* [is limited] to nonmonetary relief. . . ." The disposition of the case on these grounds isolates the remedial question for our consideration. The rejection of appellant's allegations did not rest on the view that they were false. . . . Nor did the court rely on the theory that regulatory measures such as Ordinance No. 11,855 may never constitute a taking in the constitutional sense. Instead, the claims were deemed irrelevant solely because of the California Supreme Court's decision in *Agins* that damages are unavailable to redress a "temporary" regulatory taking. The California Court of Appeal has thus held that regardless of the correctness of appellants' claim that the challenged ordinance denies it "all use of Lutherglen" appellant may not recover damages until the ordinance is finally declared unconstitutional, and then only for any period after that declaration for which the county seeks to enforce it. The constitutional question pretermitted in our earlier cases is therefore squarely presented here.

We reject appellee's suggestion that, regardless of the state court's treatment of the question, we must independently evaluate the adequacy of the complaint and resolve the takings claim on the merits before we can reach the remedial question. However "cryptic"—to use appellee's description—the allegations with respect to the taking were, the California courts deemed them sufficient to present the issue. We accordingly have no occasion to decide whether the ordinance at issue actually denied appellant all use of its property or whether the county might avoid the conclusion that a compensable taking had occurred by establishing that the denial of all use was insulated as a part of the State's authority to enact safety regulations. See e.g., Goldblatt v. Hempstead, 369 U.S. 590 (1962); Hadacheck v. Sebastian, 239 U.S. 394 (1915); Mugler v. Kansas, 123 U.S. 623 (1887). These questions, of course, remain open for decision on the remand we direct today. We now turn to the question of whether the Just Compensation Clause requires the government to pay for "temporary" regulatory takings.

II

Consideration of the compensation question must begin with direct reference to the language of the Fifth Amendment, which provides in relevant part that "private property [shall not] be taken for public use, without just compensation." As its language indicates, and as the Court has frequently noted, this provision does not prohibit the taking of private property, but instead places a condition on the exercise of that power. . . . This basic understanding of the Amendment makes clear that it is designed not to limit the governmental interference with property rights *per se,* but rather to secure *compensation* in the event of otherwise proper interference amounting to a taking. Thus, government action that works a taking of property rights necessarily implicates the "constitutional obligation to pay just compensation." Armstrong v. United States, 364 U.S. 40, 49 (1960).

We have recognized that a landowner is entitled to bring an action in inverse condemnation as a result of " 'the self-executing character of the constitutional provision with respect to compensation. . . .' " United States v. Clarke, 445 U.S. 253, 257 (1980), quoting 6 P. Nichols, Eminent Domain § 25.41 (3d rev. ed. 1972). . . . [T]he Court has frequently repeated the view that, in the event of a taking, the compensation remedy is required by the Constitution. . . .

It has also been established doctrine at least since Justice Holmes' opinion for the Court in Pennsylvania Coal Co. v. Mahon, 260 U.S. 393 (1922) that "[t]he general rule at least is, that while property may be regulated to a certain extent, if regulation goes too far it will be recognized as a taking." While the typical taking occurs when the government acts to condemn property in the exercise of its power of eminent domain, the entire doctrine of inverse condemnation is predicated on the proposition that a taking may occur without such formal proceedings. . . .

While the Supreme Court of California may not have actually disavowed this general rule in *Agins,* we believe that it has truncated the rule by disallowing damages that occurred prior to the ultimate invalidation of the challenged regulation. The Supreme Court of California justified its conclusion at length in the *Agins* opinion, concluding that:

"In combination, the need for preserving a degree of freedom in the land-use planning function, and the inhibiting financial force which inheres in the inverse condemnation remedy, persuade us that on balance mandamus or declaratory relief rather than inverse condemnation is the appropriate relief under the circumstances." Agins v. Tiburon, 24 Cal.3d, at 276–277, 598 P.2d, at 31.

We, of course, are not unmindful of these considerations, but they must be evaluated in the light of the command of the Just Compensation Clause of the Fifth Amendment. The Court has recognized in more than one case that the government may elect to abandon its intrusion or discontinue regulations. See e.g., Kirby Forest Industries, Inc. v. United States, 467 U.S. 1 (1984); United States v. Dow, 357 U.S. 17, 26 (1958). Similarly, a governmental body may acquiesce in a judicial declaration that one of its ordinances has affected an unconstitutional taking of property; the landowner has no right under the Just Compensation Clause to insist that a "temporary" taking be deemed a permanent taking. But we have not resolved whether abandonment by the government requires payment of compensation for the period of time during which regulations deny a landowner all use of his land.

In considering this question, we find substantial guidance in cases where the government has only temporarily exercised its right to use private property. . . .

These cases reflect the fact that "temporary" takings which, as here, deny a landowner all use of his property, are not different in kind from permanent takings, for which the Constitution clearly requires compensation. Cf. San Diego Gas & Electric Co., 450 U.S., at 657 (Brennan, J., dissenting) ("Nothing in the Just Compensation Clause suggests that 'takings' must be permanent and irrevocable"). It is axiomatic that the Fifth Amendment's just compensation provision is "designed to bar Government from forcing some people alone to bear public burdens which, in all fairness and justice, should be borne by the public as a whole." Armstrong v. United States, 364 U.S., at 49. See also Penn Central Transportation Co. v. New York City, 438 U.S., at 123–125; Monongahela Navigation Co. v. United States, 148 U.S., at 325. In the present case the interim ordinance was adopted by the county of Los Angeles in January 1979, and became effective immediately. Appellant filed suit within a month after the effective date of the ordinance and yet when the Supreme Court of California denied a hearing in the case on October 17, 1985, the merits of appellant's claim had yet to be determined. The United States has been required to pay compensation for leasehold interests of shorter duration than this. The value of a leasehold interest in property for a period of years may be substantial, and the burden on the property owner in extinguishing such an interest for a period of years may be great indeed. See, e.g., United States v. General Motors, supra. Where this burden results from governmental action that amounted to a taking, the Just Compensation Clause of the Fifth Amendment requires that the government pay the landowner for the value of the use of the land during this period. Cf. United States v. Causby, 328 U.S., at 261 ("It is the owner's loss, not the taker's gain, which is the measure of the value of the property taken"). Invalidation of the ordinance or its successor ordinance after this period of time, though converting the taking into a "temporary" one, is not a sufficient remedy to meet the demands of the Just Compensation Clause.

Appellee argues that requiring compensation for denial of all use of land prior to invalidation is inconsistent with this Court's decisions in Danforth v. United States, 308 U.S. 271 (1939), and Agins v. Tiburon, 447 U.S. 255 (1980). In *Danforth,* the landowner contended that the "taking" of his property had occurred prior to the institution of condemnation proceedings, by reason of the enactment of the Flood Control Act itself. He claimed that the passage of that Act had diminished the value of his property because the plan embodied in the Act required condemnation of a flowage easement across his property. The Court held that in the context of condemnation proceedings a taking does not occur until compensation is determined and paid, and went on to say that "[a] reduction or increase in the value of property may occur by reason of legislation for or the beginning or completion of a project," but "[s]uch changes in value are incidents of ownership. They cannot be considered as a 'taking' in the constitutional sense." *Danforth,* supra, at 285. *Agins* likewise rejected a claim that the city's preliminary activities constituted a taking, saying that "[m]ere fluctuations in value during the process of governmental decisionmaking, absent extraordinary delay, are 'incidents of ownership.' " See 447 U.S., at 263, n. 9.

But these cases merely stand for the unexceptional proposition that the valuation of property which has been taken must be calculated as of the time of the taking, and that depreciation in value of the property by reason of preliminary activity is not chargeable to the government. Thus, in *Agins,* we concluded that the preliminary activity did not work a taking. It would require a considerable extension of these decisions to say that no compensable regulatory taking may occur until a challenged ordinance has ultimately been held invalid.

Nothing we say today is intended to abrogate the principle that the decision to exercise the power of eminent domain is a legislative function, " 'for Congress and Congress alone to determine.' " Hawaii Housing Authority v. Midkiff, 467 U.S. 229, 240 (1984), quoting Berman v. Parker, 348 U.S. 26, 33 (1954). Once a court determines that a taking has occurred, the government retains the whole range of options already available—amendment of the regulation, withdrawal of the invalidated regulation, or exercise of eminent domain. Thus we do not, as the Solicitor General suggests, "permit a court, at the behest of a private person, to require the . . . Government to exercise the power of eminent domain. . . ." We merely hold that where the government's activities have already worked a taking of all use of property, no subsequent action by the government can relieve it of the duty to provide compensation for the period during which the taking was effective.

We also point out that the allegation of the complaint which we treat as true for purposes of our decision was that the ordinance in question denied appellant all use of its property. We limit our holding to the facts presented, and of course do not deal with the quite different questions that would arise in the case of normal delays in obtaining building permits, changes in zoning ordinances, variances, and the like which are not before us. We realize that even our present holding will undoubtedly lessen to some extent the freedom and flexibility of land-use planners and governing bodies of municipal corporations when enacting land-use regulations. But such consequences necessarily flow from any decision upholding a claim of constitutional right; many of the provisions of the Constitution are designed to limit the flexibility and freedom of governmental authorities and the Just Compensation Clause of the Fifth Amendment is one of them. As Justice Holmes aptly noted more than 50 years ago, "a strong public desire to improve the public condition is not enough to warrant achieving the desire by a shorter cut than the constitutional way of paying for the change." Pennsylvania Coal Co. v. Mahon, 260 U.S., at 416.

Here we must assume that the Los Angeles County ordinances have denied appellant all use of its property for a considerable period of years, and we hold that invalidation of the ordinance without payment of fair value for the use of the property during this period of time would be a constitutionally insufficient remedy. The judgment of the California Court of Appeals is therefore reversed, and the case is remanded for further proceedings not inconsistent with this opinion.

It is so ordered.

————

Justice Stevens, with whom Justice Blackmun and Justice O'Connor join as to Parts I and III, dissenting.

One thing is certain. The Court's decision today will generate a great deal of litigation. Most of it, I believe, will be unproductive. But the mere duty to defend the actions that today's decision will spawn will undoubtedly have a significant adverse impact on the land-use regulatory process. The Court has reached out to address an issue not actually presented in this case, and has then answered that self-imposed question in a superficial and, I believe, dangerous way.

Four flaws in the Court's analysis merit special comment. First, the Court unnecessarily and imprudently assumes that appellant's complaint alleges an unconstitutional taking of Lutherglen. Second, the Court distorts our precedents in the area of regulatory takings when it concludes that all ordinances which would constitute takings if allowed to remain in effect permanently, necessarily also constitute takings if they are in effect for only a limited period of time. Third, the Court incorrectly assumes that the California Supreme Court has already decided that it will never allow a state court to grant monetary relief for a temporary regulatory taking, and then uses that conclusion to reverse a judgment which is correct under the Court's own theories. Finally, the Court errs in concluding that it is the Takings Clause, rather than the Due Process Clause, which is the primary constraint on the use of unfair and dilatory procedures in the land-use area.

I

. . .

This Court clearly has the authority to decide this case by ruling that the complaint did not allege a taking under the Federal Constitution, and therefore to avoid the novel constitutional issue that it addresses. Even though I believe the Court's lack of self-restraint is imprudent, it is imperative to stress that the Court does not hold that appellant is entitled to compensation as a result of the flood protection regulation that the County enacted. No matter whether the regulation is treated as one that deprives appellant of its property on a permanent or temporary basis, this Court's precedents demonstrate that the type of regulatory program at issue here cannot constitute a taking.

. . .

In this case, the legitimacy of the County's interest in the enactment of Ordinance No. 11,855 is apparent from the face of the ordinance and has never been challenged. . . .

Thus, although the Court uses the allegations of this complaint as a springboard for its discussion of a discrete legal issue, it does not, and could not under our precedents, hold that the allegations sufficiently alleged a taking or that the County's effort to preserve life and property could ever constitute a taking. As far as the United States Constitution is concerned, the claim that the ordinance was a taking of Lutherglen should be summarily rejected on its merits.

II

There is no dispute about the proposition that a regulation which goes "too far" must be deemed a taking. See Pennsylvania Coal Co. v. Mahon, 260 U.S. 393, 415 (1922). When that happens, the Government has a choice: it may abandon the regulation or it may continue to regulate and compensate those whose property it takes. In the usual case, either of these options is wholly satisfactory. Paying compensation for the property is, of course, a constitutional prerogative of the sovereign. Alternatively, if the sovereign chooses not to retain the regulation, repeal will, in virtually all cases, mitigate the overall effect of the regulation so substantially that the slight diminution in value that the regulation caused while in effect cannot be classified as a taking of property. We may assume, however, that this may not always be the case. There may be some situations in which even the temporary existence of a regulation has such severe consequences that invalidation or repeal will not mitigate the damage enough to remove the "taking" label. This hypothetical situation is what the Court calls a "temporary taking." But, contrary to the Court's implications, the fact that a regulation would constitute a taking if allowed to remain in effect permanently is by no means dispositive of the question whether the effect that the regulation has already had on the property is so severe that a taking occurred during the period before the regulation was invalidated.

. . .

In my opinion, the question whether a "temporary taking" has occurred should not be answered by simply looking at the reason a temporary interference with an owner's use of his property is terminated. Litigation challenging the validity of a land-use restriction gives rise to a delay that is just as "normal" as an administrative procedure seeking a variance or an approval of a controversial plan. Just because a plaintiff can prove that a land-use restriction would constitute a taking if allowed to remain in effect permanently does not mean that he or she can also prove that its temporary application rose to the level of a constitutional taking.

III

The Court recognizes that the California courts have the right to adopt invalidation of an excessive regulation as the appropriate remedy for the permanent effects of overburdensome regulations, rather than allowing the regulation to stand and ordering the government to afford compensation for the permanent taking. . . . The difference between these two remedies is less substantial than one might assume. When a court invalidates a regulation, the Legislative or Executive Branch must then decide whether to condemn the property in order to proceed with the regulatory scheme. On the other hand, if the court requires compensation for a permanent taking, the Executive or Legislative Branch may still repeal the regulation and thus prevent the permanent taking. The difference, therefore, is only in what will happen in the case of Legislative or Executive inertia. Many scholars have debated the respective merits of the alternate approaches in light of separation of powers concerns, but our only concern is with a *state court's* decision on which procedure it considers more appropriate. California is fully competent to decide how it wishes to deal with the separation of powers implications of the remedy it routinely uses.

Once it is recognized that California may deal with the permanent taking problem by invalidating objectionable regulations, it becomes clear that the California Court of Appeal's decision in this case should be affirmed. Even if this Court is correct in stating that one who makes out a claim for a permanent taking is automatically entitled to some compensation for the temporary aspect of the taking as well, the States still have the right to deal with the permanent aspect of a taking by invalidating the regulation. That is all that the California courts have done in this case. They have refused to proceed upon a complaint which sought only damages, and which did not contain a request for a declaratory invalidation of the regulation, as clearly required by California precedent.

. . .

The appellant should not be permitted to circumvent that requirement by omitting any prayer for equitable relief from its complaint. I believe the California Supreme Court is justified in insisting that the owner recover as much of its property as possible before foisting any of it on an unwilling governmental purchaser. The Court apparently agrees with this proposition. Thus, even on the Court's own radical view of temporary regulatory takings announced today, the California courts had the right to strike this complaint.

IV

There is, of course, a possibility that land-use planning, like other forms of regulation, will unfairly deprive a citizen of the right to develop his property at the time and in the manner that will best serve his economic interests. The "regulatory taking" doctrine announced in *Pennsylvania Coal* places a limit on the permissible scope of land-use restrictions. In my opinion, however, it is the Due Process Clause rather than that doctrine that protects the property owner from improperly motivated, unfairly conducted, or unnecessarily protracted governmental decisionmaking. Violation of the procedural safeguards mandated by the Due Process Clause will give rise to actions for damages under 42 U.S.C. § 1983, but I am not persuaded that delays in the development of property that are occasioned by fairly conducted administrative or judicial proceedings are compensable, except perhaps in the most unusual circumstances. On the contrary, I am convinced that the public interest in having important governmental decisions made in an orderly, fully informed way amply justifies the temporary burden on the citizen that is the inevitable by-product of democratic government.

.   .   .

SECTION 2. PROTECTION OF PERSONAL LIBERTIES

———

B. PERSONAL AUTONOMY

———

Page 617. Add ahead of C. Family Relationships:

THORNBURGH v. AMERICAN COLLEGE OF OBSTETRICIANS AND GYNECOLOGISTS

476 U.S. 747, 106 S.Ct. 2169, 90 L.Ed.2d 779 (1986).

Justice Blackmun delivered the opinion of the Court.

This is an appeal from a judgment of the United States Court of Appeals for the Third Circuit reviewing the District Court's rulings upon a motion for a preliminary injunction. The Court of Appeals held unconstitutional several provisions of Pennsylvania's current Abortion Control Act, 1982 Pa. Laws, Act No. 138, now codified as 18 Pa.Cons. Stat. § 3201 et seq. (1983) (Act). Among the provisions ruled invalid by the Court of Appeals were portions of § 3205, relating to "informed consent"; § 3208, concerning "printed information"; §§ 3210(b) and (c), having to do with postviability abortions; and § 3211(a) and §§ 3214(a) and (h), regarding reporting requirements.

I

The Abortion Control Act was approved by the Governor of the Commonwealth on June 11, 1982. By its own terms, however, see § 7 of the Act, it was to become effective only 180 days thereafter, that is, on the following December 8. It had been offered as an amendment to a pending bill to regulate paramilitary training.

. . .

After the passage of the Act, but before its effective date, the present litigation was instituted in the United States District Court for the Eastern District of Pennsylvania. The plaintiffs, who are the appellees here, were the American College of Obstetricians and Gynecologists, Pennsylvania Section; certain physicians licensed in Pennsylvania; clergymen; an individual who purchases from a Pennsylvania insurer health-care and disability insurance extending to abortions; and Pennsylvania abortion counselors and providers. Alleging that the Act violated the United States Constitution, the plaintiffs, pursuant to 42 U.S.C. § 1983, sought declaratory and injunctive relief. The defendants named in the complaint were the Governor of the Commonwealth, other Commonwealth officials, and the District Attorney for Montgomery County, Pa.

. . .

[The plaintiffs filed a motion for preliminary injunction. Based on affidavits submitted with the motion, a comprehensive opposing memorandum, and a stipulation of facts, the district court concluded that the plaintiffs had failed to establish a likelihood of success on the merits and denied them preliminary injunction.

[On appeal the court of appeals reached the merits and ruled that various sections of the statute were unconstitutional.

[The Supreme Court first held that they had no appellate jurisdiction but treating the appeal papers as a petition for certiorari, they granted the writ.

[The Supreme Court then held that the normal rule restricting the court of appeals to determining whether the trial court abused its discretion in finding the presence or absence of irreparable harm and a probability that the plaintiffs would succeed on the merits should not apply here. That rule is one of orderly judicial administration, and not a limit on judicial power. The court of appeals acted properly in reaching the issues here when there was an ample record and the unconstitutionality of the state action was clear.]

IV

This case, as it comes to us, concerns the constitutionality of six provisions of the Pennsylvania Act that the Court of Appeals struck down as facially invalid: § 3205 ("informed consent"); § 3208 ("printed information"); §§ 3214(a) and (h) (reporting requirements); § 3211(a) (determination of viability); § 3210(b) (degree of care required in postviability abortions); and § 3210(c) (second-physician requirement).

We have no reason to address the validity of the other sections of the Act challenged in the District Court.

A

Less than three years ago, this Court, in *Akron, Ashcroft,* and *Simopoulos,* reviewed challenges to state and municipal legislation regulating the performance of abortions. In *Akron,* the Court specifically reaffirmed Roe v. Wade, 410 U.S. 113 (1973). See 462 U.S., at 420, 426–431. Again today, we reaffirm the general principles laid down in *Roe* and in *Akron.*

In the years since this Court's decision in *Roe,* States and municipalities have adopted a number of measures seemingly designed to prevent a woman, with the advice of her physician, from exercising her freedom of choice. *Akron* is but one example. But the constitutional principles that led this Court to its decisions in 1973 still provide the compelling reason for recognizing the constitutional dimensions of a woman's right to decide whether to end her pregnancy. "[I]t should go without saying that the vitality of these constitutional principles cannot be allowed to yield simply because of disagreement with them." Brown v. Board of Education, 349 U.S. 294, 300 (1955). The States are not free, under the guise of protecting maternal health or potential life, to intimidate women into continuing pregnancies. Appellants claim that the statutory provisions before us today further legitimate compelling interests of the Commonwealth. Close analysis of those provisions, however, shows that they wholly subordinate constitutional privacy interests and concerns with maternal health in an effort to deter a woman from making a decision that, with her physician, is hers to make.

B

We turn to the challenged statutes:

1. Section 3205 ("informed consent") and § 3208 (printed information). Section 3205(a) requires that the woman give her "voluntary and informed consent" to an abortion. Failure to observe the provisions of § 3205 subjects the physician to suspension or revocation of his license, and subjects any other person obligated to provide information relating to informed consent to criminal penalties. § 3205(c). A requirement that the woman give what is truly a voluntary and informed consent, as a general proposition, is, of course, proper and is surely not unconstitutional. See *Danforth,* 428 U.S., at 67. But the State may not require the delivery of information designed "to influence the woman's informed choice between abortion or childbirth." *Akron,* 462 U.S., at 443–444.

. . .

. . . We conclude that . . . §§ 3205 and 3208 fail the *Akron* measurement. The two sections prescribe in detail the method for securing "informed consent." Seven explicit kinds of information must be delivered to the woman at least 24 hours before her consent is given, and five of these must be presented by the woman's physician. The five are: (a) the name of the physician who will perform the abortion, (b) the "fact that there may be detrimental physical and psychological effects which are not accurately foreseeable," (c) the "particular medical risks associated with the particular abortion procedure to be employed," (d) the probable gestational age, and (e) the "medical risks associated with carrying her child to term." The remaining two categories are (f) the "fact that medical assistance benefits may be available for prenatal care, childbirth and neonatal care," and (g) the "fact that the father is liable to assist" in the child's support, "even in instances where the father has offered to pay for the abortion." §§ 3205(a)(1) and (2). The woman also must be informed that materials printed and supplied by the Commonwealth that describe the fetus and that list agencies offering alternatives to abortion are available for her review. If she chooses to review the materials but is unable to read, the materials "shall be read to her," and any answer she seeks must be "provided her in her own language." § 3205(a)(2)(iii). She must certify in writing, prior to the abortion, that all this has been done. § 3205(a) (3). The printed materials "shall include the following statement":

> "There are many public and private agencies willing and able to help you to carry your child to term, and to assist you and your child after your child is born, whether you choose to keep your child or place her or him for adoption. The Commonwealth of Pennsylvania strongly urges you to contact them before making a final decision about abortion. The law requires that your physician or his agent give you the opportunity to call agencies like these before you undergo an abortion." § 3208(a)(1).

The materials must describe the "probable anatomical and physiological characteristics of the unborn child at two-week gestational increments from fertilization to full term, including any relevant information on the possibility of the unborn child's survival." § 3208(a)(2).

. . .

The informational requirements in the *Akron* ordinance were invalid for two "equally decisive" reasons. Id., at 445. The first was that "much of the information required is designed not to inform the woman's consent but rather to persuade her to withhold it altogether." Id., at 444. The second was that a rigid requirement that a specific body of information be given in all cases, irrespective of the particular needs of the patient, intrudes upon the discretion of the pregnant woman's physician and thereby imposes the " 'undesired and uncomfortable straitjacket' " with which the Court in *Danforth*, 428 U.S., at 67, n. 8, was concerned.

These two reasons apply with equal and controlling force to the specific and intrusive informational prescriptions of the Pennsylvania statutes. The printed materials required by §§ 3205 and 3208 seem to us to be nothing less than an outright attempt to wedge the Commonwealth's message discouraging abortion into the privacy of the informed-consent dialogue between the woman and her physician. The mandated description of fetal characteristics at 2-week intervals, no matter how objective, is plainly overinclusive. This is not medical information that is always relevant to the woman's decision, and it may serve only to confuse and punish her and to heighten her anxiety, contrary to accepted medical practice. Even the listing of agencies in the printed Pennsylvania form presents serious problems; it contains names of agencies that well may be out of step with the needs of the particular woman and thus places the physician in an awkward position and infringes upon his or her professional responsibilities. Forcing the physician or counselor to present the materials and the list to the woman makes him or her in effect an agent of the State in treating the woman and places his or her imprimatur upon both the materials and the list. See Women's Medical Center of Providence, Inc. v. Roberts, 530 F.Supp. 1136, 1154 (RI 1982). All this is, or comes close to being, state medicine imposed upon the woman, not the professional medical guidance she seeks, and it officially structures—as it obviously was intended to do—the dialogue between the woman and her physician.

The requirements of §§ 3205(a)(2)(i) and (ii) that the woman be advised that medical assistance benefits may be available, and that the father is responsible for financial assistance in the support of the child similarly are poorly disguised elements of discouragement for the abortion decision. Much of this would be nonmedical information beyond the physician's area of expertise and, for many patients, would be irrelevant and inappropriate. For a patient with a life-threatening pregnancy, the "information" in its very rendition may be cruel as well as destructive of the physician-patient relationship. As any experienced social worker or other counsellor knows, theoretical financial responsibility often does not equate with fulfillment. And a victim of rape should not have to hear gratuitous advice that an unidentified perpetrator is liable for support if she continues the pregnancy to term. Under the guise of informed consent, the Act requires the dissemination of information that is not relevant to such consent, and, thus, it advances no legitimate state interest.

The requirements of §§ 3205(a)(1)(ii) and (iii) that the woman be informed by the physician of "detrimental physical and psychological effects" and of all "particular medical risks" compound the problem of medical attendance, increase the patient's anxiety, and intrude upon the physician's exercise of proper professional judgment. This type of compelled information is the antithesis of informed consent. That the Commonwealth does not, and surely would not, compel similar disclosure of every possible peril of necessary surgery or of simple vaccination, reveals the anti-abortion character of the statute and its real purpose. Pennsylvania, like Akron, "has gone far beyond merely describing the general subject matter relevant to informed consent." *Akron,* 462 U.S., at 445. In addition, the Commonwealth would require the physician to recite its litany "regardless of whether in his judgment the information is relevant to [the patient's] personal decision." Ibid. These statutory defects cannot be saved by any facts that might be forthcoming at a subsequent hearing. Section 3205's informational requirements therefore are facially unconstitutional.

. . . .

2. Sections 3214(a) and (h) (reporting) and § 3211(a) (determination of viability). Section 3214(a)(8), part of the general reporting section, incorporates § 3211(a). Section 3211(a) requires the physician to report the basis for his determination "that a child is not viable." It applies only after the first trimester. The report required by §§ 3214(a) and (h) is detailed and must include, among other things, identification of the performing and referring physicians and of the facility or agency; information as to the woman's political subdivision and State of residence, age, race, marital status, and number of prior pregnancies; the date of her last menstrual period and the probable gestational age; the basis for any judgment that a medical emergency existed; the basis for any determination of nonviability; and the method of payment for the abortion. The report is to be signed by the attending physician. § 3214(b).

Despite the fact that § 3214(e)(2) provides that such reports "shall not be deemed public records," within the meaning of the Commonwealth's "Right-to-Know Law," Pa.Stat.Ann., Tit. 65, § 66.1 et seq. (Purdon 1959 and Supp.1985), each report "shall be made available for public inspection and copying within 15 days of receipt in a form which will not lead to the disclosure of the identity of any person filing a report." Similarly, the report of complications, required by § 3214(h), "shall be open to public inspection and copying." A willful failure to file a report required under § 3214 is "unprofessional conduct" and the noncomplying physician's license "shall be subject to suspension or revocation." § 3214(i)(1).

The scope of the information required and its availability to the public belie any assertions by the Commonwealth that it is advancing any legitimate interest. In Planned Parenthood of Central Mo. v. Danforth, 428 U.S. 52, 80 (1976), we recognized that recordkeeping and reporting provisions "that are reasonably directed to the preservation of maternal health and that properly respect a patient's confidentiality and privacy are permissible." But the reports required under the Act before us today go well beyond the health-related interests that served to justify the Missouri reports under consideration in *Danforth*. Pennsylvania would require, as Missouri did not, information as to method of payment, as to the woman's personal history, and as to the bases for medical judgments. The Missouri reports were to be used "only for statistical purposes." See id., at 87. They were to be maintained in confidence, with the sole exception of public health officers. In *Akron*, the Court explained its holding in *Danforth* when it said: "The decisive factor was that the State met its burden of demonstrating that these regulations furthered important health-related state concerns." 462 U.S., at 430.

The required Pennsylvania reports, on the other hand, while claimed not to be "public," are available nonetheless to the public for copying. Moreover, there is no limitation on the use to which the Commonwealth or the public copiers may put them. The elements that proved persuasive for the ruling in *Danforth* are absent here. The decision to terminate a pregnancy is an intensely private one that must be protected in a way that assures anonymity. . . .

A woman and her physician will necessarily be more reluctant to choose an abortion if there exists a possibility that her decision and her identity will become known publicly. Although the statute does not specifically require the reporting of the woman's name, the amount of information about her and the circumstances under which she had an abortion are so detailed that identification is likely. Identification is the obvious purpose of these extreme reporting requirements. The "impermissible limits" that *Danforth* mentioned and that Missouri approached, see 428 U.S., at 81, have been exceeded here.

We note, as we reach this conclusion, that the Court consistently has refused to allow government to chill the exercise of constitutional rights by requiring disclosure of protected, but sometimes unpopular, activities. See, e.g., Lamont v. Postmaster General, 381 U.S. 301 (1965) (invalidating Post Office requirement that addressee affirmatively request delivery of "communist" materials in order to receive them); Talley v. California, 362 U.S. 60, 64–65 (1960) (striking down municipal ban on unsigned handbills); NAACP v. Alabama ex rel. Patterson, 357 U.S. 449, 462–465 (1958) (invalidating compelled disclosure of NAACP membership list). Pennsylvania's reporting requirements raise the spectre of public exposure and harassment of women who choose to exercise their personal, intensely private, right, with their physician, to end a pregnancy. Thus, they pose an unacceptable danger of deterring the exercise of that right, and must be invalidated.

3. Section 3210(b) (degree of care for postviability abortions) and § 3210(c) (second-physician requirement when the fetus is possibly viable). Section 3210(b) sets forth two independent requirements for a postviability abortion. First, it demands the exercise of that degree of care "which such person would be required to exercise in order to preserve the life and health of any unborn child intended to be born and not aborted." Second, "the abortion technique employed shall be that which would provide the best opportunity for the unborn child to be aborted alive unless," in the physician's good-faith judgment, that technique "would present a significantly greater medical risk to the life or health of the pregnant woman." An intentional, knowing, or reckless violation of this standard is a felony of the third degree, and subjects the violator to the possibility of imprisonment for not more than seven years and to a fine of not more than $15,000. See 18 Pa. Cons.Stat. §§ 1101(2) and 1103(3) (1983).

The Court of Appeals ruled that § 3210(b) was unconstitutional because it required a "trade-off" between the woman's health and fetal survival, and failed to require that maternal health be the physician's paramount consideration. . . .

. . . We agree with the Court of Appeals and therefore find the statute to be facially invalid.

Section 3210(c) requires that a second physician be present during an abortion performed when viability is possible. The second physician is to "take control of the child and . . . provide immediate medical care for the child, taking all reasonable steps necessary, in his judgment, to preserve the child's life and health." Violation of this requirement is a felony of the third degree.

In Planned Parenthood Assn. v. Ashcroft, 462 U.S. 476 (1983), the Court, by a 5–4 vote, but not by a controlling single opinion, ruled that a Missouri statute requiring the presence of a second physician during an abortion performed after viability was constitutional. Justice Powell, joined by The Chief Justice, concluded that the State had a compelling interest in protecting the life of a viable fetus and that the second physician's presence provided assurance that the State's interest was protected more fully than with only one physician in attendance. Id., at 482–486. Justice Powell recognized that, to pass constitutional muster, the statute must contain an exception for the situation where the health of the mother was endangered by delay in the arrival of the second physician. Recognizing that there was "no clearly expressed exception" on the face of the Missouri statute for the emergency situation, Justice Powell found the exception implicit in the statutory requirement that action be taken to preserve the fetus "provided it does not pose an increased risk to the life or health of the woman." Id., at 485, n. 8.

Like the Missouri statute, § 3210(c) of the Pennsylvania statute contains no express exception for an emergency situation. . . .

. . . We necessarily conclude that the legislature's failure to provide a medical-emergency exception in § 3210(c) was intentional. All the factors are here for chilling the performance of a late abortion, which, more than one performed at an earlier date, perhaps tends to be under emergency conditions.

V

Constitutional rights do not always have easily ascertainable boundaries, and controversy over the meaning of our Nation's most majestic guarantees frequently has been turbulent. As judges, however, we are sworn to uphold the law even when its content gives rise to bitter dispute. See Cooper v. Aaron, 358 U.S. 1 (1958). We recognized at the very beginning of our opinion in *Roe*, 410 U.S., at 116, that abortion raises moral and spiritual questions over which honorable persons can disagree sincerely and profoundly. But those disagreements did not then and do not now relieve us of our duty to apply the Constitution faithfully.

Our cases long have recognized that the Constitution embodies a promise that a certain private sphere of individual liberty will be kept largely beyond the reach of government. See, e.g., Carey v. Population Services International, 431 U.S. 678 (1977); Moore v. East Cleveland, 431 U.S. 494 (1977); Eisenstadt v. Baird, 405 U.S. 438 (1972); Griswold v. Connecticut, 381 U.S. 479 (1965); Pierce v. Society of Sisters, 268 U.S. 510 (1925); Meyer v. Nebraska, 262 U.S. 390 (1923). See also Whalen v. Roe, 429 U.S. 589, 598–600 (1977). That promise extends to women as well as to men. Few decisions are more personal and intimate, more properly private, or more basic to individual dignity and autonomy, than a woman's decision—with the guidance of her physician and within the limits specified in *Roe*—whether to end her pregnancy. A woman's right to make that choice freely is fundamental. Any other result, in our view, would protect inadequately a central part of the sphere of liberty that our law guarantees equally to all.

The Court of Appeals correctly invalidated the specified provisions of Pennsylvania's 1982 Abortion Control Act. Its judgment is affirmed.

It is so ordered.

Justice Stevens, concurring.

The scope of the individual interest in liberty that is given protection by the Due Process Clause of the Fourteenth Amendment is a matter about which conscientious judges have long disagreed. Although I believe that that interest is significantly broader than Justice White does, I have always had the highest respect for his views on this subject. In this case, although our ultimate conclusions differ, it may be useful to emphasize some of our areas of agreement in order to ensure that the clarity of certain fundamental propositions not be obscured by his forceful rhetoric.

. . .

In the final analysis, the holding in Roe v. Wade presumes that it is far better to permit some individuals to make incorrect decisions than to deny all individuals the right to make decisions that have a profound effect upon their destiny. Arguably a very primitive society would have been protected from evil by a rule against eating apples; a majority familiar with Adam's experience might favor such a rule. But the lawmakers who placed a special premium on the protection of individual liberty have recognized that certain values are more important than the will of a transient majority.

Chief Justice Burger, dissenting.

I agree with much of Justice White's and Justice O'Connor's dissents. In my concurrence in the companion case to Roe v. Wade in 1973, I noted that

> "I do not read the Court's holdings today as having the sweeping consequences attributed to them by the dissenting Justices; the dissenting views discount the reality that the vast majority of physicians observe the standards of their profession, and act only on the basis of carefully deliberated medical judgments relating to life and health. Plainly, the Court today rejects any claim that the Constitution requires abortions on demand." Doe v. Bolton, 410 U.S. 179, 208 (1973).

Later, in Maher v. Roe, 432 U.S. 464, 481 (1977), I stated my view that

> "[t]he Court's holdings in *Roe* . . . and Doe v. Bolton . . . simply require that a State not create an absolute barrier to a woman's decision to have an abortion."

I based my concurring statements in *Roe* and *Maher* on the principle expressed in the Court's opinion in *Roe* that the right to an abortion "is not unqualified and must be considered against important state interests in regulation." 410 U.S., at 154–155. In short, every member of the *Roe* Court rejected the idea of abortion on demand. The Court's opinion today, however, plainly undermines that important principle, and I regretfully conclude that some of the concerns of the dissenting Justices in *Roe,* as well as the concerns I expressed in my separate opinion, have now been realized.

. . .

In discovering constitutional infirmities in state regulations of abortion that are in accord with our history and tradition, we may have lured judges into "roaming at large in the constitutional field." Griswold v. Connecticut, 381 U.S. 479, 502 (1965) (Harlan, J., concurring). The soundness of our holdings must be tested by the decisions that purport to follow them. If *Danforth* and today's holding really mean what they seem to say, I agree we should reexamine *Roe.*

Justice White, with whom Justice Rehnquist joins, dissenting.

Today the Court carries forward the "difficult and continuing venture in substantive due process," Planned Parenthood of Missouri v. Danforth, 428 U.S. 52 (1976) (White, J., dissenting), that began with the decision in Roe v. Wade, 410 U.S. 113 (1973), and has led the Court further and further afield in the 13 years since that decision was handed down. I was in dissent in Roe v. Wade and am in dissent today. In Part I below, I state why I continue to believe that this venture has been fundamentally misguided since its inception. In Part II, I submit that even accepting Roe v. Wade, the concerns underlying that decision by no means command or justify the results reached today. Indeed, in my view, our precedents in this area, applied in a manner consistent with sound principles of constitutional adjudication, require reversal of the Court of Appeals on the ground that the provisions before us are facially constitutional.[1]

I

The rule of *stare decisis* is essential if case-by-case judicial decisionmaking is to be reconciled with the principle of the rule of law, for when governing legal standards are open to revision in every case, deciding cases becomes a mere exercise of judicial will, with arbitrary and unpredictable results. But *stare decisis* is not the only constraint upon judicial decisionmaking. Cases—like this one—that involve our assumed power to set aside on grounds of unconstitutionality a State or federal statute representing the democratically expressed will of the people call other considerations into play. Because the Constitution itself is ordained and established by the people of the United States, constitutional adjudication by this Court does not, in theory at any rate, frustrate the authority of the people to govern themselves through institutions of their own devising and in accordance with principles of their own choosing. But decisions that find in the Constitution principles or values that cannot fairly be read into that document usurp the people's authority, for such decisions represent choices that the people have never made and that they cannot disavow through corrective

[1] I shall, for the most part, leave to one side the Court's somewhat extraordinary procedural rulings. . . .

legislation. For this reason, it is essential that this Court maintain the power to restore authority to its proper possessors by correcting constitutional decisions that, on reconsideration, are found to be mistaken. . . .

In my view, the time has come to recognize that Roe v. Wade, . . . "departs from a proper understanding" of the Constitution and to overrule it. I do not claim that the arguments in support of this proposition are new ones or that they were not considered by the Court in *Roe* or in the cases that succeeded it. Cf. Akron v. Akron Center for Reproductive Health, 462 U.S. 416, 419–420 (1983). But if an argument that a constitutional decision is erroneous must be novel in order to justify overruling that precedent, the Court's decisions in Lochner v. New York, 198 U.S. 45 (1905), and Plessy v. Ferguson, 163 U.S. 537 (1896), would remain the law, for the doctrines announced in those decisions were nowhere more eloquently or incisively criticized than in the dissenting opinions of Justices Holmes (in *Lochner*) and Harlan (in both cases). That the flaws in an opinion were evident at the time it was handed down is hardly a reason for adhering to it.

A

Roe v. Wade posits that a woman has a fundamental right to terminate her pregnancy, and that this right may be restricted only in the service of two compelling state interests: the interest in maternal health (which becomes compelling only at the stage in pregnancy at which an abortion becomes more hazardous than carrying the pregnancy to term) and the interest in protecting the life of the fetus (which becomes compelling only at the point of viability). A reader of the Constitution might be surprised to find that it encompassed these detailed rules, for the text obviously contains no references to abortion, nor, indeed, to pregnancy or reproduction generally; and, of course, it is highly doubtful that the authors of any of the provisions of the Constitution believed that they were giving protection to abortion. As its prior cases clearly show, however, this Court does not subscribe to the simplistic view that constitutional interpretation can possibly be limited to the "plain meaning" of the Constitution's text or to the subjective intention of the Framers. The Constitution is not a deed setting forth the precise metes and bounds of its subject matter; rather, it is a document announcing fundamental principles in value-laden terms that leave ample scope for the exercise of normative judgment by those charged with interpreting and applying it. In particular, the Due Process Clause of the Fourteenth Amendment, which forbids the deprivation of "life, liberty, or property without due process of law," has been read by the majority of the Court to be broad enough to provide substantive protection against State infringement of a broad range of individual interests. See Moore v. City of East Cleveland, 431 U.S. 494, 541–552 (White, J., dissenting).

In most instances, the substantive protection afforded the liberty or property of an individual by the Fourteenth Amendment is extremely limited: State action impinging on individual interests need only be rational to survive scrutiny under the Due Process Clause, and the determination of rationality is to be made with a heavy dose of deference to the policy choices of the legislature. Only "fundamental" rights are entitled to the added protection provided by strict judicial scrutiny of legislation that impinges upon them. . . . I can certainly agree with the proposition—which I deem indisputable—that a woman's ability to choose an abortion is a species of "liberty" that is subject to the general protections of the Due Process Clause. I cannot agree, however, that this liberty is so "fundamental" that restrictions upon it call into play anything more than the most minimal judicial scrutiny.

Fundamental liberties and interests are most clearly present when the Constitution provides specific textual recognition of their existence and importance. Thus, the Court is on relatively firm ground when it deems certain of the liberties set forth in the Bill of Rights to be fundamental and therefore finds them incorporated in the Fourteenth Amendment's guarantee that no State may deprive any person of liberty without due process of law. When the Court ventures further and defines as "fundamental" liberties that are nowhere mentioned in the Constitution (or that are present only in the so-called "penumbras" of specifically enumerated rights), it must, of necessity, act with more caution, lest it open itself to the accusation that, in the name of identifying constitutional principles to which the people have consented in framing their Constitution, the Court has done nothing more than impose its own controversial choices of value upon the people.

Attempts to articulate the constraints that must operate upon the Court when it employs the Due Process Clause to protect liberties not specifically enumerated in the text of the Constitution have produced varying definitions of "fundamental liberties." One approach has been to limit the class of fundamental liberties to those interests that are "implicit in the concept of ordered liberty" such that "neither liberty nor justice would exist if [they] were sacrificed." Palko v. Connecticut, 302 U.S. 319, 325, 326 (1937); see Moore v. City of East Cleveland, supra, 431 U.S., at 537 (Stewart, J., joined by Rehnquist, J., dissenting). Another, broader approach is to define fundamental liberties as those that are "deeply rooted in this Nation's history and tradition." Id., at 503 (opinion of Powell, J.); see also Griswold v. Connecticut, 381 U.S., at 501 (Harlan, J., concurring). These distillations of the possible approaches to the identification of unenumerated fundamental rights are not and do not purport to be precise legal tests or "mechanical yardstick[s]," Poe v. Ullman, 367 U.S., at 544 (1961) (Harlan, J., dissenting). Their utility lies in their effort to identify some source of constitutional value that reflects not the philosophical predilections of individual judges, but basic choices made by the people themselves in constituting their system of government—*"the balance struck by this country,"* id., at 542 (emphasis added)—and they seek to achieve this end through locating fundamental rights either in the traditions and consensus of our society as a whole or in the logical implications of a system that recognizes both individual liberty and democratic order. Whether either of these approaches can, as Justice Harlan hoped, prevent "judges from roaming at large in the constitutional field," *Griswold,* 381 U.S., at 502, is debatable. What for me is not subject to debate, however, is that either of the basic definitions of fundamental liberties, taken seriously, indicates the illegitimacy of the Court's decision in Roe v. Wade.

The Court has justified the recognition of a woman's fundamental right to terminate her pregnancy by invoking decisions upholding claims of personal autonomy in connection with the conduct of family life, the rearing of children, marital privacy and the use of contraceptives, and the preservation of the individual's capacity to procreate. See Carey v. Population Services International, 431 U.S. 678 (1977); Moore v. City of East Cleveland, supra; Eisenstadt v. Baird, 405 U.S. 438 (1972); Griswold v. Connecticut, supra; Skinner v. Oklahoma, 316 U.S. 535 (1942); Pierce v. Society of Sisters, 268 U.S. 510 (1925); Meyer v. Nebraska, 262 U.S. 390 (1923). Even if each of these cases was correctly decided and could be properly grounded in rights that are "implicit in the concept of ordered liberty" or "deeply rooted in this Nation's history and tradition," the issues in the cases cited differ from those at stake where abortion is concerned. As the Court appropriately recognized in Roe v. Wade, "[t]he pregnant woman cannot be isolated in her privacy," 410 U.S., at 159; the termination of a pregnancy typically involves the destruction of another entity: the fetus. However one answers the metaphysical or theological question whether the fetus is a "human being" or the legal question whether it is a "person" as that term is used in the Constitution, one must at least recognize, first, that the fetus is an entity that bears in its cells all the genetic information that characterizes a member of the species *homo sapiens* and distinguishes an individual member of that species from all others, and second, that there is no nonarbitrary line separating a fetus from a child or, indeed, an adult human being. Given that the continued existence and development—that is to say, the *life*—of such an entity are so directly at stake in the woman's decision whether or not to terminate her pregnancy, that decision must be recognized as *sui generis,* different in kind from the others that the Court has protected under the rubric of personal or family privacy and autonomy. Accordingly, the decisions cited by the Court both in *Roe* and in its opinion today as precedent for the fundamental nature of the liberty to choose abortion do not, even if all are accepted as valid, dictate the Court's classification.

If the woman's liberty to choose an abortion is fundamental, then, it is not because any of our precedents (aside from *Roe* itself) commands or justifies that result; it can only be because protection for this unique choice is itself "implicit in the concept of ordered liberty" or, perhaps, "deeply rooted in this Nation's history and tradition." It seems clear to me that it is neither. The Court's opinion in *Roe* itself convincingly refutes the notion that the abortion liberty is deeply rooted in the history or tradition of our people, as does the continuing and deep division of the people themselves over the question of abortion. As for the notion that choice in the matter of abortion is implicit in the concept of ordered liberty, it seems apparent to me that a free, egalitarian, and democratic society does not presuppose any particular rule or set of rules with respect to abortion. And again, the fact that many men and women of good will and high commitment to constitutional government place themselves on both sides of the abortion controversy strengthens my own conviction that the values animating the Constitution do not compel recognition of the abortion liberty as fundamental. In so denominating that liberty, the Court engages not in constitutional interpretation, but in the unrestrained imposition of its own, extraconstitutional value preferences.

B

A second, equally basic error infects the Court's decision in *Roe v. Wade.* The detailed set of rules governing state restrictions on abortion that the Court first articulated in *Roe* and has since refined and elaborated presupposes not only that the woman's liberty to choose an abortion is fundamental, but also that the state's countervailing interest in protecting fetal life (or, as the Court would have it, "potential human life," 410 U.S., at 159) becomes "compelling" only at the point at which the fetus is viable. As Justice O'Connor pointed out three years ago in her dissent in Akron v. Akron Center for Reproductive Health, 462 U.S. 416, 461 (1983), the Court's choice of viability as the point at which the state's interest becomes compelling is entirely arbitrary. The Court's "explanation" for the line it has drawn is that the state's interest becomes compelling at viability "because the fetus then presumably has the capacity of meaningful life outside the mother's womb." 410 U.S., at 163. As one critic of *Roe* has observed, this argument "mistakes a definition for a syllogism." Ely, The Wages of Crying Wolf: A Comment on Roe v. Wade, 82 Yale L.J. 920, 924 (1973).

The governmental interest at issue is in protecting those who will be citizens if their lives are not ended in the womb. The substantiality of this interest is in no way dependent on the probability that the fetus may be capable of surviving outside the womb at any given point in its development, as the possibility of fetal survival is contingent on the state of medical practice and technology, factors that are in essence morally and constitutionally irrelevant. The State's interest is in the fetus as an entity in itself, and the character of this entity does not change at the point of viability under conventional medical wisdom. Accordingly, the State's interest, if compelling after viability, is equally compelling before viability.

C

Both the characterization of the abortion liberty as fundamental and the denigration of the State's interest in preserving the lives of nonviable fetuses are essential to the detailed set of constitutional rules devised by the Court to limit the States' power to regulate abortion. If either or both of these facets of *Roe v. Wade* were rejected, a broad range of limitations on abortion (including outright prohibition) that are now unavailable to the States would again become constitutional possibilities.

In my view, such a state of affairs would be highly desirable from the standpoint of the Constitution. Abortion is a hotly contested moral and political issue. Such issues, in our society, are to be resolved by the will of the people, either as expressed through legislation or through the general principles they have already incorporated into the Constitution they have adopted. *Roe v. Wade* implies that the people have already resolved the debate by weaving into the Constitution the values and principles that answer the issue. As I have argued, I believe it is clear that the people have never—not in 1787, 1791, 1868, or at any time since—done any such thing. I would return the issue to the people by overruling *Roe v. Wade*.

II

As it has evolved in the decisions of this Court, the freedom recognized by the Court in *Roe v. Wade* and its progeny is essentially a negative one, based not on the notion that abortion is a good in itself, but only on the view that the legitimate goals that may be served by state coercion of private choices regarding abortion are, at least under some circumstances, outweighed by the damage to individual autonomy and privacy that such coercion entails. In other words, the evil of abortion does not justify the evil of forbidding it. Cf. Stanley v. Georgia, 394 U.S. 557 (1969). But precisely because *Roe v. Wade* is not premised on the notion that abortion is itself desirable (either as a matter of constitutional entitlement or of social policy), the decision does not command the States to fund or encourage abortion, or even to approve of it. Rather, we have recognized that the States may legitimately adopt a policy of encouraging normal childbirth rather than abortion so long as the measures through which that policy is implemented do not amount to direct compulsion of the woman's choice regarding abortion. Harris v. McRae, 448 U.S. 297 (1980); Maher v. Roe, 432 U.S. 464 (1977); Beal v. Doe, 432 U.S. 438 (1977). The provisions before the Court today quite obviously represent the State's effort to implement such a policy.

The majority's opinion evinces no deference toward the State's legitimate policy. Rather, the majority makes it clear from the outset that it simply disapproves of any attempt by Pennsylvania to legislate in this area. . . . The result is a decision that finds no justification in the Court's previous holdings, departs from sound principles of constitutional and statutory interpretation, and unduly limits the state's power to implement the legitimate (and in some circumstances compelling) policy of encouraging normal childbirth in preference to abortion.

A

The Court begins by striking down statutory provisions designed to ensure that the woman's choice of an abortion is fully informed—that is, that she is aware not only of the reasons for having an abortion, but also of the risks associated with an abortion and the availability of assistance that might make the alternative of normal childbirth more attractive than it might otherwise appear. At first blush, the Court's action seems extraordinary: after all, *Roe v. Wade* purports to be about freedom of choice, and statutory provisions requiring that a woman seeking an abortion be afforded information regarding her decision not only do not limit her ability to choose abortion, but would also appear to enhance her freedom of choice by helping to ensure that her decision whether or not to terminate her pregnancy is an informed one. Indeed, maximization of the patient's freedom of choice—not restriction of his or her liberty—is generally perceived to be the principal value justifying the imposition of disclosure requirements upon physicians: . . .

One searches the majority's opinion in vain for a convincing reason why the apparently laudable policy of promoting informed consent becomes unconstitutional when the subject is abortion.

Why, then, is the statute unconstitutional? The majority's argument, while primarily rhetorical, appears to offer three answers. First, the information that must be provided will in some cases be irrelevant to the woman's decision. This is true. Its pertinence to the question of the statute's constitutionality, however, is beyond me. . . . Indeed, I fail to see how providing a woman with accurate information—whether relevant or irrelevant—could ever be deemed to impair any constitutionally protected interest (even if, as the majority hypothesizes, the information may upset her). Thus, the majority's observation that the statute may require the provision of irrelevant information in some cases is itself an irrelevancy.

Second, the majority appears to reason that the informed consent provisions are invalid because the information they require may increase the woman's "anxiety" about the procedure and even "influence" her in her choice. Again, both observations are undoubtedly true; but they by no means cast the constitutionality of the provisions into question. It is in the very nature of informed consent provisions that they may produce some anxiety in the patient and influence her in her choice. This is in fact their reason for existence, and—provided that the information required is accurate and nonmisleading—it is an entirely salutary reason. . . .

Third, the majority concludes that the informed consent provisions are invalid because they "intrud[e] upon the discretion of the pregnant woman's physician," violate "the privacy of the informed-consent dialogue between the woman and her physician," and "officially structur[e]" that dialogue. The provisions thus constitute "state medicine" that "infringes upon [the physician's] professional responsibilities." This is nonsensical. I can concede that the Constitution extends its protection to certain zones of personal autonomy and privacy, see Griswold v. Connecticut, 381 U.S. 479, 502 (1965) (White, J., concurring in judgment), and I can understand, if not share, the notion that that protection may extend to a woman's decision regarding abortion. But I cannot concede the possibility that the Constitution provides more than minimal protection for the manner in which a physician practices his or her profession or for the "dialogues" in which he or she chooses to participate in the course of treating patients. I had thought it clear that regulation of the practice of medicine, like regulation of other professions and of economic affairs generally, was a matter peculiarly within the competence of legislatures, and that such regulation was subject to review only for rationality. See, e.g., Williamson v. Lee Optical of Oklahoma, Inc., 348 U.S. 483 (1955).

.   .   .

I do not really believe that the Court's invocation of professional freedom signals a retreat from the principle that the Constitution is largely unconcerned with the substantive aspects of governmental regulation of professional and business relations. Clearly, the majority is uninterested in undermining the edifice of post-New Deal constitutional law by extending its holding to cases that do not concern the issue of abortion. But if one assumes, as I do, that the majority is unwilling to commit itself to the implications of that part of its rhetoric which smacks of economic due process rights for physicians, it becomes obvious that the talk of "infringement of professional responsibility" is mere window-dressing for a holding that must stand or fall on other grounds. And because the informed-consent provisions do not infringe the essential right at issue—the right of the woman to choose to have an abortion—the majority's conclusion that the provisions are unconstitutional is without foundation.

B

The majority's decision to strike down the reporting requirements of the statute is equally extraordinary. The requirements obviously serve legitimate purposes. The information contained in the reports is highly relevant to the State's efforts to enforce § 3210(a) of the statute, which forbids abortion of viable fetuses except when necessary to the mother's health. The information concerning complications plainly serves the legitimate goal of advancing the state of medical knowledge concerning maternal and fetal health. See Planned Parenthood of Central Mo. v. Danforth, 428 U.S., at 80. Given that the subject of abortion is a matter of considerable public interest and debate (constrained to some extent, of course, by the pre-emptive effect of this Court's ill-conceived constitutional decisions), the collection and dissemination of demographic information concerning abortions is clearly a legitimate goal of public policy. Moreover, there is little reason to believe that the required reports, though fairly detailed, would impose an undue burden on physicians and impede the ability of their patients to obtain abortions, as all of the information required would necessarily be readily available to a physician who had performed an abortion. Accordingly, under this Court's prior decisions in this area, the reporting requirements are constitutional. Planned Parenthood Assn. of Kansas City, Mo., Inc. v. Ashcroft, 462 U.S. 476, 486–490 (1983) (opinion of Powell, J.); id., at 505 (opinion of O'Connor, J.); Planned Parenthood of Central Missouri v. Danforth, supra, 428 U.S., at 79–81.

.   .   .

C

The majority resorts to linguistic nit-picking in striking down the provision requiring physicians aborting viable fetuses to use the method of abortion most likely to result in fetal survival unless that method would pose a "significantly greater medical risk to the life or health of the pregnant woman" than would other available methods. The majority concludes that the statute's use of the word "significantly" indicates that the statute represents an unlawful "trade-off" between the woman's health and the chance of fetal survival. Not only is this conclusion based on a wholly unreasonable interpretation of the statute, but the statute would also be constitutional even if it meant what the majority says it means.

. . . .

The framework of rights and interests devised by the Court in *Roe v. Wade* indicates that just as a State may prohibit a post-viability abortion unless it is necessary to protect the life or health of the woman, the State may require that postviability abortions be conducted using the ethod most protective of the fetus unless a less protective method is necessary to protect the life or health of the woman. Under this standard, the Pennsylvania statute—which does not require the woman to accept any significant health risks to protect the fetus—is plainly constitutional.

D

The Court strikes down the statute's second-physician requirement because, in its view, the existence of a medical emergency requiring an immediate abortion to save the life of the pregnant woman would not be a defense to a prosecution under the statute. The Court does not question the proposition, established in the *Ashcroft* case, that a second-physician requirement accompanied by an exception for emergencies is a permissible means of vindicating the compelling state interest in protecting the lives of viable fetuses. Accordingly, the majority's ruling on this issue does not on its face involve a substantial departure from the Court's previous decisions.

What is disturbing about the Court's opinion on this point is not the general principle on which it rests, but the manner in which that principle is applied. . . .

The Court's rejection of a perfectly plausible reading of the statute flies in the face of the principle—which until today I had thought applicable to abortion statutes as well as to other legislative enactments—that "[w]here fairly possible, courts should construe a statute to avoid a danger of unconstitutionality." Planned Parenthood Assn. v. Ashcroft, 462 U.S., at 493. The Court's reading is obviously based on an entirely different principle: that in cases involving abortion, a permissible reading of a statute is to be avoided at all costs. Not sharing this viewpoint, I cannot accept the majority's conclusion that the statute does not provide for the equivalent of a defense of emergency.

. . . .

III

The decision today appears symptomatic of the Court's own insecurity over its handiwork in Roe v. Wade and the cases following that decision. Aware that in *Roe* it essentially created something out of nothing and that there are many in this country who hold that decision to be basically illegitimate, the Court responds defensively. Perceiving, in a statute implementing the State's legitimate policy of prefering childbirth to abortion, a threat to or criticism of the decision in Roe v. Wade, the majority indiscriminately strikes down statutory provisions that in no way contravene the right recognized in *Roe.* I do not share the warped point of view of the majority, nor can I follow the tortuous path the majority treads in proceeding to strike down the statute before us. I dissent.

Justice O'Connor, with whom Justice Rehnquist joins, dissenting.

This Court's abortion decisions have already worked a major distortion in the Court's constitutional jurisprudence. See Akron v. Akron Center for Reproductive Health, Inc., 462 U.S. 416, 452 (1983) (O'Connor, J., dissenting). Today's decision goes further, and makes it painfully clear that no legal rule or doctrine is safe from ad hoc nullification by this Court when an occasion for its application arises in a case involving state regulation of abortion. The permissible scope of abortion regulation is not the only constitutional issue on which this Court is divided, but—except when it comes to abortion—the Court has generally refused to let such disagreements, however longstanding or deeply felt, prevent it from evenhandedly applying uncontroversial legal doctrines to cases that come before it. See Heckler v. Chaney, 470 U.S. ___, ___ (1985); id., at ___, n. 2 (Brennan, J., concurring) (differences over the validity of the death penalty under the Eighth Amendment should not influence the Court's consideration of a question of statutory administrative law). That the Court's unworkable scheme for constitutionalizing the regulation of abortion has had this institutionally debilitating effect should not be surprising, however, since the Court is not suited to the expansive role it has claimed for itself in the series of cases that began with Roe v. Wade, 410 U.S. 113 (1973).

The Court today holds that "[t]he Court of Appeals correctly invalidated the specified provisions of Pennsylvania's 1982 Abortion Control Act." Ante, at ___. In so doing, the Court prematurely decides serious constitutional questions on an inadequate record, in contravention of settled principles of constitutional adjudication and procedural fairness. The constitutionality of the challenged provisions was not properly before the Court of Appeals, and is not properly before this Court. There has been no trial on the merits, and appellants have had no opportunity to develop facts that might have a bearing on the constitutionality of the statute. The only question properly before the

Court is whether or not a preliminary injunction should have been issued to restrain enforcement of the challenged provisions pending trial on the merits. This Court's decisions in Akron v. Akron Center for Reproductive Health, supra, Planned Parenthood Assn. of Kansas City, Mo., Inc. v. Ashcroft, 462 U.S. 476 (1983), and Simopoulos v. Virginia, 462 U.S. 506 (1983), do not establish a likelihood that appellees would succeed on the merits of their constitutional claims sufficient to warrant overturning the District Court's denial of a preliminary injunction. Under the approach to abortion regulation outlined in my dissenting opinion in *Akron,* to which I adhere, it is even clearer that no preliminary injunction should have issued. I therefore dissent.

. . .

I agree with much of what Justice White has written in Part II of his dissenting opinion, and the arguments he has framed might well suffice to show that the provisions at issue are facially constitutional. Nonetheless, I believe the proper course is to decide this case as the Court of Appeals should have decided it, lest appellees suffer the very prejudice the Court sees fit to inflict on appellants. For me, then, the question is not one of "success" but of the "likelihood of success." In addition, because Pennsylvania has not asked the Court to reconsider or overrule Roe v. Wade, 410 U.S. 113 (1973), I do not address that question.

I do, however, remain of the views expressed in my dissent in *Akron,* 462 U.S., at 459–466. . . .

. . .

In my view, today's decision makes bad constitutional law and bad procedural law. The " 'undesired and uncomfortable straitjacket' " in this case, is not the one the Court purports to discover in Pennsylvania's statute; it is the one the Court has tailored for the 50 States. I respectfully dissent.

BOWERS v. HARDWICK

478 U.S. 186, 106 S.Ct. 2841, 92 L.Ed.2d 140 (1986).

Justice White delivered the opinion of the Court.

In August 1982, respondent was charged with violating the Georgia statute criminalizing sodomy [1] by committing that act with another adult male in the bedroom of respondent's home. After a preliminary hearing, the District Attorney decided not to present the matter to the grand jury unless further evidence developed.

Respondent then brought suit in the Federal District Court, challenging the constitutionality of the statute insofar as it criminalized

---

[1] Ga.Code Ann. § 16–6–2 (1984) provides, in pertinent part, as follows:

"(a) A person commits the offense of sodomy when he performs or submits to any sexual act involving the sex organs of one person and the mouth or anus of another. . . .

"(b) A person convicted of the offense of sodomy shall be punished by imprisonment for not less than one nor more than 20 years. . . ."

consensual sodomy.[2] He asserted that he was a practicing homosexual, that the Georgia sodomy statute, as administered by the defendants, placed him in imminent danger of arrest, and that the statute for several reasons violates the Federal Constitution. The District Court granted the defendants' motion to dismiss for failure to state a claim . . .

A divided panel of the Court of Appeals for the Eleventh Circuit reversed. 760 F.2d 1202 (1985). . . . Relying on our decisions in Griswold v. Connecticut, 381 U.S. 479 (1965), Eisenstadt v. Baird, 405 U.S. 438 (1972), Stanley v. Georgia, 394 U.S. 557 (1969), and Roe v. Wade, 410 U.S. 113 (1973), the court went on to hold that the Georgia statute violated respondent's fundamental rights because his homosexual activity is a private and intimate association that is beyond the reach of state regulation by reason of the Ninth Amendment and the Due Process Clause of the Fourteenth Amendment. The case was remanded for trial, at which, to prevail, the State would have to prove that the statute is supported by a compelling interest and is the most narrowly drawn means of achieving that end.

Because other Courts of Appeals have arrived at judgments contrary to that of the Eleventh Circuit in this case we granted the State's petition for certiorari questioning the holding that its sodomy statute violates the fundamental rights of homosexuals. We agree with the State that the Court of Appeals erred, and hence reverse its judgment.

This case does not require a judgment on whether laws against sodomy between consenting adults in general, or between homosexuals in particular, are wise or desirable. It raises no question about the right or propriety of state legislative decisions to repeal their laws that criminalize homosexual sodomy, or of state court decisions invalidating those laws on state constitutional grounds. The issue presented is whether the Federal Constitution confers a fundamental right upon homosexuals to engage in sodomy and hence invalidates the laws of the many States that still make such conduct illegal and have done so for a very long time. The case also calls for some judgment about the limits of the Court's role in carrying out its constitutional mandate.

We first register our disagreement with the Court of Appeals and with respondent that the Court's prior cases have construed the Constitution to confer a right of privacy that extends to homosexual sodomy and for all intents and purposes have decided this case. The reach of this line of cases was sketched in Carey v. Population Services Interna-

---

[2] John and Mary Doe were also plaintiffs in the action. They alleged that they wished to engage in sexual activity proscribed by § 16–6–2 in the privacy of their home, and that they had been "chilled and deterred" from engaging in such activity by both the existence of the statute and Hardwick's arrest. The District Court held, however, that because they had neither sustained, nor were in immediate danger of sustaining, any direct injury from the enforcement of the statute, they did not have proper standing to maintain the action. The Court of Appeals affirmed the District Court's judgment dismissing the Does' claim for lack of standing, 760 F.2d 1202, 1206–1207 (1985), and the Does do not challenge that holding in this Court.

The only claim properly before the Court, therefore, is Hardwick's challenge to the Georgia statute as applied to consensual homosexual sodomy. We express no opinion on the constitutionality of the Georgia statute as applied to other acts of sodomy.

tional, 431 U.S. 678, 685 (1977). Pierce v. Society of Sisters, 268 U.S. 510 (1925), and Meyer v. Nebraska, 262 U.S. 390 (1923), were described as dealing with child rearing and education; Prince v. Massachusetts, 321 U.S. 158 (1944), with family relationships; Skinner v. Oklahoma ex rel. Williamson, 316 U.S. 535 (1942), with procreation; Loving v. Virginia, 388 U.S. 1 (1967), with marriage; Griswold v. Connecticut, supra, and Eisenstadt v. Baird, supra, with contraception; and Roe v. Wade, 410 U.S. 113 (1973), with abortion. The latter three cases were interpreted as construing the Due Process Clause of the Fourteenth Amendment to confer a fundamental individual right to decide whether or not to beget or bear a child. Carey v. Population Services International, supra, at 688–689.

Accepting the decisions in these cases and the above description of them, we think it evident that none of the rights announced in those cases bears any resemblance to the claimed constitutional right of homosexuals to engage in acts of sodomy that is asserted in this case. No connection between family, marriage, or procreation on the one hand and homosexual activity on the other has been demonstrated, either by the Court of Appeals or by respondent. Moreover, any claim that these cases nevertheless stand for the proposition that any kind of private sexual conduct between consenting adults is constitutionally insulated from state proscription is unsupportable. Indeed, the Court's opinion in *Carey* twice asserted that the privacy right, which the *Griswold* line of cases found to be one of the protections provided by the Due Process Clause, did not reach so far. 431 U.S., at 688, n. 5, 694, n. 17.

Precedent aside, however, respondent would have us announce, as the Court of Appeals did, a fundamental right to engage in homosexual sodomy. This we are quite unwilling to do. It is true that despite the language of the Due Process Clauses of the Fifth and Fourteenth Amendments, which appears to focus only on the processes by which life, liberty, or property is taken, the cases are legion in which those Clauses have been interpreted to have substantive content, subsuming rights that to a great extent are immune from federal or state regulation or proscription. Among such cases are those recognizing rights that have little or no textual support in the constitutional language. *Myers, Prince,* and *Pierce* fall in this category, as do the privacy cases from *Griswold* to *Carey.*

Striving to assure itself and the public that announcing rights not readily identifiable in the Constitution's text involves much more than the imposition of the Justices' own choice of values on the States and the Federal Government, the Court has sought to identify the nature of the rights qualifying for heightened judicial protection. In Palko v. Connecticut, 302 U.S. 319, 325, 326 (1937), it was said that this category includes those fundamental liberties that are "implicit in the concept of ordered liberty," such that "neither liberty nor justice would exist if [they] were sacrificed." A different description of fundamental liberties appeared in Moore v. East Cleveland, 431 U.S. 494, 503 (1977) (opinion of Powell, J.), where they are characterized as those liberties that are "deeply rooted in this Nation's history and tradition." Id., at 503 (Powell, J.). See also Griswold v. Connecticut, 381 U.S., at 506.

It is obvious to us that neither of these formulations would extend a fundamental right to homosexuals to engage in acts of consensual sodomy. Proscriptions against that conduct have ancient roots. See generally, Survey on the Constitutional Right to Privacy in the Context of Homosexual Activity, 40 Miami U.L.Rev. 521, 525 (1986). Sodomy was a criminal offense at common law and was forbidden by the laws of the original thirteen States when they ratified the Bill of Rights. In 1868, when the Fourteenth Amendment was ratified, all but 5 of the 37 States in the Union had criminal sodomy laws. In fact, until 1961, all 50 States outlawed sodomy, and today, 24 States and the District of Columbia continue to provide criminal penalties for sodomy performed in private and between consenting adults. Survey, Miami U.L.Rev., supra, at 524, n. 9. Against this background, to claim that a right to engage in such conduct is "deeply rooted in this Nation's history and tradition" or "implicit in the concept of ordered liberty" is, at best, facetious.

Nor are we inclined to take a more expansive view of our authority to discover new fundamental rights imbedded in the Due Process Clause. The Court is most vulnerable and comes nearest to illegitimacy when it deals with judge-made constitutional law having little or no cognizable roots in the language or design of the Constitution. That this is so was painfully demonstrated by the face-off between the Executive and the Court in the 1930's, which resulted in the repudiation of much of the substantive gloss that the Court had placed on the Due Process Clause of the Fifth and Fourteenth Amendments. There should be, therefore, great resistance to expand the substantive reach of those Clauses, particularly if it requires redefining the category of rights deemed to be fundamental. Otherwise, the Judiciary necessarily takes to itself further authority to govern the country without express constitutional authority. The claimed right pressed on us today falls far short of overcoming this resistance.

Respondent, however, asserts that the result should be different where the homosexual conduct occurs in the privacy of the home. He relies on Stanley v. Georgia, 394 U.S. 557 (1969), where the Court held that the First Amendment prevents conviction for possessing and reading obscene material in the privacy of his home: "If the First Amendment means anything, it means that a State has no business telling a man, sitting alone in his house, what books he may read or what films he may watch." Id., at 565.

Stanley did protect conduct that would not have been protected outside the home, and it partially prevented the enforcement of state obscenity laws; but the decision was firmly grounded in the First Amendment. The right pressed upon us here has no similar support in the text of the Constitution, and it does not qualify for recognition under the prevailing principles for construing the Fourteenth Amendment. Its limits are also difficult to discern. Plainly enough, otherwise illegal conduct is not always immunized whenever it occurs in the home. Victimless crimes, such as the possession and use of illegal drugs do not escape the law where they are committed at home. *Stanley* itself recognized that its holding offered no protection for the possession in the home of drugs, firearms, or stolen goods. Id., at 568, n. 11. And if respondent's submission is limited to the voluntary sexual conduct between consenting adults, it would be difficult, except by fiat, to limit the claimed right to homosexual conduct while leaving exposed to prosecution adultery, incest, and other sexual crimes even though they are committed in the home. We are unwilling to start down that road.

Even if the conduct at issue here is not a fundamental right, respondent asserts that there must be a rational basis for the law and that there is none in this case other than the presumed belief of a majority of the electorate in Georgia that homosexual sodomy is immoral and unacceptable. This is said to be an inadequate rationale to support the law. The law, however, is constantly based on notions of morality, and if all laws representing essentially moral choices are to be invalidated under the Due Process Clause, the courts will be very busy indeed. Even respondent makes no such claim, but insists that majority sentiments about the morality of homosexuality should be declared inadequate. We do not agree, and are unpersuaded that the sodomy laws of some 25 States should be invalidated on this basis.[8]

Accordingly, the judgment of the Court of Appeals is reversed.

Chief Justice Burger, concurring.

I join the Court's opinion, but I write separately to underscore my view that in constitutional terms there is no such thing as a fundamental right to commit homosexual sodomy.

As the Court notes, the proscriptions against sodomy have very "ancient roots." Decisions of individuals relating to homosexual conduct have been subject to state intervention throughout the history of Western Civilization. Condemnation of those practices is firmly rooted in Judeao-Christian moral and ethical standards. Homosexual sodomy was a capital crime under Roman law. See Code Theod. 9.7.6; Code Just. 9.9.31. See also D. Bailey, Homosexuality in the Western Christian Tradition 70–81 (1975). During the English Reformation when powers of the ecclesiastical courts were transferred to the King's Courts, the first English statute criminalizing sodomy was passed. 25 Hen. VIII, c. 6. Blackstone described "the infamous crime against nature" as an offense of "deeper malignity" than rape, an heinous act "the very mention of which is a disgrace to human nature," and "a crime not fit to be named." Blackstone's Commentaries *215. The common law of England, including its prohibition of sodomy, became the received law of Georgia and the other Colonies. In 1816 the Georgia Legislature passed the statute at issue here, and that statute has been continuously in force in one form or another since that time.

---

[8] Respondent does not defend the judgment below based on the Ninth Amendment, the Equal Protection Clause or the Eighth Amendment.

To hold that the act of homosexual sodomy is somehow protected as a fundamental right would be to cast aside millennia of moral teaching.

This is essentially not a question of personal "preferences" but rather that of the legislative authority of the State. I find nothing in the Constitution depriving a State of the power to enact the statute challenged here.

Justice Powell, concurring.

I join the opinion of the Court. I agree with the Court that there is no fundamental right—i.e., no substantive right under the Due Process Clause—such as that claimed by respondent, and found to exist by the Court of Appeals. This is not to suggest, however, that respondent may not be protected by the Eighth Amendment of the Constitution. The Georgia statute at issue in this case, Ga. Code Ann. § 16–6–2, authorizes a court to imprison a person for up to 20 years for a single private, consensual act of sodomy. In my view, a prison sentence for such conduct—certainly a sentence of long duration—would create a serious Eighth Amendment issue. Under the Georgia statute a single act of sodomy, even in the private setting of a home, is a felony comparable in terms of the possible sentence imposed to serious felonies such as aggravated battery, § 16–5–24, first degree arson, § 16–7–60 and robbery, § 16–8–40.

In this case, however, respondent has not been tried, much less convicted and sentenced. Moreover, respondent has not raised the Eighth Amendment issue below. For these reasons this constitutional argument is not before us.

Justice Blackmun, with whom Justice Brennan, Justice Marshall, and Justice Stevens join, dissenting.

This case is no more about "a fundamental right to engage in homosexual sodomy," as the Court purports to declare than Stanley v. Georgia, 394 U.S. 557 (1969), was about a fundamental right to watch obscene movies, or Katz v. United States, 389 U.S. 347 (1967), was about a fundamental right to place interstate bets from a telephone booth. Rather, this case is about "the most comprehensive of rights and the right most valued by civilized men," namely, "the right to be let alone." Olmstead v. United States, 277 U.S. 438, 478 (1928) (Brandeis, J., dissenting).

The statute at issue, Ga. Code Ann. § 16–6–2, denies individuals the right to decide for themselves whether to engage in particular forms of private, consensual sexual activity. The Court concludes that § 16–6–2 is valid essentially because "the laws of . . . many States . . . still make such conduct illegal and have done so for a very long time." But the fact that the moral judgments expressed by statutes like § 16–6–2 may be "natural and familiar . . . ought not to conclude our judgment upon the question whether statutes embodying them conflict with the Constitution of the United States." Roe v. Wade, 410

U.S. 113, 117 (1973), quoting Lochner v. New York, 198 U.S. 45, 76 (1905) (Holmes, J., dissenting). Like Justice Holmes, I believe that "[i]t is revolting to have no better reason for a rule of law than that so it was laid down in the time of Henry IV. It is still more revolting if the grounds upon which it was laid down have vanished long since, and the rule simply persists from blind imitation of the past." Holmes, The Path of the Law, 10 Harv.L.Rev. 457, 469 (1897). I believe we must analyze respondent's claim in the light of the values that underlie the constitutional right to privacy. If that right means anything, it means that, before Georgia can prosecute its citizens for making choices about the most intimate aspects of their lives, it must do more than assert that the choice they have made is an " 'abominable crime not fit to be named among Christians.' " Herring v. State, 119 Ga. 709, 721, 46 S.E. 876, 882 (1904).

I

In its haste to reverse the Court of Appeals and hold that the Constitution does not "confe[r] a fundamental right upon homosexuals to engage in sodomy," the Court relegates the actual statute being challenged to a footnote and ignores the procedural posture of the case before it. A fair reading of the statute and of the complaint clearly reveals that the majority has distorted the question this case presents.

First, the Court's almost obsessive focus on homosexual activity is particularly hard to justify in light of the broad language Georgia has used. Unlike the Court, the Georgia Legislature has not proceeded on the assumption that homosexuals are so different from other citizens that their lives may be controlled in a way that would not be tolerated if it limited the choices of those other citizens. Rather, Georgia has provided that "[a] person commits the offense of sodomy when he performs or submits to any sexual act involving the sex organs of one person and the mouth or anus of another." Ga. Code Ann. § 16–6–2(a). The sex or status of the persons who engage in the act is irrelevant as a matter of state law. In fact, to the extent I can discern a legislative purpose for Georgia's 1968 enactment of § 16–6–2, that purpose seems to have been to broaden the coverage of the law to reach heterosexual as well as homosexual activity. I therefore see no basis for the Court's decision to treat this case as an "as applied" challenge to § 16–6–2, or for Georgia's attempt, both in its brief and at oral argument, to defend § 16–6–2 solely on the grounds that it prohibits homosexual activity. Michael Hardwick's standing may rest in significant part on Georgia's apparent willingness to enforce against homosexuals a law it seems not to have any desire to enforce against heterosexuals. . . . But his claim that § 16–6–2 involves an unconstitutional intrusion into his privacy and his right of intimate association does not depend in any way on his sexual orientation.

Second, I disagree with the Court's refusal to consider whether § 16–6–2 runs afoul of the Eighth or Ninth Amendments or the Equal Protection Clause of the Fourteenth Amendment. . . .

II

"Our cases long have recognized that the Constitution embodies a promise that a certain private sphere of individual liberty will be kept largely beyond the reach of government." Thornburgh v. American Coll. of Obst. & Gyn., 476 U.S. 747, 772 (1986). In construing the right to privacy the Court has proceeded along two somewhat distinct, albeit complementary, lines. First, it has recognized a privacy interest with reference to certain *decisions* that are properly for the individual to make. E.g., Roe v. Wade, 410 U.S. 113 (1973); Pierce v. Society of Sisters, 268 U.S. 510 (1925). Second, it has recognized a privacy interest with reference to certain *places* without regard for the particular activities in which the individuals who occupy them are engaged. E.g., United States v. Karo, 468 U.S. 705 (1984); Payton v. New York, 445 U.S. 573 (1980); Rios v. United States, 364 U.S. 253 (1960). The case before us implicates both the decisional and the spatial aspects of the right to privacy.

A

The Court concludes today that none of our prior cases dealing with various decisions that individuals are entitled to make free of governmental interference "bears any resemblance to the claimed constitutional right of homosexuals to engage in acts of sodomy that is asserted in this case." While it is true that these cases may be characterized by their connection to protection of the family, see Roberts v. United States Jaycees, 468 U.S. 609, 619 (1984), the Court's conclusion that they extend no further than this boundary ignores the warning in Moore v. East Cleveland, 431 U.S. 494, 501 (1977) (plurality opinion), against "clos[ing] our eyes to the basic reasons why certain rights associated with the family have been accorded shelter under the Fourteenth Amendment's Due Process Clause." We protect those rights not because they contribute, in some direct and material way, to the general public welfare, but because they form so central a part of an individual's life. "[T]he concept of privacy embodies the 'moral fact that a person belongs to himself and not others nor to society as a whole.'" Thornburgh v. American Coll. of Obst. & Gyn., 476 U.S. at 777, n. 5 (Stevens, J., concurring), quoting Fried, Correspondence, 6 Phil. & Pub. Affairs 288–289 (1977). And so we protect the decision whether to marry precisely because marriage "is an association that promotes a way of life, not causes; a harmony in living, not political faiths; a bilateral loyalty, not commercial or social projects." Griswold v. Connecticut, 381 U.S., at 486. We protect the decision whether to have a child because parenthood alters so dramatically an individual's self-definition, not because of demographic considerations or the Bible's command to be fruitful and multiply. Cf. Thornburgh v. American Coll. of Obst. & Gyn., supra, at 778, n. 6 (Stevens, J., concurring). And we protect the family because it contributes so powerfully to the happiness of individuals, not because of a preference for stereotypical households. Cf. Moore v. East Cleveland, 431 U.S., at 500–506 (plurality opinion). The Court recognized in *Roberts*, 468 U.S., at 619, that the "ability independently to define one's identity that is central to any concept of liberty" cannot truly be exercised in a vacuum; we all depend on the "emotional enrichment of close ties with others." Ibid.

Only the most willful blindness could obscure the fact that sexual intimacy is "a sensitive, key relationship of human existence, central to family life, community welfare, and the development of human personality," Paris Adult Theatre I v. Slayton, 413 U.S. 49, 63 (1973); see also Carey v. Population Services International, 431 U.S. 678, 685 (1977). The fact that individuals define themselves in a significant way through their intimate sexual relationships with others suggests, in a Nation as diverse as ours, that there may be many "right" ways of conducting those relationships, and that much of the richness of a relationship will come from the freedom an individual has to *choose* the form and nature of these intensely personal bonds. See Karst, The Freedom of Intimate Association, 89 Yale L.J. 624, 637 (1980); cf. Eisenstadt v. Baird, 405 U.S. 438, 453 (1972); Roe v. Wade, 410 U.S., at 153.

In a variety of circumstances we have recognized that a necessary corollary of giving individuals freedom to choose how to conduct their lives is acceptance of the fact that different individuals will make different choices. For example, in holding that the clearly important state interest in public education should give way to a competing claim by the Amish to the effect that extended formal schooling threatened their way of life, the Court declared: "There can be no assumption that today's majority is 'right' and the Amish and others like them are 'wrong.' A way of life that is odd or even erratic but interferes with no rights or interests of others is not to be condemned because it is different." Wisconsin v. Yoder, 406 U.S. 205, 223–224 (1972). The Court claims that its decision today merely refuses to recognize a fundamental right to engage in homosexual sodomy; what the Court really has refused to recognize is the fundamental interest all individuals have in controlling the nature of their intimate associations with others.

B

The behavior for which Hardwick faces prosecution occurred in his own home, a place to which the Fourth Amendment attaches special significance. The Court's treatment of this aspect of the case is symptomatic of its overall refusal to consider the broad principles that have informed our treatment of privacy in specific cases. Just as the right to privacy is more than the mere aggregation of a number of entitlements to engage in specific behavior, so too, protecting the physical integrity of the home is more than merely a means of protecting specific activities that often take place there. Even when our understanding of the contours of the right to privacy depends on "reference to a 'place,'" Katz v. United States, 389 U.S., at 361 (Harlan, J., concurring), "the essence of a Fourth Amendment violation is 'not the breaking of [a person's] doors, and the rummaging of his drawers,' but rather is 'the invasion of his indefeasible right of personal security, personal liberty and private property.' " California v. Ciraolo, ___ U.S. ___, ___ (1986) (Powell, J., dissenting) quoting Boyd v. United States, 116 U.S. 616, 630 (1886).

The Court's interpretation of the pivotal case of Stanley v. Georgia, 394 U.S. 557 (1969), is entirely unconvincing. . . .

. . . Indeed, the right of an individual to conduct intimate relationships in the intimacy of his or her own home seems to me to be the heart of the Constitution's protection of privacy.

III

The Court's failure to comprehend the magnitude of the liberty interests at stake in this case leads it to slight the question whether petitioner, on behalf of the State, has justified Georgia's infringement on these interests. I believe that neither of the two general justifications for § 16–6–2 that petitioner has advanced warrants dismissing respondent's challenge for failure to state a claim.

First, petitioner asserts that the acts made criminal by the statute may have serious adverse consequences for "the general public health and welfare," such as spreading communicable diseases or fostering other criminal activity. Inasmuch as this case was dismissed by the District Court on the pleadings, it is not surprising that the record before us is barren of any evidence to support petitioner's claim. In light of the state of the record, I see no justification for the Court's attempt to equate the private, consensual sexual activity at issue here with the "possession in the home of drugs, firearms, or stolen goods," ante, at 9, to which *Stanley* refused to extend its protection. . . .

. . . .

Nor can § 16–6–2 be justified as a "morally neutral" exercise of Georgia's power to "protect the public environment," *Paris Adult Theatre I,* 413 U.S., at 68–69. Certainly, some private behavior can affect the fabric of society as a whole. Reasonable people may differ about whether particular sexual acts are moral or immoral, but "we have ample evidence for believing that people will not abandon morality, will not think any better of murder, cruelty and dishonesty, merely because some private sexual practice which they abominate is not punished by the law." H.L.A. Hart, Immorality and Treason, reprinted in The Law as Literature 220, 225 (L.Blom-Cooper ed. 1961). Petitioner and the Court fail to see the difference between laws that protect public sensibilities and those that enforce private morality. Statutes banning public sexual activity are entirely consistent with protecting the individual's liberty interest in decisions concerning sexual relations: the same recognition that those decisions are intensely private which justifies protecting them from governmental interference can justify protecting individuals from unwilling exposure to the sexual activities of others. But the mere fact that intimate behavior may be punished when it takes place in public cannot dictate how States can regulate intimate behavior that occurs in intimate places. . . .

This case involves no real interference with the rights of others, for the mere knowledge that other individuals do not adhere to one's value system cannot be a legally cognizable interest, cf. Diamond v. Charles, ___ U.S. ___, ___ (1986), let alone an interest that can justify invading the houses, hearts, and minds of citizens who choose to live there lives differently.

IV

It took but three years for the Court to see the error in its analysis in Minersville School District v. Gobitis, 310 U.S. 586 (1940), and to recognize that the threat to national cohesion posed by a refusal to salute the flag was vastly outweighed by the threat to those same values posed by compelling such a salute. See West Virginia Board of Education v. Barnette, 319 U.S. 624 (1943). I can only hope that here, too, the Court soon will reconsider its analysis and conclude that depriving individuals of the right to choose for themselves how to conduct their intimate relationships poses a far greater threat to the values most deeply rooted in our Nation's history than tolerance of nonconformity could ever do. Because I think the Court today betrays those values, I dissent.

————

Justice Stevens, with whom Justice Brennan and Justice Marshall join, dissenting.

Like the statute that is challenged in this case, the rationale of the Court's opinion applies equally to the prohibited conduct regardless of whether the parties who engage in it are married or unmarried, or are of the same or different sexes. Sodomy was condemned as an odious and sinful type of behavior during the formative period of the common law. That condemation was equally damning for heterosexual and homosexual sodomy. Moreover, it provided no special exemption for married couples. The license to cohabit and to produce legitimate offspring simply did not include any permission to engage in sexual conduct that was considered a "crime against nature."

The history of the Georgia statute before us clearly reveals this traditional prohibition of heterosexual, as well as homosexual, sodomy. Indeed, at one point in the 20th century, Georgia's law was construed to permit certain sexual conduct between homosexual women even though such conduct was prohibited between heterosexuals. The history of the statutes cited by the majority as proof for the proposition that sodomy is not constitutionally protected, similarly reveals a prohibition on heterosexual, as well as homosexual, sodomy.

Because the Georgia statute expresses the traditional view that sodomy is an immoral kind of conduct regardless of the identity of the persons who engage in it, I believe that a proper analysis of its constitutionality requires consideration of two questions: First, may a State totally prohibit the described conduct by means of a neutral law applying without exception to all persons subject to its jurisdiction? If not, may the State save the statute by announcing that it will only enforce the law against homosexuals? The two questions merit separate discussion.

I

Our prior cases make two propositions abundantly clear. First, the fact that the governing majority in a State has traditionally viewed a particular practice as immoral is not a sufficient reason for upholding a law prohibiting the practice; neither history nor tradition could save a law prohibiting miscegenation from constitutional attack. Second, individual decisions by married persons, concerning the intimacies of their physical relationship, even when not intended to produce offspring, are a form of "liberty" protected by the Due Process Clause of the Fourteenth Amendment. Griswold v. Connecticut, 381 U.S. 479 (1965). Moreover, this protection extends to intimate choices by unmarried as well as married persons. Carey v. Population Services International, 431 U.S. 678 (1977); Eisenstadt v. Baird, 405 U.S. 438 (1972).

. . .

II

If the Georgia statute cannot be enforced as it is written—if the conduct it seeks to prohibit is a protected form of liberty for the vast majority of Georgia's citizens—the State must assume the burden of justifying a selective application of its law. Either the persons to whom Georgia seeks to apply its statute do not have the same interest in "liberty" that others have, or there must be a reason why the State may be permitted to apply a generally applicable law to certain persons that it does not apply to others.

The first possibility is plainly unacceptable. Although the meaning of the principle that "all men are created equal" is not always clear, it surely must mean that every free citizen has the same interest in "liberty" that the members of the majority share. From the standpoint of the individual, the homosexual and the heterosexual have the same interest in deciding how he will live his own life, and, more narrowly, how he will conduct himself in his personal and voluntary associations with his companions. State intrusion into the private conduct of either is equally burdensome.

The second possibility is similarly unacceptable. A policy of selective application must be supported by a neutral and legitimate interest—something more substantial than a habitual dislike for, or ignorance about, the disfavored group. Neither the State not the Court has identified any such interest in this case. The Court has posited as a justification for the Georgia statute "the presumed belief of a majority of the electorate in Georgia that homosexual sodomy is immoral and unacceptable." But the Georgia electorate has expressed no such belief—instead, its representatives enacted a law that presumably reflects the belief that *all sodomy* is immoral and unacceptable. Unless the Court is prepared to conclude that such a law is constitutional, it may not rely on the work product of the Georgia Legislature to support its holding. For the Georgia statute does not single out homosexuals as a separate class meriting special disfavored treatment.

Nor, indeed, does the Georgia prosecutor even believe that all homosexuals who violate this statute should be punished. This conclusion is evident from the fact that the respondent in this very case has formally acknowledged in his complaint and in court that he has engaged, and intends to continue to engage, in the prohibited conduct, yet the State has elected not to process criminal charges against him. As Justice Powell points out, moreover, Georgia's prohibition on private, consensual sodomy has not been enforced for decades. The record of nonenforcement, in this case and in the last several decades, belies the Attorney General's representations about the importance of the State's selective application of its generally applicable law.

Both the Georgia statute and the Georgia prosecutor thus completely fail to provide the Court with any support for the conclusion that homosexual sodomy, *simpliciter*, is considered unacceptable conduct in that State, and that the burden of justifying a selective application of the generally applicable law has been met.

III

The Court orders the dismissal of respondent's complaint even though the State's statute prohibits all sodomy; even though that prohibition is concededly unconstitutional with respect to heterosexuals; and even though the State's *post hoc* explanations for selective application are belied by the State's own actions. At the very least, I think it clear at this early stage of the litigation that respondent has alleged a constitutional claim sufficient to withstand a motion to dismiss.

I respectfully dissent.

TURNER v. SAFLEY
__ U.S. __, 107 S.Ct. 2254, 96 L.Ed.2d 64 (1987).

Justice O'Connor delivered the opinion of the Court.

This case requires us to determine the constitutionality of regulations promulgated by the Missouri Division of Corrections relating to inmate marriages and inmate-to-inmate correspondence. The Court of Appeals for the Eighth Circuit, applying a strict scrutiny analysis, concluded that the regulations violate respondents' constitutional rights. We hold that a lesser standard of scrutiny is appropriate in determining the constitutionality of the prison rules. Applying that standard, we uphold the validity of the correspondence regulation, but we conclude that the marriage restriction cannot be sustained.

I

Respondents brought this class action for injunctive relief and damages in the United States District Court for the Western District of

Missouri. The regulations challenged in the complaint were in effect at all prisons within the jurisdiction of the Missouri Division of Corrections. This litigation focused, however, on practices at the Renz Correctional Institution (Renz), located in Cedar City, Missouri. The Renz prison population includes both male and female prisoners of varying security levels. Most of the female prisoners at Renz are classified as medium or maximum security inmates, while most of the male prisoners are classified as minimum security offenders. Renz is used on occasion to provide protective custody for inmates from other prisons in the Missouri system. The facility originally was built as a minimum security prison farm, and it still has a minimum security perimeter without guard towers or walls.

Two regulations are at issue here. The first of the challenged regulations relates to correspondence between inmates at different institutions. It permits such correspondence "with immediate family members who are inmates in other correctional institutions," and it permits correspondence between inmates "concerning legal matters." Other correspondence between inmates, however, is permitted only if "the classification/treatment team of each inmate deems it in the best interest of the parties involved." . . .

The challenged marriage regulation, which was promulgated while this litigation was pending, permits an inmate to marry only with the permission of the superintendent of the prison, and provides that such approval should be given only "when there are compelling reasons to do so." The term "compelling" is not defined, but prison officials testified at trial that generally only a pregnancy or the birth of an illegitimate child would be considered a compelling reason. See 586 F.Supp., at 592. Prior to the promulgation of this rule, the applicable regulation did not obligate Missouri Division of Corrections officials to assist an inmate who wanted to get married, but it also did not specifically authorize the superintendent of an institution to prohibit inmates from getting married. . . .

The District Court issued a memorandum opinion and order finding both the correspondence and marriage regulations unconstitutional. The court, relying on Procunier v. Martinez, 416 U.S. 396, 413–414 (1974), applied a strict scrutiny standard. It held the marriage regulation to be an unconstitutional infringement upon the fundamental right to marry because it was far more restrictive than was either reasonable or essential for the protection of the State's interests in security and rehabilitation. 586 F.Supp., at 594. The correspondence regulation also was unnecessarily broad, the court concluded, because prison officials could effectively cope with the security problems raised by inmate-to-inmate correspondence through less restrictive means, such as scanning the mail of potentially troublesome inmates. Id., at 596. The District Court also held that the correspondence regulation had been applied in an arbitrary and capricious manner.

The Court of Appeals for the Eighth Circuit affirmed. 777 F.2d 1307 (1985). The Court of Appeals held that the District Court properly used strict scrutiny in evaluating the constitutionality of the Missouri correspondence and marriage regulations. . . .

We granted certiorari, 476 U.S. ___ (1986).

II

We begin, as did the courts below, with our decision in Procunier v. Martinez, supra, which described the principles that necessarily frame our analysis of prisoners' constitutional claims. The first of these principles is that federal courts must take cognizance of the valid constitutional claims of prison inmates. Prison walls do not form a barrier separating prison inmates from the protections of the Constitution. Hence, for example, prisoners retain the constitutional right to petition the Government for the redress of grievances, Johnson v. Avery, 393 U.S. 483 (1969); they are protected against invidious racial discrimination by the Equal Protection Clause of the Fourteenth Amendment, Lee v. Washington, 390 U.S. 333 (1968); and they enjoy the protections of due process, Wolff v. McDonnell, 418 U.S. 539 (1974), Haines v. Kerner, 404 U.S. 519 (1972). Because prisoners retain these rights, "[w]hen a prison regulation or practice offends a fundamental constitutional guarantee, federal courts will discharge their duty to protect constitutional rights." Procunier v. Martinez, 416 U.S., at 405–406.

A second principle identified in *Martinez*, however, is the recognition that "courts are ill equipped to deal with the increasingly urgent problems of prison administration and reform." As the *Martinez* Court acknowledged, "the problems of prisons in America are complex and intractable, and, more to the point, they are not readily susceptible of resolution by decree." Running a prison is an inordinately difficult undertaking that requires expertise, planning, and the commitment of resources, all of which are peculiarly within the province of the Legislative and Executive Branches of Government. Prison administration is, moreover, a task that has been committed to the responsibility of those branches, and separation of powers concerns counsel a policy of judicial restraint. Where a state penal system is involved, federal courts have, as we indicated in *Martinez*, additional reason to accord deference to the appropriate prison authorities.

Our task, then, as we stated in *Martinez*, is to formulate a standard of review for prisoners' constitutional claims that is responsive both to the "policy of judicial restraint regarding prisoner complaints and [to] the need to protect constitutional rights." As the Court of Appeals acknowledged, *Martinez* did not itself resolve the question that it framed. *Martinez* involved mail censorship regulations proscribing statements that "unduly complain," "magnify grievances," or express "inflammatory political, racial, religious or other views." In that case, the Court determined that the proper standard of review for prison restrictions on correspondence between prisoners and members of the general public could be decided without resolving the "broad questions of 'prisoners' rights.' " . . . We expressly reserved the question of the proper standard of review to apply in cases "involving questions of 'prisoners' rights.' "

In four cases following *Martinez,* this Court has addressed such "questions of 'prisoners' rights.' " The first of these, Pell v. Procunier, 417 U.S. 817 (1974), decided the same Term as *Martinez,* involved a constitutional challenge to a prison regulation prohibiting face-to-face media interviews with individual inmates. The Court rejected the inmates' First Amendment challenge to the ban on media interviews, noting that judgments regarding prison security "are peculiarly within the province and professional expertise of corrections officials, and, in the absence of substantial evidence in the record to indicate that the officials have exaggerated their response to these considerations, courts should ordinarily defer to their expert judgment in such matters."

The next case to consider a claim of prisoners' rights was Jones v. North Carolina Prisoners' Union, 433 U.S. 119 (1977). There the Court considered prison regulations that prohibited meetings of a "prisoners' labor union," inmate solicitation of other inmates to join the union, and bulk mailings concerning the union from outside sources. Noting that the lower court in *Jones* had "got[ten] off on the wrong foot . . . by not giving appropriate deference to the decisions of prison administrators and appropriate recognition to the peculiar and restrictive circumstances of penal confinement," the Court determined that the First and Fourteenth Amendment rights of prisoners were "barely implicated" by the prohibition on bulk mailings and that the regulation was "reasonable" under the circumstances. The prisoners' constitutional challenge to the union meeting and solicitation restrictions was also rejected, because "[t]he ban on inmate solicitation and group meetings . . . was rationally related to the reasonable, indeed to the central, objectives of prison administration."

Bell v. Wolfish, 441 U.S. 520 (1979) concerned a First Amendment challenge to a Bureau of Prisons rule restricting inmates' receipt of hardback books unless mailed directly from publishers, book clubs, or bookstores. The rule was upheld as a "rational response" to a clear security problem. Because there was "no evidence" that officials had exaggerated their response to the security problem, the Court held that "the considered judgment of these experts must control in the absence of prohibitions far more sweeping than those involved here." And in Block v. Rutherford, 468 U.S. 576 (1984), a ban on contact visits was upheld on the ground that "responsible, experienced administrators have determined, in their sound discretion, that such visits will jeopardize the security of the facility," and the regulation was "reasonably related" to these security concerns.

In none of these four "prisoners' rights" cases did the Court apply a standard of heightened scrutiny, but instead inquired whether a prison regulation that burdens fundamental rights is "reasonably related" to legitimate penological objectives, or whether it represents an "exaggerated response" to those concerns. The Court of Appeals in this case nevertheless concluded that *Martinez* provided the closest analogy for determining the appropriate standard of review for resolving respondents' constitutional complaints. The Court of Appeals distinguished this Court's decisions in *Pell, Jones, Bell,* and *Block* as variously involving "time, place, or manner" regulations, or regulations that restrict "presumptively dangerous" inmate activities. See 777 F.2d, at 1310–1312. The Court of Appeals acknowledged that *Martinez* had expressly reserved the question of the appropriate standard of review based on inmates' constitutional claims, but it nonetheless believed that the *Martinez* standard was the proper one to apply to respondents' constitutional claims.

We disagree with the Court of Appeals that the reasoning in our cases subsequent to *Martinez* can be so narrowly cabined. . . .

. . .

If *Pell, Jones,* and *Bell* have not already resolved the question posed in *Martinez,* we resolve it now: when a prison regulation impinges on inmates' constitutional rights, the regulation is valid if it is reasonably related to legitimate penological interests. In our view, such a standard is necessary if "prison administrators . . ., and not the courts, [are] to make the difficult judgments concerning institutional operations." Jones v. North Carolina Prisoners' Union, 433 U.S., at 128. Subjecting the day-to-day judgments of prison officials to an inflexible strict scrutiny analysis would seriously hamper their ability to anticipate security problems and to adopt innovative solutions to the intractable problems of prison administration. The rule would also distort the decisionmaking process, for every administrative judgment would be subject to the possibility that some court somewhere would conclude that it had a less restrictive way of solving the problem at hand. Courts inevitably would become the primary arbiters of what constitutes the best solution to every administrative problem, thereby "unnecessarily perpetuat[ing] the involvement of the federal courts in affairs of prison administration." Procunier v. Martinez, 416 U.S., at 407.

As our opinions in *Pell, Bell,* and *Jones* show, several factors are relevant in determining the reasonableness of the regulation at issue. First, there must be a "valid, rational connection" between the prison regulation and the legitimate governmental interest put forward to justify it. Block v. Rutherford, 468 U.S., at 586. Thus, a regulation cannot be sustained where the logical connection between the regulation and the asserted goal is so remote as to render the policy arbitrary or irrational. Moreover, the governmental objective must be a legitimate and neutral one. We have found it important to inquire whether prison regulations restricting inmates' First Amendment rights operated in a neutral fashion, without regard to the content of the expression. See Pell v. Procunier, 417 U.S., at 828; Bell v. Wolfish, 441 U.S., at 551.

A second factor relevant in determining the reasonableness of a prison restriction, as *Pell* shows, is whether there are alternative means of exercising the right that remain open to prison inmates. Where "other avenues" remain available for the exercise of the asserted right, see Jones v. North Carolina Prisoners' Union, supra, at 131, courts should be particularly conscious of the "measure of judicial deference owed to corrections officials . . . in gauging the validity of the regulation." Pell v. Procunier, supra, at 827.

A third consideration is the impact accommodation of the asserted constitutional right will have on guards and other inmates, and on the allocation of prison resources generally. In the necessarily closed environment of the correctional institution, few changes will have no ramifications on the liberty of others or on the use of the prison's limited resources for preserving institutional order. When accommodation of an asserted right will have a significant "ripple effect" on fellow inmates or on prison staff, courts should be particularly deferential to the informed discretion of corrections officials. Cf. Jones v. North Carolina Prisoners' Union, supra, at 132–133.

Finally, the absence of ready alternatives is evidence of the reasonableness of a prison regulation. See Block v. Rutherford, 468 U.S., at 587. By the same token, the existence of obvious, easy alternatives may be evidence that the regulation is not reasonable, but is an "exaggerated response" to prison concerns. This is not a "least restrictive alternative" test: prison officials do not have to set up and then shoot down every conceivable alternative method of accommodating the claimant's constitutional complaint. But if an inmate claimant can point to an alternative that fully accommodates the prisoner's rights at *de minimis* cost to valid penological interests, a court may consider that as evidence that the regulation does not satisfy the reasonable relationship standard.

III

Applying our analysis to the Missouri rule barring inmate-to-inmate correspondence, we conclude that the record clearly demonstrates that the regulation was reasonably related to legitimate security interests. We find that the marriage restriction, however, does not satisfy the reasonable relationship standard, but rather constitutes an exaggerated response to petitioners' rehabilitation and security concerns.

A

According to the testimony at trial, the Missouri correspondence provision was promulgated primarily for security reasons. Prison officials testified that mail between institutions can be used to communicate escape plans and to arrange assaults and other violent acts. Witnesses stated that the Missouri Division of Corrections had a growing problem with prison gangs, and that restricting communications among gang members, both by transferring gang members to different institutions and by restricting their correspondence, was an important element in combating this problem. Officials also testified that the use of Renz as a facility to provide protective custody for certain inmates could be compromised by permitting correspondence between inmates at Renz and inmates at other correctional institutions.

The prohibition on correspondence between institutions is logically connected to these legitimate security concerns. Undoubtedly, communication with other felons is a potential spur to criminal behavior: this sort of contact frequently is prohibited even after an inmate has been released on parole. See, e.g., 28 CFR § 2.40(a)(10) (1986) (federal parole conditioned on non-association with known criminals, unless permission is granted by the parole officer). In Missouri prisons, the danger of such coordinated criminal activity is exacerbated by the presence of prison gangs. The Missouri policy of separating and isolating gang members . . . logically is furthered by the restriction on prisoner-to-prisoner correspondence. Moreover, the correspondence regulation does not deprive prisoners of all means of expression. Rather, it bars communication only with a limited class of other people with whom prison officials have particular cause to be concerned—inmates at other institutions within the Missouri prison system.

We also think that the Court of Appeals' analysis overlooks the impact of respondents' asserted right on other inmates and prison personnel. Prison officials have stated that in their expert opinion, correspondence between prison institutions facilitates the development of informal organizations that threaten the core functions of prison administration, maintaining safety and internal security. As a result, the correspondence rights asserted by respondents, like the organizational activities at issue in Jones v. North Carolina Prisoners' Union, 433 U.S. 119 (1977), can be exercised only at the cost of significantly less liberty and safety for everyone else, guards and other prisoners alike. Indeed, the potential "ripple effect" is even broader here than in *Jones*, because exercise of the right affects the inmates and staff of more than one institution. Where exercise of a right requires this kind of trade-off, we think that the choice made by corrections officials— which is, after all, a judgment "peculiarly within [their] province and professional expertise," Pell v. Procunier, 417 U.S., at 827—should not be lightly set aside by the courts.

Finally, there are no obvious, easy alternatives to the policy adopted by petitioners. Other well-run prison systems, including the Federal Bureau of Prisons, have concluded that substantially similar restrictions on inmate correspondence were necessary to protect institutional order and security. See, e.g., 28 CFR § 540.17 (1986). As petitioners have shown, the only alternative proffered by the claimant prisoners, the monitoring of inmate correspondence, clearly would impose more than a *de minimis* cost on the pursuit of legitimate corrections goals. Prison officials testified that it would be impossible to read every piece of inmate-to-inmate correspondence and consequently there would be an appreciable risk of missing dangerous messages. In any event, prisoners could easily write in jargon or codes to prevent detection of their real messages. . . . The risk of missing dangerous communications, taken together with the sheer burden on staff resources required to conduct item-by-item censorship support the judgment of prison officials that this alternative is not an adequate alternative to restricting correspondence.

The prohibition on correspondence is reasonably related to valid corrections goals. The rule is content-neutral, it logically advances the goals of institutional security and safety identified by Missouri prison officials, and it is not an exaggerated response to those objectives. On that basis, we conclude that the regulation does not unconstitutionally abridge the First Amendment rights of prison inmates.*

B

In support of the marriage regulation, petitioners first suggest that the rule does not deprive prisoners of a constitutionally protected right. They concede that the decision to marry is a fundamental right under *Zablocki v. Redhail*, 434 U.S. 374 (1976), and *Loving v. Virginia*, 388 U.S. 1 (1967), but they imply that a different rule should obtain "in . . . a prison forum." Petitioners then argue that even if the regulation burdens inmates' constitutional rights, the restriction should be tested under a reasonableness standard. They urge that the restriction is reasonably related to legitimate security and rehabilitation concerns.

We disagree with petitioners that *Zablocki* does not apply to prison inmates. It is settled that a prison inmate "retains those [constitutional] rights that are not inconsistent with his status as a prisoner or with the legitimate penological objectives of the corrections system." *Pell v. Procunier*, 417 U.S., at 822. The right to marry, like many other rights, is subject to substantial restrictions as a result of incarceration. Many important attributes of marriage remain, however, after taking into account the limitations imposed by prison life. First, inmate marriages, like others, are expressions of emotional support and public commitment. These elements are an important and significant aspect of the marital relationship. In addition, many religions recognize marriage as having spiritual significance; for some inmates and their spouses, therefore, the commitment of marriage may be an exercise of religious faith as well as an expression of personal dedication. Third, most inmates eventually will be released by parole or commutation, and therefore most inmate marriages are formed in the expectation that they ultimately will be fully consummated. Finally, marital

---

* Suggesting that there is little difference between the "unnecessarily sweeping" standard applied by the District Court in reaching its judgment and the reasonableness standard described in Part II; Justice Stevens complains that we have "ignore[d] the findings of fact that were made by the District Court," and have improperly "encroach[ed] into the fact-finding domain of the District Court."

The District Court's inquiry as to whether the regulations were "needlessly broad" is not just semantically different from the standard we have articulated in Part II: it is the least-restrictive alternative test of *Procunier v. Martinez*, 416 U.S. 396 (1974). As *Martinez* states, in a passage quoted by the District Court:

"[T]he limitation of First Amendment freedoms must be no greater than is necessary or essential to the protection of the particular governmental interest involved. Thus a restriction on inmate correspondence . . . will . . . be invalid *if its sweep is unnecessarily broad*."

The District Court's judgment that the correspondence regulation was "unnecessarily sweeping," 586 F.Supp. 589, 596 (WD Mo.1984), thus was a judgment based on application of an erroneous legal standard. . . .

. . . .

status often is a pre-condition to the receipt of government benefits (e.g., Social Security benefits), property rights (e.g., tenancy by the entirety, inheritance rights), and other, less tangible benefits (e.g., legitimation of children born out of wedlock). These incidents of marriage, like the religious and personal aspects of the marriage commitment, are unaffected by the fact of confinement or the pursuit of legitimate corrections goals.

Taken together, we conclude that these remaining elements are sufficient to form a constitutionally protected marital relationship in the prison context. . . .

The Missouri marriage regulation prohibits inmates from marrying unless the prison superintendent has approved the marriage after finding that there are compelling reasons for doing so. As noted previously, generally only pregnancy or birth of a child is considered a "compelling reason" to approve a marriage. In determining whether this regulation impermissibly burdens the right to marry, we note initially that the regulation prohibits marriages between inmates and civilians, as well as marriages between inmates. Although not urged by respondents, this implication of the interests of nonprisoners may support application of the *Martinez* standard, because the regulation may entail a "consequential restriction on the [constitutional] rights of those who are not prisoners." See Procunier v. Martinez, 416 U.S., at 409. We need not reach this question, however, because even under the reasonable relationship test, the marriage regulation does not withstand scrutiny.

Petitioners have identified both security and rehabilitation concerns in support of the marriage prohibition. The security concern emphasized by petitioners is that "love triangles" might lead to violent confrontations between inmates. With respect to rehabilitation, prison officials testified that female prisoners often were subject to abuse at home or were overly dependent on male figures, and that this dependence or abuse was connected to the crimes they had committed. The superintendent at Renz, petitioner William Turner, testified that in his view, these women prisoners needed to concentrate on developing skills of self-reliance, and that the prohibition on marriage furthered this rehabilitative goal. Petitioners emphasize that the prohibition on marriage should be understood in light of Superintendent Turner's experience with several ill-advised marriage requests from female inmates.

We conclude that on this record, the Missouri prison regulation, as written, is not reasonably related to these penological interests. No doubt legitimate security concerns may require placing reasonable restrictions upon an inmate's right to marry, and may justify requiring approval of the superintendent. The Missouri regulation, however, represents an exaggerated response to such security objectives. There are obvious, easy alternatives to the Missouri regulation that accommodate the right to marry while imposing a *de minimis* burden on the pursuit of security objectives. See, e.g., 28 CFR § 551.10 (1986) (marriage by inmates in federal prison generally permitted, but not if warden finds that it presents a threat to security or order of institution, or to public safety). We are aware of no place in the record where prison officials testified that such ready alternatives would not fully satisfy their security concerns. Moreover, with respect to the security concern emphasized in petitioners' brief—the creation of "love triangles"—petitioners have pointed to nothing in the record suggesting that the marriage regulation was viewed as preventing such entanglements. Common sense likewise suggests that there is no logical connection between the marriage restriction and the formation of love triangles: surely in prisons housing both male and female prisoners, inmate rivalries are as likely to develop without a formal marriage ceremony as with one. Finally, this is not an instance where the "ripple effect" on the security of fellow inmates and prison staff justifies a broad restriction on inmates' rights—indeed, where the inmate wishes to marry a civilian, the decision to marry (apart from the logistics of the wedding ceremony) is a completely private one.

Nor, on this record, is the marriage restriction reasonably related to the articulated rehabilitation goal. First, in requiring refusal of permission absent a finding of a compelling reason to allow the marriage, the rule sweeps much more broadly than can be explained by petitioners' penological objectives. Missouri prison officials testified that generally they had experienced no problem with the marriage of male inmates, and the District Court found that such marriages had routinely been allowed as a matter of practice at Missouri correctional institutions prior to adoption of the rule, 586 F.Supp., at 592. The proffered justification thus does not explain the adoption of a rule banning marriages by these inmates. Nor does it account for the prohibition on inmate marriages to civilians. Missouri prison officials testified that generally they had no objection to inmate-civilian marriages and Superintendent Turner testified that he usually did not object to the marriage of either male or female prisoners to civilians. The rehabilitation concern appears from the record to have been centered almost exclusively on female inmates marrying other inmates or ex-felons; it does not account for the ban on inmate-civilian marriages.

. . .

It is undisputed that Missouri prison officials may regulate the time and circumstances under which the marriage ceremony itself takes place. On this record, however, the almost complete ban on the decision to marry is not reasonably related to legitimate penological objectives. We conclude, therefore, that the Missouri marriage regulation is facially invalid.

IV

We uphold the facial validity of the correspondence regulation, but we conclude that the marriage rule is constitutionally infirm. We read petitioners' additional challenge to the District Court's findings of fact to be a claim that the District Court erred in holding that the correspondence regulation had been applied by prison officials in an arbitrary and capricious manner. Because the Court of Appeals did not address this question, we remand the issue to the Court of Appeals for its consideration.

Accordingly, the judgment of the Court of Appeals striking down the Missouri marriage regulation is affirmed; its judgment invalidating the correspondence rule is reversed; and the case is remanded to the Court of Appeals for further proceedings consistent with this opinion.

It is so ordered.

———

Justice Stevens, with whom Justice Brennan, Justice Marshall, and Justice Blackmun join, concurring in part and dissenting in part.

How a court describes its standard of review when a prison regulation infringes fundamental constitutional rights often has far less consequence for the inmates than the actual showing that the court demands of the State in order to uphold the regulation. This case provides a prime example.

There would not appear to be much difference between the question whether a prison regulation that burdens fundamental rights in the quest for security is "needlessly broad"—the standard applied by the District Court and the Court of Appeals—and this Court's requirement that the regulation must be "reasonably related to legitimate penological interests" and may not represent "an 'exaggerated response' to those concerns." But if the standard can be satisfied by nothing more than a "*logical* connection" between the regulation and any legitimate penological concern perceived by a cautious warden it is virtually meaningless. Application of the standard would seem to permit disregard for inmates' constitutional rights whenever the imagination of the warden produces a plausible security concern and a deferential trial court is able to discern a logical connection between that concern and the challenged regulation. Indeed, there is a logical connection between prison discipline and the use of bullwhips on prisoners; and security is logically furthered by a total ban on inmate communication, not only with other inmates but also with outsiders who conceivably might be interested in arranging an attack within the prison or an escape from it. Thus, I dissent from Part II of the Court's opinion.[1]

I am able to join Part III–B because the Court's invalidation of the marriage regulation does not rely on a rejection of a standard of review more stringent than the one announced in Part II. The Court in Part III–B concludes after careful examination that, even applying a "rea-

———

[1] The Court's rather open-ended "reasonableness" standard makes it much too easy to uphold restrictions on prisoners' First Amendment rights on the basis of administrative concerns and speculation about possible security risks rather than on the basis of evidence that the restrictions are needed to further an important governmental interest. Judge Kaufman's opinion in Abdul Wali v. Coughlin, 754 F.2d 1015, 1033 (CA2 1985), makes a more careful attempt to strike a fair balance between legitimate penological concerns and the well-settled proposition that inmates do not give up all constitutional rights by virtue of incarceration.

sonableness" standard, the marriage regulation must fail because the justifications asserted on its behalf lack record support. Part III–A, however, is not only based on an application of the Court's newly minted standard, but also represents the product of a plainly improper appellate encroachment into the fact-finding domain of the District Court. . . . Indeed, a fundamental difference between the Court of Appeals and this Court in this case—and the principal point of this dissent—rests in the respective ways the two courts have examined and made use of the trial record. In my opinion the Court of Appeals correctly held that the trial court's findings of fact adequately supported its judgment sustaining the inmates' challenge to the mail regulation as it has been administered at the Renz Correctional Center in Cedar City, Missouri. In contrast, this Court sifts the trial testimony on its own in order to uphold a general prohibition against correspondence between unrelated inmates.

. . .

III

The contrasts between the Court's acceptance of the challenge to the marriage regulation as overbroad and its rejection of the challenge to the correspondence rule are striking and puzzling. The Court inexplicably expresses different views about the security concerns common to prison marriages and prison mail. In the marriage context expert speculation about the security problems associated with "love triangles" is summarily rejected, while in the mail context speculation about the potential "gang problem" and the possible use of codes by prisoners receives virtually total deference. Moreover, while the Court correctly dismisses as a defense to the marriage rule the speculation that the inmate's spouse, once released from incarceration, would attempt to aid the inmate in escaping, the Court grants virtually total credence to similar speculation about escape plans concealed in letters.

In addition, the Court disregards the same considerations it relies on to invalidate the marriage regulation when it turns to the mail regulation. The marriage rule is said to sweep too broadly because it is more restrictive than the routine practices at other Missouri correctional institutions, but the mail rule at Renz is not an "exaggerated response" even though it is more restrictive than practices in the remainder of the state. The Court finds the rehabilitative value of marriage apparent, but dismisses the value of corresponding with a friend who is also an inmate for the reason that communication with the outside world is not totally prohibited. The Court relies on the District Court's finding that the marriage regulation operated on the basis of "excessive paternalism" toward female inmates, but rejects the same court's factual findings on the correspondence regulation. Unfathomably, while rejecting the Superintendent's concerns about love triangles as an insufficient and invalid basis for the marriage regulation, the Court apparently accepts the same concerns as a valid basis for the mail regulation.

In pointing out these inconsistencies, I do not suggest that the Court's treatment of the marriage regulation is flawed; as I stated, I concur fully in that part of its opinion. I do suggest that consistent application of the Court's reasoning necessarily leads to a finding that the mail regulation applied at Renz is unconstitutional.

IV

To the extent that this Court affirms the judgment of the Court of Appeals, I concur in its opinion. I respectfully dissent from the Court's partial reversal of that judgment on the basis of its own selective forays into the record. When all the language about deference and security is set to one side, the Court's erratic use of the record to affirm the Court of Appeals only partially may rest on an unarticulated assumption that the marital state is fundamentally different from the exchange of mail in the satisfaction, solace, and support it affords to a confined inmate. Even if such a difference is recognized in literature, history or anthropology, the text of the Constitution more clearly protects the right to communicate than the right to marry. In this case, both of these rights should receive constitutional recognition and protection.

NOTE

In O'Lone v. Estate of Shabazz, 107 S.Ct. 2400 (1987) the Court by a vote of 5 to 4 applied the lower standard of review adopted in Turner v. Safley and upheld a prison regulation which prevented certain prisoners from attending Islamic religious services.

E. PROVISION OF ESSENTIAL GOVERNMENTAL BENEFITS AND SERVICES TO THE POOR

Page 626. Add ahead of Access of the Poor to the Courts in Civil Cases:

In Pennsylvania v. Finley, 107 S.Ct. 1990 (1987) the Court reaffirmed Ross v. Moffitt, holding that the state has no constitutional duty under either the due process or equal protection clauses to provide counsel to a defendant in postconviction proceedings.

Chapter 11

THE EQUAL PROTECTION CLAUSE AND THE REVIEW OF THE REASONABLENESS OF LEGISLATION

SECTION 2. SOCIAL AND ECONOMIC REGULATORY LEGISLATION

Page 652. Add ahead of Scope and Legitimacy of Judicial Review of the Rationality of Legislation Under Equal Protection:

METROPOLITAN LIFE INSURANCE CO. v. WARD

470 U.S. 869, 105 S.Ct. 1676, 84 L.Ed.2d 751 (1985).

Justice Powell delivered the opinion of the Court.

This case presents the question whether Alabama's domestic preference tax statute, Ala.Code §§ 27–4–4 and 27–4–5 (1975), that taxes out-of-state insurance companies at a higher rate than domestic insurance companies, violates the Equal Protection Clause.

I

Since 1955, the State of Alabama has granted a preference to its domestic insurance companies by imposing a substantially lower gross premiums tax rate on them than on out-of-state (foreign) companies. Under the current statutory provisions, foreign life insurance companies pay a tax on their gross premiums received from business conducted in Alabama at a rate of 3 percent, and foreign companies selling other types of insurance pay at a rate of 4 percent. Ala.Code § 27–4–4(a) (1975). All domestic insurance companies, in contrast, pay at a rate of only 1 percent on all types of insurance premiums. § 27–4–5(a). As a result, a foreign insurance company doing the same type and volume of business in Alabama as a domestic company generally will pay three to four times as much in gross premiums taxes as its domestic competitor.

. . .

II

Appellants, a group of insurance companies incorporated outside of the State of Alabama, filed claims with the Alabama Department of Insurance in 1981, contending that the domestic preference tax statute, as applied to them, violated the Equal Protection Clause. They sought

194

refunds of taxes paid for the tax years 1977 through 1980. The Commissioner of Insurance denied all of their claims on July 8, 1981.

Appellants appealed to the Circuit Court for Montgomery County, seeking a judgment declaring the statute to be unconstitutional and requiring the Commissioner to make the appropriate refunds. Several domestic companies intervened, and the court consolidated all of the appeals, selecting two claims as lead cases to be tried and binding on all claimants. On cross-motions for summary judgment, the court ruled on May 17, 1982, that the statute was constitutional. Relying on this Court's opinion in Western & Southern Life Ins. Co. v. State Board of Equalization of California, 451 U.S. 648 (1981), the court ruled that the Alabama statute did not violate the Equal Protection Clause because it served "at least two purposes, in addition to raising revenue: (1) encouraging the formation of new insurance companies in Alabama, and (2) encouraging capital investment by foreign insurance companies in the Alabama assets and governmental securities set forth in the statute." The court also found that the distinction the statute created between foreign and domestic companies was rationally related to those two purposes and that the Alabama Legislature reasonably could have believed that the classification would have promoted those purposes.

After their motion for a new trial was denied, appellants appealed to the Court of Civil Appeals. It affirmed the Circuit Court's rulings as to the existence of the two legitimate state purposes, but remanded for an evidentiary hearing on the issue of rational relationship, concluding that summary judgment was inappropriate on that question because the evidence was in conflict. 437 So.2d 535 (1983). Appellants petitioned the Supreme Court of Alabama for certiorari on the affirmance of the legitimate state purpose issue, and the State and the intervenors petitioned for review of the remand order. Appellants then waived their right to an evidentiary hearing on the issue whether the statute's classification bore a rational relationship to the two purposes found by the Circuit Court to be legitimate, and they requested a final determination of the legal issues with respect to their equal protection challenge to the statute. The Supreme Court denied certiorari on all claims. Appellants again waived their rights to an evidentiary hearing on the rational relationship issue and filed a joint motion with the other parties seeking rehearing and entry of a final judgment. The motion was granted, and judgment was entered for the State and the intervenors. . . .

III

Prior to our decision in Western & Southern Life Ins. Co. v. State Board of Equalization of California, supra, the jurisprudence of the applicability of the Equal Protection Clause to discriminatory tax statutes had a somewhat checkered history. Lincoln National Life Ins. Co. v. Read, 325 U.S. 673 (1945), held that so-called "privilege" taxes, required to be paid by a foreign corporation before it would be permitted to do business within a State, were immune from equal protection challenge. That case stood in stark contrast, however, to the Court's prior decisions in Southern R. Co. v. Greene, 216 U.S. 400, 30 S.Ct. 287 (1910), and Hanover Fire Ins. Co. v. Harding, 272 U.S. 494 (1926), as well as to later decisions, in which the Court had recognized that the Equal Protection Clause placed limits on other forms of discriminatory taxation imposed on out-of-state corporations solely because of their residence. See, e.g., WHYY, Inc. v. Glassboro, 393 U.S. 117 (1968); Allied Stores of Ohio, Inc. v. Bowers, 358 U.S. 522 (1959); Wheeling Steel Corp. v. Glander, 337 U.S. 562 (1949).

In *Western & Southern,* supra, we reviewed all of these cases for the purpose of deciding whether to permit an equal protection challenge to a California statute imposing a retaliatory tax on foreign insurance companies doing business within the State, when the home States of those companies imposed a similar tax on California insurers entering their borders. We concluded that *Lincoln* was no more than "a surprising throwback" to the days before enactment of the Fourteenth Amendment and in which incorporation of a domestic corporation or entry of a foreign one had been granted only as a matter of privilege by the State in its unfettered discretion. 451 U.S., at 665. We therefore rejected the longstanding but "anachronis[tic]" rule of *Lincoln* and explicitly held that the Equal Protection Clause imposes limits upon a State's power to condition the right of a foreign corporation to do business within its borders. Id., at 667. We held that "[w]e consider it now established that, whatever the extent of a State's authority to exclude foreign corporations from doing business within its boundaries, that authority does not justify imposition of more onerous taxes or other burdens on foreign corporations than those imposed on domestic corporations, unless the discrimination between foreign and domestic corporations bears a rational relation to a legitimate state purpose." Id., at 667–668.

Because appellants waived their right to an evidentiary hearing on the issue whether the classification in the Alabama domestic preference tax statute bears a rational relation to the two purposes upheld by the Circuit Court, the only question before us is whether those purposes are legitimate.[5]

A

(1)

The first of the purposes found by the trial court to be a legitimate reason for the statute's classification between foreign and domestic corporations is that it encourages the formation of new domestic insurance companies in Alabama. The State, agreeing with the Court of Civil Appeals, contends that this Court has long held that the promotion of domestic industry, in and of itself, is a legitimate state

[5] The State and the intervenors advanced some 15 additional purposes in support of the Alabama statute. As neither the Circuit Court nor the Court of Civil Appeals ruled on the legitimacy of those purposes, that question is not before us, and we express no view as to it. On remand, the State will be free to advance again its arguments relating to the legitimacy of those purposes.

. . .

purpose that will survive equal protection scrutiny. In so contending, it relies on a series of cases, including *Western & Southern,* that are said to have upheld discriminatory taxes. . . .

The cases cited lend little or no support to the State's contention. In *Western & Southern,* the case principally relied upon, we did not hold as a general rule that promotion of domestic industry is a legitimate state purpose under equal protection analysis.[6] Rather, we held that California's purpose in enacting the retaliatory tax—to promote the *interstate* business of domestic insurers by deterring *other States* from enacting discriminatory or excessive taxes—was a legitimate one. 451 U.S., at 668. In contrast, Alabama asks us to approve its purpose of promoting the business of its domestic insurers *in Alabama* by penalizing foreign insurers who also want to do business in the State. Alabama has made no attempt, as California did, to influence the policies of other States in order to enhance its domestic companies' ability to operate interstate; rather, it has erected barriers to foreign companies who wish to do interstate business in order to improve its domestic insurers' ability to compete at home.

The crucial distinction between the two cases lies in the fact that Alabama's aim to promote domestic industry is purely and completely discriminatory, designed only to favor domestic industry within the State, no matter what the cost to foreign corporations also seeking to do business there. Alabama's purpose, contrary to California's, constitutes the very sort of parochial discrimination that the Equal Protection Clause was intended to prevent . . .. Unlike the retaliatory tax involved in *Western & Southern,* which only burdens residents of a State that imposes its own discriminatory tax on outsiders, the domestic preference tax gives the "home team" an advantage by burdening *all* foreign corporations seeking to do business within the State, no matter what they or their States do.

The validity of the view that a State may not constitutionally favor its own residents by taxing foreign corporations at a higher rate solely because of their residence is confirmed by a long line of this Court's cases so holding. WHYY, Inc. v. Glassboro, 393 U.S., at 119–120; Wheeling Steel Corp. v. Glander, 337 U.S., at 571; Hanover Fire Ins. Co. v. Harding, 272 U.S., at 511; Southern R. Co. v. Greene, 216 U.S., at 417. See Reserve Life Ins. Co. v. Bowers, 380 U.S. 258 (1965) (per curiam). As the Court stated in *Hanover Fire Ins. Co.,* with respect to general tax burdens on business, "the foreign corporation stands equal, and is to be classified with domestic corporations of the same kind." 272 U.S., at 511. In all of these cases, the discriminatory tax was

---

[6] We find the other cases on which the State relies also to be inapposite to this inquiry. *Bacchus Imports, Pike,* and *Parker* discussed whether promotion of local industry is a valid state purpose under the Commerce Clause. The Commerce Clause, unlike the Equal Protection Clause, is integrally concerned with whether a state purpose implicates local or national interests. The Equal Protection Clause, in contrast, is concerned with whether a state purpose is impermissibly discriminatory; whether the discrimination involves local or other interests is not central to the inquiry to be made. Thus, the fact that promotion of local industry is a legitimate state interest in the Commerce Clause context says nothing about its validity under equal protection analysis. . . .

. . . .

imposed by the State on foreign corporations doing business within the State solely because of their residence, presumably to promote domestic industry within the State. In relying on these cases and rejecting *Lincoln* in *Western & Southern,* we reaffirmed the continuing viability of the Equal Protection Clause as a means of challenging a statute that seeks to benefit domestic industry within the State only by grossly discriminating against foreign competitors.

. . .

(2)

The State argues nonetheless that it is impermissible to view a discriminatory tax such as the one at issue here as violative of the Equal Protection Clause. This approach, it contends, amounts to no more than "Commerce Clause rhetoric in equal protection clothing." The State maintains that because Congress, in enacting the McCarran-Ferguson Act, 15 U.S.C. §§ 1011–1015, intended to authorize States to impose taxes that burden interstate commerce in the insurance field, the tax at issue here must stand. Our concerns are much more fundamental than as characterized by the State. Although the McCarran-Ferguson Act exempts the insurance industry from Commerce Clause restrictions, it does not purport to limit in any way the applicability of the Equal Protection Clause. As noted above, our opinion in *Western & Southern* expressly reaffirmed the viability of equal protection restraints on discriminatory taxes in the insurance context.

Moreover, the State's view ignores the differences between Commerce Clause and equal protection analysis and the consequent different purposes those two constitutional provisions serve. Under Commerce Clause analysis, the State's interest, if legitimate, is weighed against the burden the state law would impose on interstate commerce. In the equal protection context, however, if the State's purpose is found to be legitimate, the state law stands as long as the burden it imposes is found to be rationally related to that purpose, a relationship that is not difficult to establish. See *Western & Southern,* 451 U.S., at 674, (if purpose is legitimate, equal protection challenge may not prevail so long as the question of rational relationship is " 'at least debatable' " (quoting United States v. Carolene Products Co., 304 U.S. 144, 154 (1938)).

The two constitutional provisions perform different functions in the analysis of the permissible scope of a State's power—one protects interstate commerce, and the other protects persons from unconstitutional discrimination by the States. . . . The effect of the statute at issue here is to place a discriminatory tax burden on foreign insurers who desire to do business within the State, thereby also incidentally placing a burden on interstate commerce. Equal protection restraints are applicable even though the effect of the discrimination in this case is similar to the type of burden with which the Commerce Clause also would be concerned. We reaffirmed the importance of the Equal Protection Clause in the insurance context in *Western & Southern* and see no reason now for reassessing that view.

In whatever light the State's position is cast, acceptance of its contention that promotion of domestic industry is always a legitimate state purpose under equal protection analysis would eviscerate the Equal Protection Clause in this context. A State's natural inclination frequently would be to prefer domestic business over foreign. If we accept the State's view here, then any discriminatory tax would be valid if the State could show it reasonably was intended to benefit domestic business.[10] A discriminatory tax would stand or fall depending primarily on how a State framed its purpose—as benefiting one group or as harming another. This is a distinction without a difference, and one that we rejected last term in an analogous context arising under the Commerce Clause. Bacchus Imports, Ltd. v. Dias, 468 U.S., at ___. We hold that under the circumstances of this case, promotion of domestic business by discriminating against nonresident competitors is not a legitimate state purpose.

B

The second purpose found by the courts below to be legitimate was the encouragement of capital investment in the Alabama assets and governmental securities specified in the statute. We do not agree that this is a legitimate state purpose when furthered by discrimination. Domestic insurers remain entitled to the more favorable rate of tax regardless of whether they invest in Alabama assets. Moreover, the investment incentive provision of the Alabama statute does not enable foreign insurance companies to eliminate the discriminatory effect of the statute. No matter how much of their assets they invest in Alabama, foreign insurance companies are still required to pay a higher gross premiums tax than domestic companies. The State's investment incentive provision therefore does not cure, but reaffirms, the statute's impermissible classification based solely on residence. We hold that encouraging investment in Alabama assets and securities in this plainly discriminatory manner serves no legitimate state purpose.

IV

We conclude that neither of the two purposes furthered by the Alabama domestic preference tax statute and addressed by the Circuit Court for Montgomery County, see supra, at 1679, is legitimate under the Equal Protection Clause to justify the imposition of the discriminatory tax at issue here. The judgment of the Alabama Supreme Court accordingly is reversed, and the case is remanded for further proceedings not inconsistent with this opinion.

It is so ordered.

[10] Indeed, under the State's analysis, *any* discrimination subject to the rational relation level of scrutiny could be justified simply on the ground that it favored one group at the expense of another. This case does not involve or question, as the dissent suggests, the broad authority of a State to promote and regulate its own economy. We hold only that such regulation may not be accomplished by imposing discriminatorily higher taxes on nonresident corporations solely because they are nonresidents.

Justice O'Connor, with whom Justice Brennan, Justice Marshall and Justice Rehnquist join, dissenting.

This case presents a simple question: Is it legitimate for a state to use its taxing power to promote a domestic insurance industry and to encourage capital investment within its borders? In a holding that can only be characterized as astonishing, the Court determines that these purposes are illegitimate. This holding is unsupported by precedent and subtly distorts the constitutional balance, threatening the freedom of both state and federal legislative bodies to fashion appropriate classifications in economic legislation. Because I disagree with both the Court's method of analysis and its conclusion, I respectfully dissent.

I

Alabama's legislature has chosen to impose a higher tax on out-of-state insurance companies and insurance companies incorporated in Alabama that do not maintain their principal place of business or invest assets within the State. Ala.Code § 27–4–4 et seq. (1975). This tax seeks to promote both a domestic insurance industry and capital investment in Alabama. Metropolitan Life Insurance Company, joined by many other out-of-state insurers, alleges that this discrimination violates its rights under the Equal Protection Clause of the Fourteenth Amendment, which provides that a State shall not "deny to any person within its jurisdiction the equal protection of the laws." Appellants rely on the Equal Protection Clause because, as corporations, they are not "citizens" protected by the privileges and immunities clauses of the Constitution. Hemphill v. Orloff, 277 U.S. 537, 548–550 (1928). Similarly, they cannot claim Commerce Clause protection because Congress in the McCarran-Ferguson Act, 59 Stat. 33, 15 U.S.C. § 1011 et seq., explicitly suspended Commerce Clause restraints on state taxation of insurance and placed insurance regulation firmly within the purview of the several States. Western & Southern Life Ins. Co. v. State Board of Equalization, 451 U.S. 648, 655 (1981).

Our precedents impose a heavy burden on those who challenge local economic regulation solely on Equal Protection Clause grounds. In this context, our long-established jurisprudence requires us to defer to a legislature's judgment if the classification is rationally related to a legitimate state purpose. Yet the Court evades this careful framework for analysis, melding the proper two-step inquiry regarding the State's purpose and the classification's relationship to that purpose into a single unarticulated judgment. This tactic enables the Court to characterize State goals that have been legitimated by Congress itself as improper solely because it disagrees with the concededly rational means of differential taxation selected by the legislature. This unorthodox approach leads to further error. The Court gives only the most cursory attention to the factual and legal bases supporting the State's purposes and ignores both precedent and significant evidence in the record establishing their legitimacy. Most troubling, the Court discovers in the Equal Protection Clause an implied prohibition against classifications whose purpose is to give the "home team" an advantage over interstate competitors even where Congress has authorized such advantages.

The Court overlooks the unequivocal language of our prior decisions. "Unless a classification trammels fundamental personal rights or is drawn upon inherently suspect distinctions such as race, religion, or alienage, our decisions presume the constitutionality of the statutory discriminations and require only that the classification challenged be rationally related to a legitimate state interest." New Orleans v. Dukes, 427 U.S. 297, 303 (1976). See, e.g., Lehnhausen v. Lake Shore Auto Parts Co., 410 U.S. 356 (1973). Judicial deference is strongest where a tax classification is alleged to infringe the right to equal protection. "[I]n taxation, even more than in other fields, legislatures possess the greatest freedom in classification." Madden v. Kentucky, 309 U.S. 83, 88 (1940). "Where the public interest is served one business may be left untaxed and another taxed, in order to promote the one or to restrict or suppress the other." Carmichael v. Southern Coal & Coke Co., 301 U.S. 495, 512 (1937) (citations omitted). As the Court emphatically noted in *Allied Stores of Ohio, Inc. v. Bowers:*

> "[I]t has repeatedly been held and appears to be entirely settled that a statute which encourages the location within the State of needed and useful industries by exempting them, though not also others, from its taxes is not arbitrary and does not violate the Equal Protection Clause of the Fourteenth Amendment. Similarly, it has long been settled that a classification, though discriminatory, is not arbitrary or violative of the Equal Protection Clause of the Fourteenth Amendment if any state of facts reasonably can be conceived that would sustain it." 358 U.S. 522 (1959) (citations omitted).

See also Western & Southern Life Ins. Co. v. State Board of Equalization, supra, 451 U.S., at 674; Minnesota v. Clover Leaf Creamery Co., 449 U.S. 456, 464 (1981).

. . .

III

. . .

. . . Alabama does *not* tax at a higher rate solely on the basis of residence; it taxes insurers, domestic as well as foreign, who do not maintain a principal place of business or substantial assets in Alabama, based on conceded distinctions in the contributions of these insurers *as a class* to the State's insurance objectives. The majority obscures the issue by observing that a given "foreign insurance company doing the same type and volume of business in Alabama as a domestic company" will pay a higher tax. Under our precedents, tax classifications need merely "res[t] upon some reasonable consideration of difference or policy." Allied Stores of Ohio, Inc. v. Bowers, supra, 358 U.S., at 527. Rational basis scrutiny does not require that the classification be mathematically precise or that *every* foreign insurer or *every* domestic company fit to perfection the general profile on which the classification is based. "[T]he Equal Protection Clause does not demand a surveyor's precision" in fashioning classifications.   Hughes v. Alexandria Scrap Corp., 426 U.S., at 814.

IV

Because Alabama's classification bears a rational relationship to a legitimate purpose, our precedents demand that it be sustained.   The Court avoids this clear directive by a remarkable evasive tactic.   It simply declares that the ends of promoting a domestic insurance industry and attracting investments to the State *when accomplished through the means of discriminatory taxation* are not legitimate state purposes.   This bold assertion marks a drastic and unfortunate departure from established equal protection doctrine.   By collapsing the two prongs of the rational basis test into one, the Court arrives at the ultimate issue—whether the *means* are constitutional—without ever engaging in the deferential inquiry we have adopted as a brake on judicial impeachment of legislative policy choices.   In addition to unleashing an undisciplined form of Equal Protection Clause scrutiny, the Court's approach today has serious implications for the authority of Congress under the Commerce Clause.   . . .

. . .

. . . Favoring local business as an end in itself might be "rational" but would be antithetical to federalism.   Accepting arguendo this interpretation, we have shown that the measure at issue here does not benefit local business as an end in itself but serves important ulterior goals.   Moreover, any federalism component of equal protection is fully vindicated where Congress has explicitly validated a parochial focus.   Surely the Equal Protection Clause was not intended to supplant the Commerce Clause, foiling Congress' decision under its commerce powers to "affirmatively permit [some measure of] parochial favoritism" when necessary to a healthy federation.   White v. Massachusetts Council of Construction Employers, 460 U.S. 204, 312 (1983).   Such a view of the Equal Protection Clause cannot be reconciled with the McCarran-Ferguson Act and our decisions in *Western & Southern* and *Benjamin.*

Western & Southern established that a state may validly tax out-of-state corporations at a higher rate if its goal is to promote the ability of its domestic businesses to compete in *interstate* markets.   Nevertheless, the Court today concludes that the converse policy is forbidden, striking down legislation whose purpose is to encourage the *intrastate* activities of local business concerns by permitting them to compete effectively on their home turf.   In essence, the Court declares "We will excuse an unequal burden on foreign insurers if the State's purpose is to foster its domestic insurers activities in *other* States, but the same unequal burden will be unconstitutional when employed to further a policy that places a higher social value on the domestic insurer's *homestate* than interstate activities."   This conclusion is not drawn from the Commerce Clause, the textual source of constitutional restrictions on State interference with interstate competition.   Reliance on the Commerce Clause would, of course, be unavailing here in view of the McCarran-Ferguson Act.   Instead the Court engrafts its own economic values on the Equal

Protection Clause. Beyond guarding against arbitrary or irrational discrimination, as interpreted by the Court today this Clause now prohibits the effectuation of economic policies, even where sanctioned by Congress, that elevate local concerns over interstate competition. "But a constitution is not intended to embody a particular economic theory . . .. It is made for people of fundamentally differing views." Lochner v. New York, 198 U.S. 45, 75–76 (1905) (Holmes, J., dissenting). In the heyday of economic due process, Justice Holmes warned:

> "Courts should be careful not to extend [the express] prohibitions [of the Constitution] beyond their obvious meaning by reading into them conceptions of public policy that the particular Court may happen to entertain." Tyson & Brother v. Banton, 273 U.S. 418, 445–446 (1927) (Holmes, J., dissenting, joined by Brandeis, J.) (emphasis added).

Ignoring the wisdom of this observation, the Court fashions its own brand of economic equal protection. In so doing, it supplants a legislative policy endorsed by both Congress and the individual States that explicitly sanctioned the very parochialism in regulation and taxation of insurance that the Court's decision holds illegitimate. This newly unveiled power of the Equal Protection Clause would come as a surprise to the Congress that passed the McCarran-Ferguson Act and the Court that sustained the Act against constitutional attack. In the McCarran-Ferguson Act, Congress expressly sanctioned such economic parochialism in the context of state regulation and taxation of insurance.

The doctrine adopted by the majority threatens the freedom not only of the States but also of the Federal Government to formulate economic policy. The dangers in discerning in the Equal Protection Clause a prohibition against barriers to interstate business irrespective of the Commerce Clause should be self-evident. The Commerce Clause is a flexible tool of economic policy that Congress may use as it sees fit, letting it lie dormant or invoking it to limit as well as promote the free flow of commerce. Doctrines of equal protection are constitutional limits that constrain the acts of federal and state legislatures alike. See, e.g., Califano v. Webster, 430 U.S. 313 (1977); Cohen, Congressional Power to Validate Unconstitutional State Laws: A Forgotten Solution to an Old Enigma, 35 Stan.L.Rev. 387, 400–413 (1983). The Court's analysis casts a shadow over numerous congressional enactments that adopted as federal policy "the type of parochial favoritism" the Court today finds unconstitutional. White v. Massachusetts Council of Construction Employers, 460 U.S., at 213. Contrary to the reasoning in *Benjamin,* the Court today indicates the Equal Protection Clause stands as an independent barrier if courts should determine that either Congress or a State has ventured the "wrong" direction down what has become, by judicial fiat, the one-way street of the Commerce Clause. Nothing in the Constitution or our past decisions supports forcing such an economic straight-jacket on the federal system.

V

Today's opinion charts an ominous course. I can only hope this unfortunate adventure away from the safety of our precedents will be an isolated episode. I had thought the Court had finally accepted that

"the judiciary may not sit as a superlegislature to judge the wisdom or desirability of legislative policy determinations made in areas that neither affect fundamental rights nor proceed along suspect lines; in the local economic sphere, it is only the invidious discrimination, the wholly arbitrary act, which cannot stand consistently with the Fourteenth Amendment. New Orleans v. Dukes, 427 U.S., at 303–304 (citations omitted).

Because I believe that the Alabama law at issue here serves legitimate State purposes through concededly rational means, and thus is neither invidious nor arbitrary, I would affirm the court below. I respectfully dissent.

————

WILLIAMS v. VERMONT, 472 U.S. 14 (1985). Vermont has a motor vehicle purchase and use tax the proceeds from which are used to improve and maintain highways. Under this statute a use tax is collected when cars are registered in Vermont with two exemptions. It does not apply if the car was purchased in Vermont and a sales tax paid. Nor does it apply when a resident of Vermont has paid a sales or use tax purchasing the car outside of Vermont if the state collecting the tax would afford a credit for taxes paid to Vermont in similar circumstances.

Williams purchased a new car in Illinois, paying a five percent sales tax. Three months later he moved to Vermont, bringing the car with him, and attempted to register it without paying the use tax. Levine bought a car in New York paying a seven percent sales tax. A year later she moved to Vermont and sought to register the car without paying the use tax. In each case the tax was collected and they brought suit in the state courts seeking a refund. The refund was denied and the case came to the Supreme Court from the Vermont Supreme Court.

Justice White, delivering the opinion of the Court, held that the failure of the statute to give a credit to the plaintiffs was a denial of equal protection of the laws. There was dispute over the meaning of the statute. Did it exempt a resident of Vermont who purchased a car in another state, registered it there, and then brought it to Vermont or did it exempt only the resident who purchased a car in another state and first registered it in Vermont? The record in the state court was not clear but Justice White decided that the resident of Vermont would get a credit in either case and so the question was whether giving a credit to a resident who bought and registered a car out of state but not giving the same credit to a nonresident who purchased a car out of state and then moved to Vermont violated equal protection. He said, in part:

"This Court has expressly reserved the question whether a State must credit a sales tax paid to another State against its own use tax. Southern Pacific Co. v. Gallagher, 306 U.S. 167, 172 (1939); Henneford v. Silas Mason Co., 300 U.S. 577, 587 (1937). The District of Columbia and all but three States with sales and use taxes do provide such a credit, although reciprocity may be required. CCH, State Tax Guide 6013 (1984). As noted above, Vermont provides a credit with regard to its general use tax. Such a requirement has been endorsed by at least one state court, Montgomery Ward & Co. v. State Board of Equalization, 272 Cal. App.2d 728, 78 Cal.Rptr. 373 (1969), cert. denied, 396 U.S. 1040 (1970), was advocated 20 years ago in the much-cited Report of the Willis Subcommittee, H.R.Rep. No. 565, 89th Cong., 1st Sess., 1136, 1177–1178 (1965), is adopted in the Multistate Tax Compact, Art. V, § 1, and has significant support in the commentary, e.g., J. Hellerstein & W. Hellerstein, State and Local Taxation 637–638 (1978); Developments in the Law: Federal Limits on State Taxation of Interstate Business, 75 Harv.L.Rev. 953, 999–1000 (1962). Appellants urge us to hold that it is a constitutional requirement. Once again, however, we find it unnecessary to reach this question. Whatever the general rule may be, to provide a credit only to those who were residents at the time they paid the sales tax to another State is an arbitrary distinction that violates the Equal Protection Clause.

"This Court has many times pointed out that in structuring internal taxation schemes 'the States have large leeway in making classifications and drawing lines which in their judgment produce reasonable systems of taxation.' Lehnhausen v. Lake Shore Auto Parts Co., 410 U.S. 356, 359 (1973). It has been reluctant to interfere with legislative policy decisions in this area. See Regan v. Taxation with Representation of Washington, 461 U.S. 540, 547–548 (1983); San Antonio Independent School District v. Rodriguez, 411 U.S. 1, 40–41 (1973); Allied Stores of Ohio, Inc. v. Bowers, 358 U.S. 522, 526–527 (1959). An exemption such as that challenged here 'will be sustained if the legislature could have reasonably concluded that the challenged classification would promote a legitimate state purpose.' Exxon Corp. v. Eagerton, 462 U.S. 176, 196 (1983). See generally Schweiker v. Wilson, 450 U.S. 221, 234–235 (1981).

"We perceive no legitimate purpose, however, that is furthered by this discriminatory exemption. As we said in holding that the use tax base cannot be broader than the sales tax base, 'equal treatment for in-state and out-of-state taxpayers similarly situated is the condition precedent for a valid use tax on goods imported from out-of-state.' Halliburton Oil Well Co. v. Reily, 373 U.S. 64, 70 (1963).[7] A State may not treat those within its borders unequally solely on the basis of their different residences or States of

[7] Halliburton was decided under the Commerce Clause and is not dispositive. We do not consider in what way, if any, the failure to give appellants a credit might burden interstate commerce. The critical point is the Court's emphasis on the need for equal

incorporation. WHYY v. Glassboro, 393 U.S. 117, 119 (1968); Wheeling Steel Corp. v. Glander, 337 U.S. 562, 571–572 (1949). In the present case, residence at the time of purchase is a wholly arbitrary basis on which to distinguish among present Vermont registrants—at least among those who used their cars elsewhere before coming to Vermont.[8] Having registered a car in Vermont they are similarly situated for all relevant purposes. Each is a Vermont resident, using a car in Vermont, with an equal obligation to pay for the maintenance and improvement of Vermont's roads. The purposes of the statute would be identically served, and with an identical burden, by taxing each. The distinction between them bears no relation to the statutory purpose. See Zobel v. Williams, 457 U.S. 55, 61 (1982); cf. Texaco, Inc. v. Short, 454 U.S. 516, 540 (1982). As the Court said in *Wheeling*, appellants have not been 'accorded equal treatment, and the inequality is not because of the slightest difference in [Vermont's] relation to the decisive transaction, but solely because of the[ir] different residence.' 337 U.S., at 572.

"In sum, we can see no relevant difference between motor vehicle registrants who purchased their cars out-of-state while they were Vermont residents and those who only came to Vermont after buying a car elsewhere. To free one group and not the other from the otherwise applicable tax burden violates the Equal Protection Clause."

Justice Powell took no part in the decision of the case. Justice Brennan concurred, stating:

"I join the Court's opinion for the reasons stated therein and in my concurring opinion in Zobel v. Williams, 457 U.S. 55, 65 (1982). General application of distinctions of the kind made by the Vermont statute would clearly, though indirectly, threaten the 'federal interest in free interstate migration.' Id., at 66. In addition, the statute makes distinctions among residents that are not 'supported by a valid state interest independent of the discrimination itself.' Id., at 70."

Justice Blackmun, joined by Justice Rehnquist and Justice O'Connor, dissented. He opened his opinion with the following paragraph:

"The Court in this case draws into question the constitutionality of a statute that was not intended to discriminate against anyone, does not discriminate against appellants, and, for all that appears, never has been applied in a discriminatory fashion against

treatment of taxpayers who can be distinguished only on the basis of residence. See also Henneford v. Silas Mason Co., 300 U.S. 577, 583–584 (1937).

[8] The dissent does not disagree that such people are similarly situated, nor does it identify any justification for preferential treatment of the resident. It merely argues that the inequity is the acceptable result of the imprecision of a generally rational classification. Under rational-basis scrutiny, legislative classifications are of course allowed some play in the joints. But the choice of a proxy criterion—here, residence for State of use—cannot be so casual as this, particularly when a more precise and direct classification is easily drawn.

anyone else. Nevertheless, the Court has imagined a fanciful hypothetical discrimination, and then has threatened that the statute will violate equal protection unless the Vermont Supreme Court or the Vermont Legislature rejects the Court's conjecture."

Later in the opinion, he said:

"The reason nonresidents who purchase cars out-of-state are taxed if they subsequently relocate in Vermont, while resident out-of-state purchasers are not, is that it was presumed that people will use their cars primarily in the States in which they reside. Most people who do not reside in Vermont and do not purchase their cars in that State, will not use their cars primarily in Vermont. If at some time in the future they move to Vermont and register their automobiles there, the assumption is that they will have used their cars in two different States. On the other hand, most people who reside in Vermont and purchase their cars out-of-state will return to Vermont immediately with their cars. Thus, the out-of-state purchaser is taxed, while the Vermont purchaser is exempted to the extent that he already has paid a sales tax. This distinction is hardly irrational, and the fact that there may be a Vermont resident who both purchases and uses his car out-of-state, and is therefore situated similarly to Mr. Williams, surely does not render the scheme irrational. A tax classification does not violate the demands of equal protection simply because it may not perfectly identify the class of people it wishes to single out. A State 'is not required to resort to close distinctions or to maintain a precise, scientific uniformity with reference to composition, use or value.' Allied Stores of Ohio, Inc. v. Bowers, 358 U.S. 522, 527 (1959).

"The Court disagrees, and finds that 'residence at the time of purchase is a wholly arbitrary basis on which to distinguish among present Vermont registrants—at least among those who used their cars elsewhere before coming to Vermont.' The Court, however, ignores the purpose of the tax and of the classification. Vermont does not wish to 'distinguish among present Vermont registrants,' but to distinguish those who will likely use Vermont's roads immediately after they have purchased cars out-of-state from those who will not. Residency is not an irrational way to enact such a classification. Moreover, the Court's qualification misstates the language of the statute, for, as indicated, § 8911(9) does not distinguish among residents depending upon where they first *used* their cars, but upon where they *acquired* their cars. A classification based on the assumption that people will use their cars in the States where they live, rather than in the States where they acquire them, is far from the kind of 'palpably arbitrary' classification that the Court previously has struck down on equal protection grounds. See Allied Stores of Ohio, Inc. v. Bowers, 358 U.S., at 527."

NORTHEAST BANCORP, INC. v. BOARD OF GOVERNORS OF THE FEDERAL RESERVE SYSTEM, 472 U.S. 159 (1985). Congress enacted in 1965 the Bank Holding Company Act which prohibits the approval of an application of a bank holding company or a bank located in one state to acquire a bank or a bank holding company located in another state unless the acquisition "is specifically authorized by the statute laws of the State in which such bank is located by language to that effect and not merely by implication." In 1982 Massachusetts enacted a statute permitting an out-of-state bank holding company with its principal place of business in one of the other New England states to establish or acquire a Massachusetts based bank or bank holding company, provided that the other New England state accords equivalent reciprocal privileges to Massachusetts banking organizations. Connecticut enacted a similar statute in 1983. A Connecticut bank holding company sought permission from the Federal Reserve Board to purchase a bank holding company in Massachusetts and a Massachusetts bank holding company sought permission to acquire a Connecticut bank holding company. The Board approved the acquisitions and the court of appeals affirmed.

Justice Rehnquist, writing for the Court, said first that there was no commerce clause objection because Congress had specifically consented to the kind of state regulations involved here. He also looked at the contention that under the decision in *Metropolitan Life Insurance Co. v. Ward* it was a denial of equal protection to permit the states to favor banks from the New England region as opposed to those outside of that region. On this he said:

"In *Metropolitan Life* we held that encouraging the formation of new domestic insurance companies within a State and encouraging capital investment in the State's assets and governmental securities were not, standing alone, legitimate state purposes which could permissibly be furthered by discriminating against out-of-state corporations in favor of local corporations. There we said:

This case does not involve or question, as the dissent suggests, the broad authority of a State, to promote and regulate its own economy. We hold only that such regulation may not be accomplished by imposing discriminatorily higher taxes on nonresident corporations solely because they are nonresidents.

"Here the States in question—Massachusetts and Connecticut—are not favoring local corporations at the expense of out-of-state corporations. They are favoring out-of-state corporations domiciled within the New England region over out-of-state corporations from other parts of the country, and to this extent their laws may be said to 'discriminate' against the latter. But with respect to the business of banking, we do not write on a clean slate; recently in Lewis v. B.T. Investment Managers, Inc., 447 U.S., at 38, we said that 'banking and related financial activities are of profound local concern.' This statement is a recognition of the historical fact that our country traditionally has favored widely dispersed control of banking. While many other western nations are dominated by a handful of centralized banks, we have some 15,000 commercial banks attached to a greater or lesser degree to the communities in which they are located. The Connecticut legislative Commission that recommended adoption of the Connecticut statute in question considered interstate banking on a regional basis to combine the beneficial effect of increasing the number of banking competitors with the need to preserve a close relationship between those in the community who need credit and those who provide credit. The debates in the Connecticut Legislature preceding the enactment of the Connecticut law evince concern that immediate acquisition of Connecticut banks by holding companies headquartered outside the New England region would threaten the independence of local banking institutions. No doubt similar concerns motivated the Massachusetts Legislature.

"We think that the concerns which spurred Massachusetts and Connecticut to enact the statutes here challenged, different as they are from those which motivated the enactment of the Alabama statute in *Metropolitan,* meet the traditional rational basis for judging equal protection claims under the Fourteenth Amendment. Barry v. Barchi, 443 U.S. 55, 67 (1979); Vance v. Bradley, 440 U.S. 93, 97 (1979)."

Justice O'Connor, concurring said:

"I agree that the state banking statutes at issue here do not violate the Commerce Clause, the Compact Clause, or the Equal Protection Clause. I write separately to note that I see no meaningful distinction for Equal Protection Clause purposes between the Massachusetts and Connecticut statutes we uphold today and the Alabama statute at issue in Metropolitan Life Insurance Co. v. Ward, 470 U.S. 869 (1985).

"The Court distinguishes this case from Metropolitan Life on the ground that Massachusetts and Connecticut favor neighboring out-of-state banks over all other out-of-state banks. It is not clear to me why completely barring the banks of 44 States from doing business is less discriminatory than Alabama's scheme of taxing the insurance companies from 49 States at a slightly higher rate. Nor is it clear why the Equal Protection clause should tolerate a regional 'home team' when it condemns a state 'home team.'

"The Court emphasizes that here we do not write on a clean slate as the business of banking is 'of profound local concern.' The business of insurance is also of uniquely local concern. Prudential Insurance Co. v. Benjamin, 328 U.S. 408, 415–416 (1946). Both industries historically have been regulated by the States in recognition of the critical part they play in securing the financial well-being of local citizens and businesses. . . . States have regulated insurance since 1851. Like the local nature of banking, the local nature of insurance is firmly ensconced in federal law. . . .

. . . .

"Especially where Congress has sanctioned the barriers to commerce that fostering of local industries might engender, this Court has no authority under the Equal Protection Clause to invalidate classifications designed to encourage local businesses because of their special contributions. Today's opinion is consistent with the longstanding doctrine that the Equal Protection Clause permits economic regulation that distinguishes between groups that *are* legitimately different—as local institutions so often are—in ways relevant to the proper goals of the State."

Justice Powell took no part in the decision of the case.

PENNELL v. SAN JOSE, 108 S.Ct. 849 (1988). The city of San Jose enacted a rent control ordinance the allowed a hearing officer to consider, among other factors, the "hardship to a tenant" when determining whether to approve a rent increase proposed by a landlord. Apartment owners sued seeking a declaration that, among other things, the ordinance on its face violated the equal protection clause. The Court unanimously (except for Justice Kennedy who took no part) rejected this claim, saying:

"We also find that the Ordinance does not violate the Amendment's Equal Protection Clause. Here again, the standard is deferential; appellees need only show that the classification scheme embodied in the Ordinance is 'rationally related to a legitimate state interest.' New Orleans v. Dukes, 427 U.S. 297, 303, 96 S.Ct. 2513, 2517, 49 L.Ed.2d 511 (1976). . . . In light of our conclusion above that the Ordinance's tenant hardship provisions are designed to serve the legitimate purpose of protecting tenants, we can hardly conclude that it is irrational for the Ordinance to treat certain landlords differently on the basis of whether or not they have hardship tenants. The Ordinance distinguishes between landlords because doing so furthers the purpose of ensuring that individual tenants do not suffer 'unreasonable' hardship; it would be inconsistent to state that hardship is a legitimate factor to be considered but then hold that appellees could not tailor the Ordinance so that only legitimate hardship cases are redressed. . . . We recognize, as appellants point out, that in general it is difficult to say that the landlord 'causes' the tenant's hardship. But this is beside the point—if a landlord does have a hardship tenant, regardless of the reason why, it is rational for appellees to take that fact into consideration under § 5703.28 of the Ordinance when establishing a rent that is 'reasonable under the circumstances.' "

LYNG v. INTERNATIONAL UNION, UNITED AUTOMOBILE, AEROSPACE AND AGRICULTURAL IMPLEMENT WORKERS OF AMERICA, UAW
___ U.S. ___, 108 S.Ct. 1184, 99 L.Ed.2d 380 (1988).

Justice White delivered the opinion of the Court.

A 1981 amendment to the Food Stamp Act states that no household shall become eligible to participate in the food stamp program during the time that any member of the household is on strike or shall increase the allotment of food stamps that it was receiving already because the income of the striking member has decreased. We must decide whether this provision is valid under the First and the Fifth Amendments.

. . .

III

Because the statute challenged here has no substantial impact on any fundamental interest and does not "affect with particularity any protected class," *Hodory*, supra, 431 U.S. at 489, we confine our consideration to whether the statutory classification "is rationally related to a legitimate governmental interest." Department of Agriculture v. Moreno, 413 U.S. 528, 533 (1973). We have stressed that this standard of review is typically quite deferential; legislative classifications are "presumed to be valid," Massachusetts Board of Retirement v. Murgia, 427 U.S. 307, 314 (1976), largely for the reason that "the drawing of lines that create distinctions is peculiarly a legislative task and an unavoidable one." See Dandridge v. Williams, 397 U.S. 471, 485 (1970).

The Government submits that this statute serves three objectives. Most obvious, given its source in OBRA, is to cut federal expenditures. Second, the limited funds available were to be used when the need was likely to be greatest, an approach which Congress thought did not justify food stamps for strikers. Third was the concern that the food stamp program was being used to provide one-sided support for labor strikes; the Senate Report indicated that the amendment was intended to remove the basis for that perception and criticism.

We have little trouble in concluding that § 109 is rationally related to the legitimate governmental objective of avoiding undue favoritism to one side or the other in private labor disputes. The Senate Report declared: "Public policy demands an end to the food stamp subsidization of all strikers who become eligible for the program solely through the temporary loss of income during a strike. Union strike funds should be responsible for providing support and benefits to strikers during labor-management disputes." It was no part of the purposes of the Food Stamp Act to establish a program that would serve as a weapon in labor disputes; the Act was passed to alleviate hunger and malnutrition and to strengthen the agricultural economy. 7 U.S.C. § 2011. The Senate Report stated that "allowing strikers to be eligible for food stamps has damaged the program's public integrity" and thus endangers these other goals served by the program. Congress acted in response to these problems.

It would be difficult to deny that this statute works at least some discrimination against strikers and their households. For the duration of the strike, those households cannot increase their allotment of food stamps even though the loss of income occasioned by the strike may well be enough to qualify them for food stamps or to increase their allotment if the fact of the strike itself were ignored. Yet Congress was in a difficult position when it sought to address the problems it had identified. Because a striking individual faces an immediate and often total drop in income during a strike, a single controversy pitting an employer against its employees can lead to a large number of claims for food stamps for as long as the controversy endures. It is the disburse-ment of food stamps in response to such a controversy that constitutes the source of the concern, and of the dangers to the program, that Congress believed it was important to remedy. We are not free in this instance to reject Congress' views about "what constitutes wise econom-ic or social policy." *Dandridge,* supra, 397 U.S. at 486.

It is true that in terms of the scope and extent of their ineligibility for food stamps, § 109 is harder on strikers than on "voluntary quit-ters." . . . But the concern about neutrality in labor disputes does not arise with respect to those who, for one reason or another, simply quit their jobs. . . . Congress need not draw a statutory classification to the satisfaction of the most sharp-eyed observers in order to meet the limitations that the Constitution imposes in this setting. And we are not authorized to ignore Congress' considered efforts to avoid favoritism in labor disputes, which are evidenced also by the two significant provisos contained in the statute. The first proviso preserves eligibility for the program of any household that was eligible to receive stamps "immediately prior to such strike." 7 U.S.C. § 2015(d)(3). The second proviso makes clear that the statutory ineligibility for food stamps does not apply "to any household that does not contain a member on strike, if any of its members refuses to accept employment at a plant or site because of a strike or lockout." In light of all this, the statute is rationally related to the stated objective of maintaining neutrality in private labor disputes.

In view of the foregoing, we need not determine whether either of the other two proffered justifications for § 109 would alone suffice. But it is relevant to note that protecting the fiscal integrity of govern-ment programs, and of the Government as a whole, "is a legitimate concern of the State." *Hodory,* supra, at 493, 97 S.Ct., at 1910. This does not mean that Congress can pursue the objective of saving money by discriminating against individuals or groups. But our review of distinctions that Congress draws in order to make allocations from a finite pool of resources must be deferential, for the discretion about how best to spend money to improve the general welfare is lodged in Congress rather than the courts. . . . In OBRA Congress had already found it necessary to restrict eligibility in the food stamp program and to reduce the amount of deductions that were allowed to recipients. Rather than undertaking further budget cuts in these or other areas, and in order to avoid favoritism in labor disputes, Congress judged that it would do better to pass this statute along with its provisos. The Constitution does not permit us to disturb that judgment in this case.

Appellees contend and the District Court held that the legislative classification is irrational because of the "critical" fact that it "imper-missibly strikes at the striker through his family." 648 F.Supp., at 1240. This, however, is nothing more than a description of how the food stamp program operates as a general matter, a fact that was acknowledged by the District Court. Whenever an individual takes any action that hampers his or her ability to meet the program's eligibility requirements, such as quitting a job or failing to comply with the work-registration requirements, the entire household suffers accordingly.

We have never questioned the constitutionality of the entire Act on this basis, and we just recently upheld the validity of the Act's definition of "household" even though that definition embodies the basic fact that the Act determines benefits "on a 'household' rather than an individual basis." *Lyng,* 477 U.S., at 636, 106 S.Ct., at 2728. That aspect of the program does not violate the Constitution any more so today.

The decision of the District Court is therefore

Reversed.

Justice Kennedy took no part in the consideration or decision of this case.

Justice Marshall, with whom Justice Brennan and Justice Blackmun join, dissenting.

The Court today declares that it has "little trouble" in concluding that Congress's denial of food stamps to the households of striking workers is rationally related to a legitimate governmental objective. The ease with which the Court reaches this conclusion is reflected in the brevity of its Fifth Amendment analysis: the Court gives short shrift to appellees' Equal Protection challenge to the striker amendment even though this argument was the centerpiece of appellees' case in their briefs and at oral argument. I believe that the Court's dismissive approach has caused it to fail to register the full force of appellees' claim. After canvassing the many absurdities that afflict the striker amendment, I conclude that it fails to pass constitutional muster under even the most deferential scrutiny. I therefore would affirm the judgment below.

I

The thrust of appellees' Equal Protection challenge is that the striker amendment to the Food Stamp Act—§ 109 of the Omnibus Budget Reconciliation Act of 1981, codified at 7 U.S.C. § 2015(d)(3)— singles them out for special punitive treatment without reasonable justification. As the Court observes, this Fifth Amendment challenge to an allegedly arbitrary legislative classification implicates our least intrusive standard of review—the so-called "rational basis" test, which requires that legislative classifications be " 'rationally related to a legitimate governmental interest.' " . . . The Court fails to note, however, that this standard of review, although deferential, " 'is not a toothless one.' " Mathews v. De Castro, 429 U.S. 181, 185 (1976), quoting Mathews v. Lucas, 427 U.S. 495, 510 (1976). The rational basis test contains two substantive limitations on legislative choice: legislative enactments must implicate legitimate goals, and the means chosen by the legislature must bear a rational relationship to those goals. In an alternative formulation, the Court has explained that these limitations amount to a prescription that "all persons similarly situated should be treated alike." City of Cleburne v. Cleburne Living Center, Inc., 473 U.S. 432, 439 (1985). . . .

In recent years, the Court has struck down a variety of legislative enactments using the rational basis test. In some cases, the Court found that the legislature's goal was not legitimate. See, e.g., Hooper v. Bernalillo County Assessor, 472 U.S. 612 (1985); Zobel v. Williams, 457 U.S. 55 (1982). In other cases, the Court found that the classification employed by the legislature did not rationally further the legislature's goal. See, e.g., Lindsey v. Normet, 405 U.S. 56 (1972); Reed v. Reed, supra, 404 U.S. at 76–77. In addition, the Court on occasion has combined these two approaches, in essence, concluding that the lack of a rational relationship between the legislative classification and the purported legislative goal suggests that the true goal is illegitimate. See, e.g., City of Cleburne v. Cleburne Living Center, Inc., supra, 473 U.S. at 450; Department of Agriculture v. Moreno, supra, 413 U.S. at 534. The Court's failure today to take seriously appellees' challenge or to address systematically the irrationalities they identify in the striker amendment is difficult to reconcile with these precedents.

. . .

C

Unable to explain completely the striker amendment by the "willingness to work" rationale, the Secretary relies most heavily on yet a third rationale: the promotion of governmental neutrality in labor disputes. Indeed, the Court relies solely on this explanation in rejecting appellees' Equal Protection challenge to the amendment. According to the Secretary and the Court, this last goal rationalizes the discrepancies in the treatment of strikers and voluntary quitters, and of strikers and non-strikers unwilling to cross a picket line. As the Court explains it, excluding strikers from participation in the food stamp program avoids "undue favoritism to one side or the other in private labor disputes" by preventing governmental " 'subsidization' " of strikes. The Court notes that we accepted a version of this governmental neutrality argument "in a related context" in Ohio Bureau of Employment Services v. Hodory, 431 U.S. 471 (1977).

. . .

More important, the "neutrality" argument on its merits is both deceptive and deeply flawed. Even on the most superficial level, the striker amendment does not treat the parties to a labor dispute evenhandedly: forepersons and other management employees who may become temporarily unemployed when a business ceases to operate during a strike remain eligible for food stamps. Management's burden during the course of the dispute is thus lessened by the receipt of public funds, whereas labor must struggle unaided. This disparity cannot be justified by the argument that the strike is labor's "fault," because strikes are often a direct response to illegal practices by management, such as failure to abide by the terms of a collective bargaining agreement or refusal to bargain in good faith.

On a deeper level, the "neutrality" argument reflects a profoundly inaccurate view of the relationship of the modern federal government to the various parties to a labor dispute. Both individuals and businesses are connected to the government by a complex web of supports and incentives. On the one hand, individuals may be eligible to receive a wide variety of health, education, and welfare-related benefits. On the other hand, businesses may be eligible to receive a myriad of tax subsidies through deductions, depreciation, and credits, or direct subsidies in the form of government loans through the Small Business Administration (SBA). Businesses also may receive lucrative government contracts and invoke the protections of the Bankruptcy Act against their creditors. None of these governmental subsidies to businesses is made contingent on the businesses' abstention from labor disputes, even if a labor dispute is the direct cause of the claim to a subsidy. For example, a small business in need of financial support because of labor troubles may seek a loan from the SBA. See 15 U.S.C. § 661 et seq. And a business that claims a net operating loss as a result of a strike or a lockout presumably may carry the loss back three years and forward five years in order to maximize its tax advantage. See 26 U.S.C. §§ 172, 381, 382. In addition, it appears that businesses may be eligible for special tax credits for hiring replacement workers during a strike under the Targeted Jobs Tax Credit program. See BNA Daily Labor Report No. 68, p. A–6 (April 10, 1987). When viewed against the network of governmental support of both labor and management, the withdrawal of the single support of food stamps—a support critical to the continued life and health of an individual worker and his or her family—cannot be seen as a "neutral" act. Altering the backdrop of governmental support in this one-sided and devastating way amounts to a penalty on strikers, not neutrality.

. . .

II

I agree with the Court that "[i]t was no part of the purposes of the Food Stamp Act to establish a program that would serve as a weapon in labor disputes." The striker amendment under consideration today, however, seems to have precisely that purpose—one admittedly irreconcilable with the legitimate goals of the food stamp program. No other purpose can adquately explain the especially harsh treatment reserved for strikers and their families by the 1981 enactment. Because I conclude that the striker amendment cannot survive even rational basis scrutiny, I would affirm the District Court's invalidation of the amendment. I dissent.

BANKERS LIFE AND CASUALTY CO. v. CRENSHAW, 108 S.Ct. 1645 (1988). A Mississippi statute imposed a 15% penalty on parties who appeal unsuccessfully from a money judgment or other judgments whose value may readily be determined. An insurance company which lost on appeal from a money judgment claimed that this penalty provision violated the equal protection clause. The seven Justices sitting (Justices Stevens and Kennedy did not take part) unanimously rejected this claim, saying:

"Appellant argues that the penalty statute violates the Equal Protection Clause of the Fourteenth Amendment because it singles out appellants from money judgments, and because it penalizes all such

appellants who are unsuccessful, regardless of the merit of their appeal.
. . .

"Under this Court's equal protection jurisprudence, Mississippi's statute is 'presumed to be valid and will be sustained if the classification . . . is rationally related to a legitimate state interest.' Cleburne v. Cleburne Living Center, Inc., 473 U.S. 432, 440 (1985). The state interests assertedly served by the Mississippi statute were detailed by the Mississippi Supreme Court in Walters v. Inexco Oil Co., 440 So.2d 268 (1983). The penalty statute, some version of which has been part of Mississippi law since 1857, 'expresses the state's interest in discouraging frivolous appeals. It likewise expresses a bona fide interest in providing a measure of compensation for the successful appellee, compensation for his having endured the slings and arrows of successful appellate litigation.' In a similar vein, the statute protects the integrity of judgments by discouraging appellant-defendants from prolonging the litigation merely to 'squeeze a favorable settlement out of an impecunious' appellee. Also, the penalty statute tells the litigants that the trial itself is a momentous event, the centerpiece of the litigation, not just a first step weighing station en route to endless rehearings and reconsiderations. Finally, in part because it serves these other goals, the penalty statute furthers the State's interest in conserving judicial resources.

"The legitimacy of these state interests cannot seriously be doubted, and this Court has upheld statutes that serve similar interests. . . . The statute therefore offends the Equal Protection Clause only if the legislative means that Mississippi has chosen are not rationally related to these legitimate interests.

"In arguing that § 11–3–23 violates equal protection, appellant seeks to draw support from the Court's opinion in *Lindsey v. Normet,* [405 U.S. 56 (1972)] *Lindsey* addressed the constitutionality of an Oregon statute that required tenants challenging eviction proceedings to post a bond of twice the amount of rent expected to accrue pending appellate review. The bond was forfeited to the landlord if the lower court decision was affirmed. We agreed with the appellants that the double-bond requirement violated the Equal Protection Clause. We noted that the requirement was 'unrelated to actual rent accrued or to specific damage sustained by the landlord.' 405 U.S., at 77. Moreover, the requirement, which burdened only tenants, including tenants whose appeals were nonfrivolous, erected 'a substantial barrier to appeal faced by no other civil litigant in Oregon.' We therefore concluded that the requirement bore 'no reasonable relationship to any valid state objective' and that it discriminated against the class of tenants appealing from adverse decisions in wrongful-detainer actions in an 'arbitrary and irrational' fashion.

"As *Lindsey* demonstrates, arbitrary and irrational discrimination violates the Equal Protection Clause under even our most deferential standard of review. Unlike the statute in *Lindsey,* however, Mississippi's penalty statute does not single out a class of appellants in an arbitrary and irrational fashion. First, whereas the statute in *Lindsey* singled out the narrow class of defendant-tenants for discriminatory treatment, the sweep of § 11–3–23 is far broader: the penalty applies both to plaintiffs and defendants, and it also applies to all money judgments as well as to a long list of judgments whose money value may readily be determined. Second, and more generally, there is a rational connection between the statute's objective and Mississippi's choice to impose a penalty only on appellants from money judgments or judgments the money value of which can readily be determined. If Mississippi wanted similarly to deter frivolous appeals from other kinds of judgments, it either would have to erect a fixed bond that bore no relation to the value of the underlying suit, or else it would have to set appropriate penalties in each case using some kind of individualized procedure, which would impose a considerable cost in judicial resources, exactly what the statute aims to avoid. Mississippi instead has chosen a partial solution that will deter many, though not all, frivolous appeals without requiring a significant commitment of governmental resources. Appellants from money judgments, and from the other types of judgments delineated in the statute, are a rational target of this scheme because the value of their claims, and thus of a proportional penalty, may be readily computed without substantial judicial intervention. . . . The Constitution does not forbid Mississippi from singling out a group of litigants that it rationally concludes is most likely to be deterred from bringing meritless claims at the least cost to the State.

"In addition, Mississippi's statute is less likely than was the statute in *Lindsey* to discourage substantial appeals along with insubstantial ones. Because the penalty operates only after a judgment has been affirmed without modification, there is less risk than in *Lindsey* of discouraging appellants who believe they have meritorious appeals but simply lack the funds to post a substantial bond during the appellate process. And whereas the assessment in *Lindsey* 'automatically doubled the stakes,' 405 U.S. at 79, the 15% penalty here is a relatively modest additional assessment. . . . Although Mississippi may not have succeeded in eliminating all danger of deterring meritorious claims, we cannot say that the residual danger is sufficient to render the statutory scheme irrational.

"In short, unlike the double-bond provision condemned in *Lindsey*, the means chosen in § 11–3–23 are reasonably related to the achievement of the State's objectives of discouraging frivolous appeals, compensating appellees for the intangible costs of litigation, and conserving judicial resources. See *Lindsey*, supra, at 70. It of course is possible that Mississippi might have enacted a statute that more precisely serves these goals and these goals only; as we frequently have explained, however, a state statute need not be so perfectly calibrated in order to pass muster under the rational basis test. See, e.g., Vance v. Bradley, 440 U.S. 93, 108 (1979). We are satisfied that the means that the State has chosen are 'reasonably tailored to achieve [the State's legitimate] ends.' *Lindsey*, supra, at 78. We therefore affirm the judgment of the Mississippi Supreme Court denying appellant's equal protection challenge to § 11–3–23."

SECTION 3. SUSPECT CLASSIFICATIONS

D. CLASSIFICATIONS DISADVANTAGING NON–MARITAL CHILDREN

Page 706. Add ahead of note, "Parental Rights of Fathers of Illegitimate Children":

CLARK v. JETER, 108 S.Ct. 1910 (1988). Under Pennsylvania law an illegitimate child must prove paternity before seeking support from his or her father, and a suit to establish paternity normally must be brought within six years of an illegitimate child's birth. A legitimate child, by contrast, may seek support from his or her parents at any time. The Supreme Court unanimously held that the six year limitation on paternity suits by illegitimate children was invalid as a denial of the equal protection of the laws. The Court said that discriminatory classifications based on sex or illegitimacy are reviewed under a level of intermediate scrutiny and that to withstand that scrutiny "a statutory classification must be substantially related to an important government objective." The Court said that the six year limit here was invalid, relying on Pickett v. Brown which overturned a two-year limit. The court did not directly address the question of what limit would be held valid.

F. ARE THERE OTHER SUSPECT CLASSIFICATIONS?

Page 750. Add ahead of Wealth Classifications:

CITY OF CLEBURNE v. CLEBURNE LIVING CENTER
473 U.S. 432, 105 S.Ct. 3249, 87 L.Ed.2d 313 (1985).

Justice White delivered the opinion of the Court.

A Texas city denied a special use permit for the operation of a group home for the mentally retarded, acting pursuant to a municipal zoning ordinance requiring permits for such homes. The Court of Appeals for the Fifth Circuit held that mental retardation is a "quasi-suspect" classification and that the ordinance violated the Equal Protection Clause because it did not substantially further an important governmental purpose. We hold that a lesser standard of scrutiny is appropriate, but conclude that under that standard the ordinance is invalid as applied in this case.

I

In July, 1980, respondent Jan Hannah purchased a building at 201 Featherston Street in the city of Cleburne, Texas, with the intention of leasing it to Cleburne Living Centers, Inc. (CLC), for the operation of a group home for the mentally retarded. It was anticipated that the home would house 13 retarded men and women, who would be under the constant supervision of CLC staff members. The house had four bedrooms and two baths, with a half bath to be added. CLC planned to comply with all applicable state and federal regulations.

The city informed CLC that a special use permit would be required for the operation of a group home at the site, and CLC accordingly submitted a permit application. In response to a subsequent inquiry from CLC, the city explained that under the zoning regulations applicable to the site, a special use permit, renewable annually, was required for the construction of "[h]ospitals for the insane or feeble-minded, or alcoholic [sic] or drug addicts, or penal or correctional institutions." The city had determined that the proposed group home should be classified as a "hospital for the feeble-minded." After holding a public hearing on CLC's application, the city council voted three to one to deny a special use permit.

CLC then filed suit in Federal District Court against the city and a number of its officials, alleging, *inter alia,* that the zoning ordinance was invalid on its face and as applied because it discriminated against the mentally retarded in violation of the equal protection rights of CLC and its potential residents. . . . The court deemed the ordinance, as written and applied, to be rationally related to the City's legitimate interests in "the legal responsibility of CLC and its residents, . . . the safety and fears of residents in the adjoining neighborhood," and the number of people to be housed in the home.

The Court of Appeals for the Fifth Circuit reversed, determining that mental retardation was a quasi-suspect classification and that it should assess the validity of the ordinance under intermediate-level scrutiny. . . . Applying the test that it considered appropriate, the court held that the ordinance was invalid on its face because it did not substantially further any important governmental interests. The Court of Appeals went on to hold that the ordinance was also invalid as applied. . . .

II

. . . When social or economic legislation is at issue, the Equal Protection Clause allows the states wide latitude, United States Railroad Retirement Board v. Fritz, supra, at 174; New Orleans v. Dukes, supra, at 303, and the Constitution presumes that even improvident decisions will eventually be rectified by the democratic processes.

The general rule gives way, however, when a statute classifies by race, alienage or national origin. These factors are so seldom relevant to the achievement of any legitimate state interest that laws grounded in such considerations are deemed to reflect prejudice and antipathy—a view that those in the burdened class are not as worthy or deserving as others. . . .

Legislative classifications based on gender also call for a heightened standard of review. . . . Rather than resting on meaningful considerations, statutes distributing benefits and burdens between the sexes in different ways very likely reflect outmoded notions of the relative capabilities of men and women . . .. Because illegitimacy is beyond the individual's control and bears "no relation to the individual's ability to participate in and contribute to society," Mathews v. Lucas, 427 U.S. 495, 505 (1976), official discriminations resting on that characteristic are also subject to somewhat heightened review. . . .

We have declined, however, to extend heightened review to differential treatment based on age . . ..

. . .

The lesson of *Murgia* is that where individuals in the group affected by a law have distinguishing characteristics relevant to interests the state has the authority to implement, the courts have been very reluctant, as they should be in our federal system and with our respect for the separation of powers, to closely scrutinize legislative choices as to whether, how and to what extent those interests should be pursued. In such cases, the Equal Protection Clause requires only a rational means to serve a legitimate end.

III

Against this background, we conclude for several reasons that the Court of Appeals erred in holding mental retardation a quasi-suspect classification calling for a more exacting standard of judicial review than is normally accorded economic and social legislation. First, it is undeniable, and it is not argued otherwise here, that those who are mentally retarded have a reduced ability to cope with and function in the everyday world. Nor are they all cut from the same pattern: as the testimony in this record indicates, they range from those whose disability is not immediately evident to those who must be constantly cared for. They are thus different, immutably so, in relevant respects, and the states' interest in dealing with and providing for them is plainly a legitimate one.[10] How this large and diversified group is to be treated under the law is a difficult and often a technical matter, very much a task for legislators guided by qualified professionals and not by the perhaps ill-informed opinions of the judiciary. Heightened scrutiny inevitably involves substantive judgments about legislative decisions, and we doubt that the predicate for such judicial oversight is present where the classification deals with mental retardation.

Second, the distinctive legislative response, both national and state, to the plight of those who are mentally retarded demonstrates not only that they have unique problems, but also that the lawmakers have been addressing their difficulties in a manner that belies a continuing

[10] As Dean Ely has observed:

"Surely one has to feel sorry for a person disabled by something he or she can't do anything about, but I'm not aware of any reason to suppose that elected officials are unusually unlikely to share that feeling. Moreover, classifications based on physical disability and intelligence are typically accepted as legitimate, even by judges and commentators who assert that immutability is relevant. The explanation, when one is given, is that *those* characteristics (unlike the one the commentator is trying to render suspect) are often relevant to legitimate purposes. At that point there's not much left of the immutability theory, is there?" J. Ely, Democracy and Distrust 150 (1980) (footnote omitted). See also id., at 154–155.

antipathy or prejudice and a corresponding need for more intrusive oversight by the judiciary. Thus, the federal government has not only outlawed discrimination against the mentally retarded in federally funded programs, see § 504 of the Rehabilitation Act of 1973, 29 U.S.C. § 794, but it has also provided the retarded with the right to receive "appropriate treatment, services, and habilitation" in a setting that is "least restrictive of [their] personal liberty." Developmental Disabilities Assistance and Bill of Rights Act, 42 U.S.C. §§ 6010(1), (2). In addition, the government has conditioned federal education funds on a State's assurance that retarded children will enjoy an education that, "to the maximum extent appropriate," is integrated with that of non-mentally retarded children. Education of the Handicapped Act, 20 U.S.C. § 1412(5)(B). The government has also facilitated the hiring of the mentally retarded into the federal civil service by exempting them from the requirement of competitive examination. See 5 CFR § 213.3102(t) (1984). The State of Texas has similarly enacted legislation that acknowledges the special status of the mentally retarded by conferring certain rights upon them, such as "the right to live in the least restrictive setting appropriate to [their] individual needs and abilities," including "the right to live . . . in a group home." Mentally Retarded Persons Act of 1977, Tex.Rev.Civ.Stat.Ann., Art. 5547–300, § 7 (Vernon Supp.1985).

Such legislation thus singling out the retarded for special treatment reflects the real and undeniable differences between the retarded and others. That a civilized and decent society expects and approves such legislation indicates that governmental consideration of those differences in the vast majority of situations is not only legitimate but desirable. It may be, as CLC contends, that legislation designed to benefit, rather than disadvantage, the retarded would generally withstand examination under a test of heightened scrutiny. The relevant inquiry, however, is whether heightened scrutiny is constitutionally mandated in the first instance. Even assuming that many of these laws could be shown to be substantially related to an important governmental purpose, merely requiring the legislature to justify its efforts in these terms may lead it to refrain from acting at all. Much recent legislation intended to benefit the retarded also assumes the need for measures that might be perceived to disadvantage them. The Education of the Handicapped Act, for example, requires an "appropriate" education, not one that is equal in all respects to the education of non-retarded children; clearly, admission to a class that exceeded the abilities of a retarded child would not be appropriate. Similarly, the Developmental Disabilities Assistance Act and the Texas act give the retarded the right to live only in the "least restrictive setting" appropriate to their abilities, implicitly assuming the need for at least some restrictions that would not be imposed on others. Especially given the wide variation in the abilities and needs of the retarded themselves, governmental bodies must have a certain amount of flexibility and freedom from judicial oversight in shaping and limiting their remedial efforts.

Third, the legislative response, which could hardly have occurred and survived without public support, negates any claim that the mentally retarded are politically powerless in the sense that they have no ability to attract the attention of the lawmakers. Any minority can be said to be powerless to assert direct control over the legislature, but if that were a criterion for higher level scrutiny by the courts, much economic and social legislation would now be suspect.

Fourth, if the large and amorphous class of the mentally retarded were deemed quasi-suspect for the reasons given by the Court of Appeals, it would be difficult to find a principled way to distinguish a variety of other groups who have perhaps immutable disabilities setting them off from others, who cannot themselves mandate the desired legislative responses, and who can claim some degree of prejudice from at least part of the public at large. One need mention in this respect only the aging, the disabled, the mentally ill, and the infirm. We are reluctant to set out on that course, and we decline to do so.

Doubtless, there have been and there will continue to be instances of discrimination against the retarded that are in fact invidious, and that are properly subject to judicial correction under constitutional norms. But the appropriate method of reaching such instances is not to create a new quasi-suspect classification and subject all governmental action based on that classification to more searching evaluation. Rather, we should look to the likelihood that governmental action premised on a particular classification is valid as a general matter, not merely to the specifics of the case before us. Because mental retardation is a characteristic that the government may legitimately take into account in a wide range of decisions, and because both state and federal governments have recently committed themselves to assisting the retarded, we will not presume that any given legislative action, even one that disadvantages retarded individuals, is rooted in considerations that the Constitution will not tolerate.

Our refusal to recognize the retarded as a quasi-suspect class does not leave them entirely unprotected from invidious discrimination. To withstand equal protection review, legislation that distinguishes between the mentally retarded and others must be rationally related to a legitimate governmental purpose. This standard, we believe, affords government the latitude necessary both to pursue policies designed to assist the retarded in realizing their full potential, and to freely and efficiently engage in activities that burden the retarded in what is essentially an incidental manner. . . ..

IV

We turn to the issue of the validity of the zoning ordinance insofar as it requires a special use permit for homes for the mentally retarded.[14] We inquire first whether requiring a special use permit for the Featherston home in the circumstances here deprives respondents of the equal protection of the laws. If it does, there will be no occasion to

[14] It goes without saying that there is nothing before us with respect to the validity of requiring a special use permit for the other uses listed in the ordinance.

decide whether the special use permit provision is facially invalid where the mentally retarded are involved, or to put it another way, whether the city may never insist on a special use permit for a home for the mentally retarded in an R-3 zone. This is the preferred course of adjudication since it enables courts to avoid making unnecessarily broad constitutional judgments. . . .

The constitutional issue is clearly posed. The City does not require a special use permit in an R-3 zone for apartment houses, multiple dwellings, boarding and lodging houses, fraternity or sorority houses, dormitories, apartment hotels, hospitals, sanitariums, nursing homes for convalescents or the aged (other than for the insane or feeble-minded or alcoholics or drug addicts), private clubs or fraternal orders, and other specified uses. It does, however, insist on a special permit for the Featherston home, and it does so, as the District Court found, because it would be a facility for the mentally retarded. May the city require the permit for this facility when other care and multiple dwelling facilities are freely permitted?

It is true, as already pointed out, that the mentally retarded as a group are indeed different from others not sharing their misfortune, and in this respect they may be different from those who would occupy other facilities that would be permitted in an R-3 zone without a special permit. But this difference is largely irrelevant unless the Featherston home and those who would occupy it would threaten legitimate interests of the city in a way that other permitted uses such as boarding houses and hospitals would not. Because in our view the record does not reveal any rational basis for believing that the Feather-ston home would pose any special threat to the city's legitimate interests, we affirm the judgment below insofar as it holds the ordinance invalid as applied in this case.

The District Court found that the City Council's insistence on the permit rested on several factors. First, the Council was concerned with the negative attitude of the majority of property owners located within 200 feet of the Featherston facility, as well as with the fears of elderly residents of the neighborhood. But mere negative attitudes, or fear, unsubstantiated by factors which are properly cognizable in a zoning proceeding, are not permissible bases for treating a home for the mentally retarded differently from apartment houses, multiple dwellings, and the like. It is plain that the electorate as a whole, whether by referendum or otherwise, could not order city action violative of the Equal Protection Clause, Lucas v. Forty-Fourth General Assembly of Colorado, 377 U.S. 713, 736-737 (1964), and the City may not avoid the strictures of that Clause by deferring to the wishes or objections of some fraction of the body politic. "Private biases may be outside the reach of the law, but the law cannot, directly or indirectly, give them effect." Palmore v. Sidoti, 466 U.S. 429, 433 (1984).

Second, the Council had two objections to the location of the facility. It was concerned that the facility was across the street from a junior high school, and it feared that the students might harass the occupants of the Featherston home. But the school itself is attended by about 30 mentally retarded students, and denying a permit based on such vague, undifferentiated fears is again permitting some portion of the community to validate what would otherwise be an equal protection violation. The other objection to the home's location was that it was located on "a five hundred year flood plain." This concern with the possibility of a flood, however, can hardly be based on a distinction between the Featherston home and, for example, nursing homes, homes for convalescents or the aged, or sanitariums or hospitals, any of which could be located on the Featherston site without obtaining a special use permit. The same may be said of another concern of the Council— doubts about the legal responsibility for actions which the mentally retarded might take. If there is no concern about legal responsibility with respect to other uses that would be permitted in the area, such as boarding and fraternity houses, it is difficult to believe that the groups of mildly or moderately mentally retarded individuals who would live at 201 Featherston would present any different or special hazard.

Fourth, the Council was concerned with the size of the home and the number of people that would occupy it. The District Court found, and the Court of Appeals repeated, that "[i]f the potential residents of the Featherston Street home were not mentally retarded, but the home was the same in all other respects, its use would be permitted under the city's zoning ordinance." Given this finding, there would be no restrictions on the number of people who could occupy this home as a boarding house, nursing home, family dwelling, fraternity house, or dormitory. The question is whether it is rational to treat the mentally retarded differently. It is true that they suffer disability not shared by others; but why this difference warrants a density regulation that others need not observe is not at all apparent. At least this record does not clarify how, in this connection, the characteristics of the intended occupants of the Featherston home rationally justify denying to those occupants what would be permitted to groups occupying the same site for different purposes. Those who would live in the Featherston home are the type of individuals who, with supporting staff, satisfy federal and state standards for group housing in the community; and there is no dispute that the home would meet the federal square-footage-per-resident requirement for facilities of this type. See 42 CFR § 442.447 (1984). In the words of the Court of Appeals, "The City never justifies its apparent view that other people can live under such 'crowded' conditions when mentally retarded persons cannot."

In the courts below the city also urged that the ordinance is aimed at avoiding concentration of population and at lessening congestion of the streets. These concerns obviously fail to explain why apartment houses, fraternity and sorority houses, hospitals and the like, may freely locate in the area without a permit. So, too, the expressed worry about fire hazards, the serenity of the neighborhood, and the avoidance of danger to other residents fail rationally to justify singling out a home such as 201 Featherston for the special use permit, yet imposing no such restrictions on the many other uses freely permitted in the neighborhood.

The short of it is that requiring the permit in this case appears to us to rest on an irrational prejudice against the mentally retarded, including those who would occupy the Featherston facility and who would live under the closely supervised and highly regulated conditions expressly provided for by state and federal law.

The judgment of the Court of Appeals is affirmed insofar as it invalidates the zoning ordinance as applied to the Featherston home. The judgment is otherwise vacated.

It is so ordered.

Justice Stevens, with whom The Chief Justice joins, concurring.

The Court of Appeals disposed of this case as if a critical question to be decided were which of three clearly defined standards of equal protection review should be applied to a legislative classification discriminating against the mentally retarded. In fact, our cases have not delineated three—or even one or two—such well defined standards. Rather, our cases reflect a continuum of judgmental responses to differing classifications which have been explained in opinions by terms ranging from "strict scrutiny" at one extreme to "rational basis" at the other. I have never been persuaded that these so called "standards" adequately explain the decisional process. Cases involving classifications based on alienage, illegal residency, illegitimacy, gender, age, or—as in this case—mental retardation, do not fit well into sharply defined classifications.

. . .

Every law that places the mentally retarded in a special class is not presumptively irrational. The differences between mentally retarded persons and those with greater mental capacity are obviously relevant to certain legislative decisions. An impartial lawmaker—indeed, even a member of a class of persons defined as mentally retarded—could rationally vote in favor of a law providing funds for special education and special treatment for the mentally retarded. A mentally retarded person could also recognize that he is a member of a class that might need special supervision in some situations, both to protect himself and to protect others. Restrictions on his right to drive cars or to operate hazardous equipment might well seem rational even though they deprived him of employment opportunities and the kind of freedom of travel enjoyed by other citizens. . . .

Even so, the Court of Appeals correctly observed that through ignorance and prejudice the mentally retarded "have been subjected to a history of unfair and often grotesque mistreatment." The discrimination against the mentally retarded that is at issue in this case is the city's decision to require an annual special use permit before property in an apartment house district may be used as a group home for persons who are mildly retarded. The record convinces me that this permit was required because of the irrational fears of neighboring property owners, rather than for the protection of the mentally retarded persons who would reside in respondent's home.

Although the city argued in the Court of Appeals that legitimate interests of the neighbors justified the restriction, the court unambiguously rejected that argument. In this Court, the city has argued that the discrimination was really motivated by a desire to protect the mentally retarded from the hazards presented by the neighborhood. Zoning ordinances are not usually justified on any such basis, and in this case, for the reasons explained by the Court, I find that justification wholly unconvincing. I cannot believe that a rational member of this disadvantaged class could ever approve of the discriminatory application of the city's ordinance in this case.

Accordingly, I join the opinion of the Court.

Justice Marshall, with whom Justice Brennan and Justice Blackmun join, concurring in the judgment in part and dissenting in part.

The Court holds that all retarded individuals cannot be grouped together as the "feebleminded" and deemed presumptively unfit to live in a community. Underlying this holding is the principle that mental retardation per se cannot be a proxy for depriving retarded people of their rights and interests without regard to variations in individual ability. With this holding and principle I agree. The equal protection clause requires attention to the capacities and needs of retarded people as individuals.

I cannot agree, however, with the way in which the Court reaches its result or with the narrow, as-applied remedy it provides for the City of Cleburne's equal protection violation. The Court holds the ordinance invalid on rational basis grounds and disclaims that anything special, in the form of heightened scrutiny, is taking place. Yet Cleburne's ordinance surely would be valid under the traditional rational basis test applicable to economic and commercial regulation. In my view, it is important to articulate, as the Court does not, the facts and principles that justify subjecting this zoning ordinance to the searching review— the heightened scrutiny—that actually leads to its invalidation. Moreover, in invalidating Cleburne's exclusion of the "feebleminded" only as applied to respondents, rather than on its face, the Court radically departs from our equal protection precedents. Because I dissent from this novel and truncated remedy, and because I cannot accept the Court's disclaimer that no "more exacting standard" than ordinary rational basis review is being applied, I write separately.

I

. . .

. . . [H]owever labelled, the rational basis test invoked today is most assuredly not the rational basis test of Williamson v. Lee Optical, 348 U.S. 483 (1955), Allied Stores v. Bowers, 358 U.S. 522 (1959), and their progeny.

. . .

I share the Court's criticisms of the overly broad lines that Cleburne's zoning ordinance has drawn. But if the ordinance is to be invalidated for its imprecise classifications, it must be pursuant to more powerful scrutiny than the minimal rational-basis test used to review classifications affecting only economic and commercial matters. The same imprecision in a similar ordinance that required opticians but not optometrists to be licensed to practice, see Williamson v. Lee Optical Co., supra, or that excluded new but not old businesses from parts of a community, see New Orleans v. Dukes, supra, would hardly be fatal to the statutory scheme.

The refusal to acknowledge that something more than minimum rationality review is at work here is, in my view, unfortunate in at least two respects. The suggestion that the traditional rational basis test allows this sort of searching inquiry creates precedent for this Court and lower courts to subject economic and commercial classifications to similar and searching "ordinary" rational basis review—a small and regrettable step back toward the days of Lochner v. New York, 198 U.S. 75 (1905). Moreover, by failing to articulate the factors that justify today's "second order" rational basis review, the Court provides no principled foundation for determining when more searching inquiry is to be invoked. Lower courts are thus left in the dark on this important question, and this Court remains unaccountable for its decisions employing, or refusing to employ, particularly searching scrutiny. Candor requires me to acknowledge the particular factors that justify invalidating Cleburne's zoning ordinance under the careful scrutiny it today receives.

II

I have long believed the level of scrutiny employed in an equal protection case should vary with "the constitutional and societal importance of the interest adversely affected and the recognized invidiousness of the basis upon which the particular classification is drawn." San Antonio Independent School District v. Rodriguez, 411 U.S. 1, 99 (1973) (Marshall, J., dissenting). . . . When a zoning ordinance works to exclude the retarded from all residential districts in a community, these two considerations require that the ordinance be convincingly justified as substantially furthering legitimate and important purposes.

. . .

First, the interest of the retarded in establishing group homes is substantial. The right to "establish a home" has long been cherished as one of the fundamental liberties embraced by the Due Process Clause. See Meyer v. Nebraska, 262 U.S. 390, 399 (1923). For retarded adults, this right means living together in group homes, for as deinstitutionalization has progressed, group homes have become the primary means by which retarded adults can enter life in the community.

. . .

Second, the mentally retarded have been subject to a "lengthy and tragic history," University of California Regents v. Bakke, 438 U.S. 265, 303 (1978) (opinion of Powell, J.), of segregation and discrimination that can only be called grotesque. During much of the nineteenth century, mental retardation was viewed as neither curable nor dangerous and the retarded were largely left to their own devices. By the latter part of the century and during the first decades of the new one, however, social views of the retarded underwent a radical transformation. Fueled by the rising tide of Social Darwinism, the "science" of eugenics, and the extreme xenophobia of those years, leading medical authorities and others began to portray the "feeble minded" as a "menace to society and civilization . . . responsible in a large degree for many, if not all, of our social problems." A regime of state-mandated segregation and degradation soon emerged that in its virulence and bigotry rivaled, and indeed paralleled, the worst excesses of Jim Crow. Massive custodial institutions were built to warehouse the retarded for life; the aim was to halt reproduction of the retarded and "nearly extinguish their race." Retarded children were categorically excluded from public schools, based on the false stereotype that all were ineducable and on the purported need to protect nonretarded children from them. State laws deemed the retarded "unfit for citizenship."

Segregation was accompanied by eugenic marriage and sterilization laws that extinguished for the retarded one of the "basic civil rights of man"—the right to marry and procreate. Skinner v. Oklahoma, 316 U.S. 535, 541 (1942). Marriages of the retarded were made, and in some states continue to be, not only voidable but also often a criminal offense. The purpose of such limitations, which frequently applied only to women of child bearing age, was unabashedly eugenic: to prevent the retarded from propagating. To assure this end, 29 states enacted compulsory eugenic sterilization laws between 1907 and 1931. J. Landman, Human Sterilization 302–303 (1932). See Buck v. Bell, 274 U.S. 200, 207 (1927) (Holmes, J.); cf. Plessy v. Ferguson, 163 U.S. 537 (1896); Bradwell v. Illinois, 16 Wall. 130, 141 (1873) (Bradley, J., concurring in judgment).

Prejudice, once let loose, is not easily cabined. . . . As of 1979, most states still categorically disqualified "idiots" from voting, without regard to individual capacity and with discretion to exclude left in the hands of low-level election officials. Not until Congress enacted the Education of the Handicapped Act, 84 Stat. 175, as amended 20 U.S.C. § 1401 et seq. (1976 and Supp. IV) were "the door[s] of public education" opened wide to handicapped children. Hendrick Hudson District Board of Education v. Rowley, 458 U.S. 176, 192 (1982). But most important, lengthy and continuing isolation of the retarded has perpetuated the ignorance, irrational fears, and stereotyping that long have plagued them.

In light of the importance of the interest at stake and the history of discrimination the retarded have suffered, the Equal Protection Clause requires us to do more than review the distinctions drawn by Cleburne's zoning ordinance as if they appeared in a taxing statute or in economic or commercial legislation.[17] The searching scrutiny I would give to restrictions on the ability of the retarded to establish

---

[17] This history of discrimination may well be directly relevant to the issue before the Court. Cleburne's current exclusion of the "feeble minded" in its 1965 zoning ordinance appeared as a similar exclusion of the "feeble minded" in the City's 1947 ordinance, see Act of Sept. 26, 1947 § 5; the latter tracked word for word a similar exclusion in the 1929

community group homes leads me to conclude that Cleburne's vague generalizations for classifying the "feeble minded" with drug addicts, alcoholics, and the insane, and excluding them where the elderly, the ill, the boarder, and the transient are allowed, are not substantial or important enough to overcome the suspicion that the ordinance rests on impermissible assumptions or outmoded and perhaps invidious stereotypes. . . .

III

. . .

The Court downplays the lengthy "history of purposeful unequal treatment" of the retarded, . . . by pointing to recent legislative action that is said to "beli[e] a continuing antipathy or prejudice." Building on this point, the Court similarly concludes that the retarded are not "politically powerless" and deserve no greater judicial protection than "any minority" that wins some political battles and loses others. The import of these conclusions, it seems, is that the only discrimination courts may remedy is the discrimination they alone are perspicacious enough to see. Once society begins to recognize certain practices as discriminatory, in part because previously stigmatized groups have mobilized politically to lift this stigma, the Court would refrain from approaching such practices with the added skepticism of heightened scrutiny.

Courts, however, do not sit or act in a social vacuum. Moral philosophers may debate whether certain inequalities are absolute wrongs, but history makes clear that constitutional principles of equality, like constitutional principles of liberty, property, and due process, evolve over time; what once was a "natural" and "self-evident" ordering later comes to be seen as an artificial and invidious constraint on human potential and freedom. . . . Shifting cultural, political, and social patterns at times come to make past practices appear inconsistent with fundamental principles upon which American society rests, an inconsistency legally cognizable under the Equal Protection Clause. It is natural that evolving standards of equality come to be embodied in legislation. When that occurs, courts should look to the fact of such change as a source of guidance on evolving principles of equality. . . .

. . .

comprehensive zoning ordinance for the nearby City of Dallas. See Dallas Ordinance, No. 2052, § 4, passed Sept. 11, 1929.

Although we have been presented with no legislative history for Cleburne's zoning ordinances, this genealogy strongly suggests that Cleburne's current exclusion of the "feeble minded" was written in the darkest days of segregation and stigmatization of the retarded and simply carried over to the current ordinance. Recently we held that extant laws originally motivated by a discriminatory purpose continue to violate the Equal Protection Clause, even if they would be permissible were they reenacted without a discriminatory motive. See Hunter v. Underwood, —— U.S. ——, —— (1985). But in any event, the roots of a law that by its terms excludes from a community the "feeble minded" are clear. As the examples above attest, "feeble minded" was the defining term for all retarded people in the era of overt and pervasive discrimination.

Moreover, even when judicial action *has* catalyzed legislative change, that change certainly does not eviscerate the underlying constitutional principle. The Court, for example, has never suggested that race-based classifications became any less suspect once extensive legislation had been enacted on the subject. See Palmore v. Sidoti, 466 U.S. 429 (1984).

For the retarded, just as for Negroes and women, much has changed in recent years, but much remains the same; out-dated statutes are still on the books, and irrational fears or ignorance, traceable to the prolonged social and cultural isolation of the retarded, continue to stymie recognition of the dignity and individuality of retarded people. Heightened judicial scrutiny of action appearing to impose unnecessary barriers to the retarded is required in light of increasing recognition that such barriers are inconsistent with evolving principles of equality embedded in the Fourteenth Amendment.

The Court also offers a more general view of heightened scrutiny, a view focused primarily on when heightened scrutiny does *not* apply as opposed to when it does apply. Two principles appear central to the Court's theory. First, heightened scrutiny is said to be inapplicable where *individuals* in a group have distinguishing characteristics that legislatures properly may take into account in some circumstances. Heightened scrutiny is also purportedly inappropriate when many legislative classifications affecting the *group* are likely to be valid. . . .

If the Court's first principle were sound, heightened scrutiny would have to await a day when people could be cut from a cookie mold. Women are hardly alike in all their characteristics, but heightened scrutiny applies to them because legislatures can rarely use gender itself as a proxy for these other characteristics. . . . Similarly, that some retarded people have reduced capacities in some areas does not justify using retardation as a proxy for reduced capacity in areas where relevant individual variations in capacity do exist.

The Court's second assertion—that the standard of review must be fixed with reference to the number of classifications to which a characteristic would validly be relevant—is similarly flawed. Certainly the assertion is not a logical one; that a characteristic may be relevant under some or even many circumstances does not suggest any reason to presume it relevant under other circumstances where there is reason to suspect it is not. A sign that says "men only" looks very different on a bathroom door than a courthouse door. . . .

. . .

Potentially discriminatory classifications exist only where some constitutional basis can be found for presuming that equal rights are required. Discrimination, in the Fourteenth Amendment sense, connotes a substantive constitutional judgment that two individuals or groups are entitled to be treated equally with respect to some thing. With regard to economic and commercial matters, no basis for such a conclusion exists, for as Justice Holmes urged the *Lochner* Court, the Fourteenth Amendment was not "intended to embody a particular economic theory . . .". Lochner v. New York, 198 U.S. 75 (1905) (Holmes, J., dissenting). As a matter of substantive policy, therefore, government is free to move in any direction, or to change directions, in the economic and commercial sphere. The structure of economic and commercial life is a matter of political compromise, not constitutional principle, and no norm of equality requires that there be as many opticians as optometrists, see Williamson v. Lee Optical, supra, or new businesses as old, see New Orleans v. Dukes, supra.

. . .

IV

In light of the scrutiny that should be applied here, Cleburne's ordinance sweeps too broadly to dispel the suspicion that it rests on a bare desire to treat the retarded as outsiders, pariahs who do not belong in the community. The Court, while disclaiming that special scrutiny is necessary or warranted, reaches the same conclusion. Rather than striking the ordinance down, however, the Court invalidates it merely as applied to respondents. I must dissent from the novel proposition that "the preferred course of adjudication" is to leave standing a legislative act resting on "irrational prejudice" thereby forcing individuals in the group discriminated against to continue to run the act's gauntlet.

. . .

Invalidating on its face the ordinance's special treatment of the "feebleminded", in contrast, would place the responsibility for tailoring and updating Cleburne's unconstitutional ordinance where it belongs: with the legislative arm of the City of Cleburne. If Cleburne perceives a legitimate need for requiring a certain well-defined subgroup of the retarded to obtain special permits before establishing group homes, Cleburne will, after studying the problem and making the appropriate policy decisions, enact a new, more narrowly tailored ordinance. That ordinance might well look very different from the current one; it might separate group homes (presently treated nowhere in the ordinance) from hospitals, and it might define a narrow sub-class of the retarded for whom even group homes could legitimately be excluded. Special treatment of the retarded might be ended altogether. But whatever the contours such an ordinance might take, the city should not be allowed to keep its ordinance on the books intact and thereby shift to the courts the responsibility to confront the complex empirical and policy questions involved in updating statutes affecting the mentally retarded. A legislative solution would yield standards and provide the sort of certainty to retarded applicants and administrative officials that case-by-case judicial rulings cannot provide. Retarded applicants should not have to continue to attempt to surmount Cleburne's vastly overbroad ordinance.

. . .

V

The Court's opinion approaches the task of principled equal protection adjudication in what I view as precisely the wrong way. The formal label under which an equal protection claim is reviewed is less important than careful identification of the interest at stake and the extent to which society recognizes the classification as an invidious one. Yet in focusing obsessively on the appropriate label to give its standard of review, the Court fails to identify the interests at stake or to articulate the principle that classifications based on mental retardation must be carefully examined to assure they do not rest on impermissible assumptions or false stereotypes regarding individual ability and need. No guidance is thereby given as to when the Court's freewheeling, and potentially dangerous, "rational basis standard" is to be employed, nor is attention directed to the invidiousness of grouping all retarded individuals together. Moreover, the Court's narrow, as-applied remedy fails to deal adequately with the overbroad presumption that lies at the heart of this case. Rather than leaving future retarded individuals to run the gauntlet of this overbroad presumption, I would affirm the judgment of the Court of Appeals in its entirety and would strike down on its face the provision at issue. I therefore concur in the judgment in part and dissent in part.

G. THE REQUIREMENT OF A DISCRIMINATORY PURPOSE—THE RELEVANCE OF DISCRIMINATORY IMPACT

Page 772. Add ahead of City of Memphis v. Greene:

HUNTER v. UNDERWOOD, 471 U.S. 222 (1985). Section 182 of the Alabama Constitution, adopted at a convention in 1901, disenfranchised persons convicted of, among other offenses, "any crime . . . involving moral turpitude." Edwards, a black, and Underwood, a white, have been blocked from the voter roles because they each have been convicted of presenting a worthless check. They brought suit in the federal district court contending that § 182 had been intentionally adopted to disenfranchise blacks on account of their race. On this issue the district court treated Edwards as the representative of a class of black members and ruled for the defendants. The court of appeals reversed, holding that the evidence showed that § 182 had disenfranchised 10 times as many blacks as whites, and that it had been adopted for the purpose of preventing blacks from voting. The Supreme Court affirmed, all joining an opinion by Justice Rehnquist, except for Justice Powell who took no part in the case.

The Court said first that a neutral state law that produces disproportionate effects along racial lines will be invalidated only if it is shown that racially discriminatory intent or purpose was a substantial factor behind enacting the law.

"Proving the motivation behind official action is often a problematic undertaking. See Rogers v. Lodge, 458 U.S. 613 (1982). When we move from an examination of a board of county commissioners such as was involved in *Rogers* to a body the size of the Alabama Constitutional Convention of 1901, the difficulties in determining the actual motivations of the various legislators that produced a given decision increase." But no such difficulties were present here. Evidence from historians and from speeches at the Convention make it clear that zeal for white supremacy ran rampant at the convention. Indeed, the appellants did not seriously dispute that fact. What appellants did argue was that the real purpose behind § 182 was to disenfranchise both poor whites and blacks.

"Even were we to accept this explanation as correct, it hardly saves § 182 from invalidity. The explanation concedes both that discrimination against blacks, as well as against poor whites, was a motivating factor for the provision and that § 182 certainly would not have been adopted by the convention or ratified by the electorate in the absence of the racially discriminatory motivation.

"Citing Palmer v. Thompson, 403 U.S., at 224, and Michael M. v. Superior Court of Sonoma County, 450 U.S. 464, 472, n. 7 (1981) (plurality opinion), appellants make the further argument that the existence of a permissible motive for § 182, namely the disenfranchisement of poor whites, trumps any proof of a parallel impermissible motive. Whether or not intentional disenfranchisement of poor whites would qualify as a 'permissible motive' within the meaning of *Palmer* and *Michael M.,* it is clear that where both impermissible racial motivation and racially discriminatory impact are demonstrated, *Arlington Heights* and *Mt. Healthy* supply the proper analysis. Under the view that the Court of Appeals could properly take of the evidence, an additional purpose to discriminate against poor whites would not render nugatory the purpose to discriminate against all blacks, and it is beyond peradventure that the latter was a 'but-for' motivation for the enactment of § 182.

. . .

"At oral argument in this Court, the State suggested that, regardless of the original purpose of § 182, events occurring in the succeeding 80 years had legitimated the provision. . . . Without deciding whether § 182 would be valid if enacted today without any impermissible motivation, we simply observe that its original enactment was motivated by a desire to discriminate against blacks on account of race and the section continues to this day to have that effect. As such, it violates equal protection under *Arlington Heights.*

"Finally, appellants contend that the State is authorized by the Tenth Amendment and § 2 of the Fourteenth Amendment to deny the franchise to persons who commit misdemeanors involving moral turpitude. For the reasons we have stated, the enactment of § 182 violated the Fourteenth Amendment, and the Tenth Amendment cannot save legislation prohibited by the subsequently enacted Fourteenth Amendment. The single remaining question is whether § 182 is excepted from the operation of the Equal Protection Clause of § 1 of the Fourteenth Amendment by the 'other crime' provision of § 2 of that Amendment. Without again considering the implicit authorization of § 2 to deny the vote to citizens 'for participation in rebellion, or other crime,' see Richardson v. Ramirez, 418 U.S. 24 (1974), we are confident that § 2 was not designed to permit the purposeful racial discrimination attending the enactment and operation of § 182 which otherwise violates § 1 of the Fourteenth Amendment. Nothing in our opinion in Richardson v. Ramirez, supra, suggests the contrary."

. . .

THORNBURG v. GINGLES, 478 U.S. 30 (1986). In this case a legislative redistricting plan using multimember districts was held to be in violation of the Voting Rights Act of 1965. No constitutional issues were decided. The Court concluded that the 1982 amendments to the Act eliminated any requirement of establishing that the contested electoral practice was adopted or maintained with the intent to discriminate against minority voters. The opinions in the case contain elaborate discussion of the problems involved in showing that multimember districts operate to prejudice the voting rights of minorities and should be seen by one interested in such problems.

H.   "BENIGN" DISCRIMINATION: AFFIRMATIVE ACTION, QUOTAS, PREFERENCES BASED ON GENDER OR RACE

---

1.   CLASSIFICATIONS ADVANTAGING FEMALES

Page 786.   Add ahead of 2.   Classifications Advantaging Racial Minorities:

JOHNSON v. TRANSPORTATION AGENCY, SANTA CLARA COUNTY, 107 S.Ct. 1442 (1987). In this case a white male who had been passed over for promotion in favor of a female employee with lower test scores, brought a suit under Title VII of the Civil Rights Act of 1942. He did not raise any constitutional issues and the Court decided the case entirely under Title VII. After much discussion the Court held "that the Agency appropriately took into account as one factor the sex of Diane Joyce in determining that she should be promoted to the road dispatcher position. The decision to do so was made pursuant to an affirmative action plan that represents a moderate, flexible, case-by-case approach to affecting a gradual improvement in the representation of minorities and women in the Agency's work force." Three justices dissented.

---

2. CLASSIFICATIONS ADVANTAGING RACIAL MINORITIES

Page 835. Add at end of page:

WYGANT v. JACKSON BOARD OF EDUCATION

476 U.S. 267, 106 S.Ct. 1842, 90 L.Ed.2d 260 (1986).

Justice Powell announced the judgment of the Court and delivered an opinion in which The Chief Justice and Justice Rehnquist joined, and which Justice O'Connor joined in parts I, II, III–A, III–B, and V.

This case presents the question whether a school board, consistent with the Equal Protection Clause, may extend preferential protection against layoffs to some of its employees because of their race or national origin.

I

In 1972 the Jackson Board of Education, because of racial tension in the community that extended to its schools, considered adding a layoff provision to the Collective Bargaining Agreement (CBA) between the Board and the Jackson Education Association (the Union) that would protect employees who were members of certain minority groups against layoffs. The Board and the Union eventually approved a new provision, Article XII of the CBA, covering layoffs. It stated:

> "In the event that it becomes necessary to reduce the number of teachers through layoff from employment by the Board, teachers with the most seniority in the district shall be retained, except that at no time will there be a greater percentage of minority personnel laid off than the current percentage of minority personnel employed at the time of the layoff. In no event will the number given notice of possible layoff be greater than the number of positions to be eliminated. Each teacher so affected will be called back in reverse order for positions for which he is certificated maintaining the above minority balance." [2]

When layoffs became necessary in 1974, it was evident that adherence to the CBA would result in the layoff of tenured nonminority teachers while minority teachers on probationary status were retained. Rather than complying with Article XII, the Board retained the tenured teachers and laid off probationary minority teachers, thus failing to maintain the percentage of minority personnel that existed at the time of the layoff. The Union, together with two minority teachers who had been laid off, brought suit in federal court, . . . Following trial, the District Court *sua sponte* concluded that it lacked jurisdiction over the case . . .

Rather than taking an appeal, the plaintiffs instituted a suit in state court, Jackson Education Assn. v. Board of Education, . . . (*Jackson II*), raising in essence the same claims that had been raised in

---

[2] Article VII of the CBA defined "minority group personnel" as "those employees who are Black, American Indian, Oriental, or of Spanish descendancy." App. 15.

Jackson I. In entering judgment for the plaintiffs, the state court found that the Board had breached its contract with the plaintiffs, and that Article XII did not violate the Michigan Teacher Tenure Act. In rejecting the Board's argument that the layoff provision violated the Civil Rights Act of 1964, the state court found that it "ha[d] not been established that the board had discriminated against minorities in its hiring practices. The minority representation on the faculty was the result of societal racial discrimination." The state court also found that "[t]here is no history of overt past discrimination by the parties to this contract." Nevertheless, the court held that Article XII was permissible, despite its discriminatory effect on nonminority teachers, as an attempt to remedy the effects of societal discrimination.

After *Jackson II*, the Board adhered to Article XII. As a result, during the 1976–1977 and 1981–1982 school years, nonminority teachers were laid off, while minority teachers with less seniority were retained. The displaced nonminority teachers, petitioners here, brought suit in Federal District Court, alleging violations of the Equal Protection Clause, Title VII, 42 U.S.C. § 1983, and other federal and state statutes. On cross motions for summary judgment, the District Court dismissed all of petitioners' claims. With respect to the equal protection claim, the District Court held that the racial preferences granted by the Board need not be grounded on a finding of prior discrimination. Instead, the court decided that the racial preferences were permissible under the Equal Protection Clause as an attempt to remedy societal discrimination by providing "role models" for minority schoolchildren, and upheld the constitutionality of the layoff provision.

The Court of Appeals for the Sixth Circuit affirmed, largely adopting the reasoning and language of the District Court. 746 F.2d 1152 (1984). We granted certiorari, ... to resolve the important issue of the constitutionality of race-based layoffs by public employers. We now reverse.

II

Petitioners' central claim is that they were laid off because of their race in violation of the Equal Protection Clause of the Fourteenth Amendment. Decisions by faculties and administrators of public schools based on race or ethnic origin are reviewable under the Fourteenth Amendment. This Court has "consistently repudiated '[d]istinctions between citizens solely because of their ancestry' as being 'odious to a free people whose institutions are founded upon the doctrine of equality,'" Loving v. Virginia, 388 U.S. 1, 11 (1967) quoting Hirabayashi v. United States, 320 U.S. 81, 100 (1943). "Racial and ethnic distinctions of any sort are inherently suspect and thus call for the most exacting judicial examination." Regents of University of California v. Bakke, 438 U.S. 265, 291 (1978) (opinion of Powell, J., joined by White, J.).

The Court has recognized that the level of scrutiny does not change merely because the challenged classification operates against a group that historically has not been subject to governmental discrimination.

Mississippi University for Women v. Hogan, 458 U.S. 718, 724 n. 9 (1982); Bakke, 438 U.S., at 291–299; see Shelley v. Kraemer, 334 U.S. 1, 22 (1948); see also A. Bickel, The Morality of Consent 133 (1975). In this case, Article XII of the CBA operates against whites and in favor of certain minorities, and therefore constitutes a classification based on race. "Any preference based on racial or ethnic criteria must necessarily receive a most searching examination to make sure that it does not conflict with constitutional guarantees." Fullilove v. Klutznick, 448 U.S. 448, 491 (1980) (opinion of Burger, C.J.). There are two prongs to this examination. First, any racial classification "must be justified by a compelling governmental interest." Palmore v. Sidoti, 466 U.S. 429, 432 (1984); see Loving v. Virginia, 388 U.S. 1, 11 (1967); cf. Graham v. Richardson, 403 U.S. 365, 375 (1971) (alienage). Second, the means chosen by the State to effectuate its purpose must be "narrowly tailored to the achievement of that goal." *Fullilove*, 448 U.S., at 480. We must decide whether the layoff provision is supported by a compelling state purpose and whether the means chosen to accomplish that purpose are narrowly tailored.

III

A

The Court of Appeals, relying on the reasoning and language of the District Court's opinion, held that the Board's interest in providing minority role models for its minority students, as an attempt to alleviate the effects of societal discrimination, was sufficiently important to justify the racial classification embodied in the layoff provision. . . . The court discerned a need for more minority faculty role models by finding that the percentage of minority teachers was less than the percentage of minority students.

This Court never has held that societal discrimination alone is sufficient to justify a racial classification. Rather, the Court has insisted upon some showing of prior discrimination by the governmental unit involved before allowing limited use of racial classifications in order to remedy such discrimination. This Court's reasoning in Hazelwood School District v. United States, 433 U.S. 299 (1977), illustrates that the relevant analysis in cases involving proof of discrimination by statistical disparity focuses on those disparities that demonstrate such prior governmental discrimination. In *Hazelwood* the Court concluded that, absent employment discrimination by the school board, " 'nondiscriminatory hiring practices will in time result in a work force more or less representative of the racial and ethnic composition of the population in the community from which the employees are hired.' " . . . [T]he Court in *Hazelwood* held that the proper comparison for determining the existence of actual discrimination by the school board was "between the racial composition of [the school's] teaching staff and the racial composition of the qualified public school teacher population in the relevant labor market." *Hazelwood* demonstrates this Court's focus on prior discrimination as the justification for, and the limitation on, a State's adoption of race-based remedies. See also Swann v. Charlotte-Mecklenburg Board of Education, 402 U.S. 1 (1971).

Unlike the analysis in *Hazelwood*, the role model theory employed by the District Court has no logical stopping point. The role model theory allows the Board to engage in discriminatory hiring and layoff practices long past the point required by any legitimate remedial purpose. Indeed, by tying the required percentage of minority teachers to the percentage of minority students, it requires just the sort of year-to-year calibration the Court stated was unnecessary in *Swann*, 402 U.S., at 31–32. . . .

Moreover, because the role model theory does not necessarily bear a relationship to the harm caused by prior discriminatory hiring practices, it actually could be used to escape the obligation to remedy such practices by justifying the small percentage of black teachers by reference to the small percentage of black students. . . . Carried to its logical extreme, the idea that black students are better off with black teachers could lead to the very system the Court rejected in Brown v. Board of Education, 347 U.S. 483 (1954) (*Brown I*).

Societal discrimination, without more, is too amorphous a basis for imposing a racially classified remedy. The role model theory announced by the District Court and the resultant holding typify this indefiniteness. There are numerous explanations for a disparity between the percentage of minority students and the percentage of minority faculty, many of them completely unrelated to discrimination of any kind. In fact, there is no apparent connection between the two groups. Nevertheless, the District Court combined irrelevant comparisons between these two groups with an indisputable statement that there has been societal discrimination, and upheld state action predicated upon racial classifications. No one doubts that there has been serious racial discrimination in this country. But as the basis for imposing discriminatory *legal* remedies that work against innocent people, societal discrimination is insufficient and over expansive. In the absence of particularized findings, a court could uphold remedies that are ageless in their reach into the past, and timeless in their ability to affect the future.

B

Respondents also now argue that their purpose in adopting the layoff provision was to remedy prior discrimination against minorities by the Jackson School District in hiring teachers. Public schools, like other public employers, operate under two interrelated constitutional duties. They are under a clear command from this Court, starting with Brown v. Board of Education, 349 U.S. 294 (1955), to eliminate every vestige of racial segregation and discrimination in the schools. Pursuant to that goal, race-conscious remedial action may be necessary. North Carolina State Board of Education v. Swann, 402 U.S. 43, 46 (1971). On the other hand, public employers, including public schools, also must act in accordance with a "core purpose of the Fourteenth Amendment" which is to "do away with all governmentally imposed distinctions based on race." Palmore v. Sidoti, 466 U.S., at 432. These related constitutional duties are not always harmonious; reconciling them requires public employers to act with extraordinary care. In particular, a public employer like the Board must ensure that, before it embarks on an affirmative action program, it has convincing evidence that remedial action is warranted. That is, it must have sufficient evidence to justify the conclusion that there has been prior discrimination.

Evidentiary support for the conclusion that remedial action is warranted becomes crucial when the remedial program is challenged in court by nonminority employees. In this case, for example, petitioners contended at trial that the remedial program—Article XII—had the purpose and effect of instituting a racial classification that was not justified by a remedial purpose. . . . In such a case, the trial court must make a factual determination that the employer had a strong basis in evidence for its conclusion that remedial action was necessary. The ultimate burden remains with the employees to demonstrate the unconstitutionality of an affirmative action program. But unless such a determination is made, an appellate court reviewing a challenge to remedial action by nonminority employees cannot determine whether the race-based action is justified as a remedy for prior discrimination.

Despite the fact that Article XII has spawned years of litigation and three separate lawsuits, no such determination ever has been made. Although its litigation position was different, the Board in *Jackson I* and *Jackson II* denied the existence of prior discriminatory hiring practices. This precise issue was litigated in both those suits. Both courts concluded that any statistical disparities were the result of general societal discrimination, not of prior discrimination by the Board. The Board now contends that, given another opportunity, it could establish the existence of prior discrimination. Although this argument seems belated at this point in the proceedings, we need not consider the question since we conclude below that the layoff provision was not a legally appropriate means of achieving even a compelling purpose.[5]

[5] Justice Marshall contends that "the majority has too quickly assumed the absence of a legitimate factual predicate for affirmative action in the Jackson schools." In support of that assertion, he engages in an unprecedented reliance on non-record documents that respondent has "lodged" with this Court. This selective citation to factual materials not considered by the District Court of the Court of Appeals below is unusual enough by itself. My disagreement with Justice Marshall, however, is more fundamental than any disagreement over the heretofore unquestioned rule that this Court decides cases based on the record before it. Justice Marshall does not define what he means by "legitimate factual predicate," nor does he demonstrate the relationship of these non-record materials to his undefined predicate. If, for example, his dissent assumes that general societal discrimination is a sufficient factual predicate, then there is no need to refer to respondents' lodgings as to its own employment history. No one disputes that there has been race discrimination in this country. If that fact alone can justify race-conscious action by the State, despite the Equal Protection Clause, then the dissent need not rely on non-record materials to show a "legitimate factual predicate." If, on the other hand, Justice Marshall is assuming that the necessary factual predicate is prior discrimination by the Board, there is no escaping the need for a factual determination below—a determination that does not exist.

IV

The Court of Appeals examined the means chosen to accomplish the Board's race-conscious purposes under a test of "reasonableness." That standard has no support in the decisions of this Court. As demonstrated in Part II above, our decisions always have employed a more stringent standard—however articulated—to test the validity of the means chosen by a state to accomplish its race-conscious purposes. See, e.g., Palmore, 466 U.S., at 432 ("to pass constitutional muster, [racial classifications] must be necessary . . . to the accomplishment of their legitimate purpose") (quoting McLaughlin v. Florida, 379 U.S. 184, 196 (1964); Fullilove, 448 U.S., at 480 (opinion of Burger, C.J.) ("We recognize the need for careful judicial evaluation to assure that any . . . program that employs racial or ethnic criteria to accomplish the objective of remedying the present effects of past discrimination is narrowly tailored to the achievement of that goal").[6] Under strict scrutiny the means chosen to accomplish the State's asserted purpose must be specifically and narrowly framed to accomplish that purpose. *Fullilove*, 448 U.S., at 480 (opinion of Burger, C.J.).[7] "Racial classifica-

The real dispute, then, is not over the state of the record. It is disagreement as to what constitutes a "legitimate factual predicate." If the necessary factual predicate is *prior discrimination*—that is, that race-based state action is taken to remedy prior discrimination by the governmental unit involved—then the very nature of appellate review requires that a factfinder determine whether the employer was justified in instituting a remedial plan. Nor can the respondent unilaterally insulate itself from this key constitutional question by conceding that it has discriminated in the past, now that it is in its interest to make such a concession. Contrary to the dissent's assertion, the requirement of such a determination by the trial court is not some arbitrary barrier set up by today's opinion. Rather, it is a necessary result of the requirement that race-based state action be remedial.

. . .

[6] The term "narrowly tailored," so frequently used in our cases, has acquired a secondary meaning. More specifically, as commentators have indicated, the term may be used to require consideration whether lawful alternative and less restrictive means could have been used. Or, as Professor Ely has noted, the classification at issue must "fit" with greater precision than any alternative means. Ely, The Constitutionality of Reverse Racial Discrimination, 41 U.Chi.L.Rev. 723, 727, n. 26 (1974) (hereinafter Ely). "[Courts] should give particularly intense scrutiny to whether a nonracial approach or a more narrowly tailored racial classification could promote the substantial interest about as well and at tolerable administrative expense." Greenawalt, Judicial Scrutiny of "Benign" Racial Preference in Law School Admissions, 75 Colum.L.Rev. 559, 578–579 (1975) (hereinafter Greenawalt).

[7] Several commentators have emphasized, no matter what the weight of the asserted governmental purpose, that the *means* chosen to accomplish the purpose should be narrowly tailored. In arguing for a form of intermediate scrutiny, Professor Greenawalt contends that, "while benign racial classifications call for some weighing of the importance of ends they call for even more intense scrutiny of means, especially of the administrability of less onerous alternative classifications." Greenawalt 565. Professor Ely has suggested that "special scrutiny in the suspect classification context has in fact consisted not in weighing ends but rather in insisting that the classification in issue fit a constitutional permissible state goal with greater precision than any available alternative." Ely 727, n. 26. Professor Gunther argues that judicial scrutiny of legislative means is more appropriate than judicial weighing of the importance of the legislative purpose. Gunther, Foreward: In Search of Evolving Doctrine on a Changing Court: A Model For a Newer Equal Protection, 86 Harv.L.Rev. 1, 20–21 (1972).

tions are simply too pernicious to permit any but the most exact connection between justification and classification." Id., at 537 (Stevens, J., dissenting).

We have recognized, however, that in order to remedy the effects of prior discrimination, it may be necessary to take race into account. As part of this Nation's dedication to eradicating racial discrimination, innocent persons may be called upon to bear some of the burden of the remedy. "When effectuating a limited and properly tailored remedy to cure the effects of prior discrimination, such a 'sharing of the burden' by innocent parties is not impermissible." Id., at 484, quoting Franks v. Bowman Transportation Co., 424 U.S. 747 (1976).[8] In *Fullilove*, the challenged statute required at least 10 percent of federal public works funds to be used in contracts with minority-owned business enterprises. This requirement was found to be within the remedial powers of Congress in part because the "actual burden shouldered by nonminority firms is relatively light." 448 U.S., at 484.

Significantly, none of the cases discussed above involved layoffs. Here, by contrast, the means chosen to achieve the Board's asserted purposes is that of laying off nonminority teachers with greater seniority in order to retain minority teachers with less seniority. We have previously expressed concern over the burden that a preferential layoffs scheme imposes on innocent parties. See Firefighters v. Stotts, 467 U.S. 561, 574–576, 578–579 (1984); see also *Weber*, n. 9, supra this page, at 208 ("The plan does not require the discharge of white workers and

---

[8] Of course, when a state implements a race-based plan that requires such a sharing of the burden, it cannot justify the discriminatory effect on some individuals because other individuals had approved the plan. Any "waiver" of the right not to be dealt with by the government on the basis of one's race must be made by those affected. Yet Justice Marshall repeatedly contends that the fact that Article XII was approved by a majority vote of the Union somehow validates this plan. He sees this case not in terms of individual constitutional rights, but as an allocation of burdens "between two racial groups." Thus, Article XII becomes a political compromise that "avoided placing the entire burden of layoffs on either the white teachers as a group or the minority teachers as a group." But the petitioners before us today are not "the white teachers as a group." They are Wendy Wygant and other individuals who claim that they were fired from their jobs because of their race. That claim cannot be waived by petitioners' more senior colleagues. In view of the way union seniority works, it is not surprising that while a straight freeze on minority layoffs was overwhelmingly rejected, a "compromise" eventually was reached that placed the entire burden of the compromise on the most junior union members. The more senior union members simply had nothing to lose from such a compromise. ("To petitioners, at the bottom of the seniority scale among white teachers, fell the lot of bearing the white group's proportionate share of layoffs that became necessary in 1982.") The fact that such a painless accommodation was approved by the more senior union members six times since 1972 is irrelevant. The Constitution does not allocate constitutional rights to be distributed like bloc grants within discrete racial groups; and until it does, petitioners' more senior union colleagues cannot vote away petitioners' rights.

Justice Marshall also attempts to portray the layoff plan as one that has no real invidious effect, stating that "within the confines of constant minority proportions, it preserves the hierarchy of seniority in the selection of individuals for layoff." That phrase merely expresses the tautology that layoffs are based on seniority except as to those nonminority teachers who are displaced by minority teachers with less seniority. This is really nothing more than group-based analysis: "each group would shoulder a portion of [the layoff] burden equal to its portion of the faculty." The constitutional problem remains: the decision that petitioners would be laid off was based on their race.

their replacement with new black hirees"). In cases involving valid *hiring* goals, the burden to be borne by innocent individuals is diffused to a considerable extent among society generally. Though hiring goals may burden some innocent individuals, they simply do not impose the same kind of injury that layoffs impose. Denial of a future employment opportunity is not as intrusive as loss of an existing job.

Many of our cases involve union seniority plans with employees who are typically heavily dependent on wages for their day-to-day living. Even a temporary layoff may have adverse financial as well as psychological effects. A worker may invest many productive years in one job and one city with the expectation of earning the stability and security of seniority. "At that point, the rights and expectations surrounding seniority make up what is probably the most valuable capital asset that the worker 'owns,' worth even more than the current equity in his home." Fallon & Weiler, Conflicting Models of Racial Justice, 1984 S.Ct.Rev. 1, 58. Layoffs disrupt these settled expectations in a way that general hiring goals do not.

While hiring goals impose a diffuse burden, often foreclosing only one of several opportunities, layoffs impose the entire burden of achieving racial equality on particular individuals, often resulting in serious disruption of their lives. That burden is too intrusive. We therefore hold that, as a means of accomplishing purposes that otherwise may be legitimate, the Board's layoff plan is not sufficiently narrowly tailored. Other, less intrusive means of accomplishing similar purposes—such as the adoption of hiring goals—are available. For these reasons, the Board's selection of layoffs as the means to accomplish even a valid purpose cannot satisfy the demands of the Equal Protection Clause.[13]

V

We accordingly reverse the judgment of the Court of Appeals for the Sixth Circuit.

It is so ordered.

———

Justice O'Connor, concurring in part and concurring in the judgment.

This case requires us to define and apply the standard required by the Equal Protection Clause when a governmental agency agrees to give preferences on the basis of race or national origin in making layoffs of employees. The specific question posed is, as Justice Marshall puts it, "whether the Constitution prohibits a union and a local school board from developing a collective-bargaining agreement that

[13] The Board's definition of minority to include blacks, Orientals, American Indians, and persons of Spanish descent, n. 2, supra, further illustrates the undifferentiated nature of the plan. There is no explanation of why the Board chose to favor these particular minorities or how in fact members of some of the categories can be identified. Moreover, respondents have never suggested—much less formally found—that they have engaged in prior, purposeful discrimination against members of each of these minority groups.

apportions layoffs between two racially determined groups as a means of preserving the effects of an affirmative hiring policy." There is no issue here of the interpretation and application of Title VII of the Civil Rights Act; accordingly, we have only the constitutional issue to resolve.

The Equal Protection Clause standard applicable to racial classifications that work to the disadvantage of "nonminorities" has been articulated in various ways. Justice Powell now would require that: (1) the racial classification be justified by a " 'compelling governmental interest,' " and (2) the means chosen by the State to effectuate its purpose be "narrowly tailored." This standard reflects the belief, apparently held by all members of this Court, that racial classifications of any sort must be subjected to "strict scrutiny," however defined. . . . Justices Marshall, Brennan, and Blackmun, however, seem to adhere to the formulation of the "strict" standard that they authored, with Justice White, in *Bakke*: "remedial use of race is permissible if it serves 'important governmental objectives' and is 'substantially related to achievement of those objectives.' " (Marshall, J., dissenting), quoting *Bakke*, supra, at 359 (opinion of Brennan, White, Marshall, and Blackmun, JJ.).

I subscribe to Justice Powell's formulation because it mirrors the standard we have consistently applied in examining racial classifications in other contexts. . . . Although Justice Powell's formulation may be viewed as more stringent than that suggested by Justices Brennan, White, Marshall, and Blackmun, the disparities between the two tests do not preclude a fair measure of consensus. In particular, as regards certain state interests commonly relied upon in formulating affirmative action programs, the distinction between a "compelling" and an "important" governmental purpose may be a negligible one. The Court is in agreement that, whatever the formulation employed, remedying past or present racial discrimination by a state actor is a sufficiently weighty state interest to warrant the remedial use of a carefully constructed affirmative action program. This remedial purpose need not be accompanied by contemporaneous findings of actual discrimination to be accepted as legitimate as long as the public actor has a firm basis for believing that remedial action is required. Additionally, although its precise contours are uncertain, a state interest in the promotion of racial diversity has been found sufficiently "compelling," at least in the context of higher education, to support the use of racial considerations in furthering that interest. See, e.g., *Bakke*, 438 U.S., at 311–315 (opinion of Powell, J.). And certainly nothing the Court has said today necessarily forecloses the possibility that the Court will find other governmental interests which have been relied upon in the lower courts but which have not been passed on here to be sufficiently "important" or "compelling" to sustain the use of affirmative action policies.

It appears, then, that the true source of disagreement on the Court lies not so much in defining the state interests which may support affirmative action efforts as in defining the degree to which the means employed must "fit" the ends pursued to meet constitutional standards.

Yet even here the Court has forged a degree of unanimity; it is agreed that a plan need not be limited to the remedying of specific instances of identified discrimination for it to be deemed sufficiently "narrowly tailored," or "substantially related," to the correction of prior discrimination by the state actor.

In the final analysis, the diverse formulations and the number of separate writings put forth by various members of the Court in these difficult cases do not necessarily reflect an intractable fragmentation in opinion with respect to certain core principles. Ultimately, the Court is at least in accord in believing that a public employer, consistent with the Constitution, may undertake an affirmative action program which is designed to further a legitimate remedial purpose and which implements that purpose by means that do not impose disproportionate harm on the interests, or unnecessarily trammel the rights, of innocent individuals directly and adversely affected by a plan's racial preference.

. . .

In sum, I do not think that the layoff provision was constitutionally infirm simply because the School Board, the Commission or a court had not made particularized findings of discrimination at the time the provision was agreed upon. But when the plan was challenged, the District Court and the Court of Appeals did not make the proper inquiry into the legitimacy of the Board's asserted remedial purpose; instead, they relied upon governmental purposes that we have deemed insufficient to withstand strict scrutiny, and therefore failed to isolate a sufficiently important governmental purpose that could support the challenged provision.

There is, however, no need to inquire whether the provision actually had a legitimate remedial purpose based on the record, such as it is, because the judgment is vulnerable on yet another ground: the courts below applied a "reasonableness" test in evaluating the relationship between the ends pursued and the means employed to achieve them that is plainly incorrect under any of the standards articulated by this Court. Nor is it necessary, in my view, to resolve the troubling questions of whether any layoff provision could survive strict scrutiny or whether this particular layoff provision could, when considered without reference to the hiring goal it was intended to further, pass the onerous "narrowly tailored" requirement. Petitioners have met their burden of establishing that this layoff provision is not "narrowly tailored" to achieve its asserted remedial purpose by demonstrating that the provision is keyed to a hiring goal that itself has no relation to the remedying of employment discrimination.

Although the constitutionality of the hiring goal as such is not before us, it is impossible to evaluate the necessity of the layoff provision as a remedy for the apparent prior employment discrimination absent reference to that goal. In this case, the hiring goal that the layoff provision was designed to safeguard was tied to the percentage of minority students in the school district, not to the percentage of qualified minority teachers within the relevant labor pool. The disparity between the percentage of minorities on the teaching staff and the percentage of minorities in the student body is not probative of employment discrimination; it is only when it is established that the availability of minorities in the relevant labor pool substantially exceeded those hired that one may draw an inference of deliberate discrimination in employment. See Hazelwood School District v. United States, 433 U.S. 299, 308 (1977) (Title VII context). Because the layoff provision here acts to maintain levels of minority hiring that have no relation to remedying employment discrimination, it cannot be adjudged "narrowly tailored" to effectuate its asserted remedial purpose.

I therefore join in parts I, II, III–A, III–B, and V of the Court's opinion, and concur in the judgment.

Justice White, concurring in the judgment.

The school board's policy when layoffs are necessary is to maintain a certain proportion of minority teachers. This policy requires laying off non-minority teachers solely on the basis of their race, including teachers with seniority, and retaining other teachers solely because they are black, even though some of them are in probationary status. None of the interests asserted by the board, singly or together, justify this racially discriminatory layoff policy and save it from the structures of the Equal Protection Clause. Whatever the legitimacy of hiring goals or quotas may be, the discharge of white teachers to make room for blacks, none of whom has been shown to be a victim of any racial discrimination, is quite a different matter. I cannot believe that in order to integrate a work force, it would be permissible to discharge whites and hire blacks until the latter comprised a suitable percentage of the work force. None of our cases suggest that this would be permissible under the Equal Protection Clause. Indeed, our cases look quite the other way. The layoff policy in this case—laying off whites who would otherwise be retained in order to keep blacks on the job— has the same effect and is equally violative of the Equal Protection Clause. I agree with the plurality that this official policy is unconstitutional and hence concur in the judgment.

Justice Marshall, with whom Justice Brennan and Justice Blackmun join, dissenting.

When this Court seeks to resolve far-ranging constitutional issues, it must be especially careful to ground its analysis firmly in the facts of the particular controversy before it. Yet in this significant case, we are hindered by a record that is informal and incomplete. Both parties now appear to realize that the record is inadequate to inform the Court's decision. Both have lodged with the Court voluminous "submissions" containing factual material that was not considered by the District Court or the Court of Appeals. Petitioners have submitted 21 separate items, predominantly statistical charts, which they assert are relevant to their claim of discrimination. Respondents have submitted public documents that tend to substantiate the facts alleged in the brief accompanying their motion for summary judgment in the District

Court. These include transcripts and exhibits from two prior proceedings, in which certain questions of discrimination in the Jackson schools were litigated. . . .

We should not acquiesce in the parties' attempt to try their case before this Court. Yet it would be just as serious a mistake simply to ignore altogether, as the plurality has done, the compelling factual setting in which this case evidently has arisen. No race-conscious provision that purports to serve a remedial purpose can be fairly assessed in a vacuum.

The haste with which the District Court granted summary judgment to respondents, without seeking to develop the factual allegations contained in respondents' brief, prevented the full exploration of the facts that are now critical to resolution of the important issue before us. Respondents' acquiescence in a premature victory in the District Court should not now be used as an instrument of their defeat. Rather, the District Court should have the opportunity to develop a factual record adequate to resolve the serious issue raised by the case. I believe, therefore, that it is improper for this Court to resolve the constitutional issue in its current posture. But, because I feel that the plurality has also erred seriously in its legal analysis of the merits of this case, I write further to express my disagreement with the conclusions that it has reached.

I, too, believe that layoffs are unfair. But unfairness ought not be confused with constitutional injury. Paying no heed to the true circumstances of petitioners' plight, the plurality would nullify years of negotiation and compromise designed to solve serious educational problems in the public schools of Jackson, Michigan. Because I believe that a public employer, with the full agreement of its employees, should be permitted to preserve the benefits of a legitimate and constitutional affirmative-action hiring plan even while reducing its work force, I dissent.

. . .

II

From the outset, it is useful to bear in mind what this case is not. There has been no court order to achieve racial balance, which might require us to reflect upon the existence of judicial power to impose obligations on parties not proven to have committed a wrong. See Swann v. Charlotte-Mecklenburg Board of Education, 402 U.S. 1, 16 (1971). There is also no occasion here to resolve whether a white worker may be required to give up his or her job in order to be replaced by a black worker. See Steelworkers v. Weber, 443 U.S. 193, 208 (1979). Nor are we asked to order parties to suffer the consequences of an agreement that they had no role in adopting. See Firefighters v. Stotts, 467 U.S. 561, 575 (1984). Moreover, this is not a case in which a party to a collective-bargaining agreement has attempted unilaterally to achieve racial balance by refusing to comply with a contractual, seniority-based layoff provision. Cf. Teamsters v. United States, 431 U.S. 324, 350, 352 (1977).

The sole question posed by this case is whether the Constitution prohibits a union and a local school board from developing a collective-bargaining agreement that apportions layoffs between two racially determined groups as a means of preserving the effects of an affirmative hiring policy, the constitutionality of which is unchallenged.

III

Agreement upon a means for applying the Equal Protection Clause to an affirmative-action program has eluded this Court every time the issue has come before us. . . .

. . .

Despite the Court's inability to agree on a route, we have reached a common destination in sustaining affirmative action against constitutional attack. In *Bakke*, we determined that a state institution may take race into account as a factor in its decisions, 438 U.S., at 326, and in *Fullilove*, the Court upheld a congressional preference for minority contractors because the measure was legitimately designed to ameliorate the present effects of past discrimination, 448 U.S., at 520.

In this case, it should not matter which test the Court applies. What is most important, under any approach to the constitutional analysis, is that a reviewing court genuinely consider the circumstances of the provision at issue. The history and application of Article XII, assuming verification upon a proper record, demonstrate that this provision would pass constitutional muster, no matter which standard the Court should adopt.

. . .

VII

The narrow question presented by this case, if indeed we proceed to the merits, offers no occasion for the Court to issue broad proclamations of public policy concerning the controversial issue of affirmative action. Rather, this case calls for calm, dispassionate reflection upon exactly what has been done, to whom, and why. If one honestly confronts each of those questions against the factual background suggested by the materials submitted to us, I believe the conclusion is inescapable that Article XII meets, and indeed surpasses, any standard for ensuring that race-conscious programs are necessary to achieve remedial purposes. When an elected school board and a teachers' union collectively bargain a layoff provision designed to preserve the effects of a valid minority recruitment plan by apportioning layoffs between two racial groups, as a result of a settlement achieved under the auspices of a supervisory state agency charged with protecting the civil rights of all citizens, that provision should not be upset by this Court on constitutional grounds.

The alleged facts that I have set forth above evince, at the very least, a wealth of plausible evidence supporting the Board's position that Article XII was a legitimate and necessary response both to racial discrimination and to educational imperatives. To attempt to resolve the constitutional issue either with no historical context whatever, as the plurality has done, or on the basis of a record devoid of established facts, is to do a grave injustice not only to the Board and teachers of Jackson and to the State of Michigan, but also to individuals and governments committed to the goal of eliminating all traces of segregation throughout the country. Most of all, it does an injustice to the aspirations embodied in the Fourteenth Amendment itself. I would vacate the judgment of the Court of Appeals and remand with instructions that the case be remanded to the District Court for further proceedings consistent with the views I have expressed.

Justice Stevens, dissenting.

In my opinion, it is not necessary to find that the Board of Education has been guilty of racial discrimination in the past to support the conclusion that it has a legitimate interest in employing more black teachers in the future. Rather than analyzing a case of this kind by asking whether minority teachers have some sort of special entitlement to jobs as a remedy for sins that were committed in the past, I believe that we should first ask whether the Board's action advances the public interest in educating children for the future. If so, I believe we should consider whether that public interest, and the manner in which it is pursued, justifies any adverse effects on the disadvantaged group.

I

The Equal Protection Clause absolutely prohibits the use of race in many governmental contexts. To cite only a few: the government may not use race to decide who may serve on juries, who may use public services, who may marry, and who may be fit parents. The use of race in these situations is "utterly irrational" because it is completely unrelated to any valid public purpose; moreover, it is particularly pernicious because it constitutes a badge of oppression that is unfaithful to the central promise of the Fourteenth Amendment.

Nevertheless, in our present society, race is not always irrelevant to sound governmental decisionmaking. To take the most obvious example, in law enforcement, if an undercover agent is needed to infiltrate a group suspected of ongoing criminal behavior—and if the members of the group are all of the same race—it would seem perfectly rational to employ an agent of that race rather than a member of a different racial class. Similarly, in a city with a recent history of racial unrest, the superintendent of police might reasonably conclude that an integrated police force could develop a better relationship with the community and thereby do a more effective job of maintaining law and order than a force composed only of white officers.

In the context of public education, it is quite obvious that a school board may reasonably conclude that an integrated faculty will be able to provide benefits to the student body that could not be provided by an all white, or nearly all white, faculty. For one of the most important lessons that the American public schools teach is that the diverse ethnic, cultural, and national backgrounds that have been brought together in our famous "melting pot" do not identify essential differences among the human beings that inhabit our land. It is one thing for a white child to be taught by a white teacher that color, like beauty, is only "skin deep"; it is far more convincing to experience that truth on a day to day basis during the routine, ongoing learning process.

In this case, the collective-bargaining agreement between the Union and the Board of Education succinctly stated a valid public purpose—"recognition of the desirability of multi-ethnic representation on the teaching faculty," and thus "a policy of actively seeking minority group personnel." Nothing in the record—not a shred of evidence—contradicts the view that the Board's attempt to employ, and to retain, more minority teachers in the Jackson public school system served this completely sound educational purpose. Thus, there was a rational and unquestionably legitimate basis for the Board's decision to enter into the collective-bargaining agreement that petitioners have challenged, even though the agreement required special efforts to recruit and retain minority teachers.

. . .

IV

We should not lightly approve the government's use of a race-based distinction. History teaches the obvious dangers of such classifications. Our ultimate goal must, of course, be "to eliminate entirely from governmental decisionmaking such irrelevant factors as a human being's race." In this case, however, I am persuaded that the decision to include more minority teachers in the Jackson, Michigan, school system served a valid public purpose, that it was adopted with fair procedures and given a narrow breadth, that it transcends the harm to petitioners, and that it is a step toward that ultimate goal of eliminating entirely from governmental decisionmaking such irrelevant factors as a human being's race. I would therefore affirm the judgment of the Court of Appeals.

LOCAL NO. 93, INTERNATIONAL ASS'N OF FIREFIGHTERS v. CLEVELAND, 478 U.S. 501 (1986). An organization of Black and Hispanic firefighters employed by the City of Cleveland filed a complaint in the federal district court charging that the city had discriminated against them in the hiring, assignment, and promotion of firefighters. Local 93 of the International Association of Firefighters, which represented a majority of Cleveland's firefighters intervened. The city decided to negotiate a consent decree with the minority organization. After several attempts and over the objection of Local 93 the city and the minority firefighters agreed to a consent decree and the court entered a judgment based on it. The decree provided that 66 promotions to lieutenant be made, with half going to minority firefighters, and that with respect to 52 promotions to be made to higher positions all minorities who had qualified (10) should be appointed. Local 93 contended that section 706(g) of the Civil Rights Act of 1964, as amended, prevented a court from making an order such as this one based on race without a showing that the persons benefited had been discriminated against. The trial court rejected this contention and the Supreme Court, by a vote of 6 to 3, agreed with the district court's order. They said that a consent decree was essentially a contract between the parties rather than an order by the court and that the statute encouraged rather than discouraged voluntary resolution of these problems.

No constitutional issue was decided in the case and it was stated that Local 93 could pursue any claims it might have that the action of the city in joining this consent decree violated the fourteenth amendment.

LOCAL 28 OF THE SHEET METAL WORKERS' INTERNATIONAL ASS'N v. EQUAL EMPLOYMENT OPPORTUNITY COMMISSION, 478 U.S. 421 (1986): The EEOC brought suit against Local 28 of the Sheet Metal Workers' Ass'n charging the union with violating Title VII of the Civil Rights Act of 1964 by engaging in a pattern and practice of discrimination against Black and Hispanic individuals. In 1975 the court concluded that the union had violated the statute and entered an order requiring the union to achieve a goal of 29% nonwhite membership by 1981. This order was basically upheld on appeal to the court of appeals but remanded for certain modifications. On remand the 29% goal was maintained and affirmed on appeal.

Contempt proceedings were brought against the union in 1982 and 1983. In the latter proceeding the court found the union guilty of intentional violations of the judgment and ordered the union to support a fund to aid in increasing the pool of qualified nonwhite applicants and to achieve a 29.23% goal of nonwhite members by 1987. This judgment was affirmed by the court of appeals and the Supreme Court granted certiorari. By a series of split votes it upheld the action below against both statutory and constitutional challenges. Only the constitutional issues are considered here.

Justice Brennan, joined by Justices Marshall, Blackmun, and Stevens said:

"Petitioners also allege that the membership goal and Fund order contravene the equal protection component of the Due Process Clause of the Fifth Amendment because they deny benefits to white individuals based on race. We have consistently recognized that government bodies constitutionally may adopt racial classifications as a remedy for past discrimination. . . . We have not agreed, however, on the proper test to be applied in analyzing the constitutionality of race-conscious remedial measures. . . . We need not resolve this dispute here, since we conclude that the relief ordered in this case passes even the most rigorous test—it is narrowly tailored to further the Government's compelling interest in remedying past discrimination.

"In this case, there is no problem, as there was in *Wygant*, with a proper showing of prior discrimination that would justify the use of remedial racial classifications. Both the District Court and Court of Appeals have repeatedly found petitioners guilty of egregious violations of Title VII, and have determined that affirmative measures were necessary to remedy their racially discriminatory practices. More importantly, the District Court's orders were properly tailored to accomplish this objective. First, the District Court considered the efficacy of alternative remedies, and concluded that, in light of petitioners' long record of resistance to official efforts to end their discriminatory practices, stronger measures were necessary. . . . The court devised the temporary membership goal and the Fund as tools for remedying past discrimination. More importantly, the District Court's orders will have only a marginal impact on the interests of white workers. . . . Again, petitioners concede that the District Court's orders did not disadvantage *existing* union members. While white applicants for union membership may be denied certain benefits available to their nonwhite counterparts, the court's orders do not stand as an absolute bar to the admission of such individuals; again, a majority of those entering the union after entry of the court's orders have been white. We therefore conclude that the District Court's orders do not violate the equal protection safeguards of the Constitution."

. . . .

Justice Powell concurred in the judgment with respect to the constitutional issue, stating:

"There remains for consideration the question whether the Fund order and membership goal contravene the equal protection component of the Due Process Clause of the Fifth Amendment because they may deny benefits to white individuals based on race. . . .

"The finding by the District Court and the Court of Appeals that petitioners have engaged in egregious violations of Title VII establishes, without doubt, a compelling governmental interest sufficient to justify the imposition of a racially classified remedy. It would be difficult to find defendants more determined to discriminate against minorities. My inquiry, therefore, focuses on whether the District Court's remedy is 'narrowly tailored,' to the goal of eradicating the discrimination engaged in by petitioners. I believe it is.

"The Fund order is supported not only by the governmental interest in eradicating petitioners' discriminatory practices, it also is supported by the societal interest in compliance with the judgments of federal courts. Cf. United States v. Mine Workers, 330 U.S. 258, 303 (1947). The Fund order was not imposed until *after* petitioners were held in contempt. In requiring the Union to create the Fund, the District Court expressly considered ' "the consequent seriousness of the burden" to the defendants'. Moreover, the focus of the Fund order was to give minorities opportunities that for years had been available informally only to nonminorities. The burden this imposes on nonminorities is slight. Under these circumstances, I have little difficulty concluding that the Fund order was carefully structured to vindicate the compelling governmental interests present in this case.

"The percentage goal raises a different question. In Fullilove v. Klutznick, 448 U.S. 448, (1980) . . . I relied on four factors that had been applied by courts of appeals when considering the proper scope of race-conscious hiring remedies. Those factors were: (i) the efficacy of alternative remedies; (ii) the planned duration of the remedy; (iii) the relationship between the percentage of minority workers to be employed and the percentage of minority group members in the relevant population or work force; and (iv) the availability of waiver provisions if the hiring plan could not be met. Id., at 510–511 (Powell, J., concurring). A final factor of primary importance that I considered in *Fullilove*, as well as in *Wygant*, was 'the effect of the [remedy] upon innocent third-parties.' 448 U.S., at 514. Application of those factors demonstrates that the goal in this case comports with constitutional requirements.

"First, it is doubtful, given petitioners' history in this litigation, that the District Court had available to it any other effective remedy. That court, having had the parties before it over a period of time, was in the best position to judge whether an alternative remedy, such as a simple injunction, would have been effective in ending petitioners' discriminatory practices. Here, the court imposed the 29% goal in 1975 only after declaring that '[i]n light of Local 28's and JAC's failure to "clean house" this court concludes that the imposition of a remedial racial goal . . . is essential to place the defendants in a position of compliance with the 1964 Civil Rights Act.' EEOC v. Local 638, 401 F.Supp. 467, 488 (SDNY 1975). On these facts, it is fair to conclude that absent authority to set a goal as a benchmark against which it could measure progress in eliminating discriminatory practices, the District Court may have been powerless to provide an effective remedy. Second, the goal was not imposed as a permanent requirement, but is of limited duration. Third, the goal is directly related to the percentage of nonwhites in the relevant workforce.

"As a fourth factor, my concurring opinion in *Fullilove* considered whether waiver provisions were available in the event that the hiring goal could not be met. The requirement of a waiver provision or, more generally, of flexibility with respect to the imposition of a numerical goal reflects a recognition that neither the Constitution nor Title VII requires a particular racial balance in the workplace. Indeed, the Constitution forbids such a requirement if imposed for its own sake. *Fullilove*, supra, at 507. 'We have recognized, however, that in order to remedy the effects of prior discrimination, it may be necessary to take race into account.' *Wygant*, supra. Thus, a court may not choose a remedy for the purpose of attaining a particular racial balance; rather, remedies properly are confined to the elimination of proven discrimination. A goal is a means, useful in limited circumstances, to assist a court in determining whether discrimination has been eradicated.

"The flexible application of the goal requirement in this case demonstrates that it is not a means to achieve racial balance. The contempt order was not imposed for the Union's failure to achieve the goal, but for its failure to take the prescribed steps that would facilitate achieving the goal. Additional flexibility is evidenced by the fact that this goal, originally set to be achieved by 1981, has been twice delayed and is now set for 1987.

"It is also important to emphasize that on the record before us, it does not appear that nonminorities will be burdened directly, if at all. Petitioners' counsel conceded at oral argument that imposition of the goal would not require the layoff of nonminority union workers, and that therefore the District Court's order did not disadvantage existing union members. This case is thus distinguishable from *Wygant* where the plurality opinion noted that 'layoffs impose the entire burden of achieving racial equality on particular individuals, often resulting in serious disruption of their lives.' 476 U.S., at ___ – ___. In contrast to the layoff provision in *Wygant*, the goal at issue here is akin to a hiring goal. . . .

"My view that the imposition of flexible goals as a remedy for past discrimination may be permissible under the Constitution is not an endorsement of their indiscriminate use. Nor do I imply that the adoption of such a goal will always pass constitutional muster."

Justice O'Connor concurred in part and dissented in part. Justice White wrote a dissenting opinion as did Justice Rehnquist joined by Chief Justice Burger. None of these justices reached the constitutional issue.

UNITED STATES v. PARADISE
___ U.S. ___, 107 S.Ct. 1053, 94 L.Ed.2d 203 (1987).

Justice Brennan announced the judgment of the Court and delivered an opinion in which Justice Marshall, Justice Blackmun, and Justice Powell join.

The question we must decide is whether relief awarded in this case, in the form of a one-black-for-one-white promotion requirement to be applied as an interim measure to state trooper promotions in the Alabama Department of Public Safety (Department), is permissible under the Equal Protection guarantee of the Fourteenth Amendment.

In 1972 the United States District Court for the Middle District of Alabama held that the Department had systematically excluded blacks from employment in violation of the Fourteenth Amendment. Some 11 years later, confronted with the Department's failure to develop promotion procedures that did not have an adverse impact on blacks, the District Court ordered the promotion of one black trooper for each white trooper elevated in rank, as long as qualified black candidates were available, until the Department implemented an acceptable promotion procedure. The United States challenges the constitutionality of this order.

I

Because the Department's prior employment practices and conduct during this lawsuit bear directly on the constitutionality of any race-conscious remedy imposed upon it, we must relate the tortuous course of this litigation in some detail.

A

In 1972 the National Association for the Advancement of Colored People (NAACP) brought this action challenging the Department's long-standing practice of excluding blacks from employment. The United States was joined as a party plaintiff, and Phillip Paradise, Jr., intervened on behalf of a class of black plaintiffs. District Judge Frank M. Johnson, Jr., . . . [determined that the defendants had engaged in blatant and continuous discrimination in the hiring of blacks for both troopers and supporting personnel. As a result, the court said it had the authority to order an end to discriminatory practices and to order practices designed to eliminate the present effects of past discrimination.]

As a result, the court issued an order (1972 order), enjoining the Department to hire one black trooper for each white trooper hired until blacks constituted approximately 25% of the state trooper force. Judge Johnson also enjoined the Department from "engaging in any employment practices, including recruitment, examination, appointment, training, *promotion,* retention or any other personnel action, for the purpose or with the effect of discriminating against any employee, or actual or potential applicant for employment, on the ground of race or color." (emphasis added). . . .

The defendants appealed, but the Fifth Circuit upheld the hiring requirement: . . .

In 1974, only shortly after the Court of Appeals' decision, the plaintiffs found it necessary to seek further relief from the District Court. . . . The court reaffirmed the 1972 hiring order, enjoining any further attempts by the Department to delay or frustrate compliance.

B

In September 1977 the plaintiffs again had to return to the District Court for supplemental relief, this time specifically on the question of the Department's *promotion* practices. Following extensive discovery, the parties entered into a Partial Consent Decree (1979 Decree), approved by the court in February 1979. In this decree, the Department agreed to develop within one year a promotion procedure that would be fair to all applicants and have "little or no adverse impact upon blacks seeking promotion to corporal." In the decree, the Department also agreed that the promotion procedure would conform with the 1978 Uniform Guidelines on Employee Selection Procedures, 28 CFR § 50.14 (1978). Once such a procedure was in place for the rank of corporal, the decree required the defendants to develop similar procedures for the other upper ranks—sergeant, lieutenant, captain, and major. The decree expressly provided that the plaintiffs might apply to the court for enforcement of its terms or for other appropriate relief.

Five days after approval of the 1979 Decree, the defendants sought clarification of the 1972 *hiring* order. The Department maintained that its goal—a 25% black trooper force—applied only to officers in entry-level positions and not to the upper ranks. The court responded:

"On this point, there is no ambiguity. The Court's [1972] order required that one-to-one hiring be carried out until approximately twenty-five percent of the *state trooper force* is black. It is perfectly clear that the order did not distinguish among troopers by rank." Paradise v. Shoemaker, 470 F.Supp. 439, 440 (MD Ala.1979) (emphasis in original).

The Department also argued that because the 25% objective could not be achieved unless 37.5% of entry-level positions were held by blacks, "more qualified white applicants" were passed over than was constitutionally permissible. The District Court rejected the argument,

. . . .

In April 1981, more than a year after the deadline set in the 1979 Decree, the Department proposed a selection procedure for promotion to corporal and sought approval from the District Court. The United States and the plaintiff class both objected to implementation of the procedure, arguing that it had not been validated and that its use would be impermissible if it had an adverse impact on blacks. To resolve this dispute the parties executed a second consent decree (1981 Decree) which the District Court approved on August 18, 1981.

In the 1981 Decree, the Department reaffirmed its commitment made in 1979 to implement a promotion procedure with little or no adverse impact on blacks. The parties then agreed to the administration of the proposed promotion procedure and that its results would be "reviewed to determine whether the selection procedure has an adverse impact against black applicants."

The defendants administered the test to 262 applicants of whom 60 (23%) were black. Of the 60 blacks who took the test, only 5 (8.3%) were listed in the top half of the promotion register; the highest ranked black candidate was number 80. In response to an inquiry from the United States, the Department indicated that there was an immediate need to make between 8 and 10 promotions to corporal and announced its intention to elevate between 16 and 20 individuals before construction of a new list.

The United States objected to any rank-ordered use of the list, stating that such use "would result in substantial adverse impact against black applicants" and suggested that the defendants submit an alternative proposal that would comply with the requirements of the 1979 and 1981 decrees. No proposal was submitted, and no promotions were made during the next nine months.

In April 1983, plaintiffs returned to District Court and sought an order enforcing the terms of the two consent decrees. Specifically, they requested that defendants be required to *promote* blacks to corporal "at the same rate at which they have been hired, 1 for 1, until such time as the defendants implement a valid promotional procedure." The plaintiff class contended that such an order would "encourage defendants to develop a valid promotional procedure as soon as possible," and would "help to alleviate the gross underrepresentation of blacks in the supervisory ranks of the Department"—an underrepresentation caused by the Department's past discrimination and exacerbated by its continuing refusal to implement a fair procedure.

Although it opposed the one-for-one promotion requirement, the United States agreed that the consent decrees should be enforced. It stated that defendants had failed to offer "any reason[s] why promotions should not be made," nor had they offered an explanation as to why they had halted "progress towards remedying the effects of past discrimination." The United States further observed that the Department's failure to produce a promotion plan in compliance with the 1979 and 1981 decrees "suggests that a pattern of discrimination against blacks in the Department . . . may be continuing."

After the motion to enforce was filed, four white applicants for promotion to corporal sought to intervene on behalf of a class composed of those white applicants who took the proposed corporal's examination and ranked # 1 through # 79. They argued that the 1979 and 1981 Decrees and the relief proposed by the plaintiffs in their motion to enforce were "unreasonable, illegal, unconstitutional or against public policy."

In an order entered October 28, 1983, the District Court held that the Department's selection procedure had an adverse impact on blacks. Paradise v. Prescott, 580 F.Supp. 171, 174 (MD Ala.). Observing that even if 79 corporals were promoted in rank order, rather than the 15 contemplated, none would be black, the court concluded that "[s]hort of outright exclusion based on race, it is hard to conceive of a selection procedure which would have a greater discriminatory impact." The Department was ordered to submit, by November 10, 1983, "a plan to promote to corporal, from qualified candidates, at least 15 persons in a manner that will not have an adverse racial impact."

The Department subsequently submitted a proposal to promote 15 persons to the rank of corporal, of whom four would be black. In addition, the Department requested that the Department of Personnel be given more time to develop and submit for court approval a nondiscriminatory promotion procedure.

The United States did not oppose the Department's proposal, but plaintiffs did. They argued that the proposal "totally disregards the injury plaintiffs have suffered due to the defendants' four-and-a-half year delay [since the 1979 Decree] and fails to provide any mechanism that will insure the present scenario will not reoccur."

On December 15, 1983, the District Court granted plaintiffs' motion to enforce the 1979 and 1981 Decrees. Paradise v. Prescott, 585 F.Supp. 72 (MD Ala.). Confronted with the Department's immediate need to promote 15 troopers to corporal and the parties' inability to agree, the court was required by the 1979 and 1981 Decrees to fashion a promotion procedure. The District Judge summarized the situation:

> "On February 10, 1984, less than two months from today, twelve years will have passed since this court condemned the

racially discriminatory policies and practices of the Alabama Department of Public Safety. Nevertheless, the effects of these policies and practices remain pervasive and conspicuous at all ranks above the entry-level position. Of the 6 majors, *there is still not one black.* Of the 25 captains, *there is still not one black.* Of the 35 lieutenants, *there is still not one black.* Of the 65 sergeants, *there is still not one black.* Of the 66 corporals, *only four are black.* Thus, the department *still* operates an upper rank structure in which almost every trooper obtained his position through procedures that totally excluded black persons. Moreover, the department is *still* without acceptable procedures for advancement of black troopers into this structure, and it does not appear that any procedures will be in place within the near future. The preceding scenario is intolerable and must not continue. The time has now arrived for the department to take affirmative and substantial steps to open the upper ranks to black troopers." (emphasis in original).

The court then fashioned the relief at issue here. It held that "for a period of time," at least 50% of the promotions to corporal must be awarded to black troopers, if qualified black candidates were available. The court also held that "if there is to be within the near future an orderly path for black troopers to enter the upper ranks, any relief fashioned by the court must address the department's delay in developing acceptable promotion procedures for all ranks." Thus, the court imposed a 50% promotional quota in the upper ranks, but only *if* there were qualified black candidates, *if* the rank were less than 25% black, and *if* the Department had not developed and implemented a promotion plan without adverse impact for the relevant rank. The court concluded that the effects of past discrimination in the Department "will not wither away of their own accord" and that "without promotional quotas the continuing effects of this discrimination cannot be eliminated." The court highlighted the temporary nature and flexible design of the relief ordered, stating that it was "specifically tailored" to eliminate the lingering effects of past discrimination, to remedy the delayed compliance with the consent decrees, and to ensure prompt implementation of lawful procedures.

Finally, the Department was ordered to submit within 30 days a schedule for the development of promotion procedures for all ranks above the entry-level. The schedule was to be "based upon realistic expectations" as the court intended that "the use of the quotas . . . be a one-time occurrence." The District Court reasoned that, under the order it had entered, the Department had "the prerogative to end the promotional quotas at any time, simply by developing acceptable promotion procedures."

Numerous motions for reconsideration of the court's order and for the alteration or amendment of the court's judgment were denied by the District Court. . . . In February 1984, the Department promoted eight blacks and eight whites to corporal pursuant to the District Court's order enforcing the consent decrees.

Four months later, the Department submitted for the court's approval its proposed procedure for promotions to the rank of corporal. The District Court ruled that the Department could promote up to 13 troopers utilizing this procedure and suspended application of the one-for-one requirement for that purpose. In October 1984, following approval of the Department's new selection procedure for promotion to sergeant, the court similarly suspended application of the quota at that rank.[15]

On appeal the Court of Appeals for the Eleventh Circuit affirmed the District Court's order. The Court of Appeals concluded that the relief at issue was designed to remedy the present effects of past discrimination—"effects which, as the history of this case amply demonstrates, 'will not wither away of their own accord.' " Paradise v. Prescott, 767 F.2d 1514, 1533 (1985) (quoting 585 F.Supp., at 75). In addition, the relief awarded was deemed to "exten[d] no further than necessary to accomplish the objective of remedying the 'egregious' and long-standing racial imbalances in the upper ranks of the Department." 767 F.2d, at 1532–1533.

. . .

II

The United States maintains that the race-conscious relief ordered in this case violates the Equal Protection Clause of the Fourteenth Amendment to the Constitution of the United States.

It is now well established that government bodies, including courts, may constitutionally employ racial classifications essential to remedy unlawful treatment of racial or ethnic groups subject to discrimination. See Sheet Metal Workers v. EEOC, 478 U.S. 421, __ (1986), and cases cited therein. See also Wygant v. Jackson Board of Education, 476 U.S. 267, __ (1986) ("The Court is in agreement that . . . remedying past or present racial discrimination . . . is a sufficiently weighty state interest to warrant the remedial use of a carefully constructed affirmative action program") (O'Connor, J., concurring in part and concurring in judgment). But although this Court has consistently held that some elevated level of scrutiny is required when a racial or ethnic distinction is made for remedial purposes, it has yet to reach consensus on the appropriate constitutional analysis.[17] We need not do so in this case,

---

[15] In addition, the Department has been permitted to promote only white troopers to lieutenant and captain because no blacks have qualified, as of yet, for promotion to those ranks. Paradise v. Prescott, 767 F.2d 1514, 1538, n. 19 (CA11 1985).

[17] See Wygant v. Jackson Board of Education, 476 U.S. 267, __ (1986) (opinion of Powell, J.) (the means chosen must be "narrowly tailored" to achieve a "compelling government interest"); id., at __ (O'Connor, J., concurring) (same); id., at __ (Marshall, J., dissenting, joined by Brennan, J. and Blackmun, J.) (remedial use of race permissible if it serves " 'important governmental objectives' " and is " 'substantially related to achievement of those objectives' ") (quoting University of California Regents v. Bakke, 438 U.S. 265, 359 (1978)); 476 U.S., at __ (Stevens, J., dissenting) (both public interest served by racial classification and means employed must justify adverse effects on the disadvantaged group); Fullilove v. Klutznick, 448 U.S. 448, 507 (1980) (Powell, J., concurring) (expressing concern first articulated in *Bakke,* supra, at 362, that review not be " 'strict' in theory and fatal in fact").

however, because we conclude that the relief ordered survives even strict scrutiny analysis: it is "narrowly tailored" to serve a "compelling governmental purpose." (opinion of Powell, J.).

The government unquestionably has a compelling interest in remedying past and present discrimination by a state actor. . . . In 1972 the District Court found, and the Court of Appeals affirmed, that for almost four decades the Department had excluded blacks from all positions, including jobs in the upper ranks. Such egregious discriminatory conduct was "unquestionably a violation of the Fourteenth Amendment." NAACP v. Allen, 340 F.Supp., at 705. As the United States concedes, the pervasive, systematic, and obstinate discriminatory conduct of the Department created a profound need and a firm justification for the race-conscious relief ordered by the District Court.

The Department and the intervenors, however, maintain that the Department was found guilty only of discrimination in hiring, and not in its promotional practices. They argue that no remedial relief is justified in the promotion context because the intentional discrimination in hiring was without effect in the upper ranks, and because the Department's promotional procedure was not discriminatory. There is no merit in either premise.

Discrimination at the entry-level necessarily precluded blacks from competing for promotions, and resulted in a departmental hierarchy dominated exclusively by nonminorities. The lower courts determined that this situation was explicable only by reference to the Department's past discriminatory conduct.[19] In 1972 the Department was "not just found guilty of discriminating against blacks in hiring to entry-level positions. The Court found that in thirty-seven years there had never been a black trooper at any rank." Paradise v. Shoemaker, 470 F.Supp., at 442. In 1979 the District Judge stated that one continuing effect of the Department's historical discrimination was that, "as of November 1, 1978, out of 232 state troopers at the rank of corporal or above, *there is still not one black.*" The court explained that the *hiring* quota it had fashioned was intended to provide "an impetus to promote blacks into those positions" and that "[t]o focus only on the entry-level positions would be to ignore that past discrimination by the Department was pervasive, that its effects persist, and that they are manifest." The District Court crafted the relief it did due to "the department's failure after almost twelve years to eradicate the continuing effects of its own discrimination." 585 F.Supp., at 75, n. 1. It is too late for the Department to attempt to segregate the results achieved by its hiring practices and those achieved by its promotional practices.

The argument that the Department's promotion procedure was not discriminatory is belied by the record. In 1979, faced with additional allegations of discrimination, the Department agreed to adopt promotion procedures without an adverse impact on black candidates within

---

[19] Compare this situation with that described in *Wygant,* supra, at ___ (opinion of Powell, J.) ("There are numerous explanations for a disparity between the percentage of minority students and the percentage of minority faculty, many of them completely unrelated to discrimination of any kind").

one year. See 767 F.2d, at 1532. By 1983 the Department had promoted only four blacks, and these promotions had been made pursuant to the 1979 Decree, and "not the voluntary action of the Department." Id., at 1533, n. 16. In December 1983, the District Court found, despite the commitments made in the consent decrees, that the Department's proposed promotion plan would have an adverse impact upon blacks, 580 F.Supp., at 174, and that "the department *still* operate[d] an upper rank structure in which almost every trooper obtained his position through procedures that totally excluded black persons." 585 F.Supp., at 74 (emphasis in original). On appeal, the Eleventh Circuit summarily rejected the argument of the Department and the intervenors:

> "[I]t is no answer in this case to say that plaintiffs have not proven that the Department has discriminated against blacks above the entry-level seeking promotions. . . . [I]t cannot be gainsaid that white troopers promoted *since 1972* were the specific beneficiaries of *an official policy which systematically excluded all blacks.*" 767 F.2d, at 1533, n. 16 (emphasis added).

Promotion, like hiring, has been a central concern of the District Court since the commencement of this action; since 1972, the relief crafted has included strictures against promotion procedures that have a discriminatory purpose or effect. The race-conscious relief at issue here is justified by a compelling interest in remedying the discrimination that permeated entry-level hiring practices and the promotional process alike.

Finally, in this case, as in Sheet Metal Workers, 478 U.S., at ___ (Powell, J., concurring in part and concurring in judgment), the District Court's enforcement order is "supported not only by the governmental interest in eradicating [the Department's] discriminatory practices, it is also supported by the societal interest in compliance with the judgments of federal courts." The relief at issue was imposed upon a defendant with a consistent history of resistance to the District Court's orders, and only *after* the Department failed to live up to its court-approved commitments.

III

While conceding that the District Court's order serves a compelling interest, the Government insists that it was not narrowly tailored to accomplish its purposes—to remedy past discrimination and eliminate its lingering effects, to enforce compliance with the 1979 and 1981 Decrees by bringing about the speedy implementation of a promotion procedure that would not have an adverse impact on blacks, and to eradicate the ill effects of the Department's delay in producing such a procedure. We cannot agree.

In determining whether race-conscious remedies are appropriate, we look to several factors, including the necessity for the relief and the efficacy of alternative remedies, the flexibility and duration of the relief, including the availability of waiver provisions; the relationship of the numerical goals to the relevant labor market; and the impact of the relief on the rights of third parties. . . . When considered in light of these factors, it was amply established, and we find that the one-for-one promotion requirement was narrowly tailored to serve its several purposes, both as applied to the initial set of promotions to the rank of corporal and as a continuing contingent order with respect to the upper ranks.

A

To evaluate the District Court's determination that it was *necessary* to order the promotion of eight whites and eight blacks to the rank of corporal at the time of the motion to enforce, we must examine the purposes the order was intended to serve. First, the court sought to eliminate the effects of the Department's "long term, open, and pervasive" discrimination, including the absolute exclusion of blacks from its upper ranks. Second, the judge sought to ensure expeditious compliance with the 1979 and 1981 Decrees by inducing the Department to implement a promotion procedure that would not have an adverse impact on blacks. Finally, the court needed to eliminate so far as possible the effects of the Department's delay in producing such a procedure. Confronted by the Department's urgent need to promote at least 15 troopers to corporal, see Paradise v. Prescott, 580 F.Supp., at 173, the District Court determined that all of its purposes could be served only by ordering the promotion of eight blacks and eight whites, as requested by the plaintiff class.

The options proffered by the Government and the Department would not have served the court's purposes. The Department proposed, as a stop-gap measure, to promote four blacks and eleven whites and requested additional time to allow the Department of Personnel to develop and submit a nondiscriminatory promotion procedure. The United States argues that the Department's proposal would have allowed this round of promotions to be made without adverse impact on black candidates.

The Department's proposal was inadequate because it completely failed to address two of the purposes cited above. The Department's ad hoc offer to make one round of promotions without an adverse impact ignored the court's concern that an acceptable procedure be adopted with alacrity. As early as 1972, the Department had been enjoined from engaging in any promotional practices "for the purpose or with the effect of discriminating against any employee . . . on the ground of race or color." NAACP v. Allen, 340 F.Supp., at 706. In 1979, the Department had promised in a court-approved consent decree to develop and implement a *procedure* without adverse impact by 1980. By 1983, such a procedure still had not been established, and Paradise sought enforcement of the consent decrees. Given the record of delay, we find it astonishing that the Department should suggest that in 1983 the District Court was constitutionally required to settle for yet another promise that such a procedure would be forthcoming "as soon as possible."

Moreover, the Department's proposal ignored the injury to the plaintiff class that resulted from its delay in complying with the terms of the 1972 order and the 1979 and 1981 Decrees. As the Fifth Circuit pointed out, no blacks were promoted between 1972 and 1979; the four blacks promoted in 1979 were elevated pursuant to the 1979 Decree and not as a result of the voluntary action of the Department; and, finally, the whites promoted *since* 1972 "were the specific beneficiaries of an official policy which systematically excluded all blacks." 767 F.2d, at 1533, n. 16. To permit ad hoc decisionmaking to continue and allow only four of fifteen slots to be filled by blacks would have denied relief to black troopers who had irretrievably lost promotion opportunities. Thus, adoption of the Department's proposal would have fallen far short of the remedy necessary to eliminate the effects of the Department's past discrimination, would not have ensured adoption of a procedure without adverse impact, and would not have vitiated the effects of the defendant's delay.

The Government suggests that the trial judge could have imposed heavy fines and fees on the Department pending compliance. This alternative was never proposed to the District Court. Furthermore, the Department had been ordered to pay the plaintiffs' attorney's fees and costs throughout this lengthy litigation; these court orders had done little to prevent future foot-dragging. . . . In addition, imposing fines on the defendant does nothing to compensate the plaintiffs for the long delays in implementing acceptable promotion procedures. Finally, the Department had expressed an immediate and urgent need to make 15 promotions, and the District Court took this need into consideration in constructing its remedy. As we observed only last Term, "a district court may find it necessary to order interim hiring or promotional goals pending the development of nondiscriminatory hiring or promotion procedures. In these cases, the use of numerical goals provides a compromise between two unacceptable alternatives: an outright ban on hiring or promotions . . . continued use of a discriminatory selection procedure," or, we might add, use of no selection procedure at all. Sheet Metal Workers, 478 U.S., at ___ (opinion of Brennan, J.).

By 1984 the District Court was plainly justified in imposing the remedy chosen. Any order allowing further delay by the Department was entirely unacceptable. . . . Not only was the immediate promotion of blacks to the rank of corporal essential, but, if the need for continuing judicial oversight was to end, it was also essential that the Department be required to develop a procedure without adverse impact on blacks, and that the effect of past delays be eliminated.

We conclude that in 1983, when the District Judge entered his order, "it is doubtful, given [the Department's] history in this litigation, that the District Court had available to it any other effective remedy." Sheet Metal Workers, supra, at ___ (Powell, J., concurring in part and concurring in judgment).

B

The features of the one-for-one requirement and its actual operation indicate that it is flexible in application at all ranks. The requirement may be waived if no qualified black candidates are available. The Department has, for example, been permitted to promote only white troopers to the ranks of lieutenant and captain since no black troopers have qualified for those positions. Further, it applies only when the Department needs to make promotions. Thus, if external forces, such as budget cuts, necessitate a promotion freeze, the Department will not be required to make gratuitous promotions to remain in compliance with the court's order.

Most significantly, the one-for-one requirement is ephemeral; the term of its application is contingent upon the Department's own conduct. The requirement endures only until the Department comes up with a procedure that does not have a discriminatory impact on blacks—something the Department was enjoined to do in 1972 and expressly promised to do by 1980. [T]he court has taken into account the difficulty of validating a test and does not require validation as a prerequisite for suspension of the promotional requirement. The one-for-one requirement evaporated at the ranks of corporal and sergeant upon implementation of promotion procedures without an adverse impact, demonstrating that it is not a disguised means to achieve racial balance. . . .

Finally, the record reveals that this requirement was flexible, waivable, and temporary in application. When the District Court imposed the provision, the judge expressed the hope that its use would be "a one-time occurrence." 585 F.Supp., at 76. The court believed that this hope would be fulfilled: at the January 15, 1984, hearing on the plaintiffs' motion to enforce the consent decrees, "the Personnel Department pledged that it would *now* devote its full resources to assisting the Public Safety Department in not only developing acceptable promotion procedures as required by the two consent decrees, but in doing so within the near future." The Department has since timely submitted procedures for promotions to corporal and sergeant, and the court has consequently suspended application of the promotional order with respect to those ranks. In the higher ranks, the Department has been permitted to promote only white troopers. It now appears that the effect of the order enforcing the decrees will be "the development of acceptable promotion procedures for all ranks and the nullification of the promotion quota." 767 F.2d, at 1538, n. 19. The remedy chosen has proven both effective and flexible.

C

We must also examine the relationship between the numerical relief ordered and the percentage of nonwhites in the relevant workforce. The original hiring order of the District Court required the Department to hire 50% black applicants until 25% of the state trooper force was composed of blacks; the latter figure reflects the percentage of blacks in the relevant labor market. 585 F.Supp., at 75, n. 2. The enforcement order at issue here is less restrictive: it requires the Department to promote 50% black candidates until 25% of the rank in question is black, but *only* until a promotion procedure without an adverse impact on blacks is in place. Thus, had the promotion order remained in effect for the rank of corporal, it would have survived only until 25% of the Department's corporals were black.

The Government suggests that the one-for-one requirement is arbitrary because it bears no relationship to the 25% minority labor pool relevant here. This argument ignores that the 50% figure is not itself the goal; rather it represents the speed at which the goal of 25% will be achieved. The interim requirement of one-for-one promotion (had it continued) would simply have determined how quickly the Department progressed toward this ultimate goal. This requirement is therefore analogous to the imposition in *Sheet Metal Workers* of an end date, which regulated the speed of progress toward fulfillment of the hiring goal. Sheet Metal Workers, 478 U.S., at ___ (Powell, J., concurring in part and concurring in judgment).

To achieve the goal of 25% black representation in the upper ranks, the court was not limited to ordering the promotion of only 25% blacks at any one time. Some promptness in the administration of relief was plainly justified in this case, and use of deadlines or end-dates had proven ineffective. In these circumstances, the use of a temporary requirement of 50% minority promotions, which, like the end date in *Sheet Metal Workers,* was crafted and applied flexibly, was constitutionally permissible.

The District Court did not accept the argument that in order to achieve a goal of 25% representation, it could order only 25% of any particular round of promotions to be awarded to minorities. Had it done so, the court would have implemented the Department's proposal to promote 4 blacks and 11 whites when it issued its order enforcing the consent decree, because this proposal approximated the 25% figure.[30] Again, however, this proposal completely ignores the fact and the effects of the Department's past discrimination and its delay in implementing the necessary promotion procedure. Here the District Court considered both the Department's proposal and the possibility of promoting blacks to all 15 corporal positions "[i]n light of the department's failure after almost twelve years to eradicate the continuing effects of its own discrimination and to develop acceptable promotion procedures and in light of the severity of the existing racial imbalances." 585 F.Supp., at 75, n. 1. The court rejected both of these alternatives and, upon consideration of the Department's behavior and of the interests

[30] Following adoption of the plaintiffs' proposal that 8 blacks and 8 whites should be promoted, the corporal rank was composed of 14 black and 73 white troopers (16% black). Under the Department's proposal that 4 blacks and 11 whites should be promoted, the corporal rank would have been composed of 8 black and 79 white troopers (9.2% black). Neither proposal would have raised the percentage of blacks in the corporal rank to the 25% mark set as an alternate goal by the District Court (the other alternative being the adoption of a promotion procedure without adverse impact). Obviously, however, the plaintiffs' proposal provided an accelerated approach to achieving that goal to compensate for past delay.

and the purposes to be served, arrived at an intermediate figure. Although the appropriate ratio here "necessarily involve[d] a degree of approximation and imprecision," Teamsters v. United States, 431 U.S. 324, 372 (1977), the District Court, with its first-hand experience of the parties and the potential for resistance, imposed the requirement that it determined would compensate for past delay and prevent future recalcitrance, while not unduly burdening the interests of white troopers.

It would have been improper for the District Judge to ignore the effects of the Department's delay and its continued default of its obligation to develop a promotion procedure, and to require only that, commencing in 1984, the Department promote one black for every three whites promoted. The figure selected to compensate for past discrimination and delay necessarily involved a delicate calibration of the rights and interests of the plaintiff class, the Department, and the white troopers. The Government concedes that a one-to-three requirement would have been lawful; the District Court determined that more stringent measures were necessary. This Court should not second-guess the lower court's carefully considered choice of the figure necessary to achieve its many purposes, especially when that figure is hedged about with specific qualifying measures designed to prevent any unfair impact that might arise from rigid application.[32]

D

The one-for-one requirement did not impose an unacceptable burden on innocent third parties. As stated above, the temporary and extremely limited nature of the requirement substantially limits any potential burden on white applicants for promotion. It was used only once at the rank of corporal and may not be utilized at all in the upper ranks. Nor has the court imposed an "absolute bar" to white advancement. *Sheet Metal Workers*, 478 U.S., at ___. In the one instance in which the quota was employed, 50% of those elevated were white.

The one-for-one requirement does not require the layoff and discharge of white employees and therefore does not impose burdens of the sort that concerned the plurality in *Wygant*, 476 U.S., at ___ (opinion of Powell, J.) ("layoffs impose the entire burden of achieving racial equality on particular individuals, often resulting in serious disruption of their lives") id., at ___ (White, J., concurring) (same). Because the one-for-one requirement is so limited in scope and duration, it only postpones the promotions of qualified whites. Consequently, like a hiring goal, it "impose[s] a diffuse burden, . . . foreclosing only one of several opportunities." Id., at ___. "Denial of a future employment

---

[32] The dissent suggests that the percentage of minority individuals benefited by this race-conscious remedial order should not exceed the percentage of minority groups members in the relevant population or work force. We disagree. Even within the narrow confines of strict scrutiny, there remains the requirement that the district court not only *refrain* from ordering relief that violates the Constitution, but also that it *order* the relief necessary to cure past violations and to obtain compliance with its mandate. There will be cases—this is one—where some accelerated relief is plainly justified. To say that it is not overlooks the history of this litigation.

opportunity is not as intrusive as loss of an existing job," *Wygant,* 476 U.S., at ___ (opinion of Powell, J.), and plainly postponement imposes a lesser burden still.

Finally, the basic limitation, that black troopers promoted must be qualified, remains. Qualified white candidates simply have to compete with qualified black candidates. To be sure, should the District Court's promotion requirement be applied, black applicants would receive some advantage. But this situation is only temporary, and is subject to amelioration by the action of the Department itself.

Accordingly, the one-for-one promotion requirement imposed in this case does not disproportionately harm the interests, or unnecessarily trammel the rights, of innocent individuals.

E

In determining whether this order was "narrowly tailored," we must acknowledge the respect owed a District Judge's judgment that specified relief is essential to cure a violation of the Fourteenth Amendment. A district court has "not merely the power but the duty to render a decree which will so far as possible eliminate the discriminatory effects of the past as well as bar like discrimination in the future." Louisiana v. United States, 380 U.S. 145, 154 (1965). "Once a right and a violation have been shown, the scope of a district court's equitable powers to remedy past wrongs is broad, for breadth and flexibility are inherent in equitable remedies." Swann v. Charlotte-Mecklenburg Bd. of Education, 402 U.S. 1, 15 (1971).

Nor have we in all situations "required remedial plans to be limited to the least restrictive means of implementation. We have recognized that the choice of remedies to redress racial discrimination is 'a balancing process left, within appropriate constitutional or statutory limits, to the sound discretion of the trial court.'" *Fullilove,* supra, at 508 (Powell, J., concurring) (quoting Franks v. Bowman Transportation Co., 424 U.S., at 794 (Powell, J., concurring in part and dissenting in part)). . . .

The district court has first-hand experience with the parties and is best qualified to deal with the "flinty, intractable realities of day-to-day implementation of constitutional commands." *Swann,* supra, at 6. In this case, as in *Sheet Metal Workers,* "th[e] court having had the parties before it over a period of time, was in the best position to judge whether an alternative remedy, such as a simple injunction, would have been effective in ending [the] discriminatory practices." 478 U.S., at ___ (Powell, J., concurring). The District Judge determined that the record demonstrated that "without promotional quotas the continuing effects of [the Department's] discrimination cannot be eliminated." 585 F.Supp., at 76. His proximate position and broad equitable powers mandate substantial respect for this judgment.

Plainly the District Court's discretion in remedying the deeply-rooted Fourteenth Amendment violations here was limited by the rights and interests of the white troopers seeking promotion to corporal. But we conclude that the District Judge properly balanced the individual and collective interests at stake, including the interests of the white troopers eligible for promotion, in shaping this remedy. . . . While a remedy must be narrowly tailored, that requirement does not operate to remove all discretion from the District Court in its construction of a remedial decree.

IV

The remedy imposed here is an effective, temporary and flexible measure. It applies only if qualified blacks are available, only if the Department has an objective need to make promotions, and only if the Department fails to implement a promotion procedure that does not have an adverse impact on blacks. The one-for-one requirement is the product of the considered judgment of the District Court which, with its knowledge of the parties and their resources, properly determined that strong measures were required in light of the Department's long and shameful record of delay and resistance.

The race-conscious relief imposed here was amply justified, and narrowly tailored to serve the legitimate and laudable purposes of the District Court. The judgment of the Court of Appeals, upholding the order of the District Court, is

Affirmed.

Justice Powell, concurring.

. . .

I . . . agree with the Court that the protracted history of this litigation justifies the conclusion that the "one-for-one" promotion to corporal was appropriate. It is reasonable to conclude that the District Court would have been "powerless to provide an effective remedy" if it had lacked authority to establish a benchmark against which to measure progress in remedying the effects of the discrimination.

In determining whether an affirmative action remedy is narrowly drawn to achieve its goal, I have thought that five factors may be relevant: (i) the efficacy of alternative remedies; (ii) the planned duration of the remedy; (iii) the relationship between the percentage of minority workers to be employed and the percentage of minority group members in the relevant population or work force; (iv) the availability of waiver provisions if the hiring plan could not be met; and (v) the effect of the remedy upon innocent third parties. Id., at ___; Fullilove v. Klutznick, 448 U.S. 448, 510–511, 514 (1980) (opinion of Powell, J.). The Court's opinion today makes clear that the affirmative action ordered by the District Court and approved by the Court of Appeals for the Eleventh Circuit was narrowly drawn to achieve the goal of remedying the proven and continuing discrimination. . . .

In view of the purpose and indeed the explicit language of the Equal Protection Clause, court-ordered or government-adopted affirmative action plans must be most carefully scrutinized. The Court, in its opinion today, has done this. I therefore join the opinion.

_____

Justice Stevens, concurring in the judgment.

In 1971, one year before the District Court found in this case that the State of Alabama had persistently maintained a deliberately segregated police force, this Court issued a unanimous opinion setting forth the guidelines for district judges in fashioning remedies to eliminate the effects of racial segregation in public schools. Swann v. Charlotte-Mecklenburg Bd. of Education, 402 U.S. 1 (1971). The central theme of that opinion is that race-conscious remedies are obviously required to remedy racially discriminatory actions by the State that violate the Fourteenth Amendment.

Because *Swann* explained the appropriate governing standard, it must have provided guidance to the District Court in this case and it should now guide our deliberations. Chief Justice Burger wrote:

"Once a right and a violation have been shown, the scope of a district court's equitable powers to remedy past wrongs is broad, for breadth and flexibility are inherent in equitable remedies. . . ."

In this case, the record discloses an egregious violation of the Equal Protection Clause. It follows, therefore, that the District Court had broad and flexible authority to remedy the wrongs resulting from this violation—exactly the opposite of the Solicitor General's unprecedented suggestion that the judge's discretion is constricted by a "narrowly tailored to achieve a compelling governmental interest" standard.

The notion that this Court should craft special and narrow rules for reviewing judicial decrees in racial discrimination cases was soundly rejected in *Swann*. . . .

The Court was equally unambiguous in its rejection of the argument that a different standard of review is required when a remedial decree employs mathematical ratios. . . .

A party who has been found guilty of repeated and persistent violations of the law bears the burden of demonstrating that the chancellor's efforts to fashion effective relief exceed the bounds of "reasonableness." The burden of proof in a case like this is precisely the opposite of that in cases such as Wygant v. Jackson Board of Education, 476 U.S. ___ (1986), and Fullilove v. Klutznick, 448 U.S. 448 (1980), which did not involve any proven violations of law. In such cases the governmental decisionmaker who would make race-conscious decisions must overcome a strong presumption against them. No such burden rests on a federal district judge who has found that the governmental unit before him is guilty of racially discriminatory conduct that violates the Constitution.

The relief that the district judge has a duty to fashion must unavoidably consider race. . . .

The District Court, like the school authority in North Carolina State Board of Education v. Swann, may, and in some instances must, resort to race-conscious remedies to vindicate federal constitutional guarantees. Because the instant employment discrimination case "does not differ fundamentally from other cases involving the framing of equitable remedies to repair the denial of a constitutional right," Swann v. Charlotte-Mecklenburg Board of Education, supra, at 15–16, and because there has been no showing that the District Judge abused his discretion in shaping a remedy, I concur in the Court's judgment.

Justice O'Connor, with whom The Chief Justice and Justice Scalia join, dissenting.

In Wygant v. Jackson Board of Education, 476 U.S. ___, ___ (1986), we concluded that the level of Fourteenth Amendment "scrutiny does not change merely because the challenged classification operates against a group that historically has not been subject to governmental discrimination." Thus, in evaluating the constitutionality of the District Court order in this case under the Fourteenth Amendment, we must undertake a two-part inquiry. First, we must decide whether the order is "supported by a compelling [governmental] purpose." Second, we must scrutinize the order to ensure that "the means chosen to accomplish that purpose are narrowly tailored."

One cannot read the record in this case without concluding that the Alabama Department of Public Safety had undertaken a course of action that amounted to "pervasive, systematic, and obstinate discriminatory conduct."

Because the Federal Government has a compelling interest in remedying past and present discrimination by the Department, the District Court unquestionably had the authority to fashion a remedy designed to end the Department's egregious history of discrimination. In doing so, however, the District Court was obligated to fashion a remedy that was narrowly tailored to accomplish this purpose. The Court today purports to apply strict scrutiny, and concludes that the order in this case was narrowly tailored for its remedial purpose. Because the Court adopts a standardless view of "narrowly tailored" far less stringent than that required by strict scrutiny, I dissent.

As Justice Powell notes, this case is similar to Sheet Metal Workers v. EEOC, 478 U.S. ___ (1986). In *Sheet Metal Workers,* I observed that "it is completely unrealistic to assume that individuals of each race will gravitate with mathematical exactitude to each employer or union absent unlawful discrimination." Thus, a rigid quota is impermissible because it adopts "an unjustified conclusion about the precise extent to which past discrimination has lingering effects, or . . . an unjustified prediction about what would happen in the future in the absence of continuing discrimination." Even more flexible "goals," however, also may trammel unnecessarily the rights of nonminorities. Racially preferential treatment of nonvictims, therefore, should only be ordered "where such remedies are truly necessary." Thus, "the creation of racial preferences by courts, even in the more limited form of goals rather than quotas, must be done sparingly and only where manifestly necessary."

In my view, whether characterized as a goal or a quota, the District Court's order was not "manifestly necessary" to achieve compliance with that court's previous orders. The order at issue in this case clearly had one purpose, and one purpose only—to compel the Department to develop a promotion procedure that would not have an adverse impact on blacks. Although the Court and the courts below suggest that the order also had the purpose of "eradicat[ing] the ill effects of the Department's delay in producing" such a promotion procedure, the District Court's subsequent implementation of the order makes clear that the order cannot be defended on the basis of such a purpose.

The order imposed the promotion quota only until the Department developed a promotion procedure that complied with the consent decrees. If the order were truly designed to eradicate the effects of the Department's delay, the District Court would certainly have continued the use of the one-for-one quota even after the Department had complied with the consent decrees. Consistent with the terms of the order, once the Department developed a promotion procedure that did not have an adverse impact on blacks, the District Court suspended application of the quota. Under the approved promotion procedure, 13 troopers were promoted to corporal, of whom 3 (23.1%) were black. The result of this new procedure was the promotion of a *lower* percentage of blacks than the purported goal of 25% black representation in the upper ranks, and the promotion of *fewer* blacks than even the Department's promotion proposal rejected by the District Court. To say the least, it strains credibility to view the one-for-one promotion quota as designed to eradicate the past effects of the Department's delay when the quota was suspended once the Department developed a promotion procedure that promoted a *lower* percentage of blacks than the 25% black representation goal.

Moreover, even if the one-for-one quota had the purpose of eradicating the effects of the Department's delay, this purpose would not justify the quota imposed in this case. "[T]he relationship between the percentage of minority workers to be [promoted] and the percentage of minority group members in the relevant population or work force" is of vital importance in considering the validity of a racial goal. Sheet Metal Workers v. EEOC, supra, at __ (Powell, J., concurring in part and concurring in judgment). The one-for-one promotion quota used in this case far exceeded the percentage of blacks in the trooper force, and there is no evidence in the record that such an extreme quota was necessary to eradicate the effects of the Department's delay. The Court attempts to defend this one-for-one promotion quota as merely affecting the speed by which the Department attains the goal of 25% black representation in the upper ranks. Such a justification, however, necessarily eviscerates any notion of "narrowly tailored" because it has no stopping point; even a 100% quota could be defended on the ground that it merely "determined how quickly the Department progressed toward" some ultimate goal.

If strict scrutiny is to have any meaning, therefore, a promotion goal must have a closer relationship to the percentage of blacks eligible for promotions. This is not to say that the percentage of minority individuals benefited by a racial goal may never exceed the percentage of minority group members in the relevant work force. But protection of the rights of nonminority workers demands that a racial goal not substantially exceed the percentage of minority group members in the relevant population or work force absent compelling justification. In this case the District Court—and indeed this Court—provide no such compelling justification for the choice of a one-for-one promotion quota rather than a lower quota. In my view, therefore, the order in this case must stand or fall on its stated purpose of coercing the Department to develop a promotion procedure without an adverse impact on black troopers.

Given the singular *in terrorem* purpose of the District Court order, it cannot survive strict scrutiny. There is simply no justification for the use of racial preferences if the purpose of the order could be achieved without their use because "[r]acial classifications are simply too pernicious to permit any but the most exact connection between justification and classification." Fullilove v. Klutznick, 448 U.S. 448, 537 (1980) (Stevens, J., dissenting). Thus, to survive strict scrutiny, the District Court order must fit with greater precision than any alternative remedy. See Ely, The Constitutionality of Reverse Racial Discrimination, 41 U.Chi.L.Rev. 723, 727, n. 26 (1974). The District Court had available several alternatives that would have achieved full compliance with the consent decrees without trammeling on the rights of nonminority troopers. The court, for example, could have appointed a trustee to develop a promotion procedure that would satisfy the terms of the consent decrees. By imposing the trustee's promotion procedure on the Department until the Department developed an alternative promotion procedure that complied with the consent decrees, the District Court could have enforced the decrees without the use of racial preferences. Alternatively, the District Court could have found the recalcitrant Department in contempt of court, and imposed stiff fines or other penalties for the contempt. Surely, some combination of penalties could have been designed that would have compelled compliance with the consent decrees.

The District Court, however, did not discuss these options or *any* other alternatives to the use of racial quota. Not a single alternative method of achieving compliance with the consent decrees is even mentioned in the District Court's opinion—with the exception of an even more objectionable 100% *racial quota.* See Paradise v. Prescott, 585 F.Supp. 72, 75, n. 1 (MD Ala. 1983). What is most disturbing about the District Court's order, therefore, is not merely that it implicitly or explicitly rejected two particular options, but that the District Court imposed the promotion quota *without consideration of any of the available alternatives.* Even in Sheet Metal Workers v. EEOC, 478 U.S. ___ (1986), the District Court had "considered the efficacy of alternative remedies" before imposing a racial quota. Thus, the Court was able to evaluate the claim that the racial quota was "necessary." Without any exploration of the available alternatives in the instant case, no such evaluation is possible. Remarkably, however, the Court—purporting to apply "strict scrutiny"—concludes that the order in this case was narrowly tailored for a remedial purpose.

Although the Court states that it is merely "respect[ing]" the "balancing process" of the District Court, it wholly ignores the fact that no such "balancing process" took place in this case. For even if, as the Court insists, the District Court " 'was in the best position to judge whether an alternative remedy, such as a simple injunction, would have been effective in ending [the] discriminatory practices,' " the *least* that strict scrutiny requires is that the District Court expressly evaluate the available alternative remedies. If a District Court order that is imposed after no evident consideration of the available alternatives can survive strict scrutiny as narrowly tailored, the requirement that a racial classification be "narrowly tailored" for a compelling governmental purpose has lost most of its meaning.

I have no quarrel with the Court's conclusion that the recalcitrance of the Department of Public Safety in complying with the consent decrees was reprehensible. In its understandable frustration over the Department's conduct, however, the District Court imposed a racial quota without first considering the effectiveness of alternatives that would have a lesser effect on the rights of nonminority troopers. Because the District Court did not even consider the available alternatives to a one-for-one promotion quota, and because these alternatives would have successfully compelled the Department to comply with the consent decrees, I must respectfully dissent.

Justice White, dissenting.

Agreeing with much of what Justice O'Connor has written in this case, I find it evident that the District Court exceeded its equitable powers in devising a remedy in this case. I therefore dissent from the judgment of affirmance.

SECTION 4. PROTECTION OF PERSONAL LIBERTIES

B. VOTING AND ELECTIONS

---

2. LEGISLATIVE DISTRICTING

Page 865. Add ahead of Reynolds and Local Government Units:

DAVIS v. BANDEMER
478 U.S. 109, 106 S.Ct. 2797, 92 L.Ed.2d 85 (1986).

Justice White announced the judgment of the Court and delivered the opinion of the Court as to Part II and an opinion in which Justice Brennan, Justice Marshall, and Justice Blackmun joined as to Parts I, III, and IV.

In this case, we review a judgment from a three-judge District Court, which sustained an equal protection challenge to Indiana's 1981 state apportionment on the basis that the law unconstitutionally diluted the votes of Indiana Democrats. 603 F.Supp. 1479 (1984). Although we find such political gerrymandering to be justiciable, we conclude that the District Court applied an insufficiently demanding standard in finding unconstitutional vote dilution. Consequently, we reverse.

I

The Indiana Legislature, also known as the "General Assembly," consists of a House of Representatives and a Senate. There are 100 members of the House of Representatives, and 50 members of the Senate. The members of the House serve two-year terms, with elections held for all seats every 2 years. The members of the Senate serve 4-year terms, and Senate elections are staggered so that half of the seats are up for election every two years. The members of both Houses are elected from legislative districts; but, while all Senate members are elected from single-member districts, House members are elected from a mixture of single-member and multi-member districts. The division of the State into districts is accomplished by legislative enactment, which is signed by the Governor into law. Reapportionment is required every 10 years and is based on the federal decennial census. There is no prohibition against more frequent reapportionments.

In early 1981, the General Assembly initiated the process of reapportioning the State's legislative districts pursuant to the 1980 census. At this time, there were Republican majorities in both the House and the Senate, and the Governor was Republican. Bills were introduced in both Houses, and a reapportionment plan was duly passed and approved by the Governor. This plan provided 50 single-member districts for the Senate; for the House, it provided 7 triple-member, 9 double-member, and 61 single-member districts. In the Senate plan, the population deviation between districts was 1.15%; in the House plan, the deviation was 1.05%. The multi-member districts generally included the more metropolitan areas of the State, although not every metropolitan area was in a multi-member district. Marion County, which includes Indianapolis, was combined with portions of its neighboring counties to form five triple-member districts. Fort Wayne was divided into two parts, and each part was combined with portions of the surrounding county or counties to make two double-member districts. On the other hand, South Bend was divided and put partly into a double-member district and partly into a single-member district (each part combined with part of the surrounding county or counties). Although county and city lines were not consistently followed, township lines generally were. The two plans, the Senate and the House, were not nested; that is, each Senate district was not divided exactly into two House districts. There appears to have been little relation between the lines drawn in the two plans.

In early 1982, this suit was filed by several Indiana Democrats (here the appellees) against various state officials (here the appellants), alleging that the 1981 reapportionment plans constituted a political gerrymander intended to disadvantage Democrats. Specifically, they contended that the particular district lines that were drawn and the mix of single- and multi-member districts were intended to and did violate their right, as Democrats, to equal protection under the Fourteenth Amendment. A three-judge District Court was convened to hear these claims.

In November 1982, before the case went to trial, elections were held under the new districting plan. All of the House seats and half of the Senate seats were up for election. Over all the House races statewide, Democratic candidates received 51.9% of the vote. Only 43 Democrats, however, were elected to the House. Over all the Senate races statewide, Democratic candidates received 53.1% of the vote. Thirteen (of 25) Democrats were elected. In Marion and Allen Counties, both divided into multi-member House districts, Democratic candidates drew 46.6% of the vote, but only 3 of the 21 House seats were filled by Democrats.

On December 13, 1984, a divided District Court issued a decision declaring the reapportionment to be unconstitutional, enjoining the appellants from holding elections pursuant to the 1981 redistricting, ordering the General Assembly to prepare a new plan, and retaining jurisdiction over the case. See 603 F.Supp. 1479 (1984).

To the District Court majority, the results of the 1982 elections seemed "to support an argument that there is a built-in bias favoring the majority party, the Republicans, which instituted the reapportionment plan." Although the court thought that these figures were unreliable predictors of future elections, it concluded that they warranted further examination of the circumstances surrounding the passage of the reapportionment statute. In the course of this further examination, the court noted the irregular shape of some district lines, the peculiar mix of single- and multi-member districts, and the failure of the district lines to adhere consistently to political subdivision boundaries to define communities of interest. The court also found inadequate the other explanations given for the configuration of the districts, such as adherence to the one-person, one-vote imperative and the Voting Right Act's no retrogression requirement. These factors, concluded the court, evidenced an intentional effort to favor Republican incumbents and candidates and to disadvantage Democratic voters. This was achieved by "stacking" Democrats into districts with large Democratic majorities and "splitting" them in other districts so as to give Republicans safe but not excessive majorities in those districts. Because the 1982 elections indicated that the plan also had a discriminatory effect in that the proportionate voting influence of Democratic voters had been adversely affected and because any scheme "which purposely inhibit[s] or prevent[s] proportional representation cannot be tolerated" the District Court invalidated the statute.

The defendants appealed, seeking review of the District Court's rulings that the case was justiciable and that, if justiciable, an equal protection violation had occurred. . . .

II

We address first the question whether this case presents a justiciable controversy or a nonjusticiable political question. Although the District Court never explicitly stated that the case was justiciable, its holding clearly rests on such a finding. The appellees urge that this Court has in the past acknowledged and acted upon the justiciability of purely political gerrymandering claims. The appellants contend that we have affirmed on the merits decisions of lower courts finding such claims to be nonjusticiable.

A

Since Baker v. Carr, 369 U.S. 186 (1962), we have consistently adjudicated equal protection claims in the legislative districting context regarding inequalities in population between districts. In the course of these cases, we have developed and enforced the "one person, one vote" principle. See, e.g., Reynolds v. Sims, 377 U.S. 533 (1964).

Our past decisions also make clear that even where there is no population deviation among the districts, racial gerrymandering presents a justiciable equal protection claim. In the multi-member district context, we have reviewed, and on occasion rejected, districting plans that unconstitutionally diminished the effectiveness of the votes of racial minorities. See Rogers v. Lodge, 458 U.S. 613 (1982); Mobile v. Bolden, 446 U.S. 55 (1980); White v. Regester, 412 U.S. 755 (1973); Whitcomb v. Chavis, 403 U.S. 124 (1971); Burns v. Richardson, 384 U.S. 73 (1966); Fortson v. Dorsey, 379 U.S. 433 (1965). We have also adjudicated claims that the configuration of single-member districts violated equal protection with respect to racial and ethnic minorities, although we have never struck down an apportionment plan because of such a claim. See United Jewish Organizations of Williamsburgh, Inc. v. Carey, 430 U.S. 144 (1977); Wright v. Rockefeller, 376 U.S. 52 (1964).

In the multi-member district cases, we have also repeatedly stated that districting that would "operate to minimize or cancel out the voting strength of racial *or political* elements of the voting population" would raise a constitutional question. *Fortson,* supra, at 439 (emphasis added). See also Gaffney v. Cummings, 412 U.S. 735, 751 (1973); Whitcomb v. Chavis, supra, at 143; Burns v. Richardson, supra, at 88. Finally, in Gaffney v. Cummings, supra, we upheld against an equal protection political gerrymandering challenge a state legislative single-member redistricting scheme that was formulated in a bipartisan effort to try to provide political representation on a level approximately proportional to the strength of political parties in the State. In that case, we adjudicated the type of purely political equal protection claim that is brought here, although we did not, as a threshold matter, expressly hold such a claim to be justiciable. Regardless of this lack of a specific holding, our consideration of the merits of the claim in *Gaffney* in the face of a discussion of justiciability in appellant's brief, combined with our repeated reference in other opinions to the constitutional deficiencies of plans that dilute the vote of political groups, at the least supports an inference that these cases are justiciable.

In the years since Baker v. Carr, both before and after *Gaffney,* however, we have also affirmed a number of decisions in which the lower courts rejected the justiciability of purely political gerrymandering claims. In WMCA, Inc. v. Lomenzo, 382 U.S. 4 (1985), summarily aff'g 238 F.Supp. 916 (SDNY), the most frequently cited of these cases, we affirmed the decision of a three-judge District Court upholding a temporary apportionment plan for the State of New York. The District Court had determined that political gerrymandering equal protection challenges to this plan were nonjusticiable. See id., at 925–926. Justice Harlan, in his opinion concurring in the Court's summary affirmance, expressed his understanding that the affirmance was based on the Court's approval of the lower court's finding of nonjusticiability. See 382 U.S., at 6. See also Jimenez v. Hidalgo County Water Improvement District No. 2, 424 U.S. 950 (1976), summarily aff'g 68 F.R.D. 668 (SD Tex.1975); Ferrell v. Hall, 406 U.S. 939 (1972), summarily aff'g 339 F.Supp. 73 (WD Okla.); Wells v. Rockefeller, 398 U.S. 901 (1970), summarily aff'g 311 F.Supp. 48 (SDNY). Although these summary affirmances arguably support an inference that these claims are not justiciable, there are other cases in which federal or state courts adjudicated political gerrymandering claims and we summarily affirmed or dismissed for want of a substantial federal question. See, e.g., Wiser v. Hughes, 459 U.S. 962 (1982), dismissing for want of a substantial federal question an appeal from In re Legislative Districting, 299 Md. 658, 475 A.2d 428; Kelly v. Bumpers, 413 U.S. 901 (1973), summarily aff'g 340 F.Supp. 568 (ED Ark. 1972); Archer v. Smith, 409 U.S. 808 (1972), summarily aff'g Graves v. Barnes, 343 F.Supp. 704, 734 (WD Tex.).

These sets of cases may look in different directions, but to the extent that our summary affirmances indicate the nonjusticiability of political gerrymander cases, we are not bound by those decisions. As we have observed before, "[i]t is not at all unusual for the Court to find it appropriate to give full consideration to a question that has been the subject of previous summary action." Washington v. Yakima Indian Nation, 439 U.S. 463, 477, n. 20 (1979). See also Edelman v. Jordan, 415 U.S. 651, 670–671 (1974). The issue that the appellants would have us find to be precluded by these summary dispositions is an important one, and it deserves further consideration.

B

The outlines of the political question doctrine were described and to a large extent defined in Baker v. Carr. The synthesis of that effort is found in the following passage in the Court's opinion:

> "It is apparent that several formulations which vary slightly according to the settings in which the questions arise may describe a political question, although each has one or more elements which identify it as essentially a function of the separation of powers. Prominent on the surface of any case held to involve a political

question is found a textually demonstrable constitutional commitment of the issue to a coordinate political department; or a lack of judicially discoverable and manageable standards for resolving it; or the impossibility of deciding without an initial policy determination of a kind clearly for nonjudicial discretion; or the impossibility of a court's undertaking independent resolution without expressing lack of the respect due coordinate branches of government; or an unusual need for unquestioning adherence to a political decision already made; or the potentiality of embarrassment from multifarious pronouncements by various departments on one question.

"Unless one of these formulations is inextricable from the case at bar, there should be no dismissal for nonjusticiability on the ground of a political question's presence. The doctrine of which we treat is one of 'political questions,' not one of 'political cases.' The courts cannot reject as 'no law suit' a bona fide controversy as to whether some action denominated 'political' exceeds constitutional authority. The cases we have reviewed show the necessity for discriminating inquiry into the precise facts and posture of the particular case, and the impossibility of resolution by any semantic cataloguing." 369 U.S., at 217.

In *Baker,* the Court applied this analysis to an equal protection claim based on a state legislative apportionment that allowed substantial disparities in the number of voters represented by each state representative. See id., at 253–258 (Clark, J., concurring). In holding that claim to be justiciable, the Court concluded that none of the identifying characteristics of a political question were present:

"The question here is the consistency of state action with the Federal Constitution. We have no question decided, or to be decided, by a political branch of government coequal with this Court. Nor do we risk embarrassment of our government abroad, or grave disturbance at home if we take issue with Tennessee as to the constitutionality of her action here challenged. Nor need the appellants, in order to succeed in this action, ask the Court to enter upon policy determinations for which judicially manageable standards are lacking. Judicial standards under the Equal Protection Clause are well developed and familiar, and it has been open to courts since the enactment of the Fourteenth Amendment to determine, if on the particular facts they must, that a discrimination reflects *no* policy, but simply arbitrary and capricious action." Id., at 226.

This analysis applies equally to the question now before us. Disposition of this question does not involve us in a matter more properly decided by a coequal branch of our Government. There is no risk of foreign or domestic disturbance, and in light of our cases since *Baker* we are not persuaded that there are no judicially discernible and manageable standards by which political gerrymander cases are to be decided.

It is true that the type of claim that was presented in Baker v. Carr was subsequently resolved in this Court by the formulation of the "one

person, one vote" rule. See, e.g., Reynolds v. Sims, 377 U.S., at 557–
561. The mere fact, however, that we may not now similarly perceive a
likely arithmetic presumption in the instant context does not compel a
conclusion that the claims presented here are nonjusticiable. The one
person, one vote principle had not yet been developed when *Baker* was
decided. At that time, the Court did not rely on the potential for such
a rule in finding justiciability. Instead, as the language quoted above
clearly indicates, the Court contemplated simply that legislative linedrawing in the districting context would be susceptible of adjudication
under the applicable constitutional criteria.

Furthermore, in formulating the one-person, one-vote formula, the
Court characterized the question posed by election districts of disparate
size as an issue of fair representation. In such cases, it is not that
anyone is deprived of a vote or that any person's vote is not counted.
Rather, it is that one electoral district elects a single representative and
another district of the same size elects two or more—the elector's vote
in the former district having less weight in the sense that he may vote
for and his district be represented by only one legislator, while his
neighbor in the adjoining district votes for and is represented by two or
more. *Reynolds* accordingly observed:

> "Since the achieving of fair and effective representation for all
> citizens is concededly the basic aim of legislative apportionment,
> we conclude that the Equal Protection Clause guarantees the
> opportunity for equal participation by all voters in the election of
> State legislators. Diluting the weight of votes because of place of
> residence impairs basic constitutional rights under the Fourteenth
> Amendment just as much as invidious discriminations based upon
> factors such as race . . . ." 377 U.S., at 565–566.

Reynolds surely indicates the justiciability of claims going to the
adequacy of representation in state legislatures.

The issue here is of course different from that adjudicated in
Reynolds. It does not concern districts of unequal size. Not only does
everyone have the right to vote and to have his vote counted, but each
elector may vote for and be represented by the same number of
lawmakers. Rather, the claim is that each political group in a State
should have the same chance to elect representatives of its choice as
any other political group. Nevertheless, the issue is one of representation, and we decline to hold that such claims are never justiciable.

Our racial gerrymander cases such as White v. Regester and
Whitcomb v. Chavis indicate as much. In those cases, there was no
population variation among the districts, and no one was precluded
from voting. The claim instead was that an identifiable racial or
ethnic group had an insufficient chance to elect a representative of its
choice and that district lines should be redrawn to remedy this alleged
defect. In both cases, we adjudicated the merits of such claims,
rejecting the claim in *Whitcomb* and sustaining it in *Regester*. Just as
clearly, in Gaffney v. Cummings, where the districts also passed muster
under the *Reynolds* formula, the claim was that the legislature had
manipulated district lines to afford political groups in various districts

an enhanced opportunity to elect legislators of their choice. Although advising caution, we said that "we *must* . . . respond to [the] claims . . . that even if acceptable populationwise, the . . . plan was invidiously discriminatory because a 'political fairness principle' was followed . . . ." 412 U.S., at 751–752 (emphasis added). We went on to hold that the statute at issue did not violate the Equal Protection Clause.

These decisions support a conclusion that this case is justiciable. As *Gaffney* demonstrates, that the claim is submitted by a political group, rather than a racial group, does not distinguish it in terms of justiciability. That the characteristics of the complaining group are not immutable or that the group has not been subject to the same historical stigma may be relevant to the manner in which the case is adjudicated, but these differences do not justify a refusal to entertain such a case.

In fact, Justice O'Connor's attempt to distinguish this political gerrymandering claim from the racial gerrymandering claims that we have consistently adjudicated demonstrates the futility of such an effort. Her conclusion that the claim in this case is not justiciable seems to rest on a dual concern that no judicially manageable standards exist and that adjudication of such claims requires an initial policy decision that the judiciary should not make. Yet she does not point out how the standards that we set forth here for adjudicating this political gerrymandering claim are less manageable than the standards that have been developed for racial gerrymandering claims. Nor does she demonstrate what initial policy decision—regarding, for example, the desirability of fair group representation—we have made here that we have not made in the race cases.[9] She merely asserts that because race has historically been a suspect classification individual minority voters' rights are more immediately related to a racial minority group's voting strength. This, in combination with "the greater warrant the Equal Protection Clause gives the federal courts to intervene for protection against racial discrimination, suffice to render racial gerrymandering claims justiciable."

Reliance on these assertions to determine justiciability would transform the narrow categories of "political questions" that Baker v. Carr carefully defined into an ad hoc litmus test of this Court's reactions to the desirability of and need for judicial application of constitutional or statutory standards to a given type of claim. Justice O'Connor's own discussion seems to reflect such an approach: She

[9] As to the illegitimate policy determinations that Justice O'Connor believes that we have made, she points to two. The first is a preference for nonpartisan as opposed to partisan gerrymanders, and the second is a preference for proportionality. On a group level, however, which must be our focus in this type of claim, neither of these policy determinations is "of a kind clearly for nonjudicial discretion." Baker v. Carr, 369 U.S., at 217. The first merely recognizes that nonpartisan gerrymanders in fact are aimed at guaranteeing rather than infringing fair group representation. The second, which is not a preference for proportionality *per se* but a preference for a level of parity between votes and representation sufficient to ensure that significant minority voices are heard and that majorities are not consigned to minority status, is hardly an illegitimate extrapolation from our general majoritarian ethic and the objective of fair and adequate representation recognized in Reynolds v. Sims, 377 U.S. 533 (1964).

concludes that because political gerrymandering may be a "self-limiting enterprise" there is no need for judicial intervention. She also expresses concern that our decision today will lead to "political instability and judicial malaise," *post*, at 3, because nothing will prevent members of other identifiable groups from bringing similar claims. To begin with, Justice O'Connor's factual assumptions are by no means obviously correct: It is not clear that political gerrymandering *is* a self-limiting enterprise or that other groups will have any great incentive to bring gerrymandering claims, given the requirement of a showing of discriminatory intent. At a more fundamental level, however, Justice O'Connor's analysis is flawed because it focuses on the perceived need for judicial review and on the potential practical problems with allowing such review. Validation of the consideration of such amorphous and wide-ranging factors in assessing justiciability would alter substantially the analysis the Court enunciated in Baker v. Carr, and we decline Justice O'Connor's implicit invitation to rethink that approach.

III

Having determined that the political gerrymandering claim in this case is justiciable, we turn to the question whether the District Court erred in holding that appellees had alleged and proved a violation of the Equal Protection Clause.

A

Preliminarily, we agree with the District Court that the claim made by the appellees in this case is a claim that the 1981 apportionment discriminates against Democrats on a statewide basis. Both the appellees and the District Court have cited instances of individual districting within the State which they believe exemplify this discrimination, but the appellees' claim as we understand it is that Democratic voters over the State as a whole, not Democratic voters in particular districts, have been subjected to unconstitutional discrimination. Although the statewide discrimination asserted here was allegedly accomplished through the manipulation of individual district lines, the focus of the equal protection inquiry is necessarily somewhat different from that involved in the review of individual districts.

We also agree with the District Court that in order to succeed the Bandemer plaintiffs were required to prove both intentional discrimination against an identifiable political group and an actual discriminatory effect on that group. See, e.g., Mobile v. Bolden, 446 U.S., at 67–68. Further, we are confident that if the law challenged here had discriminatory effects on Democrats, this record would support a finding that the discrimination was intentional. Thus, we decline to overturn the District Court's finding of discriminatory intent as clearly erroneous.

Indeed, quite aside from the anecdotal evidence, the shape of the House and Senate Districts, and the alleged disregard for political boundaries, we think it most likely that whenever a legislature redistricts, those responsible for the legislation will know the likely political composition of the new districts and will have a prediction as to whether a particular district is a safe one for a Democratic or Republican candidate or is a competitive district that either candidate might win. . . . As long as redistricting is done by a legislature, it should not be very difficult to prove that the likely political consequences of the reapportionment were intended.

B

We do not accept, however, the District Court's legal and factual bases for concluding that the 1981 Act visited a sufficiently adverse effect on the appellees' constitutionally protected rights to make out a violation of the Equal Protection Clause. The District Court held that because any apportionment scheme that purposely prevents proportional representation is unconstitutional, Democratic voters need only show that their proportionate voting influence has been adversely affected. Our cases, however, clearly foreclose any claim that the Constitution requires proportional representation or that legislatures in reapportioning must draw district lines to come as near as possible to allocating seats to the contending parties in proportion to what their anticipated statewide vote will be. Whitcomb v. Chavis, 403 U.S., at 153, 156, 160; White v. Regester, 412 U.S., at 765–766.

The typical election for legislative seats in the United States is conducted in described geopraphical districts, with the candidate receiving the most votes in each district winning the seat allocated to that district. If all or most of the districts are competitive—defined by the District Court in this case as districts in which the anticipated split in the party vote is within the range of 45% to 55%—even a narrow statewide preference for either party would produce an overwhelming majority for the winning party in the state legislature. This consequence, however, is inherent in winner-take-all, district-based elections, and we cannot hold that such a reapportionment law would violate the Equal Protection Clause because the voters in the losing party do not have representation in the legislature in proportion to the statewide vote received by their party candidates. As we have said: "[W]e are unprepared to hold that district-based elections decided by plurality vote are unconstitutional in either single- or multi-member districts simply because the supporters of losing candidates have no legislative seats assigned to them." Whitcomb v. Chavis, supra, at 160. This is true of a racial as well as a political group. White v. Regester, supra, at 765–766. It is also true of a statewide claim as well as an individual district claim.

To draw district lines to maximize the representation of each major party would require creating as many safe seats for each party as the demographic and predicted political characteristics of the State would permit. This in turn would leave the minority in each safe district without a representative of its choice. We upheld this "political fairness" approach in Gaffney v. Cummings, despite its tendency to deny safe district minorities any realistic chance to elect their own representatives. But *Gaffney* in no way suggested that the Constitution requires the approach that Connecticut had adopted in that case.

In cases involving individual multi-member districts, we have required a substantially greater showing of adverse effects than a mere lack of proportional representation to support a finding of unconstitutional vote dilution. Only where there is evidence that excluded groups have "less opportunity to participate in the political processes and to elect candidates of their choice" have we refused to approve the use of multi-member districts. Rogers v. Lodge, 458 U.S., at 624. . . . In these cases, we have also noted the lack of responsiveness by those elected to the concerns of the relevant groups. See Rogers v. Lodge, supra, at 625–627; White v. Regester, supra, at 766–767.[12]

These holdings rest on a conviction that the mere fact that a particular apportionment scheme makes it more difficult for a particular group in a particular district to elect the representatives of its choice does not render that scheme constitutionally infirm. This conviction, in turn, stems from a perception that the power to influence the political process is not limited to winning elections. An individual or a group of individuals who votes for a losing candidate is usually deemed to be adequately represented by the winning candidate and to have as much opportunity to influence that candidate as other voters in the district. We cannot presume in such a situation, without actual proof to the contrary, that the candidate elected will entirely ignore the interests of those voters. This is true even in a safe district where the losing group loses election after election. Thus, a group's electoral power is not unconstitutionally diminished by the simple fact of an apportionment scheme that makes winning elections more difficult, and a failure of proportional representation alone does not constitute impermissible discrimination under the Equal Protection Clause. See Mobile v. Bolden, 446 U.S., at 111, n. 7 (Marshall, J., dissenting).

As with individual districts, where unconstitutional vote dilution is alleged in the form of statewide political gerrymandering, the mere lack of proportional representation will not be sufficient to prove unconstitutional discrimination. Again, without specific supporting evidence, a court cannot presume in such a case that those who are elected will disregard the disproportionately underrepresented group. Rather, unconstitutional discrimination occurs only when the electoral system is arranged in a manner that will consistently degrade a voter's or a group of voters' influence on the political process as a whole.

Although this is a somewhat different formulation than we have previously used in describing unconstitutional vote dilution in an individual district, the focus of both of these inquiries is essentially the same. In both contexts, the question is whether a particular group has been unconstitutionally denied its chance to effectively influence the political process. In a challenge to an individual district, this inquiry

[12] Although these cases involved racial groups, we believe that the principles developed in these cases would apply equally to claims by political groups in individual districts. We note, however, that the elements necessary to a successful vote dilution claim may be more difficult to prove in relation to a claim by a political group. For example, historical patterns of exclusion from the political processes, evidence which would support a vote dilution claim, are in general more likely to be present for a racial group than for a political group.

focuses on the opportunity of members of the group to participate in party deliberations in the slating and nomination of candidates, their opportunity to register and vote, and hence their chance to directly influence the election returns and to secure the attention of the winning candidate. Statewide, however, the inquiry centers on the voters' direct or indirect influence on the elections of the state legislature as a whole. And, as in individual district cases, an equal protection violation may be found only where the electoral system substantially disadvantages certain voters in their opportunity to influence the political process effectively. In this context, such a finding of unconstitutionality must be supported by evidence of continued frustration of the will of a majority of the voters or effective denial to a minority of voters of a fair chance to influence the political process.

Based on these views, we would reject the District Court's apparent holding that *any* interference with an opportunity to elect a representative of one's choice would be sufficient to allege or make out an equal protection violation, unless justified by some acceptable state interest that the State would be required to demonstrate. In addition to being contrary to the above-described conception of an unconstitutional political gerrymander, such a low threshold for legal action would invite attack on all or almost all reapportionment statutes. District-based elections hardly ever produce a perfect fit between votes and representation. The one-person, one-vote imperative often mandates departure from this result as does the no-retrogression rule required by § 5 of the Voting Rights Act. Inviting attack on minor departures from some supposed norm would too much embroil the judiciary in second-guessing what has consistently been referred to as a political task for the legislature, a task that should not be monitored too closely unless the express or tacit goal is to effect its removal from legislative halls. We decline to take a major step toward that end, which would be so much at odds with our history and experience.

The view that a prima facie case of illegal discrimination in reapportionment requires a showing of more than a *de minimis* effect is not unprecedented. Reapportionment cases involving the one-person, one-vote principle such as Gaffney v. Cummings and White v. Regester provide support for such a requirement. In the present, considerably more complex context, it is also appropriate to require allegations and proof that the challenged legislative plan has had or will have effects that are sufficiently serious to require intervention by the federal courts in state reapportionment decisions.[14]

C

The District Court's findings do not satisfy this threshold condition to stating and proving a cause of action. In reaching its conclusion, the District Court relied primarily on the results of the 1982 elections.

[14] The requirement of a threshold showing is derived from the peculiar characteristics of these political gerrymandering claims. We do not contemplate that a similar requirement would apply to our Equal Protection cases outside of this particular context.

Relying on a single election to prove unconstitutional discrimination is unsatisfactory. The District Court observed, and the parties do not disagree, that Indiana is a swing State. Voters sometimes prefer Democratic candidates, and sometimes Republican. The District Court did not find that because of the 1981 Act the Democrats could not in one of the next few elections secure a sufficient vote to take control of the assembly. Indeed, the District Court declined to hold that the 1982 election results were the predictable consequences of the 1981 Act and expressly refused to hold that those results were a reliable prediction of future ones. The District Court did not ask by what percentage the statewide Democratic vote would have had to increase to control either the House or the Senate. The appellants argue here, without a persuasive response from appellees, that had the Democratic candidates received an additional few percentage points of the votes cast statewide, they would have obtained a majority of the seats in both houses. Nor was there any finding that the 1981 reapportionment would consign the Democrats to a minority status in the Assembly throughout the 1980's or that the Democrats would have no hope of doing any better in the reapportionment that would occur after the 1990 census. Without findings of this nature, the District Court erred in concluding that the 1981 Act violated the Equal Protection Clause.

The District Court's discussion of the multi-member districts created by the 1981 Act does not undermine this conclusion. For the purposes of the statewide political gerrymandering claim, these districts appear indistinguishable from safe Republican and safe Democratic single-member districts. Simply showing that there are multi-member districts in the State and that those districts are constructed so as to be safely Republican or Democratic in no way bolsters the contention that there has been *statewide* discrimination against Democratic voters. It could be, were the necessary threshold effect to be shown, that multi-member districts could be demonstrated to be suspect on the ground that they are particularly useful in attaining impermissibly discriminatory ends; at this stage of the inquiry, however, the multi-member district evidence does not materially aid the appellees' case.

. . .

This participatory approach to the legality of individual multi-member districts is not helpful where the claim is that such districts discriminate against Democrats, for it could hardly be said that Democrats, any more than Republicans, are excluded from participating in the affairs of their own party or from the processes by which candidates are nominated and elected. For constitutional purposes, the Democratic claim in this case, insofar as it challenges *vel non* the legality of the multi-member districts in certain counties, is like that of the Negroes in *Whitcomb* who failed to prove a racial gerrymander, for it boils down to a complaint that they failed to attract a majority of the voters in the challenged multi-member districts.

D

In response to our approach, Justice Powell suggests an alternative method for evaluating equal protection claims of political gerrymandering. In his view, courts should look at a number of factors in considering these claims: the nature of the legislative procedures by which the challenged redistricting was accomplished and the intent behind the redistricting; the shapes of the districts and their conformity with political subdivision boundaries; and "evidence concerning population disparities and statistics tending to show vote dilution." The District Court in this case reviewed these factors in reaching its ultimate conclusion that unconstitutional vote dilution had occurred, and Justice Powell concludes that its findings on these factors—and on the ultimate question of vote discrimination—should be upheld. According to Justice Powell, those findings adequately support a conclusion that "the boundaries of the voting districts have been distorted deliberately and arbitrarily to achieve illegitimate ends." This deliberate and arbitrary distortion of boundaries, in turn, apparently distinguishes gerrymandering in a "loose" sense, "the common practice of the party in power to choose the redistricting plan that gives it an advantage at the polls" from gerrymandering in an "unconstitutional" sense.

Although we are not completely clear as to the distinction between these two categories of gerrymander, the crux of Justice Powell's analysis seems to be that—at least in some cases—the intentional drawing of district boundaries for partisan ends and for no other reason violates the Equal Protection Clause in and of itself. We disagree, however, with this conception of a constitutional violation. Specifically, even if a state legislature redistricts with the specific intention of disadvantaging one political party's election prospects, we do not believe that there has been an unconstitutional discrimination against members of that party unless the redistricting does in fact disadvantage it at the polls.

Moreover, as we discussed above, a mere lack of proportionate results in one election cannot suffice in this regard. We have reached this conclusion in our cases involving challenges to individual multi-member districts, and it applies equally here. In the individual multi-member district cases, we have found equal protection violations only where a history of disproportionate results appeared in conjunction with strong indicia of lack of political power and the denial of fair representation. In those cases, the racial minorities asserting the successful equal protection claims had essentially been shut out of the political process. In the statewide political gerrymandering context, these prior cases lead to the analogous conclusion that equal protection violations may be found only where a history (actual or projected) of disproportionate results appears in conjunction with similar indicia. The mere lack of control of the General Assembly after a single election does not rise to the requisite level.

This requirement of more than a showing of possibly transitory results is where we appear to depart from Justice Powell. Stripped of its "factors" verbiage, Justice Powell's analysis turns on a determination that a lack of proportionate election results can support a finding of an equal protection violation, at least in some circumstances. Here, the only concrete effect on the Democrats in Indiana in terms of election results that the District Court had before it was one election in which the percentage of Democrats elected was lower than the percentage of total Democratic votes cast. In Justice Powell's view, this disproportionality, when combined with clearly discriminatory intent on the part of the 1981 General Assembly and the manipulation of district lines in the apportionment process, is sufficient to conclude that fair representation has been denied.

The factors other than disproportionate election results, however, do not contribute to a finding that Democratic voters have been disadvantaged in fact. They support a finding that an intention to discriminate was present and that districts were drawn in accordance with that intention, but they do not show any actual disadvantage beyond that shown by the election results: It surely cannot be an actual disadvantage in terms of fair representation on a group level just to be placed in a district with a supermajority of other Democratic voters or a district that departs from preexisting political boundaries. Only when such placement affects election results and political power statewide has an actual disadvantage occurred.

Consequently, Justice Powell's view would allow a constitutional violation to be found where the only proven effect on a political party's electoral power was disproportionate results in one (or possibly two) elections. This view, however, contains no explanation of why a lack of proportionate election results should suffice in these political gerrymandering cases while it does not in the cases involving racial gerrymandering. In fact, Justice Powell's opinion is silent as to the relevance of the substantive standard developed in the multi-member district cases to these political gerrymandering cases.

In rejecting Justice Powell's approach, we do not mean to intimate that the factors he considers are entirely irrelevant. The election results obviously are relevant to a showing of the effects required to prove a political gerrymandering claim under our view. And the district configurations may be combined with vote projections to predict future election results, which are also relevant to the effects showing. The other factors, even if not relevant to the effects issue, might well be relevant to an equal protection claim. The equal protection argument would proceed along the following lines: If there were a discriminatory effect and a discriminatory intent, then the legislation would be examined for valid underpinnings. Thus, evidence of exclusive legislative process and deliberate drawing of district lines in accordance with accepted gerrymandering principles would be relevant to intent, and evidence of valid and invalid configuration would be relevant to whether the districting plan met legitimate state interests.

This course is consistent with our equal protection cases generally and is the course we follow here: We assumed that there was discriminatory intent, found that there was insufficient discriminatory effect to constitute an equal protection violation and therefore did not reach the question of the state interests (legitimate or otherwise) served by the particular districts as they were created by the legislature. Consequently, the valid or invalid configuration of the districts was an issue we did not need to consider.

It seems inappropriate, however, to view these separate components of an equal protection analysis as "factors" to be considered together without regard for their separate functions or meaning. This undifferentiated consideration of the various factors confuses the import of each factor and disguises the essential conclusion of Justice Powell's opinion: that disproportionate election results alone are a sufficient effect to support a finding of a constitutional violation.

In sum, we decline to adopt the approach enunciated by Justice Powell. In our view, that approach departs from our past cases and invites judicial interference in legislative districting whenever a political party suffers at the polls. We recognize that our own view may be difficult of application. Determining when an electoral system has been "arranged in a manner that will consistently degrade a voter's or a group of voters' influence on the political process as a whole", is of necessary a difficult inquiry. Nevertheless, we believe that it recognizes the delicacy of intruding on this most political of legislative functions and is at the same time consistent with our prior cases regarding individual multi-member districts, which have formulated a parallel standard.

IV

In sum, we hold that political gerrymandering cases are properly justiciable under the Equal Protection Clause. We also conclude, however, that a threshold showing of discriminatory vote dilution is required for a prima facie case of an equal protection violation. In this case, the findings made by the District Court of an adverse effect on the appellees do not surmount the threshold requirement. Consequently, the judgment of the District Court is reversed.

Chief Justice Burger, concurring in the judgment.

I join Justice O'Connor's opinion.

. . .

Justice O'Connor, with whom The Chief Justice and Justice Rehnquist join, concurring in the judgment.

Today the Court holds that claims of political gerrymandering lodged by members of one of the political parties that make up our two-party system are justiciable under the Equal Protection Clause of the Fourteenth Amendment. Nothing in our precedents compels us to take this step, and there is every reason not to do so. I would hold that the partisan gerrymandering claims of major political parties raise a non-justiciable political question that the judiciary should leave to the legislative branch as the Framers of the Constitution unquestionably intended. Accordingly, I would reverse the District Court's judgment on the grounds that appellees' claim is nonjusticiable.

. . .

Of course, in one sense a requirement of proportional representation, whether loose or absolute, is judicially manageable. If this Court were to declare that the Equal Protection Clause required proportional representation within certain fixed tolerances, I have no doubt that district courts would be able to apply this edict. The flaw in such a pronouncement, however, would be the use of the Equal Protection Clause as the vehicle for making a fundamental policy choice that is contrary to the intent of its Farmers and to the traditions of this republic. The political question doctrine as articulated in Baker v. Carr rightly requires that we refrain from making such policy choices in order to evade what would otherwise be a lack of judicially manageable standards. See 369 U.S., at 217.

Unfortunately, a drift towards proportional representation is apparent even in the plurality opinion. Although at times the plurality seems to require that the political party be "essentially . . . shut out of the political process" before a constitutional violation will be found, the plurality's explanation of the deficiencies in the District Court's approach focuses not on access to the political process as a whole, but entirely on statewide electoral success. Thus, the critical inquiry appears to be into whether the complaining political party could be expected to regain control of the state legislature in the next few elections if backed by a majority of voters. As an aid in this inquiry, courts must apparently also ask "by what percentage the statewide . . . vote" for the complaining political party would have to increase to control the legislature or one of its Houses. Ibid.

Under the plurality's approach, where it is shown that under a challenged apportionment plan one party will consistently fail to gain control of the legislature even if it wins a majority of the votes, a court would be justified in finding the "threshold showing" met, at which point "the legislation would be examined for valid underpinnings." It may fairly be doubted that this last step is anything more than a formality, except perhaps in the case of bipartisan gerrymanders that have proved unexpectedly favorable to one party. Consequently, although the plurality criticizes Justice Powell for effectively concluding "that disproportionate short-term election results alone are a sufficient effect to support a finding of a constitutional violation," the plurality itself arrives at the conclusion that foreseeable, disproportionate *long-term* election results suffice to prove a constitutional violation.

Thus, the plurality opinion ultimately rests on a political preference for proportionality—not an outright claim that proportional results are required, but a conviction that the greater the departure from proportionality, the more suspect an apportionment plan becomes. This preference for proportionality is in serious tension with essential features of state legislative elections. Districting itself represents a middle ground between winner-take-all statewide elections and proportional representation for political parties. If there is a constitutional preference for proportionality, the legitimacy of districting itself is called into question: the voting strength of less evenly distributed groups will invariably be diminished by districting as compared to at-large proportional systems for electing representatives. Moreover, one implication of the districting system is that voters cast votes for candidates in their districts, not for a statewide slate of legislative candidates put forward by the parties. Consequently, efforts to determine party voting strength presuppose a norm that does not exist—statewide elections for representatives along party lines.

The plurality's theory is also internally inconsistent. The plurality recognizes that, given a normal dispersion of party strength and winner-take-all district-based elections, it is likely that even a narrow statewide preference for one party will give that party a disproportionately large majority in the legislature. The plurality is prepared to tolerate this effect, because not to do so would spell the end of district-based elections, or require reverse gerrymandering to ensure greater proportionality for the minority party. But this means that the plurality would extend greater protection to a party that can command a majority of the statewide vote than to a party that cannot: the explanation, once again, is that the plurality has made a political judgment—in this instance, that district-based elections must be taken as a given.

Because a statewide majority for a party's candidates will frequently result only if the "winning" party attracts independent voters and voters from the other party, under the plurality's approach a great deal will turn on whether the support of these voters is included as part of the party's voting strength. The plurality would reserve this question, but, however it is ultimately answered anomalies will result. To measure a party's voting strength by including voters who only occasionally vote for that party's candidates is arbitrary; to ignore the role these voters play will be to further discriminate against parties that do not command a permanent majority of the electorate in a given State.

I would avoid the difficulties generated by the plurality's efforts to confine the effects of a generalized group right to equal representation by not recognizing such a right in the first instance. To allow district courts to strike down apportionment plans on the basis of their prognostications as to the outcome of future elections or future apportionments invites "findings" on matters as to which neither judges nor anyone else can have any confidence. Once it is conceded that "a group's electoral power is not unconstitutionally diminished by the simple fact of an apportionment scheme that makes winning elections more difficult," the virtual impossibility of reliability predicting how difficult it will be to win an election in 2, or 4, or 10 years should, in my view, weigh in favor of holding such challenges nonjusticiable. Racial gerrymandering should remain justiciable, for the harms it engenders run counter to the central thrust of the Fourteenth Amendment. But no such justification can be given for judicial intervention on behalf of mainstream political parties, and the risks such intervention poses to our political institutions are unacceptable. "Political affiliation is the keystone of the political trade. Race, ideally, is not." United Jewish Organizations of Williamsburgh, Inc. v. Carey, 430 U.S. 144, 171 n. 1 (1977) (Brennan, J., concurring).

Justice Powell, with whom Justice Stevens joins, concurring in Part II, and dissenting.

This case presents the question whether a state legislature violates the Equal Protection Clause by adopting a redistricting plan designed solely to preserve the power of the dominant political party, when the plan follows the doctrine of "one person, one vote" but ignores all other neutral factors relevant to the fairness of redistricting.

In answering this question, the plurality expresses the view, with which I agree, that a partisan political gerrymander violates the Equal Protection Clause only on proof of "both intentional discrimination against an identifiable political group and an actual discriminatory effect on that group." The plurality acknowledges that the record in this case supports a finding that the challenged redistricting plan was adopted for the purpose of discriminating against Democratic voters. Ante, at 15–16. The plurality argues, however, that appellees failed to establish that their voting strength was diluted statewide despite uncontradicted proof that certain key districts were grotesquely gerrymandered to enhance the election prospects of Republican candidates. This argument appears to rest solely on the ground that the legislature accomplished its gerrymander consistent with "one person, one vote," in the sense that the legislature designed voting districts of approximately equal population and erected no direct barriers to Democratic voters' exercise of the franchise. Since the essence of a gerrymandering claim is that the members of a political party as a group have been denied their right to "fair and effective representation," Reynolds v. Sims, 377 U.S. 533, 565 (1964), I believe that the claim cannot be tested solely by reference to "one person, one vote." Rather, a number of other relevant neutral factors must be considered. Because the plurality ignores such factors and fails to enunciate standards by which to determine whether a legislature has enacted an unconstitutional gerrymander, I dissent.

. . .

II

A

Gerrymandering is "the deliberate and arbitrary distortion of district boundaries and populations for partisan or personal political purposes." Kirkpatrick v. Preisler, 394 U.S. 526, 538 (1969) (Fortas, J., concurring). As Justice Stevens correctly observed, gerrymandering violates the Equal Protection Clause only when the redistricting plan serves "no purpose other than to favor one segment—whether racial, ethnic, religious, economic, or political—that may occupy a position of strength at a particular time, or to disadvantage a politically weak segment of the community." Karcher v. Daggett, 462 U.S. 725, 748 (1983) (Stevens, J., concurring).

The term "gerrymandering," however, is also used loosely to describe the common practice of the party in power to choose the redistricting plan that gives it an advantage at the polls. An intent to discriminate in this sense may be present whenever redistricting occurs. See Gaffney v. Cummings, 412 U.S. 735, 753 (1973); Cousins v. City Council of Chicago, 466 F.2d 830, 847 (CA7) (Stevens, J., dissenting), cert. denied, 409 U.S. 893 (1972). Moreover, since legislative bodies rarely reflect accurately the popular voting strength of the principal political parties, the effect of any particular redistricting may be perceived as unfair. See id., at 752–754. Consequently, only a sensitive and searching inquiry can distinguish gerrymandering in the "loose" sense from gerrymandering that amounts to unconstitutional discrimination. Because it is difficult to develop and apply standards that will identify the unconstitutional gerrymander, courts may seek to avoid their responsibility to enforce the Equal Protection Clause by finding that a claim of gerrymandering is nonjusticiable. I agree with the plurality that such a course is mistaken, and that the allegations in this case raise a justiciable issue.

Moreover, I am convinced that appropriate judicial standards can and should be developed. Justice Fortas' definition of unconstitutional gerrymandering properly focuses on whether the boundaries of the voting districts have been distorted deliberately and arbitrarily to achieve illegitimate ends. Kirkpatrick v. Preisler, 394 U.S., at 538. Under this definition, the merits of a gerrymandering claim must be determined by reference to the configurations of the districts, the observance of political subdivision lines, and other criteria that have independent relevance to the fairness of redistricting. See Karcher v. Daggett, 462 U.S., at 755–759 (Stevens, J., concurring). In this case, the District Court examined the redistricting in light of such factors and found, among other facts, that the boundaries of a number of districts were deliberately distorted to deprive Democratic voters of an equal opportunity to participate in the State's legislative processes. The plurality makes no reference to any of these findings of fact. It rejects the District Court's ultimate conclusion with no explanation of the respects in which appellees' proof fell short of establishing discriminatory effect. A brief review of the Court's jurisprudence in the context of another kind of challenge to redistricting, a claim of malapportionment, demonstrates the pressing need for the Court to enunciate standards to guide legislators who redistrict and judges who determine the constitutionality of the legislative effort.

. . . .

V

In conclusion, I want to make clear the limits of the standard that I believe the Equal Protection Clause imposes on legislators engaged in redistricting. Traditionally, the determination of electoral districts within a State has been a matter left to the legislative branch of the state government. Apart from the doctrine of separation of powers and the federal system prescribed by the Constitution, federal judges are ill-equipped generally to review legislative decisions respecting redistricting. As the plurality opinion makes clear, however, our precedents hold that a colorable claim of discriminatory gerrymandering presents a justiciable controversy under the Equal Protection Clause. Federal courts in exercising their duty to adjudicate such claims should impose a heavy burden of proof on those who allege that a redistricting plan violates the Constitution. In light of Baker v. Carr, Reynolds v. Sims, and their progeny, including such comparatively recent decisions as Gaffney v. Cummings, this case presents a paradigm example of unconstitutional discrimination against the members of a political party that happened to be out of power. The well-grounded findings of the District Court to this effect have not been, and I believe cannot be, held clearly erroneous.

Accordingly, I would affirm the judgment of the District Court.[25]

C. TRAVEL AND INTERSTATE MIGRATION

Page 895. Add ahead of D. Welfare:

ATTORNEY GENERAL OF NEW YORK v. SOTO–LOPEZ
476 U.S. 898, 106 S.Ct. 2317, 90 L.Ed.2d 899 (1986).

Justice Brennan announced the judgment of the Court and delivered an opinion in which Justice Marshall, Justice Blackmun, and Justice Powell joined.

The question presented by this appeal is whether a preference in civil service employment opportunities offered by the State of New York solely to resident veterans who lived in the State at the time they entered military service violates the constitutional rights of resident veterans who lived outside the State when they entered military service.

I

The State of New York, through its Constitution, N.Y.Const., Art. V, § 6, and its Civil Service Law, N.Y.Civ.Serv.Law § 85 (McKinney 1983 and Supp.1986), grants a civil service employment preference, in the form of points added to examination scores, to New York residents who are honorably-discharged veterans of the United States armed forces, who served during time of war, and who were residents of New York when they entered military service. This preference may be

---

[25] As is evident from the several opinions filed today, there is no "Court" for a standard that properly should be applied in determining whether a challenged redistricting plan is an unconstitutional partisan political gerrymander. The standard proposed by the plurality is explicitly rejected by two Justices, and three Justices also have expressed the view that the plurality's standard will "prove unmanagement and arbitrary." Ante, at 12 (O'Connor, J., joined by Burger, C.J., and Rehnquist, J., concurring in the judgment).

exercised only once, either for original hiring or for one promotion. N.Y.Const., Art. V, § 6.

Appellees, Eduardo Soto-Lopez and Eliezer Baez-Hernandez, are veterans of the United States Army and long-time residents of New York. Both men claim to have met all the eligibility criteria for the New York State civil service preference except New York residence when they entered the Army. Both Soto-Lopez and Baez-Hernandez passed New York City civil service examinations, but were denied the veterans' preference by the New York City Civil Service Commission because they were residents of Puerto Rico at the time they joined the military. Appellees sued the City in Federal District Court, alleging that the requirement of residence when they joined the military violated the Equal Protection Clause of the Fourteenth Amendment and the constitutionally protected right to travel. The Attorney General of the State of New York intervened as a defendant.

The District Court dismissed appellees' complaint . . . .. The Court of Appeals for the Second Circuit reversed. . . . It . . . held that the prior residence requirement of the New York civil service preference offends both the Equal Protection Clause and the right to travel. . . . We noted probable jurisdiction of this appeal of the Attorney General of New York. . . . We affirm.

" '[F]reedom to travel throughout the United States has long been recognized as a basic right under the Constitution.' " Dunn v. Blumstein, 405 U.S. 330, 338 (1972) (quoting United States v. Guest, 383 U.S. 745, 758 (1966). . . . And, it is clear that the freedom to travel includes the " 'freedom to enter and abide in any State in the Union.' " *Dunn,* supra, at 338 . . .

The textual source of the constitutional right to travel, or, more precisely, the right of free interstate migration, though, has proven elusive. It has been variously assigned to the Privileges and Immunities Clause of Art. IV, . . . to the Commerce Clause, . . . and to the Privileges and Immunities Clause of the Fourteenth Amendment, ... The right has also been inferred from the federal structure of government adopted by our Constitution. . . . However, in light of the unquestioned historic acceptance of the principle of free interstate migration, and of the important role that principle has played in transforming many States into a single Nation, we have not felt impelled to locate this right definitively in any particular constitutional provision. . . . Whatever its origin, the right to migrate is firmly established and has been repeatedly recognized by our cases. See, e.g., Hooper v. Bernalillo County Assessor, 472 U.S. 612, 618, n. 6 (1985); *Zobel,* [457 U.S. 55] at 60, n. 6; . . .

A state law implicates the right to travel when it actually deters such travel, . . ., when impeding travel is its primary objective, . . ., or when it uses " 'any classification which serves to penalize the exercise of that right.' " . . . Our right to migrate cases have principally involved the latter, indirect manner of burdening the right. More particularly, our recent cases have dealt with state laws that, by classifying residents according to the time they established residence, resulted in the unequal distribution of rights and benefits among otherwise qualified bona fide residents.[3]

Because the creation of different classes of residents raises equal protection concerns, we have also relied upon the Equal Protection Clause in these cases. Whenever a state law infringes a constitutionally protected right, we undertake intensified equal protection scrutiny of that law. . . . Thus, in several cases, we asked expressly whether the distinction drawn by the State between older and newer residents burdens the right to migrate. Where we found such a burden, we required the State to come forward with a compelling justification. . . . In other cases, where we concluded that the contested classifications did not survive even rational basis scrutiny, we had no occasion to inquire whether enhanced scrutiny was appropriate. *Hooper,* supra; *Zobel,* supra. The analysis in all of these cases, however, is informed by the same guiding principle—the right to migrate protects residents of a State from being disadvantaged, or from being treated differently, simply because of the timing of their migration, from other similarly situated residents.[4] . . .

New York's eligibility requirements for its civil service preference conditions a benefit on New York residence at a particular past time in an individual's life. It favors those veterans who were New York residents at a past fixed point over those who were not New York residents at the same point in their lives. Our cases have established that similar methods of favoring "prior" residents over "newer" ones, such as limiting a benefit to those who resided in the State by a fixed past date, *Hooper,* supra; granting incrementally greater benefits for each year of residence, *Zobel,* supra; and conditioning eligibility for certain benefits on completion of a fixed period of residence, see, e.g., *Memorial Hospital,* supra; Dunn v. Blumstein, 405 U.S. 330 (1972); *Shapiro,* supra, warrant careful judicial review.[5] But, our cases have also established that only where a State's law " 'operates to penalize those persons . . . who have exercised their constitutional right of

[3] We have always carefully distinguished between bona fide residence requirements, which seek to differentiate between residents and nonresidents, and residence requirements, such as durational, fixed date, and fixed point residence requirements, which treat established residents differently based on the time they migrated into the State. . . .

[4] Of course, regardless of the label we place on our analysis—right to migrate or equal protection—once we find a burden on the right to migrate the standard of review is the same. Laws which burden that right must be necessary to further a compelling state interest. See, e.g., *Memorial Hospital,* supra; *Dunn,* supra; *Shapiro,* supra.

[5] We have cautioned, however, that not all waiting periods are impermissible. See, e.g., *Memorial Hospital,* supra, at 258–259; *Shapiro,* supra, at 638, n. 21. Indeed, in Sosna v. Iowa, 419 U.S. 393 (1975), we upheld a 1-year residency condition for maintaining an action for divorce. We noted the State's strong, traditional interest in setting the terms of and procedures for marriage and divorce. Weighing the fact that appellant's access to the desired state procedure was only temporarily delayed, against the State's important interest, we concluded that her right to migrate was not violated.

We have also sustained domicile requirements, which incorporated 1-year waiting periods, for resident tuition at state universities. Starns v. Malkerson, 401 U.S. 985 (1971), summarily aff'g 326 F.Supp. 234 (Minn.1970) (three-judge court); Sturgis v. Washington, 414 U.S. 1057 (1973), summarily aff'g 368 F.Supp. 38 (WD Wash.) (three-judge court). See also Vlandis v. Kline, 412 U.S. 441, 452–454 (1973).

interstate migration'" is heightened scrutiny triggered. *Memorial Hospital,* supra, at 258, ...

Our task in this case, then, is first to determine whether the New York's restriction of its civil service preference to veterans who entered the armed forces while residing in New York operates to penalize those persons who have exercised their right to migrate. If we find that it does, appellees must prevail unless New York can demonstrate that its classification is necessary to accomplish a compelling state interest.[6]

. . .

III

A

In previous cases, we have held that even temporary deprivations of very important benefits and rights can operate to penalize migration. For example, in *Shapiro,* supra, and in *Memorial Hospital,* supra, we found that recently arrived indigent residents were deprived of life's necessities by durational residence requirements for welfare assistance and for free, nonemergency medical care, respectively, which were available to other poor residents. In *Dunn,* supra, we held that new residents were denied a basic right by a durational residence requirement for establishing eligibility to vote. The fact that these deprivations were temporary did not offset the Court's conclusions that they were so severe and worked such serious inequities among otherwise qualified residents that they effectively penalized new residents for the exercise of their rights to migrate.

More recently, in Hooper v. Bernalillo, 472 U.S. 612 (1985), and Zobel v. Williams, supra, we struck down state laws that created permanent distinctions among residents based on the length or timing of their residence in the State. At issue in *Hooper* was a New Mexico statute that granted a tax exemption to Vietnam veterans who resided in the State before May 8, 1976. *Zobel* concerned an Alaska statute granting residents one state mineral income dividend unit for each year of residence subsequent to 1959. Because we employed rational basis equal protection analysis in those cases, we did not face directly the question whether the contested laws operated to penalize interstate migration. Nonetheless, the conclusion that they did penalize migration may be inferred from our determination that "the Constitution will not tolerate a state benefit program that 'creates fixed, permanent

---

[6] In his concurrence, The Chief Justice takes the Court to task for asking in the first instance what is the appropriate standard of review to employ in evaluating New York's laws. The Chief Justice argues that we should initially run the laws through a rational basis analysis and then, if they survive that level of scrutiny, ask whether a higher level is appropriate.

We disagree. The logical first question to ask when presented with an equal protection claim, and the one we usually ask first, is what level of review is appropriate. . . .

It is true, as The Chief Justice suggests, that in *Hooper,* supra, and *Zobel,* supra, the Court did not follow this same logical sequence of analysis. We think that the better approach is that which the Court has employed in other equal protection cases—to inquire first as to the proper level of scrutiny and then to apply it.

distinctions . . . between . . . classes of concededly bona fide residents, based on how long they have been in the State.' " *Hooper*, supra, at ___, (quoting *Zobel*, 457 U.S., at 59). See also *Zobel*, supra, at 64.

Soto-Lopez and Baez-Hernandez have been denied a significant benefit that is granted to all veterans similarly situated except for state of residence at the time of their entry into the military. While the benefit sought here may not rise to the same level of importance as the necessities of life and the right to vote, it is unquestionably substantial. The award of bonus points can mean the difference between winning or losing civil service employment, with its attendant job security, decent pay, and good benefits. . . . Furthermore, appellees have been permanently deprived of the veterans' credits that they seek. As the Court of Appeals observed, "[t]he veteran's ability to satisfy the New York residence requirement is . . . fixed. He either was a New York resident at the time of his initial induction or he was not; he cannot earn a change in status." 755 F.2d, at 275. Such a permanent deprivation of a significant benefit, based only on the fact of nonresidence at a past point in time, clearly operates to penalize appellees' for exercising their rights to migrate.

B

New York offers four interests in justification of its fixed point residence requirement: (1) the encouragement of New York residents to join the armed services; (2) the compensation of residents for service in time of war by helping these veterans reestablish themselves upon coming home; (3) the inducement of veterans to return to New York after wartime service; and (4) the employment of a "uniquely valuable class of public servants" who possess useful experience acquired through their military service. All four justifications fail to withstand heightened scrutiny on a common ground—each of the State's asserted interests could be promoted fully by granting bonus points to *all* otherwise qualified veterans. New York residents would still be encouraged to join the services. Veterans who served in time of war would be compensated. And, both former New Yorkers and prior residents of other States would be drawn to New York after serving the Nation, thus providing the State with an even larger pool of potentially valuable public servants.

. . . .

IV

In sum, the provisions of New York's Constitution, Art. V, § 6, and Civil Service Law § 85, which limit the award of a civil service employment preference to resident veterans who lived in New York at the time they entered the armed forces effectively penalize otherwise qualified resident veterans who do not meet the prior residence requirement for their exercise of the right to migrate. The State has not met its heavy burden of proving that it has selected a means of pursuing a compelling state interest which does not impinge unnecessarily on constitutionally protected interests. Consequently, we conclude that

New York's veterans' preference violates appellees' constitutionally protected rights to migrate and to equal protection of the law.

. . .

Affirmed.

Chief Justice Burger, concurring in the judgment.

In this case the Court of Appeals held that New York's civil service veterans' preference violated both equal protection and the right to travel, relying on Zobel v. Williams, 457 U.S. 55 (1982). Shortly after the Court of Appeals' decision was issued, we struck down New Mexico's property tax veterans' preference in Hooper v. Bernalillo County Assessor, 472 U.S. 612 (1985). Both *Zobel* and *Hooper* held that the classifications used by the States to award preferences to certain citizens failed to pass a rational basis test *under the Equal Protection Clause.* As a result, we had no occasion to reach the issues whether the classifications would survive heightened scrutiny or whether the right to travel was violated. See *Hooper,* supra, at 618, and n. 6; *Zobel,* supra, at 60–61, and n. 6.

The classification held invalid on equal protection grounds in *Hooper* was remarkably similar to the one at issue here; *Hooper,* therefore would appear to be controlling. The Court's opinion, however, instead *begins* the analysis by addressing the "right to migrate." Moreover, heightened scrutiny is employed without first determining whether the challenged New York classification would survive even rational basis analysis. But as we observed in *Zobel,* supra, at 60, n. 6, and reiterated only last Term in *Hooper,* supra, at 618, n. 6, "[r]ight to travel cases have examined, in equal protection terms, state distinctions between newcomers and longer term residents." This follows because "[i]n reality, right to travel analysis refers to little more than a particular application of equal protection analysis." *Zobel,* supra, at 60, n. 6.

I believe the appropriate framework for reviewing New York's preference scheme is the one dictated by *Zobel* and followed in *Hooper* —both very recent cases. Because "[t]his case involves a distinction between residents based on when they first established residence in the State," just as in *Hooper,* "we [must] subject this case to equal protection analysis." *Hooper,* 472 U.S., at 618, n. 6. The first question is whether the law survives rational basis analysis under the Equal Protection Clause. "[I]f the statutory scheme cannot pass even the minimum rationality test, our inquiry ends." Id., at 618. Under *Hooper,* it seems clear that New York's provision is invalid on equal protection grounds.

. . .

I would affirm the judgment of the Court of Appeals based on our reasoning and holdings in *Hooper* and *Zobel,* rather than adding dicta concerning the right to travel.

Justice White, concurring in the judgment.

I agree with Justice O'Connor that the right to travel is not sufficiently implicated in this case to require heightened scrutiny.

Hence, I differ with Justice Brennan in this respect. But I agree with The Chief Justice that the New York statute at issue denies equal protection of the laws because the classification it employs is irrational. I therefore concur in the judgment.

Justice Stevens, dissenting.

Justice O'Connor has explained why the Court's decision is erroneous. I add these comments to explain why I do not feel constrained by the decision in Hooper v. Bernalillo County Assessor, 472 U.S. 612 (1985), to join the Court's judgment.

. . .

I respectfully dissent.

Justice O'Connor, with whom Justice Rehnquist and Justice Stevens join, dissenting.

The Court today holds unconstitutional the preference in public employment opportunities New York offers to resident war-time veterans who resided in New York when they entered military service. Because I believe that New York's veterans' preference scheme is not constitutionally offensive under the Equal Protection Clause, does not penalize some free-floating "right to migrate," and does not violate the Privileges and Immunities Clause of Art. IV, § 2, of the Constitution, I dissent.

I

The Court's constitutional analysis runs generally as follows: because the classification imposed by New York's limited, one-time veterans' civil service preference "penalizes" appellees' constitutional "right to migrate," the preference program must be subjected to heightened scrutiny, which it does not survive because it is insufficiently narrowly tailored to serve its asserted purposes. On the strength of this reasoning, the Court concludes that the preference program violates both appellees' constitutional "right to migrate" and their right to equal protection of the law, although it does not make clear how much of its analysis is necessary or sufficient to find a violation of the "right to migrate" independently of an Equal Protection Clause violation.

In pursuing this new dual analysis, the Court simply rejects the equal protection approach the Court has previously employed in similar cases, see, e.g., Hooper v. Bernalillo County Assessor, 472 U.S. 612 (1985), without bothering to explain why its novel use of both "right to migrate" analysis and strict equal protection scrutiny is more appropriate, necessary or doctrinally coherent. Cf. Jones v. Helms, 452 U.S. 412, 426–427 (1981) (White, J., concurring). Indeed, the Court does not even feel "impelled to locate ['the right to migrate'] definitively in any particular constitutional provision," despite the fact that its ruling rests in major part on its determination that the preference scheme penalizes that right. . . .

. . .

It is unfortunate that the Court has once again failed to articulate and justify by reference to textual sources a single constitutional principle or analysis upon which it can rely in deciding cases such as this. I adhere to my belief that the Privileges and Immunities Clause of Art. IV, § 2, of the Constitution supplies the relevant basis for analysis in evaluating claims like appellees', where the principal allegation is that the state scheme impermissibly distinguishes between state residents, allegedly imposing a relative burden on those who have more recently exercised their right to establish residence in the State. See Zobel v. Williams, 457 U.S., at 74–75 (O'Connor, J., concurring in judgment). I also continue to believe that a State's desire to compensate its citizens for their prior contributions is "neither inherently invidious nor irrational," either under the Court's "right to migrate" or under some undefined, substantive component of the Equal Protection Clause. Id., at 72. This case presents one of those instances in which the recognition of state citizens' past sacrifices constitutes a valid state interest that does not infringe any constitutionally protected interest, including the fundamental right to settle in another State which is protected by the Privileges and Immunities Clause of Art. IV, § 2. See id., at 72, n. 1.

II

In my view, the New York veterans' preference scheme weathers constitutional scrutiny under any of the theories propounded by the Court. The Court acknowledges that heightened scrutiny is appropriate only if the statutory classification "penalize[s]," "actually deters" or is primarily intended to "imped[e]" the exercise of the right to travel. In finding that the New York preference program imposes a "penalty" on appellees' right to migrate, the Court likens the New York scheme to the permanent state property tax exemption for veterans struck down in Hooper v. Bernalillo County Assessor, supra, and the durational residency requirements for essential governmental services invalidated in Memorial Hospital v. Maricopa County, 415 U.S. 250 (1974), and Shapiro v. Thompson, supra.

. . .

The New York law certainly does not directly restrict or burden appellees' freedom to move to New York and to establish residence there by imposing discriminatory fees, taxes, or other direct restraints.

. . .

Finally, the New York scheme does not effectively penalize those who exercise their fundamental right to settle in the State of their choice by requiring newcomers to accept a status inferior to that of all oldtime residents of New York upon their arrival. Cf. Zobel v. Williams, 457 U.S., at 74 (O'Connor, J., concurring in judgment). Those veterans who were not New York residents when they joined the United States Armed Forces, who subsequently move to New York, and who endeavor to secure civil service employment are treated exactly the same as the vast majority of New York citizens; they are in no sense regarded as "second-class citizens" when compared with the vast majority of New Yorkers or even the majority of the candidates against whom they must compete in obtaining civil employment. Cf. Hicklin v.

Orbeck, 437 U.S. 518 (1978). To the extent that persons such as appellees labor under any practical disability, it is a disability that they share in equal measure with countless other New York residents, including New York residents who joined the Armed Forces from New York but are ineligible for the veterans' preference for other reasons.

The only persons who arguably have an advantage based on their prior residency in New York in relation to persons in appellees' position are a discrete group of veterans who joined the Armed Forces while New York residents, who served during war time, who returned to New York, and who elected to seek public employment. Even that group does not enjoy an unqualified advantage over appellees based on their prior residence. New York's veterans' preference scheme requires that veterans satisfy a number of preconditions, of which prior residency is only one, before they qualify for the preference. Moreover, the preference only increases the possibility of securing a civil service appointment; it does not guarantee it. Those newly arrived veterans who achieve a sufficiently high score on the exam may not be disadvantaged at all by the preference program; conversely, the chances of those who receive a very low score may not be affected by the fact that their competitors received bonus points. Finally, the bonus program is a one-time benefit. Veterans who join the service in New York, who satisfy the other statutory requirements, and who achieve a sufficiently high score on the exam to bring them within range of securing employment may only use the bonus points on one examination for appointment and in one job for promotion. Thus, persons such as appellees are not forced to labor under a "continuous disability" by comparison even to this discrete group of New York citizens. Zobel v. Williams, supra, at 75 (O'Connor, J., concurring in judgment).

Certainly the New York veterans' preference program imposes a less direct burden on a less "significant" interest than many resident-preference programs that this Court has upheld without difficulty.

In sum, finding that this scheme in theory or practical effect constitutes a "penalty" on appellees' fundamental right to settle in New York or on their "right to migrate" seems to me ephemeral, and completely unnecessary to safeguard the constitutional purpose of "maintaining a Union rather than a mere 'league of States.'" Zobel v. Williams, supra, at 73 (O'Connor, J., concurring in judgment). . . . Thus, heightened scrutiny, either under the "right to migrate" or the Equal Protection Clause is inappropriate.

Under rational basis review, New York's program plainly passes constitutional muster. . . .

. . .

Whether this issue is tested under the "right to migrate," the Equal Protection Clause, or the Privileges and Immunities Clause of Art. IV, § 2, something more than the minimal effect on the right to travel or migrate that exists in this case must be required to trigger heightened scrutiny or the Court's right to travel analysis will swallow all the traditional deference shown to state economic and social regulation. The modest scheme at issue here does not penalize in a constitutional sense veterans who joined the Armed Forces in other States for choosing to eventually settle in New York, and does not deny them equal protection. I would reverse the judgment of the Court of Appeals for the Second Circuit.

D. WELFARE

Page 899. Add after Dandridge v. Williams

LYNG v. CASTILLO

477 U.S. 635, 106 S.Ct. 2727, 91 L.Ed.2d 527 (1986).

Justice Stevens delivered the opinion of the Court.

Eligibility and benefit levels in the Federal Food Stamp Program are determined on a "household" rather than an individual basis. The statutory definition of the term "household," as amended in 1981 and 1982, generally treats parents, children, and siblings who live together as a single household, but does not treat more distant relatives, or groups of unrelated persons who live together, as a single household unless they also customarily purchase food and prepare meals together.[1] Although there are variations in the facts of the four cases that were consolidated in the District Court, they all raise the question whether the statutory distinction between parents, children, and siblings, and all other groups of individuals violates the guarantee of equal treatment in the Due Process Clause of the Fifth Amendment.

I

Appellees are families who generally buy their food and prepare their meals as separate economic units; each family will either lose its benefits or have its food stamp allotment decreased as a result of the 1981 and 1982 amendments. Moreover, as appellees' counsel eloquently explained, in each case the loss or reduction of benefits will impose a severe hardship on a needy family, and may be especially harmful to the affected young children for whom an adequate diet is essential.

Appellees accordingly filed these lawsuits to invalidate the 1981 and 1982 amendments and to be treated as separate household for the purpose determining eligibility and allotment of food stamps. On cross-motions for summary judgment, the District Court considered the merits of appellees' challenge to the constitutionality of the "household" definition.

---

[1] Section 3(i) of the Food Stamp Act of 1964, as amended, 7 U.S.C. § 2012(i), provides in part:

" 'Household' means (1) an individual who lives alone or who, while living with others, customarily purchases foods and prepares meals for home consumption separate and apart from the others, or (2) a group of individuals who live together and customarily purchase food and prepare meals together for home consumption; *except that parents and children,* **or siblings,** *who live together shall be treated as a group of individuals who customarily purchase and prepare meals together for home consumption even if they do not do so, unless one of the parents,* **or siblings,** *is an elderly or disabled member.*"

. . .

The District Court was persuaded that the statutory definition had a rational basis. It observed that the amendment made it more difficult for individuals who live together to "manipulate" the rules "so as to obtain separate household status and receive greater benefits"; that the administrative burden of "attempting to make individual household determinations as to 'household' status" was time-consuming; and that unrelated persons who live together for reasons of economy or health are more likely " 'to actually be separate households' " than related families who live together. It held, however, that "a stricter standard of review than the 'rational basis' test" was required. Relying primarily on United States Department of Agriculture v. Moreno, 413 U.S. 528, 534 (1973), a case which it construed as holding that a "congressional desire to harm a politically unpopular group" could not justify the exclusion of household groups which contained unrelated persons, the District Court reasoned that "if the Supreme Court is willing to protect unpopular political groups it should even be more willing to protect the traditional family value of living together."

We noted probable jurisdiction and now reverse.

II

The District Court erred in judging the constitutionality of the statutory distinction under "heightened scrutiny." The disadvantaged class is that comprised by parents, children, and siblings. Close relatives are not a "suspect" or "quasi-suspect" class. As a historical matter, they have not been subjected to discrimination; they do not exhibit obvious, immutable, or distinguishing characteristics that define them as a discrete group; and they are not a minority or politically powerless. See, e.g., Massachusetts Board of Retirement v. Murgia, 427 U.S. 307, 313–314 (1976) (per curiam). In fact, quite the contrary is true.

Nor does the statutory classification "directly and substantially" interfere with family living arrangements and thereby burden a fundamental right. Zablocki v. Redhail, 434 U.S. 374, 386–387, and n. 12 (1978). . . . The "household" definition does not order or prevent any group of persons from dining together. Indeed, in the overwhelming majority of cases it probably has no effect at all. It is exceedingly unlikely that close relatives would choose to live apart simply to increase their allotment of food stamps, for the cost of separate housing would almost certainly exceed the incremental value of the additional stamps. See 50 Fed.Reg. 36641, 36642 (1985). Thus, just as in United States Department of Agriculture v. Moreno—the decision which the District Court read to require "heightened scrutiny"—the "legislative classification must be sustained if the classification itself is rationally related to a legitimate governmental interest." 413 U.S., at 533. See id., at 533–538.[3]

---

[3] In United States Department of Agriculture v. Moreno, 413 U.S. 528 (1973), we held that the definition of the term "household" in the Food Stamp Act as amended in 1971, 84 Stat. 2048, was unconstitutional. That definition drew a distinction between house-

Under the proper standard of review, we agree with the District Court that Congress had a rational basis both for treating parents, children and siblings who live together as a single "household," and for applying a different standard in determining whether groups of more distant relatives and unrelated persons living together constitute a "household."

As a general matter, the economies of scale that may be realized in group purchase and preparation of food surely justified Congress in providing additional food stamp benefits to households that could not achieve such efficiencies.[4] Moreover, the Legislature's recognition of the potential for mistake and fraud and the cost-ineffectiveness of case-by-case verification of claims that individuals ate as separate households unquestionably warrants the use of general definitions in this area.

The question that remains is whether Congress could accommodate the wishes of distant relatives and unrelated individuals to dine separately without invidiously discriminating against close relatives. The question, in other words, is whether Congress could "[l]imi[t] the availability of the 'purchase and prepare food separately' rule to those most likely to actually be separate households, although living together with others for reasons of economy or health (i.e., [distant relatives and] unrelated persons)." S.Rep. No. 97–504, p. 25 (1982).

So stated, the justification for the statutory classification is obvious. Congress could reasonably determine that close relatives sharing a home—almost by definition—tend to purchase and prepare meals together while distant relatives and unrelated individuals might not be so inclined. In that event, even though close relatives are undoubtedly as honest as other food stamp recipients, the potential for mistaken or misstated claims of separate dining would be greater in the case of close relatives than would be true for those with weaker communal ties, simply because a greater percentage of the former category in fact prepare meals jointly than the comparable percentage in the latter category. The additional fact that close relatives represent by far the largest proportion of food stamp recipients, might well have convinced Congress that limited funds would not permit the accommodation given

holds composed entirely of persons who are related to one another and households containing one or more members who are unrelated to the rest. Unlike the present statute, the 1971 definition completely disqualified all households in the latter category. Not only were all groups of unrelated persons ineligible for benefits, but even groups of related persons would lose their benefits if they admitted one nonrelative to their household. We concluded that this definition did not further the interest in preventing fraud, or any other legitimate purpose of the Food Stamp Program. . . .

The 1971 definition was, therefore, "wholly without any rational basis" and "invalid under the Due Process Clause of the Fifth Amendment." 413 U.S., at 538.

[4] See S.Rep. No. 97–504, p. 24 (1982) ("Because of economics of scale, small (one-, two-, and three-person) households are provided more food stamps per person than larger households. For example, current benefit levels are $70 for 1-, $128 for 2-, $183 for 3-person households"); S.Rep. No. 97–128, p. 31 (1981) ("It should be noted that because of economics of scale, small (one, two, or three persons) households are provided more food stamps per person than larger households—for example, $70 for one, $128 for two, $183 for three, and $233 for four").

distant relatives and unrelated persons to be stretched to embrace close relatives as well. Finally, Congress might have reasoned that it would be somewhat easier for close relatives—again, almost by definition—to accommodate their living habits to a federal policy favoring common meal preparation than it would be for more distant relatives or unrelated persons to do so. Because of these differences, we are persuaded that Congress could rationally conclude that the two categories merited differential treatment. Neither the decision to take "one step" in 1981—when the rule was applied to parents and children—nor the decision to take a second step in 1982, when the rule was extended to siblings as well—was irrational because Congress did not simultaneously take a third step that would apply to the entire food stamp program.

The judgment of the District Court is therefore reversed.

Justice Brennan, dissenting.

I would affirm on the ground that the challenged classifications violate the Equal Protection Clause because they fail the rational-basis test.

Justice White, dissenting.

For the reasons given in the last three paragraphs of Justice Marshall's dissenting opinion, the classification at issue in this case is irrational. Accordingly, I dissent.

Justice Marshall, dissenting.

This case demonstrates yet again the lack of vitality in this Court's recent equal protection jurisprudence. . . . In my view, when analyzing classifications affecting the receipt of governmental benefits, a court must consider "the character of the classification in question, the relative importance to individuals in the class discriminated against of the governmental benefits that they do not receive, and the asserted state interests in support of the classification." Dandridge v. Williams, 397 U.S. 471, 521 (1970) (Marshall, J., dissenting). By contrast, the Court's rigid, bipolar approach, which purports to apply rational basis scrutiny unless a suspect classification is involved or the exercise of a fundamental right is impeded puts legislative classifications impinging upon sensitive issues of family structure and survival on the same plane as a refusal to let a merchant hawk his wares on a particular street corner. I do not believe the equal protection component of the Due Process Clause could become such a blunt instrument.

The importance of the interests involved in his case can hardly be denied. The Court concludes that the challenged statute does not directly and substantially interfere with family living arrangements, cf. Moore v. East Cleveland, 431 U.S. 494 (1977) (plurality opinion), because it "does not order or prevent any group of persons from dining together." The Court relies, apparently, on the fact that the statute does not use criminal sanctions, but merely the loss of benefits, to influence family living decisions. It is a bit late in the day, however, to cut off due process analysis—be it procedural or substantive—by simply invoking such a distinction. See Goldberg v. Kelly, 397 U.S. 254, 262 (1970); Shapiro v. Thompson, 394 U.S. 618, 627 (1969).

The food stamp benefits at issue are necessary for the affected families' very survival, and the Federal Government denies that benefit to families who do not, by preparing their meals together, structure themselves in a manner that the Government believes will minimize unnecessary expenditures. The importance of that benefit belies any suggestion that the Government is not directly and substantially influencing the living arrangements of families whose resources are so low that they must rely on their relatives for shelter. The Government has thus chosen to intrude into the family dining room—a place where I would have thought the right to privacy exists in its strongest form. What possible interest can the Government have in preventing members of a family from dining as they choose? It is simply none of the Government's business.

The challenged classifications amount to a conclusive presumption that related families living under the same roof do all of their cooking together. Thus the regulation does not merely affect the important privacy interest in family living arrangements recognized in *Moore*, but the even more vital interest in survival. As Congress itself recognized, some separate families live in the same house but cannot prepare meals together because of different work schedules. See S.Rep. No. 97–504, p. 25 (1982). Others may lack sufficient plates and utensils to accommodate more than a few persons at once, or may have only one burner on their stove. These extended families simply lack the option of cooking and eating together. For them, the legislative presumption in this case does far greater damage than merely prescribing with whom they must dine. By assuming that they realize economies of scale that they in fact cannot achieve, the regulation threatens their lives and health by denying them the minimal benefits provided to all other families of similar income and needs.

Balanced against these vital interests is Congress' undeniably legitimate desire to prevent fraud and waste in the food stamp program. The legislative presumption that Congress used, however, is related at best tenuously to the achievement of those goals. While I believe that our standard of review must take into consideration the importance of the individual interests affected, I have some doubt that the classification used here could pass even a rational-basis test. In United States Dept. of Agriculture v. Moreno, 413 U.S. 528 (1973), we held that a definition of "household" that excluded any living group containing an individual unrelated to any other member of the group did not rationally further the Government's interest in preventing fraud in the food stamp program. Despite the Court's attempts to distinguish this case from *Moreno*, the critical fact in both cases is that the statute drew a distinction that bears no necessary relation to the prevention of fraud. See id., at 535–536 ("denial of essential federal food assistance to *all* otherwise eligible households containing unrelated members" not rationally related to fraud prevention). In the present case, the Government has provided no justification for the conclusion that related individuals living together are more likely to lie about their living arrangements than are unrelated individuals. Nor has it demonstrated that fraudulent conduct by related households is more difficult to detect than similar abuses by unrelated households.

Congress stressed its desire to prevent fraud in the food stamp program, . . . and it classified the "household consolidation" provision as an antifraud measure. Nevertheless, the Committee Reports cite no hard evidence that related persons living together were in fact significant sources of fraud; the committees merely determined that the Government could save money by "tighten[ing] the definition of an eligible food stamp household." . . . The House did hypothesize, in the course of considering the 1981 amendments, that an 18-year old child living with his parents could declare himself a separate household for food stamp purposes, ... If indeed that abuse widely existed, the resulting legislation, which lumped together all nonelderly parents and their offspring living under one roof as a "household," provided a more than sufficient cure. Nevertheless, Congress proceeded to restrict eligibility even further the following year.

When it moved beyond the rule that merely grouped parents and children, and in the 1982 amendments grouped siblings together as well, Congress interfered substantially with the desires of demonstrably separate families to remain separate families. It did so, moreover, while recognizing that distinct families living together often are genuinely separate households, and that the food stamp program should permit separate families that are not related to live together but maintain separate households. . . . Congress nevertheless assumed that related families are less likely to be genuinely separate households than are unrelated families, and failed even to provide related families a chance to rebut the legislative presumption. In view of the importance to the affected families of their family life and their very survival, the Court's extreme deference to this untested assumption is simply inappropriate. I respectfully dissent.

BOWEN v. GILLIARD, 107 S.Ct. 3008 (1987): The facts in this case involving a challenge to a change in the AFDC are summarized supra, p. 133. On the equal protection challenge the Court divided 6 to 3. Justice Stevens, writing for the majority, found the statute constitutional, saying, in part:

"The precepts that govern our review of appellees' due process and equal protection challenges to this program are similar to those we have applied in reviewing challenges to other parts of the Social Security Act: 'Our review is deferential.' Governmental decisions to spend money to improve the general public welfare in one way and not another are 'not confided to the courts. The discretion belongs to Congress unless the choice is clearly wrong, a display of arbitrary power, not an exercise of judgment.' Mathews v. De Castro, 429 U.S.

181, 185 (1976), quoting Helvering v. Davis, 301 U.S. 619, 640 (1937). Bowen v. Owens, 476 U.S. ___, ___ (1986).

"This standard of review is premised on Congress' 'plenary power to define the scope and the duration of the entitlement to . . . benefits, and to increase, to decrease, or to terminate those benefits based on its appraisal of the relative importance of the recipients' needs and the resources available to fund the program.' Atkins v. Parker, 472 U.S. 115, 129 (1985); . . .

"The District Court had before it evidence that the DEFRA amendments were severely impacting some families. For example, some noncustodial parents stopped making their support payments because they believed that their payments were helping only the State, and not their children. 633 F.Supp., at 1542–1543. It is clear, however, that in the administration of a fund that is large enough to have a significant impact on the Nation's deficit, general rules must be examined in light of the broad purposes they are intended to serve. The challenged amendment unquestionably serves Congress' goal of decreasing federal expenditures. . . . The evidence that a few noncustodial parents were willing to violate the law by not making court-ordered support payments does not alter the fact that the entire program has resulted in saving huge sums of money.

"The rationality of the amendment denying a family the right to exclude a supported child from the filing unit is also supported by the Government's separate interest in distributing benefits among competing needy families in a fair way. Given its perceived need to make cuts in the AFDC budget, Congress obviously sought to identify a group that would suffer less than others as a result of a reduction in benefits. When considering the plight of two five-person families, one of which receives no income at all while the other receives regular support payments for some of the minor children, it is surely reasonable for Congress to conclude that the former is in greater need than the latter. . . .

"Appellees argue (and the District Court ruled), however, that finding that Congress acted rationally is not enough to sustain this legislation. Rather, they claim that some form of 'heightened scrutiny' is appropriate because the amendment interferes with a family's fundamental right to live in the type of family unit it chooses. We conclude that the District Court erred in subjecting the DEFRA amendment to any form of heightened scrutiny. That some families may decide to modify their living arrangements in order to avoid the effect of the amendment, does not transform the amendment into an act whose design and direct effect is to 'intrude on choices concerning family living arrangements.' Moore v. East Cleveland, 431 U.S. 494, 499 (1977). As was the case with the marriage-related provision upheld in Califano v. Jobst, 434 U.S. 47 (1977), 'Congress adopted this rule in the course of constructing a complex social welfare system that necessarily deals with the intimacies of family life. This is not a case in which government seeks to foist orthodoxy on the unwilling.'

"Last Term we rejected a constitutional challenge to a provision in the Federal Food Stamp Program, which determines eligibility and benefit levels on a 'household' rather than an individual basis. Lyng v. Castillo, 477 U.S. ___ (1986). We held that the guarantee of equal treatment in the Due Process Clause of the Fifth Amendment was not violated by the statutory requirement that generally treated parents, children, and siblings who lived together as a single household, ...

"In light of this, we concluded in Lyng that the 'District Court erred in judging the constitutionality of the statutory distinction under "heightened scrutiny." ' In this case the District Court committed the same error. As in Lyng, the standard of review here is whether 'Congress had a rational basis' for its decision. And as in Lyng, 'the justification for the statutory classification is obvious.' Id., at ___. The provisions at issue do not violate the Due Process Clause."

Justice Brennan, joined by Justice Marshall, filed a lengthy dissent. Justice Blackmun, dissenting, indicated his agreement with much of what Justice Brennan wrote. Justice Brennan's opinion opened with the following paragraphs:

"Government in the modern age has assumed increasing responsibility for the welfare of its citizens. This expansion of responsibility has been accompanied by an increase in the scale and complexity of the activities that Government conducts. Respect for the enormity of the administrative task that confronts the modern welfare state, as well as for the scarcity of Government resources, counsels that public officials enjoy discretion in determining the most effective means of fulfilling their responsibilities.

The very pervasiveness of modern Government, however, creates an unparalleled opportunity for intrusion on personal life. In a society in which most persons receive some form of Government benefit, Government has considerable leverage in shaping individual behavior. In most cases, we acknowledge that Government may wield its power even when its actions likely influence choices involving personal behavior. On certain occasions, however, Government intrusion into private life is so direct and substantial that we must deem it intolerable if we are to be true to our belief that there is a boundary between the public citizen and the private person.

"This is such a case. The Government has told a child who lives with a mother receiving public assistance that it cannot both live with its mother and be supported by its father. The child must either leave the care and custody of the mother, or forgo the support of the father and become a Government client. The child is put to this choice not because it seeks Government benefits for itself, but because of a fact over which it has no control: the need of *other* household members for public assistance. A child who lives with one parent has, under the best of circumstances, a difficult time sustaining a relationship with both its parents. A crucial bond between a child and its parent outside the home, usually the father, is the father's commitment to care for the material needs of the child, and the expectation of the child that it may look to its father for such care. The Government has thus decreed that a condition of welfare eligibility for a mother is that her child surrender a vital connection with either the father or the mother.

"The Court holds that the Government need only show a rational basis for such action. This standard of review has regularly been used in evaluating the claims of applicants for Government benefits, since 'a noncontractual claim to receive funds from the public treasury enjoys no constitutionally protected status.' Weinberger v. Salfi, 422 U.S. 749, 772 (1975). Plaintiff child support recipients in this case, however, are children who wish *NOT* to receive public assistance, but to continue to be supported by their noncustodial parent. Their claim is *NOT* that the Government has unfairly denied them benefits, but that it has intruded deeply into their relationship with their parents. More than a mere rational basis is required to withstand this challenge, and, as the following analysis shows, the Government can offer no adequate justification for doing such damage to the parent-child relationship."

E. EDUCATION

Page 931. Add at end of page:

PAPASAN v. ALLAIN, 478 U.S. 265 (1986). When Mississippi became a state the federal government provided for the sale of lands, except that the sixteenth section of each township was reserved for the support of schools. The lands were given to the state to hold in trust for the benefit of the public schools. This provision, however, did not extend to the portion of the state held by the Chickasaw Indian Nation—an area now including the 23 northern counties of the state. Later when the Indians ceded the land to the federal government it was put up for sale without reservation of the sixteenth sections. Later the federal government selected land and gave it to the state in lieu of the sixteenth section land to support the schools in the northern counties. Still later the Congress permitted the state to sell these lands and invest the proceeds in loans to railroads. The railroads and the state's investment in them were destroyed during the Civil War and never replaced.

Currently, the funds derived from the sixteenth section lands in the southern part of the state are allocated to schools in the districts in which the lands exist and provide an average income of $75.34 per pupil. With respect to the northern 23 counties, however, the state has done no more than pay interest on the principal lost during the Civil War—an amount which provides only $.63 for each pupil in the northern 23 counties.

Local school officials and school children in the northern 23 counties filed suit in the federal district court charging that the variation in the funding support constituted a denial of equal protection of the laws.

Justice White, delivering the opinion of the Court, said:

III

"The question remains whether the petitioners' equal protection claim, although not barred by the Eleventh Amendment, is legally insufficient and was properly dismissed for failure to state a claim. See Fed.Rule Civ.Proc. 12(b)(6). We are bound for the purposes of this review to take the well-pleaded factual allegations in the complaint as true. . . . Construing these facts and relevant facts obtained from the public record in the light most favorable to the petitioners, we must ascertain whether they state a claim on which relief could be granted.

A

"In [San Antonio Independent School District v.] Rodriguez, the Court upheld against an equal protection challenge Texas' system of financing its public schools, under which funds for the public schools were derived from two main sources. Approximately half of the funds came from the Texas Minimum Foundation School Program, a state program aimed at guaranteeing a certain level of minimum education for all children in the State. 411 U.S., at 9. Most of the remainder of the funds came from local sources—in particular local property taxes. Id., at 9, n. 21. As a result of this dual funding system, most specifically as a result of differences in amounts collected from local property taxes, 'substantial interdistrict disparities in school expenditures [were] found . . . in varying degrees throughout the State.' Id., at 15.

"In examining the equal protection status of these disparities, the Court declined to apply any heightened scrutiny based either on wealth as a suspect classification or on education as a fundamental right. As to the latter, the Court recognized the importance of public education but noted that education 'is not among the rights afforded explicit protection under our Federal Constitution.' Id., at 35. The Court did not, however, foreclose the possibility 'that some identifiable quantum of education is a constitutionally protected prerequisite to the meaningful exercise of either [the right to speak or the right to vote].' Id., at 36. Given the absence of such radical denial of educational opportunity, it was concluded that the State's school financing scheme would be constitutional if it bore 'some rational relationship to a legitimate state purpose.' Id., at 44.

"Applying this standard, the dual Texas system was deemed reasonably structured to accommodate two separate forces:

'[T]he desire by members of society to have educational opportunity for all children, and the desire of each family to provide the best education it can afford for its own children.'

'. . . While assuring a basic education for every child in the State, it permits and encourages a large measure of participation in and control of each district's schools at the local level.' Id., at 49 (quoting J. Coleman, Foreword to G. Strayer & R. Haig, The Financing of Education in the State of New York vii (1923)).

"Given this rational basis, the Court concluded that the mere 'happenstance' that the quality of education might vary from district to district because of varying property values within the districts did not render the system 'so irrational as to be invidiously discriminatory.' 411 U.S., at 55. In particular, the Court found that 'any scheme of local taxation—indeed the very existence of identifiable local governmental units—requires the establishment of jurisdictional boundaries that are inevitably arbitrary.' Id., at 53–54.

"Almost 10 years later, the Court again considered the equal protection status of the administration of the Texas public schools—this time in relation to the State's decision not to expend any state funds on the education of children who were not 'legally admitted' to the United States. Plyler v. Doe, 457 U.S. 202 (1982). The Court did not, however, measurably change the approach articulated in *Rodriguez*. It reiterated that education is not a fundamental right and concluded that undocumented aliens were not a suspect class. Id., at 223–224. Nevertheless, it concluded that the justifications for the discrimination offered by the State were 'wholly insubstantial in light of the costs involved to these children, the State, and the Nation.' Id., at 230.

B

"The complaint in this case asserted not simply that the petitioners had been denied their right to a minimally adequate education but also that such a right was fundamental and that because that right had been infringed the State's action here should be reviewed under strict scrutiny. As *Rodriguez* and *Plyler* indicate, this Court has not yet definitively settled the questions whether a minimally adequate education is a fundamental right and whether a statute alleged to discriminatorily infringe that right should be accorded heightened equal protection review.

"Nor does this case require resolution of these issues. Although for the purposes of this motion to dismiss we must take all the factual allegations in the complaint as true, we are not bound to accept as true a legal conclusion couched as a factual allegation. . . . Petitioners' allegation that, by reason of the funding disparities relating to the Sixteenth Section Lands, they have been deprived of a minimally adequate education is just such an allegation. Petitioners do not allege that schoolchildren in the Chickasaw Counties are not taught to read or write; they do not allege that they receive no instruction on even the educational basics; they allege no actual facts in support of their assertion that they have been deprived of a minimally adequate education. As we see it, we are not bound to credit and may disregard the allegation that petitioners have been denied a minimally adequate education.

"Concentrating instead on the disparities in terms of Sixteenth Section Lands benefits that the complaint in fact alleged and that are documented in the public record, we are persuaded that the Court of Appeals properly determined that *Rodriguez* dictates the applicable standard of review. The differential treatment alleged here constitutes an equal protection violation only if it is not rationally related to a legitimate state interest.

"Applying this test, the Court of Appeals concluded that, historical roots aside, the essence of the petitioners' claim was an attack on Mississippi's system of financing public education. And it reasoned that the inevitability of disparities in income derived from real estate managed and administered locally, as in *Rodriguez,* supplied a rationale for the disparities alleged. To begin with, we disagree with the Court of Appeals' apparent understanding of the crux of the petitioners' claim. As we read their complaint, the petitioners do not challenge the overall organization of the Mississippi public school financing program. Instead, their challenge is restricted to one aspect of that program: The Sixteenth Section and Lieu Lands funding. All of the allegations in the complaint center around disparities in the distribution of these particular benefits, and no allegations concerning disparities in other public school funding programs are included.

"Consequently, this is a very different claim than the claim made in *Rodriguez.* In *Rodriguez* the contention was that the State's overall system of funding was unconstitutionally discriminatory. There, the Court examined the basic structure of that system and concluded that it was rationally related to a legitimate state purpose. In reaching that conclusion, the Court necessarily found that funding disparities resulting from differences in local taxes were acceptable because related to the state goal of allowing a measure of effective local control over school funding levels. *Rodriguez* did not, however, purport to validate all funding variations that might result from a State's public school funding decisions. It held merely that the variations that resulted from allowing local control over local property tax funding of the public schools were constitutionally permissible in that case.

"Here, the petitioners' claim goes neither to the overall funding system nor to the local ad valorem component of that system. Instead, it goes solely to the Sixteenth Section and Lieu Lands portion of the State's public school funding. And, as to this claim, we are unpersuaded that *Rodriguez* resolves the equal protection question in favor of the State. The allegations of the complaint are that the State is distributing the income from Sixteenth Section lands or from lieu lands or funds unequally among the school districts, to the detriment of the Chickasaw Cession schools and their students. The Sixteenth Section and Lieu Lands in Mississippi were granted to and held by the State itself. Under state law, these lands 'constitute property held in trust for the benefit of the public schools and must be treated as such,' Miss.Code Ann. § 29–3–1(1) (Supp.1985), but in carrying out the trust, the State has vested the management of these lands in the local school boards throughout the State, under the supervision of the Secretary of State, and has credited the income from these lands to the 'school districts of the township in which such sixteenth section lands may be located, or to which any sixteenth section lieu lands may belong,' such income to be used for the purpose of educating the children of the school district or as otherwise may be provided by law. Miss.Code Ann. § 29–3–109 (Supp.1985). This case is therefore very different from *Rodriguez,* where the differential financing available to school districts was traceable to school district funds available from local real estate taxation, not to a state decision to divide state resources unequally among school districts. The rationality of the disparity in *Rodriguez,* therefore, which rested on the fact that funding disparities based on differing local wealth were a necessary adjunct of allowing meaningful local control over school funding, does not settle the constitutionality of disparities alleged in this case, and we differ with the Court of Appeals in this respect.

"Nevertheless, the question remains whether the variations in the benefits received by school districts from Sixteenth Section or Lieu Lands are, on the allegations in the complaint and as a matter of law, rationally related to a legitimate state interest. We believe, however, that we should not pursue this issue here but should instead remand the case for further proceedings. Neither the Court of Appeals nor the parties have addressed the equal protection issue as we think it is posed by this case: Given that the State has title to assets granted to it by the Federal Government for the use of the State's schools, does the Equal Protection Clause permit it to distribute the benefit of these assets unequally among the school districts as it now does?

"A crucial consideration in resolving this issue is whether the federal law requires the State to allocate the economic benefits of school lands to schools in the townships in which those lands are located. If, as a matter of federal law, the State has no choice in the matter, whether the complaint states an equal protection claim depends on whether the federal policy is itself violative of the Clause. If it is, the State may properly be enjoined from implementing such policy. Contrariwise, if the federal law is valid and the State is bound by it, then it provides a rational reason for the funding disparity. Neither the courts below nor the parties have addressed the equal protection issue in these terms. Another possible consideration in resolving the equal protection issue is that school lands require management and that the State has assigned this task to the individual districts in which the lands are located, subject to supervision by the State. The significance, if any, in equal protection terms of this allocation of duties in justifying assigning the income exclusively to those who perform the management function and none of it to those districts that have no lands to manage is a matter that is best addressed by the lower courts in the first instance.

". . . With respect to the affirmance of the District Court's dismissal of the equal protection claim, the judgment of the Court of Appeals is vacated, and the case is remanded to that court for further proceedings consistent with this opinion."

Justice Powell, joined by Chief Justice Burger and Justice Rehnquist dissented on the equal protection issue, stating:

"The public record refutes petitioners' equal protection claims that the disparities in funding from various school lands detrimentally affects students and schools in school districts within the Chickasaw Cession. Statistics from Mississippi's State Department of Education show the statewide ranking of school districts in terms of expenditures per pupil. In this ranking, the Chickasaw Cession districts are scattered widely among the State's 154 school districts. Moreover, far from being a 'critical element of school funding in Mississippi,' as alleged by petitioners, the Sixteenth Section lands account for only 1½% of overall funds provided for schools. I therefore find no basis for the assumption that petitioners can prove that students in Chickasaw Cession districts have been detrimentally affected by this differential, and I do not believe that petitioners have asserted an equal protection claim that can survive a motion to dismiss under Federal Rule of Civil Procedure 12(b)(6).

. . .

"It is alleged—and here accepted as true—that there is a disparity between the payments from the Sixteenth Section Lands in the Chocktaw districts and the payments from the state of Mississippi's trust fund to Chickasaw districts. The complaint characterizes this disparity as an 'unjust, inequitable and unconstitutional deprivation of the rights of the children of the Chickasaw Cession counties.' The Court reads the complaint as alleging that this unequal distribution of such funds acts 'to the detriment of the Chickasaw Cession schools and their students.' The complaint, however, contains no factual assertions other than this disparity to support these conclusory allegations, nor is there any basis for believing a detriment could ever be proven. As shown in Table A, the various per pupil expenditures in petitioners' school districts are comparable to, and in some cases higher than, the average for districts within the Chocktaw area. And the Sixteenth Section payments—as the figures in Table B demonstrate beyond argument—are an insignificant part of the total payments from all sources made to Mississippi's school districts.

"The Court does not question these data. It instead states that petitioners 'have limited themselves to challenging discrimination in the Sixteenth Section' program, and, relying on that limitation, 'decline[s] the dissent's invitation to look at school receipts overall.' The Court thereby ignores the undisputed facts concerning the funding of public education in the State of Mississippi, and instead bases its equal protection analysis on 1½% of the overall funds provided for public secondary and elementary schools in the State. The Equal Protection Clause, at least in the context of a state funding of schools, is concerned with *substance,* not with the *de minimis* variations of funding among the districts."

KADRMAS v. DICKINSON PUBLIC SCHOOLS
—— U.S. ——, 108 S.Ct. 2481, —— L.Ed.2d —— (1988).

Justice O'Connor delivered the opinion of the Court.

Appellants urge us to hold that the Equal Protection Clause forbids a State to allow some local school boards, but not others, to assess a fee for transporting pupils between their homes and the public schools. Applying well-established equal protection principles, we reject this claim and affirm the constitutionality of the challenged statute.

I

North Dakota is a sparsely populated State, with many people living on isolated farms and ranches. One result has been that some children, as late as the mid-20th century, were educated in "the one-room school where, in many cases, there [we]re twenty or more pupils with one teacher attempting in crowded conditions and under other disadvantages to give instructions in all primary grades." Herman v. Medicine Lodge School Dist. No. 8, 71 N.W.2d 323, 328 (N.D.1955). The State has experimented with various ameliorative devices at different times in its history. Beginning in 1907, for example, it has adopted a series of policies that "in certain circumstances required and in other circumstances merely authorized [local public] school districts to participate in transporting or providing compensation for transporting students to school." 402 N.W.2d 897, 900 (N.D.1987) (opinion below).

Since 1947, the legislature has authorized and encouraged thinly populated school districts to consolidate or "reorganize" themselves into larger districts so that education can be provided more efficiently. See *Herman, supra,* at 328; N.D. Cent. Code, ch. 15-27.3 (Supp.1987). Reorganization proposals, which obviously must contemplate an increase in the distance that some children travel to school, are required by law to include provisions for transporting students back and forth from their homes. See § 15-27.3-10. The details of these provisions may vary from district to district, but once a reorganization plan is adopted the transportation provisions can be changed only with the approval of the voters. See §§ 15-27.3-10 and 15-27.3-19.

Appellee Dickinson Public Schools, which serves a relatively populous area, has chosen not to participate in such a reorganization. Until 1973, this school system provided free bus service to students in outlying areas, but the "pickup points" for this service were often at considerable distances from the students' homes. After a plebiscite of the bus users, Dickinson's school board instituted door-to-door bus service and began charging a fee. During the period relevant to this case, about 13% of the students rode the bus; their parents were charged $97.00 per year for one child or $150.00 per year for two children. 402 N.W.2d, at 898. Such fees covered approximately 11% of the cost of providing the bus service, and the remainder was provided from state and local tax revenues.

In 1979, the State enacted the legislation at issue in this case. This statute expressly indicates that nonreorganized school districts, like Dickinson, may charge a fee for transporting students to school; such fees, however, may not exceed the estimated cost to the school district of providing the service. See N.D. Cent. Code § 15-34.2-06.1 (1981 and Supp.1987). . . .

Appellants are a Dickinson school child, Sarita Kadrmas, and her mother, Paula. The Kadrmas family, which also includes Mrs. Kadrmas' husband and two preschool children, lives about 16 miles from Sarita's school. Mr. Kadrmas works sporadically in the North Dakota oil fields, and the family's annual income at the time of trial was at or near the officially defined poverty level. Until 1985, the Kadrmas family had agreed each year to pay the fee for busing Sarita to school. Having fallen behind on these and other bills, however, the family refused to sign a contract obligating them to pay $97.00 for the 1985 school year. Accordingly, the school bus no longer stopped for

Sarita, and the family arranged to transport her to school privately. The costs they incurred that year for Sarita's transportation exceeded $1,000.00, or about 10 times the fee charged by the school district for bus service. This arrangement continued until the Spring of 1987, when Paula Kadrmas signed a bus service contract for the remainder of the 1986 school year and paid part of the fee. Mrs. Kadrmas later signed another contract for the 1987 school year, and paid about half of the fee for that period.

In September 1985, appellants, along with others who have since withdrawn from the case, filed an action in state court seeking to enjoin appellees—the Dickinson Public Schools and various school district officials—from collecting any fee for the bus service. The action was dismissed on the merits, and an appeal was taken to the Supreme Court of North Dakota. After rejecting a state-law challenge, which is not at issue here, the court considered appellants' claim that the busing fee violates the Equal Protection Clause of the Fourteenth Amendment. The court characterized the 1979 statute as "purely economic legislation," which "must be upheld unless it is patently arbitrary and fails to bear a rational relationship to any legitimate government purpose." 402 N.W.2d at 902. The court then concluded "that the charges authorized [by the statute] are rationally related to the legitimate governmental objective of allocating limited resources and that the statute does not discriminate on the basis of wealth so as to violate federal or state equal protection rights." Id., at 903. The court also rejected the contention that the distinction drawn by the statute between reorganized and nonreorganized school districts violates the Equal Protection Clause. The distinction, the court found, serves the legitimate objective of promoting reorganization "by alleviating parental concerns regarding the cost of student transportation in the reorganized district." Ibid. Three justices dissented on state-law grounds. We noted probable jurisdiction, . . . and now affirm.

II

. . .

B

Unless a statute provokes "strict judicial scrutiny" because it interferes with a "fundamental-right" or discriminates against a "suspect class," it will ordinarily survive an equal protection attack so long as the challenged classification is rationally related to a legitimate governmental purpose. See, e.g., San Antonio School Dist. v. Rodriguez, 411 U.S. 1, 16–17 (1973); Plyler v. Doe, 457 U.S. 202, 216–217 (1982); Lyng v. Automobile Workers, 485 U.S. ___, ___ (1988). Appellants contend that Dickinson's user fee for bus service unconstitutionally deprives those who cannot afford to pay it of "minimum access to education." Sarita Kadrmas, however, continued to attend school during the time that she was denied access to the school bus. Appellants must therefore mean to argue that the busing fee unconstitutionally places a greater obstacle to education in the path of the poor than it does in the path of wealthier families. Alternatively, appellants may mean to suggest that the Equal Protection Clause affirmatively requires government to provide free transportation to school, at least for some class of students that would include Sarita Kadrmas. Under either interpretation of appellants' position, we are evidently being urged to apply a form of strict or "heightened" scrutiny to the North Dakota statute. Doing so would require us to extend the requirements of the Equal Protection Clause beyond the limits recognized in our cases, a step we decline to take.

We have previously rejected the suggestion that statutes having different effects on the wealthy and the poor should on that account alone be subjected to strict equal protection scrutiny. See, e.g., Harris v. McRae, 448 U.S. 297, 322–323 (1980); Ortwein v. Schwab, 410 U.S. 656, 660 (1973). Nor have we accepted the proposition that education is a "fundamental right," like equality of the franchise, which should trigger strict scrutiny when government interferes with an individual's access to it. See Papasan v. Allain, 478 U.S. 265, 284 (1986); Plyler v. Doe, supra, at 223; San Antonio School Dist. v. Rodriguez, supra, at 16, 33–36.

Relying primarily on Plyler v. Doe, supra, however, appellants suggests that North Dakota's 1979 statute should be subjected to "heightened" scrutiny. This standard of review, which is less demanding than "strict scrutiny" but more demanding than the standard rational relation test, has generally been applied only in cases that involved discriminatory classifications based on sex or illegitimacy. See, e.g., Clark v. Jeter, ___ U.S. ___, ___ (1988); Mississippi University for Women v. Hogan, 458 U.S. 718, 723–724, and n. 9 (1982); Mills v. Habluetzel, 456 U.S. 91, 101, and n. 8 (1982); Craig v. Boren, 429 U.S. 190, 197 (1976). In Plyler, which did not fit this pattern, the State of Texas had denied to the children of illegal aliens the free public education that it made available to other residents. Applying a heightened level of equal protection scrutiny, the Court concluded that the State had failed to show that its classification advanced a substantial state interest. 457 U.S., at 217–218, and n. 16, 224, 230. We have not extended this holding beyond the "unique circumstances," id., at 239 (Powell, J., concurring), that provoked its "unique confluence of theories and rationales," id., at 243 (Burger, C.J., dissenting). Nor do we think that the case before us today is governed by the holding in *Plyler.* Unlike the children in that case, Sarita Kadrmas has not been penalized by the government for illegal conduct by her parents. See id., at 220; id., at 238 (Powell, J., concurring). On the contrary, Sarita was denied access to the school bus only because her parents would not agree to pay the same user fee charged to all other families that took advantage of the service. Nor do we see any reason to suppose that this user fee will "promot[e] the creation and perpetuation of a subclass of illiterates within our boundaries, surely adding to the problems and costs of unemployment, welfare, and crime." Id., at 230; see also id., at 239 (Powell, J., concurring). Cf., N.D.Cent.Code § 15–43–11.2 (1981) ("A [school] board may waive any fee if any pupil or his parent or guardian shall be unable to pay such fees. No pupil's rights or privileges, including the receipt of grades or diplomas, may be denied or abridged for nonpayment of fees"). The case before us does not resemble *Plyler,* and we decline to extend the rationale of that decision to cover this case.

Appellants contend, finally, that whatever label is placed on the standard of review, this case is analogous to decisions in which we have held that government may not withhold certain especially important services from those who are unable to pay for them. Appellants cite Griffin v. Illinois, 351 U.S. 12 (1956) (right to appellate review of a criminal conviction conditioned on the purchase of a trial transcript); Smith v. Bennett, 365 U.S. 708 (1961) (application for writ of habeas corpus accepted only when accompanied by a filing fee); Boddie v. Connecticut, 401 U.S. 371 (1971) (action for dissolution of marriage could be pursued only upon payment of court fees and costs for service of process); Lindsey v. Normet, 405 U.S. 56 (1972) (appeal from civil judgments in certain landlord-tenant disputes conditioned on the posting of a bond for twice the amount of rent expected to accrue during the appellate process); and Little v. Streater, 452 U.S. 1 (1981) (fee for blood test in quasi-criminal paternity action brought against the putative father of a child receiving public assistance).

Leaving aside other distinctions that might be found between these cases and the one before us today, each involved a rule that barred indigent litigants from using the judicial process in circumstances where they had no alternative to that process. Decisions invalidating such rules are inapposite here. In contrast to the "utter exclusiveness of court access and court remedy," United States v. Kras, 409 U.S. 434, 445 (1973), North Dakota does not maintain a legal or a practical monopoly on the means of transporting children to school. Thus, unlike the complaining parties in all the cases cited by appellants, the Kadrmas family could and did find a private alternative to the public school bus service for which Dickinson charged a fee. That alternative was more expensive, to be sure, and we have no reason to doubt that genuine hardships were endured by the Kadrmas family when Sarita was denied access to the bus. Such facts, however, do not imply that the Equal Protection Clause has been violated. In upholding a filing fee for voluntary bankruptcy actions, for example, we observed: "[B]ankruptcy is not the only method available to a debtor for the adjustment of his legal relationship with his creditors. . . . However unrealistic the remedy may be in a particular situation, a debtor, in theory, and often in actuality, may adjust his debts by negotiated agreement with his creditors." Ibid. Similarly, we upheld a statute that required indigents to pay a filing fee for appellate review of adverse welfare benefits decisions. Ortwein v. Schwab, 410 U.S. 656 (1973). Noting that the case did not involve a "suspect classification," we held that the "applicable standard is that of rational justification." Id., at 660. It is plain that the busing fee in this case more closely resembles the fees that were upheld in *Kras* and *Ortwein* than it resembles the fees that were invalidated in the cases on which appellants rely. Those cases therefore do not support the suggestion that North Dakota's 1979 statute violates the Equal Protection Clause.

Applying the appropriate test—under which a statute is upheld if it bears a rational relation to a legitimate government objective—we think it is quite clear that a State's decision to allow local school boards the option of charging patrons a user fee for bus service is constitutionally permissible. The Constitution does not require that such service be provided at all, and it is difficult to imagine why choosing to offer the service should entail a constitutional obligation to offer it for free. No one denies that encouraging local school districts to provide school bus service is a legitimate state purpose or that such encouragement would be undermined by a rule requiring that general revenues be used to subsidize an optional service that will benefit a minority of the district's families. It is manifestly rational for the State to refrain from undermining its legitimate objective with such a rule.

C

Appellants contend that, even without the application of strict or heightened scrutiny, the 1979 statute violates equal protection because it permits user fees for bus service *only* in nonreorganized school districts. This distinction, they say, can be given no rational justification whatsoever. The principles governing our review of this claim are well established. " 'The Fourteenth Amendment does not prohibit legislation merely because it is special, or limited in its application to a particular geographical or political subdivision of the state.' Fort Smith Light Co. v. Paving Dist., 274 U.S. 387, 391 (1927). Rather, the Equal Protection Clause is offended only if the statute's classification 'rests on grounds wholly irrelevant to the achievement of the State's objective.' McGowan v. Maryland, 366 U.S. 420, 425 (1961); Kotch v. Board of River Port Pilot Comm'rs, 330 U.S. 552, 556 (1947)." Holt Civic Club v. Tuscaloosa, 439 U.S. 60, 71 (1978). Social and economic legislation like the statute at issue in this case, moreover, "carries with it a presumption of rationality that can only be overcome by a clear showing of arbitrariness and irrationality." Hodel v. Indiana, 452 U.S. 314, 331–332 (1981). "[W]e will not overturn such a statute unless the varying treatment of different groups or persons is so unrelated to the achievement of any combination of legitimate purposes that we can only conclude that the legislature's actions were irrational." Vance v. Bradley, 440 U.S. 93, 97 (1979). In performing this analysis, we are not bound by explanations of the statute's rationality that may be offered by litigants or other courts. Rather, those challenging the legislative judgment must convince us "that the legislative facts on which the classification is apparently based could not reasonably be conceived to be true by the governmental decisionmaker." Id., at 111.

Applying these principles to the present case, we conclude that appellants have failed to carry the "heavy burden" of demonstrating that the challenged statute is both arbitrary and irrational. Hodel v. Indiana, supra, at 332. The court below offered the following justification for the distinction drawn between reorganized and nonreorganized districts:

"The obvious purpose of [statutes treating reorganized and nonreorganized schools differently] is to encourage school district reorganization with a concomitant tax base expansion and an enhanced and more effective school system. The legislation provides incentive for the people to approve school district reorganization by alleviating parental concerns regarding the cost of student transportation in the reorganized district." 402 N.W.2d, at 903.

Appellees offer a more elaborate, but not incompatible, explanation:

"[T]he authorization of the bus fee to be charged by districts such as Dickinson has nothing to do with the reorganization of school districts. The reasoning for it is to simply have the few that use the service pay a small portion of that cost in exchange for the substantial benefits received.

"The only reason that the fee authorization was not extended to reorganized districts is that those districts, prior to the passage of the statute permitting fees, were already committed on an individual district basis to some type of transportation system which had been submitted to and approved by the voters in each separate district. To permit the 1979 statute authorizing fees to be retroactively effective in reorganized districts would have been an obvious impairment of existing legal relationships since the already established transportation systems in the various reorganized districts did not include any authority to charge a fee." Brief for Appellees 16.

The State of North Dakota informs us that the 1979 legislation was proposed to the legislature by the Dickinson School District itself, which had for several years been charging transportation fees and which "became concerned when it appeared that the 1979 Legislature would enact a statute prohibiting charging the fee." The State's account of the reason for confining the express authorization of fees to nonreorganized school districts is the same as the account offered by appellees.

The explanation offered by appellees and the State is adequate to rebut appellants' contention that the distinction drawn between reorganized and nonreorganized districts is arbitrary and irrational. The Supreme Court of North Dakota has said, and the State agrees, that all reorganized school districts are presently required to furnish or pay for transportation for students living as far away from school as Sarita Kadrmas does. See 402 N.W.2d, at 903 (citing N.D.Cent.Code § 15–27.3–10 (Supp.1987)); Tr. of Oral Arg. 32. This requirement, however, is not imposed directly by statute, but rather by the reorganization plans that are statutorily required in the reorganization process. With certain specified exceptions (not including the transportation provisions), those reorganization plans may be changed by the voters in the affected districts. N.D.Cent.Code § 15–27.3–19 (Supp.1987). Although it appears that no reorganized district has ever used this mechanism to adopt a user fee like Dickinson's, we have not been informed that such a step could not legally be taken. Thus, the one definitely established difference between reorganized and nonreorganized districts is this: in the latter, local school boards may impose a bus service user fee on their own authority, while the direct approval of the voters would be required in reorganized districts. That difference, however, simply reflects voluntary agreements made during the history of North Dakota's reorganization process, and it could scarcely be thought to make the State's laws arbitrary or irrational.

Even if we assume, as appellants apparently do, that the State has forbidden reorganized school districts to charge user fees for bus service under any circumstances, it is evident that the legislature could conceivably have believed that such a policy would serve the legitimate purpose of fulfilling the reasonable expectations of those residing in districts with free busing arrangements imposed by reorganization plans. Because this purpose could have no application to nonreorganized districts, the legislature could just as rationally conclude that those districts should have the option of imposing user fees on those who take advantage of the service they are offered.

In sum, the statute challenged in this case discriminates against no suspect class and interferes with no fundamental right. Appellants have failed to carry the heavy burden of demonstrating that the statute is arbitrary and irrational. The Supreme Court of North Dakota correctly concluded that the statute does not violate the Equal Protection Clause of the Fourteenth Amendment, and its judgment is

Affirmed.

Justice Marshall, with whom Justice Brennan joins, dissenting.

In San Antonio Independent School Dist. v. Rodriguez, 411 U.S. 1 (1973), I wrote that the Court's holding was a "retreat from our historic commitment to equality of educational opportunity and [an] unsupportable acquiescence in a system which deprives children in their earliest years of the chance to reach their full potential." Id., at 71 (Marshall, J., dissenting). Today, the Court continues the retreat from the promise of equal educational opportunity by holding that a school district's refusal to allow an indigent child who lives 16 miles from the nearest school to use a schoolbus service without paying a fee does not violate the Fourteenth Amendment's Equal Protection Clause. Because I do not believe that this Court should sanction discrimination against the poor with respect to "perhaps the most important function of state and local governments," Brown v. Board of Education, 347 U.S. 483, 493 (1954), I dissent.

The Court's opinion suggests that this case does not concern state action that discriminates against the poor with regard to the provision of a basic education. The Court notes that the particular governmental action challenged in this case involves the provision of transportation, rather than the provision of educational services. Moreover, the Court stresses that the denial of transportation to Sarita Kadrmas did not in fact prevent her from receiving an education; notwithstanding the denial of bus service, Sarita's family ensured that she attended school each day. To the Court, then, this case presents no troublesome questions; indeed, the Court's facile analysis suggests some perplexity as to why this case ever reached this Court.

I believe the Court's approach forgets that the Constitution is concerned with "sophisticated as well as simple-minded modes of discrimination." Lane v. Wilson, 307 U.S. 268, 275 (1939). This case involves state action that places a special burden on poor families in their pursuit of education. Children living far from school can receive a public education only if they have access to transportation; as the state court noted in this case, "a child must reach the schoolhouse door as a prerequisite to receiving the educational opportunity offered therein." 402 N.W.2d 897, 901 (N.D.1987). Indeed, for children in Sarita's position, imposing a fee for transportation is no different in practical effect from imposing a fee directly for education. Moreover, the fee involved in this case discriminated against Sarita's family because it necessarily fell more heavily upon the poor than upon wealthier members of the community. Cf. Bullock v. Carter, 405 U.S. 134, 144 (1972) (voting system based on flat fees "falls with unequal weight on voters, as well as candidates, according to their economic status"); Griffin v. Illinois, 351 U.S. 12, 17, n. 11 (1956) (opinion of Black, J.) (state law imposing flat fee for trial transcript is "nondiscriminatory on its face," but "grossly discriminatory in its operation"). This case therefore presents the question whether a State may discriminate against the poor in providing access to education. I regard this question as one of great urgency.

As I have stated on prior occasions, proper analysis of equal protection claims depends less on choosing the "formal label" under which the claim should be reviewed than upon identifying and carefully analyzing the real interests at stake. Cleburne v. Cleburne Living Center, Inc., 473 U.S. 432, 478 (1985) (Marshall, J., dissenting); see Selective Service System v. Minnesota Public Interest Research Group, 468 U.S. 841, 876 (1984) (Marshall, J., dissenting). In particular, the Court should focus on "the character of the classification in question, the relative importance to individuals in the class discriminated against of the governmental benefits that they do not receive, and the asserted state interests in support of the classification." Dandridge v. Williams, 397 U.S. 471, 521 (1970) (Marshall, J., dissenting); see San Antonio Independent School Dist. v. Rodriguez, supra, at 98–99 (Marshall, J., dissenting). Viewed from this perspective, the discrimination inherent in the North Dakota statute fails to satisfy the dictates of the Equal Protection Clause.

The North Dakota statute discriminates on the basis of economic status. This Court has determined that classifications based on wealth are not automatically suspect. See, e.g., Maher v. Roe, 432 U.S. 464, 470–471 (1977). Such classifications, however, have a measure of special constitutional significance. See, e.g., McDonald v. Board of Election Comm'rs of Chicago, 394 U.S. 802, 807 (1969) ("a careful examination on our part is especially warranted where lines are drawn on the basis of wealth . . . ."); Harper v. Virginia Bd. of Elections, 383 U.S. 663, 668 (1966) ("Lines drawn on the basis of wealth or property . . .

are traditionally disfavored"). This Court repeatedly has invalidated statutes, on their face or as applied, that discriminated against the poor. See, e.g., Little v. Streater, 452 U.S. 1 (1981); Bullock v. Carter, supra; Harper v. Virginia Bd. of Elections, supra; Griffin v. Illinois, supra. The Court has proved most likely to take such action when the laws in question interfered with the access of the poor to the political and judicial processes. One source of these decisions, in my view, is a deep distrust of policies that specially burden the access of disadvantaged persons to the governmental institutions and processes that offer members of our society an opportunity to improve their status and better their lives. The intent of the Fourteenth Amendment was to abolish caste legislation. See Plyler v. Doe, 457 U.S. 202, 213 (1982). When state action has the predictable tendency to entrap the poor and create a permanent underclass, that intent is frustrated. See id., at 234 (Blackmun, J., concurring). Thus, to the extent that a law places discriminatory barriers between indigents and the basic tools and opportunities that might enable them to rise, exacting scrutiny should be applied.

The statute at issue here burdens a poor person's interest in an education. The extraordinary nature of this interest cannot be denied. . . . A statute that erects special obstacles to education in the path of the poor naturally tends to consign such persons to their current disadvantaged status. By denying equal opportunity to exactly those who need it most, the law not only militates against the ability of each poor child to advance herself, but also increases the likelihood of the creation of a discrete and permanent underclass. Such a statute is difficult to reconcile with the framework of equality embodied in the Equal Protection Clause.

This Court's decision in Plyler v. Doe, supra, supports these propositions. The Court in *Plyler* upheld the right of the children of illegal aliens to receive the free public education that the State of Texas made available to other residents. The Court in that case engaged in some discussion of alienage, a classification not relevant here. The decision, however, did not rest upon this basis. Rather, the Court made clear that the infirmity of the Texas law stemmed from its differential treatment of a discrete and disadvantaged group of children with respect to the provision of education. . . . The *Plyler* Court's reasoning is fully applicable here. As in *Plyler*, the State in this case has acted to burden the educational opportunities of a disadvantaged group of children, who need an education to become full participants in society.

The State's rationale for this policy is based entirely on fiscal considerations. The State has allowed Dickinson and certain other school districts to charge a nonwaivable flat fee for bus service so that these districts may recoup part of the costs of the service. The money that Dickinson collects from applying the busing fee to indigent families, however, represents a miniscule proportion of the costs of the bus service. As the Court notes, all of the fees collected by Dickinson amount to only 11% of the cost of providing the bus service, and the fees collected from poor families represent a small fraction of the total fees. Exempting indigent families from the busing fee therefore would not require Dickinson to make any significant adjustments in either the operation or the funding of the bus service. Indeed, as the Court states, most school districts in the State provide full bus service without charging any fees at all. The state interest involved in this case is therefore insubstantial; it does not begin to justify the discrimination challenged here.

The Court's decision to the contrary "demonstrates once again a 'callous indifference to the realities of life for the poor.'" Selective Service System v. Minnesota Public Interest Research Group, 468 U.S., at 876 (Marshall, J., dissenting), quoting Flagg Bros., Inc. v. Brooks, 436 U.S. 149, 166 (1978) (Marshall, J., dissenting). These realities may not always be obvious from the Court's vantage point, but the Court fails in its constitutional duties when it refuses, as it does today, to make even the effort to see. For the poor, education is often the only route by which to become full participants in our society. In allowing a State to burden the access of poor persons to an education, the Court denies equal opportunity and discourages hope. I do not believe the Equal Protection Clause countenances such a result. I therefore dissent.

Justice Stevens, with whom Justice Blackmun joins, dissenting.

When the sovereign applies different rules to different segments of its jurisdiction, it must have a rational basis for doing so. "The term 'rational,' of course, includes a requirement that an impartial lawmaker could logically believe that the classification would serve a legitimate public purpose that transcends the harm to the members of the disadvantaged class." Cleburne v. Cleburne Living Center, Inc., 473 U.S. 432, 452 (1985) (Stevens, J., concurring) (footnote omitted). In this case, Justice Marshall accurately explicates the harm to certain members of the disadvantaged class. And since the Supreme Court of the State of North Dakota has unequivocally identified the actual purpose of the geographic discrimination, I would not second guess that conclusion that presume that the harm Justice Marshall describes has been imposed for other reasons.

The State Supreme Court explained:

"The obvious purpose of such legislation is to encourage school district reorganization with a concomitant tax base expansion and an enhanced and more effective school system. The legislation provides incentive for the people to approve school district reorganization by alleviating parental concerns regarding the cost of student transportation in the reorganized district." 402 N.W.2d 897, 903 (N.D.1987).

This explanation of the state legislative purpose makes two propositions perfectly clear. First, free bus transportation is an important component of public education in a sparsely populated State; otherwise the alleviation of parental concerns regarding the cost of student transportation in a reorganized district could not have been expected to motivate a significant number of voters. Second, after the voters in a school district have had a fair opportunity to decide whether or not to reorganize, there is no longer any justification at all for allowing the nonreorganized districts to place an obstacle in the paths of poor children seeking an education in some parts of the State that has been removed in other parts of the State. Cf. G.D. Searle & Co. v. Cohn, 455 U.S. 404, 420 (1982) (Stevens, J., dissenting) ("the Constitution requires a rational basis for the special burden imposed on the disfavored class as well as a reason for treating that class differently").

Thus, the State Supreme Court's explanation of the purpose of this discrimination does not include the "elements of legitimacy and neutrality that must always characterize the performance of the sovereign's duty to govern impartially." Cleburne, supra, at 452 (footnote omitted). Accordingly, I respectfully dissent.

Chapter 12

DEFINING THE SCOPE OF "LIBERTY" AND "PROPERTY" PROTECTED BY THE DUE PROCESS CLAUSE—THE PROCEDURAL DUE PROCESS CASES

SECTION 1. WHAT CONSTITUTES A DEPRIVATION OF LIBERTY OR PROPERTY WHICH MANDATES THE PROVISION OF A HEARING?

Page 948. Add ahead of Hudson v. Palmer:

DANIELS v. WILLIAMS
474 U.S. 327, 106 S.Ct. 662, 88 L.Ed.2d 662 (1986).

Justice Rehnquist delivered the opinion of the Court.

In Parratt v. Taylor, 451 U.S. 527 (1981), a state prisoner sued under 42 U.S.C. § 1983, claiming that prison officials had negligently deprived him of his property without due process of law. After deciding that § 1983 contains no independent state-of-mind requirement, we concluded that although petitioner had been "deprived" of property within the meaning of the Due Process Clause of the Fourteenth Amendment, the State's postdeprivation tort remedy provided the process that was due. Petitioner's claim in this case, which also rests on an alleged Fourteenth Amendment "deprivation" caused by the negligent conduct of a prison official, leads us to reconsider our statement in *Parratt* that "the alleged loss, even though negligently caused, amounted to a deprivation." Id., at 536–537. We conclude that the Due Process Clause is simply not implicated by a *negligent* act of an official causing unintended loss of or injury to life, liberty or property.

In this § 1983 action, petitioner seeks to recover damages for back and ankle injuries allegedly sustained when he fell on a prison stairway. He claims that, while an inmate at the city jail in Richmond, Virginia, he slipped on a pillow negligently left on the stairs by respondent, a correctional deputy stationed at the jail. Respondent's negligence, the argument runs, "deprived" petitioner of his "liberty" interest in freedom from bodily injury, . . . because respondent maintains that he is entitled to the defense of sovereign immunity in a state tort suit, petitioner is without an "adequate" state remedy. . . . Accordingly, the deprivation of liberty was without "due process of law."

. . .

326

In *Parratt*, before concluding that Nebraska's tort remedy provided all the process that was due, we said that the loss of the prisoner's hobby kit, "even though negligently caused, amounted to a deprivation [under the Due Process Clause]." 451 U.S., at 536–537. Justice Powell, concurring in the result, criticized the majority for "pass[ing] over" this important question of the state of mind required to constitute a "deprivation" of property. Id., at 547. He argued that negligent acts by state officials, though causing loss of property, are not actionable under the Due Process Clause. To Justice Powell, mere negligence could not "wor[k] a deprivation in the *constitutional sense*." Id., at 548, (emphasis in original). Not only does the word "deprive" in the Due Process Clause connote more than a negligent act, but we should not "open the federal courts to lawsuits where there has been no affirmative abuse of power." Id., at 548–549, . . . Upon reflection, we agree and overrule *Parratt* to the extent that it states that mere lack of due care by a state official may "deprive" an individual of life, liberty or property under the Fourteenth Amendment.

The Due Process Clause of the Fourteenth Amendment provides: "[N]or shall any State deprive any person of life, liberty, or property, without due process of law." Historically, this guarantee of due process has been applied to *deliberate* decisions of government officials to deprive a person of life, liberty or property. . . . No decision of this Court before *Parratt* supported the view that negligent conduct by a state official, even though causing injury, constitutes a deprivation under the Due Process Clause. This history reflects the traditional and common-sense notion that the Due Process Clause, like its forebear in the Magna Carta, . . . was " 'intended to secure the individual from the arbitrary exercise of the powers of government,' " Hurtado v. California, 110 U.S. 516, 527 (1884). By requiring the government to follow appropriate procedures when its agents decide to "deprive any person of life, liberty, or property," the Due Process Clause promotes fairness in such decisions. And by barring certain government actions regardless of the fairness of the procedures used to implement them, . . . it serves to prevent governmental power from being "used for purposes of oppression," Murray's Lessee v. Hoboken Land & Improvement Co., 18 How. (59 U.S.) 272, 277 (1856) (discussing Due Process Clause of Fifth Amendment).

We think that the actions of prison custodians in leaving a pillow on the prison stairs, or mislaying an inmate's property, are quite remote from the concerns just discussed. Far from an abuse of power, lack of due care suggests no more than a failure to measure up to the conduct of a reasonable person. To hold that injury caused by such conduct is a deprivation within the meaning of the Fourteenth Amendment would trivialize the centuries-old principle of due process of law.

The Fourteenth Amendment is a part of a constitution generally designed to allocate governing authority among the branches of the Federal Government and between that Government and the States, and to secure certain individual rights against both State and Federal Government. When dealing with a claim that such a document creates a right in prisoners to sue a government official because he negligently created an unsafe condition in the prison, we bear in mind Chief Justice Marshall's admonition that "we must never forget, that it is *a constitution* we are expounding," McCulloch v. Maryland, 4 Wheat. (17 U.S.) 316, 407, 4 L.Ed. 579 (1819) (emphasis in original). Our Constitution deals with the large concerns of the governors and the governed, but it does not purport to supplant traditional tort law in laying down rules of conduct to regulate liability for injuries that attend living together in society. We have previously rejected reasoning that "would make of the Fourteenth Amendment a font of tort law to be superimposed upon whatever systems may already be administered by the States," Paul v. Davis, 424 U.S. 693, 701 (1976), quoted in Parratt v. Taylor, 451 U.S., at 544.

The only tie between the facts of this case and anything governmental in nature is the fact that respondent was a sheriff's deputy at the Richmond city jail and petitioner was an inmate confined in that jail. But while the Due Process Clause of the Fourteenth Amendment obviously speaks to some facets of this relationship, see e.g., Wolff v. McDonnell, 418 U.S. 539 (1974), we do not believe its protections are triggered by lack of due care by prison officials. "Medical malpractice does not become a constitutional violation merely because the victim is a prisoner," Estelle v. Gamble, 429 U.S. 97, 106 (1976), and "false imprisonment does not become a violation of the Fourteenth Amendment merely because the defendant is a state official." Baker v. McCollan, 443 U.S. 137, 146 (1979). Where a government official's act causing injury to life, liberty or property is merely negligent, "no procedure for compensation is *constitutionally* required." *Parratt*, 451 U.S., at 548 (Powell, J., concurring in result) (emphasis added.) [1]

That injuries inflicted by governmental negligence are not addressed by the United States Constitution is not to say that they may not raise significant legal concerns and lead to the creation of protectible legal interests. The enactment of tort claim statutes, for example, reflects the view that injuries caused by such negligence should generally be redressed. It is no reflection on either the breadth of the United States Constitution or the importance of traditional tort law to say that they do not address the same concerns.

In support of his claim that negligent conduct can give rise to a due process "deprivation," petitioner makes several arguments, none of which we find persuasive. . . .

.   .   .

Affirmed.

Justice Marshall concurs in the result.

Justice Blackmun, concurring in the judgment.

I concur in the result. . . .

----

[1] Accordingly, we need not decide whether, as petitioner contends, the possibility of a sovereign immunity defense in a Virginia tort suit would render that remedy "inadequate" under *Parratt* and Hudson v. Palmer, 468 U.S. 517 (1984).

Justice Stevens also concurred in the judgment, see Davidson v. Cannon, noted below.

DAVIDSON v. CANNON, 474 U.S. 344 (1986). A prisoner sent a note to prison authorities reporting a threat made against him by another prisoner. The note was put aside and forgotten and the prisoner was assaulted. He brought suit under 42 U.S.C. § 1983. The Court, in an opinion by Justice Rehnquist, treated the case as involving simply negligence by prison officials and hence not involving any denial of due process of law. "Respondents' lack of due care in this case led to serious injury, but that lack of care simply does not approach the sort of abusive government conduct that the Due Process Clause was designed to prevent." The Court had said in a footnote in Daniels v. Williams that the case "affords us no occasion to consider whether something less than intentional conduct, such as recklessness or "gross negligence," is enough to trigger the protections of the Due Process Clause." It did not discuss the issue in *Davidson.*

Justice Brennan dissented, arguing that "official conduct which causes personal injury due to recklessness or deliberate indifference, does deprive the victim of liberty within the meaning of the Fourteenth Amendment." He urged that the judgment be vacated and the case remanded for review of the district court's holding that the conduct involved was not reckless.

Justices Blackmun and Marshall dissented. They contended first that negligence is a violation of due process in the setting when the state assumes sole responsibility for one's physical security and then ignores one's call for help. They also agreed with Justice Brennan that in any event recklessness constituted a violation of due process and the case should be sent back for review on that issue.

Justice Stevens concurred in the judgment. He argued in both *Daniels* and *Davidson* that negligence was sufficient to deprive a person of due process of law. He concurred in the judgments on the ground that in each case the state had provided adequate procedure for vindication of the plaintiff's claims.

Page 949. Add ahead of The Interrelationship of Substantive and Procedural Due Process:

CLEVELAND BOARD OF EDUCATION v. LOUDERMILL, 470 U.S. 532 (1985). An Ohio statute provided that classified civil service employees were entitled to retain their positions "during good behavior and efficient service" and could not be dismissed except for "misfeasance, malfeasance, or nonfeasance in office." It also provided that an employee dismissed for cause was to be provided with an order of removal giving the reasons therefor which could be appealed to a state administrative board, and that board's judgment could be reviewed in the state trial court.

A state security guard stated on his job application that he had never been convicted of a felony. Several months after he was hired the Board of Education discovered that he had been convicted of grand larceny and discharged him. He was given a letter stating this reason. He appealed to the Civil Service Commission, and his dismissal was upheld. He then filed this case in the federal district court, arguing that the state statute was unconstitutional on its face because it did not give him a chance to respond to charges before dismissal. The district court rejected that claim, but the court of appeals reversed and the Supreme Court affirmed.

The Court, by a vote of 8 to 1, rejected an argument based on the plurality opinion in Arnett v. Kennedy. After discussing that case and those following it, the Court said:

"In light of these holdings, it is settled that the 'bitter with the sweet' approach misconceives the constitutional guarantee. If a clearer holding is needed, we provide it today. The point is straightforward: the Due Process Clause provides that certain substantive rights—life, liberty, and property—cannot be deprived except pursuant to constitutionally adequate procedures. The categories of substance and procedure are distinct. Were the rule otherwise, the Clause would be reduced to a mere tautology. 'Property' cannot be defined by the procedures provided for its deprivation any more than can life or liberty. The right to due process 'is conferred, not by legislative grace, but by constitutional guarantee. While the legislature may elect not to confer a property interest in [public] employment, it may not constitutionally authorize the deprivation of such an interest, once conferred, without appropriate procedural safeguards.' Arnett v. Kennedy, supra, 416 U.S., at 167 (Powell, J., concurring in part and concurring in result in part); see id., at 185 (White, J., concurring in part and dissenting in part).

"In short, once it is determined that the Due Process Clause applies, 'the question remains what process is due.' Morrissey v. Brewer, 408 U.S. 471, 481 (1972). The answer to that question is not to be found in the Ohio statute."

The Court then went on to hold that an employee must have some kind of hearing prior to discharge when he has a constitutionally protected property interest in his employment. But as to the required hearing, the Court said that in a situation like this, with a full administrative hearing and judicial review after termination, the employee does not have a right to a hearing prior to discharge. "The tenured public employee is entitled to oral or written notice of the charges against him, an explanation of the employer's evidence, and an opportunity to present his side of the story. . . . To require more than this prior to termination would intrude to an unwarranted extent on the government's interest in quickly removing an unsatisfactory employee."

Justice Marshall argued that the employee should receive a pre-termination hearing. Justice Rehnquist dissented, arguing that the employee got only the hearing prescribed in the Act which defined his tenure in office.

————

In Walters v. National Association of Radiation Survivors, 105 S.Ct. 3180 (1985) the Court held that a federal statute limiting to $10 the fee that may be paid an attorney or agent who represents a veteran seeking benefits from the Veterans' Administration for service-connected death or disability did not deny procedural due process.

Chapter 13

APPLICATION OF THE POST CIVIL WAR AMENDMENTS TO PRIVATE CONDUCT: CONGRESSIONAL POWER TO ENFORCE THE AMENDMENTS

___

SECTION 2. APPLICATION OF THE CONSTITUTION TO PRIVATE CONDUCT

___

A. PRIVATE PERFORMANCE OF "GOVERNMENT" FUNCTIONS

___

Page 974. Add at end of subsection:

SAN FRANCISCO ARTS & ATHLETICS, INC. v. UNITED STATES OLYMPIC COMMITTEE, 107 S.Ct. 2971 (1987). Section 110 of the Amateur Sports Act of 1978 grants the Committee the right to prohibit commercial and promotional uses of the word "Olympic." The Court rejected an argument that the Committee violated the equal protection component of the Fifth Amendment by discriminatory enforcement of its exclusive right. The Committee was not a governmental actor and did not perform functions that have been traditionally the exclusive prerogative of the federal government. There was no evidence of governmental involvement in the Committee's choice of how it enforced its right. Four dissenters argued that the Committee was a governmental actor because there was a "symbiotic relationship" between the Committee and the Federal Government in coordinating amateur athletics in international competition. Two of the four dissenters argued, in addition, that the Committee performed a public function in governing international amateur athletics.

C. GOVERNMENT FINANCING, REGULATION AND AUTHORIZATION OF PRIVATE CONDUCT

___

2. Government Financial Assistance to Private Activities

Page 988. Add after Rendell–Baker v. Kohn:

WEST v. ATKINS, 108 S.Ct. 2250 (1988). The Court held that a prison inmate could bring suit, under 42 U.S.C. § 1983, against a private physician who treated prisoners on a part-time basis under contract with the state. The Court distinguished Polk County v. Dodson, 454 U.S. 312 (1981), where the Court had held that a public defender did not act under color of state law. *Dodson* was the only case where the Court had decided that a person employed by the state, and allegedly abusing that position in performing assigned tasks, was not acting under color of state law. *Dodson* was not based simply on the proposition that professionals as a class have independence and integrity. Rather, the public defender does not act under color of state law because a defense attorney is the State's adversary. A physician providing medical services to prisoners does not function as an adversary to prison authorities.

SECTION 3. FEDERAL CIVIL RIGHTS LEGISLATION

A. THE RECONSTRUCTION LEGACY

Page 1005. Add to end of footnote 7:

For a modern case construing 18 U.S.C. § 1584, which forbids holding another person in "involuntary servitude," see United States v. Kosminski, 108 S.Ct. ___ (1988).

SECTION 4. FEDERAL POWER TO REGULATE PRIVATE CONDUCT UNDER THE THIRTEENTH AMENDMENT

Page 1013. Add to the end of Note (1):

On April 25, 1988, the Court ordered a reargument on the question "[w]hether or not the interpretation of 42 U.S.C. section 1981 adopted by this Court in Runyon v. McCrary, 427 U.S. 160 (1976), should be reconsidered?" Patterson v. McLean Credit Union, 108 S.Ct. 1419 (1988). Justice Stevens' dissent, joined by Justices Brennan, Marshall and Blackmun, stated:

> "The Court's spontaneous decision to reexamine our holding in Runyon v. McCrary . . . is certain to engender widespread concern in those segments of our population that must rely on a federal rule of law as a protection against invidious private discrimination. . . . The Court's order today will, by itself, have a deleterious effect on the faith reposed by racial minorities in the continuing stability of a rule of law that guarantees them the 'same right' as 'white citizens.' To recognize an equality right—a right that 12 years ago we thought 'well established'—and then to declare unceremoniously that perhaps we were wrong and had better reconsider our prior judgment, is to replace what is ideally a sense of guaranteed right with the uneasiness of unsecured privilege. Time alone will tell whether the erosion in faith is unneces-

sarily precipitous, but in the meantime, some of the harm that will flow from today's order may never be completely undone."

In a *per curiam* opinion, the Court responded:

"[T]he dissents intimate that the statutory question involved in Runyon v. McCrary should not be subject to the same principles of stare decisis as other decisions because it benefited civil rights plaintiffs by expanding liability under the statute. We do not believe that the Court may recognize any such exception to the abiding rule that it treat all litigants equally: that is, that the claim of any litigant for the application of a rule to its case should not be influenced by the Court's view of the worthiness of the litigant in terms of extralegal criteria."

Page 1015. Add to the end of Note (7):

The Court also relied on the legislative history of the 1866 Act in Shaare Tefila Congregation v. Cobb, 107 S.Ct. 2019 (1987) and Saint Francis College v. Al-Khazraji, 107 S.Ct. 2022 (1987). Sections 1981 and 1982 are limited to "racial" discrimination, and do not reach discrimination on the basis of national origin or religion. The concept of "race" used by Congress in 1866, however, was not based on the modern scientific understanding of the term. Thus, the Court held that actions by an Arab under § 1981 and by Jews under § 1982 stated claims for "racial" discrimination. "Congress intended to protect from discrimination identifiable classes of persons who are subjected to intentional discrimination solely because of their ancestry or ethnic characteristics."

Part IV

CONSTITUTIONAL PROTECTION OF EXPRESSION AND CONSCIENCE

Chapter 14

GOVERNMENTAL CONTROL OF THE CONTENT OF EXPRESSION

SECTION 2. INTERMEZZO: AN INTRODUCTION TO THE CONCEPTS OF VAGUENESS, OVERBREADTH AND PRIOR RESTRAINT

A. VAGUENESS AND OVERBREADTH

Page 1097. Add at end of subsection:

BROCKETT v. SPOKANE ARCADES, INC., 472 U.S. 491 (1985). The Court concluded that a state obscenity statute was overbroad because it used the term "lust" in defining obscene matter. The Court of Appeals had decided that the definition included materials that appealed to "only normal sexual appetites," and were thus constitutionally protected. The Court decided, however, that the lower federal court had erred in declaring the statute invalid as a whole. On this issue, the Court's opinion said:

"For its holding that in First Amendment cases an overbroad statute must be stricken down on its face, the Court of Appeals relied on that line of cases exemplified by Thornhill v. Alabama, 310 U.S. 88 (1940), and more recently by Village of Schaumburg v. Citizens for a Better Environment, 444 U.S. 620 (1980). In those cases, an individual whose own speech or expressive conduct may validly be prohibited or sanctioned is permitted to challenge a statute on its face because it also threatens others not before the court—those who desire to engage in legally protected expression but who may refrain from doing so rather than risk prosecution or undertake to have the law declared partially invalid. If the over-

335

breadth is 'substantial,' [12] the law may not be enforced against anyone, including the party before the court, until it is narrowed to reach only unprotected activity, whether by legislative action or by judicial construction or partial invalidation. Broadrick v. Oklahoma, 413 U.S. 601 (1973).

"It is otherwise where the parties challenging the statute are those who desire to engage in protected speech that the overbroad statute purports to punish, or who seek to publish both protected and unprotected material. There is then no want of a proper party to challenge the statute, no concern that an attack on the statute will be unduly delayed or protected speech discouraged. The statute may forthwith be declared invalid to the extent that it reaches too far, but otherwise left intact.

"The cases before us are ones governed by the normal rule that partial, rather than facial, invalidation is the required course. The Washington statute was faulted by the Court of Appeals only because it reached material that incited normal as well as unhealthy interest in sex, and appellees, or some of them, desiring to publish this sort of material, claimed that they faced punishment if they did so. Unless there are countervailing considerations, the Washington law should have been invalidated only insofar as the word 'lust' is to be understood as reaching protected materials.

"The Court of Appeals was of the view that the term 'lust' did not lend itself to a limiting construction and that it would not be feasible to separate its valid and invalid applications. Even accepting the Court of Appeals' construction of 'lust,' however, we are unconvinced that the identified overbreadth is incurable and would taint all possible applications of the statute, as was the case in Secretary of State of Maryland v. Joseph H. Munson Co., 467 U.S. 947 (1984). . . . If, as we have held, prurience may be constitutionally defined for the purposes of identifying obscenity as that which appeals to a shameful or morbid interest in sex, Roth v. United States, 354 U.S. 476 (1957), it is equally certain that if the statute at issue here is invalidated only insofar as the word 'lust' is taken to include normal interest in sex, the statute would pass constitutional muster and would validly reach the whole range of obscene publications. Furthermore, had the Court of Appeals thought that 'lust' refers *only* to normal sexual appetites, it could have excised the word from the statute entirely, since the statutory definition of prurience referred to 'lasciviousness' as well as 'lust.' Even if the statute had not defined prurience at all, there would have been no satisfactory ground for striking the statute down in its entirety because of invalidity in all of its applications.

[12] The Court of Appeals erred in holding that the Broadrick substantial overbreadth requirement is inapplicable where pure speech rather than conduct is at issue. New York v. Ferber, 458 U.S. 747, 772 (1982), specifically held to the contrary. Because of our disposition of this case, we do not address the issue whether the overbreadth of the Washington statute, in relation to its legitimate reach, is substantial and warrants a declaration of facial invalidity. See Secretary of State of Maryland v. Joseph H. Munson Co., 467 U.S. 947 (1984); CSC v. Letter Carriers, 413 U.S. 548, 580–581 (1973).

"Partial invalidation would be improper if it were contrary to legislative intent in the sense that the legislature had passed an inseverable Act or would not have passed it had it known the challenged provision was invalid . . . .. It would be frivolous to suggest, and no one does, that the Washington Legislature, if it could not proscribe materials that appealed to normal as well as abnormal sexual appetites, would have refrained from passing the moral nuisance statute. And it is quite evident that the remainder of the statute retains its effectiveness as a regulation of obscenity. In these circumstances, the issue of severability is no obstacle to partial invalidation, which is the course the Court of Appeals should have pursued."

SECTION 3. SPEECH CONFLICTING WITH OTHER COMMUNITY VALUES: GOVERNMENT CONTROL OF THE CONTENT OF SPEECH

A. PROTECTION OF INDIVIDUAL REPUTATION AND PRIVACY

Page 1121. Add after Hutchinson v. Proxmire:

McDONALD v. SMITH, 472 U.S. 479 (1985). Defendant wrote two letters to President Reagan concerning plaintiff, who was seeking an appointment as United States Attorney. Lower federal courts, in a libel action, granted defendant judgment on the pleadings, reasoning that the petition clause of the first amendment provided absolute immunity. The Supreme Court reversed. Rights granted by the first amendment's petition clause are indistinguishable from other first amendment rights. Damages for libel could be imposed under the standards of New York Times v. Sullivan.

HUSTLER MAGAZINE v. FALWELL, 108 S.Ct. 876 (1988). Falwell is a nationally known minister and political activist. Hustler magazine published an advertisement parody, portraying Falwell as committing incest with his mother in an outhouse. In a libel action, the jury found against Falwell on the ground that the parody could not be understood as describing actual facts. Lower federal courts, however, entered judgment on the jury award of damages for emotional distress. The Supreme Court reversed in an opinion by Chief Justice Rehnquist. Public officials and public figures could not recover damages for media publications without showing false statement of fact made with "actual malice" under the *New York Times* standard. The common law tort of intentional infliction of emotional distress requires, among other things, that the defendant's publication be "outrageous." An outrageousness standard does not supply a standard for allowing damages that would distinguish the advertisement in this case from traditional political cartoons. While all expression is not of equal first amendment importance, speech concerning public officials and public figures can not be inhibited merely because it is offensive or has an adverse emotional impact on the audience.

DUN & BRADSTREET, INC. v. GREENMOSS BUILDERS, INC.

472 U.S. 749, 105 S.Ct. 2939, 86 L.Ed.2d 593 (1985).

Justice Powell announced the judgment of the Court and delivered an opinion, in which Justice Rehnquist and Justice O'Connor joined.

In Gertz v. Robert Welch, Inc., 418 U.S. 323 (1974), we held that the First Amendment restricted the damages that a private individual could obtain from a publisher for a libel that involved a matter of public concern. More specifically, we held that in these circumstances the First Amendment prohibited awards of presumed and punitive damages for false and defamatory statements unless the plaintiff shows "actual malice," that is, knowledge of falsity or reckless disregard for the truth. The question presented in this case is whether this rule of *Gertz* applies when the false and defamatory statements do not involve matters of public concern.

I

Petitioner Dun & Bradstreet, a credit reporting agency, provides subscribers with financial and related information about businesses. All the information is confidential; under the terms of the subscription agreement the subscribers may not reveal it to anyone else. On July 26, 1976, petitioner sent a report to five subscribers indicating that respondent, a construction contractor, had filed a voluntary petition for bankruptcy. This report was false and grossly misrepresented respondent's assets and liabilities. That same day, while discussing the possibility of future financing with its bank, respondent's president was told that the bank had received the defamatory report. He immediately called petitioner's regional office, explained the error, and asked for a correction. In addition, he requested the names of the firms that had received the false report in order to assure them that the company was solvent. Petitioner promised to look into the matter but refused to divulge the names of those who had received the report.

After determining that its report was indeed false, petitioner issued a corrective notice on or about August 3, 1976 to the five subscribers who had received the initial report. The notice stated that one of respondent's former employees, not respondent itself, had filed for bankruptcy and that respondent "continued in business as usual." Respondent told petitioner that it was dissatisfied with the notice and it again asked for a list of subscribers who had seen the initial report. Again petitioner refused to divulge their names.

Respondent then brought this defamation action in Vermont state court. It alleged that the false report had injured its reputation and sought both compensatory and punitive damages. The trial established that the error in petitioner's report had been caused when one of its employees, a seventeen year old high school student paid to review Vermont bankruptcy pleadings, had inadvertently attributed to respondent a bankruptcy petition filed by one of respondent's former employees. Although petitioner's representative testified that it was routine practice to check the accuracy of such reports with the businesses themselves, it did not try to verify the information about respondent before reporting it.

After trial, the jury returned a verdict in favor of respondent and awarded $50,000 in compensatory or presumed damages and $300,000 in punitive damages. Petitioner moved for a new trial. It argued that in Gertz v. Robert Welch, Inc., supra, at 349, this Court had ruled broadly "that the States may not permit recovery of presumed or punitive damages, at least when liability is not based on a showing of knowledge of falsity or reckless disregard for the truth," and it argued that the judge's instructions in this case permitted the jury to award such damages on a lesser showing. The trial court indicated some doubt as to whether *Gertz* applied to "non-media cases," but granted a new trial "[b]ecause of . . . dissatisfaction with its charge and . . . conviction that the interests of justice require[d]" it.

The Vermont Supreme Court reversed. . . . [T]he court held "that as a matter of federal constitutional law, the media protections outlined in *Gertz* are inapplicable to nonmedia defamation actions."

Recognizing disagreement among the lower courts about when the protections of *Gertz* apply, we granted certiorari. We now affirm, although for reasons different from those relied upon by the Vermont Supreme Court.

. . .

IV

We have never considered whether the *Gertz* balance obtains when the defamatory statements involve no issue of public concern. To make this determination, we must employ the approach approved in *Gertz* and balance the State's interest in compensating private individuals for injury to their reputation against the First Amendment interest in protecting this type of expression. This state interest is identical to the one weighed in *Gertz* . . ..

. . .

The First Amendment interest, on the other hand, is less important than the one weighed in *Gertz*. We have long recognized that not all speech is of equal First Amendment importance. It is speech on "'matters of public concern'" that is "at the heart of the First Amendment's protection." First National Bank of Boston v. Bellotti, 435 U.S. 765, 776 (1978), quoting Thornhill v. Alabama, 310 U.S. 88, 101 (1940) . . .. In contrast, speech on matters of purely private concern is of less First Amendment concern. 461 U.S., at 146–147. As a number of state courts, including the court below, have recognized, the role of the Constitution in regulating state libel law is far more limited when the concerns that activated *New York Times* and *Gertz* are absent. In such a case,

> "[t]here is no threat to the free and robust debate of public issues; there is no potential interference with a meaningful dialogue of ideas concerning self-government; and there is no threat of liability causing a reaction of self-censorship by the press. The facts of the present case are wholly without the First Amendment concerns with which the Supreme Court of the United States has been struggling." Harley-Davidson Motorsports, Inc. v. Markley, 279 Or. 361, 366, 568 P.2d 1359, 1363 (1977) . . ..

While such speech is not totally unprotected by the First Amendment, see Connick v. Myers, 461 U.S., at 147, its protections are less stringent. In *Gertz,* we found that the state interest in awarding presumed and punitive damages was not "substantial" in view of their effect on speech at the core of First Amendment concern. 418 U.S., at 349. This interest, however, is "substantial" relative to the incidental effect these remedies may have on speech of significantly less constitutional interest. The rationale of the common law rules has been the experience and judgment of history that "proof of actual damage will be impossible in a great many cases where, from the character of the defamatory words and the circumstances of publication, it is all but certain that serious harm has resulted in fact." W. Prosser, Law of Torts § 112, p. 765 (4th ed. 1971); . . . As a result, courts for centuries have allowed juries to presume that some damage occurred from many defamatory utterances and publications. Restatement of Torts § 568, comment b, at 162 (1938) (noting that Hale announced that damages were to be presumed for libel as early as 1670). This rule furthers the state interest in providing remedies for defamation by ensuring that those remedies are effective. In light of the reduced constitutional value of speech involving no matters of public concern, we hold that the state interest adequately supports awards of presumed and punitive damages—even absent a showing of "actual malice."

V

The only remaining issue is whether petitioner's credit report involved a matter of public concern. In a related context, we have held that "[w]hether . . . speech addresses a matter of public concern must be determined by [the expression's] content, form, and context . . . as revealed by the whole record." Connick v. Myers, 461 U.S., at 147–148. These factors indicate that petitioner's credit report concerns no public issue. It was speech solely in the individual interest of the speaker and its specific business audience. Cf. Central Hudson Gas & Elec. v. Public Service Comm., 447 U.S. 557, 561 (1980). This particular interest warrants no special protection when—as in this case—the speech is wholly false and clearly damaging to the victim's business reputation. Cf. id., at 566; Virginia Pharmacy Board v. Virginia Consumer Council, 425 U.S. 748, 771–772 (1976). Moreover, since the credit report was made available to only five subscribers, who, under the terms of the subscription agreement, could not disseminate it further, it cannot be said that the report involves any "strong interest in the free flow of commercial information." Id., at 764. There is simply no credible argument that this type of credit reporting requires special protection to ensure that "debate on public issues [will] be uninhibited, robust, and wide-open." New York Times Co. v. Sullivan, 376 U.S., at 270.

In addition, the speech here, like advertising, is hardy and unlikely to be deterred by incidental state regulation. See Virginia Pharmacy Board v. Virginia Consumer Council, supra, at 771–772. It is solely motivated by the desire for profit, which, we have noted, is a force less likely to be deterred than others. Ibid. Arguably, the reporting here was also more objectively verifiable than speech deserving of greater protection. See ibid. In any case, the market provides a powerful incentive to a credit reporting agency to be accurate, since false credit reporting is of no use to creditors. Thus, any incremental "chilling" effect of libel suits would be of decreased significance.

VI

We conclude that permitting recovery of presumed and punitive damages in defamation cases absent a showing of "actual malice" does not violate the First Amendment when the defamatory statements do not involve matters of public concern. Accordingly, we affirm the judgment of the Vermont Supreme Court.

It is so ordered.

Chief Justice Burger, concurring in the judgment.

. . .

. . . The plurality opinion holds that *Gertz* does not apply because, unlike the challenged expression in *Gertz,* the alleged defamatory expression in this case does not relate to a matter of public concern. I agree that *Gertz* is limited to circumstances in which the alleged defamatory expression concerns a matter of general public importance, and that the expression in question here relates to a matter of essentially private concern. I therefore agree with the plurality opinion to the extent that it holds that *Gertz* is inapplicable in this case for the two reasons indicated. No more is needed to dispose of the present case.

I continue to believe, however, that *Gertz* was ill-conceived, and therefore agree with Justice White that *Gertz* should be overruled. I also agree generally with Justice White's observations concerning *New York Times v. Sullivan.* *New York Times,* however, equates "reckless disregard of the truth" with malice; this should permit a jury instruction that malice may be found if the defendant is shown to have published defamatory material which, in the exercise of reasonable care, would have been revealed as untrue. But since the Court has not applied the literal language of *New York Times* in this way, I agree with Justice White that it should be reexamined. The great rights guaranteed by the First Amendment carry with them certain responsibilities as well.

. . .

Justice White, concurring in the judgment.

. . .

I joined the judgment and opinion in *New York Times.* I also joined later decisions extending the *New York Times* standard to other situations. But I came to have increasing doubts about the soundness of the Court's approach and about some of the assumptions underlying it. I could not join the plurality opinion in *Rosenbloom,* and I dissented in *Gertz,* asserting that the common-law remedies should be retained for private plaintiffs. I remain convinced that *Gertz* was erroneously decided. I have also become convinced that the Court struck an improvident balance in the *New York Times* case between the public's interest in being fully informed about public officials and public affairs and the competing interest of those who have been defamed in vindicating their reputation.

. . .

The *New York Times* rule . . . countenances two evils: first, the stream of information about public officials and public affairs is polluted and often remains polluted by false information; and second, the reputation and professional life of the defeated plaintiff may be destroyed by falsehoods that might have been avoided with a reasonable effort to investigate the facts. In terms of the First Amendment and reputational interests at stake, these seem grossly perverse results.

. . .

I still believe the common-law rules should have been retained where plaintiff is not a public official or public figure. As I see it, the Court undervalued the reputational interest at stake in such cases. I have also come to doubt the easy assumption that the common-law rules would muzzle the press. But even accepting the *Gertz* premise that the press also needed protection in suits by private parties, there was no need to modify the common-law requirements for establishing liability and to increase the burden of proof that must be satisfied to secure a judgment authorizing at least nominal damages and the recovery of additional sums within the limitations that the Court might have set.

It is interesting that Justice Powell declines to follow the *Gertz* approach in this case. I had thought that the decision in *Gertz* was intended to reach cases that involve any false statements of fact injurious to reputation, whether the statement is made privately or publicly and whether or not it implicates a matter of public importance. Justice Powell, however, distinguishes *Gertz* as a case that involved a matter of public concern, an element absent here. Wisely, in my view, Justice Powell does not rest his application of a different rule here on a distinction drawn between media and non-media defendants. On that issue, I agree with Justice Brennan that the First Amendment gives no more protection to the press in defamation suits than it does to others exercising their freedom of speech. None of our cases affords such a distinction; to the contrary, the Court has rejected it at every turn. It should be rejected again, particularly in this context, since it makes no sense to give the most protection to those publishers who reach the most readers and therefore pollute the channels of communication with the most misinformation and do the most damage to private reputation. If *Gertz* is to be distinguished from this case, on the ground that it applies only where the allegedly false publication deals with a matter of general or public importance, then where the false publication does not deal with such a matter, the common-law rules would apply whether the defendant is a member of the media or other public disseminator or a non-media individual publishing privately. Although Justice Powell speaks only of the inapplicability of the *Gertz* rule with respect to presumed and punitive damages, it must be that the *Gertz* requirement of some kind of fault on the part of the defendant is also inapplicable in cases such as this.

As I have said, I dissented in *Gertz,* and I doubt that the decision in that case has made any measurable contribution to First Amendment or reputational values since its announcement. Nor am I sure that it has saved the press a great deal of money. Like the *New York Times* decision, the burden that plaintiffs must meet invites long and complicated discovery involving detailed investigation of the workings of the press, how a news story is developed, and the state of mind of the reporter and publisher. See Herbert v. Lando, 441 U.S. 153 (1979). That kind of litigation is very expensive. I suspect that the press would be no worse off financially if the common-law rules were to apply and if the judiciary was careful to insist that damages awards be kept within bounds. A legislative solution to the damages problem would also be appropriate. Moreover, since libel plaintiffs are very likely more interested in clearing their names than in damages, I doubt that limiting recoveries would deter or be unfair to them. In any event, I cannot assume that the press, as successful and powerful as it is, will be intimidated into withholding news that by decent journalistic standards it believes to be true.

The question before us is whether *Gertz* is to be applied in this case. For either of two reasons, I believe that it should not. First, I am unreconciled to the *Gertz* holding and believe that it should be overruled. Second, as Justice Powell indicates, the defamatory publication in this case does not deal with a matter of public importance. Consequently, I concur in the Court's judgment.

Justice Brennan, with whom Justice Marshall, Justice Blackmun and Justice Stevens join, dissenting.

. . .

II

The question presented here is narrow. Neither the parties nor the courts below have suggested that Respondent Greenmoss Builders should be required to show actual malice to obtain a judgment and actual compensatory damages. Nor do the parties question the requirement of *Gertz* that respondent must show fault to obtain a judgment and actual damages. The only question presented is whether a jury award of presumed and punitive damages based on less than a showing of actual malice is constitutionally permissible. *Gertz* provides a forthright negative answer. To preserve the jury verdict in this case, therefore, the opinions of Justice Powell and Justice White have cut away the protective mantle of *Gertz.*

A

Relying on the analysis of the Vermont Supreme Court, Respondent urged that this pruning be accomplished by restricting the applicability of *Gertz* to cases in which the defendant is a "media" entity. Such a distinction is irreconcilable with the fundamental First Amendment principle that "[t]he inherent worth of . . . speech in terms of its capacity for informing the public does not depend upon the identity of its source, whether corporation, association, union, or individual." First National Bank of Boston v. Bellotti, 435 U.S. 765, 777 (1978). First Amendment difficulties lurk in the definitional questions such an approach would generate. . . . Perhaps most importantly, the argument that *Gertz* should be limited to the media misapprehends our cases. We protect the press to ensure the vitality of First Amendment guarantees. This solicitude implies no endorsement of the principle that speakers other than the press deserve lesser First Amendment protection . . ..

The free speech guarantee gives each citizen an equal right to self-expression and to participation in self-government. . . . This guarantee also protects the rights of listeners to "the widest possible dissemination of information from diverse and antagonistic sources." Associated Press v. United States, 326 U.S. 1, 20 (1945). Accordingly, at least six Members of this Court (the four who join this opinion and Justice White and The Chief Justice) agree today that, in the context of defamation law, the rights of the institutional media are no greater and no less than those enjoyed by other individuals or organizations engaged in the same activities.[10]

B

Eschewing the media/nonmedia distinction, the opinions of both Justice White and Justice Powell focus primarily on the content of the credit report as a reason for restricting the applicability of *Gertz* . . . .

. . . Without explaining what *is* a "matter of public concern," the plurality opinion proceeds to serve up a smorgasbord of reasons why the speech at issue here is not, and on this basis affirms the Vermont courts' award of presumed and punitive damages.

. . .

. . . The credit reporting at issue here surely involves a subject matter of sufficient public concern to require the comprehensive protections of *Gertz.* Were this speech appropriately characterized as a matter of only private concern, moreover, the elimination of the *Gertz* restrictions on presumed and punitive damages would still violate basic First Amendment requirements.

---

[10] Justice Powell's opinion does not expressly reject the media/nonmedia distinction, but does expressly decline to apply that distinction to resolve this case.

. . .

Even if the subject matter of credit reporting were properly considered—in the terms of Justice White and Justice Powell—as purely a matter of private discourse, this speech would fall well within the range of valuable expression for which the First Amendment demands protection. Much expression that does not directly involve public issues receives significant protection. Our cases do permit some diminution in the degree of protection afforded one category of speech about economic or commercial matters. "Commercial speech"—defined as advertisements that "do no more than propose a commercial transaction," Pittsburgh Press Co. v. Human Relations Comm'n, 413 U.S. 376, 385 (1973)—may be more closely regulated than other types of speech. Even commercial speech, however, receives substantial First Amendment protection . . ..

. . .

The credit reports of Dun & Bradstreet bear few of the earmarks of commercial speech that might be entitled to somewhat less rigorous protection. In *every* case in which we have permitted more extensive state regulation on the basis of a commercial speech rationale the speech being regulated was pure advertising—an offer to buy or sell goods and services or encouraging such buying and selling. Credit reports are not commercial advertisements for a good or service or a proposal to buy or sell such a product. We have been extremely chary about extending the "commercial speech" doctrine beyond this narrowly circumscribed category of advertising because often vitally important speech will be uttered to advance economic interests and because the profit motive making such speech hardy dissipates rapidly when the speech is not advertising. Compare Central Hudson Gas & Elec. Corp. v. Public Service Comm., 447 U.S. 557 (1980) with Consolidated Edison Co. v. Public Service Comm'n, 447 U.S. 530 (1980).

It is worth noting in this regard that the common law of most states, although apparently not of Vermont, 461 A.2d, at 419, recognizes a qualified privilege for reports like that at issue here. See Maurer, Common Law Defamation and the Fair Credit Reporting Act, 72 Geo.L.Rev. 95, 99–105 (1983). The privilege typically precludes recovery for false and defamatory credit information without a showing of bad faith or malice, a standard of proof which is often defined according to the *New York Times* formulation. See, e.g., Datacon, Inc. v. Dun & Bradstreet, 465 F.Supp. 706, 708 (ND Tex.1979). The common law thus recognizes that credit reporting is quite susceptible to libel's chill; this accumulated learning is worthy of respect.

Even if Justice Powell's characterization of the credit reporting at issue here were accepted in its entirety, his opinion would have done no more than demonstrate that this speech is the equivalent of commercial speech. The opinion, after all, relies on analogy to advertising. Credit reporting is said to be hardy, motivated by desire for profit, and relatively verifiable. But this does not justify the elimination of restrictions on presumed and punitive damages. State efforts to regulate commercial speech in the form of advertising must abide by the requirement that the regulatory means chosen be narrowly tailored so as to avoid any unnecessary chilling of protected expression . . ..

. . .

Of course, the commercial context of Dun & Bradstreet's reports is relevant to the constitutional analysis insofar as it implicates the strong state interest "in protecting consumers and regulating commercial transactions," Ohralik v. Ohio State Bar Ass'n, 436 U.S. 447, 460 (1978). Cf. Bolger v. Young Drug Products Corp., 463 U.S. 60, ___ (1983) (Stevens, J., concurring in the judgment). The special harms caused by inaccurate credit reports, the lack of public sophistication about or access to such reports, and the fact that such reports by and large contain statements that are fairly readily susceptible of verification, all may justify appropriate regulation designed to prevent the social losses caused by false credit reports. And in the libel context, the states' regulatory interest in protecting reputation is served by rules permitting recovery for actual compensatory damages upon a showing of fault. Any further interest in deterring potential defamation through case-by-case judicial imposition of presumed and punitive damage awards on less than a showing of actual malice simply exacts too high a toll on First Amendment values. Accordingly, Greenmoss Builders should be permitted to recover for any actual damage it can show resulted from Dun & Bradstreet's negligently false credit report, but should be required to show actual malice to receive presumed or punitive damages. Because the jury was not instructed in accordance with these principles, we would reverse and remand for further proceedings not inconsistent with this opinion.

PHILADELPHIA NEWSPAPERS, INC. v. HEPPS, 475 U.S. 767 (1986). Hepps was the principal stockholder of a corporation that franchised a chain of convenience stores. The Philadelphia Inquirer published a series of articles stating that Hepps, his corporation, and corporation franchisees had links to organized crime. Hepps' state court libel suit resulted in a defense verdict after the jury was instructed that plaintiff bore the burden of proving that the articles were false. The Pennsylvania Supreme Court reversed, holding that the jury instruction was erroneous. The Supreme Court reversed. "To ensure that true speech on matters of public concern is not deterred, we hold that the common law presumption that defamatory speech is false cannot stand when a plaintiff seeks damages against a media defendant for speech of public concern." (In a footnote, the Court reserved the question whether its holding would apply to suits against nonmedia defendants.)

While previous Supreme Court cases had concentrated on the nature of a defendant's fault required for recovery in a defamation case, the Court concluded that it had also been established that public officials or public figures must prove falsity of the defamatory statements under the *New York Times* standard. Private figures seeking recovery for statements of public concern under the *Gertz* standard should similarly bear the burden of showing falsity, as well as fault, before recovering damages.

Justice Stevens dissented, joined by the Chief Justice and Justices White and Rehnquist.

Page 1122. Add to end of note:

In Anderson v. Liberty Lobby, Inc., 477 U.S. 242 (1986), the Court dismissed the dictum in the *Hutchison* footnote as "simply an acknowledgment of our general reluctance" to grant special procedural protections to libel defendants. The Court concluded that summary judgment for defendant in a libel action was appropriate unless plaintiff had presented evidence on the issue of actual malice that a jury could find was "clear and convincing."

B. CONTROL OF OBSCENITY

1. THE RATIONALE FOR PROHIBITING OBSCENITY

Page 1131. Add at end of subsection:

AMERICAN BOOKSELLERS ASSOCIATION, INC. v. HUDNUT

771 F.2d 323 (7th Cir.1985).

Before Cudahy and Easterbrook, Circuit Judges, and Swygert, Senior Circuit Judge.

Easterbrook, Circuit Judge.

Indianapolis enacted an ordinance defining "pornography" as a practice that discriminates against women. "Pornography" is to be redressed through the administrative and judicial methods used for other discrimination. The City's definition of "pornography" is considerably different from "obscenity," which the Supreme Court has held is not protected by the First Amendment.

To be "obscene" under Miller v. California, 413 U.S. 15 (1973), "a publication must, taken as a whole, appeal to the prurient interest, must contain patently offensive depictions or descriptions of specified sexual conduct, and on the whole have no serious literary, artistic, political, or scientific value." Brockett v. Spokane Arcades, Inc., ____ U.S. ____ (1985). Offensiveness must be assessed under the standards of the community. Both offensiveness and an appeal to something other than "normal, healthy sexual desires" . . . are essential elements of "obscenity."

"Pornography" under the ordinance is "the graphic sexually explicit subordination of women, whether in pictures or in words, that also includes one or more of the following:

(1) Women are presented as sexual objects who enjoy pain or humiliation; or

(2) Women are presented as sexual objects who experience sexual pleasure in being raped; or

(3) Women are presented as sexual objects tied up or cut up or mutilated or bruised or physically hurt, or as dismembered or truncated or fragmented or severed into body parts; or

(4) Women are presented as being penetrated by objects or animals; or

(5) Women are presented in scenarios of degradation, injury, abasement, torture, shown as filthy or inferior, bleeding, bruised, or hurt in a context that makes these conditions sexual; or

(6) Women are presented as sexual objects for domination, conquest, violation, exploitation, possession, or use, or through postures or positions of servility or submission or display." Indianapolis Code § 16–3(q).

The statute provides that the "use of men, children, or transsexuals in the place of women in paragraphs (1) through (6) above shall also constitute pornography under this section." The ordinance as passed in April 1984 defined "sexually explicit" to mean actual or simulated intercourse or the uncovered exhibition of the genitals, buttocks or anus. An amendment in June 1984 deleted this provision, leaving the term undefined.

The Indianapolis ordinance does not refer to the prurient interest, to offensiveness, or to the standards of the community. It demands attention to particular depictions, not to the work judged as a whole. It is irrelevant under the ordinance whether the work has literary, artistic, political, or scientific value. The City and many amici point to these omissions as virtues. They maintain that pornography influences attitudes, and the statute is a way to alter the socialization of men and women rather than to vindicate community standards of offensiveness. And as one of the principal drafters of the ordinance has asserted, "if a woman is subjected, why should it matter that the work has other value?" Catharine A. MacKinnon, Pornography, Civil Rights, and Speech, 20 Harv.Civ.Rts.—Civ.Lib.L.Rev. 1, 21 (1985).

Civil rights groups and feminists have entered this case as amici on both sides. Those supporting the ordinance say that it will play an important role in reducing the tendency of men to view women as sexual objects, a tendency that leads to both unacceptable attitudes and discrimination in the workplace and violence away from it. Those opposing the ordinance point out that much radical feminist literature is explicit and depicts women in ways forbidden by the ordinance and that the ordinance would reopen old battles. It is unclear how Indianapolis would treat works from James Joyce's *Ulysses* to Homer's *Iliad;* both depict women as submissive objects for conquest and domination.

We do not try to balance the arguments for and against an ordinance such as this. The ordinance discriminates on the ground of the content of the speech. Speech treating women in the approved way—in sexual encounters "premised on equality" (MacKinnon, supra, at 22)—is lawful no matter how sexually explicit. Speech treating women in the disapproved way—as submissive in matters sexual or as enjoying humiliation—is unlawful no matter how significant the literary, artistic, or political qualities of the work taken as a whole. The state may not ordain preferred viewpoints in this way. The Constitution forbids the state to declare one perspective right and silence opponents.

I

The ordinance contains four prohibitions. People may not "traffic" in pornography, "coerce" others into performing in pornographic works, or "force" pornography on anyone. Anyone injured by someone who has seen or read pornography has a right of action against the maker or seller.

Trafficking is defined in § 16–3(g)(4) as the "production, sale, exhibition, or distribution of pornography." The offense excludes exhibition in a public or educational library, but a "special display" in a library may be sex discrimination. Section 16–3(g)(4)(C) provides that the trafficking paragraph "shall not be construed to make isolated passages or isolated parts actionable."

"Coercion into pornographic performance" is defined in § 16–3(g)(5) as "[c]oercing, intimidating or fraudulently inducing any person . . . into performing for pornography. . . ." The ordinance specifies that proof of any of the following "shall not constitute a defense: I. That the person is a woman; . . . VI. That the person has previously posed for sexually explicit pictures . . . with anyone . . .; . . . VIII. That the person actually consented to a use of the performance that is changed into pornography; . . . IX. That the person knew that the purpose of the acts or events in question was to make pornography; . . . XI. That the person signed a contract, or made statements affirming a willingness to cooperate in the production of pornography; XII. That no physical force, threats, or weapons were used in the making of the pornography; or XIII. That the person was paid or otherwise compensated."

"Forcing pornography on a person," according to § 16–3(g)(5), is the "forcing of pornography on any woman, man, child, or transsexual in any place of employment, in education, in a home, or in any public place." The statute does not define forcing, but one of its authors states that the definition reaches pornography shown to medical students as part of their education or given to language students for translation. MacKinnon, supra, at 40–41.

Section 16–3(g)(7) defines as a prohibited practice the "assault, physical attack, or injury of any woman, man, child, or transsexual in a way that is directly caused by specific pornography."

For purposes of all four offenses, it is generally "not . . . a defense that the respondent did not know or intend that the materials were pornography. . . ." Section 16–3(g)(8). But the ordinance provides that damages are unavailable in trafficking cases unless the complainant proves "that the respondent knew or had reason to know that the materials were pornography." It is a complete defense to a trafficking case that all of the materials in question were pornography only by virtue of category (6) of the definition of pornography. In cases of assault caused by pornography, those who seek damages from "a seller, exhibitor or distributor" must show that the defendant knew or had reason to know of the material's status as pornography. By implication, those who seek damages from an author need not show this.

A woman aggrieved by trafficking in pornography may file a complaint "as a woman acting against the subordination of women" with the office of equal opportunity. Section 16–17(b). A man, child, or transsexual also may protest trafficking "but must prove injury in the same way that a woman is injured. . . ." Ibid. Subsection (a) also provides, however, that "any person claiming to be aggrieved" by trafficking, coercion, forcing, or assault may complain against the "perpetrators." We need not decide whether § 16–17(b) qualifies the right of action in § 16–17(a).

. . .

The district court held the ordinance unconstitutional. . . .

II

The plaintiffs are a congeries of distributors and readers of books, magazines, and films. The American Booksellers Association comprises about 5,200 bookstores and chains. The Association for American Publishers includes most of the country's publishers. Video Shack, Inc., sells and rents video cassettes in Indianapolis. Kelly Bentley, a resident of Indianapolis, reads books and watches films. There are many more plaintiffs. Collectively the plaintiffs (or their members, whose interests they represent) make, sell, or read just about every kind of material that could be affected by the ordinance, from hard-core films to W.B. Yeats's poem "Leda and the Swan" (from the myth of Zeus in the form of a swan impregnating an apparently subordinate Leda), to the collected works of James Joyce, D.H. Lawrence, and John Cleland.

. . .

III

"If there is any fixed star in our constitutional constellation, it is that no official, high or petty, can prescribe what shall be orthodox in politics, nationalism, religion, or other matters of opinion or force citizens to confess by word or act their faith therein." West Virginia State Board of Education v. Barnette, 319 U.S. 624 (1943). Under the First Amendment the government must leave to the people the evaluation of ideas. Bald or subtle, an idea is as powerful as the audience allows it to be. A belief may be pernicious—the beliefs of Nazis led to the death of millions, those of the Klan to the repression of millions. A pernicious belief may prevail. Totalitarian governments today rule much of the planet, practicing suppression of billions and spreading dogma that may enslave others. One of the things that separates our society from theirs is our absolute right to propagate opinions that the government finds wrong or even hateful.

The ideas of the Klan may be propagated. Brandenburg v. Ohio, 395 U.S. 444 (1969). Communists may speak freely and run for office. DeJonge v. Oregon, 299 U.S. 353 (1937). The Nazi Party may march through a city with a large Jewish population. Collin v. Smith, 578 F.2d 1197 (7th Cir.), cert. denied, 439 U.S. 916 (1978). . . . People may teach religions that others despise. People may seek to repeal laws guaranteeing equal opportunity in employment or to revoke the constitutional amendments granting the vote to blacks and women. They may do this because "above all else, the First Amendment means that government has no power to restrict expression because of its message [or] its ideas. . . ." Police Department v. Mosley, 408 U.S. 92, 95 (1972). See also Geoffrey R. Stone, Content Regulation and the First Amendment, 25 William & Mary L.Rev. 189 (1983); Paul B. Stephan, The First Amendment and Content Discrimination, 68 Va.L.Rev. 203, 233–36 (1982).

Under the ordinance graphic sexually explicit speech is "pornography" or not depending on the perspective the author adopts. Speech that "subordinates" women and also, for example, presents women as enjoying pain, humiliation, or rape, or even simply presents women in "positions of servility or submission or display" is forbidden, no matter how great the literary or political value of the work taken as a whole. Speech that portrays women in positions of equality is lawful, no matter how graphic the sexual content. This is thought control. It establishes an "approved" view of women, of how they may react to sexual encounters, of how the sexes may relate to each other. Those who espouse the approved view may use sexual images; those who do not, may not.

Indianapolis justifies the ordinance on the ground that pornography affects thoughts. Men who see women depicted as subordinate are more likely to treat them so. Pornography is an aspect of dominance. It does not persuade people so much as change them. It works by socializing, by establishing the expected and the permissible. In this view pornography is not an idea; pornography is the injury. There is much to this perspective. Beliefs are also facts. People often act in accordance with the images and patterns they find around them. People raised in a religion tend to accept the tenets of that religion, often without independent examination. People taught from birth that black people are fit only for slavery rarely rebelled against that creed; beliefs coupled with the self-interest of the masters established a social structure that inflicted great harm while enduring for centuries. Words and images act at the level of the subconscious before they persuade at the level of the conscious. Even the truth has little chance unless a statement fits within the framework of beliefs that may never have been subjected to rational study.

Therefore we accept the premises of this legislation. Depictions of subordination tend to perpetuate subordination. The subordinate status of women in turn leads to affront and lower pay at work, insult and injury at home, battery and rape on the streets. In the language of the legislature, "(p)ornography is central in creating and maintaining sex as a basis of discrimination. Pornography is a systematic practice of exploitation and subordination based on sex which differentially harms women. The bigotry and contempt it produces, with the acts of aggression it fosters, harm women's opportunities for equality and rights [of all kinds]." Indianapolis Code § 16–1(a)(2).

Yet this simply demonstrates the power of pornography as speech. All of these unhappy effects depend on mental intermediation. Pornography affects how people see the world, their fellows, and social relations. If pornography is what pornography does, so is other speech. . . . The Alien and Sedition Acts passed during the administration of John Adams rested on a sincerely held belief that disrespect for the government leads to social collapse and revolution—a belief with support in the history of many nations. Most governments of the world act on this empirical regularity, suppressing critical speech. In the United States, however, the strength of the support for this belief is irrelevant. . . .

Racial bigotry, anti-semitism, violence on television, reporters' biases—these and many more influence the culture and shape our socialization. None is directly answerable by more speech, unless that speech too finds its place in the popular culture. Yet all is protected as speech, however insidious. Any other answer leaves the government in control of all of the institutions of culture, the great censor and director of which thoughts are good for us.

Sexual responses often are unthinking responses, and the association of sexual arousal with the subordination of women therefore may have a substantial effect. But almost all cultural stimuli provoke unconscious responses. Religious ceremonies condition their participants. Teachers convey messages by selecting what not to cover; the implicit message about what is off limits or unthinkable may be more powerful than the messages for which they present rational argument. Television scripts contain unarticulated assumptions. People may be conditioned in subtle ways. If the fact that speech plays a role in a process of conditioning were enough to permit governmental regulation, that would be the end of freedom of speech.

It is possible to interpret the claim that the pornography is the harm in a different way. Indianapolis emphasizes the injury that models in pornographic films and pictures may suffer. The record contains materials depicting sexual torture, penetration of women by red-hot irons and the like. These concerns have nothing to do with written materials subject to the statute, and physical injury can occur with or without the "subordination" of women. As we discuss in Part IV, a state may make injury in the course of producing a film unlawful independent of the viewpoint expressed in the film.

The more immediate point, however, is that the image of pain is not necessarily pain. In *Body Double,* a suspense film directed by Brian DePalma, a woman who has disrobed and presented a sexually explicit display is murdered by an intruder with a drill. The drill runs through the woman's body. The film is sexually explicit and a murder occurs—yet no one believes that the actress suffered pain or died. In *Barbarella* a character played by Jane Fonda is at times displayed in sexually explicit ways and at times shown "bleeding, bruised, [and] hurt in a context that makes these conditions sexual"—and again no one believes that Fonda was actually tortured to make the film. In *Carnal Knowledge* a woman grovels to please the sexual whims of a character played by Jack Nicholson; no one believes that there was a real sexual submission, and the Supreme Court held the film protected by the First Amendment. Jenkins v. Georgia, 418 U.S. 153 (1974). And this works both ways. The description of women's sexual domination of men in *Lysistrata* was not real dominance. Depictions may affect slavery, war, or sexual roles, but a book about slavery is not itself slavery, or a book about death by poison a murder.

Much of Indianapolis's argument rests on the belief that when speech is "unanswerable," and the metaphor that there is a "marketplace of ideas" does not apply, the First Amendment does not apply either. The metaphor is honored; Milton's *Aeropagitica* and John Stewart Mill's *On Liberty* defend freedom of speech on the ground that the truth will prevail, and many of the most important cases under the First Amendment recite this position. The Framers undoubtedly believed it. As a general matter it is true. But the Constitution does not make the dominance of truth a necessary condition of freedom of speech. To say that it does would be to confuse an outcome of free speech with a necessary condition for the application of the amendment.

A power to limit speech on the ground that truth has not yet prevailed and is not likely to prevail implies the power to declare truth. At some point the government must be able to say (as Indianapolis has said): "We know what the truth is, yet a free exchange of speech has not driven out falsity, so that we must now prohibit falsity." If the government may declare the truth, why wait for the failure of speech? Under the First Amendment, however, there is no such thing as a false idea, Gertz v. Robert Welch, Inc., 418 U.S. 323, 339 (1974), so the government may not restrict speech on the ground that in a free exchange truth is not yet dominant.

At any time, some speech is ahead in the game; the more numerous speakers prevail. Supporters of minority candidates may be forever "excluded" from the political process because their candidates never win, because few people believe their positions. This does not mean that freedom of speech has failed.

. . .

We come, finally, to the argument that pornography is "low value" speech, that it is enough like obscenity that Indianapolis may prohibit it. Some cases hold that speech far removed from politics and other subjects at the core of the Framers' concerns may be subjected to special regulation. E.g., FCC v. Pacifica Foundation, 438 U.S. 726 (1978); Young v. American Mini Theatres, Inc., 427 U.S. 50, 67–70 (1976) (plurality opinion); Chaplinsky v. New Hampshire, 315 U.S. 568, 571–72 (1942). These cases do not sustain statutes that select among viewpoints, however. In *Pacifica* the FCC sought to keep vile language off the air during certain times. The Court held that it may; but the Court would not have sustained a regulation prohibiting scatological descriptions of Republicans but not scatological descriptions of Democrats, or any other form of selection among viewpoints. . . .

At all events, "pornography" is not low value speech within the meaning of these cases. Indianapolis seeks to prohibit certain speech because it believes this speech influences social relations and politics on a grand scale, that it controls attitudes at home and in the legislature. This precludes a characterization of the speech as low value. True, pornography and obscenity have sex in common. But Indianapolis left out of its definition any reference to literary, artistic, political, or scientific value. The ordinance applies to graphic sexually explicit subordination in works great and small.[3] The Court sometimes balances the value of speech against the costs of its restriction, but it does this by category of speech and not by the content of particular works. . . . Indianapolis has created an approved point of view and so loses the support of these cases.

Any rationale we could imagine in support of this ordinance could not be limited to sex discrimination. Free speech has been on balance an ally of those seeking change. Governments that want stasis start by restricting speech. Culture is a powerful force of continuity; Indianapolis paints pornography as part of the culture of power. Change in any complex system ultimately depends on the ability of outsiders to challenge accepted views and the reigning institutions. Without a strong guarantee of freedom of speech, there is no effective right to challenge what is.

IV

The definition of "pornography" is unconstitutional. No construction or excision of particular terms could save it. The offense of trafficking in pornography necessarily falls with the definition. We express no view on the district court's conclusions that the ordinance is vague and that it establishes a prior restraint. Neither is necessary to our judgment. We also express no view on the argument presented by

---

[3] Indianapolis briefly argues that Beauharnais v. Illinois, 343 U.S. 250 (1952), which allowed a state to penalize "group libel," supports the ordinance. In Collin v. Smith, 578 F.2d at 1205, we concluded that cases such as New York Times v. Sullivan had so washed away the foundations of *Beauharnais* that it could not be considered authoritative. If we are wrong in this, however, the case still does not support the ordinance. It is not clear that depicting women as subordinate in sexually explicit ways, even combined with a depiction of pleasure in rape, would fit within the definition of a group libel. The well received film Swept Away used explicit sex, plus taking pleasure in rape, to make a political statement, not to defame. Work must be an insult or slur for its own sake to come within the ambit of *Beauharnais,* and a work need not be scurrilous at all to be "pornography" under the ordinance.

several amici that the ordinance is itself a form of discrimination on account of sex.

Section 8 of the ordinance is a strong severability clause, and Indianapolis asks that we parse the ordinance to save what we can. If a court could do this by surgical excision, this might be possible. . . . But a federal court may not completely reconstruct a local ordinance, and we conclude that nothing short of rewriting could save anything.

The offense of coercion to engage in a pornographic performance, for example, has elements that might be constitutional. Without question a state may prohibit fraud, trickery, or the use of force to induce people to perform—in pornographic films or in any other films. Such a statute may be written without regard to the viewpoint depicted in the work. New York v. Ferber, 458 U.S. 747 (1982), suggests that when a state has a strong interest in forbidding the conduct that makes up a film (in *Ferber* sexual acts involving minors), it may restrict or forbid dissemination of the film in order to reinforce the prohibition of the conduct. A state may apply such a rule to non-sexual coercion (although it need not). We suppose that if someone forced a prominent political figure, at gunpoint, to endorse a candidate for office, a state could forbid the commercial sale of the film containing that coerced endorsement. . . .

. . .

The offense of forcing pornography on unwilling recipients is harder to assess. Many kinds of forcing (such as giving texts to students for translation) may themselves be protected speech. Rowan v. Post Office, 397 U.S. 728 (1970), shows that a state may permit people to insulate themselves from categories of speech—in *Rowan* sexual mail—but that the government must leave the decision about what items are forbidden in the hands of the potentially offended recipients. . . . Exposure to sex is not something the government may prevent, see Erznoznik v. City of Jacksonville, 422 U.S. 205 (1975). We therefore could not save the offense of "forcing" by redefining "pornography" as all sexually-offensive speech or some related category. The statute needs a definition of "forcing" that removes the government from the role of censor. . . .

The section creating remedies for injuries and assaults attributable to pornography also is salvageable in principle, although not by us. The First Amendment does not prohibit redress of all injuries caused by speech. Injury to reputation is redressed through the law of libel, which is constitutional subject to strict limitations. Cases such as Brandenburg v. Ohio and NAACP v. Claiborne Hardware hold that a state may not penalize speech that does not cause immediate injury. But we do not doubt that if, immediately after the Klan's rally in *Brandenburg,* a mob had burned to the ground the house of a nearby black person, that person could have recovered damages from the speaker who whipped the crowd into a frenzy. All of the Justices assumed in *Claiborne Hardware* that if the threats in Charles Evers's incendiary speech had been a little less veiled and had led directly to an assault against a person shopping in a store owned by a white merchant, the victim of the assault and even the merchant could have recovered damages from the speaker.

.   .   .

Again, however, the assault statute is tied to "pornography," and we cannot find a sensible way to repair the defect without seizing power that belongs elsewhere. Indianapolis might choose to have no ordinance if it cannot be limited to viewpoint-specific harms, or it might choose to extend the scope to all speech, just as the law of libel applies to all speech. An attempt to repair this ordinance would be nothing but a blind guess. No amount of struggle with particular words and phrases in this ordinance can leave anything in effect. The district court came to the same conclusion. Its judgment is therefore

Affirmed.

Swygert, Senior Circuit Judge, concurring.

I concur in Parts I, II, and III of the court's opinion except for the following strictures.   .   .   .

I . . . believe that the majority's questionable and broad assertions regarding how human behavior can be conditioned by certain teachings and beliefs are unnecessary. For even if this court accepts the City of Indianapolis' basic contention that pornography does condition unfavorable responses to women, the ordinance is still unconstitutional.

As to Part IV of the opinion, I agree that the ordinance is unconstitutional on first amendment grounds and that there is no need to discuss vagueness or prior restraint. I do, however, disassociate myself from the extensive statements with respect to how the Indianapolis City Council could fashion an ordinance dealing with pornography that might pass constitutional muster. Indianapolis has asked us to sever the ordinance and save those parts that are not unconstitutional, if we can. All then that this court is required to do is to rule that the ordinance is not severable. Statements regarding which portions of the ordinance may be constitutional are merely advisory and are not the function of this court.*

2.   THE PROBLEM OF DEFINITION

Page 1136. Add ahead of Jenkins v. Georgia:

BROCKETT v. SPOKANE ARCADES, INC., 472 U.S. 491 (1985). A state obscenity statute defined obscene matter as that appealing to a prurient interest. "Prurient" was, in turn, defined as "that which incites lasciviousness or lust." The Court concluded that the statutory definition was constitutionally defective. On this issue, the Court's opinion said:

---

* The decision was summarily affirmed by the Supreme Court without argument or opinion. (Chief Justice Burger, and Justices Rehnquist and O'Connor dissented, stating that the case should be set for argument.) 475 U.S. 1001 (1986).

"Under *Roth*, obscenity was equated with prurience and was not entitled to First Amendment protection. Nine years later, however, the decision in Memoirs v. Massachusetts, 383 U.S. 413 (1966), established a much more demanding three-part definition of obscenity, a definition that was in turn modified in Miller v. California, 413 U.S. 15 (1973). The *Miller* guidelines for identifying obscenity are:

'(a) whether "the average person, applying contemporary community standards" would find that the work, taken as a whole, appeals to the prurient interest, Kois v. Wisconsin, [408 U.S.,] at 230, quoting Roth v. United States, supra, at 489; (b) whether the work depicts or describes, in a patently offensive way, sexual conduct specifically defined by the applicable state law; and (c) whether the work, taken as a whole, lacks serious literary, artistic, political, or scientific value.' Id., at 24.

Miller thus retained, as had *Memoirs*, the *Roth* formulation as the first part of this test, without elaborating on or disagreeing with the definition of 'prurient interest' contained in the *Roth* opinion.

"The Court of Appeals was aware that *Roth* had indicated in footnote 20 that material appealing to the prurient interest was 'material having a tendency to excite lustful thoughts' but did not believe that *Roth* had intended to characterize as obscene material that provoked only normal, healthy sexual desires. We do not differ with that view. As already noted, material appealing to the 'prurient interest' was itself the definition of obscenity announced in *Roth*; and we are quite sure that by using the words 'lustful thoughts' in footnote 20, the Court was referring to sexual responses over and beyond those that would be characterized as normal. At the end of that footnote, as the Court of Appeals observed, the *Roth* opinion referred to the Model Penal Code definition of obscenity—material whose predominate appeal is to 'a shameful or morbid interest in nudity, sex, or excretion' and indicated that it perceived no significant difference between that definition and the meaning of obscenity developed in the case law. This effectively negated any inference that 'lustful thoughts' as used earlier in the footnote was limited to or included normal sexual responses. It would require more than the possible ambiguity in footnote 20 to lead us to believe that the Court intended to characterize as obscene and exclude from the protection of the First Amendment any and all speech that aroused any sexual responses, whether normal or morbid."

POPE v. ILLINOIS, 107 S.Ct. 1918 (1987). The jury instruction in a state obscenity prosecution told the jury to apply community standards to the third aspect of the tripartite *Miller* test. The Court held that it was inappropriate to apply community standards to the question whether the work lacks serious value. Only the first two elements of the *Miller* inquiry—appeal to prurient interest and patent offensiveness—are issues for the jury to determine according to contemporary community standards. Justice White's opinion for the Court stated:

> "Just as the ideas a work represents need not obtain majority approval to merit protection, neither, insofar as the First Amendment is concerned, does the value of the work vary from community to community based on the degree of local acceptance it has won. The proper inquiry is not whether an ordinary member of any given community would find serious literary, artistic, political or scientific value in allegedly obscene material, but whether a reasonable person would find such value in the material, taken as a whole."

Justice Stevens, joined by Justices Brennan and Marshall, argued that the reasonable person standard might lead a jury to convict if it concluded "that the majority of the population who find no value . . . are more reasonable than the minority who do." The dissenters argued that sexually oriented material should be constitutionally protected if "some reasonable persons could" conclude that it had serious value. Justice Scalia's concurrence explained that he joined the Court's opinion because the Court had not been asked to reconsider the *Miller* test, but argued that there was a need for reexamination.

> "Just as there is no use arguing about taste, there is no use litigating about it. For the law courts to decide 'What is Beauty' is a novelty even by today's standards."

C. CONTROL OF "FIGHTING WORDS" AND OFFENSIVE SPEECH

Page 1153. Add at end of subsection:

BETHEL SCHOOL DISTRICT NO. 403 v. FRASER
478 U.S. 675, 106 S.Ct. 3159, 92 L.Ed.2d 549 (1986).

Chief Justice Burger delivered the opinion of the Court.

We granted certiorari to decide whether the First Amendment prevents a school district from disciplining a high school student for giving a lewd speech at a school assembly.

I

A

On April 26, 1983, respondent Matthew N. Fraser, a student at Bethel High School in Bethel, Washington, delivered a speech nominating a fellow student for student elective office. Approximately 600 high school students, many of whom were 14-year-olds, attended the assembly. Students were required to attend the assembly or to report to the study hall. The assembly was part of a school-sponsored educational program in self-government. Students who elected not to attend the assembly were required to report to study hall. During the entire speech, Fraser referred to his candidate in terms of an elaborate, graphic, and explicit sexual metaphor.

Two of Fraser's teachers, with whom he discussed the contents of his speech in advance, informed him that the speech was "inappropriate and that he probably should not deliver it," and that his delivery of the speech might have "severe consequences."

During Fraser's delivery of the speech, a school counselor observed the reaction of students to the speech. Some students hooted and yelled; some by gestures graphically simulated the sexual activities pointedly alluded to in respondent's speech. Other students appeared to be bewildered and embarrassed by the speech. One teacher reported that on the day following the speech, she found it necessary to forgo a portion of the scheduled class lesson in order to discuss the speech with the class.

A Bethel High School disciplinary rule prohibiting the use of obscene language in the school provides:

"Conduct which materially and substantially interferes with the educational process is prohibited, including the use of obscene, profane language or gestures."

The morning after the assembly, the Assistant Principal called Fraser into her office and notified him that the school considered his speech to have been a violation of this rule. Fraser was presented with copies of five letters submitted by teachers, describing his conduct at the assembly; he was given a chance to explain his conduct, and he admitted to having given the speech described and that he deliberately used sexual innuendo in the speech. Fraser was then informed that he would be suspended for three days, and that his name would be removed from the list of candidates for graduation speaker at the school's commencement exercises.

Fraser sought review of this disciplinary action through the School District's grievance procedures. The hearing officer determined that the speech given by respondent was "indecent, lewd, and offensive to the modesty and decency of many of the students and faculty in attendance at the assembly." The examiner determined that the speech fell within the ordinary meaning of "obscene," as used in the disruptive-conduct rule, and affirmed the discipline in its entirety. Fraser served two days of his suspension, and was allowed to return to school on the third day.

B

Respondent, by his father as guardian ad litem, then brought this action in the United States District Court for the Western District of Washington. Respondent alleged a violation of his First Amendment right to freedom of speech and sought both injunctive relief and monetary damages under 42 U.S.C. section 1983. The District Court held that the school's sanctions violated respondent's right to freedom of speech under the First Amendment to the United States Constitution

. . ..

The Court of Appeals for the Ninth Circuit affirmed the judgment of the District Court . . ..

. . . We reverse.

II

This Court acknowledged in Tinker v. Des Moines Independent Community School Dist., [393 U.S. 503 (1969)], that students do not "shed their constitutional rights to freedom of speech or expression at the schoolhouse gate." Id., at 506. The Court of Appeals read that case as precluding any discipline of Fraser for indecent speech and lewd conduct in the school assembly. That court appears to have proceeded on the theory that the use of lewd and obscene speech in order to make what the speaker considered to be a point in a nominating speech for a fellow student was essentially the same as the wearing of an armband in *Tinker* as a form of protest or the expression of a political position.

The marked distinction between the political "message" of the armbands in *Tinker* and the sexual content of respondent's speech in this case seems to have been given little weight by the Court of Appeals. In upholding the students' right to engage in a nondisruptive, passive expression of a political viewpoint in *Tinker,* this Court was careful to note that the case did "not concern speech or action that intrudes upon the work of the schools or the rights of other students." Id., at 508.

It is against this background that we turn to consider the level of First Amendment protection accorded to Fraser's utterances and actions before an official high school assembly attended by 600 students.

III

The role and purpose of the American public school system was well described by two historians, saying "public education must prepare pupils for citizenship in the Republic . . ... It must inculcate the habits and manners of civility as values in themselves conducive to happiness and as indispensable to the practice of self-government in the community and the nation." C. Beard & M. Beard, New Basic History of the United States 228 (1968). In Ambach v. Norwick, 441 U.S. 68, 76–77 (1979), we echoed the essence of this statement of the objectives of public education as the "inculcation of fundamental values necessary to the maintenance of a democratic political system."

These fundamental values of "habits and manners of civility" essential to a democratic society must, of course, include tolerance of divergent political and religious views, even when the views expressed may be unpopular. But these "fundamental values" must also take into account consideration of the sensibilities of others, and, in the case of a school, the sensibilities of fellow students. The undoubted freedom to advocate unpopular and controversial views in schools and classrooms must be balanced against the society's countervailing interest in teaching students the boundaries of socially appropriate behavior. Even the most heated political discourse in a democratic society requires consideration for the personal sensibilities of the other participants and audiences.

In our Nation's legislative halls, where some of the most vigorous political debates in our society are carried on, there are rules prohibiting the use of expressions offensive to other participants in the debate. . . . Can it be that what is proscribed in the halls of Congress is beyond the reach of school officials to regulate?

The First Amendment guarantees wide freedom in matters of adult public discourse. A sharply divided Court upheld the right to express an antidraft viewpoint in a public place, albeit in terms highly offensive to most citizens. See Cohen v. California, 403 U.S. 15 (1971). It does not follow, however, that simply because the use of an offensive form of expression may not be prohibited to adults making what the speaker considers a political point, that the same latitude must be permitted to children in a public school. . . .

Surely it is a highly appropriate function of public school education to prohibit the use of vulgar and offensive terms in public discourse. Indeed, the "fundamental values necessary to the maintenance of a democratic political system" disfavor the use of terms of debate highly offensive or highly threatening to others. Nothing in the Constitution prohibits the states from insisting that certain modes of expression are inappropriate and subject to sanctions. The inculcation of these values is truly the "work of the schools." *Tinker,* 393 U.S., at 508 . . . The determination of what manner of speech in the classroom or in school assembly is inappropriate properly rests with the school board.

The process of educating our youth for citizenship in public schools is not confined to books, the curriculum, and the civics class; schools must teach by example the shared values of a civilized social order. Consciously or otherwise, teachers—and indeed the older students—demonstrate the appropriate form of civil discourse and political expression by their conduct and deportment in and out of class. Inescapably, like parents, they are role models. The schools, as instruments of the state, may determine that the essential lessons of civil, mature conduct cannot be conveyed in a school that tolerates lewd, indecent, or offensive speech and conduct such as that indulged in by this confused boy.

The pervasive sexual innuendo in Fraser's speech was plainly offensive to both teachers and students—indeed to any mature person. By glorifying male sexuality, and in its verbal content, the speech was acutely insulting to teenage girl students. The speech could well be seriously damaging to its less mature audience, many of whom were only 14 years old and on the threshold of awareness of human sexuality. Some students were reported as bewildered by the speech and the reaction of mimicry it provoked.

This Court's First Amendment jurisprudence has acknowledged limitations on the otherwise absolute interest of the speaker in reaching an unlimited audience where the speech is sexually explicit and the audience may include children. In Ginsberg v. New York, 390 U.S. 629 (1968) this Court upheld a New York statute banning the sale of sexually oriented material to minors, even though the material in question was entitled to First Amendment protection with respect to adults. And in addressing the question whether the First Amendment places any limit on the authority of public schools to remove books from a public school library, all Members of the Court otherwise sharply divided, acknowledged that the school board has the authority to remove books that are vulgar. Board of Education v. Pico, 457 U.S. 853 . . .. These cases recognize the obvious concern on the part of parents, and school authorities acting in loco parentis to protect children—especially in a captive audience—from exposure to sexually explicit, indecent, or lewd speech.

We have also recognized an interest in protecting minors from exposure to vulgar and offensive spoken language. In FCC v. Pacifica Foundation, 438 U.S. 726 (1978), we dealt with the power of the Federal Communications Commission to regulate a radio broadcast described as "indecent but not obscene." . . .

We hold that petitioner School District acted entirely within its permissible authority in imposing sanctions upon Fraser in response to his offensively lewd and indecent speech. Unlike the sanctions imposed on the students wearing armbands in *Tinker*, the penalties imposed in this case were unrelated to any political viewpoint. The First Amendment does not prevent the school officials from determining that to permit a vulgar and lewd speech such as respondent's would undermine the school's basic educational mission. A high school assembly or classroom is no place for a sexually explicit monologue directed towards an unsuspecting audience of teenage students. Accordingly, it was perfectly appropriate for the school to disassociate itself to make the point to the pupils that vulgar speech and lewd conduct is wholly inconsistent with the "fundamental values" of public school education. . . .

IV

Respondent contends that the circumstances of his suspension violated due process because he had no way of knowing that the delivery of the speech in question would subject him to disciplinary sanctions. This argument is wholly without merit . . .. Given the school's need to be able to impose disciplinary sanctions for a wide range of unanticipated conduct disruptive of the educational process, the school disciplinary rules need not be as detailed as a criminal code which imposes criminal sanctions. . . .

The judgment of the Court of Appeals for the Ninth Circuit is reversed.

Justice Blackmun concurs in the result.

Justice Brennan, concurring in the judgment.

Respondent gave the following speech at a high school assembly in support of a candidate for student government office:

"I know a man who is firm—he's firm in his pants, he's firm in his shirt, his character is firm—but most . . . of all, his belief in you, the students of Bethel, is firm.

"Jeff Kuhlman is a man who takes his point and pounds it in. If necessary, he'll take an issue and nail it to the wall. He doesn't attack things in spurts—he drives hard, pushing and pushing until finally—he succeeds.

"Jeff is a man who will go to the very end—even the climax, for each and every one of you.

"So vote for Jeff for A.S.B. vice-president—he'll never come between you and the best our high school can be."

The Court, referring to these remarks as "obscene," "vulgar," "lewd," and "offensively lewd," concludes that school officials properly punished respondent for uttering the speech. Having read the full text of respondent's remarks, I find it difficult to believe that it is the same speech the Court describes. To my mind, the most that can be said about respondent's speech—and all that need be said—is that in light of the discretion school officials have to teach high school students how to conduct civil and effective public discourse, and to prevent disruption of school educational activities, it was not unconstitutional for school officials to conclude, under the circumstances of this case, that respondent's remarks exceeded permissible limits. Thus, while I concur in the Court's judgment, I write separately to express my understanding of the breadth of the Court's holding.

The Court today reaffirms the unimpeachable proposition that students do not "shed their constitutional rights to freedom of speech or expression at the schoolhouse gate." If respondent had given the same speech outside of the school environment, he could not have been penalized simply because government officials considered his language to be inappropriate, see Cohen v. California, 403 U.S. 15 (1971); the Court's opinion does not suggest otherwise.[1] Moreover, despite the Court's characterizations, the language respondent used is far removed from the very narrow class of "obscene" speech which the Court has held is not protected by the First Amendment. Ginsberg v. New York, 390 U.S. 629, 635 (1968); Roth v. United States, 354 U.S. 476, 485 (1957). It is true, however, that the State has interests in teaching high school students how to conduct civil and effective public discourse and in avoiding disruption of educational school activities. Thus, the Court holds that under certain circumstances, high school students may properly be reprimanded for giving a speech at a high school assembly which school officials conclude disrupted the school's educational mission. Respondent's speech may well have been protected had he given it in school but under different circumstances, where the school's

---

[1] In the course of its opinion, the Court makes certain remarks concerning the authority of school officials to regulate student language in public schools. For example, the Court notes that "nothing in the Constitution prohibits the states from insisting that certain modes of expression are inappropriate and subject to sanctions." These statements obviously do not, and indeed given our prior precedents could not, refer to the government's authority generally to regulate the language used in public debate outside of the school environment.

legitimate interests in teaching and maintaining civil public discourse were less weighty.

In the present case, school officials sought only to ensure that a high school assembly proceed in an orderly manner. There is no suggestion that school officials attempted to regulate respondent's speech because they disagreed with the views he sought to express. Cf. *Tinker,* supra. Nor does this case involve an attempt by school officials to ban written materials they consider "inappropriate" for high school students, cf. Board of Education v. Pico, 457 U.S. 853 (1982), or to limit what students should hear, read, or learn about. Thus, the Court's holding concerns only the authority that school officials have to restrict a high school student's use of disruptive language in a speech given to a high school assembly.

The authority school officials have to regulate such speech by high school students is not limitless.   . . . Under the circumstances of this case, however, I believe that school officials did not violate the First Amendment in determining that respondent should be disciplined for the disruptive language he used while addressing a high school assembly. Thus, I concur in the judgment reversing the decision of the Court of Appeals.

Justice Marshall, dissenting.

I agree with the principles that Justice Brennan sets out in his opinion concurring in the judgment. I dissent from the Court's decision, however, because in my view the school district failed to demonstrate that respondent's remarks were indeed disruptive.   . . .

Justice Stevens, dissenting.

"Frankly, my dear, I don't give a damn."

When I was a high school student, the use of those words in a public forum shocked the Nation. Today Clark Gable's four-letter expletive is less offensive than it was then. Nevertheless, I assume that high school administrators may prohibit the use of that word in classroom discussion and even in extracurricular activities that are sponsored by the school and held on school premises. For I believe a school faculty must regulate the content as well as the style of student speech in carrying out its educational mission. It does seem to me, however, that if a student is to be punished for using offensive speech, he is entitled to fair notice of the scope of the prohibition and the consequences of its violation. The interest in free speech protected by the First Amendment and the interest in fair procedure protected by the Due Process Clause of the Fourteenth Amendment combine to require this conclusion.

This respondent was an outstanding young man with a fine academic record. The fact that he was chosen by the student body to speak at the school's commencement exercises demonstrates that he was respected by his peers.   . . . [H]e was probably in a better position to determine whether an audience composed of 600 of his contemporaries would be offended by the use of a four-letter word—or a sexual metaphor—than is a group of judges who are at least two generations and 3,000 miles away from the scene of the crime.

The fact that the speech may not have been offensive to his audience—or that he honestly believed that it would be inoffensive— does not mean that he had a constitutional right to deliver it. For the school—not the student—must prescribe the rules of conduct in an educational institution. But it does mean that he should not be disciplined for speaking frankly in a school assembly if he had no reason to anticipate punitive consequences.

. . .

. . . [T]he evidence in the record, as interpreted by the District Court and the Court of Appeals, makes it perfectly clear that respondent's speech was not "conduct" prohibited by the disciplinary rule. Indeed, even if the language of the rule could be stretched to encompass the nondisruptive use of obscene or profane language, there is no such language in respondent's speech. . . .

. . .

The fact that respondent reviewed the text of his speech with three different teachers before he gave it does indicate that he must have been aware of the possibility that it would provoke an adverse reaction, but the teachers' responses certainly did not give him any better notice of the likelihood of discipline than did the student handbook itself.

. . .

. . .

It seems fairly obvious that respondent's speech would be inappropriate in certain classroom and formal social settings. On the other hand, in a locker room or perhaps in a school corridor the metaphor in the speech might be regarded as rather routine comment. If this be true, and if respondent's audience consisted almost entirely of young people with whom he conversed on a daily basis, can we—at this distance—confidently assert that he must have known that the school administration would punish him for delivering it?

. . .

I would affirm the judgment of the Court of Appeals.

———

CITY OF HOUSTON v. HILL
— U.S. —, 107 S.Ct. 2502, 96 L.Ed.2d 398 (1987).

Justice Brennan delivered the opinion of the Court.

This case presents the question whether a municipal ordinance that makes it unlawful to interrupt a police officer in the performance of his or her duties is unconstitutionally overbroad under the First Amendment.

I

Appellee Raymond Wayne Hill is a lifelong resident of Houston, Texas. At the time this lawsuit began, he worked as a paralegal and as executive director of the Houston Human Rights League. A member of the Board of the Gay Political Caucus, which he helped found in 1975, Hill was also affiliated with a Houston radio station, and had carried city and county press passes since 1975. He lived in Montrose, a "diverse and eclectic neighborhood" that is the center of gay political and social life in Houston.

The incident that sparked this lawsuit occurred in the Montrose area . . . Hill observed a friend, Charles Hill, intentionally stopping traffic on a busy street, evidently to enable a vehicle to enter traffic. Two Houston police officers, one of whom was named Kelley, approached Charles and began speaking with him. . . . Hill began shouting at the officers "in an admitted attempt to divert Kelley's attention from Charles Hill." Hill first shouted "Why don't you pick on somebody your own size?" After Officer Kelley responded "Are you interrupting me in my official capacity as a Houston police officer?" Hill then shouted, "Yes, why don't you pick on somebody my size?" Hill was arrested under Houston Municipal Code section 34–11(a) for "wilfully or intentionally interrupting a city policeman . . . by verbal challenge during an investigation." Charles Hill was not arrested. Hill was then acquitted after a nonjury trial in Municipal Court.

Houston Municipal Code section 34–11(a) (1984) reads:

"Sec. 34–11. Assaulting or interfering with policemen.

(a) It shall be unlawful for any person to assault, strike or in any manner oppose, molest, abuse or interrupt any policeman in the execution of his duty, or any person summoned to aid in making an arrest."

Following his acquittal in the Charles Hill incident, Hill brought suit in Federal District Court for the Southern District of Texas seeking (1) a declaratory judgment that section 34–11(a) was unconstitutional both on its face and as it had been applied to him . . .

At trial, Hill introduced records provided by the City regarding both the frequency with which arrests had been made for violation of the ordinance and the type of conduct with which those arrested had been charged. He also introduced evidence and testimony concerning the arrests of several reporters under the ordinance. Finally, Hill introduced evidence regarding his own experience with the ordinance, under which he has been arrested four times since 1975, but never convicted.

The District Court held that Hill's evidence did not demonstrate that the ordinance had been unconstitutionally applied. . . .

. . .

. . . [T]he Court of Appeals, by a vote of 8–7, [reversed]. . . .

. . .

. . . We . . . affirm.

II

. . .

The City's principal argument is that the ordinance does not inhibit the exposition of ideas, and that it bans "core criminal conduct" not protected by the First Amendment. In its view, the application of the ordinance to Hill illustrates that the police employ it only to prohibit such conduct, and not "as a subterfuge to control or dissuade free expression." Since the ordinance is "content-neutral," and since there is no evidence that the City has applied the ordinance to chill particular speakers or ideas, the City concludes that the ordinance is not substantially overbroad.

We disagree with the City's characterization for several reasons. First, the enforceable portion of the ordinance deals not with core criminal conduct, but with speech. As the City has conceded, the language in the ordinance making it unlawful for any person to "assault" or "strike" a police officer is preempted by the Texas Penal Code. . . . Accordingly, the enforceable portion of the ordinance makes it "unlawful for any person to . . . in any manner oppose, molest, abuse or interrupt any policeman in the execution of his duty," and thereby prohibits verbal interruptions of police officers.

Second, contrary to the City's contention, the First Amendment protects a significant amount of verbal criticism and challenge directed at police officers. "Speech is often provocative and challenging. . . . But it is nevertheless protected against censorship or punishment, unless shown likely to produce a clear and present danger of a serious substantive evil that rises far above public inconvenience, annoyance, or unrest." Terminiello v. Chicago, 337 U.S. 1, 4 (1949). In Lewis v. City of New Orleans, . . . a municipal ordinance . . . made it a crime " 'for any person wantonly to curse or revile or to use obscene or opprobrious language toward or with reference to any member of the city police while in the actual performance of his duty.' " . . . We . . . invalidated the ordinance as facially overbroad. . . . Moreover, in a concurring opinion in *Lewis,* Justice Powell suggested that even the "fighting words" exception recognized in Chaplinsky v. New Hampshire, 315 U.S. 568 (1942), might require a narrower application in cases involving words addressed to a police officer, because "a properly trained officer may reasonably be expected to 'exercise a higher degree of restraint' than the average citizen, and thus be less likely to respond belligerently to 'fighting words.' " 415 U.S., at 135 (citation omitted).

The Houston ordinance is much more sweeping than the municipal ordinance struck down in *Lewis.* It is not limited to fighting words nor even to obscene or opprobrious language, but prohibits speech that "in any manner . . . interrupts" an officer. The Constitution does not allow such speech to be made a crime.[11] The freedom of individuals verbally to oppose or challenge police action without thereby risking arrest is one of the principal characteristics by which we distinguish a free nation from a police state.

The City argues, however, that even if the ordinance encompasses some protected speech, its sweeping nature is both inevitable and essential to maintain public order. The City recalls this Court's observation in Smith v. Goguen, 415 U.S. 566, 581 (1974):

> "There are areas of human conduct where, by the nature of the problems presented, legislatures simply cannot establish standards with great precision. Control of the broad range of disorderly conduct that may inhibit a policeman in the performance of his official duties may be one such area requiring as it does an on-the-spot assessment of the need to keep order."

The City further suggests that its ordinance is comparable to the disorderly conduct statute upheld against a facial challenge in Colten v. Kentucky, 407 U.S. 104 (1972).

This Houston ordinance, however, is not narrowly tailored to prohibit only disorderly conduct or fighting words, and in no way resembles the law upheld in *Colten*. Although we appreciate the difficulties of drafting precise laws, we have repeatedly invalidated laws that provide the police with unfettered discretion to arrest individuals for words or conduct that annoy or offend them. . . . In *Lewis*, Justice Powell elaborated the basis for our concern with such sweeping, dragnet laws:

> "This ordinance, as construed by the Louisiana Supreme Court, confers on police a virtually unrestrained power to arrest and charge persons with a violation. . . . The present type of ordinance tends to be invoked only where there is no other valid basis for arresting an objectionable or suspicious person. The opportuni-

11 . . .

     . . . [T]oday's decision does not leave municipalities powerless to punish physical obstruction of police action. For example, Justice Powell states . . . "that a municipality constitutionally may punish an individual who chooses to stand near a police officer and persistently attempt to engage the officer in conversation while the officer is directing traffic at a busy intersection." We agree, however, that such conduct might constitutionally be punished under a properly tailored statute, such as a disorderly conduct statute that makes it unlawful to fail to disperse in response to a valid police order or to create a traffic hazard. E.g., Colten v. Kentucky, 407 U.S. 104 (1972). What a municipality may not do, however, and what Houston has done in this case, is to attempt to punish such conduct by broadly criminalizing speech directed to an officer—in this case, by authorizing the police to arrest a person who in any manner verbally interrupts an officer.

     Justice Powell also observes that "contentious and abusive" speech can interrupt an officer's investigation, and offers as an example a person who "runs beside an officer pursuing a felon in a public street shouting and cursing the officer." But what is of concern in that example is not simply contentious speech, but rather the possibility that by shouting and running beside the officer the person may physically obstruct the officer's investigation. Although that person might constitutionally be punished under a tailored statute that forbade individuals from physically obstructing an officer's investigation, he or she may not be punished under a broad statute aimed at speech.

ty for abuse, especially where a statute has received a virtually open-ended interpretation, is self-evident."

. . .

Houston's ordinance criminalizes a substantial amount of constitutionally protected speech, and accords the police unconstitutional discretion in enforcement. The ordinance's plain language is admittedly violated scores of times daily, yet only some individuals—those chosen by the police in their unguided discretion—are arrested. . . . We conclude that the ordinance is substantially overbroad, and that the Court of Appeals did not err in holding it facially invalid.

III

The City has also urged us not to reach the merits of Hill's constitutional challenge, but rather to abstain for reasons related to those underlying our decision in Railroad Comm'n v. Pullman Co., 312 U.S. 496 (1941). In its view, there are certain limiting constructions readily available to the state courts that would eliminate the ordinance's overbreadth.

. . . [W]e have been particularly reluctant to abstain in cases involving facial challenges based on the First Amendment. We have held that "abstention . . . is inappropriate for cases where . . . statutes are justifiably attacked on their face as abridging free expression." Dombrowski v. Pfister, 380 U.S. 479, 489–490 (1965). "In such cases to force the plaintiff who has commenced a federal action to suffer the delay of state-court proceedings might itself effect the impermissible chilling of the very constitutional right he seeks to protect." Zwickler v. Koota, 389 U.S. 241, 252 (1967).

Even if this case did not involve a facial challenge under the First Amendment, we would find abstention inappropriate. In cases involving a facial challenge to a statute, the pivotal question in determining whether abstention is appropriate is whether the statute is "fairly subject to an interpretation which will render unnecessary or substantially modify the federal constitutional question." Harman v. Forssenius, 380 U.S. 528, 534–535 (1965); . . .

This ordinance is not susceptible to a limiting construction because, as both courts below agreed, its language is plain and its meaning unambiguous. Its constitutionality cannot "turn upon a choice between one or several alternative meanings." Baggett v. Bullitt, 377 U.S. 360, 378 (1964); cf. Babbitt v. Farm Workers, 442 U.S. 289, 308 (1979). Nor can the ordinance be limited by severing discrete unconstitutional subsections from the rest. . . .

The City relies heavily on its claim that the state courts have not had an opportunity to construe the statute. Even if true, that factor would not in itself be controlling. . . . [W]hen a statute is not ambiguous, there is no need to abstain even if state courts have never interpreted the statute. . . . But in any event, the City's claim that state courts have not had an opportunity to construe the statute is misleading. Only the state *appellate* courts appear to have lacked this opportunity. It is undisputed that Houston's Municipal Courts, which have been courts of record in Texas since 1976, have had numerous opportunities to narrow the scope of the ordinance. There is no evidence that they have done so. In fact, the City's primary position throughout this litigation has been "to insist on the validity of the ordinance as literally read." We have long recognized that trial court interpretations, such as those given in jury instructions, constitute "a ruling on a question of state law that is as binding on us as though the precise words had been written into the ordinance." *Terminiello,* 337 U.S., at 4. Thus, where municipal courts have regularly applied an unambiguous statute, there is certainly no need for a federal court to abstain until state appellate courts have an opportunity to construe it.

. . .

IV

Today's decision reflects the constitutional requirement that, in the face of verbal challenges to police action, officers and municipalities must respond with restraint. We are mindful that the preservation of liberty depends in part upon the maintenance of social order. . . . But the First Amendment recognizes, wisely we think, that a certain amount of expressive disorder not only is inevitable in a society committed to individual freedom, but must itself be protected if that freedom would survive. We therefore affirm the judgment of the Court of Appeals.

It is so ordered.

Justice Blackmun, concurring.

I join the Court's opinion and its judgment except that I do not agree with any implication—if one exists—that Gooding v. Wilson, 405 U.S. 518 (1972), and Lewis v. City of New Orleans, 415 U.S. 130 (1974), are good law in the context of their facts, or that they lend any real support to the judgment under review in this case. . . .

Justice Scalia, concurring in the judgment.

For the reasons stated by Justice Powell in Part II of his opinion, I agree that abstention would not be appropriate in this case. Because I do not believe that the Houston ordinance is reasonably susceptible of a limiting construction that would avoid the constitutional question posed in this case, I agree with the Court that certification would also be inappropriate. On the merits, I agree with the views expressed by Justice Powell in Part III of his opinion. I therefore concur in the judgment and join Parts II and III of Justice Powell's opinion.

Justice Powell, with whom Justice O'Connor joins, and with whom The Chief Justice joins as to Parts I and II, and Justice Scalia joins as to Parts II and III, concurring in the judgment in part and dissenting in part.

. . . In my view, the Court should not have reached the merits of the constitutional claims, but instead should have certified a question to the Texas Court of Criminal Appeals. I also disagree with the Court's reasons for declining to abstain under the principle of Railroad

Comm'n v. Pullman Co., 312 U.S. 496 (1941). Finally, although I agree that the ordinance as interpreted by the Court violates the Fourteenth Amendment, I write separately because I cannot join the Court's reasoning.

I

. . .

The challenged ordinance does not contain an explicit intent requirement. . . . The Court apparently assumes that the requisite intent can be provided by a person's intent to utter words that constitute an interruption. But it would be plausible for the Texas Court of Criminal Appeals to construe the intent requirement differently. For example, that court could conclude that conviction under the ordinance requires proof that the person not only intended to speak, but also intended to interfere with the officer's performance of his duties.

This interpretation would change the constitutional questions in two ways: it would narrow substantially the scope of the ordinance, and possibly resolve the overbreadth question; it also would make the language of the ordinance more precise, and possibly satisfy the concern as to vagueness. At the least, such an interpretation would narrow the focus of the constitutional question and obviate the need for the Court's broad statements regarding First Amendment protections of speech directed at police officers. . . .

. . .

In my view, the ambiguity of the ordinance, coupled with the seriousness of invalidating a state law, requires that we ascertain what the ordinance means before we address appellee's constitutional claims. I therefore would vacate the judgment below and remand with instructions to certify the case to the Texas Court of Criminal Appeals, to allow it to interpret the intent requirement of this ordinance. Accordingly, I dissent.

The Court concludes, however, that the case properly is before us, and so I address the remaining issues presented.

II

. . . Although I agree with the Court that *Pullman* abstention is inappropriate in this case, I write separately because my reasons are somewhat different from those expressed by the Court.

. . .

. . . In sum, the late presentation of this claim, coupled with the doubts as to whether relief could be secured under Texas law, convinces me that *Pullman* abstention is inappropriate here.

III

I agree with the Court's conclusion that the ordinance violates the Fourteenth Amendment, but do not join the Court's reasoning.

A

. . . Lewis v. City of New Orleans, 415 U.S. 130 (1974), is clearly distinguishable. . . .

On its face, the New Orleans ordinance criminalizes only the use of language. . . . By contrast, the ordinance presented in this case could be applied to activity that involves no element of speech or communication. For example, the ordinance evidently would punish individuals who—without saying a single word—obstructed an officer's access to the scene of an ongoing public disturbance, or indeed the scene of a crime. Accordingly, I cannot agree with the Court that this ordinance punishes only speech.

I do agree that the ordinance can be applied to speech in some cases. And I also agree that the First Amendment protects a good deal of speech that may be directed at police officers. On occasion this may include verbal criticism, but I question the implication of the Court's opinion that the First Amendment generally protects verbal "challenges directed at police officers." A "challenge" often takes the form of opposition or interruption of performance of duty. In many situations, speech of this type directed at police officers will be functionally indistinguishable from conduct that the First Amendment clearly does not protect. For example, I have no doubt that a municipality constitutionally may punish an individual who chooses to stand near a police officer and persistently attempt to engage the officer in conversation while the officer is directing traffic at a busy intersection. Similarly, an individual, by contentious and abusive speech, could interrupt an officer's investigation of possible criminal conduct. A person observing an officer pursuing a person suspected of a felony could run beside him in a public street shouting at the officer. Similar tactics could interrupt a policeman lawfully attempting to interrogate persons believed to be witnesses to a crime.

In sum, the Court's opinion appears to reflect a failure to apprehend that this ordinance—however it may be construed—is intended primarily to further the public's interest in law enforcement. To be sure, there is a fine line between legitimate criticism of police and the type of criticism that interferes with the very purpose of having police officers. But the Court unfortunately seems to ignore this fine line and to extend First Amendment protection to any type of verbal molestation or interruption of an officer in the performance of his duty.

B

Despite the concerns expressed above, I nevertheless agree that the ambiguous terms of this ordinance "confer on police a virtually unrestrained power to arrest and charge persons with a violation. . . . The opportunity for abuse, especially where a statute has received a virtually open-ended interpretation, is self-evident." Lewis v. City of New Orleans, supra, at 135–136 (Powell, J., concurring in result). No Texas court has placed a limiting construction on the ordinance. Also, it is clear that Houston has made no effort to curtail the wide discretion of police officers under the present ordinance. The record contains a sampling of complaints filed under the ordinance in 1981 and 1982. People have been charged with such crimes as "Failure to remain silent and stationary," "Remaining," "Refusing to remain silent," and "Talking." Although some of these incidents may have involved unprotected conduct, the vagueness of these charges suggests that, with respect to this ordinance, Houston officials have not been acting with proper sensitivity to the constitutional rights of their citizens. When government protects society's interests in a manner that restricts some speech the law must be framed more precisely than the ordinance before us. Accordingly, I agree with the Court that the Houston ordinance is unconstitutional.

. . . In view of the difficulty of drafting precise language that never restrains speech and yet serves the public interest, the attempts of States and municipalities to draft laws of this type should be accorded some leeway. I am convinced, however, that the Houston ordinance is too vague to comport with the First and Fourteenth Amendments. . . . [I]t should be possible for the present ordinance to be reframed in a way that would limit the present broad discretion of officers and at the same time protect substantially the city's legitimate interests. For example, the ordinance could make clear that it applies to speech only if the purpose of the speech were to interfere with the performance by a police officer of his lawful duties. In this situation, the difficulties of drafting precisely should not justify upholding this ordinance.

. . .

Chief Justice Rehnquist, dissenting.

I join Parts I and II of Justice Powell's opinion concurring in the judgment in part and dissenting in part. I do not agree, however, that the Houston ordinance, in the absence of an authoritative construction by the Texas courts, is unconstitutional. . . .

D. REGULATION OF COMMERCIAL ADVERTISING

Pages 1159–1160. **Replace note on "Attorney Advertising":**

ATTORNEY ADVERTISING

Chief Justice Burger's attempt, in his concurrence, to distinguish prohibitions on professional advertising, proved to be unavailing. In Bates v. State Bar of Arizona, 433 U.S. 350 (1977), the Court held 5–4 that lawyers could not be prohibited from advertising the price of "routine legal services." In subsequent cases, a number of other lines have been drawn. The Court has distinguished between commercial solicitation and solicitation of legal employment by advocacy organizations. Ohralik v. Ohio State Bar Ass'n, 436 U.S. 447 (1978), sustained discipline of an attorney for personal solicitation of contingent fee employment, while In re Primus, 436 U.S. 412 (1978), reversed discipline of an ACLU lawyer. The Court noted that Primus' letter (offering legal assistance to a woman who had been sterilized as a condition of receiving welfare) came within the "generous zone of First Amendment protection reserved for associational freedom." The Court has also distinguished between in-person solicitation, involved in the *Ohralik* decision, and solicitation by advertisement and letter. In Zauderer v. Office of Disciplinary Counsel of the Supreme Court of Ohio, 471 U.S. 626 (1985), the Court struck down a categorical prohibition of attorney advertising containing information or advice about legal problems. In Shapero v. Kentucky State Bar, 108 S.Ct. 1916 (1988), the Court held that a state rule, prohibiting attorney mailings of advertisements "precipitated by a specific event . . . involving or relating to the addressee," was invalid. Both newspaper and direct mail advertising posed less risk of "overreaching or undue influence" than in-person solicitation.

The dissenters in *Bates* had argued that advertising of routine legal services was inherently misleading, and three Justices (Justice O'Connor, joined by Chief Justice Rehnquist and Justice Scalia) repeated that argument in *Shapero*. The Court has been divided on the question whether the contents of particular lawyer-advertisements were misleading. In *Zauderer*, a majority concluded that advertising a contingent fee was misleading because there was no disclosure that clients could be liable for significant litigation costs. In *Shapero*, a plurality concluded that a letter sent to persons against whom foreclosure suits had been filed could not be prohibited merely because it liberally used underscored, uppercase letters (e.g., "Call *NOW*, don't wait. . . . Remember it is *FREE* and there is *NO* charge for calling.") or contained subjective predictions of customer satisfaction (e.g., "It may surprise you what I may be able to do for you.")

Page 1169. Add at end of chapter:

DUN & BRADSTREET, INC. v. GREENMOSS
BUILDERS, INC.
472 U.S. 749, 105 S.Ct. 2939, 86 L.Ed.2d 593 (1985).

[The report in this case appears in this supplement, supra, p. 338.]

LOWE v. SECURITIES AND EXCHANGE COMMISSION, 472 U.S. 181 (1985). Lowe was president and principal shareholder of a corporation registered as an investment adviser under the Investment Advisers Act of 1940. He was convicted of various securities offenses, and the Securities and Exchange Commission revoked the corporation's registration, and ordered Lowe not to associate with any investment adviser. This action charged that Lowe violated the order by publishing semimonthly newsletters containing investment advice and commentary. Without reaching the question whether Lowe's publications were protected by the first amendment, the Court concluded that they fell within a statutory exclusion for "the publisher of any bona fide newspaper, news magazine, or business or financial publication of general and regular circulation."

Justice White, joined by Chief Justice Burger and Justice Rehnquist, concurred on the ground that to prevent Lowe's publication was inconsistent with the first amendment. Justice White stated that it was not necessary to decide whether Lowe's newsletters contained "fully protected speech" or commercial speech. Even if the newsletters were commercial speech, restraint on publication was not "narrowly tailored to advance a legitimate governmental interest." The government argued that, because of Lowe's past misconduct, there were reasons to fear that he would publish misleading or fraudulent advice, for which an appropriate remedy was to prevent him from publishing any advice. Justice White responded: "It cannot be plausibly maintained that investment advice from a person whose background indicates that he is unreliable is *inherently* misleading or deceptive, nor am I convinced that less drastic remedies than outright suppression (for example, application of the Act's antifraud provisions) are not available to achieve the government's asserted purpose of protecting investors. Accordingly, I would hold that the Act, as applied to prevent petitioner from publishing investment advice altogether, is too blunt an instrument to survive even the reduced level of scrutiny called for by restrictions on commercial speech."

SAN FRANCISCO ARTS & ATHLETICS, INC. v. UNITED STATES OLYMPIC COMMITTEE, 107 S.Ct. 2971 (1987). Section 110 of the Amateur Sports Act of 1978 grants the Committee the right to prohibit commercial and promotional uses of the word "Olympic." Lower federal courts granted the Committee an injunction against use of the term in connection with the proposed "Gay Olympic Games" in 1982. The Court affirmed, rejecting an argument that granting the Committee trademark rights in the term "Olympic" violated the first amendment. It was not necessary to decide whether it would be unconstitutional for Congress to grant a private entity exclusive rights in a "generic" word, because the commercial value of the word "Olympic" was the product of the Committee's talents and energy. Justice Brennan, joined by Justice Marshall in dissent, argued that the statute was overbroad because it created exclusive rights that restricted non-commercial speech (such as use of the term in promoting non-profit theatrical and athletic events), unlike conventional trademarks.

POSADAS de PUERTO RICO ASSOCIATES v. TOURISM COMPANY OF PUERTO RICO

478 U.S. 328, 106 S.Ct. 2968, 92 L.Ed.2d 266 (1986).

Justice Rehnquist delivered the opinion of the Court.

In this case we address the facial constitutionality of a Puerto Rico statute and regulations restricting advertising of casino gambling aimed at the residents of Puerto Rico. Appellant Posadas de Puerto Rico Associates, doing business in Puerto Rico as Condado Holiday Inn Hotel and Sands Casino, filed suit against appellee Tourism Company of Puerto Rico in the Superior Court of Puerto Rico, San Juan Section.

Appellant sought a declaratory judgment that the statute and regulations, both facially and as applied by the Tourism Company, impermissibly suppressed commercial speech in violation of the First Amendment and the equal protection and due process guarantees of the United States Constitution. The Superior Court held that the advertising restrictions had been unconstitutionally applied to appellant's past conduct. But the court adopted a narrowing construction of the statute and regulations and held that, based on such a construction, both were facially constitutional. The Supreme Court of Puerto Rico dismissed an appeal on the ground that it "did not present a substantial constitutional question." . . . We . . . affirm the decision of the Supreme Court of Puerto Rico with respect to the facial constitutionality of the advertising restrictions.

In 1948, the Puerto Rico Legislature legalized certain forms of casino gambling. The Games of Chance Act of 1948 . . ..

. . .

The Act also provided that "(n)o gambling room shall be permitted to advertise or otherwise offer their facilities to the public of Puerto Rico." Section 8, codified at P.R.Laws Ann., Tit. 15, section 77 (1972).

. . . Regulation 76a–1(7), as amended in 1971, provides in pertinent part:

"No concessionaire, nor his agent or employee is authorized to advertise the gambling parlors to the public in Puerto Rico. The advertising of our games of chance is hereby authorized through newspapers, magazines, radio, television and other publicity media outside Puerto Rico subject to the prior editing and approval by the Tourism Development Company of the advertisement to be submitted in draft to the Company." . . .

In 1975, appellant . . . obtained a franchise to operate a gambling casino and began doing business under the name Condado Holiday Inn Hotel and Sands Casino. In 1978, appellant was twice fined by the Tourism Company for violating the advertising restrictions in the Act and implementing regulations. Appellant protested the fines in a series of letters to the Tourism Company. On February 16, 1979, the Tourism Company issued to all casino franchise holders a memorandum setting forth the following interpretation of the advertising restrictions:

"This prohibition includes the use of the word 'casino', in matchbooks, lighters, envelopes, inter-office and/or external correspondence, invoices, napkins, brochures, menus, elevators, glasses, plates, lobbies, banners, flyers, paperholders, pencils, telephone books, directories, bulletin boards or in any hotel dependency or object which may be accessible to the public in Puerto Rico."

Pursuant to this administrative interpretation, the Tourism Company assessed additional fines against appellant. . . .

Appellant then filed a declaratory judgment action . . . seeking a declaration that the Act and implementing regulations, both facially and as applied by the Tourism Company, violated appellant's commercial speech rights under the United States Constitution. . . .

. . .

. . . [T]he court issued a narrowing construction of the statute, declaring that "the only advertisement prohibited by law originally is that which is contracted with an advertising agency, for consideration, to attract the resident to bet at the dice, card, roulette and bingo tables." The court also issued the following narrowing construction of Regulation 76a–1(7):

. . .

"We hereby allow, within the jurisdiction of Puerto Rico, advertising by the casinos addressed to tourists, provided they do not invite the residents of Puerto Rico to visit the casino, even though said announcements may incidentally reach the hands of a resident. . . . For example: an advertisement in the New York Times, an advertisement in CBS which reaches us through Cable TV, whose main objective is to reach the potential tourist."

. . .

Because this case involves the restriction of pure commercial speech which does "no more than propose a commercial transaction," Virginia Pharmacy Board v. Virginia Citizens Consumer Council, Inc., 425 U.S. 748, 762 (1976), our First Amendment analysis is guided by the general principles identified in Central Hudson Gas & Electric Corp. v. Public Service Comm'n, 447 U.S. 557 (1980). . . . Under *Central Hudson,* commercial speech receives a limited form of First Amendment protection so long as it concerns a lawful activity and is not misleading or fraudulent. Once it is determined that the First Amendment applies to the particular kind of commercial speech at issue, then the speech may be restricted only if the government's interest in doing so is substantial, the restrictions directly advance the government's asserted interest, and the restrictions are no more extensive than necessary to serve that interest. 447 U.S., at 566.

The particular kind of commercial speech at issue here, namely, advertising of casino gambling aimed at the residents of Puerto Rico, concerns a lawful activity and is not misleading or fraudulent, at least in the abstract. We must therefore proceed to the three remaining steps of the *Central Hudson* analysis in order to determine whether Puerto Rico's advertising restrictions run afoul of the First Amendment. The first of these three steps involves an assessment of the strength of the government's interest in restricting the speech. The interest at stake in this case, as determined by the Superior Court, is the reduction of demand for casino gambling by the residents of Puerto Rico. . . . These are some of the very same concerns, of course, that have motivated the vast majority of the 50 States to prohibit casino gambling. We have no difficulty in concluding that the Puerto Rico Legislature's interest in the health, safety, and welfare of its citizens constitutes a "substantial" governmental interest. . . .

The last two steps of the *Central Hudson* analysis basically involve a consideration of the "fit" between the legislature's ends and the means chosen to accomplish those ends. Step three asks the question whether the challenged restrictions on commercial speech "directly advance" the government's asserted interest. In the instant case, the answer to this question is clearly "yes." The Puerto Rico Legislature obviously believed, when it enacted the advertising restrictions at issue here, that advertising of casino gambling aimed at the residents of Puerto Rico would serve to increase the demand for the product advertised. We think the legislature's belief is a reasonable one . . . .

Appellant argues, however, that the challenged advertising restrictions are underinclusive because other kinds of gambling such as horse racing, cockfighting, and the lottery may be advertised to the residents of Puerto Rico. Appellant's argument is misplaced for two reasons. First, whether other kinds of gambling are advertised in Puerto Rico or not, the restrictions on advertising of casino gambling "directly advance" the legislature's interest in reducing demand for games of chance. . . . Second, the legislature's interest, as previously identified, is not necessarily to reduce demand for all games of chance, but to reduce demand for casino gambling. . . . In other words, the legislature felt that for Puerto Ricans the risks associated with casino gambling were significantly greater than those associated with the more traditional kinds of gambling in Puerto Rico. In our view, the legislature's separate classification of casino gambling, for purposes of the advertising ban, satisfies the third step of the *Central Hudson* analysis.

We also think it clear beyond peradventure that the challenged statute and regulations satisfy the fourth and last step of the *Central Hudson* analysis, namely, whether the restrictions on commercial speech are no more extensive than necessary to serve the government's interest. The narrowing constructions of the advertising restrictions announced by the Superior Court ensure that the restrictions will not affect advertising of casino gambling aimed at tourists, but will apply only to such advertising when aimed at the residents of Puerto Rico. . . . Appellant contends, however, that the First Amendment requires the Puerto Rico Legislature to reduce demand for casino gambling among the residents of Puerto Rico not by suppressing commercial speech that might *encourage* such gambling, but by promulgating additional speech designed to *discourage* it. We reject this contention. We think it is up to the legislature to decide whether or not such a "counterspeech" policy would be as effective in reducing the demand for casino gambling as a restriction on advertising. The legislature could conclude, as it apparently did here, that residents of Puerto Rico are already aware of the risks of casino gambling, yet would nevertheless be induced by widespread advertising to engage in such potentially harmful conduct. Cf. . . . Dunagin v. City of Oxford, Miss., 718 F.2d 738, 751 (CA5 1983) (en banc) ("We do not believe that a less restrictive time, place and manner restriction, such as a disclaimer warning of the dangers of alcohol, would be effective. The state's concern is not that the public is unaware of the dangers of alcohol . . . . The concern instead is that advertising will unduly promote alcohol consumption despite known dangers"), cert. denied, 467 U.S. 1259 (1984).

In short, we conclude that the statute and regulations at issue in this case, as construed by the Superior Court, pass muster under each prong of the *Central Hudson* test. We therefore hold that the Supreme

Court of Puerto Rico properly rejected appellant's First Amendment claim.[9]

Appellant argues, however, that the challenged advertising restrictions are constitutionally defective under our decisions in Carey v. Population Services Int'l, 431 U.S. 678 (1977), and Bigelow v. Virginia, 421 U.S. 809 (1975). In *Carey*, this Court struck down a ban on any "advertisement or display" of contraceptives, 431 U.S., at 700–702, and in *Bigelow*, we reversed a criminal conviction based on the advertisement of an abortion clinic. We think appellant's argument ignores a crucial distinction between the *Carey* and *Bigelow* decisions and the instant case. In *Carey* and *Bigelow*, the underlying conduct that was the subject of the advertising restrictions was constitutionally protected and could not have been prohibited by the State. Here, on the other hand, the Puerto Rico Legislature surely could have prohibited casino gambling by the residents of Puerto Rico altogether. In our view, the greater power to completely ban casino gambling necessarily includes the lesser power to ban advertising of casino gambling, and *Carey* and *Bigelow* are hence inapposite.

Appellant also makes the related argument that, having chosen to legalize casino gambling for residents of Puerto Rico, the First Amendment prohibits the legislature from using restrictions on advertising to accomplish its goal of reducing demand for such gambling. We disagree. In our view, appellant has the argument backwards. As we noted in the preceding paragraph, it is precisely *because* the government could have enacted a wholesale prohibition of the underlying conduct that it is permissible for the government to take the less intrusive step of allowing the conduct, but reducing the demand through restrictions on advertising. It would surely be a Pyrrhic victory for casino owners such as appellant to gain recognition of a First Amendment right to advertise their casinos to the residents of Puerto Rico, only to thereby force the legislature into banning casino gambling by residents altogether. It would just as surely be a strange constitutional doctrine which would concede to the legislature the authority to totally ban a product or activity, but deny to the legislature the authority to forbid the stimulation of demand for the product or activity through advertising on behalf of those who would profit from such increased demand. Legislative regulation of products or activities deemed harmful, such as cigarettes, alcoholic beverages, and prostitu-

---

[9] It should be apparent from our discussion of the First Amendment issue, and particularly the third and fourth prongs of the *Central Hudson* test, that appellant can fare no better under the equal protection guarantee of the Constitution. . . . If there is a sufficient "fit" between the legislature's means and ends to satisfy the concerns of the First Amendment, the same "fit" is surely adequate under the applicable "rational basis" equal protection analysis. . . . Justice Stevens, in dissent, asserts the additional equal protection claim, not raised by appellant either below or in this Court, that the Puerto Rico statute and regulations impermissibly discriminate between different kinds of publications. . . . Of course, the likelihood that a casino advertisement appearing in the New York Times will be primarily addressed to tourists, and not Puerto Rico residents, is far greater than would be the case for a similar advertisement appearing in the San Juan Star. But it is simply the demographics of the two newspapers' readerships, and not any form of "discrimination" on the part of the Puerto Rico Legislature or the Superior Court, which produces this result.

tion, has varied from outright prohibition on the one hand, . . . to legalization of the product or activity with restrictions on stimulation of its demand on the other hand . . . . To rule out the latter, intermediate kind of response would require more than we find in the First Amendment.

. . .

For the foregoing reasons, the decision of the Supreme Court of Puerto Rico that, as construed by the Superior Court, section 8 of the Games of Chance Act of 1948 and the implementing regulations do not facially violate the First Amendment or the due process or equal protection guarantees of the Constitution, is affirmed.[11]

It is so ordered.

Justice Brennan, with whom Justice Marshall and Justice Blackmun join, dissenting.

. . .

I

. . .

I see no reason why commercial speech should be afforded less protection than other types of speech where, as here, the government seeks to suppress commercial speech in order to deprive consumers of accurate information concerning lawful activity. . . . [N]o differences between commercial and other kinds of speech justify protecting commercial speech less extensively where, as here, the government seeks to manipulate private behavior by depriving citizens of truthful information concerning lawful activities.

. . .

. . . I believe that where the government seeks to suppress the dissemination of nonmisleading commercial speech relating to legal activities, for fear that recipients will act on the information provided, such regulation should be subject to strict judicial scrutiny.

II

The Court, rather than applying strict scrutiny, evalutes Puerto Rico's advertising ban under the relaxed standards normally used to test government regulation of commercial speech. Even under these standards, however, I do not believe that Puerto Rico constitutionally may suppress all casino advertising directed to its residents. . . .

---

[11] Justice Stevens claims that the Superior Court's narrowing construction creates an impermissible "prior restraint" on protected speech, because that court required the submission of certain casino advertising to appellee for its prior approval. This argument was not raised by appellant either below or in this Court, and we therefore express no view on the constitutionality of the particular portion of the Superior Court's narrowing construction cited by Justice Stevens.

A

The Court asserts that the Commonwealth has a legitimate and substantial interest in discouraging its residents from engaging in casino gambling. . . . Puerto Rico has legalized gambling casinos, and permits its residents to patronize them. Thus, the Puerto Rico legislature has determined that permitting residents to engage in casino gambling will not produce the "serious harmful effects" that have led a majority of States to ban such activity. . . .

The Court nevertheless sustains Puerto Rico's advertising ban because the legislature could have determined that casino gambling would seriously harm the health, safety, and welfare of the Puerto Rican citizens. This reasoning is contrary to this Court's long established First Amendment jurisprudence. When the government seeks to place restrictions upon commercial speech, a court may not, as the Court implies today, simply speculate about valid reasons that the government might have for enacting such restrictions. . . . In this case, appellee has not shown that "serious harmful effects" will result if Puerto Rico residents gamble in casinos, and the legislature's decision to legalize such activity suggests that it believed the opposite to be true. In short, appellees have failed to show that a substantial government interest supports Puerto Rico's ban on protected expression.

B

. . . [E]ven assuming that an advertising ban would effectively reduce residents' patronage of gambling casinos, it is not clear how it would directly advance Puerto Rico's interest in controlling the "serious harmful effects" the Court associates with casino gambling. In particular, it is unclear whether banning casino advertising aimed at residents would affect local crime, prostitution, the development of corruption, or the infiltration of organized crime. Because Puerto Rico actively promotes its casinos to tourists, these problems are likely to persist whether or not residents are also encouraged to gamble. Absent some showing that a ban on advertising aimed only at residents will directly advance Puerto Rico's interest in controlling the harmful effects allegedly associated with casino gambling, Puerto Rico may not constitutionally restrict protected expression in that way.

C

Finally, appellee has failed to show that Puerto Rico's interest in controlling the harmful effects allegedly associated with casino gambling "cannot be protected adequately by more limited regulation of appellant's commercial expression." *Central Hudson*, supra, at 570. Rather than suppressing constitutionally protected expression, Puerto Rico could seek directly to address the specific harms thought to be associated with casino gambling. . . .

The Court fails even to acknowledge the wide range of effective alternatives available to Puerto Rico, and addresses only appellant's claim that Puerto Rico's legislature might choose to reduce the demand for casino gambling among residents by "promulgating additional speech designed to discourage it." The Court rejects this alternative, asserting that "it is up to the legislature to decide whether or not such a 'counterspeech' policy would be as effective in reducing the demand for casino gambling as a restriction on advertising." This reasoning ignores the commands of the First Amendment. Where the government seeks to restrict speech in order to advance an important interest, it is not, contrary to what the Court has stated, "up to the legislature" to decide whether or not the government's interest might be protected adequately by less intrusive measures. Rather, it is incumbent upon the government to prove that more limited means are not sufficient to protect its interests, and for a *court* to decide whether or not the government has sustained this burden. . . . In this case, nothing suggests that the Puerto Rico Legislature ever considered the efficacy of measures other than suppressing protected expression. More importantly, there has been no showing that alternative measures would inadequately safeguard the Commonwealth's interest in controlling the harmful effects allegedly associated with casino gambling. Under these circumstances, Puerto Rico's ban on advertising clearly violates the First Amendment.[6]

 . . . I would hold that Puerto Rico may not suppress the dissemination of truthful information about entirely lawful activity merely to keep its residents ignorant. The Court, however, would allow Puerto Rico to do just that, thus dramatically shrinking the scope of First Amendment protection available to commercial speech, and giving government officials unprecedented authority to eviscerate constitutionally protected expression. I respectfully dissent.

Justice Stevens, with whom Justice Marshall and Justice Blackmun join, dissenting.

The Court concludes that "the greater power to completely ban casino gambling necessarily includes the lesser power to ban advertising of casino gambling." Whether a State may ban all advertising of an activity that it permits but could prohibit—such as gambling, prostitution, or the consumption of marijuana or liquor—is an elegant question of constitutional law. It is not, however, appropriate to address that question in this case because Puerto Rico's rather bizarre restraints on speech are so plainly forbidden by the First Amendment.

Puerto Rico does not simply "ban advertising of casino gambling." Rather, Puerto Rico blatantly discriminates in its punishment of speech depending on the publication, audience, and words employed. Moreover, the prohibitions, as now construed by the Puerto Rico courts, establish a regime of prior restraint . . . .

    . . .

---

[6] The Court seeks to buttress its holding by noting that some States have regulated other "harmful" products, such as cigarettes, alcoholic beverages, and legalized prostitution, by restricting advertising. While I believe that Puerto Rico may not prohibit all casino advertising directed to its residents, I reserve judgment as to the constitutionality of the variety of advertising restrictions adopted by other jurisdictions.

Chapter 15

RESTRICTIONS ON TIME, PLACE, OR MANNER OF EXPRESSION

SECTION 2. THE TRADITIONAL PUBLIC FORUM: SPEECH ACTIVITIES IN STREETS AND PARKS

A. THE CONSIDERATIONS JUSTIFYING DENIAL OF THE USE OF STREETS AND PARKS FOR SPEECH ACTIVITIES

Pages 1178–1181. Replace Kovacs v. Cooper, Cox I, Cox II, United States v. Grace and Grayned v. Rockford with the following:

FRISBY v. SCHULTZ

___ U.S. ___, 108 S.Ct. 2495, ___ L.Ed.2d ___ (1988).

Justice O'Connor delivered the opinion of the Court.

Brookfield, Wisconsin, has adopted an ordinance that completely bans picketing "before or about" any residence. This case presents a facial First Amendment challenge to that ordinance.

I

Brookfield, Wisconsin, is a residential suburb of Milwaukee with a population of approximately 4,300. The appellees, Sandra C. Schultz and Robert C. Braun, are individuals strongly opposed to abortion and wish to express their views on the subject by picketing on a public street outside the Brookfield residence of a doctor who apparently performs abortions at two clinics in neighboring towns. Appellees and others engaged in precisely that activity, assembling outside the doctor's home on at least six occasions between April 20, 1985, and May 20, 1985, for periods ranging from one to one and a half hours. The size of the group varied from 11 to more than 40. The picketing was generally orderly and peaceful; the town never had occasion to invoke any of its various ordinances prohibiting obstruction of the streets, loud and unnecessary noises, or disorderly conduct. Nonetheless, the picketing generated substantial controversy and numerous complaints.

The town Board therefore resolved to enact an ordinance to restrict the picketing. On May 7, 1985, the town passed an ordinance that prohibited all picketing in residential neighborhoods except for labor picketing. But after reviewing this Court's decision in Carey v. Brown, 447 U.S. 455 (1980), which invalidated a similar ordinance as a violation of the Equal Protection Clause, the town attorney instructed the police not to enforce the new ordinance and advised the town Board that the ordinance's labor picketing exception likely rendered it unconstitutional. This ordinance was repealed on May 15, 1985, and replaced with the following flat ban on all residential picketing:

> "It is unlawful for any person to engage in picketing before or about the residence or dwelling of any individual in the Town of Brookfield."

The ordinance itself recites the primary purpose of this ban: "the protection and preservation of the home" through assurance "that members of the community enjoy in their homes and dwellings a feeling of well-being, tranquility, and privacy." The town Board believed that a ban was necessary because it determined that "the practice of picketing before or about residences and dwellings causes emotional disturbance and distress to the occupants . . . [and] has as its object the harrassing of such occupants." The ordinance also evinces a concern for public safety, noting that picketing obstructs and interferes with "the free use of public sidewalks and public ways of travel."

. . . [A]ppellees ceased picketing in Brookfield and filed this lawsuit in United States District Court for the Eastern District of Wisconsin . . . [seeking] . . . declaratory as well as preliminary and permanent injunctive relief on the grounds that the ordinance violated the First Amendment. . . .

The District Court granted appellees' motion for a preliminary injunction[, specifying] that unless the appellants requested a trial on the merits within 60 days or appealed, the preliminary injunction would become permanent. . . .

A divided panel of the United States Court of Appeals for the Seventh Circuit affirmed. . . .

. . .

II

The antipicketing ordinance operates at the core of the First Amendment by prohibiting appellees from engaging in picketing on an issue of public concern. Because of the importance of "uninhibited, robust, and wide-open" debate on public issues, New York Times Co. v. Sullivan, 376 U.S. 254, 270 (1964), we have traditionally subjected restrictions on public issue picketing to careful scrutiny. See e.g., Boos v. Barry, 485 U.S. ___, ___ (1988); United States v. Grace, 461 U.S. 171 (1983); Carey v. Brown, 447 U.S. 455 (1980). Of course, "[e]ven protected speech is not equally permissible in all places and at all times." Cornelius v. NAACP Legal Defense and Educational Fund, Inc., 473 U.S. 788, 799 (1985).

To ascertain what limits, if any, may be placed on protected speech, we have often focused on the "place" of that speech, considering the nature of the forum the speaker seeks to employ. Our cases have recognized that the standards by which limitations on speech must be evaluated "differ depending on the character of the property at issue." Perry Education Assn. v. Perry Local Educators' Assn., 460 U.S. 37, 44 (1983). Specifically, we have identified three types of fora: "the traditional public forum, the public forum created by government designation, and the nonpublic forum." *Cornelius*, supra, at 802.

The relevant forum here may be easily identified: appellees wish to picket on the public streets of Brookfield. Ordinarily, a determination of the nature of the forum would follow automatically from this identification; we have repeatedly referred to public streets as the archetype of a traditional public forum. . . . "[T]ime out of mind" public streets and sidewalks have been used for public assembly and debate, the hallmarks of a traditional public forum. . . . Hague v. CIO, 307 U.S. 496, 515 (1939) (Roberts, J.). Appellants, however, urge us to disregard these "cliches." They argue that the streets of Brookfield should be considered a nonpublic forum. Pointing to the physical narrowness of Brookfield's streets as well as to their residential character, appellants contend that such streets have not by tradition or designation been held open for public communication.

We reject this suggestion. Our prior holdings make clear that a public street does not lose its status as a traditional public forum simply because it runs through a residential neighborhood. In Carey v. Brown—which considered a statute similar to the one at issue here, ultimately striking it down as a violation of the Equal Protection Clause because it included an exception for labor picketing—we expressly recognized that "public streets and sidewalks in residential neighborhoods," were "public for[a]." 447 U.S., at 460–461. This rather ready identification virtually forecloses appellants' argument. See also *Perry*, supra, at 54–55 (noting that the "key" to *Carey* "was the presence of a public forum").

In short, our decisions identifying public streets and sidewalks as traditional public fora are not accidental invocations of a "cliche," but recognition that "[w]herever the title of streets and parks may rest, they have immemorially been held in trust for the use of the public." Hague v. CIO, supra, at 515 (Roberts, J.). No particularized inquiry into the precise nature of a specific street is necessary; all public streets are held in the public trust and are properly considered traditional public fora. Accordingly, the streets of Brookfield are traditional public fora. The residential character of those streets may well inform the application of the relevant test, but it does not lead to a different test; the antipicketing ordinance must be judged against the stringent standards we have established for restrictions on speech in traditional public fora:

"In these quintessential public for[a], the government may not prohibit all communicative activity. For the State to enforce a content-based exclusion it must show that its reglation is necessary to serve a compelling state interest and that it is narrowly drawn to achieve that end. . . . The State may also enforce regulations of the time, place, and manner of expression which are content-neutral, are narrowly tailored to serve a significant government interest, and leave open ample alternative channels of communication." *Perry*, 460 U.S., at 45 (citations omitted).

As *Perry* makes clear, the appropriate level of scrutiny is initially tied to whether the statute distinguishes between prohibited and permitted speech on the basis of content. . . . [W]e accept the lower courts' conclusion that the Brookfield ordinance is content-neutral. Accordingly, we turn to consider whether the ordinance is "narrowly tailored to serve a significant government interest" and whether it "leave[s] open ample alternative channels of communication." *Perry*, 460 U.S., at 45.

Because the last question is so easily answered, we address it first. Of course, before we are able to assess the available alternatives, we must consider more carefully the reach of the ordinance. The precise scope of the ban is not further described within the text of the ordinance, but in our view the ordinance is readily subject to a narrowing construction that avoids constitutional difficulties. . . . To the extent they endorsed a broad reading of the ordinance, the lower courts ran afoul of the well-established principle that statutes will be interpreted to avoid constitutional difficulties. . . . Thus, . . . we are unable to accept their potentially broader view of the ordinance's scope. We instead construe the ordinance more narrowly. This narrow reading is supported by the representations of counsel for the town at oral argument, which indicate that the town takes, and will enforce, a limited view of the "picketing" proscribed by the ordinance. Thus, generally speaking, "picketing would be having the picket proceed on a definite course or route in front of a home." The picket need not be carrying a sign, but in order to fall within the scope of the ordinance the picketing must be directed at a single residence. General marching through residential neighborhoods, or even walking a route in front of an entire block of houses, is not prohibited by this ordinance. Accordingly, we construe the ban to be a limited one; only focused picketing taking place solely in front of a particular residence is prohibited.

So narrowed, the ordinance permits the more general dissemination of a message. As appellants explain, the limited nature of the prohibition makes it virtually self-evident that ample alternatives remain:

> "Protestors have not been barred from the residential neighborhoods. They may enter such neighborhoods, alone or in groups, even marching. . . . They may go door-to-door to proselytize their views. They may distribute literature in this manner . . . or through the mails. They may contact residents by telephone, short of harassment."

We readily agree that the ordinance preserves ample alternative channels of communication and thus move on to inquire whether the ordinance serves a significant government interest. We find that such an interest is identified within the text of the ordinance itself: the protection of residential privacy.

"The State's interest in protecting the well-being, tranquility, and privacy of the home is certainly of the highest order in a free and civilized society." Carey v. Brown, 447 U.S., at 471. Our prior decisions have often remarked on the unique nature of the home, "the last citadel of the tired, the weary, and the sick," Gregory v. Chicago, 394 U.S. 111, 125 (1969) (Black J., concurring), and have recognized that "[p]reserving the sanctity of the home, the one retreat to which men and women can repair to escape from the tribulations of their daily pursuits, is surely an important value." *Carey*, supra, at 471.

One important aspect of residential privacy is protection of the unwilling listener. Although in many locations, we expect individuals simply to avoid speech they do not want to hear, cf. Erznoznik v. Jacksonville, supra, at 210–211; Cohen v. California, 403 U.S. 15, 21–22 (1971), the home is different. "That we are often 'captives' outside the sanctuary of the home and subject to objectionable speech . . . does not mean we must be captives everywhere." Rowan v. Post Office Dept., 397 U.S. 728, 738 (1970). Instead, a special benefit of the privacy all citizens enjoy within their own walls, which the State may legislate to protect, is an ability to avoid intrusions. Thus, we have repeatedly held that individuals are not required to welcome unwanted speech into their own homes and that the government may protect this freedom. See, e.g., FCC v. Pacifica Foundation, 438 U.S. 726, 748–749 (1978) (offensive radio broadcasts); id., at 759–760 (Powell, J., concurring in part and concurring in judgment) (same); *Rowan*, supra (offensive mailings); Kovacs v. Cooper, 336 U.S. 77, 86–87 (1949) (sound trucks).

This principle is reflected even in prior decisions in which we have invalidated complete bans on expressive activity, including bans operating in residential areas. See, e.g., Schneider v. State, 308 U.S. 147, 162–163 (1939) (handbilling); Martin v. Struthers, 319 U.S. 141 (1943) (door-to-door solicitation). In all such cases, we have been careful to acknowledge that unwilling listeners may be protected when within their own homes. In *Schneider*, for example, in striking down a complete ban on handbilling, we spoke of a right to distribute literature only "to one willing to receive it." Similarly, when we invalidated a ban on door-to-door solicitation in *Martin*, we did so on the basis that the "home owner could protect himself from such intrusion by an appropriate sign 'that he is unwilling to be disturbed.' " *Kovacs*, supra, at 86. We have "never intimated that the visitor could insert a foot in the door and insist on a hearing." Ibid. There simply is no right to force speech into the home of an unwilling listener.

It remains to be considered, however, whether the Brookfield ordinance is narrowly tailored to protect only unwilling recipients of the communications. A statute is narrowly tailored if it targets and eliminates no more than the exact source of the "evil" it seeks to remedy. . . .

. . . The type of focused picketing prohibited by the Brookfield ordinance is fundamentally different from more generally directed means of communication that may not be completely banned in residential areas. See, e.g., *Schneider*, supra, at 162–163 (handbilling); *Martin*, supra (solicitation); Murdock v. Pennsylvania, 319 U.S. 105 (1943) (solicitation). See also Gregory v. Chicago, supra (marching). Cf. *Perry*, 460 U.S., at 45 (in traditional public forum, "the government may not prohibit all communicative activity"). In such cases "the flow of information [is not] into . . . household[s], but to the public." Organization for a Better Austin v. Keefe, 402 U.S. 415, 420 (1971). Here, in contrast, the picketing is narrowly directed at the household, not the public. The type of picketers banned by the Brookfield ordinance generally do not seek to disseminate a message to the general public, but to intrude upon the targeted resident, and to do so in an especially offensive way. Moreover, even if some such picketers have a broader communicative purpose, their activity nonetheless inherently and offensively intrudes on residential privacy. The devastating effect of targeted picketing on the quiet enjoyment of the home is beyond doubt. . . .

In this case, for example, appellees subjected the doctor and his family to the presence of a relatively large group of protestors on their doorstep in an attempt to force the doctor to cease performing abortions. But the actual size of the group is irrelevant; even a solitary picket can invade residential privacy. . . . The offensive and disturbing nature of the form of the communication banned by the Brookfield ordinance thus can scarely be questioned. . . .

The First Amendment permits the government to prohibit offensive speech as intrusive when the "captive" audience cannot avoid the objectionable speech. See Consolidated Edison Co. v. Public Service Comm'n of New York, 447 U.S. 530, 542 (1980). Cf. Bolger v. Youngs Drug Products Corp., supra, at 72. The target of the focused picketing banned by the Brookfield ordinance is just such a "captive." The resident is figuratively, and perhaps literally, trapped within the home, and because of the unique and subtle impact of such picketing is left with no ready means of avoiding the unwanted speech. Cf. Cohen v. California, 403 U.S., at 21–22 (noting ease of avoiding unwanted speech in other circumstances). . . . Accordingly, the Brookfield ordinance's complete ban of that particular medium of expression is narrowly tailored.

Of course, this case presents only a facial challenge to the ordinance. Particular hypothetical applications of the ordinance—to, for example, a particular resident's use of his or her home as a place of business or public meeting, or to picketers present at a particular home by invitation of the resident—may present somewhat different questions. Initially, the ordinance by its own terms may not apply in such circumstances, since the ordinance's goal is the protection of residential privacy, and since it speaks only of a "residence or dwelling," not a place of business. Cf. *Carey,* supra, at 457 (quoting an antipicketing ordinance expressly rendered inapplicable by use of home as a place of business or to hold a public meeting). Moreover, since our First Amendment analysis is grounded in protection of the unwilling residential listener, the constitutionality of applying the ordinance to such hypotheticals remains open to question. These are, however, questions we need not address today in order to dispose of appellees' facial challenge.

Because the picketing prohibited by the Brookfield ordinance is speech directed primarily at those who are presumptively unwilling to receive it, the State has a substantial and justifiable interest in banning it. The nature and scope of this interest make the ban narrowly tailored. The ordinance also leaves open ample alternative channels of communication and is content-neutral. Thus, largely because of its narrow scope, the facial challenge to the ordinance must fail. The contrary judgment of the Court of Appeals is

Reversed.

Justice White, concurring in the judgment.

I agree with the Court that an ordinance which only forbade picketing before a single residence would not be unconstitutional on its face. . . . I am convinced, absent more than this record indicates, that if some single-residence picketing by smaller groups could not be forbidden, the range of possibly unconstitutional application of such an ordinance would not render it substantially overbroad and thus unconstitutional on its face.

This leaves the question, however, of whether the ordinance at issue in this case forbids only single-residence picketing. . . .

. . . In my view, if the ordinance were construed to forbid all picketing in residential neighborhoods, the overbreath doctrine would render it unconstitutional on its face and hence prohibit its enforcement against those, like appellees, who engage in single-residence picketing. At least this would be the case until the ordinance is limited in some authoritative manner. Because the representations made in this Court by the Town's legal officer create sufficient doubts in my mind, however, as to how the ordinance will be enforced by the Town or construed by the state courts, I would put aside the overbreadth approach here, sustain the ordinance as applied in this case, which the Court at least does, and await further developments.

Justice Brennan, with whom Justice Marshall joins, dissenting.

The Court today sets out the appropriate legal tests and standards governing the question presented, and proceeds to apply most of them correctly. Regrettably, though, the Court errs in the final step of its analysis, and approves an ordinance banning significantly more speech than is necessary to achieve the government's substantial and legitimate goal. Accordingly, I must dissent.

. . .

Without question there are many aspects of residential picketing that, if unregulated, might easily become intrusive or unduly coercive. Indeed, some of these aspects are illustrated by this very case. As the District Court found, before the ordinance took effect up to 40 sign-carrying, slogan-shouting protestors regularly converged on Dr. Victoria's home and, in addition to protesting, warned young children not to go near the house because Dr. Victoria was a "baby killer." Further, the throng repeatedly trespassed onto the Victorias' property and at least once blocked the exists to their home. Surely it is within the government's power to enact regulations as necessary to prevent such intrusive and coercive abuses. Thus, for example, the government could constitutionally regulate the number of residential picketers, the hours during which a residential picket may take place, or the noise level of such a picket. In short, substantial regulation is permitted to neutralize the intrusive or unduly coercive aspects of picketing around the home. But to say that picketing may be substantially regulated is not to say that it may be prohibited in its entirety. Once size, time, volume, and the like have been controlled to ensure that the picket is no longer intrusive or coercive, only the speech itself remains, conveyed perhaps by a lone, silent individual, walking back and forth with a sign. . . . Such speech, which no longer implicates the heightened governmental interest in residential privacy, is nevertheless banned by the Brookfield law. Therefore, the ordinance is not narrowly tailored.

.   .   .

Justice Stevens, dissenting.

.   .   .

I do not believe we advance the inquiry by rejecting . . . the . . . argument that residential streets are something less than public fora. . . . The streets in a residential neighborhood that has no sidewalks are quite obviously a different type of forum than a stadium or a public park. Attaching the label "public forum" to the area in front of a single family dwelling does not help us decide whether the town's interest in the safe and efficient flow of traffic or its interest in protecting the privacy of its citizens justifies denying picketers the right to march up and down the streets at will.

.   .   .

In this case the overbreadth is unquestionably "real." Whether or not it is "substantial" in relation to the "plainly legitimate sweep" of the ordinance is a more difficult question. My hunch is that the town will probably not enforce its ban against friendly, innocuous, or even brief unfriendly picketing, and that the Court may be right in concluding that its legitimate sweep makes its overbreadth insubstantial. But there are two countervailing considerations that are persuasive to me. The scope of the ordinance gives the town officials far too much discretion in making enforcement decisions; while we sit by and await further developments, potential picketers must act at their peril. Second, it is a simple matter for the town to amend its ordinance and to limit the ban to conduct that unreasonably interferes with the privacy of the home and does not serve a reasonable communicative purpose. Accordingly, I respectfully dissent.

BOOS v. BARRY
___ U.S. ___, 108 S.Ct. 1157, 99 L.Ed.2d 333 (1988).

Justice O'Connor delivered the opinion of the Court, except as to Part II-A.

The question presented in this case is whether a provision of the District of Columbia Code, section 22–1115, violates the First Amendment. This section prohibits the display of any sign within 500 feet of a foreign embassy if that sign tends to bring that foreign government into "public odium" or "public disrepute." It also prohibits any congregation of three or more persons within 500 feet of a foreign embassy.

I

Petitioners are three individuals who wish to carry signs critical of the Governments of the Soviet Union and Nicaragua on the public sidewalks within 500 feet of the embassies of those Governments in Washington, D. C. Petitioners Bridget M. Brooker and Michael Boos, for example, wish to display signs stating "RELEASE SAKHAROV" and "SOLIDARITY" in front of the Soviet Embassy. Petitioner J. Michael Waller wishes to display a sign reading "STOP THE KILLING" within 500 feet of the Nicaraguan Embassy. All of the petitioners also wish to congregate with two or more other persons within 500 feet of official foreign buildings.

Asserting that D.C.Code section 22–1115 (1981) prohibited them from engaging in these expressive activities, petitioners, together with respondent Father R. David Finzer, brought a facial First Amendment challenge to that provision in the District Court for the District of Columbia. They named the respondents, the Mayor and certain other law enforcement officials of the District of Columbia, as defendants. The United States intervened as amicus curiae supporting the constitutionality of the statute.

Congress enacted section 22–1115 in 1938, S.J. Res. 191, ch. 29, section 1, 52 Stat. 30 (1938), pursuant to its authority under Article 1, section 8, Cl. 10 of the Constitution to "define and punish . . . Offenses against the Law of Nations." Section 22–1115 reads in pertinent part as follows:

> "It shall be unlawful to display any flag, banner, placard, or device designed or adapted to intimidate, coerce, or bring into public odium any foreign government, party, or organization, or any officer or officers thereof, or to bring into public disrepute political, social, or economic acts, views, or purposes of any foreign government, party or organization . . . within 500 feet of any building or premises within the District of Columbia used or occupied by any foreign government or its representative or representatives as an embassy, legation, consulate, or for other official purposes . . . or to congregate within 500 feet of any such building or premises, and refuse to disperse after having been ordered so to do by the police authorities of said District."

The first portion of this statute, the "display" clause, applies to signs tending to bring a foreign government into public odium or public disrepute, such as signs critical of a foreign government or its policies. The display clause applies only to the display of signs, not to the spoken word. . . . The second portion of the statute, the "congregation" clause, addresses a different concern. It prohibits congregation, which District of Columbia common law defines as an assemblage of three or more people. . . . Both of these prohibitions generally operate within a 500 foot zone surrounding embassies or consulates owned by foreign governments, but the statute also can extend to other buildings if foreign officials are inside for some official purpose.

The District Court granted respondents' motion for summary judgment . . . A divided panel of the Court of Appeals for the District of Columbia affirmed. Finzer v. Barry, 255 U.S.App.D.C. 19, 798 F.2d 1450 (1986). . . .

The Court of Appeals considered the two aspects of section 22–1115 separately. First, the court concluded that the display clause was a content-based restriction on speech. . . . [T]he court nonetheless found it constitutional because it was justified by a compelling governmental interest and was narrowly drawn to serve that interest. Second, the Court of Appeals concluded that the congregation clause should be construed to authorize an order to disperse "only when the police reasonably believe that a threat to the security or peace of the embassy is present," and that as construed, the congregation clause survived First Amendment scrutiny.

We . . . reverse the Court of Appeals' conclusion as to the display clause, but affirm as to the congregation clause.

II

A

Analysis of the display clause must begin with several important features of that provision. First, the display clause operates at the core of the First Amendment by prohibiting petitioners from engaging in classically political speech. We have recognized that the First Amendment reflects a "profound national commitment" to the principle that "debate on public issues should be uninhibited, robust, and wide-open," New York Times Co. v. Sullivan, 376 U.S. 254, 270 (1964), and have consistently commented on the central importance of protecting speech on public issues. See, e.g., Connick v. Myers, 461 U.S. 138, 145 (1983); NAACP v. Claiborne Hardware Co., 458 U.S. 886, 913 (1982); Carey v. Brown, supra, at 467. This has led us to scrutinize carefully any restrictions on public issue picketing. See, e.g., United States v. Grace, 461 U.S. 171 (1983); Carey v. Brown, supra; Police Department of Chicago v. Mosley, 408 U.S. 92 (1972).

Second, the display clause bars such speech on public streets and sidewalks, traditional public fora that "time out of mind, have been used for purposes of assembly, communicating thoughts between citizens, and discussing public questions." Hague v. CIO, 307 U.S. 496, 515 (1939) (Roberts, J.). In such places, which occupy a "special position in terms of First Amendment protection," United States v. Grace, 461 U.S., at 180, the government's ability to restrict expressive activity "is very limited." Id., at 177.

Third, section 22–1115 is content-based. Whether individuals may picket in front of a foreign embassy depends entirely upon whether their picket signs are critical of the foreign government or not. One category of speech has been completely prohibited within 500 feet of embassies. Other categories of speech, however, such as favorable speech about a foreign government or speech concerning a labor dispute with a foreign government, are permitted. See D.C.Code section 22–1116 (1981).

Both the majority and dissent in the Court of Appeals accepted this common sense reading of the statute and concluded that the display clause was content-based. The majority indicated, however, that it could be argued that the regulation was not content-based. Both respondents and the United States have now made such an argument in this Court. They contend that the statute is not content-based because the government is not itself selecting between viewpoints; the permissible message on a picket sign is determined solely by the policies of a foreign government.

We reject this contention, although we agree the provision is not viewpoint-based. The display clause determines which viewpoint is acceptable in a neutral fashion by looking to the policies of foreign governments. While this prevents the display clause from being directly viewpoint-based, a label with potential First Amendment ramifications of its own, see, e.g., Members of City Council of Los Angeles v. Taxpayers for Vincent, 466 U.S. 789, 804 (1984); Schacht v. United States, 398 U.S. 58, 63 (1970), it does not render the statute content-neutral. Rather, we have held that a regulation that "does not favor either side of a political controversy" is nonetheless impermissible because the "First Amendment's hostility to content-based regulation extends . . . to prohibition of public discussion of an entire topic." Consolidated Edison Co. v. Public Service Comm'n, 447 U.S. 530, 537 (1980). Here the government has determined that an entire category of speech—signs or displays critical of foreign governments—is not to be permitted.

We most recently considered the definition of a content-neutral statute in Renton v. Playtime Theatres, Inc., 475 U.S. 41 (1986). Drawing on prior decisions, we described " 'content-neutral' speech restrictions as those that 'are *justified* without reference to the content of the regulated speech.' Virginia Pharmacy Board v. Virginia Citizens Consumer Council, Inc., 425 U.S. 748, 771 (1976) (emphasis added)." Id., at 48. The regulation at issue in *Renton* described prohibited speech by reference to the type of movie theatre involved, treating "theatres that specialize in adult films differently from other kinds of theatres." Id., at 47. But while the regulation in *Renton* applied only to a particular category of speech, its justification had nothing to do with that speech. The content of the films being shown inside the theatres was irrelevant and was not the target of the regulation. Instead, the ordinance was aimed at the "*secondary effects* of such theatres in the surrounding community," Ibid., effects that are almost unique to theatres featuring sexually explicit films, i.e., prevention of crime, maintenance of property values, and protection of residential neighborhoods. In short, the ordinance in *Renton* did not aim at the suppression of free expression.

Respondents attempt to bring the display clause within *Renton* by arguing that here too the real concern is a secondary effect, namely, our international law obligation to shield diplomats from speech that offends their dignity. We think this misreads *Renton*. We spoke in that decision only of *secondary* effects of speech, referring to regulations that apply to a particular category of speech because the regulatory targets happen to be associated with that type of speech. So long as the justifications for regulation have nothing to do with content, i.e., the desire to suppress crime has nothing to do with the actual films being shown inside adult movie theatres, we concluded that the regulation was properly analyzed as content-neutral.

Regulations that focus on the direct impact of speech on its audience present a different situation. Listeners' reactions to speech are not the type of "secondary effects" we referred to in *Renton*. To take an example factually close to *Renton,* if the ordinance there was justified by the city's desire to prevent the psychological damage it felt was associated with viewing adult movies, then analysis of the measure as a content-based statute would have been appropriate. The hypothetical regulation targets the direct impact of a particular category of speech, not a secondary feature that happens to be associated with that type of speech.

Applying these principles to the case at hand leads readily to the conclusion that the display clause is content-based. The clause is justified *only* by reference to the content of speech. Respondents and the United States do not point to the "secondary effects" of picket signs in front of embassies. They do not point to congestion, to interference with ingress or egress, to visual clutter, or to the need to protect the security of embassies. Rather, they rely on the need to protect the dignity of foreign diplomatic personnel by shielding them from speech that is critical of their governments. This justification focuses *only* on the content of the speech and the direct impact that speech has on its listeners. The emotive impact of speech on its audience is not a "secondary effect." Because the display clause regulates speech due to its potential primary impact, we conclude it must be considered content-based.

B

Our cases indicate that as a *content-based* restriction on *political speech* in a *public forum,* section 22–1115 must be subjected to the most exacting scrutiny. Thus, we have required the State to show that the "regulation is necessary to serve a compelling state interest and that it is narrowly drawn to achieve that end." Perry Education Assn. v. Perry Local Educators Assn., 460 U.S., at 45. Accord Board of Airport Comm'rs of Los Angeles v. Jews for Jesus, 482 U.S. ___, ___ (1987); Cornelius v. NAACP Legal Defense and Educational Fund, Inc., 473 U.S. 788, 800 (1985); United States v. Grace, 461 U.S., at 177.

We first consider whether the display clause serves a compelling governmental interest in protecting the dignity of foreign diplomatic personnel. Since the dignity of foreign officials will be affronted by signs critical of their governments or governmental policies, we are told, these foreign diplomats must be shielded from such insults in order to fulfill our country's obligations under international law.

As a general matter, we have indicated that in public debate our own citizens must tolerate insulting, and even outrageous, speech in order to provide "adequate 'breathing space' to the freedoms protected by the First Amendment." Hustler Magazine, Inc. v. Falwell, 485 U.S. ___, ___ (1988). . . . A "dignity" standard, like the "outrageousness" standard that we rejected in *Hustler*, is so inherently subjective that it would be inconsistent with "our longstanding refusal to punish speech because the speech in question may have an adverse emotional impact on the audience." *Hustler Magazine,* 485 U.S., at ___.

We are not persuaded that the differences between foreign officials and American citizens require us to deviate from these principles here. The dignity interest is said to be compelling in this context primarily because its recognition and protection is part of the United States' obligations under international law. The Vienna Convention on Diplomatic Relations . . . imposes on host states:

> "The special duty to take all appropriate steps to protect the premises of the mission against any intrusion or damage and to prevent any disturbance of the peace of the mission or impairment of its dignity." . . .

As a general proposition, it is of course correct that the United States has a vital national interest in complying with international law. The Constitution itself attempts to further this interest by expressly authorizing Congress "to define and punish Piracies and Felonies committed on the high Seas, and Offenses against the Law of Nations." U.S.Const., Art. I, section 8, cl. 10. Cf. The Federalist No. 3, p. 43 (C. Rossiter ed. 1961) (J. Jay). Moreover, protecting foreign emissaries has a long history and noble purpose. In this country national concern for the protection of ambassadors and foreign ministers even predates the Constitution. In 1791 the Continental Congress adopted a resolution calling on the States to enact laws punishing "infractions of the immunities of ambassadors and other public ministers, authorised and received as such by the United States in Congress assembled," targeting in particular "violence offered to their persons, houses, carriages and property." 21 Journals Continental Congress 1781, pp. 1136–1137 (Hunt ed. 1912).

The need to protect diplomats is grounded in our Nation's important interest in international relations. As a leading commentator observed in 1844, "it is necessary that nations should treat and hold intercourse together, in order to promote their interests,—to avoid injuring each other,—and to adjust and terminate their disputes." E. Vattel, The Law of Nations 452 (J. Chitty ed. 1844). This observation is even more true today given the global nature of the economy and the extent to which actions in other parts of the world affect our own national security. Diplomatic personnel are essential to conduct the international affairs so crucial to the well being of this Nation. In addition, in light of the concept of reciprocity that governs much of international law in this area, see C. Wilson, Diplomatic Privileges and Immunities 32 (1967), we have a more parochial reason to protect foreign diplomats in this country. Doing so ensures that similar protections will be accorded those that we send abroad to represent the United States, and thus serves our national interest in protecting our own citizens. Recent history is replete with attempts, some unfortunately successful, to harass and harm our ambassadors and other diplomatic officials. These underlying purposes combine to make our national interest in protecting diplomatic personnel powerful indeed.

At the same time, it is well-established that "no agreement with a foreign nation can confer power on the Congress, or on any other branch of Government, which is free from the restraints of the Constitution." Reid v. Covert, 354 U.S. 1, 16 (1957). See 1 Restatement of Foreign Relations Law of the United States section 131, comment a, p. 53 (Tent. Draft No. 6, Apr. 12, 1985) ("Rules of international law and provisions of international agreements of the United States are subject to the Bill of Rights and other prohibitions, restrictions or requirements of the Constitution and cannot be given effect in violation of them").

Thus, the fact that an interest is recognized in international law does not automatically render that interest "compelling" for purposes of First Amendment analysis. We need not decide today whether, or to what extent, the dictates of international law could ever require that First Amendment analysis be adjusted to accommodate the interests of foreign officials. Even if we assume that international law recognizes a dignity interest and that it should be considered sufficiently "compelling" to support a content-based restriction on speech, we conclude that section 22–1115 is not narrowly tailored to serve that interest. . . .

The most useful starting point for assessing section 22–1115 is to compare it with an analogous statute adopted by Congress, which is the body primarily responsible for implementing our obligations under the Vienna Convention. Title 18 U.S.C. section 112(b)(2) subjects to criminal punishment willful acts or attempts to "intimidate, coerce, threaten, or harass a foreign official or an official guest or obstruct a foreign official in the performance of his duties."

Its legislative history reveals that section 112 was developed as a deliberate effort to implement our international obligations. See, e.g., 118 Cong.Rec. 27112–27113 (1972). At the same time, the history reflects a substantial concern with the effect of any such legislation on First Amendment freedoms. For example, the original provision contained a prohibition on willful acts or attempts to "intimidate, coerce, threaten, or harass . . . or obstruct a foreign official," as does the current version of section 112. In a portion with similarities to the display clause, however, it also punished anyone who

> "parades, pickets, displays any flag, banner, sign, placard, or device, or utters any word, phrase, sound, or noise, for the purpose of intimidating, coercing, threatening, or harassing any foreign official or obstructing him in the performance of his duties." Act for Protection of Foreign Official Guests of the United States, Pub.L. 92–539, Title III, section 301(c)(1), 86 Stat. 1070, 1073 (1972).

Concerned with the effects that such a provision might have on First Amendment freedoms, the Senate added a new subsection, which directed:

"Nothing contained in this section shall be construed or applied so as to abridge the exercise of rights guaranteed under the first amendment to the Constitution of the United States." Section 301(e), 86 Stat. 1073. See S.Rep. No. 92–1105, p. 19 (1972).

After the 1972 passage of section 112 in this form, congressional concerns about its impact on First Amendment freedoms apparently escalated rather than abated. In 1976, Congress revisited the area and repealed the antipicketing provision, leaving in place only the current prohibition on willful acts or attempts to "intimidate, coerce, threaten, or harass a foreign official." Section 112(b)(2). In modifying section 112, Congress was motivated by First Amendment concerns:

"This language of the original anti-picketing provision raises serious Constitutional questions because it appears to include within its purview conduct and speech protected by the First Amendment." S.Rep. No. 94–1273, p. 8, n. 9 (1976); H.R.Rep. No. 94–1614, p. 6, n. 9 (1976).

Thus, after a careful balancing of our country's international obligations with our Constitution's protection of free expression, Congress has determined that section 112 adequately satisfies the Government's interest in protecting diplomatic personnel outside the District of Columbia. It is the necessary, "appropriate" step that Congress has enacted to fulfill our international obligations. . . .

Section 112 applies to all conduct "within the United States but outside the District of Columbia." Section 112(b)(3). In the legislative history, the exclusion of the District from the statute's reach is explained with reference to section 22–1115; Congress was informed that a "similar" statute already applied inside the District. S.Rep. No. 92–1105, p. 19 (1972); H.R.Rep. No. 92–1268, p. 5 (1972). The two statutes, however, are not identical, and the differences between them are constitutionally significant. In two obvious ways, section 112 is considerably less restrictive than the display clause of section 22–1115. First and foremost, section 112 is not narrowly directed at the content of speech but at any activity, including speech, that has the prohibited effects. Moreover, section 112, unlike section 22–1115, does not prohibit picketing; it only prohibits activity undertaken to "intimidate, coerce, threaten, or harass." Indeed, unlike the display clause, even the repealed antipicketing portion of section 112 permitted peaceful picketing.

Given this congressional development of a significantly less restrictive statute to implement the Vienna Convention, there is little force to the argument that we should give deference to a supposed congressional judgment that the Convention demands the more problematic approach reflected in the display clause. If section 112 is all that is necessary in the rest of the country, petitioners contend it should be all that is necessary in District of Columbia. The only counter-argument offered by respondents is that the District has a higher concentration of foreign embassies than other locales and that a more restrictive statute is therefore necessary. But this is arguably factually incorrect . . . and logically beside the point since the need to protect "dignity" is equally present whether there is one embassy or mission or one hundred. . . .

Congressional action since the Court of Appeals' ruling in this case casts even further doubt on the validity of the display clause and causes one to doubt whether that court would have reached the same result under the law as it now stands. In section 1302 of the Omnibus Diplomatic Security and Anti-Terrorism Act of 1986, Congress said:

"(1) The District of Columbia law concerning demonstrations near foreign missions in the District of Columbia (D.C.Code, sec. 22–1115) may be inconsistent with the reasonable exercise of the rights of free speech and assembly, that law may have been selectively enforced, and peaceful demonstrators may have been unfairly arrested under the law;

"(2) the obligation of the United States to provide adequate security for the missions and personnel of foreign governments must be balanced with the reasonable exercise of the rights of free speech and assembly; and

"(3) therefore, the Council of the District of Columbia should review and, if appropriate, make revisions in the laws of the District of Columbia concerning demonstrations near foreign missions, in consultation with the Secretary of State and the Secretary of the Treasury." Pub.L. 99–399, section 1302, 100 Stat. 853, 897.

. . .

The District of Columbia government has responded to the congressional request embodied in the Omnibus Act by repealing section 22–1115. The repeal is contingent, however, on Congress' first acting to extend section 112 to the District. . . .

While this most recent round of legislative action concerning section 22–1115 has not yet led to making the repeal of that provision effective, it has undercut significantly respondents' defense of the display clause. When considered together with earlier congressional action implementing the Vienna Convention, the claim that the display clause is sufficiently narrowly tailored is gravely weakened: if ever it did so, Congress no longer considers this statute necessary to comply with our international obligations. Relying on congressional judgment in this delicate area, we conclude that the availability of alternatives such as section 112 amply demonstrates that the display clause is not crafted with sufficient precision to withstand First Amendment scrutiny. It may serve an interest in protecting the dignity of foreign missions, but it is not narrowly tailored; a less restrictive alternative is readily available. . . . Thus, even assuming for present purposes that the dignity interest is "compelling," we hold that the display clause of section 22–1115 is inconsistent with the First Amendment.

III

Petitioners initially attack the congregation clause by arguing that it confers unbridled discretion upon the police. In addressing such a facial overbreadth challenge, a court's first task is to ascertain whether the enactment reaches a substantial amount of constitutionally protected conduct. . . .

The congregation clause makes it unlawful:

"To congregate within 500 feet of any embassy, legation, or consulate and refuse to disperse after having been ordered so to do by the police." Section 22–1115.

Standing alone, this text is problematic both because it applies to *any* congregation within 500 feet of an embassy for *any* reason and because it appears to place no limits at all on the dispersal authority of the police. The Court of Appeals, however, has provided a narrowing construction that alleviates both of these difficulties.

The Court of Appeals . . . concluded that the statute permits the dispersal only of congregations that are directed at an embassy; it does not grant "police the power to disperse for reasons having nothing to do with the nearby embassy." Finally, the Court of Appeals further circumscribed police discretion by holding that the statute permits dispersal "only when the police reasonably believe that a threat to the security or peace of the embassy is present."

. . .

So narrowed, the congregation clause withstands First Amendment overbreadth scrutiny. It does not reach a substantial amount of constitutionally protected conduct; it merely regulates the place and manner of certain demonstrations. Unlike a general breach of the peace statute, see, e.g., Cox v. Louisiana, 379 U.S. 536 (1965), the congregation clause is site-specific; it applies only within 500 feet of foreign embassies. Cf. Cox. v. Louisiana, 379 U.S. 559, 568, n. 1 (1965) (ordinance prohibiting certain picketing "near" a courthouse upheld; section 22–1115 cited with approval as being less vague due to specification of 500 feet); *Grayned*, supra, at 112, 120–121 (upholding ban on picketing near a school; special nature of place relevant in judging reasonableness of restraint). Moreover, the congregation clause does not prohibit peaceful congregations; its reach is limited to groups posing a security threat. As we have noted, "where demonstrations turn violent, they lose their protected quality as expression under the First Amendment." *Grayned*, supra, at 116. These two limitations prevent the congregation clause from reaching a substantial amount of constitutionally protected conduct and make the clause consistent with the First Amendment.

Petitioners argue that even as narrowed by the Court of Appeals, the congregation clause is invalid because it is impermissibly vague. In particular, petitioners focus on the word "peace," which is not further defined or limited. We rejected an identical argument in *Grayned*, supra. That case concerned an ordinance that prohibited persons near schools from "disturbing the peace" of the schools.   408 U.S., at 107–108.   We held that given the "particular context" of the ordinance it gave fair notice of its scope: "Although the prohibited quantum of disturbance is not specified in the ordinance, it is apparent from the statute's announced purpose that the measure is whether normal school activity has been or is about to be disrupted."   Id., at 112.   Section 22–1115 presents the same situation.   It is crafted for a particular context and given that context, it is apparent that the "prohibited quantum of disturbance" is whether normal embassy activities have been or are about to be disrupted.   The statute communicates its reach in words of common understanding, ibid.; Cameron v. Johnson, 390 U.S. 611, 616 (1968), and it accordingly withstands petitioners' vagueness challenge.

IV

In addition to their First Amendment challenges to the display clause and the congregation clause, petitioners raise an equal protection argument.   Relying on Police Department of Chicago v. Mosley, 408 U.S. 92 (1972), and Carey v. Brown, 447 U.S. 455 (1980), petitioners contend that both the display clause and the congregation clause violate equal protection by virtue of section 22–1116, which excludes labor picketing from the general prohibitions of section 22–1115. . . . .

. . . [T]he Court of Appeals has already construed that provision to apply only to congregations that threaten the security or peace of an embassy.   Therefore, peaceful congregations, including peaceful labor congregations, are not prohibited.

Accordingly, only if section 22–1116 is construed to protect *violent* labor congregations, will there be any unequal treatment of nonlabor and labor picketing which could run afoul of the Equal Protection Clause.   In our view, section 22–1116 should not be interpreted in this manner . . . .   Indeed, it would be unreasonable to construe this statute in such a way that the sole purpose of section 22–1116 would be to protect violent labor congregations.

The intended function of section 22–1116 is largely pre-empted by our conclusion that the display clause is invalid.   Viewing the section in this way eliminates any potential unequal treatment of nonlabor and labor congregations.   Accordingly, in our view, section 22–1116 does not violate the Equal Protection Clause.

V

We conclude that the display clause of section 22–1115 is unconstitutional on its face.   It is a content-based restriction on political speech in a public forum, and it is not narrowly tailored to serve a compelling state interest.   We also conclude that the congregation clause, as narrowed by the Court of Appeals, is not facially unconstitutional. Accordingly, the judgment of the Court of Appeals is reversed in part and affirmed in part.

It is so ordered.

Justice Kennedy took no part in the consideration or decision of this case.

Justice Brennan, with whom Justice Marshall joins, concurring in part and concurring in the judgment.

I join all but Part II–A of Justice O'Connor's opinion. I also join Part II–A to the extent it concludes that even under the analysis set forth in Renton v. Playtime Theatres, Inc., 475 U.S. 41 (1986), the display clause constitutes a content-based restriction on speech that merits strict scrutiny. Whatever "secondary effects" means, I agree that it cannot include listeners' reactions to speech. . . . I write separately, however, to register my continued disagreement with the proposition that an otherwise content-based restriction on speech can be recast as "content-neutral" if the restriction "aims" at "secondary effects" of the speech, . . . and to object to Justice O'Connor's assumption that the *Renton* analysis applies not only outside the context of businesses purveying sexually explicit materials but even to political speech.

. . .

. . . [I]ndeterminacy is hardly *Renton*'s worst flaw, for the root problem with the *Renton* analysis is that it relies on the dubious proposition that a statute which on its face discriminates based on the content of speech aims not at content but at some secondary effect that does not itself affect the operation of the statute. But the inherently ill-defined nature of the *Renton* analysis certainly exacerbates the risk that many laws designed to suppress disfavored speech will go undetected. Although an inquiry into motive is sometimes a useful supplement, the best protection against governmental attempts to squelch opposition has never lain in our ability to assess the purity of legislative motive but rather in the requirement that the government act through content-neutral means that restrict expression the government favors as well as expression it disfavors. . . . Moreover, even if we could be confident about our ability to determine that a content-based law was intended to aim at the "secondary effects" of certain types of speech, such a law would still offend fundamental free speech interests by denying speakers the equal right to engage in speech and by denying listeners the right to an undistorted debate. These rights are all the more precious when the speech subject to unequal treatment is political speech and the debate being distorted is a political debate. And the dangers, the uncertainties, and the damage to free and equal debate caused by the *Renton* analysis are all the more regrettable given the unlikelihood of any legitimate governmental interest in a content-based restriction on speech (especially political speech) and the ample alternatives governments have for advancing content-neutral goals through content-neutral regulation. . . .

. . . True, today's application of the *Renton* analysis to political speech is dictum: the challenged statute would be treated as content-based under either *Renton* or the traditional approach, and the opinion could easily have stated simply that we need not reach the issue whether *Renton* applies to political speech because even under *Renton* the law constitutes a content-based restriction. It is nonetheless ominous dictum, for it could set the Court on a road that will lead to the evisceration of First Amendment freedoms. I can only hope that, when the Court is actually presented with a case involving a content-based regulation of political speech that allegedly aims at so-called secondary effects of that speech, the Court will recognize and avoid the pitfalls of the *Renton* approach.

Chief Justice Rehnquist, with whom Justices White and Blackmun join, concurring in part and dissenting in part.

For the reasons stated by Judge Bork in his majority opinion below, I would uphold that portion of section 22–1115 of the District of Columbia Code that prohibits the display of any sign within 500 feet of a foreign embassy if that sign tends to bring that foreign government into "public odium" or "public disrepute." . . . I join in parts III and IV of the majority opinion.

––––––––

CITY OF LAKEWOOD v. PLAIN DEALER PUBLISHING CO., 108 S.Ct. 2138 (1988). In a narrow 4–3 decision, the Court held that a municipal ordinance regulating placement of newsracks on public property was unconstitutional on its face, because it provided no standards governing the Mayor's discretion to deny permits. Justice Brennan's opinion for the Court did not reach the larger question whether a city could bar placement of newsracks on all public streets, nor did it consider the conditions that could properly be imposed upon such placement. (E.g., the Lakewood ordinance required liability insurance, and design review by the city's architectural board.) The dissent (Justice White, joined by Justices Stevens and O'Connor) argued that a facial attack on the ordinance should not be entertained if the city had the greater power to eliminate all newsracks from public property. Given interests in keeping public streets and sidewalks free for traffic, insuring safety, and aesthetics, cities would be justified in banning all newspaper dispensing devices from public property. Chief Justice Rehnquist and Justice Kennedy did not participate in the decision.

SECTION 3. THE NON–TRADITIONAL FORUM

––––––––

A. SPEECH ACTIVITIES IN PUBLIC PROPERTY OTHER THAN PARKS AND STREETS

––––––––

Page 1193. Add as a footnote to Greer v. Spock:

[1] The Court also distinguished Flower v. United States in United States v. Albertini, 472 U.S. 675 (1985). In 1972, petitioner had received a letter from the commanding officer of Hickham Air Force Base forbidding him to reenter, after he had entered the base and destroyed government property. In 1981, he entered the base during its open house, and distributed leaflets criticizing the nuclear arms race. He was convicted of violating a statute forbidding entry to a military reservation after having been ordered not to reenter by the officer in charge. The Court expressed doubt that a military base

constituted a public forum during an open house—it was not like a base open as a public street all of the time. Whether or not the base was a public forum on the day of an open house, that "respondent had received a valid bar letter distinguished him from the general public and provided a reasonable ground for excluding him from the base."

Page 1200. Add ahead of Los Angeles v. Taxpayers for Vincent:

CORNELIUS v. NAACP LEGAL DEFENSE AND EDUCATION FUND, INC.

473 U.S. 788, 105 S.Ct. 3439, 87 L.Ed.2d 567 (1985).

Justice O'Connor delivered the opinion of the Court.

This case requires us to decide whether the Federal Government violates the First Amendment when it excludes legal defense and political advocacy organizations from participation in the Combined Federal Campaign (CFC or Campaign), a charity drive aimed at federal employees. The United States District Court for the District of Columbia held that the respondent organizations could not be excluded from the CFC, and the Court of Appeals affirmed. We . . . reverse.

I

The CFC is an annual charitable fund-raising drive conducted in the federal workplace during working hours largely through the voluntary efforts of federal employees. At all times relevant to this litigation, participating organizations confined their fund-raising activities to a 30-word statement submitted by them for inclusion in the Campaign literature. Volunteer federal employees distribute to their coworkers literature describing the Campaign and the participants along with pledge cards. 5 CFR § 950.521(c) and (e) (1983). Contributions may take the form of either a payroll deduction or a lump sum payment made to a designated agency or to the general Campaign fund. § 950.523. Undesignated contributions are distributed on the local level by a private umbrella organization to certain participating organizations. § 950.509(c)(5). Designated funds are paid directly to the specified recipient. Through the CFC, the government employees contribute in excess of $100 million to charitable organizations each year.

. . .

Respondents in this case are the NAACP Legal Defense and Educational Fund, Inc., the Sierra Club Legal Defense Fund, the Puerto Rican Legal Defense and Education Fund, the Federally Employed Women Legal Defense and Education Fund, the Indian Law Resource Center, the Lawyers' Committee for Civil Rights under Law, and the Natural Resources Defense Council. Each of the respondents attempts to influence public policy through one or more of the following means: political activity, advocacy, lobbying, or litigation on behalf of others. . . .

. . .

. . . President Reagan took several steps to restore the CFC to what he determined to be its original purpose. In 1982, the President issued Executive Order No. 12353, 3 CFR 139 (1983). . . . The new

Order retained the original limitation to "national voluntary health and welfare agencies and such other national voluntary agencies as may be appropriate," and delegated to the Director of the Office of Personnel Management the authority to establish criteria for determining appropriateness. Shortly thereafter, the President amended Executive Order No. 12353 to specify the purposes of the CFC and to identify groups whose participation would be consistent with those purposes. Exec. Order No. 12404, 3 CFR 151 (1984). The CFC was designed to lessen the Government's burden in meeting human health and welfare needs by providing a convenient, nondisruptive channel for Federal employees to contribute to non-partisan agencies that directly serve those needs. Id., § 1(b), amending Exec. Order No. 12353 § 2(b)(1). The Order limited participation to "voluntary, charitable, health and welfare agencies that provide or support direct health and welfare services to individuals or their families," ibid., amending Exec. Order No. 12353 § 2(b)(2), and specifically excluded those "[a]gencies that seek to influence the outcomes of elections or the determination of public policy through political activity or advocacy, lobbying, or litigation on behalf of parties other than themselves." Ibid., amending Exec. Order No. 12353 § 2(b)(3).

. . .

II

The issue presented is whether the respondents have a First Amendment right to solicit contributions that was violated by their exclusion from the CFC. To resolve this issue we must first decide whether solicitation in the context of the CFC is speech protected by the First Amendment, for, if it is not, we need go no further. Assuming that such solicitation is protected speech, we must identify the nature of the forum, because the extent to which the Government may limit access depends on whether the forum is public or non-public. Finally, we must assess whether the justifications for exclusion from the relevant forum satisfy the requisite standard. Applying this analysis, we find that respondents' solicitation is protected speech occurring in the context of a nonpublic forum and that the Government's reasons for excluding respondents from the CFC appear, at least facially, to satisfy the reasonableness standard. We express no opinion on the question whether petitioner's explanation is merely a pretext for viewpoint discrimination. Accordingly, we reverse and remand for further proceedings consistent with this opinion.

A

Charitable solicitation of funds has been recognized by this Court as a form of protected speech. . . .

. . .

Although *Village of Schaumburg* establishes that noncommercial solicitation is protected by the First Amendment, the Government argues that solicitation within the confines of the CFC is entitled to a lesser degree of protection. This argument is premised on the inherent differences between the face-to-face solicitation involved in *Village of Schaumburg* and the 30-word written statements at issue here. In a face-to-face encounter there is a greater opportunity for the exchange of ideas and the propagation of views than is available in the CFC. The statements contained in the CFC literature are merely informative. federal standards which prohibit persuasive speech and the use of symbols "or other distractions" aimed at competing for the potential donor's attention. 5 CFR § 950.521(d) (1983).

Notwithstanding the significant distinctions between in-person solicitation and solicitation in the abbreviated context of the CFC, we find that the latter deserves First Amendment protection. The brief statements in the CFC literature directly advance the speaker's interest in informing readers about its existence and its goals. Moreover, an employee's contribution in response to a request for funds functions as a general expression of support for the recipient and its views. See Buckley v. Valeo, 424 U.S. 1, 21 (1975). Although the CFC does not entail direct discourse between the solicitor and the donor, the CFC literature facilitates the dissemination of views and ideas by directing employees to the soliciting agency to obtain more extensive information. 5 CFR § 950.521(e)(ii) (1983). Finally, without the funds obtained from solicitation in various fora, the organization's continuing ability to communicate its ideas and goals may be jeopardized. See Village of Schaumburg v. Citizens for a Better Environment, supra, at 632. Thus, the nexus between solicitation and the communication of information and advocacy of causes is present in the CFC as in other contexts. Although government restrictions on the length and content of the request are relevant to ascertaining the Government's intent as to the nature of the forum created, they do not negate the finding that the request implicates interests protected by the First Amendment.

B

. . .

To determine whether the First Amendment permits the Government to exclude respondents from the CFC, we must first decide whether the forum consists of the federal workplace, as petitioner contends, or the CFC, as respondents maintain. Having defined the relevant forum, we must then determine whether it is public or nonpublic in nature.

Petitioner contends that a First Amendment forum necessarily consists of tangible government property. Because the only "property" involved here is the federal workplace, in petitioner's view the workplace constitutes the relevant forum. Under this analysis, the CFC is merely an activity that takes place in the federal workplace. Respondents, in contrast, argue that the forum should be defined in terms of the access sought by the speaker. Under their view, the particular channel of communication constitutes the forum for First Amendment purposes. Because respondents seek access only to the CFC and do not claim a general right to engage in face-to-face solicitation in the federal workplace, they contend that the relevant forum is the CFC and its attendant literature.

We agree with respondents that the relevant forum for our purposes is the CFC. Although petitioner is correct that as an initial matter a speaker must seek access to public property or to private property dedicated to public use to evoke First Amendment concerns, forum analysis is not completed merely by identifying the government property at issue. Rather, in defining the forum we have focused on the access sought by the speaker. When speakers seek general access to public property, the forum encompasses that property. See, e.g., Greer v. Spock, supra. In cases in which limited access is sought, our cases have taken a more tailored approach to ascertaining the perimeters of a forum within the confines of the government property. For example, Perry Education Assn. v. Perry Local Educators' Assn., supra, examined the access sought by the speaker and defined the forum as a school's internal mail system and the teachers' mailboxes, notwithstanding that an "internal mail system" lacks a physical situs. Similarly, in Lehman v. City of Shaker Heights, 418 U.S. 298, 300 (1974), where petitioners sought to compel the City to permit political advertising on City-owned buses, the Court treated the advertising spaces on the buses as the forum. Here, as in *Perry Education Assn.,* respondents seek access to a particular means of communication. Consistent with the approach taken in prior cases, we find that the CFC, rather than the federal workplace, is the forum. This conclusion does not mean, however, that the Court will ignore the special nature and function of the federal workplace in evaluating the limits that may be imposed on an organization's right to participate in the CFC. . . .

Having identified the forum as the CFC, we must decide whether it is nonpublic or public in nature. . . .

. . .

Here the parties agree that neither the CFC nor the federal workplace is a traditional public forum. Respondents argue, however, that the Government created a limited public forum for use by all charitable organizations to solicit funds from federal employees. The Government contends, and we agree, that neither its practice nor its policy is consistent with an intent to designate the CFC as a public forum open to all tax-exempt organizations. In 1980, an estimated 850,000 organizations qualified for tax-exempt status. H. Godfrey, Handbook on Tax Exempt Organizations 5 (1983). In contrast, only 237 organizations participated in the 1981 CFC of the National Capitol Area. 1981 Combined Federal Campaign Contributor's Leaflet, National Capitol Area. The Government's consistent policy has been to limit participation in the CFC to "appropriate" voluntary agencies and to require agencies seeking admission to obtain permission from federal and local Campaign officials. . . .

Nor does the history of the CFC support a finding that the Government was motivated by an affirmative desire to provide an open forum for charitable solicitation in the federal workplace when it began the Campaign. The historical background indicates that the Campaign was designed to minimize the disruption to the workplace that had resulted from unlimited ad hoc solicitation activities by lessening the amount of expressive activity occurring on federal property. Indeed, the OPM stringently limited expression to the 30-word statement included in the Campaign literature. The decision of the Government to limit access to the CFC is not dispositive in itself; instead, it is relevant for what it suggests about the Government's intent in creating the forum. The Government did not create the CFC for purposes of providing a forum for expressive activity. That such activity occurs in the context of the forum created does not imply that the forum thereby becomes a public forum for First Amendment purposes. . . .

An examination of the nature of the government property involved strengthens the conclusion that the CFC is a nonpublic forum. . . . The federal workplace, like any place of employment, exists to accomplish the business of the employer. . . . It follows that the Government has the right to exercise control over access to the federal workplace in order to avoid interruptions to the performance of the duties of its employees. . . . In light of the Government policy in creating the CFC and its practice in limiting access, we conclude that the CFC is a nonpublic forum.

C

Control over access to a nonpublic forum can be based on subject matter and speaker identity so long as the distinctions drawn are reasonable in light of the purpose served by the forum and are viewpoint neutral. Perry Education Assn., supra, at 49. Although a speaker may be excluded from a nonpublic forum if he wishes to address a topic not encompassed within the purpose of the forum, see Lehman v. City of Shaker Heights, 418 U.S. 298 (1974), or if he is not a member of the class of speakers for whose especial benefit the forum was created, see *Perry Education Assn.,* supra, the Government violates the First Amendment when it denies access to a speaker solely to suppress the point of view he espouses on an otherwise includible subject. The Court of Appeals found it unnecessary to resolve whether the Government's denial of access to respondents was viewpoint based, because it determined that respondents' exclusion was unreasonable in light of the purpose served by the CFC.

Petitioner maintains that the purpose of the CFC is to provide a means for traditional health and welfare charities to solicit contributions in the federal workplace, while at the same time maximizing private support of social programs that would otherwise have to be supported by Government funds and minimizing costs to the Federal Government by controlling the time that federal employees expend on the Campaign. Petitioner posits that excluding agencies that attempt to influence the outcome of political elections or the determination of public policy is reasonable in light of this purpose. First, petitioner contends that there is likely to be a general consensus among employees that traditional health and welfare charities are worthwhile, as compared with the more diverse views concerning the goals of organizations like respondents. Limiting participation to widely accepted groups is likely to contribute significantly to employees' acceptance of the Campaign and consequently to its ultimate success. In addition, because the CFC is conducted largely through the efforts of federal employees during their working hours, any controversy surrounding the CFC would produce unwelcome disruption. Finally, the President determined that agencies seeking to affect the outcome of elections or the determination of public policy should be denied access to the CFC in order to avoid the reality and the appearance of government favoritism or entanglement with particular viewpoints. In such circumstances, petitioner contends that the decision to deny access to such groups was reasonable.

In respondents' view, the reasonableness standard is satisfied only when there is some basic incompatibility between the communication at issue and the principal activity occurring on the government property. Respondents contend that the purpose of the CFC is to permit solicitation by groups that provide health and welfare services. By permitting such solicitation to take place in the federal workplace, respondents maintain, the Government has concluded that such activity is consistent with the activities usually conducted there. Because respondents are seeking to solicit such contributions and their activities result in direct, tangible benefits to the groups they represent, the Government's attempt to exclude them is unreasonable. Respondents reject petitioner's justifications on the ground that they are unsupported by the record.

. . .

. . . The Government's decision to restrict access to a nonpublic forum need only be *reasonable;* it need not be the most reasonable or the only reasonable limitation. In contrast to a public forum, a finding of strict incompatibility between the nature of the speech or the identity of the speaker and the functioning of the nonpublic forum is not mandated. . . . Even if some incompatibility with general expressive activity were required, the CFC would meet the requirement because it would be administratively unmanageable if access could not be curtailed in a reasonable manner. Nor is there a requirement that the restriction be narrowly tailored or that the Government's interest be compelling. The First Amendment does not demand unrestricted access to a nonpublic forum merely because use of that forum may be the most efficient means of delivering the speaker's message. . . .

The reasonableness of the government's restriction of access to a nonpublic forum must be assessed in the light of the purpose of the forum and all the surrounding circumstances. Here the President could reasonably conclude that a dollar directly spent on providing food or shelter to the needy is more beneficial than a dollar spent on litigation that might or might not result in aid to the needy. Moreover, avoiding the appearance of political favoritism is a valid justification for limiting speech in a nonpublic forum. . . . In furthering this interest, the Government is not bound by decisions of other executive agencies made in other contexts. Thus, respondents' tax status, while perhaps relevant, does not determine the reasonableness of the Government's conclusion that participation by such agencies in the CFC will create the appearance of favoritism.

. . .

Finally, the record amply supports an inference that respondents' participation in the CFC jeopardized the success of the Campaign. OPM submitted a number of letters from Federal employees and managers, as well as from Chairmen of local Federal Coordinating Committees and members of Congress expressing concern about the inclusion of groups termed "political" or "nontraditional" in the CFC. More than 80 percent of this correspondence related requests that the CFC be restricted to "non-political," "non-advocacy," or "traditional" charitable organizations. In addition, OPM received approximately 1,450 telephone calls complaining about the inclusion of respondents and similar agencies in the 1983 Campaign. Many Campaign workers indicated that extra effort was required to persuade disgruntled employees to contribute. The evidence indicated that the number of contributors had declined in some areas. Other areas reported significant declines in the amount of contributions. . . . Thus, the record adequately supported petitioner's position that respondents' continued participation in the Campaign would be detrimental to the Campaign and disruptive of the federal workplace. Although the avoidance of controversy is not a valid ground for restricting speech in a public forum, a nonpublic forum by definition is not dedicated to general debate or the free exchange of ideas. The First Amendment does not forbid a viewpoint-neutral exclusion of speakers who would disrupt a nonpublic forum and hinder its effectiveness for its intended purpose.

D

On this record, the Government's posited justifications for denying respondents access to the CFC appear to be reasonable in light of the purpose of the CFC. The existence of reasonable grounds for limiting access to a nonpublic forum, however, will not save a regulation that is in reality a facade for viewpoint-based discrimination. . . .

Petitioner argues that a decision to exclude all advocacy groups, regardless of political or philosophical orientation, is by definition viewpoint neutral. Exclusion of groups advocating the use of litigation is not viewpoint based, petitioner asserts, because litigation is a means of promoting a viewpoint, not a viewpoint in itself. While we accept the validity and reasonableness of the justifications offered by the Government for excluding advocacy groups from the CFC, those justifications cannot save an exclusion that is in fact based on the desire to suppress a particular point of view. . . .

The Government contends that controversial groups must be eliminated from the CFC to avoid disruption and ensure the success of the Campaign. As noted supra, we agree that these are facially neutral and valid justifications for exclusion from the nonpublic forum created by the CFC. Nonetheless, the purported concern to avoid controversy excited by particular groups may conceal a bias against the viewpoint advanced by the excluded speakers. In addition, petitioner maintains

that limiting CFC participation to organizations that provide direct
health and welfare services to needy persons is necessary to achieve the
goals of the CFC as set forth in Executive Order 12404. Although this
concern is also sufficient to provide a reasonable grounds for excluding
certain groups from the CFC, the respondents offered some evidence to
cast doubt on its genuineness. Organizations that do not provide direct
health and welfare services, such as the World Wildlife Fund, the
Wilderness Society, and the United States Olympic Committee, have
been permitted to participate in the CFC. Although there is no
requirement that regulations limiting access to a nonpublic forum must
be precisely tailored, the issue whether the Government excluded
respondents because it disagreed with their viewpoints was neither
decided below nor fully briefed before this Court. We decline to decide
in the first instance whether the exclusion of respondents was impermissibly motivated by a desire to suppress a particular point of view.
Respondents are free to pursue this contention on remand.

III

We conclude that the Government does not violate the First
Amendment when it limits participation in the CFC in order to minimize disruption to the federal workplace, to ensure the success of the
fund-raising effort, or to avoid the appearance of political favoritism
without regard to the viewpoint of the excluded groups. Accordingly,
we reverse the judgment of the Court of Appeals that the exclusion of
respondents was unreasonable, and we remand this case for further
proceedings consistent with this opinion.

It is so ordered.

Justice Marshall took no part in the consideration or decision of
this case. Justice Powell took no part in the decision of this case.

**Justice Blackmun, with whom Justice Brennan joins, dissent-
ing.**

I agree with the Court that the Combined Federal Campaign (CFC)
is not a traditional public forum. I also agree with the Court that our
precedents indicate that the Government may create a "forum by
designation" (or, to use the term our cases have adopted, a "limited
public forum") by allowing public property that traditionally has not
been available for assembly and debate to be used as a place for
expressive activity by certain speakers or about certain subjects. I
cannot accept, however, the Court's circular reasoning that the CFC is
not a limited public forum because the Government intended to limit
the forum to a particular class of speakers. Nor can I agree with the
Court's conclusion that distinctions the Government makes between
speakers in defining the limits of a forum need not be narrowly tailored
and necessary to achieve a compelling governmental interest. Finally,
I would hold that the exclusion of the several respondents from the CFC
was, on its face, viewpoint-based discrimination. Accordingly, I dissent.

I

. . .

The Court's analysis transforms the First Amendment into a mere ban on viewpoint censorship, ignores the principles underlying the public forum doctrine, flies in the face of the decisions in which the Court has identified property as a limited public forum, and empties the limited public forum concept of all its meaning.

A

. . .

[T]he public forum, limited public forum, and nonpublic forum categories are but analytical shorthand for the principles that have guided the Court's decisions regarding claims to access to public property for expressive activity. The interests served by the expressive activity must be balanced against the interests served by the uses for which the property was intended and the interests of all citizens to enjoy the property. Where an examination of all the relevant interests indicates that certain expressive activity is not compatible with the normal uses of the property, the First Amendment does not require the Government to allow that activity.

The Court's analysis, it seems to me, turns these principles on end. Rather than recognize that a nonpublic forum is a place where expressive activity would be incompatible with the purposes the property is intended to serve, the Court states that a nonpublic forum is a place where we need not even be concerned about whether expressive activity is incompatible with the purposes of the property. Rather than taking the nature of the property into account in balancing the First Amendment interests of the speaker and society's interests in freedom of speech against the interests served by reserving the property to its normal use, the Court simply labels the property and dispenses with the balancing.

. . . The Court offers no explanation why attaching the label "nonpublic forum" to particular property frees the Government of the more stringent constraints imposed by the First Amendment in other contexts. The Government's interests in being able to use the property for the purposes for which it was intended obviously are important; that is why a compatibility requirement is imposed. But the Government's interests as property holder are hardly more important than its interests as the keeper of our military forces, as guardian of our federal elections, as administrator of our prisons, as educator, or as employer. When the Government acts in those capacities, we closely scrutinize its justifications for infringements upon expressive activity. . . . Similarly, the mere fact that the Government acts as property owner should not exempt it from the First Amendment.

Nor should tradition or governmental "designation" be completely determinative of the rights of a citizen to speak on public property. Many places that are natural sites for expressive activity have no long tradition of use for expressive activity. Airports, for example, are a relatively recent phenomenon, as are government-sponsored shopping centers. Other public places may have no history of expressive activity because only recently have they become associated with the issue that citizens wish to use the property to discuss. It is likely that the library in *Brown v. Louisiana,* supra, historically had not been used for demonstrations for the obvious reason that its association with the subject of segregation became a topic of public protest only during the civil rights movement. Another reason a particular parcel of property may have little history of expressive use is that the Government has excluded expressive activity from the property unjustifiably. . . .

. . .

B

Not only does the Court err in labeling the CFC a nonpublic forum without first engaging in a compatibility inquiry, but it errs as well in reasoning that the CFC is not a limited public forum because the Government permitted only "limited discourse," rather than "intentionally opening" the CFC for "public discourse." . . .

. . .

C

The Court's analysis empties the limited public forum concept of meaning and collapses the three categories of public forum, limited public forum, and nonpublic forum into two. The Court makes it *virtually* impossible to prove that a forum restricted to a particular class of speakers is a limited public forum. If the Government does not create a limited public forum unless it intends to provide an "open forum" for expressive activity, and if the exclusion of some speakers is evidence that the Government did not intend to create such a forum, no speaker challenging denial of access will ever be able to prove that the forum is a limited public forum. The very fact that the Government denied access to the speaker indicates that the Government did not intend to provide an open forum for expressive activity, and under the Court's analysis that fact alone would demonstrate that the forum is not a limited public forum.

. . .

II

A

The Court's strained efforts to avoid recognizing that the CFC is a limited public forum obscure the real issue in this case: what constraint does the First Amendment impose upon the Government's efforts to define the boundaries of a limited public forum? While I do not agree with the Court that the Government's consistent policy has been to limit access to the CFC to "traditional" charities through "extensive" eligibility criteria, the Government did indeed adopt eligibility criteria in 1983 specifically designed to exclude respondents. Executive Order No. 12404 of February 10, 1983, 3 CFR 151 (1984). Accordingly, the central question presented is whether those criteria need be anything more than rational.

. . .

The constraints the First Amendment imposes upon the Government's definition of the boundaries of a limited public forum follow from the principles underlying the public and limited public forum doctrine. As noted, the Government's acquiescence in the use of property for expressive activity indicates that at least some expressive activity is compatible with the intended uses of the public property. If the Government draws the boundaries of the forum to exclude expressive activity that is incompatible with the property, and to include that which is compatible, the boundaries will reflect precisely the balancing of interests the public forum doctrine was meant to encapsulate. If the Government draws the line at a point which excludes speech that would be compatible with the intended uses of the property, however, then the Government must explain how its exclusion of compatible speech is necessary to serve, and is narrowly tailored to serve, some compelling governmental interest other than preserving the property for its intended uses.

B

The Government does not even argue that its exclusion of respondents from the CFC served any compelling governmental interest; it argues merely that its exclusion was "reasonable." The Court also implicitly concedes that the justifications the Government offers would not meet anything more than the minimal "reasonable basis" scrutiny. I agree that the Government's justifications for excluding respondents neither reserve the CFC for expressive activity compatible with the property nor serve any other compelling governmental interest.

The Court would point to three "justifications" for the exclusion of respondents. First, the Court states that "the President could reasonably conclude that a dollar directly spent on providing food or shelter to the needy is more beneficial than a dollar spent on litigation that might not result in aid to the needy." I fail to see how the President's view of the relative benefits obtained by various charitable activities translates into a compelling governmental interest. The Government may have a compelling interest in increasing charitable contributions because charities provide services that the Government otherwise would have to provide. But that interest does not justify the exclusion of respondents, for respondents work to enforce the rights of minorities, women, and others through litigation, a task that various Government agencies otherwise might be called upon to undertake.

In any event, the fact that the President or his advisers may believe the money is best "directly spent on providing food or shelter to the needy" starkly fails to explain why respondents are excluded from the CFC while other groups that do not spend money to provide food or shelter directly to the needy are allowed to be included. Of the 237 groups included in the 1981–1982 CFC for the National Capital Area, only 61, or 26%, provide food, shelter, residential care, or information and referral services related to food or housing, according to the descriptions contained in the Contributor's Leaflet. Indeed, in the past few years, the CFC for the National Capital Area has included many groups that have absolutely nothing to do with the provision of food or shelter or other basic needs.

The Court next states that "avoiding the appearance of political favoritism is a valid justification for limiting speech in a nonpublic forum." The Court, however, flatly has rejected that justification in the context of limited public forums. Widmar v. Vincent, 454 U.S., at 274. In addition, the Government's proffered justification again fails to explain why respondents are excluded when other groups, such as the National Right to Life Educational Trust Fund and Planned Parenthood, at least one of which the Government presumably would wish to avoid the appearance of supporting, are allowed to participate. And the Government offers no explanation why a simple disclaimer in the brochure would not suffice to achieve its interest in avoiding the appearance of support.

Nor is the Government's "interest in avoiding controversy" a compelling state interest that would justify the exclusion of respondents. . . .

. . .

Further, even if the avoidance of controversy in the forum itself could ever serve as a legitimate governmental purpose, the record here does not support a finding that the inclusion of respondents in the CFC threatened a material and substantial disruption. In fact, the evidence shows that contributions to the CFC increased during each of the years respondents participated in the Campaign. The "hundreds" of phone calls and letters expressing a preference that groups other than "traditional" charities be excluded from the CFC reflect nothing more than the discomfort that can be expected whenever a change is made, and whenever any opinion is expressed on a topic of concern to the huge force in 1983 of some 2.7 million civilian federal employees. The letters objecting to the inclusion of respondents in the Campaign must be considered against the fact that many federal employees obviously supported their inclusion in the CFC, as is evidenced by the substantial contributions respondents received through the Campaign.

. . .

III

Even if I were to agree with the Court's determination that the CFC is a nonpublic forum, or even if I thought that the Government's exclusion of respondents from the CFC was necessary and narrowly tailored to serve a compelling governmental interest, I still would disagree with the Court's disposition, because I think the eligibility criteria, which exclude charities that "seek to influence . . . the determination of public policy," Executive Order No. 12404 of February 10, 1983, 3 CFR 151, 152 (1984), is on its face viewpoint-based. The

Government contends that the criteria are viewpoint-neutral because they apply equally to all "advocacy" groups regardless of their "political or philosophical leanings." The relevant comparison, however, is not between the individual organizations that make up the group excluded, but between those organizations allowed access to the CFC and those denied such access.

By devoting its resources to a particular activity, a charity expresses a view about the manner in which charitable goals can best be achieved. Charities working toward the same broad goal, such as "improved health," may have a variety of views about the path to that goal. Some of the "health services" charities participating in the 1982 National Capital Area CFC, for example, obviously believe that they can best achieve "improved health care" through medical research; others obviously believe that their resources are better spent on public education; others focus their energies on detection programs; and still others believe the goal is best achieved through direct care for the sick. Those of the respondents concerned with the goal of improved health, on the other hand, obviously think that the best way to achieve that goal is by changing social policy, creating new rights for various groups in society, or enforcing existing rights through litigation, lobbying, and political activism. That view cannot be communicated through the CFC, according to the Government's eligibility criteria. Instead, Government employees may hear only from those charities that think that charitable goals can best be achieved within the confines of existing social policy and the status quo. The distinction is blatantly viewpoint-based, so I see no reason to remand for a determination of whether the eligibility criteria are a "facade" for viewpoint-based discrimination.

I would affirm the judgment of the Court of Appeals.

Justice Stevens, dissenting.

The scholarly debate between Justice O'Connor and Justice Blackmun concerning the categories of public and quasi-public fora is an appropriate sequel to many of the First Amendment cases decided during the past decade. . . . I am somewhat skeptical about the value of this analytical approach in the actual decisional process. . . . At least in this case, I do not find the precise characterization of the forum particularly helpful in reaching a decision.

Everyone on the Court agrees that the exclusion of "advocacy" groups from the Combined Federal Campaign (CFC) is prohibited by the First Amendment if it is motivated by a bias against the views of the excluded groups. Moreover, everyone also recognizes that the evidence in the record, at the least, gives rise to an inference that "the purported concern to avoid controversy excited by particular groups may conceal a bias against the viewpoint advanced by the excluded speakers." The problem presented by the case is whether that inference is strong enough to support the entry of a summary judgment in favor of respondents.

Today the Court decides to remand the case for a trial to determine whether the exclusion of respondents was the product of viewpoint discrimination. That decision is supported by the rule that forecloses the entry of a summary judgment when a genuine issue of fact is present, and by the special limitations on this Court's ability to undertake its own review of trial records. . . . Nevertheless, my study of the case has persuaded me that the Court of Appeals correctly affirmed the entry of summary judgment in favor of respondents.

As the District Court found, "the CFC provides employees with two ways in which to make contributions . . . . An employee may designate that his donations be distributed to particular organizations participating in the CFC. Alternatively, if the employee does not designate any agency to benefit from the donation, the amount contributed is placed into a pool which is divided among the approved agencies in accordance with a formula set forth in the regulations."

This case does not involve the general pool that is supported by *undesignated* contributions. The respondents do not participate in that pool and do not receive, or seek to receive, any share of the federal employees' undesignated contributions. Instead, the respondents receive only those CFC contributions that are specifically designated to go to them. To phrase it in another manner, respondents only benefit from contributions that are the result of the free and voluntary choices of federal employees who make specific designations. Those federal employees who merely support the undesignated CFC fund, as well as those who designate other charities, provide no support for the respondents.

I emphasize this fact because the arguments advanced in support of the exclusion might well be sufficient to justify an exclusion from the general fund, but have manifestly less force as applied to designated contributions. Indeed, largely for the reasons that Justice Blackmun has set forth in Parts II–B and III of his opinion, the arguments advanced in support of the exclusion are so plainly without merit that they actually lend support to an inference of bias.

I am persuaded that each of the three reasons advanced in support of denying advocacy groups a right to participate in a request for *designated* contributions is wholly without merit. The Government's desire to have its workers contribute to charities that directly provide food and shelter rather than to those that do not surely cannot justify an exclusion of some but not other charities that do not do so. Moreover, any suggestion that the Government might be perceived as favoring every participant in the solicitation is belied by the diversity of the participants and by the fact that there has been no need to disclaim what must be perfectly obvious to the presumptively intelligent federal worker. Last, the supposed fear of controversy in the workplace is pure nonsense—one might as well prohibit discussions of politics, recent judicial decisions, or sporting events. In sum, the reasoning set forth in Parts II–B and III of Justice Blackmun's dissenting opinion persuades me that the judgment should be affirmed.

BOARD OF AIRPORT COMMISSIONERS v. JEWS FOR JESUS, INC., 107 S.Ct. 2568 (1987). The Board adopted a resolution banning all "First Amendment activities" in the central terminal area of the Los Angeles airport. The resolution was challenged by an organization whose members had been prevented from distributing free religious literature on a pedestrian walkway at the terminal. The Court held that the ordinance was unconstitutionally overbroad, but did not resolve the controversy concerning whether the airport was a "traditional public forum." The ordinance prohibited not merely the distribution of literature, but "even talking and reading, or the wearing of campaign buttons or symbolic clothing." "No conceivable government interest" would justify such an absolute prohibition of speech in the airport, even if the airport were a "nonpublic forum."

B. THE GOVERNMENT FORUM AND GOVERNMENT SUBSIDIES TO SPEECH

Page 1223. Add after Board of Education v. Pico:

BETHEL SCHOOL DISTRICT No. 403 v. FRASER

478 U.S. 675, 106 S.Ct. 3159, 92 L.Ed.2d 549 (1986).

[The report in this case appears, supra at p. 358.]

HAZELWOOD SCHOOL DISTRICT v. KUHLMEIER

___ U.S. ___, 108 S.Ct. 562, 98 L.Ed.2d 592 (1988).

Justice White delivered the opinion of the Court.

This case concerns the extent to which educators may exercise editorial control over the contents of a high school newspaper produced as part of the school's journalism curriculum.

I

Petitioners are the Hazelwood School District in St. Louis County, Missouri; various school officials; Robert Eugene Reynolds, the principal of Hazelwood East High School, and Howard Emerson, a teacher in the school district. Respondents are three former Hazelwood East students who were staff members of Spectrum, the school newspaper. They contend that school officials violated their First Amendment rights by deleting two pages of articles from the May 13, 1983, issue of Spectrum.

Spectrum was written and edited by the Journalism II class at Hazelwood East. The newspaper was published every three weeks or so during the 1982–1983 school year. More than 4,500 copies of the newspaper were distributed during that year to students, school personnel, and members of the community.

The Board of Education allocated funds from its annual budget for the printing of Spectrum. These funds were supplemented by proceeds from sales of the newspaper. The printing expenses during the 1982–1983 school year totaled $4,668.50; revenue from sales was $1,166.84. The other costs associated with the newspaper—such as supplies, textbooks, and a portion of the journalism teacher's salary—were borne entirely by the Board.

The Journalism II course was taught by Robert Stergos for most of the 1982–1983 academic year. Stergos left Hazelwood East to take a job in private industry on April 29, 1983, when the May 13 edition of Spectrum was nearing completion, and petitioner Emerson took his place as newspaper adviser for the remaining weeks of the term.

The practice at Hazelwood East during the spring 1983 semester was for the journalism teacher to submit page proofs of each Spectrum issue to Principal Reynolds for his review prior to publication. On May 10, Emerson delivered the proofs of the May 13 edition to Reynolds, who objected to two of the articles scheduled to appear in that edition. One of the stories described three Hazelwood East students' experiences with pregnancy; the other discussed the impact of divorce on students at the school.

Reynolds was concerned that, although the pregnancy story used false names "to keep the identity of these girls a secret," the pregnant students still might be identifiable from the text. He also believed that the article's references to sexual activity and birth control were inappropriate for some of the younger students at the school. In addition, Reynolds was concerned [with] a student identified by name in the divorce story. . . .

Reynolds believed that there was no time to make the necessary changes in the stories before the scheduled press run and that the newspaper would not appear before the end of the school year if printing were delayed to any significant extent. He concluded that his only options under the circumstances were to publish a four-page newspaper instead of the planned six-page newspaper, eliminating the two pages on which the offending stories appeared, or to publish no newspaper at all. . . .

Respondents subsequently commenced this action in the United States District Court for the Eastern District of Missouri seeking a declaration that their First Amendment rights had been violated, injunctive relief, and monetary damages. After a bench trial, the District Court denied an injunction, holding that no First Amendment violation had occurred.

.   .   .

The Court of Appeals for the Eighth Circuit reversed. . . .

.   .   .

We . . . reverse.

II

Students in the public schools do not "shed their constitutional rights to freedom of speech or expression at the schoolhouse gate." *Tinker*, at 506. They cannot be punished merely for expressing their personal views on the school premises—whether "in the cafeteria, or on the playing field, or on the campus during the authorized hours," id., at 512–513—unless school authorities have reason to believe that such expression will "substantially interfere with the work of the school or impinge upon the rights of other students." Id., at 509.

We have nonetheless recognized that the First Amendment rights of students in the public schools "are not automatically coextensive with the rights of adults in other settings," Bethel School District No. 403 v. Fraser, 478 U.S. ___, ___ (1986). . . . A school need not tolerate student speech that is inconsistent with its "basic educational mission," *Fraser*, at ___, even though the government could not censor similar speech outside the school. Accordingly, we held in *Fraser* that a student could be disciplined for having delivered a speech that was "sexually explicit" but not legally obscene at an official school assembly, because the school was entitled to "disassociate itself" from the speech in a manner that would demonstrate to others that such vulgarity is "wholly inconsistent with the 'fundamental values' of public school education." Ibid. We thus recognized that "[t]he determination of what manner of speech in the classroom or in school assembly is inappropriate properly rests with the school board," id., at ___, rather than with the federal courts. It is in this context that respondents' First Amendment claims must be considered.

A

We deal first with the question whether Spectrum may appropriately be characterized as a forum for public expression. The public schools do not possess all of the attributes of streets, parks, and other traditional public forums. . . . Hence, school facilities may be deemed to be public forums only if school authorities have "by policy or by practice" opened those facilities "for indiscriminate use by the general public," Perry Education Assn. v. Perry Local Educators' Assn., 460 U.S. 37, 47 (1983), or by some segment of the public, such as student organizations. Id., at 46, n. 7 (citing Widmar v. Vincent). If the facilities have instead been reserved for other intended purposes, "communicative or otherwise," then no public forum has been created. . . .

The policy of school officials toward Spectrum was reflected in Hazelwood School Board Policy . . . that "[s]chool sponsored publications are developed within the adopted curriculum and its educational implications in regular classroom activities." The Hazelwood East Curriculum Guide described the Journalism II course as a "laboratory situation in which the students publish the school newspaper applying skills they have learned in Journalism I." . . . Students received grades and academic credit for their performance in the course.

School officials did not deviate in practice from their policy that production of Spectrum was to be part of the educational curriculum and a "regular classroom activit[y]." . . .

. . . .

. . . Accordingly, school officials were entitled to regulate the contents of Spectrum in any reasonable manner. . . . It is this standard, rather than our decision in *Tinker*, that governs this case.

B

The question whether the First Amendment requires a school to tolerate particular student speech—the question that we addressed in *Tinker*—is different from the question whether the First Amendment requires a school affirmatively to promote particular student speech. The former question addresses educators' ability to silence a student's personal expression that happens to occur on the school premises. The latter question concerns educators' authority over school-sponsored publications, theatrical productions, and other expressive activities that students, parents, and members of the public might reasonably perceive to bear the imprimatur of the school. These activities may fairly be characterized as part of the school curriculum, whether or not they occur in a traditional classroom setting, so long as they are supervised by faculty members and designed to impart particular knowledge or skills to student participants and audiences.[3]

Educators are entitled to exercise greater control over this second form of student expression to assure that participants learn whatever lessons the activity is designed to teach, that readers or listeners are not exposed to material that may be inappropriate for their level of maturity, and that the views of the individual speaker are not erroneously attributed to the school. Hence, a school may in its capacity as publisher of a school newspaper or producer of a school play "disassociate itself," *Fraser*, 478 U.S., at __, not only from speech that would "substantially interfere with [its] work . . . or impinge upon the rights of other students," *Tinker*, 393 U.S., at 509, but also from speech that is, for example, ungrammatical, poorly written, inadequately researched, biased or prejudiced, vulgar or profane, or unsuitable for immature audiences. A school must be able to set high standards for the student speech that is disseminated under its auspices—standards that may be higher than those demanded by some newspaper publishers or theatrical producers in the "real" world—and may refuse to disseminate student speech that does not meet those standards. In addition, a school must be able to take into account the emotional maturity of the intended audience in determining whether to disseminate student speech on potentially sensitive topics, which might range from the existence of Santa Claus in an elementary school setting to the particulars of teenage sexual activity in a high school setting. A school must also retain the authority to refuse to sponsor student speech that might reasonably be perceived to advocate drug or alcohol use, irresponsible sex, or conduct otherwise inconsistent with "the shared values of a civilized social order," *Fraser*, supra, at __, or to associate the school with any position other than neutrality on matters of political controversy. . . .

Accordingly, we conclude that the standard articulated in *Tinker* for determining when a school may punish student expression need not

[3] The distinction that we draw between speech that is sponsored by the school and speech that is not is fully consistent with Papish v. Board of Curators, 410 U.S. 667 (1973) (per curiam), which involved an off-campus "underground" newspaper that school officials merely had allowed to be sold on a state university campus.

also be the standard for determining when a school may refuse to lend its name and resources to the dissemination of student expression.[5] Instead, we hold that educators do not offend the First Amendment by exercising editorial control over the style and content of student speech in school-sponsored expressive activities so long as their actions are reasonably related to legitimate pedagogical concerns.[6]

This standard is consistent with our oft-expressed view that the education of the Nation's youth is primarily the responsibility of parents, teachers, and state and local school officials, and not of federal judges. . . . It is only when the decision to censor a school-sponsored publication, theatrical production, or other vehicle of student expression has no valid educational purpose that the First Amendment require[s] judicial intervention to protect students' constitutional rights.[7]

III

We also conclude that Principal Reynolds acted reasonably in requiring the deletion from the May 13 issue of Spectrum of the pregnancy article, the divorce article, and the remaining articles that were to appear on the same pages of the newspaper.

. . .

In sum, we cannot reject as unreasonable Principal Reynolds' conclusion that neither the pregnancy article nor the divorce article was suitable for publication in Spectrum. Reynolds could reasonably have concluded that the students who had written and edited these articles had not sufficiently mastered those portions of the Journalism II curriculum that pertained to the treatment of controversial issues and personal attacks, the need to protect the privacy of individuals whose most intimate concerns are to be revealed in the newspaper, and "the legal, moral, and ethical restrictions imposed upon journalists within [a] school community" that includes adolescent subjects and readers. Finally, we conclude that the principal's decision to delete two pages of Spectrum, rather than to delete only the offending articles or to require that they be modified, was reasonable under the circumstances as he understood them. Accordingly, no violation of First Amendment rights occurred.

. . .

[5] We therefore need not decide whether the Court of Appeals correctly construed *Tinker* as precluding school officials from censoring student speech to avoid "invasion of the rights of others" except where that speech could result in tort liability to the school.

[6] We reject respondents' suggestion that school officials be permitted to exercise prepublication control over school-sponsored publications only pursuant to specific written regulations. To require such regulations in the context of a curricular activity could unduly constrain the ability of educators to educate. We need not now decide whether such regulations are required before school officials may censor publications not sponsored by the school that students seek to distribute on school grounds. . . .

[7] . . .We need not now decide whether the same degree of deference is appropriate with respect to school-sponsored expressive activities at the college and university level.

Justice Brennan, with whom Justice Marshall and Justice Blackmun join, dissenting.

. . .

In my view the principal . . . violated the First Amendment's prohibitions against censorship of any student expression that neither disrupts classwork nor invades the rights of others, and against any censorship that is not narrowly tailored to serve its purpose.

I

. . .

Free student expression undoubtedly sometimes interferes with the effectiveness of the school's pedagogical functions. Some brands of student expression do so by directly preventing the school from pursuing its pedagogical mission: The young polemic who stands on a soapbox during calculus class to deliver an eloquent political diatribe interferes with the legitimate teaching of calculus. And the student who delivers a lewd endorsement of a student-government candidate might so extremely distract an impressionable high school audience as to interfere with the orderly operation of the school. See Bethel School Dist. No. 403 v. Fraser, 478 U.S. ___ (1986). Other student speech, however, frustrates the school's legitimate pedagogical purposes merely by expressing a message that conflicts with the school's, without directly interfering with the school's expression of its message: A student who responds to a political science teacher's question with the retort, "Socialism is good," subverts the school's inculcation of the message that capitalism is better. Even the maverick who sits in class passively sporting a symbol of protest against a government policy, cf. *Tinker*, 393 U.S. 503 (1969), or the gossip who sits in the student commons swapping stories of sexual escapade could readily muddle a clear official message condoning the government policy or condemning teenage sex. Likewise, the student newspaper that, like Spectrum, conveys a moral position at odds with the school's official stance might subvert the administration's legitimate inculcation of its own perception of community values.

. . .

. . . The Court today casts no doubt on *Tinker*'s vitality. Instead it erects a taxonomy of school censorship, concluding that *Tinker* applies to one category and not another. . . .

. . .

. . . [F]rom the first sentence of its analysis . . . *Fraser* faithfully applied *Tinker*.

Nor has this Court ever intimated a distinction between personal and school-sponsored speech in any other context. Particularly telling is this Court's heavy reliance on *Tinker* in two cases of First Amendment infringement on state college campuses. See Papish v. University of Missouri Board of Curators, 410 U.S. 667, 671, n. 6 (1973) (per curiam); Healy v. James, 408 U.S. 169, 180, 189, and n. 18, 191 (1972). One involved the expulsion of a student for lewd expression in a newspaper that she sold on campus pursuant to university authorization, see *Papish*, supra, at 667–668, and the other involved the denial of university recognition and concomitant benefits to a political student organization, see *Healy*, supra, at 174, 176, 181–182. Tracking *Tinker*'s analysis, the Court found each act of suppression unconstitutional. In neither case did this Court suggest the distinction, which the Court today finds dispositive, between school-sponsored and incidental student expression.

II

Even if we were writing on a clean slate, I would reject the Court's rationale for abandoning *Tinker* in this case. . . .

. . .

. . . The educator may, under *Tinker*, constitutionally "censor" poor grammar, writing, or research because to reward such expression would "materially disrup[t]" the newspaper's curricular purpose.

The same cannot be said of official censorship designed to shield the *audience* or dissociate the *sponsor* from the expression. Censorship so motivated might well serve some other school purpose. But it in no way furthers the curricular purposes of a student *newspaper* unless one believes that the purpose of the school newspaper is to teach students that the press ought never report bad news, express unpopular views, or print a thought that might upset its sponsors. Unsurprisingly, Hazelwood East claims no such pedagogical purpose.

. . .

The mere fact of school sponsorship does not, as the Court suggests, license . . . thought control in the high school, whether through school suppression of disfavored viewpoints or through official assessment of topic sensitivity. The former would constitute unabashed and unconstitutional viewpoint discrimination . . . . Just as a school board may not purge its state-funded library of all books that " 'offen[d] [its] social, political and moral tastes.' " 457 U.S., at 858–859 (plurality opinion) (citation omitted), school officials may not, out of like motivation, discriminatorily excise objectionable ideas from a student publication. The State's prerogative to dissolve the student newspaper entirely (or to limit its subject matter) no more entitles it to dictate which viewpoints students may express on its pages, than the State's prerogative to close down the schoolhouse entitles it to prohibit the nondisruptive expression of antiwar sentiment within its gates.

. . .

SECTION 4. SPEECH ON PRIVATE PREMISES

Page 1235. Replace Young v. American Mini Theatres, Inc., and Schad v. Borough of Mount Ephraim with the following:

CITY OF RENTON v. PLAYTIME THEATRES, INC.
475 U.S. 41, 106 S.Ct. 925, 89 L.Ed.2d 29 (1986).

Justice Rehnquist delivered the opinion of the Court.

This case involves a constitutional challenge to a zoning ordinance, enacted by appellant, the city of Renton, Washington, that prohibits adult motion picture theaters from locating within 1,000 feet of any residential zone, single- or multiple-family dwelling, church, park, or school. . . .

In May 1980, the Mayor of Renton, a city of approximately 32,000 people located just south of Seattle, suggested to the Renton City Council that it consider the advisability of enacting zoning legislation dealing with adult entertainment uses. No such uses existed in the city at that time. Upon the Mayor's suggestion, the City Council referred the matter to the city's Planning and Development Committee. The committee held public hearings, reviewed the experiences of Seattle and other cities, and received a report from the City Attorney's Office advising as to developments in other cities. The City Council, meanwhile, adopted Resolution No. 2368, which imposed a moratorium on the licensing of "any business . . . which . . . has as its primary purpose the selling, renting or showing of sexually explicit materials." The resolution contained a clause explaining that such businesses "would have a severe impact upon surrounding businesses and residences."

In April 1981, acting on the basis of the Planning and Development Committee's recommendation, the City Council enacted Ordinance No. 3526. The ordinance prohibited any "adult motion picture theater" from locating within 1,000 feet of any residential zone, single- or multiple-family dwelling, church, or park, and within one mile of any school. The term "adult motion picture theater" was defined as "(a)n enclosed building used for presenting motion picture films, video cassettes, cable television, or any other such visual media, distinguished or characteri(zed) by an emphasis on matter depicting, describing or relating to 'specified sexual activities' or 'specified anatomical areas' . . . for observation by patrons therein."

In early 1982, respondents acquired two existing theaters in downtown Renton, with the intention of using them to exhibit feature-length adult films. The theaters were located within the area proscribed by Ordinance No. 3526. At about the same time, respondents filed [a] lawsuit challenging the ordinance on First and Fourteenth Amendment grounds, and seeking declaratory and injunctive relief. While the federal action was pending, the City Council amended the ordinance in several respects, adding a statement of reasons for its enactment and reducing the minimum distance from any school to 1,000 feet.

. . .

The District Court . . . entered summary judgment in favor of Renton. . . . Relying on Young v. American Mini Theatres, Inc., 427 U.S. 50 (1976), and United States v. O'Brien, 391 U.S. 367 (1968), the court held that the Renton ordinance did not violate the First Amendment.

The Court of Appeals for the Ninth Circuit reversed. . . .

In our view, the resolution of this case is largely dictated by our decision in Young v. American Mini Theatres, Inc., supra. There, although five Members of the Court did not agree on a single rationale for the decision, we held that the city of Detroit's zoning ordinance, which prohibited locating an adult theater within 1,000 feet of any two other "regulated uses" or within 500 feet of any residential zone, did not violate the First and Fourteenth Amendments. 427 U.S., at 72–73 (plurality opinion of Stevens, J., joined by Burger, C.J., and White and Rehnquist, JJ.); id., at 84 (Powell, J., concurring). The Renton ordinance, like the one in *American Mini Theatres,* does not ban adult theaters altogether, but merely provides that such theaters may not be located within 1,000 feet of any residential zone, single- or multiple-family dwelling, church, park, or school. The ordinance is therefore properly analyzed as a form of time, place, and manner regulation. . . .

Describing the ordinance as a time, place, and manner regulation is, of course, only the first step in our inquiry. This Court has long held that regulations enacted for the purpose of restraining speech on the basis of its content presumptively violate the First Amendment. . . . On the other hand, so-called "content-neutral" time, place, and manner regulations are acceptable so long as they are designed to serve a substantial governmental interest and do not unreasonably limit alternative avenues of communication. . . .

At first glance, the Renton ordinance, like the ordinance in *American Mini Theatres,* does not appear to fit neatly into either the "content-based" or the "content-neutral" category. To be sure, the ordinance treats theaters that specialize in adult films differently from other kinds of theaters. Nevertheless, as the District Court concluded, the Renton ordinance is aimed not at the *content* of the films shown at "adult motion picture theatres," but rather at the *secondary effects* of such theaters on the surrounding community. The District Court found that the City Council's *"predominate* concerns" were with the secondary effects of adult theaters, and not with the content of adult films themselves. But the Court of Appeals . . . held that this was not enough to sustain the ordinance. According to the Court of Appeals, if "a *motivating factor* " in enacting the ordinance was to restrict respondents' exercise of First Amendment rights the ordinance would be invalid, apparently no matter how small a part this motivating factor may have played in the City Council's decision. This view of the law was rejected in United States v. O'Brien, 391 U.S. 367, 382–386 (1968), the very case that the Court of Appeals said it was applying:

"It is a familiar principle of constitutional law that this Court will not strike down an otherwise constitutional statute on the basis of an alleged illicit legislative motive. . . .

. . .

". . . What motivates one legislator to make a speech about a statute is not necessarily what motivates scores of others to enact it, and the stakes are sufficiently high for us to eschew guesswork." Id., at 383–384.

The District Court's finding as to "predominate" intent, left undisturbed by the Court of Appeals, is more than adequate to establish that the city's pursuit of its zoning interests here was unrelated to the suppression of free expression. The ordinance by its terms is designed to prevent crime, protect the city's retail trade, maintain property values, and generally "protec(t) and preserv(e) the quality of (the city's) neighborhoods, commercial districts, and the quality of urban life," not to suppress the expression of unpopular views. As Justice Powell observed in *American Mini Theatres,* "(i)f (the city) had been concerned with restricting the message purveyed by adult theaters, it would have tried to close them or restrict their number rather than circumscribe their choice as to location." 427 U.S., at 82, n. 4.

. . . The ordinance does not contravene the fundamental principle that underlies our concern about "content-based" speech regulations: that "government may not grant the use of a forum to people whose views it finds acceptable, but deny use to those wishing to express less favored or more controversial views." *Mosley,* supra, 408 U.S., at 95–96.

It was with this understanding in mind that, in *American Mini Theatres,* a majority of this Court decided that, at least with respect to businesses that purvey sexually explicit materials, zoning ordinances designed to combat the undesirable secondary effects of such businesses are to be reviewed under the standards applicable to "content-neutral" time, place, and manner regulations. Justice Stevens, writing for the plurality, concluded that the city of Detroit was entitled to draw a distinction between adult theaters and other kinds of theaters "without violating the government's paramount obligation of neutrality in its regulation of protected communication," 427 U.S., at 70, noting that "(i)t is th(e) secondary effect which these zoning ordinances attempt to avoid, not the dissemination of 'offensive' speech," id., at 71, n. 34. Justice Powell, in concurrence, elaborated:

"(The) dissent misconceives the issue in this case by insisting that it involves an impermissible time, place, and manner restriction based on the content of expression. It involves nothing of the kind. We have here merely a decision by the city to treat certain movie theaters differently because they have markedly different effects upon their surroundings. . . . Moreover, even if this were a case involving a special governmental response to the content of one type of movie, it is possible that the result would be supported by a line of cases recognizing that the government can tailor its reaction to different types of speech according to the degree to which its special and overriding interests are implicated. . . ."

The appropriate inquiry in this case, then, is whether the Renton ordinance is designed to serve a substantial governmental interest and allows for reasonable alternative avenues of communication. . . . It is clear that the ordinance meets such a standard. As a majority of this Court recognized in *American Mini Theatres,* a city's "interest in attempting to preserve the quality of urban life is one that must be accorded high respect." 427 U.S., at 71 (plurality opinion); see id., at 80 (Powell, J., concurring) ("Nor is there doubt that the interests furthered by this ordinance are both important and substantial"). Exactly the same vital governmental interests are at stake here.

The Court of Appeals ruled, however, that because the Renton ordinance was enacted without the benefit of studies specifically relating to "the particular problems or needs of Renton," the city's justifications for the ordinance were "conclusory and speculative." We think the Court of Appeals imposed on the city an unnecessarily rigid burden of proof. The record in this case reveals that Renton relied heavily on the experience of, and studies produced by, the city of Seattle. In Seattle, as in Renton, the adult theater zoning ordinance was aimed at preventing the secondary effects caused by the presence of even one such theater in a given neighborhood. . . .

. . .

. . . The First Amendment does not require a city, before enacting such an ordinance, to conduct new studies or produce evidence independent of that already generated by other cities, so long as whatever evidence the city relies upon is reasonably believed to be relevant to the problem that the city addresses. That was the case here. Nor is our holding affected by the fact that Seattle ultimately chose a different method of adult theater zoning than that chosen by Renton, since Seattle's choice of a different remedy to combat the secondary effects of adult theaters does not call into question either Seattle's identification of those secondary effects or the relevance of Seattle's experience to Renton.

We also find no constitutional defect in the method chosen by Renton to further its substantial interests. Cities may regulate adult theaters by dispersing them, as in Detroit, or by effectively concentrating them, as in Renton. "It is not our function to appraise the wisdom of (the city's) decision to require adult theaters to be separated rather than concentrated in the same areas . . .. (T)he city must be allowed a reasonable opportunity to experiment with solutions to admittedly serious problems." *American Mini Theatres,* supra, 427 U.S., at 71 (plurality opinion). Moreover, the Renton ordinance is "narrowly tailored" to affect only that category of theaters shown to produce the unwanted secondary effects, thus avoiding the flaw that proved fatal to the regulations in Schad v. Mount Ephraim, 452 U.S. 61 (1981), and Erznoznik v. City of Jacksonville, 422 U.S. 205 (1975).

Respondents contend that the Renton ordinance is "under-inclusive," in that it fails to regulate other kinds of adult businesses that are likely to produce secondary effects similar to those produced by adult theaters. On this record the contention must fail. There is no evidence that, at the time the Renton ordinance was enacted, any other adult business was located in, or was contemplating moving into, Renton. In fact, Resolution No. 2368, enacted in October 1980, states that "the City of Renton does not, at the present time, have any business whose primary purpose is the sale, rental, or showing of sexually explicit materials." That Renton chose first to address the potential problems created by one particular kind of adult business in no way suggests that the city has "singled out" adult theaters for discriminatory treatment. We simply have no basis on this record for assuming that Renton will not, in the future, amend its ordinance to include other kinds of adult businesses that have been shown to produce the same kinds of secondary effects as adult theaters. See Williamson v. Lee Optical Co., 348 U.S. 483, 488–489 (1955).

Finally, turning to the question whether the Renton ordinance allows for reasonable alternative avenues of communication, we note that the ordinance leaves some 520 acres, or more than five percent of the entire land area of Renton, open to use as adult theater sites. The District Court found, and the Court of Appeals did not dispute the finding, that the 520 acres of land consists of "(a)mple, accessible real estate," including "acreage in all stages of development from raw land to developed, industrial, warehouse, office, and shopping space that is criss-crossed by freeways, highways, and roads."

Respondents argue, however, that some of the land in question is already occupied by existing businesses, that "practically none" of the undeveloped land is currently for sale or lease, and that in general there are no "commercially viable" adult theater sites within the 520 acres left open by the Renton ordinance. The Court of Appeals accepted these arguments, concluded that the 520 acres was not truly "available" land, and therefore held that the Renton ordinance "would result in a substantial restriction" on speech.

We disagree with both the reasoning and the conclusion of the Court of Appeals. That respondents must fend for themselves in the real estate market, on an equal footing with other prospective purchasers and lessees, does not give rise to a First Amendment violation. And although we have cautioned against the enactment of zoning regulations that have "the effect of suppressing, or greatly restricting access to, lawful speech," *American Mini Theatres,* 427 U.S., at 71, n. 35 (plurality opinion), we have never suggested that the First Amendment compels the Government to ensure that adult theaters, or any other kinds of speech-related businesses for that matter, will be able to obtain sites at bargain prices. . . . In our view, the First Amendment requires only that Renton refrain from effectively denying respondents a reasonable opportunity to open and operate an adult theater within the city, and the ordinance before us easily meets this requirement.

In sum, we find that the Renton ordinance represents a valid governmental response to the "admittedly serious problems" created by adult theaters. See id., at 71 (plurality opinion). Renton has not used "the power to zone as a pretext for suppressing expression," id., at 84 (Powell, J., concurring), but rather has sought to make some areas available for adult theaters and their patrons, while at the same time preserving the quality of life in the community at large by preventing those theaters from locating in other areas.   This, after all, is the essence of zoning.   Here, as in *American Mini Theatres,* the city has enacted a zoning ordinance that meets these goals while also satisfying the dictates of the First Amendment.   The judgment of the Court of Appeals is therefore

Reversed.

Justice Blackmun concurs in the result.

Justice Brennan joined by Justice Marshall, dissenting.

Renton's zoning ordinance selectively imposes limitations on the location of a movie theater based exclusively on the content of the films shown there.   The constitutionality of the ordinance is therefore not correctly analyzed under standards applied to content-neutral time, place, and manner restrictions.   But even assuming that the ordinance may fairly be characterized as content-neutral, it is plainly unconstitutional under the standards established by the decisions of this Court. Although the Court's analysis is limited to cases involving "businesses that purvey sexually explicit materials," and thus does not affect our holdings in cases involving state regulation of other kinds of speech, I dissent.

I

. . .

The fact that adult movie theaters may cause harmful "secondary" land use effects may arguably give Renton a compelling reason to regulate such establishments; it does not mean, however, that such regulations are content-neutral.   Because the ordinance imposes special restrictions on certain kinds of speech on the basis of content, I cannot simply accept, as the Court does, Renton's claim that the ordinance was not designed to suppress the content of adult movies. . . . In this case, both the language of the ordinance and its dubious legislative history belie the Court's conclusion "the city's pursuit of its zoning interests here was unrelated to the suppression of free expression."

. . .

In sum, the circumstances here strongly suggest that the ordinance was designed to suppress expression, even that constitutionally protected, and thus was not to be analyzed as a content-neutral time, place, and manner restriction.   The Court allows Renton to conceal its illicit motives, however, by reliance on the fact that other communities adopted similar restrictions.   The Court's approach largely immunizes such measures from judicial scrutiny, since a municipality can readily find other municipal ordinances to rely upon, thus always retrospectively justifying special zoning regulations for adult theaters.   Rather than speculate about Renton's motives for adopting such measures, our cases require that the ordinance, like any other content-based restriction on speech, is constitutional "only if the (city) can show that (it) is a precisely drawn means of serving a compelling (governmental) interest." Consolidated Edison Co. v. Public Service Comm'n of N.Y., 447 U.S., at 540 . . . . Only this strict approach can insure that cities will not use their zoning powers as a pretext for suppressing constitutionally protected expression.

Applying this standard to the facts of this case, the ordinance is patently unconstitutional. Renton has not shown that locating adult movie theaters in proximity to its churches, schools, parks, and residences will necessarily result in undesirable "secondary effects," or that these problems could not be effectively addressed by less intrusive restrictions.

II

Even assuming that the ordinance should be treated like a content-neutral time, place, and manner restriction, I would still find it unconstitutional. . . .

A

. . . The city made no showing as to how uses "protected" by the ordinance would be affected by the presence of an adult movie theater. Thus, the Renton ordinance is clearly distinguishable from the Detroit zoning ordinance upheld in Young v. American Mini Theatres, Inc., 427 U.S. 50 (1976). The Detroit ordinance, which was designed to disperse adult theaters throughout the city, was supported by the testimony of urban planners and real estate experts regarding the adverse effects of locating several such businesses in the same neighborhood. . . . Here, the Renton Council was aware only that some residents had complained about adult movie theaters, and that other localities had adopted special zoning restrictions for such establishments. These are not "facts" sufficient to justify the burdens the ordinance imposed upon constitutionally protected expression.

B

Finally, the ordinance is invalid because it does not provide for reasonable alternative avenues of communication. The District Court found that the ordinance left 520 acres in Renton available for adult theater sites, an area comprising about five percent of the city. However, the Court of Appeals found that because much of this land was already occupied, "(l)imiting adult theater uses to these areas is a substantial restriction on speech." Many "available" sites are also largely unsuited for use by movie theaters. Again, these facts serve to distinguish this case from *American Mini Theatres,* where there was no indication that the Detroit zoning ordinance seriously limited the locations available for adult businesses. See *American Mini Theatres,* supra, 427 U.S. at 71 n. 35 (plurality opinion) ("The situation would be quite different if the ordinance had the effect of . . . greatly restricting access to, lawful speech"). . . .

Despite the evidence in the record, the Court reasons that the fact "that respondents must fend for themselves in the real estate market, on an equal footing with other prospective purchasers and lessees, does not give rise to a First Amendment violation." However, respondents are not on equal footing with other prospective purchasers and lessees, but must conduct business under severe restrictions not imposed upon other establishments. The Court also argues that the First Amendment does not compel "the government to ensure that adult theatres, or any other kinds of speech-related businesses for that matter, will be able to obtain sites at bargain prices." However, respondents do not ask Renton to guarantee low-price sites for their businesses, but seek only a reasonable opportunity to operate adult theaters in the city. By denying them this opportunity, Renton can effectively ban a form of protected speech from its borders. . . .

Page 1255. Add at end of subsection:

RILEY v. NATIONAL FEDERATION OF THE BLIND OF NORTH CAROLINA, INC., 108 S.Ct. 2667 (1988). The Court held that three provisions of a statute regulating charitable solicitation violated the first amendment. Regulation of the maximum fees charged by professional fundraisers was invalid on the authority of *Munson.* A requirement, that professional fundraisers disclose the percentage of contributions collected that were actually turned over to charity during the past 12 months, compelled involuntary speech, and was content-related. The state's interest in informing donors was not sufficiently weighty, and the means to accomplish that interest were unduly burdensome. Thus, this requirement did not survive "exacting" scrutiny. A requirement that professional fundraisers be licensed was invalid because it did not require that the licensing authority issue the license within a brief period or take the initiative to go to court to forbid solicitation. (See Freedman v. Maryland, 380 U.S. 51 (1965), casebook page 1182.) Chief Justice Rehnquist and Justice O'Connor dissented. Justice Stevens dissented with reference to the holding that the licensing requirement was unconstitutional.

SECTION 5. LABOR PICKETING

Page 1259. Add at the end of the second paragraph of the footnote:

In Edward J. Debartolo Corp. v. Florida Gulf Coast Building and Trades Council, 108 S.Ct. 1392 (1988), the Court held that the provision of the National Labor Relations Act forbidding secondary boycotts was inapplicable to the distribution of handbills, without picketing, urging a consumer boycott of a neutral employer. The Court concluded that this construction of the statute avoided "serious" constitutional questions.

"Had the union simply been leafletting the public generally, including those entering every shopping mall in town, pursuant to an annual educational effort against substandard pay, there is little doubt that legislative proscription of such leaflets would pose a substantial issue of validity under the First Amendment. The same may well be true in this case, although here the handbills called attention to a specific situation in the mall allegedly involving the payment of unacceptably low wages by a construction contractor."

Chapter 16

PROTECTION OF PENUMBRAL FIRST AMENDMENT RIGHTS

SECTION 1. SYMBOLIC SPEECH

Page 1271. Add at end of section:

WAYTE v. UNITED STATES, 470 U.S. 598 (1985). The government adopted a policy of prosecuting for failure to register for the draft only those who advised the government they had failed to register, or were reported by others as having failed to register. The Court rejected a first amendment attack on the enforcement policy, finding that it met the four part test of United States v. O'Brien. With respect to the fourth part of the test—the restriction on first amendment freedoms is no greater than essential to the furtherance of the government's interest—the policy of prosecuting the most visible offenders was an efficient method to deter violations of the law requiring registration. Justices Marshall and Brennan dissented.

ARCARA v. CLOUD BOOKS, INC.

478 U.S. 697, 106 S.Ct. 3172, 92 L.Ed.2d 568 (1986).

Chief Justice Burger delivered the opinion of the Court

We granted certiorari to decide whether the First Amendment bars enforcement of a statute authorizing closure of a premises found to used as a place for prostitution and lewdness because the premises are also used as an adult bookstore.

I

A

Respondents own and operate the "Village Books and News Store" in Kenmore, New York. The establishment characterizes itself as an "adult" bookstore and sells sexually explicit books and magazines with booths available for the viewing of sexually explicit movies. No issue is presented with respect to whether the movies or other materials available at respondents' store are obscene pornographic materials.

During September and October 1982, the Erie County Sheriff's Department conducted an undercover investigation into reported illicit sexual activities occurring on respondents' premises. A Deputy Sheriff personally observed instances of masturbation, fondling, and fellatio by patrons on the premises of the store, all within the observation of the proprietor. He also observed instances of solicitation of prostitution, and was himself solicited on at least four occasions by men who offered to perform sexual acts in exchange for money. The Deputy Sheriff reported that the management of the "Village Books and News Store" was fully aware of the sexual activity on the premises.

B

The results of the undercover investigation formed the basis of a civil complaint against respondents seeking closure of the premises under section 2321 of the New York Public Health Law. Section 2320 of the New York Public Health Law defines places of prostitution, lewdness, and assignation as public health nuisances . . ..

Section 2329 provides for the closure of any building found to be a public health nuisance . . ..

. . .

Respondents . . . assert[ed] that a closure of the premises would impermissibly interfere with their First Amendment right to sell books on the premises. Respondents moved for partial summary judgment on these First Amendment grounds . . .. The Trial Division of the New York Supreme Court, Special Term, denied the motion for summary judgment . . ..

The Appellate Division, Fourth Department, affirmed. . . .

The New York Court of Appeals . . . agreed that the Public Health Law applied to establishments other than houses of prostitution, but reversed on First Amendment grounds. . . .

. . .

. . . We reverse.

II

This Court has applied First Amendment scrutiny to a statute regulating conduct which has the incidental effect of burdening the expression of a particular political opinion. United States v. O'Brien [391 U.S. 367 (1968)]. . . .

. . .

III

The New York Court of Appeals held that the *O'Brien* test for permissible governmental regulation was applicable to this case because the closure order sought by petitioner would also impose an incidental burden upon respondents' bookselling activities. That court ignored a crucial distinction between the circumstances presented in *O'Brien* and the circumstances of this case: unlike the symbolic draft card burning in *O'Brien*, the sexual activity carried on in this case manifests absolutely no element of protected expression. In Paris Adult Theatre I v. Slaton, 413 U.S. 49, 67 (1973), we underscored the fallacy of seeking to use the First Amendment as a cloak for obviously unlawful public sexual conduct by the diaphanous device of attributing protected expressive attributes to that conduct. First Amendment values may not be invoked by merely linking the words "sex" and "books."

Nor does the distinction drawn by the New York Public Health Law inevitably single out bookstores or others engaged in First Amendment protected activities for the imposition of its burden. . . . If the city imposed closure penalties for demonstrated Fire Code violations or health hazards from inadequate sewage treatment, the First Amendment would not aid the owner of premises who had knowingly allowed such violations to persist.

Nonetheless, respondents argue that the effect of the statutory closure remedy impermissibly burdens its First Amendment protected bookselling activities. The severity of this burden is dubious at best, and is mitigated by the fact that respondents remain free to sell the same materials at another location. In any event, this argument proves too much, since every civil and criminal remedy imposes some conceivable burden on First Amendment protected activities. . . .

. . .

The New York Court of Appeals thus misread *O'Brien*, which has no relevance to a statute directed at imposing sanctions on nonexpressive activity. The legislation providing the closure sanction was directed at unlawful conduct having nothing to do with books or other expressive activity. Bookselling in an establishment used for prostitution does not confer First Amendment coverage to defeat a valid statute aimed at penalizing and terminating illegal uses of premises. The legislature properly sought to protect the environment of the community by directing the sanction at premises knowingly used for lawless activities.[4]

The judgment of the New York Court of Appeals is reversed.

Justice O'Connor, with whom Justice Stevens joins, concurring.

. . . If . . . a city were to use a nuisance statute as a pretext for closing down a book store because it sold indecent books or because of the perceived secondary effects of having a purveyor of such books in the neighborhood, the case would clearly implicate First Amendment concerns and require analysis under the appropriate First Amendment standard of review. Because there is no suggestion in the record or opinion below of such pretextual use of the New York nuisance provision in this case, I concur in the Court's opinion and judgment.

[4] Respondents assert that closure of their premises is sought as a pretext for suppression of First Amendment protected expression. However, there is no suggestion on the record before us that the closure of respondents' bookstore was sought under the public health nuisance statute as a pretext for the suppression of First Amendment protected material. Were respondents able to establish the existence of such a speech suppressive motivation or policy on the part of the District Attorney, they might have a claim of selective prosecution. . . .

Justice Blackmun, with whom Justice Brennan and Justice Marshall join, dissenting.

. . . [T]he Court today concludes that a closure order would raise no First Amendment concerns, apparently because it would be triggered, not by respondents' sale of books, but by the nonexpressive conduct of patrons. But the First Amendment, made applicable to the States by the Fourteenth Amendment, protects against all laws "abridging the freedom of speech"—not just those specifically directed at expressive activity. . . .

. . .

At some point, of course, the impact of state regulation on First Amendment rights becomes so attenuated that it is easily outweighed by the state interest. But when a State directly and substantially impairs First Amendment activities, such as by shutting down a bookstore, I believe that the State must show, at a minimum, that it has chosen the least restrictive means of pursuing its legitimate objectives.

. . .

A State has a legitimate interest in forbidding sexual acts committed in public, including a bookstore. An obvious method of eliminating such acts is to arrest the patron committing them. . . .

. . .

SECTION 2. COMPELLED AFFIRMATION OF BELIEF

Page 1273. Add at end of section:

PACIFIC GAS AND ELECTRIC COMPANY v. PUBLIC UTILITIES COMMISSION OF CALIFORNIA

475 U.S. 1, 106 S.Ct. 903, 89 L.Ed.2d 1 (1986).

Justice Powell announced the judgment of the Court and delivered an opinion in which the Chief Justice, Justice Brennan, and Justice O'Connor joined.

The question in this case is whether the California Public Utilities Commission may require a privately owned utility company to include in its billing envelopes speech of a third party with which the utility disagrees.

I

For the past 62 years, appellant Pacific Gas and Electric Company has distributed a newsletter in its monthly billing envelope. Appellant's newsletter, called Progress, reaches over three million customers. It has included political editorials, feature stories on matters of public interest, tips on energy conservation, and straightforward information about utility services and bills.

In 1980, appellee Toward Utility Rate Normalization (TURN), an intervenor in a ratemaking proceeding before California's Public Utilities Commission, another appellee, urged the Commission to forbid appellant to use the billing envelopes to distribute political editorials, on the ground that the appellant's customers should not bear the expense of appellant's own political speech. The Commission decided that the envelope space that appellant had used to disseminate Progress is the property of the ratepayers. This "extra space" was defined as "the space remaining in the billing envelope, after inclusion of the monthly bill and any required legal notices, for inclusion of other materials up to such total envelope weight as would not result in any additional postage cost."

In an effort to apportion this "extra space" between appellant and its customers, the Commission permitted TURN to use the "extra space" four times a year for the next two years. . . . The Commission placed no limitations on what TURN or appellant could say in the envelope, except that TURN is required to state that its messages are not those of appellant. The Commission reserved the right to grant other groups access to the envelopes in the future.

Appellant appealed the Commission's order to the California Supreme Court, arguing that it has a First Amendment right not to help spread a message with which it disagrees, see Wooley v. Maynard, 430 U.S. 705 (1977), and that the Commission's order infringes that right. The California Supreme Court denied discretionary review. We . . . now reverse. . . .

II

The constitutional guarantee of free speech "serves significant societal interests" wholly apart from the speaker's interest in self-expression. First National Bank of Boston v. Bellotti, 435 U.S. 765, 776 (1978). By protecting those who wish to enter the marketplace of ideas from government attack, the First Amendment protects the public's interest in receiving information. . . . The identity of the speaker is not decisive in determining whether speech is protected. Corporations and other associations, like individuals, contribute to the "discussion, debate, and the dissemination of information and ideas" that the First Amendment seeks to foster. . . . Thus, in *Bellotti,* we invalidated a state prohibition aimed at speech by corporations that sought to influence the outcome of a state referendum. Id., at 795. Similarly, in Consolidated Edison Co. v. Public Service Comm'n of N.Y., 447 U.S. 530, 544 (1980), we invalidated a state order prohibiting a privately owned utility company from discussing controversial political issues in its billing envelopes. In both cases, the critical considerations were that the State sought to abridge speech that the First Amendment is designed to protect, and that such prohibitions limited the range of information and ideas to which the public is exposed. . . .

There is no doubt that under these principles appellant's newsletter Progress receives the full protection of the First Amendment. . . . In appearance no different from a small newspaper, Progress' contents range from energy-saving tips to stories about wildlife conservation, and from billing information to recipes. Progress thus extends well beyond speech that proposes a business transaction, . . . and includes the kind of discussion of "matters of public concern" that the First

Amendment both fully protects and implicitly encourages. . . . The Commission recognized as much, but concluded that requiring appellant to disseminate TURN's views did not infringe upon First Amendment rights. It reasoned that appellant remains free to mail its own newsletter except for the four months in which TURN is given access. The Commission's conclusion necessarily rests on one of two premises: (i) compelling appellant to grant TURN access to a hitherto private forum does not infringe appellant's right to speak; or (ii) appellant has no property interest in the relevant forum and therefore has no constitutionally protected right in restricting access to it. We now examine those propositions.

III

Compelled access like that ordered in this case both penalizes the expression of particular points of view and forces speakers to alter their speech to conform with an agenda they do not set. These impermissible effects are not remedied by the Commission's definition of the relevant property rights.

A

This Court has previously considered the question whether compelling a private corporation to provide a forum for views other than its own may infringe the corporation's freedom of speech. Miami Herald Publishing Co. v. Tornillo, 418 U.S. 241 (1974); see also PruneYard Shopping Center v. Robins, 447 U.S. 74, 85–88 (1980) . . . *Tornillo* involved a challenge to Florida's right-of-reply statute. The Florida law provided that, if a newspaper assailed a candidate's character or record, the candidate could demand that the newspaper print a reply of equal prominence and space. . . .

We found that the right-of-reply statute directly interfered with the newspaper's right to speak in two ways. . . . First, the newspaper's expression of a particular viewpoint triggered an obligation to permit other speakers, with whom the newspaper disagreed, to use the newspaper's facilities to spread their own message. The statute purported to advance free discussion, but its effect was to deter newspapers from speaking out in the first instance: by forcing the newspaper to disseminate opponents' views, the statute penalized the newspaper's own expression. . . .[6]

Second, we noted that the newspaper's "treatment of public issues and public officials—whether fair or unfair—constitute[s] the exercise of editorial control and judgment." . . . Florida's statute interfered

[6] This Court has sustained a limited government-enforced right of access to broadcast media. Red Lion Broadcasting Co. v. FCC, 395 U.S. 367 (1969). Cf. Columbia Broadcasting System, Inc. v. Democratic National Committee, 412 U.S. 94 (1973). Appellant's billing envelopes do not, however, present the same constraints that justify the result in *Red Lion*: "[A] broadcaster communicates through use of a scarce, publicly owned resource. No person can broadcast without a license, whereas all persons are free to send correspondence to private homes through the mails." Consolidated Edison Co. v. Public Service Comm'n of N.Y., 447 U.S. 530, 543 (1980).

with this "editorial control and judgment" by forcing the newspaper to tailor its speech to an opponent's agenda, and to respond to candidates' arguments where the newspaper might prefer to be silent. . . .

The concerns that caused us to invalidate the compelled access rule in *Tornillo* apply to appellant as well as to the institutional press. . . . Just as the state is not free to "tell a newspaper in advance what it can print and what it cannot," . . . the State is not free either to restrict appellant's speech to certain topics or views or to force appellant to respond to views that others may hold. . . . Under *Tornillo* a forced access rule that would accomplish these purposes indirectly is similarly forbidden.

The Court's decision in PruneYard Shopping Center v. Robins, 447 U.S. 74 (1980), is not to the contrary. . . . Notably absent from *PruneYard* was any concern that access to this area might affect the shopping center owner's exercise of his own right to speak: the owner did not even allege that he objected to the content of the pamphlets; nor was the access right content-based. *PruneYard* thus does not undercut the proposition that forced associations that burden protected speech are impermissible.[8]

B

The Commission's order is inconsistent with these principles. The order does not simply award access to the public at large; rather, it discriminates on the basis of the viewpoints of the selected speakers. Two of the acknowledged purposes of the access order are to offer the public a greater variety of views in appellant's billing envelope, and to assist groups (such as TURN) that challenge appellant in the Commission's ratemaking proceedings in raising funds. . . . Access to the envelopes thus is not content-neutral. The variety of views that the Commission seeks to foster cannot be obtained by including speakers whose speech agrees with appellant's. Similarly, the perceived need to raise funds to finance participation in ratemaking proceedings exists only where the relevant groups represent interests that diverge from appellant's interests. Access is limited to persons or groups—such as TURN—who disagree with appellant's views as expressed in Progress and who oppose appellant in Commission proceedings.

Such one-sidedness impermissibly burdens appellant's own expression. *Tornillo* illustrates the point. Access to the newspaper in that case was content-based in two senses: (i) it was triggered by a particular category of newspaper speech, and (ii) it was awarded only to those who disagreed with the newspaper's views. The Commission's order is not, in *Tornillo*'s words, a "content-based penalty" in the first sense, because TURN's access to appellant's envelopes is not conditioned on any particular expression by appellant. . . . But because access is awarded only to those who disagree with appellant's views and who are

---

[8] In addition, the relevant forum in *PruneYard* was the open area of the shopping center into which the general public was invited. This area was, almost by definition, peculiarly public in nature. . . . There is no correspondingly public aspect to appellant's billing envelopes. See post (Marshall, J., concurring in the judgment).

hostile to appellant's interests, appellant must contend with the fact that whenever it speaks out on a given issue, it may be forced—at TURN's discretion—to help disseminate hostile views. . . .

Appellant does not, of course, have the right to be free from vigorous debate. But it *does* have the right to be free from government restrictions that abridge its own rights in order to "enhance the relative voice" of its opponents. . . . The Commission's order requires *appellant* to assist in disseminating *TURN's* views; it does not equally constrain both sides of the debate about utility regulation.[10] . . .

The Commission's access order also impermissibly requires appellant to associate with speech with which appellant may disagree. The order on its face leaves TURN free to use the billing envelopes to discuss any issues it chooses.[11] Should TURN choose, for example, to urge appellant's customers to vote for a particular slate of legislative candidates, or to argue in favor of legislation that could seriously affect the utility business, appellant may be forced either to appear to agree with TURN's views or to respond. . . .[12] . . .

That kind of forced response is antithetical to the free discussion that the First Amendment seeks to foster. . . . For corporations as for individuals, the choice to speak includes within it the choice of what not to say. . . . And we have held that speech does not lose its protection because of the corporate identity of the speaker. *Bellotti,* supra, 435 U.S. at 777; *Consolidated Edison,* supra, 447 U.S. at 533. Were the government freely able to compel corporate speakers to propound political messages with which they disagree, this protection would be empty, for the government could require speakers to affirm in

[10] Justice Stevens analogizes this aspect of the Commission's order to Securities and Exchange Commission regulations that require management to transmit proposals of minority shareholders in shareholder mailings. The analogy is inappropriate. The regulations Justice Stevens cites differ from the Commission's order in two important ways. First, they allocate shareholder property between management and certain groups of shareholders. Management has no interest in corporate property except such interest as derives from the shareholders; therefore, regulations that limit management's ability to exclude some shareholders' views from corporate communications do not infringe corporate First Amendment rights. Second, the regulations govern speech by a corporation to itself. *Bellotti* and *Consolidated Edison* establish that the Constitution protects corporations' right to speak to the public based on the informational value of corporate speech. Rules that define how corporations govern themselves do not limit the range of information that the corporation may contribute to the public debate. The Commission's order, by contrast, burdens appellant's right freely to speak to the public at large.

[11] The presence of a disclaimer on TURN's messages does not suffice to eliminate the impermissible pressure on appellant to respond to TURN's speech. The disclaimer serves only to avoid giving readers the mistaken impression that TURN's words are really those of appellant. . . . It does nothing to reduce the risk that appellant will be forced to respond when there is strong disagreement with the substance of TURN's message. . . .

[12] The Commission's order is thus readily distinguishable from orders requiring appellant to carry various legal notices, such as notices of upcoming Commission proceedings or of changes in the way rates are calculated. The State, of course, has substantial leeway in determining appropriate information disclosure requirements for business corporations. See Zauderer v. Office of Disciplinary Counsel, 471 U.S. ___, ___ (1985). Nothing in *Zauderer* suggests, however, that the State is equally free to require corporations to carry the messages of third parties, where the messages themselves are biased against or are expressly contrary to the corporation's views.

one breath that which they deny in the next. It is therefore incorrect to say, as do appellees, that our decisions do not limit the government's authority to compel speech by corporations. The danger that appellant will be required to alter its own message as a consequence of the government's coercive action is a proper object of First Amendment solicitude, because the message itself is protected under our decisions in *Bellotti* and *Consolidated Edison*. Where, as in this case, the danger is one that arises from a content-based grant of access to private property, it is a danger that the government may not impose absent a compelling interest.

C

The Commission has emphasized that appellant's customers own the "extra space" in the billing envelopes. According to appellees, it follows that appellant cannot have a constitutionally protected interest in restricting access to the envelopes. This argument misperceives both the relevant property rights and the nature of the State's First Amendment violation.

The Commission expressly declined to hold that under California law appellant's customers own the entire billing envelopes and everything contained therein. It decided only that the ratepayers own the "extra space" in the envelope, defined as that space left over after including the bill and required notices, up to a weight of one ounce. The envelopes themselves, the bills, and Progress all remain appellant's property. The Commission's access order thus clearly requires appellant to use its property as a vehicle for spreading a message with which it disagrees. In Wooley v. Maynard, we held that New Hampshire could not require two citizens to display a slogan on their license plates and thereby "use their private property as a 'mobile billboard' for the State's ideological message." 430 U.S., at 715. The "private property" that was used to spread the unwelcome message was the automobile, not the license plates. Similarly, the Commission's order requires appellant to use its property—the billing envelopes—to distribute the message of another. This is so whoever is deemed to own the "extra space."

A different conclusion would necessarily imply that our decision in *Tornillo* rested on the Miami Herald's ownership of the space that would have been used to print candidate replies. Nothing in *Tornillo* suggests that the result would have been different had the Florida Supreme Court decided that the newspaper space needed to print candidates' replies was the property of the newspaper's readers, or had the court ordered the Miami Herald to distribute inserts owned and prepared by the candidates together with its newspapers. The constitutional difficulty with the right-of-reply statute was that it required the newspaper to disseminate a message with which the newspaper disagreed. This difficulty did not depend on whether the particular paper on which the replies were printed belonged to the newspaper or to the candidate.

Appellees' argument suffers from the same constitutional defect. The Commission's order forces appellant to disseminate TURN's speech in envelopes that appellant owns and that bear appellant's return address. Such forced association with potentially hostile views burdens the expression of views different from TURN's and risks forcing appellant to speak where it would prefer to remain silent. Those effects do not depend on who "owns" the "extra space."

IV

Notwithstanding that it burdens protected speech, the Commission's order could be valid if it were a narrowly tailored means of serving a compelling state interest. . . . Appellees argue that the access order does in fact further compelling state interests. . . .

A

Appellees identify two assertedly compelling state interests that the access order is said to advance. First, appellees argue that the order furthers the State's interest in effective ratemaking proceedings. TURN has been a regular participant in those proceedings, and the Commission found that TURN has aided the Commission in performing its regulatory task. Appellees argue that the access order permits TURN to continue to help the Commission by assisting TURN in raising funds from the ratepayers whose interest TURN seeks to serve.

The State's interest in fair and effective utility regulation may be compelling. The difficulty with appellees' argument is that the State can serve that interest through means that would not violate appellant's First Amendment rights, such as awarding costs and fees. . . .

Second, appellees argue that the order furthers the State's interest in promoting speech by making a variety of views available to appellant's customers. . . . We have noted above that this interest is not furthered by an order that is not content neutral. Moreover, the means chosen to advance variety tend to inhibit expression of appellant's views in order to promote TURN's. Our cases establish that the State cannot advance some points of view by burdening the expression of others. . . . It follows that the Commission's order is not a narrowly tailored means of furthering this interest.

. . . .

V

We conclude that the Commission's order impermissibly burdens appellant's First Amendment rights because it forces appellant to associate with the views of other speakers, and because it selects the other speakers on the basis of their viewpoints. The order is not a narrowly tailored means of furthering a compelling state interest,

. . . ..

For these reasons, the decision of the California Public Utilities Commission must be vacated. The case is remanded to the California

Supreme Court for further proceedings not inconsistent with this opinion. It is so ordered.

Justice Blackmun took no part in the consideration or decision of this case.

Chief Justice Burger, concurring.

I join Justice Powell's opinion, but think we need not go beyond the authority of Wooley v. Maynard, 430 U.S. 705 (1977) to decide this case. I would not go beyond the central question presented by this case, which is the infringement of Pacific's right to be free from forced association with views with which it disagrees. I would also rely on that part of Miami Herald Publishing Co. v. Tornillo, 418 U.S. 241 (1974) holding that a forced right of reply violates a newspaper's right to be free from forced dissemination of views it would not voluntarily disseminate, just as we held that Maynard must be free from being forced by the State to disseminate views with which he disagreed. . . .

Justice Marshall, concurring in the judgment.

. . . Two significant differences between the State's grant of access in this case and the grant of access in *PruneYard* lead me to find a constitutional barrier here that I did not find in the earlier case.

The first difference is the degree of intrusiveness of the permitted access. We noted in *PruneYard:* "the shopping center by choice of its owner is not limited to the personal use of [its owner]. It is instead a business establishment that is open to the public to come and go as they please." Id., at 87. The challenged rule did not permit a markedly greater intrusion onto the property than that which the owner had voluntarily encouraged, nor did it impair the commercial value of the property. . . .

In the present case, by contrast, appellant has never opened up its billing envelope to the use of the public. Appellant has not abandoned its right to exclude others from its property to the degree that the shopping center owner had done in *PruneYard*. Were appellant to use its billing envelope as a sort of community billboard, regularly carrying the messages of third parties, its desire to exclude a particular speaker would be deserving of lesser solicitude. As matters stand, however, appellant has issued no invitation to the general public to use its billing envelope, for speech or for any other purpose. Moreover, the shopping center in *PruneYard* bore a strong resemblance to the streets and parks that are traditional public forums. People routinely gathered there, at the owner's invitation, and engaged in a wide variety of activities. Adding speech to the list of those activities did not in any great way change the complexion of the property. The same is not true in this case.

The second difference between this case and *PruneYard* is that the State has chosen to give TURN a right to speak at the expense of appellant's ability to use the property in question as a forum for the exercise of its own First Amendment rights. While the shopping center owner in *PruneYard* wished to be free of unwanted expression, he nowhere alleged that his own expression was hindered in the slightest. In contrast, the present case involves a forum of inherently limited scope. By appropriating, four times a year, the space in appellant's envelope that appellant would otherwise use for its own speech, the State has necessarily curtailed petitioner's use of its own forum. The regulation in this case, therefore, goes beyond a mere infringement of appellant's desire to remain silent . . . .

. . .

. . . I do not mean to suggest that I would hold, contrary to our precedents, that the corporation's First Amendment rights are coextensive with those of individuals, or that commercial speech enjoys the same protections as individual speech. In essentially all instances, the use of business property to carry out transactions with the general public will permit the State to restrict or mandate speech in order to prevent deception or otherwise protect the public's health and welfare. In many instances, such as in *PruneYard,* business property will be open to the public to such an extent that the public's expressive activities will not interfere with the owner's use of property to a degree that offends the Constitution. The regulation at issue in this case, I believe, falls on the other side of the line. Accordingly, I join the Court's judgment.

Justice Rehnquist, with whom Justice White and Justice Stevens join as to Part I, dissenting.

. . . I do not believe that the right of access here will have any noticeable deterrent effect. Nor do I believe that negative free speech rights, applicable to individuals and perhaps the print media, should be extended to corporations generally. I believe that the right of access here is constitutionally indistinguishable from the right of access approved in PruneYard Shopping Center v. Robins, 447 U.S. 74 (1980), and therefore I dissent.

I

This Court established in First National Bank of Boston v. Bellotti, 435 U.S. 765 (1978), that the First Amendment prohibits the Government from *directly* suppressing the affirmative speech of corporations. A newspaper publishing corporation's right to express itself freely is also implicated by governmental action that penalizes speech, see Miami Herald Publishing Co. v. Tornillo, supra, because the deterrent effect of a penalty is very much like direct suppression. Our cases cannot be squared, however, with the view that the First Amendment prohibits governmental action that only *indirectly* and *remotely* affects a speaker's contribution to the overall mix of information available to society.

. . .

. . . [T]he plurality stretches *Tornillo* to stand for the general proposition that the First Amendment prohibits any regulation that deters a corporation from engaging in some expressive behavior. But the deterrent effect of any statute is an empirical question of degree.

When the potential deterrent effect of a particular state law is remote and speculative, the law simply is not subject to heightened First Amendment scrutiny. . . .

. . . The order does not prevent PG & E from using the billing envelopes in the future to distribute inserts whenever it wishes. Nor does its vitality depend on whether PG & E includes inserts in any future billing envelopes. Moreover, the central reason for the access order—to provide for an effective ratepayer voice—would not vary in importance if PG & E had never distributed the inserts or ceased distributing them tomorrow. The most that can be said about the connection between the inserts and the order is that the existence of the inserts quite probably brought to TURN's attention the possibility of requesting access.

Nor does the access order create any cognizable risk of deterring PG & E from expressing its views in the most candid fashion. Unlike the reply statute in *Tornillo,* which conditioned access upon discrete instances of certain expression, the right of access here bears no relationship to PG & E's future conduct. PG & E cannot prevent the access by remaining silent or avoiding discussion of controversial subjects. . . .

II

The plurality argues, however, that the right of access also implicates PG & E's right not to speak or to associate with the speech of others, thereby triggering heightened scrutiny. . . .

There is, however, a . . . fundamental flaw with the plurality's analysis. This Court has recognized that natural persons enjoy negative free speech rights because of their interest in self-expression; an individual's right not to speak or to associate with the speech of others is a component of the broader constitutional interest of natural persons in freedom of conscience. . . .

. . .

Extension of the individual freedom of conscience decisions to business corporations strains the rationale of those cases beyond the breaking point. To ascribe to such artificial entities an "intellect" or "mind" for freedom of conscience purposes is to confuse metaphor with reality. Corporations generally have not played the historic role of newspapers as conveyers of individual ideas and opinion. . . .

The interest in remaining isolated from the expressive activity of others, and in declining to communicate at all, is for the most part divorced from th[e] "broad public forum" purpose of the First Amendment. The right of access here constitutes an effort to facilitate and enlarge public discussion; it therefore furthers rather than abridges First Amendment values. . . . [B]ecause the interest on which the constitutional protection of corporate speech rests is the societal interest in receiving information and ideas, the constitutional interest of a corporation in not permitting the presentation of other distinct views clearly identified as those of the speaker is de minimis. . . .

This argument is bolstered by the fact that the two constitutional liberties most closely analogous to the right to refrain from speaking—the Fifth Amendment right to remain silent and the constitutional right of privacy—have been denied to corporations based on their corporate status. . . .

III

PG & E is not an individual or a newspaper publisher; it is a regulated utility. The insistence on treating identically for constitutional purposes entities that are demonstrably different is as great a jurisprudential sin as treating differently those entities which are the same. Because I think this case is governed by *PruneYard*, supra, and not by *Tornillo*, supra, or *Wooley*, supra, I would affirm the judgment of the Supreme Court of California.

Justice Stevens, dissenting.

. . . In my view, this requirement differs little from regulations applied daily to a variety of commercial communications that have rarely been challenged—and to my knowledge never invalidated—on First Amendment grounds.

. . .

I assume that the plurality would not object to a utility commission rule dictating the format of the bill, even as to required warnings and the type size of various provisos and disclaimers. Such regulation is not too different from that applicable to credit card bills, loan forms, and media advertising. . . . I assume also the plurality would permit the Commission to require the utility to disseminate legal notices of public hearings and ratemaking proceedings written by it. These compelled statements differ little from mandating disclosure of information in the bill itself, as the plurality recognizes.

Given that the Commission can require the utility to make certain statements and to carry the Commission's own messages to its customers, it seems but a small step to acknowledge that the Commission can also require the utility to act as the conduit for a public interest group's message that bears a close relationship to the purpose of the billing envelope. An analogue to this requirement appears in securities law: the Securities and Exchange Commission requires the incumbent board of directors to transmit proposals of dissident shareholders which it opposes. Presumably the plurality does not doubt the constitutionality of the SEC's requirement under the First Amendment, and yet—although the analogy is far from perfect—it performs the same function as the Commission's rule by making accessible the relevant audience, whether it be shareholders investing in the corporation or consumers served by the utility, to individuals or groups with demonstrable interests in reaching that audience for certain limited and approved purposes.

If the California Public Utility Commission had taken over company buildings and vehicles for propaganda purposes, or even engaged in viewpoint discrimination among speakers desirous of sending messages via the billing envelope, I would be concerned. But nothing in this case presents problems even remotely resembling or portending the ones just mentioned. . . .

SECTION 3. FREEDOM OF ASSOCIATION

A. THE RIGHT TO ASSOCIATE

Page 1275. Add to end of footnote 1:

In Walters v. National Association of Radiation Survivors, 473 U.S. 305 (1985), the Court upheld a Civil War era statute limiting to $10 the fee that may be paid an attorney representing a veteran seeking compensation for service-connected death or disability. The bulk of the Court's opinion answered the argument that the limitation constituted a violation of procedural due process. The Court briefly rejected a first amendment claim. The Court expressed doubt that there was any first amendment interest involved. Cases like *Mine Workers* and *Railroad Trainmen* involved a union's freedom to retain or recommend counsel, invoking "the right to associate collectively for the common good." In any event, the conclusion that there was no violation of due process because veterans had not been denied the opportunity to make a meaningful presentation necessarily controlled the first amendment claim as well.

Page 1288. Add at end of subsection:

BOARD OF DIRECTORS OF ROTARY INTERNATIONAL v. ROTARY CLUB OF DUARTE, 107 S.Ct. 1940 (1987). The Court held that application of a state antidiscrimination law to require admission of women to membership in local Rotary clubs did not deny freedom of private association or freedom of expressive association. As to freedom of private association, the critical factors were the organization's "size, purpose, selectivity, and whether others are excluded from critical aspects of the relationship." As to freedom of expressive association, Rotary clubs do not take positions on "public questions" as a matter of policy. Even if the state antidiscrimination act "does work some slight infringement" on expressive association, it was justified by the "compelling interest in eliminating discrimination against women." In a footnote, the Court noted that it had not decided the extent of First Amendment protection of associational rights "in the many clubs and other entities with selective membership." Each case would require "a careful inquiry into the objective characteristics of the particular relationship at issue."

NEW YORK STATE CLUB ASSOCIATION, INC. v. CITY OF NEW YORK

___ U.S. ___, 108 S.Ct. 2225, ___ L.Ed.2d ___ (1988).

Justice White delivered the opinion of the Court.

New York City has adopted a local law that forbids discrimination by certain private clubs. The New York Court of Appeals rejected a facial challenge to this law based on the First and Fourteenth Amendments. . . .

I

In 1965, New York City adopted a Human Rights Law that prohibits discrimination by any "place of public accommodation, resort or amusement." This term is defined broadly in the Law to cover such various places as hotels, restaurants, retail stores, hospitals, laundries, theatres, parks, public conveyances, and public halls, in addition to numerous other places that are specifically listed. N.Y.C.Admin.Code section 8–102(9) (1986). Yet the Law also exempted from its coverage various public educational facilities and "any institution, club or place of accommodation which proves that it is in its nature distinctly private." Ibid. . . .

In 1984, New York City amended its Human Rights Law. The basic purpose of the amendment is to prohibit discrimination in certain private clubs that are determined to be sufficiently "public" in nature that they do not fit properly within the exemption for "any institution, club or place of accommodation which is in its nature distinctly private." As the City Council stated at greater length:

". . . One barrier to the advancement of women and minorities in the business and professional life of the city is the discriminatory practices of certain membership organizations where business deals are often made and personal contacts valuable for business purposes, employment and professional advancement are formed. While such organizations may avowedly be organized for social, cultural, civic or educational purposes, and while many perform valuable services to the community, the commercial nature of some of the activities occurring therein and the prejudicial impact of these activities on business, professional and employment opportunities of minorities and women cannot be ignored." . . .

. . .

The specific change wrought by the amendment is to extend the antidiscrimination provisions of the Human Rights Law to any "institution, club or place of accommodation [that] has more than four hundred members, provides regular meal service and regularly receives payment for dues, fees, use of space, facilities, services, meals or beverages directly or indirectly from or on behalf of nonmembers for the furtherance of trade or business." N.Y.C.Admin.Code section 8–102(9) (1986). Any such club "shall not be considered in its nature distinctly private." Ibid. Nonetheless, the city also stated that any such club "shall be deemed to be in its nature distinctly private" if it is "a corporation incorporated under the benevolent orders law or described in the benevolent orders law but formed under any other law of this state, or a religious corporation incorporated under the education law or the religious corporations law." Ibid. The City Council explained that it drafted the amendment in this way so as to meet the specific problem confronting women and minorities in the city's business and professional world: "Because small clubs, benevolent orders and religious corporations have not been identified in testimony before the Council as places where business activity is prevalent, the Council has determined not to apply the requirements of this local law to such organizations." Local Law No. 63, section 1.

Immediately after the 1984 Law became effective, the New York State Club Association filed suit against the city and some of its officers in state court, seeking a declaration that the Law is invalid on various state grounds and is unconstitutional on its face under the First and Fourteenth Amendments and requesting that defendants be enjoined from enforcing it. On cross-motions for summary judgment, the trial court upheld the Law against all challenges, including the federal constitutional challenges. The intermediate state appellate court affirmed. . . .

The State Club Association appealed this decision to the New York Court of Appeals, which affirmed in a unanimous opinion. . . .

. . . We . . . affirm the judgment below, upholding Local Law 63 against appellant's facial attack on its constitutionality.

    . . .

                                III

    . . .

None of [the law's enforcement] procedures has come into play in this case . . . for appellant brought this suit challenging the constitutionality of the statute on its face before any enforcement proceedings were initiated against any of its member associations. Although such facial challenges are sometimes permissible and often have been entertained, especially when speech protected by the First Amendment is at stake, to prevail on a facial attack the plaintiff must demonstrate that the challenged law either "could never be applied in a valid manner" or that even though it may be validly applied to the plaintiff and others, it nevertheless is so broad that it "may inhibit the constitutionally protected speech of third parties." City Council v. Taxpayers for Vincent, 466 U.S. 789, 798 (1984). Properly understood, the latter kind of facial challenge is an exception to ordinary standing requirements, and is justified only by the recognition that free expression may be inhibited almost as easily by the potential or threatened use of power as by the actual exercise of that power. Thornhill v. Alabama, 310 U.S. 88, 97–98 (1940). Both exceptions, however, are narrow ones: the first kind of facial challenge will not succeed unless the court finds that "every application of the statute created an impermissible risk of suppression of ideas," Taxpayers for Vincent, supra, at 798, n. 15, and the second kind of facial challenge will not succeed unless the statute is "substantially" overbroad, which requires the court to find "a realistic danger that the statute itself will significantly compromise recognized First Amendment protections of parties not before the Court." 466 U.S., at 801.

We are unpersuaded that appellant is entitled to make either one of these two distinct facial challenges. Appellant conceded at oral argument, understandably we think, that the antidiscrimination provisions of the Law certainly could be constitutionally applied at least to some of the large clubs, under this Court's decisions in *Rotary* and *Roberts*. The clubs that are covered under the Law contain at least 400 members. They thus are comparable in size to the local chapters of the Jaycees that we found not to be protected private associations in *Roberts*, and they are considerably larger than many of the local clubs that were found to be unprotected in *Rotary*, some which included as few as 20 members. . . . The clubs covered by Local Law 63 also provide "regular meal service" and receive regular payments "directly or indirectly from or on behalf of nonmembers for the furtherance of trade or business." N.Y.C.Admin.Code section 8–102(9) (1986). The city found these two characteristics to be significant in pinpointing organizations which are "commercial" in nature, "where business deals are often made and personal contacts valuable for business purposes, employment and professional advancement are formed." Local Law 63, section 1.

These characteristics are at least as significant in defining the nonprivate nature of these associations, because of the kind of role that strangers play in their ordinary existence, as is the regular participation of strangers at meetings, which we emphasized in *Roberts* and *Rotary*. . . . It may well be that a considerable amount of private or intimate association occurs in such a setting, as is also true in many restaurants and other places of public accommodation . . . . Although there may be clubs that would be entitled to constitutional protection despite the presence of these characteristics, surely it cannot be said that Local Law 63 is invalid on its face because it infringes the private associational rights of each and every club covered by it.

The same may be said about the contention that the Law infringes upon every club member's right of expressive association. The ability and the opportunity to combine with others to advance one's views is a powerful practical means of ensuring the perpetuation of the freedoms the First Amendment has guaranteed to individuals as against the Government. . . . This is not to say, however, that in every setting in which individuals exercise some discrimination in choosing associates, their selective process of inclusion and exclusion is protected by the Constitution. . . .

On its face, Local Law 63 does not affect "in any significant way" the ability of individuals to form associations that will advocate public or private viewpoints. *Rotary*, supra, at ___. It does not require the clubs "to abandon or alter" any activities that are protected by the First Amendment. Ibid. If a club seeks to exclude individuals who do not share the views that the club's members wish to promote, the Law erects no obstacle to this end. Instead, the Law merely prevents an association from using race, sex, and the other specified characteristics as shorthand measures in place of what the city considers to be more legitimate criteria for determining membership. It is conceivable, of course, that an association might be able to show that it is organized for specific expressive purposes and that it will not be able to advocate its desired viewpoints nearly as effectively if it cannot confine its membership to those who share the same sex, for example, or the same religion. In the case before us, however, it seems sensible enough to believe that many of the large clubs covered by the Law are not of this kind. We could hardly hold otherwise on the record before us, which contains no specific evidence on the characteristics of *any* club covered by the Law.

The facial attack based on the claim that Local Law 63 is invalid in all of its applications must therefore fail. Appellant insists, however, that there are some clubs within the reach of the Law that are "distinctively private" and that the Law is therefore overbroad and invalid on its face. But as we have indicated, this kind of facial challenge also falls short.

The overbreadth doctrine is "strong medicine" that is used "sparingly and only as a last resort." Broadrick v. Oklahoma, 413 U.S. 601, 613 (1973). A law is constitutional unless it is "substantially overbroad." Id., at 615. To succeed in its challenge, appellant must demonstrate from the text of the Law and from actual fact that a substantial number of instances exist in which the Law cannot be applied constitutionally. Yet appellant has not identified those clubs for whom the antidiscrimination provisions will impair their ability to associate together or to advocate public or private viewpoints. . . . We therefore cannot conclude that the Law is substantially overbroad and must assume that "whatever overbreadth may exist should be cured through case-by-case analysis of the fact situations to which its sanctions, assertedly, may not be applied." Id., at 615–616.

. . .

IV

Appellant also contends that the exemption in Local Law 63 for benevolent and religious corporations, which deems them to be "distinctly private" in nature, violates the Equal Protection Clause. Since, as just discussed, it has not been demonstrated that the Law affects "in any significant way" the fundamental interests of any clubs covered by the Law, heightened scrutiny does not apply. . . . On this state of the record, the equal protection challenge must fail unless the city could not reasonably believe that the exempted organizations are different in relevant respects from appellant's members.

As written, the legislative classification on its face is not manifestly without reasoned support. . . .

Appellant contends, however, that the benevolent and religious corporations exempted in the Law are in fact no different in nature from the other clubs and associations that are now made subject to the city's antidiscrimination restrictions.   . . .

. . .

The City Council's explanation for exempting benevolent orders and religious corporations from the Law's coverage reflects a view that these associations are different in kind, at least in the crucial respect of whether business activity is prevalent among them, from the associations on whose behalf appellant has brought suit. Appellant has the burden of showing that this view is erroneous and that the issue is not truly debatable, a burden that appellant has failed to carry. . . .

We therefore affirm the judgment below.

So ordered.

Justice O'Connor, with whom Justice Kennedy joins, concurring.

I agree with the court's conclusion that the facial challenge to Local Law 63 must fail. I write separately only to note that nothing in the Court's opinion in any way undermines or denigrates the importance of any associational interest at stake.

. . .

In a city as large and diverse as New York City, there surely will be organizations that fall within the potential reach of Local Law 63 and yet are deserving of constitutional protection. For example, in such a large city a club with over 400 members may still be relatively intimate in nature, so that a constitutional right to control membership takes precedence. Similarly, there may well be organizations whose expressive purposes would be substantially undermined if they were unable to confine their membership to those of the same sex, race, religion, or ethnic background, or who share some other such common bond. The associational rights of such organizations must be respected.

But as the Court points out, . . . the existence of such protected clubs does not mean that Local Law 63 cannot be applied to other clubs. Predominately commercial organizations are not entitled to claim a First Amendment associational or expressive right to be free from the antidiscrimination provisions triggered by the law. Because Local Law 63 may be applied constitutionally to these organizations, I agree with the Court that is not invalid on its face.

Justice Scalia, concurring in part and concurring in the judgment.

I concur in the judgment of the Court, and join all except Part IV of its opinion. I note that Part III assumes for purposes of its analysis, but does not hold, the existence of a constitutional right of private association for other than expressive or religious purposes.

With respect to the equal protection issue discussed in Part IV of the opinion, I do not believe that the mere fact that benevolent orders "are unique," suffices to establish that a rational basis exits for their exemption. As forgiving as the rational basis test is, it does not go that far. There must at least be some plausible connection between the respect in which they are unique and the purpose of the law.

. . .

. . . I am content that it was rational . . . to think that such organizations did not significantly contribute to the problem the City Council was addressing. A lodge is not likely to be a club where men dine with clients and conduct business. Appellant introduced no evidence to the contrary.

B. THE RIGHT NOT TO ASSOCIATE

Page 1292. Add at end of footnote:

In Communications Workers of America v. Beck, 108 S.Ct. 2641 (1988), the Court followed Machinists v. Street, which had held that the Railway Labor Act forbids expending compulsory union fees on political causes. The Court held that the National Labor Relations Act imposed the same obligation upon non-railroad unions.

C. POLITICAL ASSOCIATION

---

1. Choosing and Electing Candidates for Public Office

Page 1294. Add ahead of Storer v. Brown:

TASHJIAN v. REPUBLICAN PARTY OF CONNECTICUT
479 U.S. 208, 107 S.Ct. 544, 93 L.Ed.2d 514 (1986).

Justice Marshall delivered the opinion of the Court.

Appellee Republican Party of the State of Connecticut (the Party) in 1984 adopted a party rule which permits independent voters—registered voters not affiliated with any political party—to vote in Republican primaries for federal and statewide offices. . . . [T]he State's election statutes . . . [require] voters in any party primary to be registered members of that party. Conn.Gen.Stat. section 9–431 (1985). Appellees . . . challenged this eligibility provision on the ground that it deprives the Party of its First Amendment right to enter into political association with individuals of its own choosing. The District Court granted summary judgment in favor of appellees. The Court of Appeals affirmed. We . . . affirm.

I

In 1955, Connecticut adopted its present primary election system. For major parties, the process of candidate selection for federal and statewide offices requires a statewide convention of party delegates; district conventions are held to select candidates for seats in the state legislature. The party convention may certify as the party-endorsed candidate any person receiving more than 20% of the votes cast in a roll-call vote at the convention. Any candidate not endorsed by the party who received 20% of the vote may challenge the party-endorsed candidate in a primary election, in which the candidate receiving the plurality of votes becomes the party's nominee. Conn.Gen.Stat. sections 9–382, 9–400, 9–444 (1985). Candidates selected by the major parties, whether through convention or primary, are automatically accorded a place on the ballot at the general election. Section 9–379. The costs of primary elections are paid out of public funds. See, e.g., section 9–441.

The statute challenged in these proceedings, section 9–431, has remained substantially unchanged since the adoption of the State's primary system. In 1976, the statute's constitutionality was upheld by a three-judge District Court against a challenge by an independent voter who sought a declaration of his right to vote in the Republican primary. Nader v. Schaffer, 417 F.Supp. 837 (Conn.), summarily aff'd, 429 U.S. 989 (1976). In that action, the Party opposed the plaintiff's efforts to participate in the Party primary.

Subsequent to the decision in *Nader,* however, the Party changed its views with respect to participation by independent voters in Party primaries. Motivated in part by the demographic importance of independent voters in Connecticut politics, in September 1983 the Party's Central Committee recommended calling a state convention to consider altering the Party's rules to allow independents to vote in Party primaries. In January 1984 the state convention adopted the Party rule now at issue, which provides:

> "Any elector enrolled as a member of the Republican Party and any elector not enrolled as a member of a party shall be eligible to vote in primaries for nomination of candidates for the offices of United States Senator, United States Representative, Governor, Lieutenant Governor, Secretary of the State, Attorney General, Comptroller and Treasurer."

During the 1984 session, the Republican leadership in the state legislature, in response to the conflict between the newly enacted Party rule and section 9–431, proposed to amend the statute to allow independents to vote in primaries when permitted by Party rules. The proposed legislation was defeated, substantially along party lines, in both houses of the legislature, which at that time were controlled by the Democratic Party.

. . .

II

We begin from the recognition that "[c]onstitutional challenges to specific provisions of a State's election laws . . . cannot be resolved by any 'litmus-paper test' that will separate valid from invalid restrictions." Anderson v. Celebrezze, 460 U.S. 780, 789 (1983) (quoting Storer v. Brown, 415 U.S. 724, 730 (1974)). "Instead, a court . . . must first consider the character and magnitude of the asserted injury to the rights protected by the First and Fourteenth Amendments that the plaintiff seeks to vindicate. It must then identify and evaluate the precise interests put forward by the State as justifications for the burden imposed by its rule. In passing judgment, the Court must not only determine the legitimacy and strength of each of these interests, it also must consider the extent to which those interests make it necessary to burden the plaintiff's rights." 460 U.S., at 789.

The nature of the appellees' First Amendment interest is evident. . . . "The right to associate with the political party of one's choice is an integral part of this basic constitutional freedom." Kusper v. Pontikes, 414 U.S. 51, 57 (1973).

The Party here contends that section 9–431 impermissibly burdens the right of its members to determine for themselves with whom they will associate, and whose support they will seek, in their quest for political success. The Party's attempt to broaden the base of public participation in and support for its activities is conduct undeniably central to the exercise of the right of association. As we have said, the freedom to join together in furtherance of common political beliefs "necessarily presupposes the freedom to identify the people who constitute the association." Democratic Party of the United States v. Wisconsin, 450 U.S. 107, 122 (1981).

. . .

Were the State to restrict by statute financial support of the Party's candidates to Party members, or to provide that only Party members might be selected as the Party's chosen nominees for public office, such a prohibition of potential association with nonmembers would clearly infringe upon the rights of the Party's members under the First Amendment to organize with like-minded citizens in support of common political goals. As we have said, " 'any interference with the freedom of a party is simultaneously an interference with the freedom of its adherents.' " *Democratic Party,* supra, at 122 (quoting *Sweezy v. New Hampshire,* 354 U.S. 234, 250 (1957)).[6] The statute here places limits upon the group of registered voters whom the Party may invite to participate in the "basic function" of selecting the Party's candidates. Kusper v. Pontikes, supra, at 58. The State thus limits the Party's associational opportunities at the crucial juncture at which the appeal to common principles may be translated into concerted action, and hence to political power in the community.

It is, of course, fundamental to appellant's defense of the State's statute that this impingement upon the associational rights of the Party and its members occurs at the ballot box, for the Constitution grants to the States a broad power to prescribe the "Times, Places and Manner of holding Elections for Senators and Representatives," Art. I,

---

[6] It is this element of potential interference with the rights of the Party's members which distinguishes the present case from others in which we have considered claims by nonmembers of a party seeking to vote in that party's primary despite the party's opposition. In this latter class of cases, the nonmember's desire to participate in the party's affairs is overborne by the countervailing and legitimate right of the party to determine its own membership qualifications. See Rosario v. Rockefeller, 410 U.S. 752 (1973); Nader v. Schaffer, 417 F.Supp. 837 (Conn.), summarily aff'd, 429 U.S. 989 (1976). Similarly, the Court has upheld the right of national political parties to refuse to seat at their conventions delegates chosen in state selection processes which did not conform to party rules. See Democratic Party of United States v. Wisconsin, 450 U.S. 107 (1981); Cousins v. Wigoda, 419 U.S. 477 (1975). These situations are analytically distinct from the present case, in which the Party and its members seek to provide enhanced opportunities for participation by willing nonmembers. Under these circumstances, there is no conflict between the associational interests of members and nonmembers. See generally Note, Primary Elections and the Collective Right of Freedom of Association, 94 Yale L.J. 117 (1984).

section 4, cl. 1, which power is matched by state control over the election process for state offices. But this authority does not extinguish the State's responsibility to observe the limits established by the First Amendment rights of the State's citizens. The power to regulate the time, place, and manner of elections does not justify, without more, the abridgment of fundamental rights, such as the right to vote, see Wesberry v. Sanders, 376 U.S. 1, 6–7 (1964), or, as here, the freedom of political association. We turn then to an examination of the interests which appellant asserts to justify the burden cast by the statute upon the associational rights of the Party and its members.

III

Appellant contends that section 9–431 is a narrowly tailored regulation which advances the State's compelling interests by ensuring the administrability of the primary system, preventing raiding, avoiding voter confusion, and protecting the responsibility of party government.

A

Although it was not presented to the Court of Appeals as a basis for the defense of the statute, appellant argues here that the administrative burden imposed by the Party rule is a sufficient ground on which to uphold the constitutionality of section 9–431. Appellant contends that the Party's rule would require the purchase of additional voting machines, the training of additional poll workers, and potentially the printing of additional ballot materials specifically intended for independents voting in the Republican primary. . . .

. . . [T]he possibility of future increases in the cost of administering the election system is not a sufficient basis here for infringing appellees' First Amendment rights. . . . While the State is of course entitled to take administrative and financial considerations into account in choosing whether or not to have a primary system at all, it can no more restrain the Republican Party's freedom of association for reasons of its own administrative convenience than it could on the same ground limit the ballot access of a new major party.

B

Appellant argues that section 9–431 is justified as a measure to prevent raiding, a practice "whereby voters in sympathy with one party designate themselves as voters of another party so as to influence or determine the results of the other party's primary." Rosario v. Rockefeller, 410 U.S. 752, 760 (1973). While we have recognized that "a State may have a legitimate interest in seeking to curtail 'raiding,' since that practice may affect the integrity of the electoral process," Kusper v. Pontikes, 414 U.S., at 59–60; Rosario v. Rockefeller, supra, at 761, that interest is not implicated here. . . . Yet a raid on the Republican Party primary by independent voters, a curious concept only distantly related to the type of raiding discussed in *Kusper* and *Rosario,* is not impeded by section 9–431. . . . Indeed, under Conn.Gen.Stat. section

9–56 (1985), which permits an independent to affiliate with the Party as late as noon on the business day preceding the primary, the State's election statutes actually *assist* a "raid" by independents, which could be organized and implemented at the eleventh hour. The State's asserted interest in the prevention of raiding provides no justification for the statute challenged here.

C

Appellant's next argument in support of section 9–431 is that the closed primary system avoids voter confusion. Appellant contends that "the legislature could properly find that it would be difficult for the general public to understand what a candidate stood for who was nominated in part by an unknown amorphous body outside the party, while nevertheless using the party name." . . .

. . . To the extent that party labels provide a shorthand designation of the views of party candidates on matters of public concern, the identification of candidates with particular parties plays a role in the process by which voters inform themselves for the exercise of the franchise. . . . [A]ppellant's concern that candidates selected under the Party rule will be the nominees of an "amorphous" group using the Party's name is inconsistent with the facts. The Party is not proposing that independents be allowed to choose the Party's nominee without Party participation; on the contrary, to be listed on the Party's primary ballot continues to require, under a statute not challenged here, that the primary candidate have obtained at least 20% of the vote at a Party convention, which only Party members may attend. Conn.Gen.Stat. section 9–400 (1985). If no such candidate seeks to challenge the convention's nominee in a primary, then no primary is held, and the convention nominee becomes the Party's nominee in the general election without any intervention by independent voters. Even assuming, however, that putative candidates defeated at the Party convention will have an increased incentive under the Party's rule to make primary challenges, hoping to attract more substantial support from independents than from Party delegates, the requirement that such challengers garner substantial minority support at the convention greatly attenuates the State's concern that the ultimate nominee will be wedded to the Party in nothing more than a marriage of convenience.

In arguing that the Party rule interferes with educated decisions by voters, appellant also disregards the substantial benefit which the Party rule provides to the Party and its members in seeking to choose successful candidates. Given the numerical strength of independent voters in the State, one of the questions most likely to occur to Connecticut Republicans in selecting candidates for public office is, how can the Party most effectively appeal to the independent voter? By inviting independents to assist in the choice at the polls between primary candidates selected at the Party convention, the Party rule is intended to produce the candidate and platform most likely to achieve that goal. The state statute is said to decrease voter confusion, yet it deprives the Party and its members of the opportunity to inform themselves as to the level of support for the Party's candidates among a critical group of electors. "A State's claim that it is enhancing the ability of its citizenry to make wise decisions by restricting the flow of information to them must be viewed with some skepticism." Anderson v. Celebrezze, supra, at 798. The State's legitimate interests in preventing voter confusion and providing for educated and responsible voter decisions in no respect "make it necessary to burden the Party's rights." 460 U.S., at 789.

D

Finally, appellant contends that section 9–431 furthers the State's compelling interest in protecting the integrity of the two-party system and the responsibility of party government. Appellant argues vigorously and at length that the closed primary system chosen by the state legislature promotes responsiveness by elected officials and strengthens the effectiveness of the political parties.

The relative merits of closed and open primaries have been the subject of substantial debate since the beginning of this century, and no consensus has as yet emerged.[11] Appellant invokes a long and distinguished line of political scientists and public officials who have been supporters of the closed primary. But our role is not to decide whether the state legislature was acting wisely in enacting the closed primary system in 1955, or whether the Republican Party makes a mistake in seeking to depart from the practice of the past 30 years.

We have previously recognized the danger that "splintered parties and unrestrained factionalism may do significant damage to the fabric of government." Storer v. Brown, 415 U.S., at 736. We upheld a California statute which denied access to the ballot to any independent candidate who had voted in a party primary or been registered as a member of a political party within one year prior to the immediately preceding primary election. . . .

The statute in *Storer* was designed to protect the parties and the party system against the disorganizing effect of independent candidacies launched by unsuccessful putative party nominees. This protection, like that accorded to parties threatened by raiding in Rosario v. Rockefeller, 410 U.S. 752 (1973), is undertaken to prevent the disruption of the political parties from without, and not, as in this case, to prevent the parties from taking internal steps affecting their own process for the selection of candidates. The forms of regulation upheld in *Storer* and *Rosario* imposed certain burdens upon the protected First and Fourteenth Amendment interests of some individuals, both voters and potential candidates, in order to protect the interests of others. In

[11] At the present time, 21 States provide for "closed" primaries of the classic sort, in which the primary voter must be registered as a member of the party for some period of time prior to the holding of the primary election. . . . Sixteen States allow a voter previously unaffiliated with any party to vote in a party primary if he affiliates with the party at the time of, or for the purpose of, voting in the primary. . . . Four States provide for nonpartisan primaries in which all registered voters may participate, . . . while nine States have adopted classical "open" primaries, in which all registered voters may choose in which party primary to vote. . . .

the present case, the state statute is defended on the ground that it protects the integrity of the Party against the Party itself.

Under these circumstances, the views of the State, which to some extent represent the views of the one political party transiently enjoying majority power, as to the optimum methods for preserving party integrity lose much of their force. The State argues that its statute is well designed to save the Republican Party from undertaking a course of conduct destructive of its own interests. But on this point "even if the State were correct, a State, or a court, may not constitutionally substitute its own judgment for that of the Party." Democratic Party of United States v. Wisconsin, 450 U.S., at 123–124 (footnote omitted). The Party's determination of the boundaries of its own association, and of the structure which best allows it to pursue its political goals, is protected by the Constitution. "And as is true of all expressions of First Amendment freedoms, the courts may not interfere on the ground that they view a particular expression as unwise or irrational." Id., at 124.[13]

We conclude that the State's enforcement, under these circumstances, of its closed primary system burdens the First Amendment rights of the Party. The interests which the appellant adduces in support of the statute are insubstantial, and accordingly the statute, as applied to the Party in this case, is unconstitutional.

IV

Appellant argues here, as in the courts below, that implementation of the Party rule would violate the Qualifications Clause of the Constitution, Art. I, section 2, cl. 1, and the Seventeenth Amendment because it would establish qualifications for voting in congressional elections which differ from the voting qualifications in elections for the more numerous house of the state legislature. The Party rule as adopted permits independent voters to vote in Party primaries for the offices of United States Senator and Member of the House of Representatives, and for statewide offices, but is silent as regards primaries held to contest nominations for seats in the state legislature. Appellant contends that the Qualifications Clause and the Seventeenth Amendment require an absolute symmetry of qualifications to vote in elections for Congress and the lower house of the state legislature, and that the Party rule, if implemented according to its terms, would require lesser qualifications for voting in Party primaries for federal office than for state legislative office.

---

[13] Our holding today does not establish that state regulation of primary voting qualifications may never withstand challenge by a political party or its membership. A party seeking, for example, to open its primary to all voters, including members of other parties, would raise a different combination of considerations. Under such circumstances, the effect of one party's broadening of participation would threaten other parties with the disorganization effects which the statutes in Storer v. Brown, 415 U.S. 724 (1974), and Rosario v. Rockefeller, 410 U.S. 752 (1973), were designed to prevent. We have observed on several occasions that a State may adopt a "policy of confining each voter to a single nominating act," a policy decision which is not involved in the present case. . . .

. . .

We recognize that the Federal Convention, in adopting the Qualifications Clause of Article I, section 2, was not contemplating the effects of that provision upon the modern system of party primaries. . . .

The fundamental purpose underlying Article I, section 2, that "the House of Representatives shall be composed of Members chosen . . . by the People of the several States," like the parallel provision of the Seventeenth Amendment, applies to the entire process by which federal legislators are chosen. . . . The constitutional goal of assuring that the Members of Congress are chosen by the people can only be secured if that principle is applicable to every stage in the selection process. If primaries were not subject to the requirements of the Qualifications Clauses contained in Article I, section 2 and the Seventeenth Amendment, the fundamental principle of free electoral choice would be subject to the sort of erosion these prior decisions were intended to prevent.

Accordingly, we hold that the Qualifications Clauses of Article I, section 2, and the Seventeenth Amendment are applicable to primary elections in precisely the same fashion that they apply to general congressional elections. Our task is then to discover whether, as appellant contends, those provisions require that voter qualifications, such as party membership, in primaries for federal office must be absolutely symmetrical with those pertaining to primaries for state legislative office.

Our inquiry begins with an examination of the Framers' purpose in enacting the first Qualifications Clause. It is clear that the clause was intended to avoid the consequences of declaring a single standard for exercise of the franchise in federal elections. The state governments represented at the Convention had established varying voter qualifications, and substantial concern was expressed by delegates as to the likely effects of a federal voting qualification which disenfranchised voters eligible to vote in the states. James Wilson argued that "it would be very hard and disagreeable for the same persons, at the same time, to vote for representatives in the State Legislature, and to be excluded from a vote for those in the National Legislature." . . .

In adopting the language of Article I, section 2, the Convention rejected the suggestion that a property qualification was necessary to restrict the availability of the federal franchise. See Madison's Journal 468–473; 2 M. Farrand, The Records of the Federal Convention of 1787, at 200–216 (1966). Far from being a device to limit the federal suffrage, the Qualifications Clause was intended by the Framers to prevent the mischief which would arise if state voters found themselves disqualified from participation in federal elections. The achievement of this goal does not require that qualifications for exercise of the federal franchise be at all times precisely equivalent to the prevailing qualifications for the exercise of the franchise in a given state. The fundamental purpose of the Qualifications Clauses contained in Article I, section 2, and the Seventeenth Amendment is satisfied if all those qualified to participate in the selection of members of the more numerous branch of the state legislature are also qualified to participate in the election of Senators and Members of the House of Representatives.

. . .

V

We conclude that section 9–431 impermissibly burdens the rights of the Party and its members protected by the First and Fourteenth Amendments. The interests asserted by appellant in defense of the statute are insubstantial. The judgment of the Court of Appeals is

Affirmed.

Justice Stevens, with whom Justice Scalia joins, dissenting.

The threshold issue by this case is whether, consistently with the Constitution, a State may permit a voter to participate in elections to the Congress while preventing that same person from voting for candidates to the most numerous branch of the state legislature. If we respect the plain language of Article I, section 2, of the Constitution and the Seventeenth Amendment, [and] the intent of the Framers, . . . we must answer that question in the negative.

. . .

The Court does not dispute the fact that the plain language of the Constitution requires that voters in congressional and senatorial elections "shall have" the qualifications of voters in elections to the state legislature. The Court nevertheless separates the federal voter qualifications from their state counterparts, inexplicably treating the mandatory "shall have" language of the Clauses as though it means only that the federal voters "may but need not have" the qualifications of state voters. In support of this freewheeling interpretation of the Constitution, the Court relies on what it describes as the Framers' purpose in enacting the first Qualification Clause. . . .

. . . [T]he draft that the Federal Convention of 1787 was considering . . . was abundantly clear—the qualifications of the federal electors "shall be the same" as the electors of the legislatures of the several States. . . . This provision would ensure uniformity of electors' qualifications within each State, but would not impose a uniform nationwide standard.

. . .

Justice Scalia, with whom The Chief Justice and Justice O'Connor join, dissenting.

. . .

In my view, the Court's opinion exaggerates the importance of the associational interest at issue, if indeed it does not see one where none exists. There is no question here of restricting the Republican Party's ability to recruit and enroll Party members by offering them the ability to select Party candidates; Conn.Gen.Stat. section 9–56 (1985) permits an independent voter to join the Party as late as the day before the primary. Cf. Kusper v. Pontikes, 414 U.S. 51 (1973). Nor is there any question of restricting the ability of the Party's members to select whatever candidate they desire. Appellees' only complaint is that the Party cannot leave the selection of its candidate to persons who are *not* members of the Party, and are unwilling to become members. It seems to me fanciful to refer to this as an interest in freedom of association between the members of the Republican Party and the putative independent voters. The Connecticut voter who, while steadfastly refusing to register as a Republican, casts a vote in the Republican primary, forms no more meaningful an "association" with the Party than does the independent or the registered Democrat who responds to questions by a Republican Party pollster. If the concept of freedom of association is extended to such casual contracts, it ceases to be of any analytical use. See Democratic Party of the United States v. Wisconsin ex rel. La Follette, 450 U.S. 107, 130–131 (1981) (Powell, J., dissenting) ("Not every conflict between state law and party rules concerning participation in the nomination process creates a burden on associational rights"; one must "look closely at the nature of the instrusion, in light of the nature of the association involved, to see whether we are presented with a real limitation on First Amendment freedoms").

The ability of the members of the Republican Party to select their own candidate, on the other hand, unquestionably implicates an associational freedom—but it can hardly be thought that that freedom is unconstitutionally impaired here. The Party is entirely free to put forward, if it wishes, that candidate who has the highest degree of support among Party members and independents combined. The State is under no obligation, however, to let its party primary be used, instead of a party-funded opinion poll, as the means by which the party identifies the relative popularity of its potential candidates among independents. Nor is there any reason apparent to me why the State cannot insist that this decision to support what might be called the independents' choice be taken *by the party membership in a democratic fashion,* rather than through a process that permits the members' votes to be diluted—and perhaps even absolutely outnumbered—by the votes of outsiders.

. . . *[E]ven if* it were the fact that the majority of the Party's members wanted its candidates to be determined by outsiders, there is no reason why the State is bound to honor that desire—any more than it would be bound to honor a party's democratically expressed desire that its candidates henceforth be selected by convention rather than by primary, or by the party's executive committee in a smoke-filled room. In other words, the validity of the state-imposed primary requirement itself, which we have hitherto considered "too plain for argument," American Party of Texas v. White, 415 U.S. 767, 781 (1974), presupposes that the State *has* the right "to protect the Party against the Party itself." Connecticut may lawfully require that significant elements of the democratic election process be democratic—whether the Party wants that or not. It is beyond my understanding why the Republican Party's delegation of its democratic choice to a Republican Convention can be proscribed, but its delegation of that choice to nonmembers of the Party cannot.

. . .

I respectfully dissent.

Page 1297.   Add after Storer v. Brown:

MUNRO v. SOCIALIST WORKERS PARTY, 479 U.S. 189
(1986). The Court upheld a Washington statute requiring minor-party
candidates for partisan offices to receive at least 1% of all votes cast for
that office in the primary election before the candidate's name would
be placed on the general election ballot. The statute imposed a valid
requirement that a candidate make a preliminary showing of substantial support in order to qualify for a place on the ballot. (Washington
conducts a "blanket primary," allowing voters to vote for any candidate
in the primary, regardless of the voter's political affiliation.) Eliminating minor party candidates without substantial voter support from the
general election ballot was supported by state interests in simplifying
the general election ballot and avoiding unrestrained factionalism at
the general election. Minor party candidates had easy access to the
primary ballot, giving them greater access to a statewide ballot than
did the statute upheld in Storer v. Brown.

---

2. POLITICAL FUNDRAISING AND EXPENDITURES

Page 1303.   Add after note, "Contributions to Ballot Measure Campaigns":

MEYER v. GRANT, 108 S.Ct. 1886 (1988). A Colorado statute,
requiring signatures of 5% of qualified voters on petitions to put an
initiative measure on the ballot, forbade paying petition circulators. A
unanimous Court concluded that the prohibition on the use of paid
petition circulators violated the First Amendment. The circulation of
an initiative petition constitutes "core political speech." Forbidding
payment burdens circulation. Asserted justifications did not survive
"exacting scrutiny." An interest in requiring grass roots support for
ballot initiatives was protected by the requirement that a specified
number of signatures be obtained. An interest in protecting integrity
of the initiative process was not served at all by the prohibition.

Page 1303.   Replace last paragraph of note on political action committees:

Federal Election Commission v. National Conservative Political
Action Committee, 470 U.S. 480 (1985) held that section 9012(f) of the
Presidential Election Campaign Fund Act was invalid under the first
amendment. That section prohibited independent political committees
from expending more than $1,000 to further the election of a presiden-
tial candidate who had opted to receive public financing. The Court
relied on that aspect of the decision in Buckley v. Valeo invalidating
limits on individual campaign expenditures. The Court rejected the
argument that PAC spending presented a greater potential for corruption because the breadth of PAC organization permitted expenditures

larger than individual expenditures. Justices White and Marshall dissented.

Page 1311. Add at end of Section:

FEDERAL ELECTION COMMISSION v. MASSACHUSETTS CITIZENS FOR LIFE, INC.
479 U.S. 238, 107 S.Ct. 616, 93 L.Ed.2d 539 (1986).

Justice Brennan delivered the opinion of the Court with respect to Parts I, II, III–B, and III–C, and an opinion with respect to Part III–A, in which Justice Marshall, Justice Powell, and Justice Scalia joined.

The questions for decision here arise under section 316 of the Federal Election Campaign Act (FECA or Act), 2 U.S.C. section 441b. The first question is whether appellee Massachusetts Citizens for Life, Inc. (MCFL), a nonprofit, nonstock corporation, by financing certain activity with its treasury funds, has violated the restriction on independent spending contained in section 441b. That section prohibits corporations from using treasury funds to make an expenditure "in connection with any election to any public office," and requires that any expenditure for such purpose be financed by voluntary contributions to a separate segregated fund. If appellee has violated section 441b, the next question is whether application of that section to MCFL's conduct is constitutional. We hold that the appellee's use of its treasury funds is prohibited by section 441b, but that section 441b is unconstitutional as applied to the activity of which the Federal Election Commission (FEC or Commission) complains.

I

A

MCFL was incorporated in January, 1973 as a nonprofit, nonstock corporation under Massachusetts law. Its corporate purpose as stated in its articles of incorporation is:

"To foster respect for human life and to defend the right to life of all human beings, born and unborn, through educational, political and other forms of activities and in addition to engage in any other lawful act or activity for which corporations may be organized . . ."

MCFL does not accept contributions from business corporations or unions. Its resources come from voluntary donations from "members," and from various fund-raising activities such as garage sales, bake sales, dances, raffles, and picnics. The corporation considers its "members" those persons who have either contributed to the organization in the past or indicated support for its activities.

Appellee has engaged in diverse educational and legislative activities designed to further its agenda. It has organized an ecumenical prayer service for the unborn in front of the Massachusetts State House; sponsored a regional conference to discuss the issues of abortion and euthanasia; provided speakers for discussion groups, debates, lectures, and media programs; and sponsored an annual March for Life. In addition, it has drafted and submitted legislation, some of which has become law in Massachusetts; sponsored testimony on proposed legislation; and has urged its members to contact their elected representatives to express their opinion on legislative proposals.

MCFL began publishing a newsletter in January 1973. It was distributed as a matter of course to contributors, and, when funds permitted, to noncontributors who had expressed support for the organization. The total distribution of any one issue has never exceeded 6,000. The newsletter was published irregularly from 1973 through 1978: three times in 1973, five times in 1974, eight times in 1975, eight times in 1976, five times in 1977, and four times in 1978. Each of the newsletters bore a masthead identifying it as the "Massachusetts Citizens for Life Newsletter," as well as a volume and issue number. The publication typically contained appeals for volunteers and contributions, and information on MCFL activities, as well as on matters such as the results of hearings on bills and constitutional amendments, the status of particular legislation, the outcome of referenda, court decisions, and administrative hearings. Newsletter recipients were usually urged to contact the relevant decision-makers and express their opinion.

B

In September 1978, MCFL prepared and distributed a "Special Election Edition" prior to the September 1978 primary elections. While the May 1978 newsletter had been mailed to 2,109 people and the October 1978 newsletter to 3,119 people, more than 100,000 copies of the "Special Election Edition" were printed for distribution. The front page of the publication was headlined "EVERYTHING YOU NEED TO KNOW TO VOTE PRO–LIFE," and readers were admonished that "no pro-life candidate can win in November without your vote in September." "VOTE PRO–LIFE" was printed in large boldfaced letters on the back page, and a coupon was provided to be clipped and taken to the polls to remind voters of the name of the "pro-life" candidates. Next to the exhortation to vote "pro-life" was a disclaimer: "This special election edition does not represent an endorsement of any particular candidate."

To aid the reader in selecting candidates, the flyer listed the candidates for each state and federal office in every voting district in Massachusetts, and identified each one as either supporting or opposing what MCFL regarded as the correct position on three issues. A "y" indicated that a candidate supported the MCFL view on a particular issue and an "n" indicated that the candidate opposed it. An asterisk was placed next to the names of those incumbents who had made a "special contribution to the unborn in maintaining a 100% pro-life voting record in the state house by actively supporting MCFL legislation." While some 400 candidates were running for office in the primary, the "Special Edition" featured the photographs of only thirteen. These thirteen had received a triple "y" rating, or were identified either as having a 100% favorable voting record or as having stated a position consistent with that of MCFL. No candidate whose photograph was featured had received even one "n" rating.

The "Special Edition" was edited by an officer of MCFL who was not part of the staff that prepared the MCFL newsletters. The "Special Edition" was mailed free of charge and without request to 5,986 contributors, and to 50,674 others whom MCFL regarded as sympathetic to the organization's purposes. The Commission asserts that the remainder of the 100,000 issues were placed in public areas for general distribution, but MCFL insists that no copies were made available to the general public. The "Special Edition" was not identified on its masthead as a special edition of the regular newsletter, although the MCFL logotype did appear at its top. The words "Volume 5, No. 3, 1978" were apparently handwritten on the Edition submitted to the FEC, but the record indicates that the actual Volume 5, No. 3 was distributed in May–June, 1977. The corporation spent $9,812.76 to publish and circulate the "Special Edition" all of which was taken from its general treasury funds.

A complaint was filed with the Commission alleging that the "Special Edition" was a violation of section 441b. The complaint maintained that the Edition represented an expenditure of funds from a corporate treasury to distribute to the general public a campaign flyer on behalf of certain political candidates. . . . [T]he Commission filed a complaint in the District Court . . .

Both parties moved for summary judgment. The District Court granted MCFL's motion, ...

. . . [T]he Court of Appeals . . . affirmed the District Court's holding that the statute as so applied was unconstitutional. We . . . affirm.

II

We agree with the Court of Appeals that the "Special Edition" is not outside the reach of section 441b. First, we find no merit in appellee's contention that preparation and distribution of the "Special Edition" does not fall within that section's definition of "expenditure." . . .

. . .

Appellee next argues that the definition of an expenditure under section 441b necessarily incorporates the requirement that a communication "expressly advocate" the election of candidates, and that its "Special Edition" does not constitute express advocacy. The argument relies on the portion of Buckley v. Valeo, 424 U.S. 1 (1976), that upheld the disclosure requirement for expenditures by individuals other than candidates and by groups other than political committees. See 2 U.S.C. section 434(c). There, in order to avoid problems of overbreadth, the Court held that the term "expenditure" encompassed "only funds used for communications that expressly advocate the election or defeat of a clearly identified candidate." 424 U.S., at 80 (footnote omitted). . . .

We agree with appellee that this rationale requires a similar construction of the more intrusive provision that directly regulates independent spending. We therefore hold that an expenditure must constitute "express advocacy" in order to be subject to the prohibition of section 441b. We also hold, however, that the publication of the "Special Edition" constitutes "express advocacy."

. . .

Finally, MCFL argues that it is entitled to the press exemption under 2 U.S.C. section 431(9)(B)(i) reserved for

"any news story, commentary, or editorial distributed through the facilities of any . . . newspaper, magazine, or other periodical publication, unless such facilities are owned or controlled by any political party, political committee, or candidate."

. . . We need not decide whether the regular MCFL newsletter is exempt under this provision, because, even assuming that it is, the "Special Edition" cannot be considered comparable to any single issue of the newsletter. . . .

A contrary position would open the door for those corporations and unions with in-house publications to engage in unlimited spending directly from their treasuries to distribute campaign material to the general public, thereby eviscerating section 441b's prohibition.

In sum, we hold that MCFL's publication and distribution of the Special Election Edition is in violation of section 441b. We therefore turn to the constitutionality of that provision as applied to appellee.

III

A

. . . We must . . . determine whether the prohibition of section 441b burdens political speech, and, if so, whether such a burden is justified by a compelling state interest. . . .

The FEC minimizes the impact of the legislation upon MCFL's First Amendment rights by emphasizing that the corporation remains free to establish a separate segregated fund, composed of contributions earmarked for that purpose by the donors, that may be used for unlimited campaign spending. However, the corporation is *not* free to use its general funds for campaign advocacy purposes. While that is not an absolute restriction on speech, it is a substantial one. Moreover, even to speak through a segregated fund, MCFL must make very significant efforts.

If it were not incorporated, MCFL's obligations under the Act would be those specified by section 434(c), the section that prescribes the duties of "every person (other than a political committee)." Section 434(c) provides that any such person that during a year makes independent expenditures exceeding $250 must: (1) identify all contributors who contribute in a given year over $200 in the aggregate in funds to influence elections, section 434(c)(1); (2) disclose the name and address of recipients of independent expenditures exceeding $200 in the aggregate, along with an indication of whether the money was used to support or oppose a particular candidate, section 434(b)(6)(B); and (3) identify any persons who make contributions over $200 that are earmarked for the purpose of furthering independent expenditures, section 434(c)(2)(C). All unincorporated organizations whose major purpose is not campaign advocacy, but who occasionally make independent expenditures on behalf of candidates, are subject only to these regulations.

Because it is incorporated, however, MCFL must establish a "separate segregated fund" if it wishes to engage in any independent spending whatsoever. Sections 441b(a), (b)(2)(C). Since such a fund is considered a "political committee" under the Act, section 431(4)(B), all MCFL independent expenditure activity is, as a result, regulated as though the organization's major purpose is to further the election of candidates. This means that MCFL must comply with several requirements in addition to those mentioned. Under section 432, it must appoint a treasurer, section 432(a); ensure that contributions are forwarded to the treasurer within 10 or 30 days of receipt, depending on the amount of contribution, section 432(b)(2); see that its treasurer keeps an account of: every contribution regardless of amount, the name and address of any person who makes a contribution in excess of $50, all contributions received from political committees, and the name and address of any person to whom a disbursement is made regardless of amount, section 432(c); and preserve receipts for all disbursements over $200 and all records for three years, sections 432(c), (d). Under section 433, MCFL must file a statement of organization containing its name, address, the name of its custodian of records, and its banks, safety deposit boxes, or other depositories, sections 433(a), (b); report any change in the above information within 10 days, section 433(c); and may dissolve only upon filing a written statement that it will no longer receive any contributions nor make disbursements, and that it has no outstanding debts or obligations, section 433(d)(1).

Under section 434, MCFL must file either monthly reports with the FEC or reports on the following schedule: quarterly reports during election years, a pre-election report no later than the twelfth day before an election, a post-election report within 30 days after an election, and reports every six months during non-election years, sections 434(a)(4) (A), (B). These reports must contain information regarding the amount of cash on hand; the total amount of receipts, detailed by ten different categories; the identification of each political committee and candidate's authorized or affiliated committee making contributions, and any persons making loans, providing rebates, refunds, dividends, or interest or any other offset to operating expenditures in an aggregate amount over $200; the total amount of all disbursements, detailed by twelve different categories; the names of all authorized or affiliated committees to whom expenditures aggregating over $200 have been made; persons to whom loan repayments or refunds have been made; the total sum of all contributions, operating expenses, outstanding debts and obligations, and the settlement terms of the retirement of any debt or obligation. Section 434(b). In addition, MCFL may solicit contributions for its separate segregated fund only from its "members," sections 441b(4)(A), (C), which does not include those persons who have merely contributed to or indicated support for the organization in the past. See FEC v. National Right to Work Committee, 459 U.S. 197, 204 (1982).

It is evident from this survey that MCFL is subject to more extensive requirements and more stringent restrictions than it would be if it were not incorporated. These additional regulations may create a disincentive for such organizations to engage in political speech. Detailed recordkeeping and disclosure obligations, along with the duty to appoint a treasurer and custodian of the records, impose administrative costs that many small entities may be unable to bear. Furthermore, such duties require a far more complex and formalized organization than many small groups could manage. Restriction of solicitation of contributions to "members" vastly reduces the sources of funding for organizations with either few or no formal members, directly limiting the ability of such organizations to engage in core political speech. It is not unreasonable to suppose that, as in this case, an incorporated group of like-minded persons might seek donations to support the dissemination of their political ideas, and their occasional endorsement of political candidates, by means of garage sales, bake sales, and raffles. Such persons might well be turned away by the prospect of complying with all the requirements imposed by the Act. Faced with the need to assume a more sophisticated organizational form, to adopt specific accounting procedures, to file periodic detailed reports, and to monitor garage sales lest nonmembers take a fancy to the merchandise on display, it would not be surprising if at least some groups decided that the contemplated political activity was simply not worth it.

Thus, while section 441b does not remove all opportunities for independent spending by organizations such as MCFL, the avenue it leaves open is more burdensome than the one it forecloses. The fact that the statute's practical effect may be to discourage protected speech is sufficient to characterize section 441b as an infringement on First Amendment activities. . . .

B

. . . The FEC first insists that justification for section 441b's expenditure restriction is provided by this Court's acknowledgment that "the special characteristics of the corporate structure require particularly careful regulation." *National Right to Work Committee,* supra, at 209–210. The Commission thus relies on the long history of regulation of corporate political activity as support for the application of section 441b to MCFL. Evaluation of the Commission's argument requires close examination of the underlying rationale for this long-standing regulation.

We have described that rationale in recent opinions as the need to restrict "the influence of political war chests funneled through the corporate form," *NCPAC,* supra, at 501 (1985); to "eliminate the effect of aggregated wealth on federal elections," *Pipefitters,* 407 U.S., at 416; to curb the political influence of "those who exercise control over large aggregations of capital," Automobile Workers, 352 U.S., at 585; and to regulate the "substantial aggregations of wealth amassed by the special advantages which go with the corporate form of organization," *National Right to Work Committee,* 459 U.S., at 207.

This concern over the corrosive influence of concentrated corporate wealth reflects the conviction that it is important to protect the integrity of the marketplace of political ideas. . . .

Direct corporate spending on political activity raises the prospect that resources amassed in the economic marketplace may be used to provide an unfair advantage in the political marketplace. Political "free trade" does not necessarily require that all who participate in the political marketplace do so with exactly equal resources. See *NCPAC,* supra (invalidating limits on independent spending by political committees); *Buckley,* 424 U.S., at 39–51 (striking down expenditure limits in 1971 Campaign Act). Relative availability of funds is after all a rough barometer of public support. The resources in the treasury of a business corporation, however, are not an indication of popular support for the corporation's political ideas. They reflect instead the economically motivated decisions of investors and customers. The availability of these resources may make a corporation a formidable political presence, even though the power of the corporation may be no reflection of the power of its ideas.

By requiring that corporate independent expenditures be financed through a political committee expressly established to engage in campaign spending, section 441b seeks to prevent this threat to the political marketplace. The resources available to this fund, as opposed to the corporate treasury, in fact reflect popular support for the political positions of the committee. . . .

Regulation of corporate political activity thus has reflected concern not about use of the corporate form per se, but about the potential for unfair deployment of wealth for political purposes. Groups such as MCFL, however, do not pose that danger of corruption. MCFL was formed to disseminate political ideas, not to amass capital. The resources it has available are not a function of its success in the economic marketplace, but its popularity in the political marketplace. While MCFL may derive some advantages from its corporate form, those are advantages that redound to its benefit as a political organization, not as a profit-making enterprise. In short, MCFL is not the type of "traditional corporation organized for economic gain," *NCPAC,* 470 U.S., at 500, that has been the focus of regulation of corporate political activity.

National Right to Work Committee, does not support the inclusion of MCFL within section 441b's restriction on direct independent spending. That case upheld the application to a non-profit corporation of a different provision of section 441b: the limitation on who can be solicited for contributions to a political committee. However, the political activity at issue in that case was contributions, as the committee had been established for the purpose of making direct contributions to political candidates. 459 U.S., at 200. We have consistently held that restrictions on contributions require less compelling justification than restrictions on independent spending. *NCPAC*, supra; *California Medical Assn. v. FEC*, 453 U.S. 182, 194, 196–197 (1981); *Buckley*, supra, at 20–22.

In light of the historical role of contributions in the corruption of the electoral process, the need for a broad prophylactic rule was thus sufficient in *National Right to Work Committee* to support a limitation on the ability of a committee to raise money for direct contributions to candidates. The limitation on solicitation in this case, however, means that non-member corporations can hardly raise any funds at all to engage in political speech warranting the highest constitutional protection. Regulation that would produce such a result demands far more precision than section 441b provides. Therefore, the desirability of a broad prophylactic rule cannot justify treating alike business corporations and appellee in the regulation of independent spending.

The Commission next argues in support of section 441b that it prevents an organization from using an individual's money for purposes that the individual may not support. We acknowledged the legitimacy of this concern as to the dissenting stockholder and union member in *National Right to Work*, 459 U.S., at 208 . . . .

This rationale for regulation is not compelling with respect to independent expenditures by appellee. Individuals who contribute to appellee are fully aware of its political purposes, and in fact contribute precisely because they support those purposes. It is true that a contributor may not be aware of the exact use to which his or her money ultimately may be put, or the specific candidate that it may be used to support. However, individuals contribute to a political organization in part because they regard such a contribution as a more effective means of advocacy than spending the money under their own personal direction. Any contribution therefore necessarily involves at least some degree of delegation of authority to use such funds in a manner that best serves the shared political purposes of the organization and contributor. In addition, an individual desiring more direct control over the use of his or her money can simply earmark the contribution for a specific purpose, an option whose availability does not depend on the applicability of section 441b. Cf. section 434(c)(2)(C) (entities other than political committees must disclose names of those persons making earmarked contributions over $200). Finally, a contributor dissatisfied with how funds are used can simply stop contributing.

. . .

Thus, the concerns underlying the regulation of corporate political activity are simply absent with regard to MCFL. The dissent is surely correct in maintaining that we should not second-guess a decision to sweep within a broad prohibition activities that differ in degree, but not kind. It is not the case, however, that MCFL merely poses less of a threat of the danger that has prompted regulation. Rather, it does not pose such a threat at all. Voluntary political associations do not suddenly present the specter of corruption merely by assuming the corporate form. Given this fact, the rationale for restricting core political speech in this case is simply the desire for a bright-line rule. This hardly constitutes the *compelling* state interest necessary to justify any infringement on First Amendment freedom. While the burden on MCFL's speech is not insurmountable, we cannot permit it to be imposed without a constitutionally adequate justification. In so holding, we do not assume a legislative role, but fulfill our judicial duty—to enforce the demands of the constitution.

C

. . .

In particular, MCFL has three features essential to our holding that it may not constitutionally be bound by section 441b's restriction on independent spending. *First,* it was formed for the express purpose of promoting political ideas, and cannot engage in business activities. If political fundraising events are expressly denominated as requests for contributions that will be used for political purposes, including direct expenditures, these events cannot be considered business activities. This ensures that political resources reflect political support. *Second,* it has no shareholders or other persons affiliated so as to have a claim on its assets or earnings. This ensures that persons connected with the organization will have no economic disincentive for disassociating with it if they disagree with its political activity. *Third,* MCFL was not established by a business corporation or a labor union, and it is its policy not to accept contributions from such entities. This prevents such corporations from serving as conduits for the type of direct spending that creates a threat to the political marketplace.

It may be that the class of organizations affected by our holding today will be small. That prospect, however, does not diminish the significance of the rights at stake. . . .

The judgment of the Court of Appeals is

Affirmed.

Justice O'Connor, concurring in part and concurring in the judgment.

I join Parts I, II, III–B, and III–C and I concur in the Court's judgment that section 316 of the Federal Election Campaign Act (Act), 2 U.S.C. section 441b, is unconstitutional as applied to the conduct of appellee Massachusetts Citizens for Life, Inc. (MCFL) at issue in this case. I write separately, however, because I am concerned that the Court's discussion of the Act's disclosure requirements may be read as moving away from the teaching of Buckley v. Valeo, 424 U.S. 1 (1976). In *Buckley,* the Court was concerned not only with the chilling effect of reporting and disclosure requirements on an organization's contributors, 424 U.S., at 66–68, but also with the potential burden of disclosure requirements on a group's own speech. Id., at 74–82. The Buckley Court concluded that disclosure of a group's independent campaign expenditures serves the important governmental interest of "shedding the light of publicity" on campaign financing, thereby helping voters to evaluate the constituencies of those who seek federal office. Id., at 81. As a result, the burden of disclosing independent expenditures generally is "a reasonable and minimally restrictive method of furthering First Amendment values by opening the basic processes of our federal election system to public view." Id., at 82.

In my view, the significant burden on MCFL in this case comes not from the disclosure requirements that it must satisfy, but from the additional organizational restraints imposed upon it by the Act. As the Court has described, engaging in campaign speech requires MCFL to assume a more formalized organizational form, and significantly reduces or eliminates the sources of funding for groups such as MCFL with few or no "members." These additional requirements do not further the Government's informational interest in campaign disclosure, and, for the reasons given by the Court, cannot be justified by any of the other interests identified by the Federal Election Commission. Although the organizational and solicitation restrictions are not invariably an insurmountable burden on speech, see, e.g., FEC v. National Right to Work Committee, 459 U.S. 197 (1982), in this case the Government has failed to show that groups such as MCFL pose any danger that would justify infringement of its core political expression. On that basis, I join in the Court's judgment that section 441b is unconstitutional as applied to MCFL.

Chief Justice Rehnquist, with whom Justice White, Justice Blackmun, and Justice Stevens join, concurring in part and dissenting in part.

In FEC v. National Right to Work Committee, 459 U.S. 197, 209–210 (1982) (NRWC), the Court unanimously endorsed the "legislative judgment that the special characteristics of the corporate structure require particularly careful regulation." I continue to believe that this judgment, as reflected in 2 U.S.C. section 441b, is constitutionally sound and entitled to substantial deference, and therefore dissent from the Court's decision to "second-guess a legislative determination as to the need for prophylactic measures where corruption is the evil feared." Id., at 210. Though I agree that the expenditures in this case violated the terms of section 441b, and accordingly join Part II of the Court's opinion, I cannot accept the conclusion that the statutory provisions are unconstitutional as applied to appellee Massachusetts Citizens for Life (MCFL).

. . .

I do not dispute that the threat from corporate political activity will vary depending on the particular characteristics of a given corporation; it is obvious that large and successful corporations with resources to fund a political war chest constitute a more potent threat to the political process than less successful business corporations or nonprofit corporations. It may also be that those supporting some nonbusiness corporations will identify with the corporations' political views more frequently than the average shareholder of General Motors would support the political activities of that corporation. These distinctions among corporations, however, are "distinctions in degree" that do not amount to "differences in kind." Buckley v. Valeo, 424 U.S. 1, 30 (1976) (per curiam). Cf. *NCPAC,* supra, at 498–499. As such, they are more properly drawn by the legislature than by the judiciary. See *Buckley,* supra, at 30. Congress expressed its judgment in section 441b that the threat posed by corporate political activity warrants a prophylactic measure applicable to all groups that organize in the corporate form. Our previous cases have expressed a reluctance to fine-tune such judgments; I would adhere to that counsel here.

I would have thought the distinctions drawn by the Court today largely foreclosed by our decision in *NRWC,* supra. . . .

The distinction between corporate and noncorporate activity was not diminished in *NCPAC,* supra, where we found fatally overbroad the $1,000 limitation in 26 U.S.C. section 9012(f) on independent expenditures by "political committees." Our conclusion rested in part on the fact that section 9012(f) regulated not only corporations but rather "indiscriminately lump[ed] with corporations any 'committee, association or organization.'" . . .

The Court explains the decisions in *NRWC* and *NCPAC* by reference to another distinction found in our decisions—that between contributions and independent expenditures. See *Buckley,* supra, at 19–23. This is admittedly a distinction between the facts of *NRWC* and those of *NCPAC,* but it does not warrant a different result in view of our longstanding approval of limitations on corporate spending and of the type of regulation involved here. The distinction between contributions and independent expenditures is not a line separating black from white. The statute here—though involving independent expenditures—is not nearly so domestic as the "wholesale restriction of clearly protected conduct" at issue in *NCPAC,* 470 U.S., at 501. It regulates instead the *form* of otherwise unregulated spending. A separate segregated fund formed by MCFL may use contributions it receives, without limit, on political expenditures. As the Court correctly notes, the regulation of section 441b is not without burdens, but it remains wholly different in character from that which we condemned in *NCPAC.* In these circumstances, I would defer to the congressional judgment that corporations are a distinct category with respect to which this sort of regulation is constitutionally permissible.

The basically legislative character of the Court's decision is dramatically illustrated by its effort to carve out a constitutional niche for "groups such as MCFL." The three-part test gratuitously announced in today's dicta, adds to a well-defined prohibition a vague and barely adumbrated exception certain to result in confusion and costly litigation. If we sat as a council of revision to modify legislative judgments, I would hesitate to join the Court's effort because of this fact alone. But we do not sit in that capacity; we are obliged to leave the drawing of lines in cases such as this to Congress if those lines are within constitutional bounds. Believing that the Act of Congress in question here passes this test, I dissent from the Court's contrary conclusion.

Justice White, while joining **The Chief Justice's** opinion, adheres to his dissenting views expressed in Buckley v. Valeo, 424 U.S. 1 (1976), First National Bank v. Bellotti, 435 U.S. 765 (1978), and Federal Election Commission v. National Conservative Political Action Committee, 470 U.S. 480 (1985).

SECTION 4. COMPELLED DISCLOSURE OF BELIEFS AND ASSOCIATIONS

A.   REGISTRATION AND REPORTING REQUIREMENTS

Page 1318. Add at end of subsection:

MEESE v. KEENE, 107 S.Ct. 1862 (1987).   The federal Foreign Agents Registration Act requires agents of foreign states to register and make certain public disclosures.   Section 611(j) requires that, in disseminating "political propaganda," the agent must label the material, disclosing that it is prepared, edited or circulated by a registered foreign agent.   Political propaganda is defined in that section to include both material that will influence the public "with reference to the political or public interests" of a foreign government, and that which "promotes racial, religious, or social dissensions" or promotes "racial, social, political, or religious disorder, civil riot" or violent conflict.   A federal district court enjoined application of the Act, on First Amendment grounds, to three films produced by the National Film Board of Canada that dealt with the subjects of nuclear war and acid rain.   The Supreme Court reversed.   The statute simply required that disseminators of the material make additional true disclosures enabling the public to evaluate the material's impact.   (It was not required that the films be publicly labeled as "propaganda.")   It had not been demonstrated that public misunderstanding, attaching a perjorative connotation to the term "political propaganda," has had an adverse impact on distribution of foreign advocacy.   Justice Blackmun, joined by Justices Brennan and Marshall, dissented.   They argued that the statutory scheme was intended to discourage communication by foreign governments, and had that effect.   The indirect burden on speech was not justified by compelling government interests.

SECTION 5. SPEECH AND ASSOCIATION RIGHTS OF GOVERNMENT EMPLOYEES

A. CONDITIONING GOVERNMENT EMPLOYMENT ON SPEECH AND POLITICAL ACTIVITY

Page 1338. Add ahead of United States Civil Service Commission v. National Association of Letter Carriers:

RANKIN v. McPHERSON, 107 S.Ct. 2891 (1987). McPherson was a clerical employee in a county constable's office. On hearing a radio report of the attempted assasination of President Reagan in March, 1981, she said to a fellow employee: "If they go for him again, I hope they get him." The Court held that McPherson's discharge violated the first amendment. The statement was speech on a matter of public concern, and did not constitute a threat to kill the President. Asserted state interests did not outweigh McPherson's first amendment rights. Her duties were clerical, and discharge was not based on an assessment that the remark demonstrated a character trait that made her unfit to perform that work. The remark did not disrupt the operation of the office, nor was there danger that it had discredited the office. Justice Marshall's opinion for the court concluded:

"We cannot believe that every employee in Constable Rankin's office, whether computer operator, electrician, or file clerk, is equally required, on pain of discharge, to avoid any statement susceptible of being interpreted by the Constable as an indication that the employee may be unworthy of employment in his law enforcement agency. At some point, such concerns are so removed from the effective function of the public employer that they cannot prevail over the free speech rights of the public employee."

Justice Powell's concurrence remarked that in the case of private speech in the workplace on matters of public concern "it will be an unusual case" where discharge can be justified.

"The risk that a single, offhand comment directed to only one other worker will lower morale, disrupt the work force, or otherwise undermine the mission of the office borders on the fanciful."

Justice Scalia, joined by Chief Justice Rehnquist and Justices White and O'Connor, dissented. The question was whether McPherson could "ride with the cops and cheer for the robbers." Although the first amendment would prohibit criminal punishment for a statement expressing approval of a serious and violent crime, such a statement is not speech on a matter of public concern. Even if the statement was speech on a matter of public concern, the discharge was justified by interests in maintaining an esprit de corps and a proper public image for a law enforcement office.

Chapter 17

FREEDOM OF THE PRESS

SECTION 1. INTRODUCTION

B. REGULATION OF THE BUSINESS OF PUBLISHING

Page 1363. Add ahead of Calder v. Jones:

ARKANSAS WRITERS' PROJECT, INC. v. RAGLAND
__ U.S. __, 107 S.Ct. 1722, 95 L.Ed.2d 209 (1987).

Justice Marshall delivered the opinion of the Court.

The question presented in this case is whether a state sales tax scheme that taxes general interest magazines, but exempts newspapers and religious, professional, trade, and sports journals violates the First Amendment's guarantee of freedom of the press.

I

Since 1935, Arkansas has imposed a tax on receipts from sales of tangible personal property. . . . Numerous items are exempt from the state sales tax, however. These include "gross receipts or gross proceeds derived from the sale of newspapers," . . . and "religious, professional, trade and sports journals and/or publications printed and published within this State . . . when sold through regular subscriptions." . . .

Appellant Arkansas Writers' Project, Inc. publishes Arkansas Times, a general interest monthly magazine with a circulation of approximately 28,000. The magazine includes articles on a variety of subjects, including religion and sports. It is printed and published in Arkansas, and is sold through mail subscriptions, coin-operated stands, and over-the-counter sales. . . .

. . . [I]n Minneapolis Star & Tribune Co. v. Minnesota Comm'r of Revenue, 460 U.S. 575 (1983), this Court held unconstitutional a Minnesota tax on paper and ink used in the production of newspapers. In January 1984, relying on this authority, appellant sought a refund of sales tax paid since October 1982, asserting that the magazine exemption must be construed to include Arkansas Times. It maintained that subjecting Arkansas Times to the sales tax, while sales of newspapers and other magazines were exempt, violated the First and Fourteenth Amendments. The Commissioner denied appellant's claim for refund.

. . .

. . . In contrast to *Minneapolis Star,* supra, and *Grosjean,* supra, the Arkansas Supreme Court concluded that the Arkansas sales tax was a permissible "ordinary form of taxation."

We . . . reverse.

II

As a threshold matter, the Commissioner argues that appellant does not have standing to challenge the Arkansas sales tax scheme. Extending the reasoning of the court below, he contends that, since appellant has conceded that Arkansas Times is neither a newspaper nor a religious, professional, trade, or sports journal, it has not asserted an injury that can be redressed by a favorable decision of this Court and therefore does not meet the requirements for standing set forth in Valley Forge Christian College v. Americans United for Separation of Church and State, Inc., 454 U.S. 464, 472 (1982).

We do not accept the Commissioner's notion of standing, for it would effectively insulate underinclusive statutes from constitutional challenge, a proposition we soundly rejected in Orr v. Orr, 440 U.S. 268, 272 (1979). The Commissioner's position is inconsistent with numerous decisions of this Court in which we have considered claims that others similarly situated were exempt from the operation of a state law adversely affecting the claimant. . . .

III

A

. . . In *Minneapolis Star,* the discrimination took two distinct forms. First, in contrast to generally applicable economic regulations to which the press can legitimately be subject, the Minnesota use tax treated the press differently from other enterprises. . . . Second, the tax targeted a small group of newspapers. This was due to the fact that the first $100,000 of paper and ink were exempt from the tax; thus "only a handful of publishers pay any tax at all, and even fewer pay any significant amount of tax." . . .

Both types of discrimination can be established even where, as here, there is no evidence of an improper censorial motive. . . .

. . .

Addressing only the first type of discrimination, the Commissioner defends the Arkansas sales tax as a generally applicable economic regulation. He acknowledges the numerous statutory exemptions to the sales tax, including those exempting newspapers and religious, trade, professional, and sports magazines. Nonetheless, apparently because the tax is nominally imposed on receipts from sales of *all* tangible personal property, . . . he insists that the tax should be upheld.

On the facts of this case, the fundamental question is not whether the tax singles out the press as a whole, but whether it targets a small group within the press. While we indicated in *Minneapolis Star* that a genuinely nondiscriminatory tax on the receipts of newspapers would be constitutionally permissible, ... the Arkansas sales tax cannot be characterized as nondiscriminatory, because it is not evenly applied to all magazines. To the contrary, the magazine exemption means that only a few Arkansas magazines pay any sales tax; in that respect, it operates in much the same way as did the $100,000 exemption to the Minnesota use tax. Because the Arkansas sales tax scheme treats some magazines less favorably than others, it suffers from the second type of discrimination identified in Minneapolis Star.

Indeed, this case involves a more disturbing use of selective taxation than *Minneapolis Star,* because the basis on which Arkansas differentiates between magazines is particularly repugnant to First Amendment principles: a magazine's tax status depends entirely on its *content* "Above all else, the First Amendment means that government has no power to restrict expression because of its message, its ideas, its subject matter, or its content." Police Dept. of Chicago v. Mosley, supra, at 95. See also Carey v. Brown, supra, at 462–463. "Regulations which permit the Government to discriminate on the basis of the content of the message cannot be tolerated under the First Amendment." Regan v. Time, Inc., 468 U.S. 641, 648–649 (1984).

If articles in Arkansas Times were uniformly devoted to religion or sports, the magazine would be exempt from the sales tax . . . . However, because the articles deal with a variety of subjects (sometimes including religion and sports), the Commissioner has determined that the magazine's sales may be taxed. In order to determine whether a magazine is subject to sales tax, Arkansas' "enforcement authorities must necessarily examine the content of the message that is conveyed. . . ." FCC v. League of Women Voters of California, 468 U.S. 364, 383 (1984). Such official scrutiny of the content of publications as the basis for imposing a tax is entirely incompatible with the First Amendment's guarantee of freedom of the press. . . .

Arkansas' system of selective taxation does not evade the strictures of the First Amendment merely because it does not burden the expression of particular *views* by specific magazines. We rejected a similar distinction between content and viewpoint restrictions in Consolidated Edison Co. v. Public Service Comm'n of New York, 447 U.S. 530 (1980). As we stated in that case, "the First Amendment's hostility to content-based regulation extends not only to restrictions on particular viewpoints, but also to prohibition of public discussion of an entire topic." Id., at 537. See FCC v. League of Women Voters of California, supra, at 383–384; Metromedia, Inc. v. San Diego, 453 U.S. 490, 518–519 (1981) (plurality opinion); Carey v. Brown, supra, at 462, n. 6.

Nor are the requirements of the First Amendment avoided by the fact that Arkansas grants an exemption to other members of the media that might publish discussions of the various subjects contained in Arkansas Times. For example, exempting *newspapers* from the tax . . . does not change the fact that the State discriminates in determining the tax status of *magazines* published in Arkansas. . . .

B

Arkansas faces a heavy burden in attempting to defend its content-based approach to taxation of magazines. In order to justify such differential taxation, the State must show that its regulation is necessary to serve a compelling state interest and is narrowly drawn to achieve that end. See Minneapolis Star, 460 U.S., at 591–592.

The Commissioner has advanced several state interests. . . .

. . .

The Commissioner . . . suggests that the exemption of religious, professional, trade and sports journals was intended to encourage "fledgling" publishers, who have only limited audiences and therefore do not have access to the same volume of advertising revenues as general interest magazines such as Arkansas Times. Even assuming that an interest in encouraging fledgling publications might be a compelling one, we do not find the exemption . . . of religious, professional, trade and sports journals narrowly tailored to achieve that end. To the contrary, the exemption is both overinclusive and underinclusive. The types of magazines enumerated . . . are exempt, regardless of whether they are "fledgling"; even the most lucrative and well-established religious, professional, trade and sports journals do not pay sales tax. By contrast, struggling general interest magazines and struggling specialty magazines on subjects other than those specified . . . are ineligible for favorable tax treatment.

Finally, the Commissioner asserted for the first time at oral argument a need to "foster communication" in the State. While this state interest might support a blanket exemption of the press from the sales tax, it cannot justify selective taxation of certain publishers. . . .

C

Appellant argues that the Arkansas tax scheme violates the First Amendment because it exempts all newspapers from the tax, but only some magazines. Appellant contends that, under applicable state regulations, the critical distinction between newspapers and magazines is not format, but rather content: newspapers are distinguished from magazines because they contain reports of current events and articles of general interest. Just as content-based distinctions between magazines are impermissible under prior decisions of this Court, appellant claims that content-based distinctions between different members of the media are also impermissible, absent a compelling justification.

Because we hold today that the State's selective application of its sales tax to magazines is unconstitutional and therefore invalid, our ruling eliminates the differential treatment of newspapers and magazines. Accordingly, we need not decide whether a distinction between different types of periodicals presents an additional basis for invalidating the sales tax, as applied to the press.

. . .

V

We stated in *Minneapolis Star* that "a tax that singles out the press, or that targets individual publications within the press, places a heavy burden on the State to justify its action." 460 U.S., at 592–593. In this case, Arkansas has failed to meet this heavy burden. It has advanced no compelling justification for selective, content-based taxation of certain magazines, and the tax is therefore invalid under the First Amendment. Accordingly, we reverse the judgment of the Arkansas Supreme Court and remand for proceedings not inconsistent with this opinion.

It is so ordered.

Justice Stevens, concurring in part and concurring in the judgment.

To the extent that the Court's opinion relies on the proposition " 'that government has no power to restrict expression because of its message, its ideas, its subject matter, or its content,' " I am unable to join it. I do, however, agree that the State has the burden of justifying its content-based discrimination and has plainly failed to do so. Accordingly, I join Parts I, II, III–B, IV and V of the Court's opinion and concur in its judgment.

Justice Scalia, with whom The Chief Justice joins, dissenting.

. . . I dissent from today's decision because it provides no rational basis for distinguishing the subsidy scheme here under challenge from many others that are common and unquestionably lawful. . . .

. . .

Here, as in the Court's earlier decision in Minneapolis Star & Tribune Co. v. Minnesota Comm'r of Revenue, 460 U.S. 575 (1983), application of the "strict scrutiny" test rests upon the premise that for First Amendment purposes denial of exemption from taxation is equivalent to regulation. That premise is demonstrably erroneous and cannot be consistently applied. Our opinions have long recognized—in First Amendment contexts as elsewhere—the reality that tax exemptions, credits, and deductions are "a form of subsidy that is administered through the tax system," and the general rule that "a legislature's decision not to subsidize the exercise of a fundamental right does not infringe the right, and thus is not subject to strict scrutiny." Regan v. Taxation With Representation of Washington, 461 U.S. 540, 544, 549 (1983) (upholding denial of tax exemption for organization engaged in lobbying even though veterans' organizations received exemption regardless of lobbying activities). See also Cammarano v. United States, 358 U.S. 498, 513 (1959) (deduction for lobbying activities); Buckley v. Valeo, 424 U.S. 1, 93–95 (1976) (declining to apply strict scrutiny to campaign finance law that excludes certain candidates); Harris v. McRae, 448 U.S. 297, 324–326 (1980) (declining to apply strict scrutiny to legislative decision not to subsidize abortions even though other medical procedures were subsidized); Maher v. Roe, 432 U.S. 464 (1977) (same).

The reason that denial of participation in a tax exemption or other subsidy scheme does not necessarily "infringe" a fundamental right is that—unlike direct restriction or prohibition—such a denial does not, as a general rule, have any significant coercive effect. It may, of course, be manipulated so as to do so, in which case the courts will be available to provide relief. But that is not remotely the case here. It is implausible that the 4% sales tax, generally applicable to all sales in the State with the few enumerated exceptions, was meant to inhibit, or had the effect of inhibiting, this appellant's publication.

Perhaps a more stringent, prophylactic rule is appropriate, and can consistently be applied, when the subsidy pertains to the expression of a particular viewpoint on a matter of political concern—a tax exemption, for example, that is expressly available only to publications that take a particular point of view on a controversial issue of foreign policy. Political speech has been accorded special protection elsewhere. See, e.g., FCC v. League of Women Voters of California, 468 U.S. 364, 375–376 (1984) (invalidating ban on editorializing by recipients of grants from the Corporation for Public Broadcasting, in part on ground that political speech "is entitled to the most exacting degree of First Amendment protection"); Connick v. Myers, 461 U.S. 138, 143–146 (1983) (discussing history of First Amendment protection for political speech by public employees); Red Lion Broadcasting Co. v. FCC, 395 U.S. 367 (1969) (upholding FCC's "fairness doctrine," which imposes special obligations upon broadcasters with regard to "controversial issues of public importance"). There is no need, however, and it is realistically quite impossible, to extend to all speech the same degree of protection against exclusion from a subsidy that one might think appropriate for opposing shades of political expression.

By seeking to do so, the majority casts doubt upon a wide variety of tax preferences and subsidies that draw distinctions based upon subject-matter. The U.S. Postal Service, for example, grants a special bulk rate to written material disseminated by certain nonprofit organizations—religious, educational, scientific, philanthropic, agricultural, labor, veterans', and fraternal organizations. See Domestic Mail Manual section 623 (1985). Must this preference be justified by a "compelling governmental need" because a nonprofit organization devoted to some other purpose—dissemination of information about boxing, for example—does not receive the special rate? The Kennedy Center, which is subsidized by the Federal Government in the amount of up to $23 million per year, see 20 U.S.C. section 76n(a), is authorized by statute to "present classical and contemporary music, opera, drama, dance, and poetry." Section 76j. Is this subsidy subject to strict scrutiny because other kinds of expressive activity, such as learned lectures and political speeches, are excluded? Are government research grant programs or the funding activities of the Corporation for Public Broadcasting, see 47 U.S.C. section 396(g)(2), subject to strict scrutiny because they provide money for the study or exposition of some subjects but not others?

Because there is no principled basis to distinguish the subsidization of speech in these areas—which we would surely uphold—from the subsidization that we strike down here, our decision today places the granting or denial of protection within our own idiosyncratic discretion. In my view, that threatens First Amendment rights infinitely more than the tax exemption at issue. I dissent.

SECTION 5. PRESS ACCESS TO GOVERNMENT INFORMATION

Page 1398. Add at end of section:

PRESS–ENTERPRISE COMPANY v. SUPERIOR COURT
478 U.S. 1, 106 S.Ct. 2735, 92 L.Ed.2d 1 (1986).

Chief Justice Burger delivered the opinion of the Court.

We granted certiorari to decide whether petitioner has a First Amendment right of access to transcripts of a preliminary hearing growing out of a criminal prosecution.

I

On December 23, 1981, the State of California filed a complaint in the Riverside County Municipal Court, charging Robert Diaz with 12 counts of murder and seeking the death penalty. The complaint alleged that Diaz, a nurse, murdered 12 patients by administering massive doses of the heart drug lidocaine. The preliminary hearing on the complaint commenced on July 6, 1982. Diaz moved to exclude the public from the proceedings under California Penal Code Ann. section 868 (West 1985), which requires such proceedings to be open unless "exclusion of the public is necessary in order to protect the defendant's right to a fair and impartial trial." The Magistrate granted the unopposed motion, finding that closure was necessary because the case had attracted national publicity and "only one side may get reported in the media."

The preliminary hearing continued for 41 days. Most of the testimony and the evidence presented by the State was medical and scientific; the remainder consisted of testimony by personnel who worked with Diaz on the shifts when the 12 patients died. Diaz did not introduce any evidence, but his counsel subjected most of the witnesses to vigorous cross-examination. Diaz was held to answer on all charges. At the conclusion of the hearing, petitioner Press-Enterprise Company asked that the transcript of the proceedings be released. The Magistrate refused and sealed the record.

On January 21, 1983, the State moved in Superior Court to have the transcripts of the preliminary hearing released to the public; petitioner later joined in support of the motion. Diaz opposed the motion, contending that release of the transcripts would result in prejudicial pretrial publicity. The Superior Court found that the information in the transcript was "as factual as it could be," and that the facts were neither "inflammatory" nor "exciting" but there was, nonetheless, "a reasonable likelihood that release of all or any part of the transcript might prejudice defendant's right to a fair and impartial trial."

. . .

The California Supreme Court thereafter denied petitioner's peremptory writ of mandate, holding that there is no general First Amendment right of access to preliminary hearings. The court reasoned that the right of access to criminal proceedings recognized in Press-Enterprise Co. v. Superior Court, 464 U.S. 501 (1984) (*Press-Enterprise I*), and Globe Newspaper Co. v. Superior Court, 457 U.S. 596 (1982), extended only to actual criminal trials. Furthermore, the reasons that had been asserted for closing the proceedings in *Press-Enterprise I* and *Globe*— the interest of witnesses and other third parties—were not the same as the right asserted in this case—the defendant's right to a fair and impartial trial by a jury uninfluenced by news accounts.

Having found no general First Amendment right of access, the court then considered the circumstances in which the closure would be proper under the California access statute, Cal. Penal Code Ann. section 868 (West 1985). Under the statute, the court reasoned, if the defendant establishes a "reasonable likelihood of substantial prejudice" the burden shifts to the prosecution or the media to show by a preponderance of the evidence that there is no such reasonable probability of prejudice.

. . . We reverse.

II

. . . . [T]his controversy is "capable of repetition, yet evading review." It can reasonably be assumed that petitioner will be subjected to a similar closure order and, because criminal proceedings are typically of short duration, such an order will likely evade review. . . . [T]his case is not moot. . . .

III

. . .

The right to an open public trial is a shared right of the accused and the public, the common concern being the assurance of fairness. Only recently, in Waller v. Georgia, 467 U.S. 39 (1984), for example, we considered whether the defendant's Sixth Amendment right to an open trial prevented the closure of a suppression hearing over the defendant's objection. We noted that the First Amendment right of access would in most instances attach to such proceedings and that "the explicit Sixth Amendment right of the accused is no less protective of a public trial than the implicit First Amendment right of the press and public." Id., at 46. When the defendant objects to the closure of a suppression hearing, therefore, the hearing must be open unless the party seeking to close the hearing advances an overriding interest that is likely to be prejudiced. Id., at 47.

Here, unlike *Waller*, the right asserted is not the defendant's Sixth Amendment right to a public trial since the defendant requested a closed preliminary hearing. Instead, the right asserted here is that of the public under the First Amendment. . . . The California Supreme Court concluded that the First Amendment was not implicated because the proceeding was not a criminal trial, but a preliminary hearing. However, the First Amendment question cannot be resolved solely on the label we give the event, i.e., "trial" or otherwise, particularly where the preliminary hearing functions much like a full scale trial.

In cases dealing with the claim of a First Amendment right of access to criminal proceedings, our decisions have emphasized two complementary considerations. First, . . . we have considered whether the place and process has historically been open to the press and general public.

. . .

Second, in this setting the Court has traditionally considered whether public access plays a significant positive role in the functioning of the particular process in question. *Globe,* supra, at 606. Although many governmental processes operate best under public scrutiny, it takes little imagination to recognize that there are some kinds of government operations that would be totally frustrated if conducted openly. A classic example is that "the proper functioning of our grand jury system depends upon the secrecy of grand jury proceedings." Douglas Oil Co. v. Petrol Stops Northwest, 441 U.S. 211, 218 (1979). Other proceedings plainly require public access. In *Press-Enterprise I,* we summarized the holdings of prior cases, noting that openness in criminal trials, including the selection of jurors, "enhances both the basic fairness of the criminal trial and the appearance of fairness so essential to public confidence in the system." 464 U.S., at 501.

. . .

IV

A

The considerations that led the Court to apply the First Amendment right of access to criminal trials in *Richmond Newspapers* and *Globe* and the selection of jurors in *Press-Enterprise I* lead us to conclude that the right of access applies to preliminary hearings as conducted in California.

First, there has been a tradition of accessibility to preliminary hearings of the type conducted in California. Although grand jury proceedings have traditionally been closed to the public and the accused, preliminary hearings conducted before neutral and detached magistrates have been open to the public. Long ago in the celebrated trail of Aaron Burr for treason, for example, with Chief Justice Marshall sitting as trial judge, the probable cause hearing was held in the Hall of the House of Delegates in Virginia, the court room being too small to accommodate the crush of interested citizens. United States v. Burr, 25 F. Cas. 1 (CC Va. 1807) (No. 14,692). From *Burr* until the present day, the near uniform practice of state and federal courts has been to conduct preliminary hearings in open court. As we noted in *Gannett,* several states following the original New York Field Code of Criminal Procedure published in 1850 have allowed preliminary hearings to be closed on the motion of the accused. 443 U.S., at 390–391. But even in these states the proceedings are presumptively open to the public and are closed only for cause shown. Open preliminary hearings, therefore, have been accorded "the favorable judgment of experience." *Globe,* supra, at 605.

The second question is whether public access to preliminary hearings as they are conducted in California plays a particularly significant positive role in the actual functioning of the process. We have already determined in *Richmond Newspapers, Globe,* and *Press-Enterprise I* that public access to criminal trials and the selection of jurors is essential to the proper functioning of the criminal justice system. California preliminary hearings are sufficiently like a trial to justify the same conclusion.

. . .

It is true that unlike a criminal trial, the California preliminary hearing cannot result in the conviction of the accused and the adjudication is before a magistrate or other judicial officer without a jury. But these features, standing alone, do not make public access any less essential to the proper functioning of the proceedings in the overall criminal justice process. Because of its entensive scope, the preliminary hearing is often the final and most important step in the criminal proceeding. . . .

Similarly, the absence of a jury . . . makes the importance of public access to a preliminary hearing even more significant. . . .

. . .

We therefore conclude that the qualified First Amendment right of access to criminal proceedings applies to preliminary hearings as they are conducted in California.

B

Since a qualified First Amendment right of access attaches to preliminary hearings in California . . ., the proceedings cannot be closed unless specific, on the record findings are made demonstrating that "closure is essential to preserve higher values and is narrowly tailored to serve that interest." *Press-Enterprise I,* supra, at 510. See also *Globe,* supra, 457 U.S., at 606–607. If the interest asserted is the right of the accused to a fair trial, the preliminary hearing shall be closed only if specific findings are made demonstrating that first, there is a substantial probability that the defendant's right to a fair trial will be prejudiced by publicity that closure would prevent and, second, reasonable alternatives to closure cannot adequately protect the defendant's free trial rights. See *Press-Enterprise I,* supra; *Richmond Newspapers,* supra, at 581.

The California Supreme Court, interpreting its access statute, concluded "that the magistrate shall close the preliminary hearing upon finding a reasonable likelihood of substantial prejudice." As the court itself acknowledged, the "reasonable likelihood" test places a lesser burden on the defendant than the "substantial probability" test which we hold is called for by the First Amendment. Moreover, that court failed to consider whether alternatives short of complete closure would have protected the interests of the accused.

. . .

. . . [The] risk of prejudice does not automatically justify refusing public access to hearings on every motion to suppress. Through voir dire, cumbersome as it is in some circumstances, a court can identify those jurors whose prior knowledge of the case would disable them from rendering an impartial verdict. And even if closure were justified for the hearings on a motion to suppress, closure of an entire 41-day proceeding would rarely be warranted. The First Amendment right of access cannot be overcome by the conclusory assertion that publicity might deprive the defendant of that right. And any limitation "must be narrowly tailored to serve that interest." *Press-Enterprise I*, supra, at 510.

The standard applied by the California Supreme Court failed to consider the First Amendment right of access to criminal proceedings. Accordingly, the judgment of the California Supreme Court is reversed.

It is so ordered.

Justice Stevens, with whom Justice Rehnquist joins as to Part II, dissenting.

. . .

I

Although perhaps obvious, it bears emphasis that the First Amendment right asserted by petitioner is not a right to publish or otherwise communicate information lawfully or unlawfully acquired. That right, which lies at the core of the First Amendment . . . may be overcome only by a governmental objective of the highest order attainable in no less intrusive way. . . . The First Amendment right asserted by petitioner in this case, in contrast, is not the right to publicize information in its possession, but the right to acquire access thereto.

. . .

. . . [I]t has always been apparent that the freedom to obtain information that the Government has a legitimate interest in not disclosing . . . is far narrower than the freedom to disseminate information . . . .. In this case, the risk of prejudice to the defendant's right to a fair trial is perfectly obvious. For me, that risk is far more significant than the countervailing interest in publishing the transcript of the preliminary hearing sooner rather than later. . . . The interest in prompt publication—in my view—is no greater than the interest in prompt publication of grand jury transcripts. . . . [W]e have always recognized the legitimacy of the governmental interest in the secrecy of grand jury proceedings, and I am unpersuaded that the difference between such proceedings and the rather elaborate procedure for determining probable cause that California has adopted strengthens the First Amendment claim to access asserted in this case.

II

. . .

In this case . . . it is uncontroverted that a common law right of access did not inhere in preliminary proceedings at the time the First Amendment was adopted, and that the Framers and ratifiers of that provision could not have intended such proceedings to remain open.
. . .

. . .

In the final analysis, the Court's lengthy historical disquisition demonstrates only that in many States preliminary proceedings are generally open to the public. In other States, numbering California and Michigan among them, . . . such proceedings have been closed.
. . . "[T]he fact that the States" have adopted different rules regarding the openness of preliminary proceedings is merely a reflection of our federal system, which demands "tolerance for a spectrum of state procedures dealing with a common problem of law enforcement," Spencer v. Texas, 385 U.S. 554, 566 (1967). . . . The Court's historical crutch cannot carry the weight of opening a preliminary proceeding that the State has ordered closed; that determination must stand or fall on whether it satisfies the second component of the Court's test.

If the Court's historical evidence proves too little, the "value of openness" on which it relies proves too much, for this measure would open to public scrutiny far more than preliminary hearings "as they are conducted in California" (a comforting phrase invoked by the Court in one form or another more than 8 times in its opinion). . . . The obvious defect in the Court's approach is that its reasoning applies to the traditionally secret grand jury with as much force as it applies to California preliminary hearings. . . .

. . .

In fact, the logic of the Court's access right extends even beyond the confines of the criminal justice system to encompass proceedings held on the civil side of the docket as well. . . .

. . .

By abjuring strict reliance on history and emphasizing the broad value of openness, the Court tacitly recognizes the importance of public access to government proceedings generally. Regrettably, the Court has taken seriously the stated requirement that the sealing of a transcript be justified by a "compelling" or "overriding" governmental interest and that the closure order be "narrowly tailored to serve that interest." . . . The cases denying access have done so on a far lesser showing than that required by a compelling governmental interest/ least restrictive-means analysis, and cases granting access have recognized as legitimate grounds for closure interests that fall far short of those traditionally thought to be "compelling," . . .

The presence of a legitimate reason for closure in this case requires an affirmance. The constitutionally-grounded fair trial interests of the accused if he is bound over for trial, and the reputational interests of the accused if he is not, provide a substantial reason for delaying access to the transcript for at least the short time before trial. By taking its own verbal formulation seriously, the Court reverses—without comment or explanation or any attempt at reconciliation—the holding in *Gannett* that a "reasonable probability of prejudice" is enough to overcome the First Amendment right of access to a preliminary proceeding. It is unfortunate that the Court neglects this opportunity to fit the result in this case into the body of precedent dealing with access rights generally. I fear that today's decision will simply further unsettle the law in this area.

I respectfully dissent.

SECTION 6.   SPECIAL PROBLEMS OF THE ELECTRONIC MEDIA

Page 1411. Add at end of chapter:

CITY OF LOS ANGELES v. PREFERRED COMMUNICATIONS, INC.

476 U.S. 488, 106 S.Ct. 2034, 90 L.Ed.2d 480 (1986).

Justice Rehnquist delivered the opinion of the Court.

Respondent Preferred Communications, Inc., sued petitioners City of Los Angeles (City) and the Department of Water and Power (DWP) in the United States District Court . . .. The complaint alleged a violation of respondent's rights under the First and Fourteenth Amendments, . . . by reason of the City's refusal to grant respondent a cable television franchise and of DWP's refusal to grant access to DWP's poles or underground conduits used for power lines. The District Court dismissed the complaint for failure to state a claim upon which relief could be granted. . . . The Court of Appeals for the Ninth Circuit . . . reversed as to the First Amendment claim. . . .

Respondent's complaint against the City and DWP alleged . . .: Respondent asked Pacific Telephone and Telegraph (PT & T) and DWP for permission to lease space on their utility poles in order to provide cable television service in the South Central area of Los Angeles. These utilities responded that they would not lease the space unless respondent first obtained a cable television franchise from the City. Respondent asked the City for a franchise, but the City refused to grant it one, stating that respondent had failed to participate in an auction that was to award a single franchise in the area.[1]

---

[1] California authorizes municipalities to limit the number of cable television operators in an area by means of a "franchise or license" system, and to prescribe "rules and

The complaint further alleged that cable operators are First Amendment speakers, that there is sufficient excess physical capacity and economic demand in the south central area of Los Angeles to accommodate more than one cable company, and that the City's auction process allowed it to discriminate among franchise applicants based on which one it deemed to be the "best." . . .

The City did not deny that there was excess physical capacity to accommodate more than one cable television system. But it argued that the physical scarcity of available space on public utility structures, the limits of economic demand for the cable medium, and the practical and esthetic disruptive effect that installing and maintaining a cable system has on the public right-of-way justified its decision to restrict access to its facilities to a single cable television company.

. . .

The Court of Appeals . . . held that, taking the allegations in the complaint as true, the City violated the First Amendment by refusing to issue a franchise to more than one cable television company when there was sufficient excess physical and economic capacity to accommodate more than one. The Court of Appeals expressed the view that the facts alleged in the complaint brought respondent into the ambit of cases such as Miami Herald Publishing Co. v. Tornillo, 418 U.S. 241 (1974), rather than of cases such as Red Lion Broadcasting Co. v. FCC, 395 U.S. 367 (1969) and Members of City Council v. Taxpayers for Vincent, 466 U.S. 789 (1984).

We agree with the Court of Appeals that respondent's complaint should not have been dismissed . . . but we do so on a narrower ground than the one taken by it. . . .

. . . We are unwilling to decide the legal questions posed by the parties without a more thoroughly developed record of proceedings in which the parties have an opportunity to prove those disputed factual assertions upon which they rely.

We do think that the activities in which respondent allegedly seeks to engage plainly implicate First Amendment interests. . . .

. . . [T]hrough original programming or by exercising editorial discretion over which stations or programs to include in its repertoire, respondent seeks to communicate messages on a wide variety of topics and in a wide variety of formats. . . . Cable television partakes of some of the aspects of speech and the communication of ideas as do the traditional enterprises of newspaper and book publishers, public speakers and pamphleteers. Respondent's proposed activities would seem to implicate First Amendment interests as do the activities of wireless broadcasters. . . .

Of course, the conclusion that respondent's factual allegations implicate protected speech does not end the inquiry. . . . [W]here speech and conduct are joined in a single course of action, the First

regulations" to protect customers of such operators. . . . Congress has recently endorsed such franchise systems. See Cable Communications Policy Act of 1984, Pub.L. 98–549, 98 Stat. 2779. . . .

Amendment values must be balanced against competing societal interests. . . . We do not think, however, that it is desirable to express any more detailed views on the proper resolution of the First Amendment question raised by the respondent's complaint and the City's responses to it without a fuller development of the disputed issues in the case. We think that we may know more than we know now about how the constitutional issues should be resolved when we know more about the present uses of the public utility poles and rights-of-way and how respondent proposes to install and maintain its facilities on them.

. . .

We affirm the judgment of the Court of Appeals reversing the dismissal of respondent's complaint by the District Court, and remand the case to the District Court so that petitioners may file an answer and the material factual disputes between the parties may be resolved.

It is so ordered.

Justice Blackmun, with whom Justice Marshall and Justice O'Connor join, concurring.

I join the Court's opinion on the understanding that it leaves open the question of the proper standard for judging First Amendment challenges to a municipality's restriction of access to cable facilities. . . . In assessing First Amendment claims concerning cable access, the Court must determine whether the characteristics of cable television make it sufficiently analogous to another medium to warrant application of an already existing standard or whether those characteristics require a new analysis. . . .

Chapter 18

RELIGION AND THE CONSTITUTION

SECTION 1. THE ESTABLISHMENT CLAUSE

B. RELIGION IN PUBLIC SCHOOLS

Page 1425. Add Ahead of Widmar v. Vincent:

WALLACE v. JAFFREE

472 U.S. 38, 105 S.Ct. 2479, 86 L.Ed.2d 29 (1985).

Justice Stevens delivered the opinion of the Court.

At an early stage of this litigation, the constitutionality of three Alabama statutes was questioned: (1) § 16–1–20, enacted in 1978, which authorized a one-minute period of silence in all public schools "for meditation"; (2) § 16–1–20.1, enacted in 1981, which authorized a period of silence "for meditation or voluntary prayer"; and (3) § 16–1–20.2, enacted in 1982, which authorized teachers to lead "willing students" in a prescribed prayer to "Almighty God . . . the Creator and Supreme Judge of the world."

At the preliminary-injunction stage of this case, the District Court distinguished § 16–1–20 from the other two statutes. It then held that there was "nothing wrong" with § 16–1–20, but that § 16–1–20.1 and 16–1–20.2 were both invalid because the sole purpose of both was "an effort on the part of the State of Alabama to encourage a religious activity." After the trial on the merits, the District Court did not change its interpretation of these two statutes, but held that they were constitutional because, in its opinion, Alabama has the power to establish a state religion if it chooses to do so.

The Court of Appeals agreed with the District Court's initial interpretation of the purpose of both §§ 16–1–20.1 and 16–1–20.2, and held them both unconstitutional. We have already affirmed the Court of Appeals' holding with respect to § 16–1–20.2. Moreover, appellees have not questioned the holding that § 16–1–20 is valid. Thus, the narrow question for decision is whether § 16–1–20.1, which authorizes a period of silence for "meditation or voluntary prayer," is a law respecting the establishment of religion within the meaning of the First Amendment.

491

I

Appellee Ishmael Jaffree is a resident of Mobile County, Alabama. On May 28, 1982, he filed a complaint on behalf of three of his minor children; two of them were second-grade students and the third was then in kindergarten. The complaint named members of the Mobile County School Board, various school officials, and the minor plaintiffs' three teachers as defendants . . ..

. . .

In its lengthy conclusions of law, the District Court reviewed a number of opinions of this Court interpreting the Establishment Clause of the First Amendment, and then embarked on a fresh examination of the question whether the First Amendment imposes any barrier to the establishment of an official religion by the State of Alabama. After reviewing at length what it perceived to be newly discovered historical evidence, the District Court concluded that "the establishment clause of the first amendment to the United States Constitution does not prohibit the state from establishing a religion." In a separate opinion, the District Court dismissed appellees' challenge to the three Alabama statutes because of a failure to state any claim for which relief could be granted. The court's dismissal of this challenge was also based on its conclusion that the Establishment Clause did not bar the States from establishing a religion.

The Court of Appeals consolidated the two cases; not surprisingly, it reversed . . ..

. . .

II

Our unanimous affirmance of the Court of Appeals' judgment concerning § 16–1–20.2 makes it unnecessary to comment at length on the District Court's remarkable conclusion that the Federal Constitution imposes no obstacle to Alabama's establishment of a state religion. Before analyzing the precise issue that is presented to us, it is nevertheless appropriate to recall how firmly embedded in our constitutional jurisprudence is the proposition that the several States have no greater power to restrain the individual freedoms protected by the First Amendment than does the Congress of the United States.

As is plain from its text, the First Amendment was adopted to curtail the power of Congress to interfere with the individual's freedom to believe, to worship, and to express himself in accordance with the dictates of his own conscience. Until the Fourteenth Amendment was added to the Constitution, the First Amendment's restraints on the exercise of federal power simply did not apply to the States. But when the Constitution was amended to prohibit any State from depriving any person of liberty without due process of law, that Amendment imposed the same substantive limitations on the States' power to legislate that the First Amendment had always imposed on the Congress' power.

This Court has confirmed and endorsed this elementary proposition of law time and time again.

. . . .[T]he Court has identified the individual's freedom of conscience as the central liberty that unifies the various clauses in the First Amendment . . . .

Just as the right to speak and the right to refrain from speaking are complementary components of a broader concept of individual freedom of mind, so also the individual's freedom to choose his own creed is the counterpart of his right to refrain from accepting the creed established by the majority. At one time it was thought that this right merely proscribed the preference of one Christian sect over another, but would not require equal respect for the conscience of the infidel, the atheist, or the adherent of a non-Christian faith such as Mohammedism or Judaism. But when the underlying principle has been examined in the crucible of litigation, the Court has unambiguously concluded that the individual freedom of conscience protected by the First Amendment embraces the right to select any religious faith or none at all. This conclusion derives support not only from the interest in respecting the individual's freedom of conscience, but also from the conviction that religious beliefs worthy of respect are the product of free and voluntary choice by the faithful, and from recognition of the fact that the political interest in forestalling intolerance extends beyond intolerance among Christian sects—or even intolerance among "religions"—to encompass intolerance of the disbeliever and the uncertain. As Justice Jackson eloquently stated in Board of Education v. Barnette, 319 U.S. 624, 642 (1943):

"If there is any fixed star in our constitutional constellation, it is that no official, high or petty, can prescribe what shall be orthodox in politics, nationalism, religion, or other matters of opinion or force citizens to confess by word or act their faith therein."

The State of Alabama, no less than the Congress of the United States, must respect that basic truth.

III

When the Court has been called upon to construe the breadth of the Establishment Clause, it has examined the criteria developed over a period of many years. Thus, in Lemon v. Kurtzman, 403 U.S. 602, 612–613 (1971), we wrote:

"Every analysis in this area must begin with consideration of the cumulative criteria developed by the Court over many years. Three such tests may be gleaned from our cases. First, the statute must have a secular legislative purpose; second, its principal or primary effect must be one that neither advances nor inhibits religion, Board of Education v. Allen, 392 U.S. 236, 243 (1968); finally, the statute must not foster 'an excessive government entanglement with religion.' Walz [v. Tax Commission, 397 U.S. 664, 674 (1970)]."

It is the first of these three criteria that is most plainly implicated by this case. As the District Court correctly recognized, no consideration of the second or third criteria is necessary if a statute does not have a clearly secular purpose. For even though a statute that is motivated in part by a religious purpose may satisfy the first criterion, see, e.g., Abington School Dist. v. Schempp, 374 U.S. 203, 296–303 (1963) (Brennan, J., concurring), the First Amendment requires that a statute must be invalidated if it is entirely motivated by a purpose to advance religion.

In applying the purpose test, it is appropriate to ask "whether government's actual purpose is to endorse or disapprove of religion." In this case, the answer to that question is dispositive. For the record not only provides us with an unambiguous affirmative answer, but it also reveals that the enactment of § 16–1–20.1 was not motivated by any clearly secular purpose—indeed, the statute had *no* secular purpose.

IV

The sponsor of the bill that became § 16–1–20.1, Senator Donald Holmes, inserted into the legislative record—apparently without dissent—a statement indicating that the legislation was an "effort to return voluntary prayer" to the public schools. Later Senator Holmes confirmed this purpose before the District Court. In response to the question whether he had any purpose for the legislation other than returning voluntary prayer to public schools, he stated, "No, I did not have no other purpose in mind." The State did not present evidence of *any* secular purpose.

The unrebutted evidence of legislative intent contained in the legislative record and in the testimony of the sponsor of § 16–1–20.1 is confirmed by a consideration of the relationship between this statute and the two other measures that were considered in this case. The District Court found that the 1981 statute and its 1982 sequel had a common, nonsecular purpose. The wholly religious character of the later enactment is plainly evident from its text. When the differences between § 16–1–20.1 and its 1978 predecessor, § 16–1–20, are examined, it is equally clear that the 1981 statute has the same wholly religious character.

There are only three textual differences between § 16–1–20.1 and § 16–1–20: (1) the earlier statute applies only to grades one through six, whereas § 16–1–20.1 applies to all grades; (2) the earlier statute uses the word "shall" whereas § 16–1–20.1 uses the word "may"; (3) the earlier statute refers only to "meditation" whereas § 16–1–20.1 refers to "meditation or voluntary prayer." The first difference is of no relevance in this litigation because the minor appellees were in kindergarten or second grade during the 1981–1982 academic year. The second difference would also have no impact on this litigation because the mandatory language of § 16–1–20 continued to apply to grades one through six. Thus, the only significant textual difference is the addition of the words "or voluntary prayer."

The legislative intent to return prayer to the public schools is, of course, quite different from merely protecting every student's right to engage in voluntary prayer during an appropriate moment of silence during the school day. The 1978 statute already protected that right, containing nothing that prevented any student from engaging in voluntary prayer during a silent minute of meditation. Appellants have not identified any secular purpose that was not fully served by § 16–1–20 before the enactment of § 16–1–20.1. Thus, only two conclusions are consistent with the text of § 16–1–20.1: (1) the statute was enacted to convey a message of State endorsement and promotion of prayer; or (2) the statute was enacted for no purpose. No one suggests that the statute was nothing but a meaningless or irrational act.

We must, therefore, conclude that the Alabama Legislature intended to change existing law and that it was motivated by the same purpose that the Governor's Answer to the Second Amended Complaint expressly admitted; that the statement inserted in the legislative history revealed; and that Senator Holmes' testimony frankly described. The Legislature enacted § 16–1–20.1 despite the existence of § 16–1–20 for the sole purpose of expressing the State's endorsement of prayer activities for one minute at the beginning of each school day. The addition of "or voluntary prayer" indicates that the State intended to characterize prayer as a favored practice. Such an endorsement is not consistent with the established principle that the Government must pursue a course of complete neutrality toward religion.

The importance of that principle does not permit us to treat this as an inconsequential case involving nothing more than a few words of symbolic speech on behalf of the political majority. For whenever the State itself speaks on a religious subject, one of the questions that we must ask is "whether the Government intends to convey a message of endorsement or disapproval of religion." The well-supported concurrent findings of the District Court and the Court of Appeals—that § 16–1–20.1 was intended to convey a message of State-approval of prayer activities in the public schools—make it unnecessary, and indeed inappropriate, to evaluate the practical significance of the addition of the words "or voluntary prayer" to the statute. Keeping in mind, as we must, "both the fundamental place held by the Establishment Clause in our constitutional scheme and the myriad, subtle ways in which Establishment Clause values can be eroded," we conclude that § 16–1–20.1 violates the First Amendment.

The judgment of the Court of Appeals is affirmed.

It is so ordered.

Justice Powell, concurring.

I concur in the Court's opinion and judgment that Ala.Code § 16–1–20.1 violates the Establishment Clause of the First Amendment. My concurrence is prompted by Alabama's persistence in attempting to institute state-sponsored prayer in the public schools by enacting three successive statutes. I agree fully with Justice O'Connor's assertion that some moment-of-silence statutes may be constitutional, a suggestion set forth in the Court's opinion as well.

I write separately to express additional views and to respond to criticism of the three-pronged *Lemon* test. Lemon v. Kurtzman, 403 U.S. 602 (1972), identifies standards that have proven useful in analyzing case after case both in our decisions and in those of other courts. It is the only coherent test a majority of the Court has ever adopted. Only once since our decision in *Lemon*, supra, have we addressed an Establishment Clause issue without resort to its three-pronged test. See Marsh v. Chambers, 463 U.S. 783 (1983). *Lemon*, supra, has not been overruled or its test modified. Yet, continued criticism of it could encourage other courts to feel free to decide Establishment Clause cases on an *ad hoc* basis.

. . .

Although we do not reach the other two prongs of the *Lemon* test, I note that the "effect" of a straightforward moment-of-silence statute is unlikely to "advanc[e] or inhibi[t] religion." See Board of Education v. Allen, 392 U.S. 236, 243 (1968). Nor would such a statute "foster 'an excessive government entanglement with religion.' " Lemon v. Kurtzman, supra, at 612–613, quoting Walz v. Tax Commissioner, 397 U.S. 664, 674 (1970).

I join the opinion and judgment of the Court.

Justice O'Connor, concurring in the judgment.

. . . I agree with the judgment of the Court that, in light of the findings of the Courts below and the history of its enactment, § 16–1–20.1 of the Alabama Code violates the Establishment Clause of the First Amendment. In my view, there can be little doubt that the purpose and likely effect of this subsequent enactment is to endorse and sponsor voluntary prayer in the public schools. I write separately to identify the peculiar features of the Alabama law that render it invalid, and to explain why moment of silence laws in other States do not necessarily manifest the same infirmity . . ..

I

. . .

Perhaps because I am new to the struggle, I am not ready to abandon all aspects of the *Lemon* test. I do believe, however, that the standards announced in *Lemon* should be reexamined and refined in order to make them more useful in achieving the underlying purpose of the First Amendment. We must strive to do more than erect a constitutional "signpost," Hunt v. McNair, 413 U.S. 734, 741 (1973), to be followed or ignored in a particular case as our predilections may dictate. Instead, our goal should be "to frame a principle for constitutional adjudication that is not only grounded in the history and language of the first amendment, but one that is also capable of consistent application to the relevant problems." Choper, Religion in the Public Schools: A Proposed Constitutional Standard, 47 Minn.L.Rev. 329, 332–333 (1963) (footnotes omitted). Last Term, I proposed a refinement of the *Lemon* test with this goal in mind. Lynch v. Donnelly, 465 U.S., at ___ (concurring opinion).

The *Lynch* concurrence suggested that the religious liberty protected by the Establishment Clause is infringed when the government makes adherence to religion relevant to a person's standing in the political community. Direct government action endorsing religion or a particular religious practice is invalid under this approach because it "sends a message to nonadherents that they are outsiders, not full members of the political community, and an accompanying message to adherents that they are insiders, favored members of the political community." Id., at ___. Under this view, *Lemon*'s inquiry as to the purpose and effect of a statute requires courts to examine whether government's purpose is to endorse religion and whether the statute actually conveys a message of endorsement.

The endorsement test is useful because of the analytic content it gives to the *Lemon*-mandated inquiry into legislative purpose and effect. In this country, church and state must necessarily operate within the same community. Because of this coexistence, it is inevitable that the secular interests of Government and the religious interests of various sects and their adherents will frequently intersect, conflict, and combine. A statute that ostensibly promotes a secular interest often has an incidental or even a primary effect of helping or hindering a sectarian belief. Chaos would ensue if every such statute were invalid under the Establishment Clause. For example, the State could not criminalize murder for fear that it would thereby promote the Biblical command against killing. The task for the Court is to sort out those statutes and government practices whose purpose and effect go against the grain of religious liberty protected by the First Amendment.

The endorsement test does not preclude government from acknowledging religion or from taking religion into account in making law and policy. It does preclude government from conveying or attempting to convey a message that religion or a particular religious belief is favored or preferred . . ..

A

Twenty-five states permit or require public school teachers to have students observe a moment of silence in their classrooms. A few statutes provide that the moment of silence is for the purpose of meditation alone . . .. The typical statute, however, calls for a moment of silence at the beginning of the school day during which students may meditate, pray, or reflect on the activities of the day . . .. Federal trial courts have divided on the constitutionality of these moment of silence laws . . ..

. . .

A state sponsored moment of silence in the public schools is different from state sponsored vocal prayer or Bible reading. First, a moment of silence is not inherently religious. Silence, unlike prayer or Bible reading, need not be associated with a religious exercise. Second, a pupil who participates in a moment of silence need not compromise his or her beliefs. During a moment of silence, a student who objects to prayer is left to his or her own thoughts, and is not compelled to listen to the prayers or thoughts of others. For these simple reasons, a moment of silence statute does not stand or fall under the Establishment Clause according to how the Court regards vocal prayer or Bible reading . . ..

By mandating a moment of silence, a State does not necessarily endorse any activity that might occur during the period . . .. The crucial question is whether the State has conveyed or attempted to convey the message that children should use the moment of silence for prayer. This question cannot be answered in the abstract, but instead requires courts to examine the history, language, and administration of a particular statute to determine whether it operates as an endorsement of religion . . ..

. . .

. . . The relevant issue is whether an objective observer, acquainted with the text, legislative history, and implementation of the statute, would perceive it as a state endorsement of prayer in public schools. . . . A moment of silence law that is clearly drafted and implemented so as to permit prayer, meditation, and reflection within the prescribed period, without endorsing one alternative over the others, should pass this test.

B

The analysis above suggests that moment of silence laws in many States should pass Establishment Clause scrutiny because they do not favor the child who chooses to pray during a moment of silence over the child who chooses to meditate or reflect. Alabama Code § 16–1–20.1 (Supp.1984) does not stand on the same footing. However deferentially one examines its text and legislative history, however objectively one views the message attempted to be conveyed to the public, the conclusion is unavoidable that the purpose of the statute is to endorse prayer in public schools . . ..

. . .

II

. . .

The solution to the conflict between the religion clauses lies not in "neutrality," but rather in identifying workable limits to the Government's license to promote the free exercise of religion. The text of the Free Exercise Clause speaks of laws that prohibit the free exercise of religion. On its face, the Clause is directed at government interference with free exercise. Given that concern, one can plausibly assert that government pursues free exercise clause values when it lifts a government-imposed burden on the free exercise of religion. If a statute falls within this category, then the standard Establishment Clause test should be modified accordingly. It is disingenuous to look for a purely secular purpose when the manifest objective of a statute is to facilitate the free exercise of religion by lifting a government-imposed burden. Instead, the Court should simply acknowledge that the religious purpose of such a statute is legitimated by the Free Exercise Clause. I would also go further. In assessing the effect of such a statute—that is, in determining whether the statute conveys the message of endorsement of religion or a particular religious belief—courts should assume that the "objective observer" is acquainted with the Free Exercise Clause and the values it promotes. Thus individual perceptions, or resentment that a religious observer is exempted from a particular government requirement, would be entitled to little weight if the Free Exercise Clause strongly supported the exemption.

While this "accommodation" analysis would help reconcile our Free Exercise and Establishment Clause standards, it would not save Alabama's moment of silence law. If we assume that the religious activity that Alabama seeks to protect is silent prayer, then it is difficult to discern any state-imposed burden on that activity that is lifted by Alabama Code § 16–1–20.1. No law prevents a student who is so inclined from praying silently in public schools. Moreover, state law already provided a moment of silence to these appellees irrespective of Alabama Code § 16–1–20.1. See Ala.Code § 16–1–20. Of course, the State might argue that § 16–1–20.1 protects not silent prayer, but rather group silent prayer under State sponsorship. Phrased in these terms, the burden lifted by the statute is not one imposed by the State of Alabama, but by the Establishment Clause as interpreted in *Engle* and *Abington*. In my view, it is beyond the authority of the State of Alabama to remove burdens imposed by the Constitution itself. I conclude that the Alabama statute at issue today lifts no state-imposed burden on the free exercise of religion, and accordingly cannot properly be viewed as an accommodation statute.

. . .

Chief Justice Burger, dissenting.

. . .

I make several points about today's curious holding.

(a) It makes no sense to say that Alabama has "endorsed prayer" . . . .. To suggest that a moment-of-silence statute that includes the word "prayer" unconstitutionally endorses religion, while one that simply provides for a moment of silence does not, manifests not neutrality but hostility toward religion . . . ..

(b) The inexplicable aspect of the foregoing opinions, however, is what they advance as support for the holding concerning the purpose of the Alabama legislature . . . ..

Curiously, the opinions do not mention that *all* of the sponsor's statements relied upon—including the statement "inserted" into the Senate Journal—were made *after* the legislature had passed the statute; indeed, the testimony that the Court finds critical was given well over a year after the statute was enacted . . . ..

. . .

The several preceding opinions conclude that the principal difference between § 16–1–20.1 and its predecessor statute proves that the sole purpose behind the inclusion of the phrase "or voluntary prayer" in § 16–1–20.1 was to endorse and promote prayer. This reasoning is simply a subtle way of focusing exclusively on the religious component of the statute rather than examining the statute as a whole. Such logic—if it can be called that—would lead the Court to hold, for example, that a state may enact a statute that provides reimbursement for bus transportation to the parents of all schoolchildren, but may not *add* parents of parochial school students to an existing program providing reimbursement for parents of public school students. Congress amended the statutory Pledge of Allegiance 31 years ago to add the words "under God." Act of June 14, 1954, Pub.L. 396, 68 Stat. 249. Do the several opinions in support of the judgment today render the Pledge unconstitutional? That would be the consequence of their method of focusing on the difference between § 16–1–20.1 and its predecessor statute rather than examining § 16–1–20.1 as a whole . . . ..

(c) The Court's extended treatment of the "test" of Lemon v. Kurtzman, 403 U.S. 602 (1971), suggests a naive preoccupation with an easy, bright-line approach for addressing constitutional issues. We have repeatedly cautioned that *Lemon* did not establish a rigid caliper capable of resolving every Establishment Clause issue, but that it sought only to provide "signposts." "In each [Establishment Clause] case, the inquiry calls for line drawing; no fixed, *per se* rule can be framed." Lynch v. Donnelly, 465 U.S. ___, ___ (1984). In any event, our responsibility is not to apply tidy formulas by rote; our duty is to determine whether the statute or practice at issue is a step toward establishing a state religion. Given today's decision, however, perhaps it is understandable that the opinions in support of the judgment all but ignore the Establishment Clause itself and the concerns that underlie it.

(d) The notion that the Alabama statute is a step toward creating an established church borders on, if it does not trespass into, the ridiculous. The statute does not remotely threaten religious liberty; it affirmatively furthers the values of religious freedom and tolerance that the Establishment Clause was designed to protect. Without pressuring those who do not wish to pray, the statute simply creates an opportunity to think, to plan, or to pray if one wishes—as Congress does by providing chaplains and chapels. It accommodates the purely private, voluntary religious choices of the individual pupils who wish to pray while at the same time creating a time for nonreligious reflection for those who do not choose to pray. The statute also provides a meaningful opportunity for schoolchildren to appreciate the absolute constitutional right of each individual to worship and believe as the individual wishes. The statute "endorses" only the view that the religious observances of others should be tolerated and, where possible, accommodated. If the government may not accommodate religious needs when it does so in a wholly neutral and noncoercive manner, the "benevolent neutrality" that we have long considered the correct constitutional standard will quickly translate into the "callous indifference" that the Court has consistently held the Establishment Clause does not require.

   . . .

Justice White, dissenting.

For the most part agreeing with the opinion of the Chief Justice, I dissent from the Court's judgment invalidating Alabama Code § 16-1-20.1. Because I do, it is apparent that in my view the First Amendment does not proscribe either (1) statutes authorizing or requiring in so many words a moment of silence before classes begin or (2) a statute that provides, when it is initially passed, for a moment of silence for meditation or prayer. As I read the filed opinions, a majority of the Court would approve statutes that provided for a moment of silence but did not mention prayer. But if a student asked whether he could pray during that moment, it is difficult to believe that the teacher could not answer in the affirmative. If that is the case, I would not invalidate a statute that at the outset provided the legislative answer to the question "May I pray?" This is so even if the Alabama statute is infirm, which I do not believe it is, because of its peculiar legislative history.

I appreciate Justice Rehnquist's explication of the history of the religion clauses of the First Amendment. Against that history, it would be quite understandable if we undertook to reassess our cases dealing with these clauses, particularly those dealing with the Establishment Clause. Of course, I have been out of step with many of the Court's decisions dealing with this subject matter, and it is thus not surprising that I would support a basic reconsideration of our precedents.

Justice Rehnquist, dissenting.

Thirty-eight years ago this Court, in Everson v. Board of Education, 330 U.S. 1, 16 (1947) summarized its exegesis of Establishment Clause doctrine thus:

> "In the words of Jefferson, the clause against establishment of religion by law was intended to erect 'a wall of separation between church and State.' Reynolds v. United States, [98 U.S. 145, 164 (1879)]."

This language from *Reynolds,* a case involving the Free Exercise Clause of the First Amendment rather than the Establishment Clause, quoted from Thomas Jefferson's letter to the Danbury Baptist Association the phrase "I contemplate with sovereign reverence that act of the whole American people which declared that their legislature should 'make no law respecting an establishment of religion, or prohibiting the free exercise thereof,' thus building a wall of separation between church and State." 8 Writings of Thomas Jefferson 113 (H. Washington ed. 1861).

It is impossible to build sound constitutional doctrine upon a mistaken understanding of constitutional history, but unfortunately the Establishment Clause has been expressly freighted with Jefferson's misleading metaphor for nearly forty years. Thomas Jefferson was of course in France at the time the constitutional amendments known as the Bill of Rights were passed by Congress and ratified by the states. His letter to the Danbury Baptist Association was a short note of courtesy, written fourteen years after the amendments were passed by Congress. He would seem to any detached observer as a less than ideal

source of contemporary history as to the meaning of the Religion
Clauses of the First Amendment.

Jefferson's fellow Virginian James Madison, with whom he was
joined in the battle for the enactment of the Virginia Statute of
Religious Liberty of 1786, did play as large a part as anyone in the
drafting of the Bill of Rights. He had two advantages over Jefferson in
this regard: he was present in the United States, and he was a leading
member of the First Congress. But when we turn to the record of the
proceedings in the First Congress leading up to the adoption of the
Establishment Clause of the Constitution, including Madison's significant contributions thereto, we see a far different picture of its purpose
than the highly simplified "wall of separation between church and
State."

. . .

It seems indisputable . . . that [Madison] saw the amendment as
designed to prohibit the establishment of a national religion, and
perhaps to prevent discrimination among sects. He did not see it as
requiring neutrality on the part of government between religion and
irreligion. Thus the Court's opinion in *Everson* —while correct in
bracketing Madison and Jefferson together in their exertions in their
home state leading to the enactment of the Virginia Statute of Religious Liberty—is totally incorrect in suggesting that Madison carried
these views onto the floor of the United States House of Representatives when he proposed the language which would ultimately become
the Bill of Rights.

. . .

. . . There is simply no historical foundation for the proposition
that the Framers intended to build the "wall of separation" that was
constitutionalized in *Everson.*

Notwithstanding the absence of an historical basis for this theory
of rigid separation, the wall idea might well have served as a useful
albeit misguided analytical concept, had it led this Court to unified and
principled results in Establishment Clause cases. The opposite, unfortunately, has been true; in the 38 years since *Everson* our Establishment Clause cases have been neither principled nor unified. Our
recent opinions, many of them hopelessly divided pluralities, have with
embarrassing candor conceded that the "wall of separation" is merely a
"blurred, indistinct, and variable barrier," which "is not wholly accurate" and can only be "dimly perceived." Lemon v. Kurtzman, 403
U.S. 602, 614 (1971); Tilton v. Richardson, 403 U.S. 672, 677–678 (1971);
Wolman v. Walter, 433 U.S. 229, 236 (1977); Lynch v. Donnelly, 465
U.S. ___ (1984).

. . .

The Framers intended the Establishment Clause to prohibit the
designation of any church as a "national" one. The Clause was also
designed to stop the Federal Government from asserting a preference
for one religious denomination or sect over others. Given the "incorporation" of the Establishment Clause as against the States via the
Fourteenth Amendment in *Everson,* States are prohibited as well from

establishing a religion or discriminating between sects. As its history abundantly shows, however, nothing in the Establishment Clause requires government to be strictly neutral between religion and irreligion, nor does that Clause prohibit Congress or the States from pursuing legitimate secular ends through nondiscriminatory sectarian means.

The Court strikes down the Alabama statute in No. 83–812, Wallace v. Jaffree, because the State wished to "endorse prayer as a favored practice." It would come as much of a shock to those who drafted the Bill of Rights as it will to a large number of thoughtful Americans today to learn that the Constitution, as construed by the majority, prohibits the Alabama Legislature from "endorsing" prayer. George Washington himself, at the request of the very Congress which passed the Bill of Rights, proclaimed a day of "public thanksgiving and prayer, to be observed by acknowledging with grateful hearts the many and signal favors of Almighty God." History must judge whether it was the father of his country in 1789, or a majority of the Court today, which has strayed from the meaning of the Establishment Clause.

The State surely has a secular interest in regulating the manner in which public schools are conducted. Nothing in the Establishment Clause of the First Amendment, properly understood, prohibits any such generalized "endorsement" of prayer. I would therefore reverse the judgment of the Court of Appeals in *Wallace v. Jaffree.*

Page 1425. Add after Widmar v. Vincent:

BENDER v. WILLIAMSPORT AREA SCHOOL DISTRICT, 475 U.S. 534 (1986). This case raised the question whether *Widmar* was applicable to student-initiated and student-led religious meetings in a public high school. A majority of the Court resolved the case on the ground that a single school board member had no standing to appeal an adverse decision of the federal district court. Four members of the Court who reached the merits (Chief Justice Burger, and Justices White, Rehnquist, and Powell) concluded that the establishment clause did not prevent such meetings, and that *Widmar* was controlling.

Page 1425: Replace Epperson v. Arkansas with the following:

EDWARDS v. AGUILLARD

___ U.S. ___, 107 S.Ct. 2573, 96 L.Ed.2d 510 (1987).

Justice Brennan delivered the opinion of the Court.

The question for decision is whether Louisiana's "Balanced Treatment for Creation-Science and Evolution-Science in Public School Instruction" Act (Creationism Act), La.Rev.Stat.Ann. sections 17:286.1–17:286.7 (West 1982), is facially invalid as violative of the Establishment Clause of the First Amendment.

I

The Creationism Act forbids the teaching of the theory of evolution in public schools unless accompanied by instruction in "creation science." Section 17:286.4A. No school is required to teach evolution or creation science. If either is taught, however, the other must also be taught. Ibid. The theories of evolution and creation science are statutorily defined as "the scientific evidences for [creation or evolution] and inferences from those scientific evidences." Sections 17:286.3(2) and (3).

Appellees, who include parents of children attending Louisiana public schools, Louisiana teachers, and religious leaders, challenged the constitutionality of the Act in District Court, seeking an injunction and declaratory relief. Appellants, Louisiana officials charged with implementing the Act, defended on the ground that the purpose of the Act is to protect a legitimate secular interest, namely, academic freedom. Appellees attacked the Act as facially invalid because it violated the Establishment Clause and made a motion for summary judgment. The District Court granted the motion. . . .

The Court of Appeals affirmed. . . . We . . . affirm.

II

The Establishment Clause forbids the enactment of any law "respecting an establishment of religion." The Court has applied a three-pronged test to determine whether legislation comports with the Establishment Clause. First, the legislature must have adopted the law with a secular purpose. Second, the statute's principal or primary effect must be one that neither advances nor inhibits religion. Third, the statute must not result in an excessive entanglement of government with religion. Lemon v. Kurtzman, 403 U.S. 602, 612–613 (1971).[4] State action violates the Establishment Clause if it fails to satisfy any of these prongs.

In this case, the Court must determine whether the Establishment Clause was violated in the special context of the public elementary and secondary school system. States and local school boards are generally afforded considerable discretion in operating public schools. . . . "At the same time . . . we have necessarily recognized that the discretion of the States and local school boards in matters of education must be exercised in a manner that comports with the transcendent imperatives

---

[4] The *Lemon* test has been applied in all cases since its adoption in 1971, except in Marsh v. Chambers, 463 U.S. 783 (1983), where the Court held that the Nebraska legislature's practice of opening a session with a prayer by a chaplain paid by the State did not violate the Establishment Clause. The Court based its conclusion in that case on the historical acceptance of the practice. Such a historical approach is not useful in determining the proper roles of church and state in public schools, since free public education was virtually nonexistent at the time the Constitution was adopted. See Wallace v. Jaffree, 472 U.S. 38, 80 (1985) (O'Connor, J., concurring in judgment) (citing Abington School Dist. v. Schempp, 374 U.S. 203, 238, and n. 7 (1963) (Brennan, J., concurring)).

of the First Amendment." Board of Education v. Pico, 457 U.S. 853, 864 (1982).

The Court has been particularly vigilant in monitoring compliance with the Establishment Clause in elementary and secondary schools. Families entrust public schools with the education of their children, but condition their trust on the understanding that the classroom will not purposely be used to advance religious views that may conflict with the private beliefs of the student and his or her family. Students in such institutions are impressionable and their attendance is involuntary. . . . The State exerts great authority and coercive power through mandatory attendance requirements, and because of the students' emulation of teachers as role models and the children's susceptibility to peer pressure.[5] . . .

. . .

Therefore, in employing the three-pronged *Lemon* test, we must do so mindful of the particular concerns that arise in the context of public elementary and secondary schools. We now turn to the evaluation of the Act under the *Lemon* test.

III

Lemon's first prong focuses on the purpose that animated adoption of the Act. . . . If the law was enacted for the purpose of endorsing religion, "no consideration of the second or third criteria [of *Lemon*] is necessary." Wallace v. Jaffree, supra, at 56. In this case, the petitioners have identified no clear secular purpose for the Louisiana Act.

True, the Act's stated purpose is to protect academic freedom. . . . This phrase might, in common parlance, be understood as referring to enhancing the freedom of teachers to teach what they will. The Court of Appeals, however, correctly concluded that the Act was not designed to further that goal. We find no merit in the State's argument that the "legislature may not [have] use[d] the terms 'academic freedom' in the correct legal sense. They might have [had] in mind, instead, a basic concept of fairness; teaching all of the evidence." Even if "academic freedom" is read to mean "teaching all of the evidence" with respect to the origin of human beings, the Act does not further this purpose. The goal of providing a more comprehensive science curriculum is not furthered either by outlawing the teaching of evolution or by requiring the teaching of creation science.

A

While the Court is normally deferential to a State's articulation of a secular purpose, it is required that the statement of such purpose be sincere and not a sham. . . .

[5] The potential for undue influence is far less significant with regard to college students who voluntarily enroll in courses. "This distinction warrants a difference in constitutional results." Abington School Dist. v. Schempp, supra, at 253 (Brennan, J., concurring). Thus, for instance, the Court has not questioned the authority of state colleges and universities to offer courses on religion or theology. See Widmar v. Vincent, 454 U.S. 263, 271 (1981) (Powell, J.); id., at 281 (Stevens, J., concurring in judgment).

It is clear from the legislative history that the purpose of the legislative sponsor, Senator Bill Keith, was to narrow the science curriculum. During the legislative hearings, Senator Keith stated: "My preference would be that neither [creationism nor evolution] be taught." Such a ban on teaching does not promote—indeed, it undermines—the provision of a comprehensive scientific education.

It is equally clear that requiring schools to teach creation science with evolution does not advance academic freedom. The Act does not grant teachers a flexibility that they did not already possess to supplant the present science curriculum with the presentation of theories, besides evolution, about the origin of life. Indeed, the Court of Appeals' found that no law prohibited Louisiana public schoolteachers from teaching any scientific theory. . . .

. . .

Furthermore, the goal of basic "fairness" is hardly furthered by the Act's discriminatory preference for the teaching of creation science and against the teaching of evolution. While requiring that curriculum guides be developed for creation science, the Act says nothing of comparable guides for evolution. . . . Similarly, research services are supplied for creation science but not for evolution. . . . Only "creation scientists" can serve on the panel that supplies the resource services. . . . The Act forbids school boards to discriminate against anyone who "chooses to be a creation-scientist" or to teach "creationism," but fails to protect those who choose to teach evolution or any other non-creation science theory, or who refuse to teach creation science. . . .

If the Louisiana legislature's purpose was solely to maximize the comprehensiveness and effectiveness of science instruction, it would have encouraged the teaching of all scientific theories about the origins of humankind. But under the Act's requirements, teachers who were once free to teach any and all facets of this subject are now unable to do so. Moreover, the Act fails even to ensure that creation science will be taught, but instead requires the teaching of this theory only when the theory of evolution is taught. Thus we agree with the Court of Appeals' conclusion that the Act does not serve to protect academic freedom, but has the distinctly different purpose of discrediting "evolution by counterbalancing its teaching at every turn with the teaching of creation science. . . ."

B

. . .

As in *Stone* and *Abington,* we need not be blind in this case to the legislature's preeminent religious purpose in enacting this statute. There is a historic and contemporaneous link between the teachings of certain religious denominations and the teaching of evolution. It was this link that concerned the Court in Epperson v. Arkansas, 393 U.S. 97 (1968), which also involved a facial challenge to a statute regulating the teaching of evolution. In that case, the Court reviewed an Arkansas statute that made it unlawful for an instructor to teach evolution or to use a textbook that referred to this scientific theory. Although the Arkansas anti-evolution law did not explicitly state its predominate religious purpose, the Court could not ignore that "[t]he statute was a product of the upsurge of 'fundamentalist' religious fervor" that has long viewed this particular scientific theory as contradicting the literal interpretation of the Bible. Id. at 106–107. After reviewing the history of anti-evolution statutes, the Court determined that "there can be no doubt that the motivation for the [Arkansas] law was the same [as other anti-evolution statutes]: to suppress the teaching of a theory which, it was thought, 'denied' the divine creation of man." Id., at 109. The Court found that there can be no legitimate state interest in protecting particular religions from scientific views "distasteful to them," id., at 107 (citation omitted), and concluded "that the First Amendment does not permit the State to require that teaching and learning must be tailored to the principles or prohibitions of any religious sect or dogma," id., at 106.

These same historic and contemporaneous antagonisms between the teachings of certain religious denominations and the teaching of evolution are present in this case. The preeminent purpose of the Louisiana legislature was clearly to advance the religious viewpoint that a supernatural being created humankind. The term "creation science" was defined as embracing this particular religious doctrine by those responsible for the passage of the Creationism Act. Senator Keith's leading expert on creation science, Edward Boudreaux, testified at the legislative hearings that the theory of creation science included belief in the existence of a supernatural creator. Senator Keith also cited testimony from other experts to support the creation-science view that "a creator [was] responsible for the universe and everything in it." The legislative history therefore reveals that the term "creation science," as contemplated by the legislature that adopted this Act, embodies the religious belief that a supernatural creator was responsible for the creation of humankind.

Furthermore, it is not happenstance that the legislature required the teaching of a theory that coincided with this religious view. The legislative history documents that the Act's primary purpose was to change the science curriculum of public schools in order to provide persuasive advantage to a particular religious doctrine that rejects the factual basis of evolution in its entirety. The sponsor of the Creationism Act, Senator Keith, explained during the legislative hearings that his disdain for the theory of evolution resulted from the support that evolution supplied to views contrary to his own religious beliefs. According to Senator Keith, the theory of evolution was consonant with the "cardinal principle[s] of religious humanism, secular humanism, theological liberalism, aetheistism [sic]." The state senator repeatedly stated that scientific evidence supporting his religious views should be included in the public school curriculum to redress the fact that the theory of evolution incidentally coincided with what he characterized as religious beliefs antithetical to his own. The legislation therefore sought to alter the science curriculum to reflect endorsement of a religious view that is antagonistic to the theory of evolution.

In this case, the purpose of the Creationism Act was to restructure the science curriculum to conform with a particular religious viewpoint. Out of many possible science subjects taught in the public schools, the legislature chose to affect the teaching of the one scientific theory that historically has been opposed by certain religious sects. As in *Epperson*, the legislature passed the Act to give preference to those religious groups which have as one of their tenets the creation of humankind by a divine creator. The "overriding fact" that confronted the Court in *Epperson* was "that Arkansas' law selects from the body of knowledge a particular segment which it proscribes for the sole reason that it is deemed to conflict with . . . a particular interpretation of the Book of Genesis by a particular religious group." 393 U.S., at 103. Similarly, the Creationism Act is designed either to promote the theory of creation science which embodies a particular religious tenet by requiring that creation science be taught whenever evolution is taught or to prohibit the teaching of a scientific theory disfavored by certain religious sects by forbidding the teaching of evolution when creation science is not also taught. The Establishment Clause, however, "forbids *alike* the preference of a religious doctrine OR the prohibition of theory which is deemed antagonistic to a particular dogma." Id., at 106–107 (emphasis added). Because the primary purpose of the Creationism Act is to advance a particular religious belief, the Act endorses religion in violation of the First Amendment.

We do not imply that a legislature could never require that scientific critiques of prevailing scientific theories be taught. Indeed, the Court acknowledged in *Stone* that its decision forbidding the posting of the Ten Commandments did not mean that no use could ever be made of the Ten Commandments, or that the Ten Commandments played an exclusively religious role in the history of Western Civilization. 449 U.S., at 42. In a similar way, teaching a variety of scientific theories about the origins of humankind to schoolchildren might be validly done with the clear secular intent of enhancing the effectiveness of science instruction. But because the primary purpose of the Creationism Act is to endorse a particular religious doctrine, the Act furthers religion in violation of the Establishment Clause.

IV

Appellants contend that genuine issues of material fact remain in dispute, and therefore the District Court erred in granting summary judgment. . . .

In this case, appellees' motion for summary judgment rested on the plain language of the Creationism Act, the legislative history and historical context of the Act, the specific sequence of events leading to the passage of the Act, the State Board's report on a survey of school superintendents, and the correspondence between the Act's legislative sponsor and its key witnesses. Appellants contend that affidavits made by two scientists, two theologians, and an education administrator raise a genuine issue of material fact and that summary judgment was therefore barred. The affidavits define creation science as "origin through abrupt appearance in complex form" and allege that such a viewpoint constitutes a true scientific theory. . . . [T]he postenactment testimony of outside experts is of little use in determining the Louisiana legislature's purpose in enacting this statute. . . . The District Court . . . properly concluded that a Monday-morning "battle of the experts" over possible technical meanings of terms in the statute would not illuminate the contemporaneous purpose of the Louisiana legislature when it made the law. We therefore conclude that the District Court did not err in finding that appellants failed to raise a genuine issue of material fact, and in granting summary judgment.

V

The Louisiana Creationism Act advances a religious doctrine by requiring either the banishment of the theory of evolution from public school classrooms or the presentation of a religious viewpoint that rejects evolution in its entirety. The Act violates the Establishment Clause of the First Amendment because it seeks to employ the symbolic and financial support of government to achieve a religious purpose. The judgment of the Court of Appeals therefore is

Affirmed.

Justice Powell, with whom Justice O'Connor joins, concurring.

I write separately to note certain aspects of the legislative history, and to emphasize that nothing in the Court's opinion diminishes the traditionally broad discretion accorded state and local school officials in the selection of the public school curriculum.

I

This Court consistently has applied the three-pronged test of Lemon v. Kurtzman, 403 U.S. 602 (1971), to determine whether a particular state action violates the Establishment Clause of the Constitution. . . .

A

. . .

A religious purpose alone is not enough to invalidate an act of a state legislature. The religious purpose must predominate. . . .

. . .

C

When, as here, "both courts below are unable to discern an arguably valid secular purpose, this Court normally should hesitate to find one." Wallace v. Jaffree, supra, at 66 (Powell, J., concurring). My examination of the language and the legislative history of the Balanced Treatment Act confirms that the intent of the Louisiana legislature was to promote a particular religious belief. The legislative history of the Arkansas statute prohibiting the teaching of evolution examined in

Epperson v. Arkansas, 393 U.S. 97 (1968), was strikingly similar to the legislative history of the Balanced Treatment Act. . . .

. . .

. . . The fact that the Louisiana legislature purported to add information to the school curriculum rather than detract from it as in *Epperson* does not affect my analysis. Both legislatures acted with the unconstitutional purpose of structuring the public school curriculum to make it compatible with a particular religious belief: the "divine creation of man."

. . .

II

Even though I find Louisiana's Balanced Treatment Act unconstitutional, I adhere to the view "that the States and locally elected school boards should have the responsibility for determining the educational policy of the public schools." Board of Education v. Pico, 457 U.S. 853, 893 (1982) (Powell, J., dissenting). A decision respecting the subject matter to be taught in public schools does not violate the Establishment Clause simply because the material to be taught " 'happens to coincide or harmonize with the tenets of some or all religions.' " Harris v. McRae, 448 U.S. 297, 319 (1980) (quoting McGowan v. Maryland, 366 U.S. 420, 442 (1961)). In the context of a challenge under the Establishment Clause, interference with the decisions of these authorities is warranted only when the purpose for their decisions is clearly religious.

. . .

As a matter of history, school children can and should properly be informed of all aspects of this Nation's religious heritage. I would see no constitutional problem if school children were taught the nature of the Founding Father's religious beliefs and how these beliefs affected the attitudes of the times and the structure of our government. Courses in comparative religion of course are customary and constitutionally appropriate. In fact, since religion permeates our history, a familiarity with the nature of religious beliefs is necessary to understand many historical as well as contemporary events. In addition, it is worth noting that the Establishment Clause does not prohibit per se the educational use of religious documents in public school education. . . . The Establishment Clause is properly understood to prohibit the use of the Bible and other religious documents in public school education only when the purpose of the use is to advance a particular religious belief.

III

In sum, I find that the language and the legislative history of the Balanced Treatment Act unquestionably demonstrate that its purpose is to advance a particular religious belief. Although the discretion of state and local authorities over public school curricula is broad, "the First Amendment does not permit the State to require that teaching and learning must be tailored to the principles or prohibitions of any religious sect or dogma." Epperson v. Arkansas, 393 U.S., at 106. Accordingly, I concur in the opinion of the Court and its judgment that the Balanced Treatment Act violates the Establishment Clause of the Constitution.

Justice White, concurring in the judgment.

As it comes to us, this is not a difficult case. . . .

. . .

Here, the District Judge, relying on the terms of the Act, discerned its purpose to be the furtherance of a religious belief, and a panel of the Court of Appeals agreed. Of those four judges, two are Louisianians. I would accept this view of the statute. Even if as an original matter I might have arrived at a different conclusion based on a reading of the statute and the record before us, I cannot say that the two courts below are so plainly wrong that they should be reversed. . . .

If the Court of Appeals' construction is to be accepted, so is its conclusion that under our prior cases the Balanced Treatment law is unconstitutional because its primary purpose is to further a religious belief by imposing certain requirements on the school curriculum. Unless, therefore, we are to reconsider the Court's decisions interpreting the Establishment Clause, I agree that the judgment of the Court of Appeals must be affirmed.

Justice Scalia, with whom The Chief Justice joins, dissenting.

Even if I agreed with the questionable premise that legislation can be invalidated under the Establishment Clause on the basis of its motivation alone, without regard to its effects, I would still find no justification for today's decision. The Louisiana legislators who passed the "Balanced Treatment for Creation-Science and Evolution-Science Act" (Balanced Treatment Act), . . . each of whom had sworn to support the Constitution, were well aware of the potential Establishment Clause problems and considered that aspect of the legislation with great care. . . . [T]he question of its constitutionality cannot rightly be disposed of on the gallop, by impugning the motives of its supporters.

I

This case arrives here in the following posture: The Louisiana Supreme Court has never been given an opportunity to interpret the Balanced Treatment Act, State officials have never attempted to implement it, and it has never been the subject of a full evidentiary hearing. We can only guess at its meaning. We know that it forbids instruction in either "creation-science" or "evolution-science" without instruction in the other, . . . but the parties are sharply divided over what creation science consists of. Appellants insist that it is a collection of educationally valuable scientific data that has been censored from classrooms by an embarrassed scientific establishment. Appellees insist it is not science at all but thinly veiled religious doctrine. Both interpretations of the intended meaning of that phrase find considerable support in the legislative history.

. . .

II

. . .

B

. . .

The Court cites three provisions of the Act which, it argues, demonstrate a "discriminatory preference for the teaching of creation science" and no interest in "academic freedom." First, the Act prohibits discrimination only against creation scientists and those who teach creation science. . . . Second, the Act requires local school boards to develop and provide to science teachers "a curriculum guide on presentation of creation-science." . . . Finally, the Act requires the governor to designate seven creation scientists who shall, upon request, assist local school boards in developing the curriculum guides. . . . But none of these provisions casts doubt upon the sincerity of the legislators' articulated purpose of "academic freedom"—unless, of course, one gives that term the obviously erroneous meanings preferred by the Court. The Louisiana legislators had been told repeatedly that creation scientists were scorned by most educators and scientists, who themselves had an almost religious faith in evolution. It is hardly surprising, then, that in seeking to achieve a balanced, "nonindoctrinating" curriculum, the legislators protected from discrimination only those teachers whom they thought were *suffering* from discrimination. (Also, the legislators were undoubtedly aware of Epperson v. Arkansas, 393 U.S. 97 (1968), and thus could quite reasonably have concluded that discrimination against evolutionists was already prohibited.) The two provisions respecting the development of curriculum guides are also consistent with "academic freedom" as the Louisiana Legislature understood the term. Witnesses had informed the legislators that, because of the hostility of most scientists and educators to creation science, the topic had been censored from or badly misrepresented in elementary and secondary school texts. In light of the unavailability of works on creation science suitable for classroom use (a fact appellees concede, and the existence of ample materials on evolution, it was entirely reasonable for the Legislature to conclude that science teachers attempting to implement the Act would need a curriculum guide on creation science, but not on evolution, and that those charged with developing the guide would need an easily accessible group of creation scientists. Thus, the provisions of the Act of so much concern to the Court *support* the conclusion that the Legislature acted to advance "academic freedom."

. . .

It is undoubtedly true that what prompted the Legislature to direct its attention to the misrepresentation of evolution in the schools (rather than the inaccurate presentation of other topics) was its awareness of the tension between evolution and the religious beliefs of many children. But even appellees concede that a valid secular purpose is not rendered impermissible simply because its pursuit is prompted by concern for religious sensitivities. If a history teacher falsely told her students that the bones of Jesus Christ had been discovered, or a physics teacher that the Shroud of Turin had been conclusively established to be inexplicable on the basis of natural causes, I cannot believe (despite the majority's implication to the contrary) that legislators or school board members would be constitutionally prohibited from taking corrective action, simply because that action was prompted by concern for the religious beliefs of the misinstructed students.

In sum, even if one concedes, for the sake of argument, that a majority of the Louisiana Legislature voted for the Balanced Treatment Act partly in order to foster (rather than merely eliminate discrimination against) Christian fundamentalist beliefs, our cases establish that that alone would not suffice to invalidate the Act, so long as there was a genuine secular purpose as well. We have, moreover, no adequate basis for disbelieving the secular purpose set forth in the Act itself, or for concluding that it is a sham enacted to conceal the legislators' violation of their oaths of office. I am astonished by the Court's unprecedented readiness to reach such a conclusion, which I can only attribute to an intellectual predisposition created by the facts and the legend of Scopes v. State, 154 Tenn. 105, 289 S.W. 363 (1927)—an instinctive reaction that any governmentally imposed requirements bearing upon the teaching of evolution must be a manifestation of Christian fundamentalist repression. In this case, however, it seems to me the Court's position is the repressive one. The people of Louisiana, including those who are Christian fundamentalists, are quite entitled, as a secular matter, to have whatever scientific evidence there may be against evolution presented in their schools, just as Mr. Scopes was entitled to present whatever scientific evidence there was for it. Perhaps what the Louisiana Legislature has done is unconstitutional because there *is* no such evidence, and the scheme they have established will amount to no more than a presentation of the Book of Genesis. But we cannot say that on the evidence before us in this summary judgment context, which includes ample uncontradicted testimony that "creation science" is a body of scientific knowledge rather than revealed belief. *Infinitely less* can we say (or should we say) that the scientific evidence for evolution is so conclusive that no one could be gullible enough to believe that there is any real scientific evidence to the contrary, so that the legislation's stated purpose must be a lie. Yet that in liberal judgment, that *Scopes* -in-reverse, is ultimately the basis on which the Court's facile rejection of the Louisiana Legislature's purpose must rest.

. . .

Because I believe that the Balanced Treatment Act had a secular purpose, which is all the first component of the *Lemon* test requires, I would reverse the judgment of the Court of Appeals and remand for further consideration.

III

I have to this point assumed the validity of the *Lemon* "purpose" test. In fact, however, I think the pessimistic evaluation that the Chief Justice made of the totality of *Lemon* is particularly applicable to the "purpose" prong: it is "a constitutional theory [that] has no basis in the history of the amendment it seeks to interpret, is difficult to apply and yields unprincipled results." Wallace v. Jaffree, 472 U.S., at 112 (Rehnquist, J., dissenting).

Our cases interpreting and applying the purpose test have made such a maze of the Establishment Clause that even the most conscientious governmental officials can only guess what motives will be held unconstitutional. We have said essentially the following: Government may not act with the purpose of advancing religion, except when forced to do so by the Free Exercise Clause (which is now and then); or when eliminating existing governmental hostility to religion (which exists sometimes); or even when merely accommodating governmentally uninhibited religious practices, except that at some point (it is unclear where) intentional accommodation results in the fostering of religion, which is of course unconstitutional.

But the difficulty of knowing what vitiating purpose one is looking for is as nothing compared with the difficulty of knowing how or where to find it. For while it is possible to discern the objective "purpose" of a statute (i.e., the public good at which its provisions appear to be directed), or even the formal motivation for a statute where that is explicitly set forth (as it was, to no avail, here), discerning the subjective motivation of those enacting the statute is, to be honest, almost always an impossible task. The number of possible motivations, to begin with, is not binary, or indeed even finite. In the present case, for example, a particular legislator need not have voted for the Act either because he wanted to foster religion or because he wanted to improve education. He may have thought the bill would provide jobs for his district, or may have wanted to make amends with a faction of his party he had alienated on another vote, or he may have been a close friend of the bill's sponsor, or he may have been repaying a favor he owed the Majority Leader, or he may have hoped the Governor would appreciate his vote and make a fundraising appearance for him, or he may have been pressured to vote for a bill he disliked by a wealthy contributor or by a flood of constituent mail, or he may have been seeking favorable publicity, or he may have been reluctant to hurt the feelings of a loyal staff member who worked on the bill, or he may have been settling an old score with a legislator who opposed the bill, or he may have been mad at his wife who opposed the bill, or he may have been intoxicated and utterly *un*motivated when the vote was called, or he may have accidentally voted "yes" instead of "no," or, of course, he may have had (and very likely did have) a combination of some of the above and many other motivations. To look for *the sole purpose* of even a single legislator is probably to look for something that does not exist.

Putting that problem aside, however, where ought we to look for the individual legislator's purpose? We cannot of course assume that every member present (if, as is unlikely, we know who or even how many they were) agreed with the motivation expressed in a particular legislator's pre-enactment floor or committee statement. . . . Can we assume, then, that they all agree with the motivation expressed in the staff-prepared committee reports they might have read—even though we are unwilling to assume that they agreed with the motivation expressed in the very statute that they voted for? Should we consider post-enactment floor statements? Or post-enactment testimony from legislators, obtained expressly for the lawsuit? Should we consider media reports on the realities of the legislative bargaining? All of these sources, of course, are eminently manipulable. Legislative histories can be contrived and sanitized, favorable media coverage orchestrated, and post-enactment recollections conveniently distorted. Perhaps most valuable of all would be more objective indications—for example, evidence regarding the individual legislators' religious affiliations. And if that, why not evidence regarding the fervor or tepidity of their beliefs?

Having achieved, through these simple means, an assessment of what individual legislators intended, we must still confront the question (yet to be addressed in any of our cases) how *many* of them must have the invalidating intent. If a state senate approves a bill by vote of 26 to 25, and only one of the 26 intended solely to advance religion, is the law unconstitutional? What if 13 of the 26 had that intent? What if 3 of the 26 had the impermissible intent, but 3 of the 25 voting against the bill were motivated by religious hostility or were simply attempting to "balance" the votes of their impermissibly motivated colleagues? Or is it possible that the intent of the bill's sponsor is alone enough to invalidate it—on a theory, perhaps, that even though everyone else's intent was pure, what they produced was the fruit of a forbidden tree?

Because there are no good answers to these questions, this Court has recognized from Chief Justice Marshall, see Fletcher v. Peck, 6 Cranch 87, 130 (1810), to Chief Justice Warren, United States v. O'Brien, supra, at 383–384, that determining the subjective intent of legislators is a perilous enterprise. See also Palmer v. Thompson, 403 U.S. 217, 224–225 (1971); Epperson v. Arkansas, 393 U.S., at 113 (Black, J., concurring). It is perilous, I might note, not just for the judges who will very likely reach the wrong result, but also for the legislators who find that they must assess the validity of proposed legislation—and risk the condemnation of having voted for an unconstitutional measure—not on the basis of what the legislation contains, nor even on the basis of what they themselves intend, but on the basis of what *others* have in mind.

Given the many hazards involved in assessing the subjective intent of governmental decisionmakers, the first prong of *Lemon* is defensible, I think, only if the text of the Establishment Clause demands it. That is surely not the case. . . . It is, in short, far from an inevitable reading of the Establishment Clause that it forbids all governmental action intended to advance religion; and if not inevitable, any reading with such untoward consequences must be wrong.

In the past we have attempted to justify our embarrassing Establishment Clause jurisprudence on the ground that it "sacrifices clarity and predictability for flexibility." Committee for Public Education & Religious Liberty v. Regan, 444 U.S., at 662. . . . I think it time that we sacrifice some "flexibility" for "clarity and predictability." Abandoning Lemon's purpose test—a test which exacerbates the tension between the Free Exercise and Establishment Clauses, has no basis in the language or history of the amendment, and, as today's decision shows, has wonderfully flexible consequences—would be a good place to start.

———

Page 1426: Delete first paragraph of note:

C. FINANCIAL AID TO CHURCH–RELATED SCHOOLS

———

1. ELEMENTARY AND SECONDARY SCHOOLS

———

Page 1445. Add ahead of 2. Higher Education:

GRAND RAPIDS SCHOOL DISTRICT v. BALL

473 U.S. 373, 105 S.Ct. 3216, 87 L.Ed.2d 267 (1985).

Justice Brennan delivered the opinion of the Court.

The School District of Grand Rapids, Michigan, adopted two programs in which classes for nonpublic school students are financed by the public school system, taught by teachers hired by the public school system, and conducted in "leased" classrooms in the nonpublic schools. Most of the nonpublic schools involved in the programs are sectarian religious schools. This case raises the question whether these programs impermissibly involve the government in the support of sectarian religious activities and thus violate the Establishment Clause of the First Amendment.

I

A

At issue in this case are the Community Education and Shared Time programs offered in the nonpublic schools of Grand Rapids, Michigan. These programs, first instituted in the 1976–1977 school year, provide classes to nonpublic school students at public expense in classrooms located in and leased from the local nonpublic schools.

The Shared Time program offers classes during the regular school day that are intended to be supplementary to the "core curriculum" courses that the State of Michigan requires as a part of an accredited school program. Among the subjects offered are "remedial" and "enrichment" mathematics, "remedial" and "enrichment" reading, art, music, and physical education. A typical nonpublic school student attends these classes for one or two class periods per week; approximately "ten percent of any given nonpublic school student's time during the academic year would consist of Shared Time instruction." Although Shared Time itself is a program offered only in the nonpublic schools, there was testimony that the courses included in that program are offered, albeit perhaps in a somewhat different form, in the public schools as well. All of the classes that are the subject of this case are taught in elementary schools, with the exception of Math Topics, a remedial math course taught in the secondary schools.

The Shared Time teachers are full-time employees of the public schools, who often move from classroom to classroom during the course of the school day. A "significant portion" of the teachers (approximately 10%) "previously taught in nonpublic schools, and many of those had been assigned to the same nonpublic school where they were previously employed." The School District of Grand Rapids hires Shared Time teachers in accordance with its ordinary hiring procedures. The public school system apparently provides all of the supplies, materials, and equipment used in connection with Shared Time instruction.

The Community Education Program is offered throughout the Grand Rapids community in schools and on other sites, for children as well as adults. The classes at issue here are taught in the nonpublic elementary schools and commence at the conclusion of the regular school day. Among the courses offered are Arts and Crafts, Home Economics, Spanish, Gymnastics, Yearbook Production, Christmas Arts and Crafts, Drama, Newspaper, Humanities, Chess, Model Building, and Nature Appreciation. The District Court found that "[a]lthough certain Community Education courses offered at nonpublic school sites are not offered at the public schools on a Community Education basis, all Community Education programs are otherwise available at the public schools, usually as a part of their more extensive regular curriculum."

Community Education teachers are part-time public school employees. Community Education courses are completely voluntary and are offered only if 12 or more students enroll. Because a well-known teacher is necessary to attract the requisite number of students, the School District accords a preference in hiring to instructors already teaching within the school. Thus, "virtually every Community Education course conducted on facilities leased from nonpublic schools has an instructor otherwise employed full time by the same nonpublic school."

Both programs are administered similarly. The Director of the program, a public school employee, sends packets of course listings to the participating nonpublic schools before the school year begins. The nonpublic school administrators then decide which courses they want to offer. The Director works out an academic schedule for each school, taking into account, *inter alia,* the varying religious holidays celebrated by the schools of different denominations.

Nonpublic school administrators decide which classrooms will be used for the programs, and the Director then inspects the facilities and consults with Shared Time teachers to make sure the facilities are satisfactory. The public school system pays the nonpublic schools for the use of the necessary classroom space by entering into "leases" at the rate of $6 per classroom per week. The "leases," however, contain no mention of the particular room, space, or facility leased and teachers' rooms, libraries, lavatories, and similar facilities are made available at no additional charge. Each room used in the programs has to be free of any crucifix, religious symbol, or artifact, although such religious symbols can be present in the adjoining hallways, corridors, and other facilities used in connection with the program. During the time that a given classroom is being used in the programs, the teacher is required to post a sign stating that it is a "public school classroom." However, there are no signs posted outside the school buildings indicating that public school courses are conducted inside or that the facilities are being used as a public school annex.

Although petitioners label the Shared Time and Community Education students as "part-time public school students," the students attending Shared Time and Community Education courses in facilities leased from a nonpublic school are the same students who attend that particular school otherwise. There is no evidence that any public school student has ever attended a Shared Time or Community Education class in a nonpublic school. The District Court found that "[t]hough Defendants claim the Shared Time program is available to all students, the record is abundantly clear that only nonpublic school students wearing the cloak of a 'public school student' can enroll in it." The District Court noted that "[w]hereas public school students are assembled at the public facility nearest to their residence, students in religious schools are assembled on the basis of religion without any consideration of residence or school district boundaries." Thus, "beneficiaries are wholly designated on the basis of religion," and these "public school" classes, in contrast to ordinary public school classes which are largely neighborhood-based, are as segregated by religion as are the schools at which they are offered.

Forty of the forty-one schools at which the programs operate are sectarian in character. The schools of course vary from one another, but substantial evidence suggests that they share deep religious purposes. For instance, the Parent Handbook of one Catholic school states the goals of Catholic education as "[a] God oriented environment which *permeates* the total educational program," "[a] Christian atmosphere which guides and encourages participation in the church's commitment to social justice," and "[a] continuous development of knowledge of the Catholic faith, its traditions, teachings and theology." A policy statement of the Christian schools similarly proclaims that "it is not sufficient that the teachings of Christianity be a separate subject in the curriculum, but *the Word of God must be an all-pervading force in the educational program.*" These Christian schools require all parents seeking to enroll their children either to subscribe to a particular doctrinal statement or to agree to have their children taught according to the doctrinal statement. The District Court found that the schools are "pervasively sectarian," and concluded "without hesitation that the purposes of these schools is to advance their particular religions," and that "a substantial portion of their functions are subsumed in the religious mission."

B

Respondents are six taxpayers who filed suit against the School District of Grand Rapids and a number of state officials. . . . After an 8-day bench trial, the District Court entered a judgment on the merits on behalf of respondents and enjoined further operation of the programs.

. . . A divided panel of the Court of Appeals affirmed. We . . . affirm.

II

A

. . .

We have noted that the three-part test first articulated in Lemon v. Kurtzman, at 612–613, guides "[t]he general nature of our inquiry in this area," Mueller v. Allen, 463 U.S. 388, 394 (1983) . . .. We have particularly relied on Lemon in every case involving the sensitive relationship between government and religion in the education of our children. The government's activities in this area can have a magnified impact on impressionable young minds, and the occasional rivalry of parallel public and private school systems offers an all-too-ready opportunity for divisive rifts along religious lines in the body politic.

. . .

As has often been true in school aid cases, there is no dispute as to the first test. Both the District Court and the Court of Appeals found that the purpose of the Community Education and Shared Time programs was "manifestly secular." We find no reason to disagree with this holding, and therefore go on to consider whether the primary or principal effect of the challenged programs is to advance or inhibit religion.

B

. . .

Given that 40 of the 41 schools in this case are . . . "pervasively sectarian," the challenged public-school programs operating in the religious schools may impermissibly advance religion in three different ways. First, the teachers participating in the programs may become involved in intentionally or inadvertently inculcating particular religious tenets or beliefs. Second, the programs may provide a crucial symbolic link between government and religion, thereby enlisting—at least in the eyes of impressionable youngsters—the powers of government to the support of the religious denomination operating the school. Third, the programs may have the effect of directly promoting religion by impermissibly providing a subsidy to the primary religious mission of the institutions affected.

(1)

Although Establishment Clause jurisprudence is characterized by few absolutes, the Clause does absolutely prohibit government-financed or government-sponsored indoctrination into the beliefs of a particular religious faith. . . .

In Meek v. Pittenger, supra, the Court invalidated a statute providing for the loan of state-paid professional staff—including teachers—to nonpublic schools to provide remedial and accelerated instruction, guidance counseling and testing, and other services on the premises of the nonpublic schools . . . The program in *Meek,* if not sufficiently monitored, would simply have entailed too great a risk of state-sponsored indoctrination.

The programs before us today share the defect that we identified in *Meek.* With respect to the Community Education Program, the District Court found that "virtually every Community Education course conducted on facilities leased from nonpublic schools has an instructor otherwise employed full time by the same nonpublic school." These instructors, many of whom no doubt teach in the religious schools precisely because they are adherents of the controlling denomination and want to serve their religious community zealously, are expected during the regular school day to inculcate their students with the tenets and beliefs of their particular religious faiths. Yet the premise of the program is that those instructors can put aside their religious convictions and engage in entirely secular Community Education instruction as soon as the school day is over. Moreover, they are expected to do so before the same religious-school students and in the same religious-school classrooms that they employed to advance religious purposes during the "official" school day. Nonetheless, as petitioners themselves asserted, Community Education classes are not specifically monitored for religious content.

. . .

The Shared Time program, though structured somewhat differently, nonetheless also poses a substantial risk of state-sponsored indoctrination. The most important difference between the programs is that most of the instructors in the Shared Time program are full-time teachers hired by the public schools. Moreover, although "virtually every" Community Education instructor is a full-time religious school teacher, only "[a] significant portion" of the Shared Time instructors previously worked in the religious schools. Nonetheless, as with the Community Education program, no attempt is made to monitor the Shared Time courses for religious content.

Thus, despite these differences between the two programs, our holding in *Meek* controls the inquiry with respect to Shared Time, as well as Community Education. Shared Time instructors are teaching academic subjects in religious schools in courses virtually indistinguishable from the other courses offered during the regular religious-school day. The teachers in this program, even more than their Community Education colleagues, are "performing important educational services in schools in which education is an integral part of the dominant sectarian mission and in which an atmosphere dedicated to the advancement of religious belief is constantly maintained." Meek v. Pittenger, 421 U.S., at 371. Teachers in such an atmosphere may well subtly (or overtly) conform their instruction to the environment in which they teach, while students will perceive the instruction provided in the context of the dominantly religious message of the institution, thus reinforcing the indoctrinating effect. As we stated in *Meek,* "[w]hether the subject is 'remedial reading,' 'advanced reading,' or simply 'reading,' a teacher remains a teacher, and the danger that religious doctrine will become intertwined with secular instruction persists." Id., at 370. Unlike types of aid that the Court has upheld, such as state-created standardized tests, Committee for Public Education v. Regan, 444 U.S. 646 (1980), or diagnostic services, Wolman v. Walter, 433 U.S., at 241–244, there is a "substantial risk" that programs operating in this environment would "be used for religious educational purposes." Committee for Public Education v. Regan, supra, at 656.

The Court of Appeals of course recognized that respondents adduced no evidence of specific incidents of religious indoctrination in this case. But the absence of proof of specific incidents is not dispositive. When conducting a supposedly secular class in the pervasively sectarian environment of a religious school, a teacher may knowingly or unwillingly tailor the content of the course to fit the school's announced goals. If so, there is no reason to believe that this kind of ideological influence would be detected or reported by students, by their parents, or by the school system itself. The students are presumably attending religious schools precisely in order to receive religious instruction. After spending the balance of their school day in classes heavily influenced by a religious perspective, they would have little motivation or ability to discern improper ideological content that may creep into a Shared Time or Community Education course. Neither their parents nor the parochial schools would have cause to complain if the effect of the publicly-supported instruction were to advance the schools' sectarian mission. And the public school system itself has no incentive to detect or report any specific incidents of improper state-sponsored indoctrination. Thus, the lack of evidence of specific incidents of indoctrination is of little significance.

(2)

Our cases have recognized that the Establishment Clause guards against more than direct, state-funded efforts to indoctrinate youngsters in specific religious beliefs. Government promotes religion as effectively when it fosters a close identification of its powers and responsibilities with those of any—or all—religious denominations as when it attempts to inculcate specific religious doctrines. If this identification conveys a message of government endorsement or disapproval of religion, a core purpose of the Establishment Clause is violated. See Lynch v. Donnelly, 465 U.S. 668, 688 (1984) (O'Connor, J., concurring); . . .

. . .

Our school-aid cases have recognized a sensitivity to the symbolic impact of the union of church and state. Grappling with problems in many ways parallel to those we face today, McCollum v. Board of Education, 333 U.S. 203 (1948), held that a public school may not permit part-time religious instruction on its premises as a part of the school program, even if participation in that instruction is entirely voluntary and even if the instruction itself is conducted only by nonpublic-school personnel. Yet in Zorach v. Clauson, 343 U.S. 306 (1952), the Court held that a similar program conducted off the premises of the public school passed constitutional muster. The difference in symbolic impact helps to explain the difference between the cases. The symbolic connection of church and state in the *McCollum* program presented the students with a graphic symbol of the "concert of union or dependency" of church and state, see Zorach, supra, at 312. This very symbolic union was conspicuously absent in the *Zorach* program.

In the programs challenged in this case, the religious school students spend their typical school day moving between religious-school and "public-school" classes. Both types of classes take place in the same religious-school building and both are largely composed of students who are adherents of the same denomination. In this environment, the students would be unlikely to discern the crucial difference between the religious-school classes and the "public-school" classes, even if the latter were successfully kept free of religious indoctrination. . . . Consequently, even the student who notices the "public school" sign temporarily posted would have before him a powerful symbol of state endorsement and encouragement of the religious beliefs taught in the same class at some other time during the day.

. . . This effect—the symbolic union of government and religion in one sectarian enterprise—is an impermissible effect under the Establishment Clause.

(3)

. . .

. . . [T]he Court has never accepted the mere possibility of subsidization . . . as sufficient to invalidate an aid program. On the other hand, this effect is not wholly unimportant for Establishment Clause purposes. If it were, the public schools could gradually take on themselves the entire responsibility for teaching secular subjects on religious school premises. The question in each case must be whether the effect of the proffered aid is "direct and substantial," Committee for Public Education v. Nyquist, supra, at 784–785, n. 39, or indirect and incidental. "The problem, like many problems in constitutional law, is one of degree." Zorach v. Clauson, 343 U.S., at 314.

We have noted in the past that the religious school has dual functions, providing its students with a secular education while it promotes a particular religious perspective. See Mueller v. Allen, 463 U.S., at 401–402; Board of Education v. Allen, supra. In *Meek* and *Wolman,* we held unconstitutional state programs providing for loans of instructional equipment and materials to religious schools, on the ground that the programs advanced the "primary, religion-oriented educational function of the sectarian school." Meek, supra, at 364; Wolman, supra, at 248–251. Cf. Wolman, supra, at 243 (upholding provision of diagnostic services, which were " 'general welfare services for children that may be provided by the State regardless of the incidental benefit that accrues to church-related schools,' " quoting Meek, supra, at 371, n. 21). The programs challenged here, which provide teachers in addition to the instructional equipment and materials, have a similar—and forbidden—effect of advancing religion. This kind of direct aid to the educational function of the religious school is indistinguishable from the provision of a direct cash subsidy to the religious school that is most clearly prohibited under the Establishment Clause.

Petitioners claim that the aid here, like the textbooks in *Allen,* flows primarily to the students, not to the religious schools. Of course, all aid to religious schools ultimately "flows to" the students, and petitioners' argument if accepted would validate all forms of nonideological aid to religious schools, including those explicitly rejected in our prior cases. Yet in *Meek,* we held unconstitutional the loan of instructional materials to religious schools and in *Wolman,* we rejected the fiction that a similar program could be saved by masking it as aid to individual students. . . . It follows *a fortiori* that the aid here, which includes not only instructional materials but also the provision of instructional services by teachers in the parochial school building, "inescapably [has] the primary effect of providing a direct and substantial advancement of the sectarian enterprise." . . . Where, as here, no meaningful distinction can be made between aid to the student and aid to the school, "the concept of a loan to individuals is a transparent fiction." . . .

Petitioners also argue that this "subsidy" effect is not significant in this case, because the Community Education and Shared Time programs supplemented the curriculum with courses not previously offered in the religious schools and not required by school rule or state regulation. Of course, this fails to distinguish the programs here from those found unconstitutional in *Meek.* See 421 U.S., at 368. As in *Meek,* we do not find that this feature of the program is controlling. First, there is no way of knowing whether the religious schools would have offered some or all of these courses if the public school system had not offered them first. The distinction between courses that "supplement" and those that "supplant" the regular curriculum is therefore not nearly as clear as petitioners allege. Second, although the precise courses offered in these programs may have been new to the participating religious schools, their general subject matter—reading, math, etc.—was surely a part of the curriculum in the past, and the concerns of the Establishment Clause may thus be triggered despite the "supplemental" nature of the courses. Cf. Meek v. Pittenger, supra, at 370–371. Third, and most important, petitioners' argument would permit the public schools gradually to take over the entire secular curriculum of the religious school, for the latter could surely discontinue existing courses so that they might be replaced a year or two later by a Community Education or Shared Time course with the same content. The average religious school student, for instance, now spends 10 percent of the school day in Shared Time classes. But there is no principled basis on which this Court can impose a limit on the percentage of the religious-school day that can be subsidized by the public school. To let the genie out of the bottle in this case would be to permit ever larger segments of the religious school curriculum to be turned over to the public school system, thus violating the cardinal principle that the State may not in effect become the prime supporter of the religious school system. See Lemon v. Kurtzman, 403 U.S., at 624–625.

III

We conclude that the challenged programs have the effect of promoting religion in three ways. The state-paid instructors, influenced by the pervasively sectarian nature of the religious schools in which they work, may subtly or overtly indoctrinate the students in particular religious tenets at public expense. The symbolic union of church and state inherent in the provision of secular, state-provided instruction in the religious school buildings threatens to convey a message of state support for religion to students and to the general public. Finally, the programs in effect subsidize the religious functions of the parochial schools by taking over a substantial portion of their responsibility for teaching secular subjects. For these reasons, the conclusion is inescapable that the Community Education and Shared Time programs have the "primary or principal" effect of advancing religion, and therefore violate the dictates of the Establishment Clause of the First Amendment.

. . . Because "the controlling constitutional standards have become firmly rooted and the broad contours of our inquiry are now well defined," Committee for Public Education v. Nyquist, 413 U.S., at 761, the position of those lines has by now become quite clear and requires affirmance of the Court of Appeals.

It is so ordered.

Chief Justice Burger, concurring in the judgment in part and dissenting in part.

I agree with the Court that, under our decisions in Lemon v. Kurtzman, 403 U.S. 602 (1971), and Earley v. DiCenso, 403 U.S. 602 (1971), the Grand Rapids Community Education program violates the Establishment Clause. As to the Shared Time program, I dissent for the reasons stated in my dissenting opinion in Aguilar v. Felton, 473 U.S. 402 (1985).

Justice O'Connor, concurring in the judgment in part and dissenting in part.

For the reasons stated in my dissenting opinion in Aguilar v. Felton, 473 U.S. 402 (1985), I dissent from the Court's holding that the Grand Rapids Shared Time program impermissibly advances religion. . . .

. . .

I agree with the Court, however, that the Community Education program violates the Establishment Clause. . . . When full-time parochial school teachers receive public funds to teach secular courses to their parochial school students under parochial school supervision, I agree that the program has the perceived and actual effect of advancing the religious aims of the church-related schools. This is particularly the case where, as here, religion pervades the curriculum and the teachers are accustomed to bring religion to play in everything they teach. I concur in the judgment of the Court that the Community Education program violates the Establishment Clause.

Justice White, dissenting.

As evidenced by my dissenting opinions in Lemon v. Kurtzman, 403 U.S. 602, 661 (1971) and Committee for Public Education v. Nyquist, 413 U.S. 756, 813 (1973), I have long disagreed with the Court's interpretation and application of the Establishment Clause in the context of state aid to private schools. For the reasons stated in those dissents, I am firmly of the belief that the Court's decisions in these cases, like its decisions in *Lemon* and *Nyquist,* are "not required by the First Amendment and [are] contrary to the long-range interests of the country." 413 U.S., at 820. For those same reasons, I am satisfied that what the States have sought to do in these cases is well within their authority and is not forbidden by the Establishment Clause. Hence, I dissent and would reverse the judgment in each of these cases.

Justice Rehnquist, dissenting.

I dissent for the reasons stated in my dissenting opinion in Wallace v. Jaffree. . . .

. . .

AGUILAR v. FELTON

473 U.S. 402, 105 S.Ct. 3232, 87 L.Ed.2d 290 (1985).

Justice Brennan delivered the opinion of the Court.

The City of New York uses federal funds to pay the salaries of public employees who teach in parochial schools. In this companion case to *School District of Grand Rapids v. Ball,* we determine whether this practice violates the Establishment Clause of the First Amendment.

I

A

The program at issue in this case, originally enacted as Title I of the Elementary and Secondary Education Act of 1965, authorizes the Secretary of Education to distribute financial assistance to local educational institutions to meet the needs of educationally deprived children from low-income families. The funds are to be appropriated in accordance with programs proposed by local educational agencies and approved by state educational agencies. 20 U.S.C. § 3805(a). "To the extent consistent with the number of educationally deprived children in the school district of the local educational agency who are enrolled in private elementary and secondary schools, such agency shall make provisions for including special educational services and arrangements . . . in which such children can participate." § 3806(a). The proposed programs must also meet the following statutory requirements: the children involved in the program must be educationally deprived, § 3804(a), the children must reside in areas comprising a high concentration of low-income families, § 3805(b), and the programs must supplement, not supplant, programs that would exist absent funding under Title I. § 3807(b).

Since 1966, the City of New York has provided instructional services funded by Title I to parochial school students on the premises of parochial schools. Of those students eligible to receive funds in 1981–1982, 13.2% were enrolled in private schools. Of that group, 84% were enrolled in schools affiliated with the Roman Catholic Archdiocese of New York and the Diocese of Brooklyn and 8% were enrolled in Hebrew day schools. With respect to the religious atmosphere of these schools, the Court of Appeals concluded that "the picture that emerges is of a system in which religious considerations play a key role in the selection of students and teachers, and which has as its substantial purpose the inculcation of religious values."

The programs conducted at these schools include remedial reading, reading skills, remedial mathematics, English as a second language, and guidance services. These programs are carried out by regular employees of the public schools (teachers, guidance counselors, psychologists, psychiatrists and social workers) who have volunteered to teach in the parochial schools. The amount of time that each professional spends in the parochial school is determined by the number of students in the particular program and the needs of these students.

The City's Bureau of Nonpublic School Reimbursement makes teacher assignments, and the instructors are supervised by field personnel, who attempt to pay at least one unannounced visit per month. The field supervisors, in turn, report to program coordinators, who also pay occasional unannounced supervisory visits to monitor Title I classes in the parochial schools. The professionals involved in the program are directed to avoid involvement with religious activities that are conducted within the private schools and to bar religious materials in their classrooms. All material and equipment used in the programs funded under Title I are supplied by the Government and are used only in those programs. The professional personnel are solely responsible for the selection of the students. Additionally, the professionals are informed that contact with private school personnel should be kept to a minimum. Finally, the administrators of the parochial schools are required to clear the classrooms used by the public school personnel of all religious symbols.

B

In 1978, six taxpayers commenced this action in the District Court for the Eastern District of New York, alleging that the Title I program administered by the City of New York violates the Establishment Clause . . . . The District Court granted the appellants' motion for summary judgment . . . .

A unanimous panel of the Court of Appeals for the Second Circuit reversed . . . [W]e affirm the judgment below.

II

. . . The New York programs challenged in this case are very similar to the programs we examined in *Ball.* . . .

The appellants attempt to distinguish this case on the ground that the City of New York, unlike the Grand Rapids Public School District, has adopted a system for monitoring the religious content of publicly funded Title I classes in the religious schools. At best, the supervision in this case would assist in preventing the Title I program from being used, intentionally or unwittingly, to inculcate the religious beliefs of the surrounding parochial school. But appellants' argument fails in any event, because the supervisory system established by the City of New York inevitably results in the excessive entanglement of church and state, an Establishment Clause concern distinct from that addressed by the effects doctrine. Even where state aid to parochial institutions does not have the primary effect of advancing religion, the provision of such aid may nonetheless violate the Establishment Clause owing to the nature of the interaction of church and state in the administration of that aid.

. . . .

The critical elements of the entanglement proscribed in *Lemon* and *Meek* are thus present in this case. First, . . . the aid is provided in a pervasively sectarian environment. Second, because assistance is provided in the form of teachers, ongoing inspection is required to ensure the absence of a religious message. . . . In short, the scope and duration of New York's Title I program would require a permanent and pervasive State presence in the sectarian schools receiving aid.

This pervasive monitoring by public authorities in the sectarian schools infringes precisely those Establishment Clause values at the root of the prohibition of excessive entanglement. Agents of the State must visit and inspect the religious school regularly, alert for the subtle or overt presence of religious matter in Title I classes. . . . In addition, the religious school must obey these same agents when they make determinations as to what is and what is not a "religious symbol" and thus off limits in a Title I classroom. In short, the religious school, which has as a primary purpose the advancement and preservation of a particular religion must endure the ongoing presence of state personnel whose primary purpose is to monitor teachers and students in an attempt to guard against the infiltration of religious thought.

The administrative cooperation that is required to maintain the educational program at issue here entangles Church and State in still another way that infringes interests at the heart of the Establishment Clause. Administrative personnel of the public and parochial school systems must work together in resolving matters related to schedules, classroom assignments, problems that arise in the implementation of the program, requests for additional services, and the dissemination of information regarding the program. Furthermore, the program necessitates "frequent contacts between the regular and the remedial teachers (or other professionals), in which each side reports on individual student needs, problems encountered, and results achieved."

. . .

III

Despite the well-intentioned efforts taken by the City of New York, the program remains constitutionally flawed owing to the nature of the aid, to the institution receiving the aid, and to the constitutional principles that they implicate—that neither the State nor Federal Government shall promote or hinder a particular faith or faith generally through the advancement of benefits or through the excessive entanglement of church and state in the administration of those benefits.

Affirmed.

Justice Powell, concurring.

I concur in the Court's opinions and judgments today in this case and in *Grand Rapids School District v. Ball,* holding that the aid to parochial schools involved in those cases violates the Establishment Clause of the First Amendment. I write to emphasize additional reasons why precedents of this Court require us to invalidate these two educational programs that concededly have "done so much good and little, if any, detectable harm." Felton v. Secretary, United States Department of Education, 739 F.2d 48, 72 (CA2 1984). . . .

. . .

[The] risk of entanglement is compounded by the additional risk of political divisiveness stemming from the aid to religion at issue here. I do not suggest that at this point in our history the Title I program or similar parochial aid plans could result in the establishment of a state religion. There likewise is small chance that these programs would result in significant religious or denominational control over our democratic processes. . . .

. . .

. . . Our cases have upheld evenhanded secular assistance to both parochial and public school children in some areas. E.g., id. (tax deductions for educational expenses); Board of Education v. Allen, 392 U.S. 236 (1968) (provision of secular textbooks); Everson v. Board of Education, 330 U.S. 1 (1947) (reimbursements for bus fare to school). I do not read the Court's opinion as precluding these types of indirect aid to parochial schools. In the cases cited, the assistance programs made funds available equally to public and nonpublic schools without entanglement. The constitutional defect in the Title I program . . . is that it provides a direct financial subsidy to be administered in significant part by public school teachers within parochial schools—resulting in both the advancement of religion and forbidden entanglement. If, for example, Congress could fashion a program of evenhanded financial assistance to both public and private schools that could be administered, without governmental supervision in the private schools, so as to prevent the diversion of the aid from secular purposes, we would be presented with a different question.

I join the opinions and judgments of the Court.

Chief Justice Burger, dissenting.

. . .

On the merits of this case, I dissent for the reasons stated in my separate opinion in Meek v. Pittenger, 421 U.S. 349 (1975). . . .

I cannot join in striking down a program that, in the words of the Court of Appeals, "has done so much good and little, if any, detectable harm." 739 F.2d 48, 72 (CA2 1984). The notion that denying these services to students in religious schools is a neutral act to protect us from an Established Church has no support in logic, experience, or history. Rather than showing the neutrality the Court boasts of, it exhibits nothing less than hostility toward religion and the children who attend church-sponsored schools.

Justice White, dissenting.

. . .

Justice Rehnquist, dissenting.

I dissent for the reasons stated in my dissenting opinion in Wallace v. Jaffree . . . [T]he Court takes advantage of the "Catch-22" paradox of its own creation, . . . whereby aid must be supervised to ensure no entanglement but the supervision itself is held to cause an entanglement. The Court in *Aguilar* strikes down nondiscriminatory nonsectarian aid to educationally deprived children from low-income families. The Establishment Clause does not prohibit such sorely needed assistance; we have indeed travelled far afield from the concerns which prompted the adoption of the First Amendment when we rely on gossamer abstractions to invalidate a law which obviously meets an entirely secular need. I would reverse.

Justice O'Connor, with whom Justice Rehnquist joins as to Parts II and III, dissenting.

Today the Court affirms the holding of the Court of Appeals that public schoolteachers can offer remedial instruction to disadvantaged students who attend religious schools "only if such instruction . . . [is] afforded at a neutral site off the premises of the religious school." 739 F.2d 48, 64 (CA2 1984). This holding rests on the theory, enunciated in Part V of the Court's opinion in Meek v. Pittenger, 421 U.S. 349, 367–373 (1975), that public schoolteachers who set foot on parochial school premises are likely to bring religion into their classes, and that the supervision necessary to prevent religious teaching would unduly entangle church and state. Even if this theory were valid in the abstract, it cannot validly be applied to New York City's 19-year-old Title I program. The Court greatly exaggerates the degree of supervision necessary to prevent public school teachers from inculcating religion, and thereby demonstrates the flaws of a test that condemns benign cooperation between church and state. I would uphold Congress' efforts to afford remedial instruction to disadvantaged schoolchildren in both public and parochial schools.

I

. . .

The Court's discussion of the effect of the New York City Title I program is even more perfunctory than its analysis of the program's purpose. . . . While addressing the effect of the Grand Rapids program at such length, the Court overlooks the effect of Title I in New York City.

One need not delve too deeply in the record to understand why the Court does not belabor the effect of the Title I program. The abstract theories explaining why on-premises instruction might possibly advance religion dissolve in the face of experience in New York. . . . Indeed, in 19 years there has never been a single incident in which a Title I instructor "subtly or overtly" attempted to "indoctrinate the students in particular religious tenets at public expense."

Common sense suggests a plausible explanation for this unblemished record. New York City's public Title I instructors are professional educators who can and do follow instructions not to inculcate religion in their classes. They are unlikely to be influenced by the sectarian nature of the parochial schools where they teach, not only because they are carefully supervised by public officials, but also because the vast majority of them visit several different schools each week and are not of the same religion as their parochial students. In light of the ample record, an objective observer of the implementation of the Title I program in New York would hardly view it as endorsing the tenets of the participating parochial schools. To the contrary, the actual and perceived effect of the program is precisely the effect intended by Congress: impoverished school children are being helped to overcome learning deficits, improving their test scores, and receiving a significant boost in their struggle to obtain both a thorough education and the opportunities that flow from it.

The only type of impermissible effect that arguably could carry over from the *Grand Rapids* decision to this litigation, then, is the effect of subsidizing "the religious functions of the parochial schools by taking over a substantial portion of their responsibility for teaching secular subjects." 473 U.S., at 397. That effect is tenuous, however, in light of the statutory directive that Title I funds may be used only to provide services that otherwise would not be available to the participating students. 20 U.S.C. § 3807(b). The Secretary of Education has vigorously enforced the requirement that Title I funds supplement rather than supplant the services of local education agencies. See Bennett v. Kentucky Dept. of Ed., 470 U.S. 656 (1985); Bennett v. New Jersey, 470 U.S. 632 (1985).

Even if we were to assume that Title I remedial classes in New York may have duplicated to some extent instruction parochial schools would have offered in the absence of Title I, the Court's delineation of this third type of effect proscribed by the Establishment Clause would be seriously flawed. Our Establishment Clause decisions have not barred remedial assistance to parochial school children, but rather remedial assistance *on the premises of the parochial school.* Under *Wolman v. Walter,* 433 U.S. 229, 244–248 (1977), the New York City classes prohibited by the Court today would have survived Establishment Clause scrutiny if they had been offered in a neutral setting off the property of the private school. Yet it is difficult to understand why a remedial reading class offered on parochial school premises is any more likely to supplant the secular course offerings of the parochial school than the same class offered in a portable classroom next door to the school. Unless *Wolman* was wrongly decided, the defect in the Title I program cannot lie in the risk that it will supplant secular course offerings.

II

Recognizing the weakness of any claim of an improper purpose or effect, the Court today relies entirely on the entanglement prong of *Lemon* to invalidate the New York City Title I program. The Court holds that the occasional presence of peripatetic public schoolteachers on parochial school grounds threatens undue entanglement of church and state because (1) the remedial instruction is afforded in a pervasively sectarian environment; (2) ongoing supervision is required to assure that the public schoolteachers do not attempt to inculcate religion; (3) the administrative personnel of the parochial and public school systems must work together in resolving administrative and scheduling problems; and (4) the instruction is likely to result in political divisiveness over the propriety of direct aid.

This analysis of entanglement, I acknowledge, finds support in some of this Court's precedents. . . . *Meek's* analysis of entanglement was reaffirmed in *Wolman* two Terms later.

I would accord these decisions the appropriate deference commanded by the doctrine of *stare decisis* if I could discern logical support for their analysis. But experience has demonstrated that the analysis in Part V of the *Meek* opinion is flawed. At the time *Meek* was decided, thoughtful dissents pointed out the absence of any record support for the notion that public school teachers would attempt to inculcate religion simply because they temporarily occupied a parochial school classroom, or that such instruction would produce political divisiveness. 421 U.S., at 385 (opinion of Burger, C.J.); *Id.,* at 387 (opinion of Rehnquist, J.). Experience has given greater force to the arguments of the dissenting opinions in *Meek.* It is not intuitively obvious that a dedicated public school teacher will tend to disobey instructions and commence proselytizing students at public expense merely because the classroom is within a parochial school. *Meek* is correct in asserting that a teacher of remedial reading "remains a teacher," but surely it is significant that the teacher involved is a professional, full-time public school employee who is unaccustomed to bringing religion into the classroom. Given that not a single incident of religious indoctrination has been identified as occurring in the thousands of classes offered in Grand Rapids and New York over the past two decades, it is time to acknowledge that the risk identified in *Meek* was greatly exaggerated.

Just as the risk that public schoolteachers in parochial classrooms will inculcate religion has been exaggerated, so has the degree of supervision required to manage that risk. In this respect the New York Title I program is instructive. What supervision has been necessary in New York to enable public school teachers to help disadvantaged children for 19 years without once proselytizing? Public officials have prepared careful instructions warning public schoolteachers of their exclusively secular mission, and have required Title I teachers to study and observe them. Under the rules, Title I teachers are not accountable to parochial or private school officials; they have sole responsibility for selecting the students who participate in their class, must administer their own tests for determining eligibility, cannot engage in team teaching or cooperative activities with parochial school teachers, must make sure that all materials and equipment they use are not otherwise used by the parochial school, and must not participate in religious activities in the schools or introduce any religious matter into their teaching. To ensure compliance with the rules, a field supervisor and a program coordinator, who are full-time public school employees, make unannounced visits to each teacher's classroom at least once a month.

. . . Even if I remained confident of the usefulness of entanglement as an Establishment Clause test, I would conclude that New York's efforts to prevent religious indoctrination in Title I classes have been adequate and have not caused excessive institutional entanglement of church and state.

The Court's reliance on the potential for political divisiveness as evidence of undue entanglement is also unpersuasive. There is little record support for the proposition that New York's admirable Title I program has ignited any controversy other than this litigation. . . .

I adhere to the doubts about the entanglement test that were expressed in *Lynch.* It is curious indeed to base our interpretation of the Constitution on speculation as to the likelihood of a phenomenon which the parties may create merely by prosecuting a lawsuit. My reservations about the entanglement test, however, have come to encompass its institutional aspects as well. As Justice Rehnquist has pointed out, many of the inconsistencies in our Establishment Clause decisions can be ascribed to our insistence that parochial aid programs with a valid purpose and effect may still be invalid by virtue of undue entanglement. For example, we permit a State to pay for bus transportation to a parochial school, Everson v. Board of Education, 330 U.S. 1 (1947), but preclude States from providing buses for parochial school field trips, on the theory such trips involve excessive state supervision of the parochial officials who lead them. *Wolman*, 433 U.S., at 254. To a great extent, the anomalous results in our Establishment Clause cases are "attributable to [the] 'entanglement' prong." Choper, The Religion Clauses of the First Amendment: Reconciling the Conflict, 41 U.Pitt.L. Rev. 673, 681 (1980).

Pervasive institutional involvement of church and state may remain relevant in deciding the *effect* of a statute which is alleged to violate the Establishment Clause, Walz v. Tax Commission, 397 U.S. 664 (1970), but state efforts to ensure that public resources are used only for nonsectarian ends should not in themselves serve to invalidate an otherwise valid statute. . . .

III

Today's ruling does not spell the end of the Title I program of remedial education for disadvantaged children. Children attending public schools may still obtain the benefits of the program. Impoverished children who attend parochial schools may also continue to benefit from Title I programs offered off the premises of their schools— possibly in portable classrooms just over the edge of school property. The only disadvantaged children who lose under the Court's holding are those in cities where it is not economically and logistically feasible to provide public facilities for remedial education adjacent to the parochial school. But this subset is significant, for it includes more than 20,000 New York City schoolchildren and uncounted others elsewhere in the country.

For these children, the Court's decision is tragic. The Court deprives them of a program that offers a meaningful chance at success in life, and it does so on the untenable theory that public schoolteachers (most of whom are of different faiths than their students) are likely to start teaching religion merely because they have walked across the threshold of a parochial school. I reject this theory and the analysis in *Meek v. Pittenger* on which it is based. I cannot close my eyes to the fact that, over almost two decades, New York's public schoolteachers have helped thousands of impoverished parochial schoolchildren to overcome educational disadvantages without once attempting to inculcate religion. Their praiseworthy efforts have not eroded and do not threaten the religious liberty assured by the Establishment Clause. The contrary judgment of the Court of Appeals should be reversed.

I respectfully dissent.

2. HIGHER EDUCATION

Page 1451. Add at end of subsection:

WITTERS v. WASHINGTON DEPARTMENT OF SERVICES FOR THE BLIND, 474 U.S. 481 (1986). Witters was a blind person studying at a private Christian college, preparing for a career as a pastor, missionary, or church youth director. He applied for a grant under a Washington statute providing funds for education and training of the visually handicapped. The Washington Supreme Court concluded that the establishment clause required denial of the aid request, because providing financial assistance would have the principal effect of aiding religion. The Supreme Court reversed. Justice Marshall's opinion for the Court concluded that providing aid to Witters to finance his education did not "advance religion in a manner inconsistent with the" establishment clause. The Court relied on three factors: the aid was paid directly to the student, and ultimately flowed to the religious institution only as a result of the recipient's choice; funding did not create financial incentives for students to seek sectarian education, but was made available for all forms of education and training; and, "importantly," no significant portion of aid under the program went to religious institutions. The Court did not rely upon Mueller v. Allen, 463 U.S. 388 (1983) (casebook page 1441). Justice Powell's concurrence, joined by Chief Justice Burger and Justice Rehnquist, and Justice O'Connor's concurrence, emphasized that *Mueller* was controlling so long as aid was provided to students without reference to what college the student chose or whether the student sought training for a religious career. Justice White, who joined the Court's opinion, stated that he agreed "with most of Justice Powell's concurring opinion with respect to the relevance of *Mueller*."

---

3. OTHER EDUCATIONAL GRANTS

BOWEN v. KENDRICK

—— U.S. ——, 108 S.Ct. 2562, —— L.Ed.2d —— (1988).

Chief Justice Rehnquist delivered the Opinion of the Court.

This case involves a challenge to a federal grant program that provides funding for services relating to adolescent sexuality and pregnancy. Considering the federal statute both "on its face" and "as applied," the District Court ruled that the statute violated the Establishment Clause of the First Amendment insofar as it provided for the involvement of religious organizations in the federally funded programs. We conclude, however, that the statute is not unconstitutional on its face, and that a determination of whether any of the grants made pursuant to the statute violate the Establishment Clause requires further proceedings in the District Court.

. . .

II

. . .

. . . [W]e turn to consider whether the District Court was correct in concluding that the AFLA was unconstitutional on its face. As in previous cases involving facial challenges on Establishment Clause grounds, . . . we assess the constitutionality of an enactment by reference to the three factors first articulated in Lemon v. Kurtzman, 403 U.S. 602 (1971). . . .

As we see it, it is clear from the face of the statute that the AFLA was motivated primarily, if not entirely, by a legitimate secular purpose—the elimination or reduction of social and economic problems caused by teenage sexuality, pregnancy, and parenthood. . . .

. . .

As usual in Establishment Clause cases, . . . the more difficult question is whether the primary effect of the challenged statute is impermissible. Before we address this question, however, it is useful to review . . . just what the AFLA sets out to do. Simply stated, it authorizes grants to institutions that are capable of providing certain care and prevention services to adolescents. Because of the complexity of the problems that Congress sought to remedy, potential grantees are required to describe how they will involve other organizations, including religious organizations, in the programs funded by the federal grants. § 300z–5(a)(21)(B); see also § 300z–2(a). There is no requirement in the Act that grantees be affiliated with any religious denomination, although the Act clearly does not rule out grants to religious organizations. The services to be provided under the AFLA are not religious in character, nor has there been any suggestion that religious institutions or organizations with religious ties are uniquely well qualified to carry out those services. Certainly it is true that a substantial part of the services listed as "necessary services" under the Act involve some sort of education or counseling, see, e.g., §§ 300z–1(a)(4)(D), (G), (H), (J), (L), (M), (O), but there is nothing inherently religious about these activities and appellees do not contend that, by themselves, the AFLA's "necessary services" somehow have the primary effect of advancing religion. Finally, it is clear that the AFLA takes a particular approach toward dealing with adolescent sexuality and pregnancy—for example, two of its stated purposes are to "promote self discipline and other prudent approaches to the problem of adolescent premarital sexual relations," § 300z(b)(1), and to "promote adoption as an alternative," 300z(b)(2)—but again, that approach is not inherently religious, although it may coincide with the approach taken by certain religions.

Given this statutory framework, there are two ways in which the statute, considered "on its face," might be said to have the impermissible primary effect of advancing religion. First, it can be argued that the AFLA advances religion by expressly recognizing that "religious organizations have a role to play" in addressing the problems associated with teenage sexuality. Senate Report, at 16. In this view, even if no religious institution receives aid or funding pursuant to the AFLA, the statute is invalid under the Establishment Clause because, among other things, it expressly enlists the involvement of religiously affiliated organizations in the federally subsidized programs, it endorses religious solutions to the problems addressed by the Act, or it creates symbolic ties between church and state. Secondly, it can be argued that the AFLA is invalid on its face because it allows religiously affiliated organizations to participate as grantees or subgrantees in AFLA programs. From this standpoint, the Act is invalid because it authorizes direct federal funding of religious organizations which, given the AFLA's educational function and the fact that the AFLA's "viewpoint" may coincide with the grantee's "viewpoint" on sexual matters, will result unavoidably in the impermissible "inculcation" of religious beliefs in the context of a federally funded program.

We consider the former objection first. As noted previously, the AFLA expressly mentions the role of religious organizations in four places. It states (1) that the problems of teenage sexuality are "best approached through a variety of integrated and essential services provided to adolescents and their families by [, among others,] religious organizations," § 300z(a)(8)(B), (2) that federally subsidized services "should emphasize the provision of support by [, among others,] religious organizations," § 300z(a)(10)(C), (3) that AFLA programs "shall use such methods as will strengthen the capacity of families . . . to make use of support systems such as . . . religious . . . organizations," § 300z–2(a), and (4) that grant applicants shall describe how they will involve religious organizations, among other groups, in the provision of services under the Act. § 300z–5(a)(21)(A).

Putting aside for the moment the possible role of religious organizations as grantees, these provisions of the statute reflect at most Congress' considered judgment that religious organizations can help solve the problems to which the AFLA is addressed. See Senate Report, at 15–16. Nothing in our previous cases prevents Congress from making such a judgment or from recognizing the important part that religion or religious organizations may play in resolving certain secular problems. Particularly when, as Congress found, "prevention of adolescent sexual activity and adolescent pregnancy depends primarily upon developing strong family values and close family ties," § 300z(a)(10)(A), it seems quite sensible for Congress to recognize that religious organizations can influence values and can have some influence on family life, including parents' relations with their adolescent children. To the extent that this Congressional recognition has any effect of advancing religion, the effect is at most "incidental and remote." . . . In addition, although the AFLA does require potential grantees to describe how they will involve religious organizations in the provision of services under the Act, it also requires grantees to describe the involvement of "charitable organizations, voluntary associations, and other groups in the private sector," § 300z–5(a)(21)(B). In our view, this reflects the statute's successful maintenance of "a course of neutrality among religions, and between religion and nonreligion," Grand Rapids School District v. Ball, 473 U.S., at 382.

This brings us to the second grounds for objecting to the AFLA: the fact that it allows religious institutions to participate as recipients of federal funds. The AFLA defines an "eligible grant recipient" as a "public or nonprofit private organization or agency" which demonstrates the capability of providing the requisite services. § 300z–1(a)(3). As this provision would indicate, a fairly wide spectrum of organizations is eligible to apply for and receive funding under the Act, and nothing on the face of the Act suggests the AFLA is anything but neutral with respect to the grantee's status as a sectarian or purely secular institution. See Senate Report, at 16 ("Religious affiliation is not a criterion for selection as a grantee . . . ."). In this regard, then, the AFLA is similar to other statutes that this Court has upheld against Establishment Clause challenges in the past. In Roemer v. Maryland Board of Public Works, 426 U.S. 736 (1976), for example, we upheld a Maryland statute that provided annual subsidies directly to qualifying colleges and universities in the State, including religiously affiliated institutions. . . . Similarly, in Tilton v. Richardson, 403 U.S. 672 (1971), we approved the federal Higher Educational Facilities Act, which was intended by Congress to provide construction grants to "all colleges and universities regardless of any affiliation with or sponsorship by a religious body." Id., at 676. And in Hunt v. McNair, 413 U.S. 734 (1973), we rejected a challenge to a South Carolina statute that made certain benefits "available to all institutions of higher education in South Carolina, whether or not having a religious affiliation." Id., at 741. In other cases involving indirect grants of state aid to religious institutions, we have found it important that the aid is made available regardless of whether it will ultimately flow to a secular or sectarian institution. See, e.g., Witters v. Washington Dept. of Services for the Blind, 474 U.S. 481, 487 (1986); Mueller v. Allen, 463 U.S., at 398; Everson v. Board of Education, supra, at 17–18; Walz v. Tax Comm'n, 397 U.S., at 676.

We note in addition that this Court has never held that religious institutions are disabled by the First Amendment from participating in publicly sponsored social welfare programs. To the contrary, in Bradfield v. Roberts, 175 U.S. 291 (1899), the Court upheld an agreement between the Commissioners of the District of Columbia and a religiously affiliated hospital whereby the Federal Government would pay for the construction of a new building on the grounds of the hospital. In effect, the Court refused to hold that the mere fact that the hospital was "conducted under the auspices of the Roman Catholic Church" was sufficient to alter the purely secular legal character of the corporation, id., at 298, particularly in the absence of any allegation that the hospital discriminated on the basis of religion or operated in any way inconsistent with its secular charter. In the Court's view, the giving of federal aid to the hospital was entirely consistent with the Establishment Clause, and the fact that the hospital was religiously affiliated was "wholly immaterial." Ibid. The propriety of this holding, and the long history of cooperation and interdependency between governments and charitable or religious organizations is reflected in the legislative history of the AFLA. . . .

Of course, even when the challenged statute appears to be neutral on its face, we have always been careful to ensure that direct government aid to religiously affiliated institutions does not have the primary effect of advancing religion. One way in which direct government aid might have that effect is if the aid flows to institutions that are "pervasively sectarian." We stated in *Hunt* that

> "[a]id normally may be thought to have a primary effect of advancing religion when it flows to an institution in which religion is so pervasive that a substantial portion of its functions are subsumed in the religious mission. . . ." 413 U.S., at 743.

The reason for this is that there is a risk that direct government funding, even if it is designated for specific secular purposes, may nonetheless advance the pervasively sectarian institution's "religious mission." . . . Accordingly, a relevant factor in deciding whether a particular statute on its face can be said to have the improper effect of advancing religion is the determination of whether, and to what extent, the statute directs government aid to pervasively sectarian institutions. . . .

In this case, nothing on the face of the AFLA indicates that a significant proportion of the federal funds will be disbursed to "pervasively sectarian" institutions. Indeed, the contention that there is a substantial risk of such institutions receiving direct aid is undercut by the AFLA's facially neutral grant requirements, the wide spectrum of public and private organizations which are capable of meeting the AFLA's requirements, and the fact that, of the eligible religious institutions, many will not deserve the label of "pervasively sectarian." This is not a case like *Grand Rapids*, where the challenged aid flowed almost entirely to parochial schools. . . . Instead, this case more closely resembles *Tilton* and *Roemer*, where it was foreseeable that some proportion of the recipients of government aid would be religiously affiliated, but that only a small portion of these, if any, could be considered "pervasively sectarian." . . . As in *Tilton* and *Roemer*, we do not think the possibility that AFLA grants may go to religious institutions that can be considered "pervasively sectarian" is sufficient to conclude that no grants whatsoever can be given under the statute to religious organizations. We think that the District Court was wrong in concluding otherwise.

Nor do we agree with the District Court that the AFLA necessarily has the effect of advancing religion because the religiously affiliated AFLA grantees will be providing educational and counseling services to adolescents. Of course, we have . . . struck down programs that entail an unacceptable risk that government funding would be used to "advance the religious mission" of the religious institution receiving aid. See, e.g., *Meek*, 421 U.S., at 370. But nothing in our prior cases warrants the presumption adopted by the District Court that religiously affiliated AFLA grantees are not capable of carrying out their functions under the AFLA in a lawful, secular manner. Only in the context of aid to "pervasively sectarian" institutions have we invalidated an aid program on the grounds that there was a "substantial" risk that aid to these religious institutions would, knowingly or unknowingly, result in religious indoctrination. E.g., *Grand Rapids,* 473 U.S., at 387–398; *Meek,* supra, at 371. In contrast, when the aid is to flow to religiously affiliated institutions that were not pervasively sectarian, as in *Roemer,* we refused to presume that it would be used in a way that would have the primary effect of advancing religion. . . . We think that the type of presumption that the District Court applied in this case is simply unwarranted. . . .

We also disagree with the District Court's conclusion that the AFLA is invalid because it authorizes "teaching" by religious grant recipients on "matters [that] are fundamental elements of religious doctrine," such as the harm of premarital sex and the reasons for choosing adoption over abortion. . . . On an issue as sensitive and important as teenage sexuality, it is not surprising that the government's secular concerns would either coincide or conflict with those of religious institutions. But the possibility or even the likelihood that some of the religious institutions who receive AFLA funding will agree with the message that Congress intended to deliver to adolescents through the AFLA is insufficient to warrant a finding that the statute on its face has the primary effect of advancing religion. . . . Nor does the alignment of the statute and the religious views of the grantees run afoul of our proscription against "fund[ing] a specifically religious activity in an otherwise substantially secular setting." *Hunt,* 413 U.S., at 743. The facially neutral projects authorized by the AFLA—including pregnancy testing, adoption counseling and referral services, prenatal and postnatal care, educational services, residential care, child care, consumer education, etc.—are not themselves "specifically religious activities," and they are not converted into such activities by the fact that they are carried out by organizations with religious affiliations.

As yet another reason for invalidating parts of the AFLA, the District Court found that the involvement of religious organizations in the Act has the impermissible effect of creating a "crucial symbolic link" between government and religion. If we were to adopt the District Court's reasoning, it could be argued that any time a government aid program provides funding to religious organizations in an area in which the organization also has an interest, an impermissible "symbolic link" could be created, no matter whether the aid was to be used solely for secular purposes. This would jeopardize government aid to religiously affiliated hospitals, for example, on the ground that patients would perceive a "symbolic link" between the hospital—part of whose "religious mission" might be to save lives—and whatever government entity is subsidizing the purely secular medical services provided to the patient. We decline to adopt the District Court's reasoning and conclude that, in this case, whatever "symbolic link" might in fact be created by the AFLA's disbursement of funds to religious institutions is not sufficient to justify striking down the statute on its face.

A final argument that has been advanced for striking down the AFLA on "effects" grounds is the fact that the statute lacks an express provision preventing the use of federal funds for religious purposes. Compare *Tilton,* supra, at 675; *Roemer,* supra, at 740–741. Clearly, if there were such a provision in this statute, it would be easier to conclude that the statute on its face could not be said to have the primary effect of advancing religion, see, e.g., *Roemer,* supra, at 760, but we have never stated that a *statutory* restriction is constitutionally required. The closest we came to such a holding was in *Tilton,* where we struck down a provision of the statute that would have eliminated government sanctions for violating the statute's restrictions on religious uses of funds after 20 years. 403 U.S., at 683. The reason we did so, however, was because the 20-year limit on sanctions created a risk that the religious institution would, after the 20 years were up, act as if there were no longer any constitutional or statutory limitations on its use of the federally funded building. This aspect of the decision in *Tilton* was thus intended to indicate that the constitutional limitations on use of federal funds, as embodied in the statutory restriction, could not simply "expire" at some point during the economic life of the benefit that the grantee received from the government. In this case, although there is no express statutory limitation on religious use of funds, there is also no intimation in the statute that at some point, or for some grantees, religious uses are permitted. To the contrary, the 1984 Senate Report on the AFLA states that "the use of Adolescent Family Life Act funds to promote religion, or to teach the religious doctrines of a particular sect, is contrary to the intent of this legislation." S.Rep. No. 98–496, p. 10 (1984). We note in addition that the AFLA requires each grantee to undergo evaluations of the services it provides, § 300z–5(b)(1), and also requires grantees to "make such reports concerning its use of Federal funds as the Secretary may require," § 300z–5(c). The application requirements of the Act, as well, require potential grantees to disclose in detail exactly what services they intend to provide and how they will be provided. § 300z–5(a). These provisions, taken together, create a mechanism whereby the Secretary can police the grants that are given out under the Act to ensure that federal funds are not used for impermissible purposes. Unlike some other grant programs, in which aid might be given out in one-time grants without ongoing supervision by the government, the programs established under the authority of the AFLA can be monitored to determine whether the funds are, in effect, being used by the grantees in such a way as to advance religion. Given this statutory scheme, we do not think that the absence of an express limitation on the use of federal funds for religious purposes means that the statute, on its face, has the primary effect of advancing religion.

This, of course, brings us to the third prong of the *Lemon* Establishment Clause "test"—the question whether the AFLA leads to " 'an excessive government entanglement with religion.' ". . . . There is no doubt that the monitoring of AFLA grants is necessary if the Secretary is to ensure that public money is to be spent in the way that Congress intended and in a way that comports with the Establishment Clause.

Accordingly, this case presents us with yet another "Catch-22" argument: the very supervision of the aid to assure that it does not further religion renders the statute invalid. . . . Most of the cases in which the Court has divided over the "entanglement" part of the *Lemon* test have involved aid to parochial schools; . . . In *Aguilar,* the Court feared that an adequate level of supervision would require extensive and permanent on-site monitoring, . . . and would threaten both the "freedom of religious belief of those who [were] not adherents of that denomination" and the "freedom of . . . the adherents of the denomination." . . .

Here, by contrast, there is no reason to assume that the religious organizations which may receive grants are "pervasively sectarian" in the same sense as the Court has held parochial schools to be. There is accordingly no reason to fear that the less intensive monitoring involved here will cause the Government to intrude unduly in the day-to-day operation of the religiously affiliated AFLA grantees. Unquestionably, the Secretary will review the programs set up and run by the AFLA grantees, and undoubtedly this will involve a review of, for example, the educational materials that a grantee proposes to use. The Secretary may also wish to have government employees visit the clinics or offices where AFLA programs are being carried out to see whether they are in fact being administered in accordance with statutory and constitutional requirements. But in our view, this type of grant monitoring does not amount to "excessive entanglement," at least in the context of a statute authorizing grants to religiously affiliated organizations that are not necessarily "pervasively sectarian." [14]

. . .

For the foregoing reasons we conclude that the AFLA does not violate the Establishment Clause "on its face."

III

. . .

On the merits of the "as applied" challenge, it seems to us that the District Court did not follow the proper approach in assessing appellees' claim that the Secretary is making grants under the Act that violate the Establishment Clause of the First Amendment. . . . The District Court did identify certain instances in which it felt AFLA funds were used for constitutionally improper purposes, but in our view the court did not adequately design its remedy to address the specific problems it found in the Secretary's administration of the statute. Accordingly, although there is no dispute that the record contains evidence of specific incidents of impermissible behavior by AFLA grantees, we feel

---

[14.] We also disagree with the District Court's conclusion that the AFLA is invalid because it is likely to create political division along religious lines. It may well be that because of the importance of the issues relating to adolescent sexuality there may be a division of opinion along religious lines as well as other lines. But the same may be said of a great number of other public issues of our day. In addition, as we said in Mueller v. Allen, 463 U.S. 388, 404 n. 11 (1983), the question of "political divisiveness" should "be regarded as confined to cases where direct financial subsidies are paid to parochial schools or to teachers in parochial schools."

that this case should be remanded to the District Court for consideration of the evidence presented by appellees insofar as it sheds light on
the manner in which the statute is presently being administered. It is
the latter inquiry to which the Court must direct itself on remand.

In particular, it will be open to appellees on remand to show that
AFLA aid is flowing to grantees that can be considered "pervasively
sectarian" religious institutions, such as we have held parochial schools
to be. . . .

The District Court should also consider on remand whether in
particular cases AFLA aid has been used to fund "specifically religious
activit[ies] in an otherwise substantially secular setting." . . . Here it
would be relevant to determine, for example, whether the Secretary has
permitted AFLA grantees to use materials that have an explicitly
religious content or are designed to inculcate the views of a particular
religious faith. As we have pointed out in our previous discussion,
evidence that the views espoused on questions such as premarital sex,
abortion, and the like happen to coincide with the religious views of the
AFLA grantee would not be sufficient to show that the grant funds are
being used in such a way as to have a primary effect of advancing
religion.

. . .

IV

We conclude, first, that the District Court erred in holding that the
AFLA is invalid on its face, and second, that the court should consider
on remand whether particular AFLA grants have had the primary
effect of advancing religion. Should the court conclude that the Secretary's current practice does allow such grants, it should devise a
remedy to insure that grants awarded by the Secretary comply with the
constitution and the statute. The judgment of the District Court is
accordingly

Reversed.

Justice O'Connor, concurring.

. . . I join [the Court's] opinion. I write separately, however, to
explain why I do not believe that the Court's approach reflects any
tolerance for the kind of improper administration that seems to have
occurred in the government program at issue here.

. . .

The need for detailed factual findings by the District Court stems
in part from the delicacy of the task given to the Executive Branch by
the Adolescent Family Life Act (AFLA). Government has a strong and
legitimate secular interest in encouraging sexual restraint among
young people. At the same time, as the dissent rightly points out,
"[t]here is a very real and important difference between running a soup
kitchen or a hospital, and counseling pregnant teenagers on how to
make the difficult decisions facing them." Using religious organizations to advance the secular goals of the AFLA, without thereby
permitting religious indoctrination, is inevitably more difficult than in

other projects, such as ministering to the poor and the sick. I nonetheless agree with the Court that the partnership between governmental and religious institutions contemplated by the AFLA need not result in constitutional violations, despite an undeniably greater risk than is present in cooperative undertakings that involve less sensitive objectives. If the District Court finds on remand that grants are being made in violation of the Establishment Clause, an appropriate remedy would take into account the history of the program's administration as well as the extent of any continuing constitutional violations.

Justice Kennedy, with whom Justice Scalia joins, concurring.

I join the Court's opinion and write this separate concurrence to discuss one feature of the proceedings on remand. The Court states that "it will be open to appellees on remand to show that AFLA aid is flowing to grantees that can be considered 'pervasively sectarian' religious institutions, such as we have held parochial schools to be." In my view, such a showing will not alone be enough, in an as-applied challenge, to make out a violation of the Establishment Clause.

Though I am not confident that the term "pervasively sectarian" is a well-founded juridical category, I recognize the thrust of our previous decisions that a statute which provides for exclusive or disproportionate funding to pervasively sectarian institutions may impermissibly advance religion and as such be invalid on its face. We hold today, however, that the neutrality of the grant requirements and the diversity of the organizations described in the statute before us foreclose the argument that it is disproportionately tied to pervasively sectarian groups. Having held that the statute is not facially invalid, the only purpose of further inquiring whether any particular grantee institution is pervasively sectarian is as a preliminary step to demonstrating that the funds are in fact being used to further religion. In sum, where, as in this case, a statute provides that the benefits of a program are to be distributed in a neutral fashion to religious and non-religious applicants alike, and the program withstands a facial challenge, it is not unconstitutional as applied solely by reason of the religious character of a specific recipient. The question in an as-applied challenge is not whether the entity is of a religious character, but how it spends its grant.

Justice Blackmun, with whom Justice Brennan, Justice Marshall, and Justice Stevens join, dissenting.

. . . .

Whatever Congress had in mind, . . . it enacted a statute that facilitated and, indeed, encouraged the use of public funds for [religious] instruction, by giving religious groups a central pedagogical and counseling role without imposing any restraints on the sectarian quality of the participation. As the record developed thus far in this litigation makes all too clear, federal tax dollars appropriated for AFLA purposes have been used, with Government approval, to support religious teaching. . . . Because I am firmly convinced that our cases require invalidating this statutory scheme, I dissent.

I

. . .

. . . By designating appellees' broad attack on the statute as a "facial" challenge, the majority justifies divorcing its analysis from the extensive record developed in the District Court, and thereby strips the challenge of much of its force and renders the evaluation of the *Lemon* "effects" prong particularly sterile and meaningless. . . .

. . .

II

. . .

The majority first skews the Establishment Clause analysis by adopting a cramped view of what constitutes a pervasively sectarian institution. Perhaps because most of the Court's decisions in this area have come in the context of aid to parochial schools, which traditionally have been characterized as pervasively sectarian, the majority seems to equate the characterization with the institution. . . . On a continuum of "sectarianism" running from parochial schools at one end to the colleges funded by the statutes upheld in *Tilton, Hunt,* and *Roemer* at the other, the AFLA grantees described by the District Court clearly are much closer to the former than to the latter.

More importantly, the majority also errs in suggesting that the inapplicability of the label is generally dispositive. While a plurality of the Court has framed the inquiry as "whether an institution is so 'pervasively sectarian' that it may receive no direct state aid of any kind," Roemer v. Maryland Public Works Board, 426 U.S., at 758, the Court never has treated the absence of such a finding as a license to disregard the potential for impermissible fostering of religion. The characterization of an institution as "pervasively sectarian" allows us to eschew further inquiry into the use that will be made of direct government aid. In that sense, it is a sufficient, but not a necessary, basis for a finding that a challenged program creates an unacceptable Establishment Clause risk. The label thus serves in some cases as a proxy for a more detailed analysis of the institution, the nature of the aid, and the manner in which the aid may be used.

. . .

III

As is often the case, it is the effect of the statute, rather than its purpose, that creates Establishment Clause problems. . . .

A

The majority's holding that the AFLA is not unconstitutional on its face marks a sharp departure from our precedents. While aid programs providing nonmonetary, verifiably secular aid have been upheld notwithstanding the indirect effect they might have on the allocation of an institution's own funds for religious activities, . . . direct cash subsidies have always required much closer scrutiny into the expected and potential uses of the funds, and much greater guarantees that the funds would not be used inconsistently with the Establishment Clause. . . .

Notwithstanding the fact that government funds are paying for religious organizations to teach and counsel impressionable adolescents on a highly sensitive subject of considerable religious significance, often on the premises of a church or parochial school and without any effort to remove religious symbols from the sites, the majority concludes that the AFLA is not facially invalid. . . .

. . .

. . . There is a very real and important difference between running a soup kitchen or a hospital, and counseling pregnant teenagers on how to make the difficult decisions facing them. The risk of advancing religion at public expense, and of creating an appearance that the government is endorsing the medium and the message, is much greater when the religious organization is directly engaged in pedagogy, with the express intent of shaping belief and changing behavior, than where it is neutrally dispensing medication, food, or shelter.

There is also, of course, a fundamental difference between government's employing religion *because* of its unique appeal to a higher authority and the transcendental nature of its message, and government's enlisting other aid of religiously committed individuals or organizations without regard to their sectarian motivation. . . .

. . .

IV

While it is evident that the AFLA does not pass muster under Lemon's "effects" prong, the unconstitutionality of the statute becomes even more apparent when we consider the unprecedented degree of entanglement between Church and State required to prevent subsidizing the advancement of religion with AFLA funds. . . .

. . .

V

The AFLA, without a doubt, endorses religion. Because of its expressed solicitude for the participation of religious organizations in all AFLA programs in one form or another, the statute creates a symbolic and real partnership between the clergy and the fisc in addressing a problem with substantial religious overtones. Given the delicate subject matter and the impressionable audience, the risk that the AFLA will convey a message of Government endorsement of religion is overwhelming. The statutory language and the extensive record established in the District Court make clear that the problem lies in the statute and its systematically unconstitutional operation, and not merely in isolated instances of misapplication. I therefore would find the statute unconstitutional without remanding to the District Court. I trust, however, that after all its labors thus far, the District Court will not grow weary prematurely and read into the Court's decision a suggestion that the AFLA has been constitutionally implemented by the Government, for the majority deliberately eschews any review of the facts. After such further proceedings as are now to be deemed appropriate, and after the District Court enters findings of fact on the basis of the testimony and documents entered into evidence, it may well decide, as I would today, that the AFLA as a whole indeed has been unconstitutionally applied.

SECTION 2. THE FREE EXERCISE OF RELIGION

B. REGULATION OF CONDUCT COMPELLED BY RELIGIOUS BELIEF

Page 1475. Add ahead of When is Objection to War Religiously Conscientious? The Seeger and Welsh Cases:

ESTATE OF THORNTON v. CALDOR, INC.

472 U.S. 703, 105 S.Ct. 2914, 86 L.Ed.2d 557 (1985).

Chief Justice Burger delivered the opinion of the Court.

We granted certiorari to decide whether a state statute that provides employees with the absolute right not to work on their chosen Sabbath violates the Establishment Clause of the First Amendment.

I

In early 1975, petitioner's decedent Donald E. Thornton began working for respondent Caldor, Inc., a chain of New England retail stores; he managed the men's and boys' clothing department in respondent's Waterbury, Connecticut, store. At that time, respondent's Connecticut stores were closed on Sundays pursuant to state law. Conn. Gen.Stat. §§ 53–300 to 53–303 (1958).

In 1977, following the state legislature's revision of the Sunday-closing laws, respondent opened its Connecticut stores for Sunday business. In order to handle the expanded store hours, respondent required its managerial employees to work every third or fourth Sunday. Thornton, a Presbyterian who observed Sunday as his Sabbath, initially complied with respondent's demand and worked a total of 31 Sundays in 1977 and 1978. In October 1978, Thornton was transferred to a management position in respondent's Torrington store; he continued to work on Sundays during the first part of 1979. In November 1979, however, Thornton informed respondent that he would no longer work on Sundays because he observed that day as his Sabbath; he invoked the protection of Conn.Gen.Stat. § 53–303e(b) (Supp.1962–1984), which provides:

"No person who states that a particular day of the week is observed as his Sabbath may be required by his employer to work on such day. An employee's refusal to work on his Sabbath shall not constitute grounds for his dismissal."

Thornton rejected respondent's offer either to transfer him to a management job in a Massachusetts store that was closed on Sundays, or to transfer him to a nonsupervisory position in the Torrington store at a lower salary. In March 1980, respondent transferred Thornton to a clerical position in the Torrington store; Thornton resigned two days later and filed a grievance with the State Board of Mediation and Arbitration alleging that he was discharged from his manager's position in violation of Conn.Gen.Stat. § 53–303e(b).

. . .

After holding an evidentiary hearing the Board evaluated the sincerity of Thornton's claim and concluded it was based on a sincere religious conviction; it issued a formal decision sustaining Thornton's grievance . . . .. The Superior Court, in affirming that ruling, concluded that the statute did not offend the Establishment Clause.

The Supreme Court of Connecticut reversed . . . .. We affirm.

II

Under the Religion Clauses, Government must guard against activity that impinges on religious freedom, and must take pains not to compel people to act in the name of any religion. In setting the appropriate boundaries in Establishment Clause cases, the Court has frequently relied on our holding in *Lemon*, supra, for guidance, and we do so here. To pass constitutional muster under *Lemon* a statute must not only have a secular purpose and not foster excessive entanglement of government with religion, its primary effect must not advance or inhibit religion.

The Connecticut statute challenged here guarantees every employee, who "states that a particular day of the week is observed as his Sabbath," the right not to work on his chosen day. Conn.Gen.Stat. § 53–303e(b). The State has thus decreed that those who observe a Sabbath any day of the week as a matter of religious conviction must be relieved of the duty to work on that day, no matter what burden or inconvenience this imposes on the employer or fellow workers. The statute arms Sabbath observers with an absolute and unqualified right not to work on whatever day they designate as their Sabbath.

In essence, the Connecticut statute imposes on employers and employees an absolute duty to conform their business practices to the particular religious practices of the employee by enforcing observance of the Sabbath the employee unilaterally designates. The State thus commands that Sabbath religious concerns automatically control over all secular interests at the workplace; the statute takes no account of the convenience or interests of the employer or those of other employees who do not observe a Sabbath. The employer and others must adjust their affairs to the command of the State whenever the statute is invoked by an employee.

There is no exception under the statute for special circumstances, such as the Friday Sabbath observer employed in an occupation with a Monday through Friday schedule—a school teacher, for example; the statute provides for no special consideration if a high percentage of an employer's workforce asserts rights to the same Sabbath. Moreover, there is no exception when honoring the dictates of Sabbath observers would cause the employer substantial economic burdens or when the employer's compliance would require the imposition of significant burdens on other employees required to work in place of the Sabbath observers.[9] Finally, the statute allows for no consideration as to whether the employer has made reasonable accommodation proposals.

This unyielding weighting in favor of Sabbath observers over all other interests contravenes a fundamental principle of the Religion Clauses, so well articulated by Judge Learned Hand:

"The First Amendment . . . gives no one the right to insist that in pursuit of their own interests others must conform their conduct to his own religious necessities." Otten v. Baltimore & Ohio R. Co., 205 F.2d 58, 61 (CA2 1953).

As such, the statute goes beyond having an incidental or remote effect of advancing religion. See, e.g., Roemer v. Maryland Public Works Board, 426 U.S. 736, 747 (1976); Board of Education v. Allen, 392 U.S. 236 (1968). The statute has a primary effect that impermissibly advances a particular religious practice.

III

We hold that the Connecticut statute, which provides Sabbath observers with an absolute and unqualified right not to work on their Sabbath, violates the Establishment Clause of the First Amendment. Accordingly, the judgment of the Supreme Court of Connecticut is affirmed.

Affirmed.

Justice Rehnquist dissents.

Justice O'Connor, with whom Justice Marshall joins, concurring.

The Court applies the test enunciated in Lemon v. Kurtzman, 403 U.S. 602, 612–613 (1971) and concludes that Conn.Gen.Stat. § 53–303e(b) has a primary effect that impermissibly advances religion. I

---

[9] Section 53–303e(b) gives Sabbath observers the valuable right to designate a particular weekly day off—typically a weekend day, widely prized as a day off. Other employees who have strong and legitimate, but nonreligious reasons for wanting a weekend day off have no rights under the statute. For example, those employees who have earned the privilege through seniority to have weekend days off may be forced to surrender this privilege to the Sabbath observer, years of service and payment of "dues" at the workplace simply cannot compete with the Sabbath observer's absolute right under the statute. Similarly, those employees who would like a weekend day off, because that is the only day their spouses are also not working, must take a back seat to the Sabbath observer.

agree, and I join the Court's opinion and judgment. In my view, the Connecticut Sabbath law has an impermissible effect because it conveys a message of endorsement of the Sabbath observance.

. . .

I do not read the Court's opinion as suggesting that the religious accommodation provisions of Title VII of the Civil Rights Act are similarly invalid. These provisions preclude employment discrimination based on a person's religion and require private employers to reasonably accommodate the religious practices of employees unless to do so would cause undue hardship to the employer's business. 42 U.S.C. §§ 2000e(j) and 2000e–2(a)(1). Like the Connecticut Sabbath law, Title VII attempts to lift a burden on religious practice that is imposed by *private* employers, and hence it is not the sort of accommodation statute specifically contemplated by the Free Exercise Clause. See Wallace v. Jaffree, __ U.S. __, __ (1985) (opinion concurring in the judgment). The provisions of Title VII must therefore manifest a valid secular purpose and effect to be valid under the Establishment Clause. In my view, a statute outlawing employment discrimination based on race, color, religion, sex, or national origin has the valid secular purpose of assuring employment opportunity to all groups in our pluralistic society. See Trans World Airlines, Inc. v. Hardison, 432 U.S. 63, 90, n. 4 (1977) (Marshall, J., dissenting). Since Title VII calls for reasonable rather than absolute accommodation and extends that requirement to all religious beliefs and practices rather than protecting only the Sabbath observance, I believe an objective observer would perceive it as an anti-discrimination law rather than an endorsement of religion or a particular religious practice.

CORPORATION OF THE PRESIDING BISHOP OF THE CHURCH OF JESUS CHRIST OF LATTER–DAY SAINTS v. AMOS

__ U.S. __, 107 S.Ct. 2862, 97 L.Ed.2d 273 (1987).

Justice White delivered the opinion of the Court.

Section 702 of the Civil Rights Act of 1964, 78 Stat. 255, as amended, 42 U.S.C. section 2000e–1, exempts religious organizations from Title VII's prohibition against discrimination in employment on the basis of religion. The question presented is whether applying the section 702 exemption to the secular nonprofit activities of religious organizations violates the Establishment Clause of the First Amendment. The District Court held that it does, . . . We reverse.

I

The Deseret Gymnasium (Gymnasium) in Salt Lake City, Utah, is a nonprofit facility, open to the public, run by the Corporation of the Presiding Bishop of The Church of Jesus Christ of Latter-day Saints (CPB), and the Corporation of the President of The Church of Jesus

Christ of Latter-day Saints (COP). The CPB and the COP are religious entities associated with The Church of Jesus Christ of Latter-day Saints (Church), an unincorporated religious association sometimes called the Mormon or LDS Church.

Appellee Mayson worked at the Gymnasium for some 16 years as an assistant building engineer and then building engineer. He was discharged in 1981 because he failed to qualify for a temple recommend, that is, a certificate that he is a member of the Church and eligible to attend its temples.

Mayson and others purporting to represent a class of plaintiffs brought an action against the CPB and the COP alleging . . . discrimination on the basis of religion in violation of section 703 of the Civil Rights Act of 1964, 42 U.S.C. section 2000e-2. The defendants moved to dismiss this claim on the ground that section 702 shields them from liability. The plaintiffs contended that if construed to allow religious employers to discriminate on religious grounds in hiring for nonreligious jobs, section 702 violates the Establishment Clause.

. . .

II

"This Court has long recognized that the government may (and sometimes must) accommodate religious practices and that it may do so without violating the Establishment Clause." Hobbie v. Unemployment Appeals Comm'n, of Fla., 480 U.S. __, __ (1987) (footnote omitted). It is well established, too, that "the limits of permissible state accommodation to religion are by no means co-extensive with the noninterference mandated by the Free Exercise Clause." Walz v. Tax Comm'n, 397 U.S. 664, 673 (1970). There is ample room under the Establishment Clause for "benevolent neutrality which will permit religious exercise to exist without sponsorship and without interference." Id., at 669. At some point, accommodation may devolve into "an unlawful fostering of religion," Hobbie, supra, at __, but this is not such a case, in our view.

The private appellants contend that we should not apply the three-part Lemon approach, which is assertedly unsuited to judging the constitutionality of exemption statutes such as section 702. The argument is that an exemption statute will always have the effect of advancing religion and hence be invalid under the second (effects) part of the Lemon test, a result claimed to be inconsistent with cases such as Walz v. Tax Comm'n, supra, which upheld property tax exemptions for religious organizations. The first two of the three Lemon factors, however, were directly taken from pre-Walz decisions, 403 U.S., at 612–613, and Walz did not purport to depart from prior Establishment Clause cases, except by adding a consideration that became the third element of the Lemon test. Id., at 613. In any event, we need not reexamine Lemon as applied in this context, for the exemption involved here is in no way questionable under the Lemon analysis.

Lemon requires first that the law at issue serve a "secular legislative purpose." Id., at 612. This does not mean that the law's purpose must be unrelated to religion—that would amount to a requirement "that the government show a callous indifference to religious groups," Zorach v. Clauson, 343 U.S. 306, 314 (1952), and the Establishment Clause has never been so interpreted. Rather, *Lemon's* "purpose" requirement aims at preventing the relevant governmental decisionmaker—in this case, Congress—from abandoning neutrality and acting with the intent of promoting a particular point of view in religious matters.

Under the *Lemon* analysis, it is a permissible legislative purpose to alleviate significant governmental interference with the ability of religious organizations to define and carry out their religious missions. Appellees argue that there is no such purpose here because section 702 provided adequate protection for religious employers prior to the 1972 amendment, when it exempted only the religious activities of such employers from the statutory ban on religious discrimination. We may assume for the sake of argument that the pre–1972 exemption was adequate in the sense that the Free Exercise Clause required no more. Nonetheless, it is a significant burden on a religious organization to require it, on pain of substantial liability, to predict which of its activities a secular court will consider religious. The line is hardly a bright one, and an organization might understandably be concerned that a judge would not understand its religious tenets and sense of mission. Fear of potential liability might affect the way an organization carried out what it understood to be its religious mission.

. . .

The second requirement under *Lemon* is that the law in question have "a principal or primary effect . . . that neither advances nor inhibits religion." 403 U.S., at 612. Undoubtedly, religious organizations are better able now to advance their purposes than they were prior to the 1972 amendment to section 702. But religious groups have been better able to advance their purposes on account of many laws that have passed constitutional muster: for example, the property tax exemption at issue in Walz v. Tax Comm'n, supra, or the loans of school books to school children, including parochial school students, upheld in Board of Education v. Allen, 392 U.S. 236 (1968). A law is not unconstitutional simply because it allows churches to advance religion, which is their very purpose. For a law to have forbidden "effects" under *Lemon*, it must be fair to say that the government itself has advanced religion through its own activities and influence. . . .

. . . [W]e do not see how any advancement of religion achieved by the gymnasium can be fairly attributed to the government, as opposed to the church.[15]

We find unpersuasive the . . . fact that section 702 singles out religious entities for a benefit. Although the Court has given weight to

---

15 . . . This is a very different case than Estate of Thornton v. Caldor, Inc., 472 U.S. 703 (1985). In *Caldor* . . . Connecticut had given the force of law to the employee's designation of a Sabbath day and required accommodation by the employer regardless of the burden which that constituted for the employer or other employees. . . . In the present case, appellee was not legally obligated to take the steps necessary to qualify for a temple recommend, and his discharge was not required by statute. . . .

this consideration in its past decisions, it has never indicated that statutes that give special consideration to religious groups are per se invalid. That would run contrary to the teaching of our cases that there is ample room for accommodation of religion under the Establishment Clause. Where, as here, government acts with the proper purpose of lifting a regulation that burdens the exercise of religion, we see no reason to require that the exemption come packaged with benefits to secular entities.

. . .

It cannot be seriously contended that section 702 impermissibly entangles church and state; the statute effectuates a more complete separation of the two and avoids the kind of intrusive inquiry into religious belief that the District Court engaged in in this case. The statute easily passes muster under the third part of the *Lemon* test.

The judgment of the District Court is reversed, and the case is remanded for further proceedings consistent with this opinion.

It is so ordered.

Justice Brennan, with whom Justice Marshall joins, concurring in the judgment.

I write separately to emphasize that my concurrence in the judgment rests on the fact that this case involves a challenge to the application of section 702's categorical exemption to the activities of a nonprofit organization. I believe that the particular character of nonprofit activity makes inappropriate a case-by-case determination whether its nature is religious or secular.

. . .

The authority to engage in [the] process of self-definition inevitably involves what we normally regard as infringement on Free Exercise rights, since a religious organization is able to condition employment in certain activities on subscription to particular religious tenets. We are willing to countenance the imposition of such a condition because we deem it vital that, if certain activities constitute part of a religious community's practice, then a religious organization should be able to require that only members of its community perform those activities.

This rationale suggests that, ideally, religious organizations should be able to discriminate on the basis of religion *only* with respect to religious activities, so that a determination should be made in each case whether an activity is religious or secular. This is because the infringement on religious liberty that results from conditioning performance of *secular* activity upon religious belief cannot be defended as necessary for the community's self-definition. . . .

. . .

Nonprofit activities . . . are most likely to present cases in which characterization of the activity as religious or secular will be a close question. . . . This substantial potential for chilling religious activity makes inappropriate a case-by-case determination of the character of a nonprofit organization, and justifies a categorical exemption for nonprofit activities. . . .

Sensitivity to individual religious freedom dictates that religious discrimination be permitted only with respect to employment in religious activities. . . .

Justice Blackmun, concurring in the judgment.

Essentially for the reasons set forth in Justice O'Connor's opinion, particularly the third and final paragraphs thereof, I too, concur in the judgment of the Court. . . .

Justice O'Connor, concurring in the judgment.

Although I agree with the judgment of the Court, I write separately to note that this action once again illustrates certain difficulties inherent in the Court's use of the test articulated in Lemon v. Kurtzman, 403 U.S. 602, 612–613 (1971). As a result of this problematic analysis, while the holding of the opinion for the Court extends only to non-profit organizations, its reasoning fails to acknowledge that the amended section 702, 42 U.S.C. section 2000e–1, raises different questions as it is applied to profit and nonprofit organizations. . . .

. . . .

. . . [T]he Court seems to suggest that the "effects" prong of the *Lemon* test is not at all implicated as long as the government action can be characterized as "allowing" religious organizations to advance religion, in contrast to government action directly advancing religion. This distinction seems to me to obscure far more than to enlighten. Almost any government benefit to religion could be recharacterized as simply "allowing" a religion to better advance itself, unless perhaps it involved actual proselytization by government agents. In nearly every case of a government benefit to religion, the religious mission would not be advanced if the religion did not take advantage of the benefit; even a direct financial subsidy to a religious organization would not advance religion if for some reason the organization failed to make any use of the funds. It is for this same reason that there is little significance to the Court's observation that it was the Church rather than the government that penalized Mayson's refusal to adhere to Church doctrine. The Church had the power to put Mayson to a choice of qualifying for a temple recommend or losing his job because the *government* had lifted from religious organizations the general regulatory burden imposed by section 702.

The necessary first step in evaluating an Establishment Clause challenge to a government action lifting from religious organizations a generally applicable regulatory burden is to recognize that such government action *does* have the effect of advancing religion. The necessary second step is to separate those benefits to religion that constitutionally accommodate the free exercise of religion from those that provide unjustifiable awards of assistance to religious organizations. . . .

. . . Because there is a probability that a nonprofit activity of a religious organization will itself be involved in the organization's religious mission, in my view the objective observer should perceive the government action as an accommodation of the exercise of religion rather than as a government endorsement of religion.

It is not clear, however, that activities conducted by religious organizations solely as profit-making enterprises will be as likely to be directly involved in the religious mission of the organization. While I express no opinion on the issue, I emphasize that under the holding of the Court, and under my view of the appropriate Establishment Clause analysis, the question of the constitutionality of the section 702 exemption as applied to for-profit activities of religious organizations remains open.

Page 1482. Add at end of chapter:

GOLDMAN v. WEINBERGER

475 U.S. 503, 106 S.Ct. 1310, 89 L.Ed.2d 478 (1986).

Justice Rehnquist delivered the opinion of the Court.

Petitioner S. Simcha Goldman contends that the Free Exercise Clause of the First Amendment to the United States Constitution permits him to wear a yarmulke while in uniform, notwithstanding an Air Force regulation mandating uniform dress for Air Force personnel. The District Court for the District of Columbia permanently enjoined the Air Force from enforcing its regulation against petitioner and from penalizing him for wearing his yarmulke. The Court of Appeals for the District of Columbia Circuit reversed on the ground that the Air Force's strong interest in discipline justified the strict enforcement of its uniform dress requirements. We granted certiorari because of the importance of the question, and now affirm.

Petitioner Goldman is an Orthodox Jew and ordained rabbi. In 1973, he was accepted into the Armed Forces Health Professions Scholarship Program and placed on inactive reserve status in the Air Force while he studied clinical psychology at Loyola University of Chicago. During his three years in the scholarship program, he received a monthly stipend and an allowance for tuition, books, and fees. After completing his Ph.D. in psychology, petitioner . . . was stationed at March Air Force Base in Riverside, California, and served as a clinical psychologist at the mental health clinic on the base.

Until 1981, petitioner was not prevented from wearing his yarmulke on the base. He avoided controversy by remaining close to his duty station in the health clinic and by wearing his service cap over the yarmulke when out of doors. But in April 1981, after he testified as a defense witness at a court-martial wearing his yarmulke but not his service cap, opposing counsel lodged a complaint with Colonel Joseph Gregory, the Hospital Commander, arguing that petitioner's practice of wearing his yarmulke was a violation of Air Force Regulation (AFR) 35–10. This regulation states in pertinent part that "(h)eadgear will not be worn . . . (w)hile indoors except by armed security police in the performance of their duties." AFR 35–10, p. 1–6.h(2)(f) (1980).

Colonel Gregory informed petitioner that wearing a yarmulke while on duty does indeed violate AFR 35–10, and ordered him not to violate this regulation outside the hospital. Although virtually all of petitioner's time on the base was spent in the hospital, he refused. Later, after petitioner's attorney protested to the Air Force General Counsel, Colonel Gregory revised his order to prohibit petitioner from wearing the yarmulke even in the hospital. Petitioner's request to report for duty in civilian clothing pending legal resolution of the issue was denied. The next day he received a formal letter of reprimand, and was warned that failure to obey AFR 35–10 could subject him to a court-martial. Colonel Gregory also withdrew a recommendation that petitioner's application to extend the term of his active service be approved, and substituted a negative recommendation.

Petitioner argues that AFR 35–10, as applied to him, prohibits religiously motivated conduct and should therefore be analyzed under the standard enunciated in Sherbert v. Verner, 374 U.S. 398, 406 (1963). . . . But we have repeatedly held that "the military is, by necessity, a specialized society separate from civilian society." Parker v. Levy, 417 U.S. 733, 743 (1974). . . .

Our review of military regulations challenged on First Amendment grounds is far more deferential than constitutional review of similar laws or regulations designed for civilian society. The military need not encourage debate or tolerate protest to the extent that such tolerance is required of the civilian state by the First Amendment; to accomplish its mission the military must foster instinctive obedience, unity, commitment, and esprit de corps. . . .

These aspects of military life do not, of course, render entirely nugatory in the military context the guarantees of the First Amendment. . . . In the context of the present case, when evaluating whether military needs justify a particular restriction on religiously motivated conduct, courts must give great deference to the professional judgment of military authorities concerning the relative importance of a particular military interest. . . . "Judicial deference . . . is at its apogee when legislative action under the congressional authority to raise and support armies and make rules and regulations for their governance is challenged." Rostker v. Goldberg, 453 U.S. 57, 70 (1981).

The considered professional judgment of the Air Force is that the traditional outfitting of personnel in standardized uniforms encourages the subordination of personal preferences and identities in favor of the overall group mission. Uniforms encourage a sense of hierarchical unity by tending to eliminate outward individual distinctions except for those of rank. The Air Force considers them as vital during peacetime as during war because its personnel must be ready to provide an effective defense on a moment's notice; the necessary habits of discipline and unity must be developed in advance of trouble. . . .

To this end, the Air Force promulgated AFR 35–10, a 190-page document, which states that "Air Force members will wear the Air Force uniform while performing their military duties, except when authorized to wear civilian clothes on duty." AFR § 35–10, ¶ 1–6 (1980). The rest of the document describes in minute detail all of the various items of apparel that must be worn as part of the Air Force uniform. It authorizes a few individualized options with respect to certain pieces of jewelry and hair style, but even these are subject to severe limitations. See AFR 35–10, Table 1–1, and ¶ 1–12.b(1)(b) (1980). In general, authorized headgear may be worn only out of doors. See AFR § 35–10, ¶ 1–6.h (1980). Indoors, "(h)eadgear (may) not be worn . . . except by armed security police in the performance of their duties." AFR 35–10, ¶ 1–6.h(2)(f) (1980). A narrow exception to this rule exists for headgear worn during indoor religious ceremonies. See AFR 35–10, ¶ 1–6.h(2)(d) (1980). In addition, military commanders may in their discretion permit visible religious headgear and other such apparel in designated living quarters and nonvisible items generally. See Department of Defense Directive 1300.17 (June 18, 1985).

Petitioner Goldman contends that the Free Exercise Clause of the First Amendment requires the Air Force to make an exception to its uniform dress requirements for religious apparel unless the accoutrements create a "clear danger" of undermining discipline and esprit de corps. He asserts that in general, visible but "unobtrusive" apparel will not create such a danger and must therefore be accommodated. He argues that the Air Force failed to prove that a specific exception for his practice of wearing an unobtrusive yarmulke would threaten discipline. He contends that the Air Force's assertion to the contrary is mere ipse dixit, with no support from actual experience or a scientific study in the record, and is contradicted by expert testimony that religious exceptions to AFR 35–10 are in fact desirable and will increase morale by making the Air Force a more humane place.

But whether or not expert witnesses may feel that religious exceptions to AFR 35–10 are desirable is quite beside the point. The desirability of dress regulations in the military is decided by the appropriate military officials, and they are under no constitutional mandate to abandon their considered professional judgment. Quite obviously, to the extent the regulations do not permit the wearing of religious apparel such as a yarmulke, a practice described by petitioner as silent devotion akin to prayer, military life may be more objectionable for petitioner and probably others. But the First Amendment does not require the military to accommodate such practices in the face of its view that they would detract from the uniformity sought by the dress regulations. The Air Force has drawn the line essentially between religious apparel which is visible and that which is not, and we hold that those portions of the regulations challenged here reasonably and evenhandedly regulate dress in the interest of the military's perceived need for uniformity. The First Amendment therefore does not prohibit them from being applied to petitioner even though their effect is to restrict the wearing of the headgear required by his religious beliefs.

The judgment of the Court of Appeals is

Affirmed.

Justice Stevens, with whom Justice White and Justice Powell join, concurring.

Captain Goldman presents an especially attractive case for an exception from the uniform regulations that are applicable to all other Air Force personnel. His devotion to his faith is readily apparent. The yarmulke is a familiar and accepted sight. In addition to its religious significance for the wearer, the yarmulke may evoke the deepest respect and admiration—the symbol of a distinguished tradition and an eloquent rebuke to the ugliness of anti-Semitism. Captain Goldman's military duties are performed in a setting in which a modest departure from the uniform regulation creates almost no danger of impairment of the Air Force's military mission. Moreover, on the record before us, there is reason to believe that the policy of strict enforcement against Captain Goldman had a retaliatory motive—he had worn his yarmulke while testifying on behalf of a defendant in a court-martial proceeding. Nevertheless, as the case has been argued, I believe we must test the validity of the Air Force's rule not merely as it applies to Captain Goldman but also as it applies to all service personnel who have sincere religious beliefs that may conflict with one or more military commands.

Justice Brennan . . . correctly points out that "turbans, saffron robes, and dreadlocks are not before us in this case," and then suggests that other cases may be fairly decided by reference to a reasonable standard based on "functional utility, health and safety considerations, and the goal of a polished, professional appearance." As the Court has explained, this approach attaches no weight to the separate interest in uniformity itself. Because professionals in the military service attach great importance to that plausible interest, it is one that we must recognize as legitimate and rational even though personal experience or admiration for the performance of the "rag-tag band of soldiers" that won us our freedom in the revolutionary war might persuade us that the Government has exaggerated the importance of that interest.

The interest in uniformity, however, has a dimension that is of still greater importance for me. It is the interest in uniform treatment for the members of all religious faiths. The very strength of Captain Goldman's claim creates the danger that a similar claim on behalf of a Sikh or a Rastafarian might readily be dismissed as "so extreme, so unusual, or so faddish an image that public confidence in his ability to perform his duties will be destroyed." If exceptions from dress code regulations are to be granted on the basis of a multifactored test such as that proposed by Justice Brennan, inevitably the decisionmaker's evaluation of the character and the sincerity of the requestor's faith— as well as the probable reaction of the majority to the favored treatment of a member of that faith—will play a critical part in the decision. For the difference between a turban or a dreadlock on the one hand, and a yarmulke on the other, is not merely a difference in "appearance"—it is also the difference between a Sikh or a Rastafarian, on the one hand, and an Orthodox Jew on the other. The Air Force has no business drawing distinctions between such persons when it is enforcing commands of universal application.

. . .

Justice Brennan, with whom Justice Marshall joins, dissenting.

. . .

II

A

. . .

Today the Court . . . adopts for review of military decisions affecting First Amendment rights a subrational-basis standard—absolute, uncritical "deference to the professional judgment of military authorities." If a branch of the military declares one of its rules sufficiently important to outweigh a service person's constitutional rights, it seems that the Court will accept that conclusion, no matter how absurd or unsupported it may be.

A deferential standard of review, however, need not, and should not, mean that the Court must credit arguments that defy common sense. . . .

In the present case, the Air Force asserts that its interests in discipline and uniformity would be undermined by an exception to the dress code permitting observant male Orthodox Jews to wear yarmulkes. The Court simply restates these assertions without offering any explanation how the exception Dr. Goldman requests reasonably could interfere with the Air Force's interests. Had the Court given actual consideration to Goldman's claim, it would have been compelled to decide in his favor.

B

. . .

Department of Defense Directive 1300.17 (June 18, 1985) grants commanding officers the discretion to permit service personnel to wear religious items and apparel that are not visible with the uniform, such as crosses, temple garments, and scapulars. Justice Stevens favors this "visibility test" because he believes that it does not involve the Air Force in drawing distinctions among faiths. He rejects functional utility, health, and safety considerations, and similar grounds as criteria for religious exceptions to the dress code, because he fears that these standards will allow some service persons to satisfy their religious dress and grooming obligations, while preventing others from fulfilling theirs. But, the visible/not visible standard has that same effect. Furthermore, it restricts the free exercise rights of a larger number of service persons. The visibility test permits only individuals whose outer garments and grooming are indistinguishable from those of mainstream Christians to fulfill their religious duties. In my view, the Constitution requires the selection of criteria that permit the greatest possible number of persons to practice their faiths freely.

. . .

III

. . .

It is not the province of the federal courts to second-guess the professional judgments of the military services, but we are bound by the Constitution to assure ourselves that there exists a rational foundation for assertions of military necessity when they interfere with the free exercise of religion. . . . Definitions of necessity are influenced by decisionmakers' experiences and values. As a consequence, in pluralistic societies such as ours, institutions dominated by a majority are inevitably, if inadvertently, insensitive to the needs and values of minorities when these needs and values differ from those of the majority. The military, with its strong ethic of conformity and unquestioning obedience, may be particularly impervious to minority needs and values. A critical function of the Religion Clauses of the First Amendment is to protect the rights of members of minority religions against quiet erosion by majoritarian social institutions that dismiss minority beliefs and practices as unimportant, because unfamiliar. It is the constitutional role of this Court to ensure that this purpose of the First Amendment be realized.

. . .

Justice Blackmun, dissenting.

I would reverse the judgment of the Court of Appeals, but for reasons somewhat different from those respectively enunciated by Justice Brennan and Justice O'Connor. I feel that the Air Force is justified in considering not only the costs of allowing Captain Goldman to cover his head indoors, but also the cumulative costs of accommodating constitutionally indistinguishable requests for religious exemptions. Because, however, the Government has failed to make any meaningful showing that either set of costs is significant, I dissent from the Court's rejection of Goldman's claim.

. . .

The Air Force argues that it has no way of distinguishing fairly between Goldman's request for an exemption and the potential requests of others whose religious practices may conflict with the appearance code, perhaps in more conspicuous ways. In theory, this argument makes some sense. . . . To allow noncombat personnel to wear yarmulkes but not turbans or dreadlocks because the latter seem more obtrusive—or, as Justice Brennan suggests, less "polished" and "professional,"—would be to discriminate in favor of this country's more established, mainstream religions, the practices of which are more familiar to the average observer. Not only would conventional faiths receive special treatment under such an approach; they would receive special treatment precisely because they are conventional. In general, I see no constitutional difficulty in distinguishing between religious practices based on how difficult it would be to accommodate them, but favoritism based on how unobtrusive a practice appears to the majority could create serious problems of equal protection and religious establishment, problems the Air Force clearly has a strong interest in avoiding by drawing an objective line at visibility.

The problem with this argument, it seems to me, is not doctrinal but empirical. The Air Force simply has not shown any reason to fear that a significant number of enlisted personnel and officers would request religious exemptions that could not be denied on neutral grounds such as safety, let alone that granting these requests would noticeably impair the overall image of the service. Cf. Thomas v. Review Board of Indiana Employment Security Div., 450 U.S., at 719; Sherbert v. Verner, 374 U.S., at 407. . . .

. . . If, in the future, the Air Force is besieged with requests for religious exemptions from the dress code, and those requests cannot be distinguished on functional grounds from Goldman's, the service may be able to argue credibly that circumstances warrant a flat rule against any visible religious apparel. That, however, would be a case different from the one at hand.

Justice O'Connor, with whom Justice Marshall joins, dissenting.

. . .

I believe that the Court should attempt to articulate and apply an appropriate standard for a free exercise claim in the military context, and should examine Captain Goldman's claim in light of that standard.

. . .

. . . One can . . . glean at least two consistent themes from this Court's precedents. First, when the government attempts to deny a Free Exercise claim, it must show that an unusually important interest is at stake, whether that interest is denominated "compelling," "of the highest order," or "overriding." Second, the government must show that granting the requested exemption will do substantial harm to that interest, whether by showing that the means adopted is the "least restrictive" or "essential," or that the interest will not "otherwise be served." These two requirements are entirely sensible in the context of the assertion of a free exercise claim. First, because the government is attempting to override an interest specifically protected by the Bill of Rights, the government must show that the opposing interest it asserts is of especial importance before there is any chance that its claim can prevail. Second, since the Bill of Rights is expressly designed to protect the individual against the aggregated and sometimes intolerant powers of the state, the government must show that the interest asserted will in fact be substantially harmed by granting the type of exemption requested by the individual.

There is no reason why these general principles should not apply in the military, as well as the civilian, context. . . .

. . .

In the rare instances where the military has not consistently or plausibly justified its asserted need for rigidity of enforcement, and where the individual seeking the exemption establishes that the assertion by the military of a threat to discipline or esprit de corps is in his or her case completely unfounded, I would hold that the Government's policy of uniformity must yield to the individual's assertion of the right of free exercise of religion. On the facts of this case, therefore, I would require the Government to accommodate the sincere religious belief of Captain Goldman. Napoleon may have been correct to assert that, in the military sphere, morale is to all other factors as three is to one, but contradicted assertions of necessity by the military do not on the scales of justice bear a similarly disproportionate weight to sincere religious beliefs of the individual.

I respectfully dissent.

BOWEN v. ROY

476 U.S. 693, 106 S.Ct. 2147, 90 L.Ed.2d 735 (1986).

Chief Justice Burger announced the judgment of the Court and delivered the opinion of the Court with respect to Parts I and II, and an opinion with respect to Part III, in which Justice Powell and Justice Rehnquist join.

The question presented is whether the Free Exercise Clause of the First Amendment compels the government to accommodate a religiously-based objection to the statutory requirements that a Social Security number be provided by an applicant seeking to receive certain welfare benefits and that the States use these numbers in administering the benefit programs.

I

Appellees Stephen J. Roy and Karen Miller applied for and received benefits under the Aid to Families with Dependent Children program and the Food Stamp program. They refused to comply, however, with the requirement, contained in 42 U.S.C. § 602(a)(25) and 7 U.S.C. § 2025(e), that participants in these programs furnish their state welfare agencies with the Social Security numbers of the members of their household as a condition of receiving benefits. Appellees contended that obtaining a Social Security number for their two-year-old daughter, Little Bird of the Snow, would violate their Native American religious beliefs. The Pennsylvania Department of Public Welfare thereafter terminated AFDC and medical benefits payable to appellees on the child's behalf and instituted proceedings to reduce the level of food stamps that appellees' household was receiving. Appellees then filed this action against the Secretary of the Pennsylvania Department of Public Welfare, the Secretary of Health and Human Services, and the Secretary of Agriculture, arguing that the Free Exercise Clause entitled them to an exemption from the Social Security number requirement. In their complaint, appellees stated that "(t)he sole basis" for the denial of welfare benefits was "Mr. Roy's refusal to obtain a Social Security Number for Little Bird of the Snow," and thus requested injunctive relief, damages, and benefits. In the statement of "undisputed facts," the parties agreed that Little Bird of the Snow did not have a Social Security number.

At trial, Roy testified that he had recently developed a religious objection to obtaining a Social Security number for Little Bird of the Snow. Roy is a Native American descended from the Abenaki Tribe, and he asserts a religious belief that control over one's life is essential to spiritual purity and indispensable to "becoming a holy person." Based on recent conversations with an Abenaki chief, Roy believes that technology is "robbing the spirit of man." In order to prepare his daughter for greater spiritual power, therefore, Roy testified to his belief that he must keep her person and spirit unique and that the uniqueness of the Social Security number as an identifier, coupled with the other uses of the number over which she has no control, will serve to "rob the spirit" of his daughter and prevent her from attaining greater spiritual power.

. . .

In Roy's own testimony, he emphasized the evil that would flow simply from obtaining a number. On the last day of trial, however, a federal officer inquired whether Little Bird of the Snow already had a Social Security number; he learned that a number had been assigned—under first name "Little", middle name "Bird of the Snow", and last name "Roy."

. . .

After hearing all of the testimony, the District Court denied appellees' request for damages and benefits, but granted injunctive relief.
. . .

. . .

We . . . reverse.

II

Appellees raise a constitutional challenge to two features of the statutory scheme here. They object to Congress's requirement that a state AFDC plan "must . . . provide (A) that, as a condition of eligibility under the plan, each applicant for or recipient of aid shall furnish to the State agency his social security account number." . . . They also object to Congress's requirement that "such State agency shall utilize such account numbers . . . in the administration of such plan." . . . We analyze each of these contentions, turning to the latter contention first.

. . . Roy objects to the statutory requirement that state agencies "shall utilize" Social Security numbers not because it places any restriction on what he may believe or what he may do, but because he believes the use of the number may harm his daughter's spirit.

Never to our knowledge has the Court interpreted the First Amendment to require the Government itself to behave in ways that the individual believes will further his or her spiritual development or that of his or her family. The Free Exercise Clause simply cannot be understood to require the Government to conduct its own internal affairs in ways that comport with the religious beliefs of particular citizens. Just as the Government may not insist that appellees engage in any set form of religious observance, so appellees may not demand that the Government join in their chosen religious practices by refraining from using a number to identify their daughter. . . .

As a result, Roy may no more prevail on his religious objection to the Government's use of a Social Security number for his daughter than he could on a sincere religious objection to the size or color of the Government's filing cabinets. The Free Exercise Clause affords an individual protection from certain forms of governmental compulsion; it does not afford an individual a right to dictate the conduct of the Government's internal procedures.

. . .

. . . We . . . hold that the portion of the District Court's injunction that permanently restrained the Secretary from making any use of the Social Security number that had been issued in the name of Little Bird of the Snow Roy must be vacated.

III

Roy also challenges Congress' requirement that a state AFDC plan "must . . . provide (A) that, as a condition of eligibility under the plan, each applicant for or recipient of aid shall furnish to the State agency his social security account number." . . .

The statutory requirement that applicants provide a Social Security number is wholly neutral in religious terms and uniformly applicable. There is no claim that there is any attempt by Congress to discriminate invidiously or any covert suppression of particular religious beliefs. The administrative requirement does not create any danger of censorship or place a direct condition or burden on the dissemination of religious views. It does not intrude on the organization of a religious institution or school. It may indeed confront some applicants for benefits with choices, but in no sense does it affirmatively compel appellees, by threat of sanctions, to refrain from religiously motivated conduct or to engage in conduct that they find objectionable for religious reasons. Rather, it is appellees who seek benefits from the Government and who assert that, because of certain religious beliefs, they should be excused from compliance with a condition that is binding on all other persons who seek the same benefits from the Government.

This is far removed from the historical instances of religious persecution and intolerance that gave concern to those who drafted the Free Exercise Clause of the First Amendment. We are not unmindful of the importance of many government benefits today or of the value of sincerely-held religious beliefs. However, while we do not believe that no government compulsion is involved, we cannot ignore the reality that denial of such benefits by a uniformly applicable statute neutral on its face is of a wholly different, less intrusive nature than affirmative compulsion or prohibition, by threat of penal sanctions, for conduct that has religious implications.

This distinction is clearly revealed in the Court's opinions. Decisions rejecting religiously-based challenges have often recited the fact that a mere denial of a governmental benefit by a uniformly applicable statute does not constitute infringement of religious liberty. In Hamilton v. Regents of the University of California, 293 U.S. 245 (1934), for example, the Court rejected a religious challenge by students to military courses required as part of their curriculum, explaining:

> "The fact that they are able to pay their way in this university but not in any other institution in California is without significance upon any constitutional or other question here involved. California has not drafted or called them to attend the university. They are seeking education offered by the State and at the same time insisting that they be excluded from the prescribed course solely upon grounds of their religious beliefs and conscientious objections to war. . . ." Id., at 262.

In cases upholding First Amendment challenges, on the other hand, the Court has often relied on the showing that compulsion of certain activity with religious significance was involved. In West Virginia Board of Education v. Barnette, 319 U.S. 624 (1943), for example, the Court distinguished the earlier *Hamilton* holding and upheld a challenge to a flag salute requirement . . ..

. . . We have repeatedly emphasized this distinction: In rejecting a Free Exercise challenge in Bob Jones University v. United States, 461 U.S. 574, 603–604 (1983), for example, we observed that the "(d)enial of tax benefits will inevitably have a substantial impact on the operation of private religious schools, but will not prevent those schools from observing their religious tenets." [16]

We conclude then that government regulation that indirectly and incidentally calls for a choice between securing a governmental benefit and adherence to religious beliefs is wholly different from governmental action or legislation that criminalizes religiously inspired activity or inescapably compels conduct that some find objectionable for religious reasons. Although the denial of government benefits over religious objection can raise serious Free Exercise problems, these two very different forms of government action are not governed by the same constitutional standard. A governmental burden on religious liberty is not insulated from review simply because it is indirect, Thomas v. Review Board, Indian Employment Security Div., 450 U.S. 707, 717–718 (1981) (citing Sherbert v. Verner, 374 U.S., at 404); but the nature of

---

[16] The dissent asserts that the Court's holding "has no basis in precedent." To the contrary, it is the history advanced by the dissenting opinions that is revisionist. The dissent characterizes our prior cases as holding that the denial of a benefit is the same, for constitutional purposes, as the imposition of a criminal sanction. In *Bob Jones University*, however, the Court upheld the denial of tax benefits to a school that prohibited interracial dating observing that the school remained wholly free to "observ(e) (its) religious tenets." 461 U.S., at 604. If denying governmental benefits is the same as imposing criminal sanctions, then the Free Exercise Clause could not prevent the Government from ordering Bob Jones University, under pain of criminal penalty, to violate its religious beliefs and permit interracial dating on its campus. But that difficult question is still an open one since "the Constitution may compel toleration of private discrimination in some circumstances." Norwood v. Harrison, 413 U.S. 455, 463 (1973).

the burden is relevant to the standard the Government must meet to justify the burden.

The general governmental interests involved here buttress this conclusion. Governments today grant a broad range of benefits; inescapably at the same time the administration of complex programs requires certain conditions and restrictions. Although in some situations a mechanism for individual consideration will be created, a policy decision by a government that it wishes to treat all applicants alike and that it does not wish to become involved in case-by-case inquiries into the genuineness of each religious objection to such condition or restrictions is entitled to substantial deference. Moreover, legitimate interests are implicated in the need to avoid any appearance of favoring religious over nonreligious applicants.

The test applied in cases like Wisconsin v. Yoder, 406 U.S. 205 (1972), is not appropriate in this setting. In the enforcement of a facially neutral and uniformly applicable requirement for the administration of welfare programs reaching many millions of people, the Government is entitled to wide latitude. The Government should not be put to the strict test applied by the District Court; that standard required the Government to justify enforcement of the use of Social Security number requirement as the least restrictive means of accomplishing a compelling state interest.[17] Absent proof of an intent to discriminate against particular religious beliefs or against religion in general, the Government meets its burden when it demonstrates that a challenged requirement for governmental benefits, neutral and uniform in its application, is a reasonable means of promoting a legitimate public interest.

We reject appellees' contention that *Sherbert* and *Thomas* compel affirmance. The statutory conditions at issue in those cases provided that a person was not eligible for unemployment compensation benefits if, "without good cause," he had quit work or refused available work. The "good cause" standard created a mechanism for individualized exemptions. If a state creates such a mechanism, its refusal to extend an exemption to an instance of religious hardship suggests a discriminatory intent. Thus, as was urged in *Thomas*, to consider a religiously motivated resignation to be "without good cause" tends to exhibit hostility, not neutrality, towards religion. . . . In those cases, therefore, it was appropriate to require the State to demonstrate a compelling reason for denying the requested exemption.

. . .

[17] It is readily apparent that virtually every action that the Government takes, no matter how innocuous it might appear, is potentially susceptible to a Free Exercise objection. For example, someone might raise a religious objection, based on Norse mythology, to filing a tax return on a Wednesday (Woden's day). Accordingly, if the dissent's interpretation of the Free Exercise Clause is to be taken seriously, then the Government will be unable to enforce any generally applicable rule unless it can satisfy a federal court that it has a "compelling government interest." While libertarians and anarchists will no doubt applaud this result, it is hard to imagine that this is what the Framers intended.

. . . We know of no case obligating the government to tolerate a slight risk of "one or perhaps a few individuals" fraudulently obtaining benefits in order to satisfy a religious objection to a requirement designed to combat that very risk. Appellees may not use the Free Exercise Clause to demand government benefits, but only on their own terms, particularly where that insistence works a demonstrable disadvantage to the Government in the administration of the programs.

As the Court has recognized before, given the diversity of beliefs in our pluralistic society and the necessity of providing governments with sufficient operating latitude, some incidental neutral restraints on the free exercise of religion are inescapable. As a matter of legislative policy, a legislature might decide to make religious accommodations to a general and neutral system of awarding benefits, "(b)ut our concern is not with the wisdom of legislation but with its constitutional limitation." Braunfeld v. Brown, 366 U.S. 599, 608 (1961) (plurality opinion). We conclude that the Congress's refusal to grant appellees a special exemption does not violate the Free Exercise Clause.

The judgment of the District Court is vacated, and the case is remanded for further proceedings.

It is so ordered.

Justice Blackmun, concurring in part.

I join only Parts I and II of the opinion written by the Chief Justice.

. . .

. . . I agree that the portion of the District Court's judgment that enjoins the Government from using or disseminating the social security number already assigned to Little Bird of the Snow must be vacated. I would also vacate the remainder of the judgment and remand the case for further proceedings, because once the injunction against use or dissemination is set aside, it is unclear on the record presently before us whether a justiciable controversy remains with respect to the rest of the relief ordered by the District Court. . . .

. . .

Since the proceedings on remand might well render unnecessary any discussion of whether appellees constitutionally may be required to provide a social security number for Little Bird of the Snow in order to obtain government assistance on her behalf, that question could be said not to be properly before us. I nonetheless address it, partly because the rest of the Court has seen fit to do so, and partly because I think it is not the kind of difficult constitutional question that we should refrain from deciding except when absolutely necessary. Indeed, for the reasons expressed by Justice O'Connor, I think the question requires nothing more than a straightforward application of *Sherbert, Thomas,* and Wisconsin v. Yoder, 406 U.S. 205 (1972). If it proves necessary to reach the issue on remand, I agree with Justice O'Connor that, on the facts as determined by the District Court, the Government may not deny assistance to Little Bird of the Snow solely because her parents' religious convictions prevent them from supplying the Government with a social security number for their daughter.

Justice Stevens, concurring in part and concurring in the result.

. . .

Once we vacate the injunction preventing the Government from making routine use of the number that has already been assigned to Little Bird of the Snow, there is nothing disclosed by the record to prevent the appellees from receiving the payments that are in dispute. . . . The only issue that prevented the case from becoming moot was the claim asserted by Roy that he was entitled to an injunction that effectively canceled the existing number. Since that issue has now been resolved, nothing remains of the case.

. . .

Consistent with our longstanding principles of constitutional adjudication, we should decide nothing more than is actually necessary to dispose of the precise dispute before the Court . . .. No matter how interesting, or how clear their answers may appear to be, however, I would not address the hypothetical questions debated by the Chief Justice and Justice O'Connor because they are not properly presented by the record in this case.

Justice O'Connor, with whom Justice Brennan and Justice Marshall join, concurring in part and dissenting in part.

I join Parts I and II of the Chief Justice's opinion and I would vacate only a portion of the injunction issued by the District Court.

I

. . .

. . . I agree with the Chief Justice that the case is not moot.

. . . The Government still refuses to concede that it should now provide welfare benefits to Little Bird of the Snow, even though it now claims to possess Little Bird of the Snow's social security number, and even though the Solicitor General has been "advised by the Social Security Administration that the agency itself assigns (social security numbers) to persons who are required by federal law to have one but decline to complete an application." Because the Government contests the District Court's decision that the Government may not deny welfare benefits to Little Bird of the Snow despite its acknowledgement of appellees' sincere religious objections, Mr. Roy may properly press his suit. . . .

II

. . .

The Government has identified its goal as preventing fraud and abuse in the welfare system, a goal that is both laudable and compelling. The District Court, however, soundly rejected the Government's assertion that provision of the social security number was necessary to prevent such fraud and abuse. Among the means for which the social security number is used to reduce such fraud is "cross-matching," in which various computerized lists are compared with the welfare rolls to detect unreported income, individuals claimed as part of more than one household, and other fraudulent practices. As now appears, the Government not only has the social security number it wants for Little Bird of the Snow, but it can also use it. But even under the erroneous assumption of the District Court that no such number was available for use, that court found as a fact that, while cross-matching is "more difficult" without social security numbers, "(t)he file on a particular benefit recipient can be identified and cross-matching performed, if the recipient's full name, date of birth, and parents' names are entered into the computerized systems." . . .

Faced with these facts, however, the Chief Justice not only believes appellees themselves must provide a social security number to the Government before receiving benefits, but he also finds it necessary to invoke a new standard to be applied to test the validity of government regulations under the Free Exercise Clause. He would uphold any facially neutral and uniformly applicable governmental requirement if the Government shows its rule to be "a reasonable means of promoting a legitimate public interest." Such a test has no basis in precedent and relegates a serious First Amendment value to the barest level of minimal scrutiny that the Equal Protection Clause already provides. I would apply our long line of precedents to hold that the Government must accommodate a legitimate free exercise claim unless pursuing an especially important interest by narrowly tailored means.

. . .

Once it has been shown that a governmental regulation burdens the free exercise of religion, "only those interests of the highest order and those not otherwise served can over-balance legitimate claims to the free exercise of religion." Wisconsin v. Yoder, 406 U.S. 205, 215 (1972). This Court has consistently asked the Government to demonstrate that unbending application of its regulation to the religious objector "is essential to accomplish an overriding governmental interest," United States v. Lee, 455 U.S. 252, 257–258 (1982), or represents "the least restrictive means of achieving some compelling state interest," Thomas v. Review Board, supra, 450 U.S., at 718. See also Braunfeld v. Brown, 366 U.S. 599, 607 (1961); Sherbert v. Verner, supra, at 406. Only an especially important governmental interest pursued by narrowly tailored means can justify exacting a sacrifice of First Amendment freedoms as the price for an equal share of the rights, benefits, and privileges enjoyed by other citizens.

Granting an exemption to Little Bird of the Snow, and to the handful of others who can be expected to make a similar religious objection to providing the social security number in conjunction with the receipt of welfare benefits, will not demonstrably diminish the Government's ability to combat welfare fraud. . . . There is therefore no reason to believe that our previous standard for determining whether the Government must accommodate a free exercise claim does not apply.

. . .

. . . It is clear that the Court in *Bob Jones University* did not adopt anything like the legitimate interest/rational means test propounded by the Chief Justice, but rather continued to require the Government to show pursuit of an especially important interest by narrowly tailored means. In addition, the interest that the Court in *Bob Jones University* balanced against asserted religious interests was not merely a compelling governmental interest but a constitutional interest. . . .

Hamilton v. Regents of the University of California, 293 U.S. 245 (1934), also fails to support the Chief Justice's construction of a new test. When the Court decided *Hamilton,* it had not yet applied, and did not in *Hamilton* apply, the Free Exercise Clause to actions of the States. . . . The Court's discussion in Hamilton of the state university's decision to require military training is therefore limited to a generalized analysis under the Fourteenth Amendment of whether the state's policy deprived the would-be students of "life, liberty, or property." See 293 U.S., at 261–262. The Court concluded that no such deprivation was involved when the state "ha(d) not drafted or called (the individuals) to . . . war." Id., at 262.

. . .

. . . The fact that appellees seek exemption from a precondition that the Government attaches to an award of benefits does not, therefore, generate a meaningful distinction between this case and one where appellees seek an exemption from the Government's imposition of penalties upon them. Even if the Founding Fathers did not live in a society with the "broad range of benefits (and) complex programs" that the Federal Government administers today, they constructed a society in which the Constitution placed express limits upon governmental actions limiting the freedoms of that society's members. The rise of the welfare state was not the fall of the Free Exercise Clause.

. . .

I would merely vacate that portion of the injunction issued by the District Court that enjoins the Government from using or disseminating the social security number already in its possession.

Justice White, dissenting.

Being of the view that Thomas v. Review Board, 450 U.S. 707 (1981), and Sherbert v. Verner, 374 U.S. 398 (1963), control this case, I cannot join the Court's opinion and judgment.

HOBBIE v. UNEMPLOYMENT APPEALS COMMISSION OF FLORIDA, 107 S.Ct. 1046 (1987). Relying on Sherbert v. Verner and Thomas v. Review Board, the Court held that it was unconstitutional to deny unemployment compensation to an employee discharged for refusing to work on her Sabbath. The Court rejected an argument that the State's justifications for denying compensation should be determined under the less rigorous standards contained in Chief Justice Burger's plurality opinion in Bowen v. Roy. In a footnote, Justice Brennan's opinion noted that the plurality in *Roy* had distinguished *Sherbert* and *Thomas*. In the text of the opinion, however, the Court concluded that five Justices in *Roy* had completely rejected the plurality's argument. Quoting Justice O'Connor's dissenting opinion in *Roy*, the Court stated: "We reject the argument again today." The Court also rejected an argument, based on Estate of Thornton v. Caldor, that requiring the State to pay unemployment compensation constituted an establishment of religion. In a footnote, the Court explained that "provision of unemployment benefits to religious observers does not single out a particular class of such persons for favorable treatment and thereby have the effect of implicitly endorsing a religious belief."

LYNG v. NORTHWEST INDIAN CEMETERY PROTECTIVE ASSOCIATION

—— U.S. ——, 108 S.Ct. 1319, 99 L.Ed.2d 534 (1988).

Justice O'Connor delivered the opinion of the Court.

This case requires us to consider whether the First Amendment's Free Exercise Clause forbids the Government from permitting timber harvesting in, or constructing a road through, a portion of a National Forest that has traditionally been used for religious purposes by members of three American Indian tribes in northwestern California. We conclude that it does not.

I

. . .

After exhausting their administrative remedies, respondents—an Indian organization, individual Indians, nature organizations and individual members of those organizations, and the State of California— challenged both the road-building and timber-harvesting decisions in the United States District Court for the Northern District of California.

. . .

After a trial, the District Court issued a permanent injunction

. . .

. . .

By a divided decision, [a panel of the Ninth Circuit affirmed] the District Court's constitutional ruling . . .

. . .

III

A

. . . It is undisputed that the Indian respondents' beliefs are sincere and that the Government's proposed actions will have severe adverse effects on the practice of their religion. Respondents contend that the burden on their religious practices is heavy enough to violate the Free Exercise Clause unless the Government can demonstrate a compelling need . . . We disagree.

In Bowen v. Roy, 476 U.S. 693 (1986), we considered a challenge to a federal statute that required the States to use Social Security numbers in administering certain welfare programs. . . .

. . .

The building of a road or the harvesting of timber on publicly owned land cannot meaningfully be distinguished from the use of a Social Security number in *Roy.* In both cases, the challenged government action would interfere significantly with private persons' ability to pursue spiritual fulfillment according to their own religious beliefs. In neither case, however, would the affected individuals be coerced by the Government's action into violating their religious beliefs; nor would either governmental action penalize religious activity by denying any person an equal share of the rights, benefits, and privileges enjoyed by other citizens.

. . .

. . . This Court cannot determine the truth of the underlying beliefs that led to the religious objections here or in *Roy,* . . . and accordingly cannot weigh the adverse effects on the Roys and compare them with the adverse effects on respondents. Without the ability to make such comparisons, we cannot say that the one form of incidental interference with an individual's spiritual activities should be subjected to a different constitutional analysis than the other. . . .

. . . It is true that this Court has repeatedly held that indirect coercion or penalties on the free exercise of religion, not just outright prohibitions, are subject to scrutiny under the First Amendment. Thus, for example, ineligibility for unemployment benefits, based solely on a refusal to violate the Sabbath, has been analogized to a fine imposed on Sabbath worship. *Sherbert,* supra, at 404. This does not and cannot imply that incidental effects of government programs, which may make it more difficult to practice certain religions but which have no tendency to coerce individuals into acting contrary to their religious beliefs, require government to bring forward a compelling justification for its otherwise lawful actions. The crucial word in the constitutional text is "prohibit": "For the Free Exercise Clause is written in terms of what the government cannot do to the individual, not in terms of what the individual can exact from the government." *Sherbert,* supra, at 412 (Douglas, J., concurring).

Whatever may be the exact line between unconstitutional prohibitions on the free exercise of religion and the legitimate conduct by government of its own affairs, the location of the line cannot depend on measuring the effects of a governmental action on a religious objector's spiritual development. . . .

. . . [G]overnment simply could not operate if it were required to satisfy every citizen's religious needs and desires. A broad range of government activities—from social welfare programs to foreign aid to conservation projects—will always be considered essential to the spiritual well-being of some citizens, often on the basis of sincerely held religious beliefs. Others will find the very same activities deeply offensive, and perhaps incompatible with their own search for spiritual fulfillment and with the tenets of their religion. The First Amendment must apply to all citizens alike, and it can give to none of them a veto over public programs that do not prohibit the free exercise of religion. The Constitution does not, and courts cannot, offer to reconcile the various competing demands on government, many of them rooted in sincere religious belief, that inevitably arise in so diverse a society as ours. That task, to the extent that it is feasible, is for the legislatures and other institutions. Cf. The Federalist No. 10 (suggesting that the effects of religious factionalism are best restrained through competition among a multiplicity of religious sects).

. . .

IV

The decision of the court below, according to which the First Amendment precludes the Government from completing the G-O road or from permitting timber harvesting in the Chimney Rock area, is reversed. . . .

. . .

Justice Kennedy took no part in the consideration or decision of this case.

Justice Brennan, with whom Justice Marshall and Justice Blackmun join, dissenting.

. . .

I . . . cannot accept the Court's premise that the form of the Government's restraint on religious practice, rather than its effect, controls our constitutional analysis. . . .

. . .

Ultimately, the Court's coercion test turns on a distinction between governmental actions that compel affirmative conduct inconsistent with religious belief, and those governmental actions that prevent conduct consistent with religious belief. In my view, such a distinction is without constitutional significance. . . .

. . .

. . . Both common sense and our prior cases teach us . . . that governmental action that makes the practice of a given faith more difficult necessarily penalizes that practice and thereby tends to prevent adherence to religious belief. The harm to the practitioners is the same regardless of the manner in which the Government restrains their religious expression, and the Court's fear that an "effects" test will permit religious adherents to challenge governmental actions they merely find "offensive" in no way justifies its refusal to recognize the constitutional injury citizens suffer when governmental action not only offends but actually restrains their religious practices. . . .

. . .

. . . In *Roy*, we repeatedly stressed the "internal" nature of the Government practice at issue. . . When the Government processes information, of course, it acts in a purely internal manner, and any free exercise challenge to such internal recordkeeping in effect seeks to dictate how the Government conducts its own affairs.

Federal land-use decisions, by contrast, are likely to have substantial external effects that government decisions concerning office furniture and information storage obviously will not, and they are correspondingly subject to public scrutiny and public challenge in a host of ways that office equipment purchases are not. . . .

. . .

EMPLOYMENT DIVISION v. SMITH, 108 S.Ct. 1444 (1988). Two drug and alcohol abuse rehabilitation counselors were discharged after they ingested peyote, a hallucinogenic drug, during a religious ceremony of the Native American Church. Both applied for and were denied unemployment compensation. The Oregon Supreme Court held that, although it was proper as a matter of Oregon statutory and constitutional law, denial of unemployment compensation violated the free exercise clause of the first amendment to the Federal Constitution. The Court remanded to the Oregon Supreme Court for determination whether sacramental use of peyote was a crime under Oregon law. Justice Stevens' opinion for the Court explained:

"The results we reached in *Sherbert, Thomas,* and *Hobbie* might well have been different if the employees had been discharged for engaging in criminal conduct. We have held that bigamy may be forbidden, even when the practice is dictated by sincere religious convictions. Reynolds v. United States, 98 U.S. 145 (1879). If a bigamist may be sent to jail despite the religious motivation for his misconduct, surely a State may refuse to pay unemployment compensation to a marriage counselor who was discharged because he or she entered into a bigamous relationship. The protection that, the First Amendment provides to *"legitimate* claims to the free exercise of religion," see *Hobbie,* 480 U.S., at ___ (emphasis added), does not extend to conduct that a State has validly proscribed.

"Neither the Oregon Supreme Court nor this Court has confronted the question whether the ingestion of peyote for sincerely held religious reasons is a form of conduct that is protected by the Federal Constitution from the reach of a State's criminal laws. It may ultimately be necessary to answer that federal question in this case, but it is inappropriate to do so without first receiving further guidance concerning the status of the practice as a matter of Oregon law."

Justice Brennan, joined by Justices Marshall and Blackmun, dissented. The Oregon Supreme Court had disavowed any state interest that might flow from the possibility that ceremonial use of peyote would be a crime. An interest that the State's supreme court has determined to be irrelevant cannot be a "compelling" interest in deciding the first amendment free exercise issue.

†